The Diary of Anne Frank: The Critical Edition

Other Books by Anne Frank:

ANNE FRANK: THE DIARY OF A YOUNG GIRL

ANNE FRANK'S TALES FROM THE SECRET ANNEX

THE WORKS OF ANNE FRANK

THE DIARY OF ANNE FRANK

The Critical Edition

Prepared by the Netherlands State Institute
for War Documentation

Introduced by
HARRY PAAPE, GERROLD VAN DER STROOM
AND DAVID BARNOUW

With a summary of the report by
the State Forensic Science Laboratory
of the Ministry of Justice
compiled by
H. J. J. HARDY

Edited by
DAVID BARNOUW AND GERROLD VAN DER STROOM

Translated by Arnold J. Pomerans
and B. M. Mooyaart-Doubleday

Doubleday
NEW YORK LONDON TORONTO SYDNEY AUCKLAND

Published by Bantam Doubleday Dell Publishing Group, Inc.
666 Fifth Avenue, New York, New York 10103

Doubleday and the portrayal of an anchor with a dolphin are trademarks of Doubleday, a division of Bantam Doubleday Dell Publishing Group, Inc.

Library of Congress Cataloging-in-Publication Data
Frank, Anne, 1929–1945.
   [Achterhuis. English]
   The diary of Anne Frank: the critical edition / prepared by the
Netherlands State Institute for War Documentation; introductions by
Harry Paape, Gerrold van der Stroom, and David Barnouw; with a
summary of the report by the State Forensic Science Laboratory of
the Ministry of Justice; compiled by H. J. J. Hardy; edited by David
Barnouw and Gerrold van der Stroom; translated by Arnold J.
Pomerans and B. M. Mooyaart-Doubleday.—1st ed.
    p.   cm.
   Translation of: Achterhuis.
   1. Frank, Anne, 1929–1945—Diaries. 2. Holocaust, Jewish
(1939–1945)—Netherlands—Amsterdam—Personal narratives. 3. Jews—
Netherlands—Amsterdam—Persecutions. 4. Amsterdam (Netherlands)—
Ethnic relations. 5. Jews—Netherlands—Amsterdam—Diaries.
I. Hardy, H. J. J. II. Barnouw, David. III. Stroom, Gerrold van
der. IV. Rijksinstituut voor Oorlogsdocumentatie (Netherlands)
V. Netherlands. Gerechtelijk Laboratorium. VI. Title.
DS135.N5A53413 1989
840.53'15'03924—dc19
[B] *949.2*   88-9678
   FRA   CIP
ISBN 0-385-24023-6

Designed by Wilma Robin

AUG 17 1989

Contents

Foreword

In November 1980 the handwritten entries Anne Frank had made in her diary between June 12, 1942, and August 1, 1944, were delivered to the Netherlands State Institute for War Documentation by a notary public from Basle in Switzerland. Otto Frank, Anne's father, who had died in August of that year, had bequeathed the material to the Institute.

The Institute had never interested itself in Anne Frank; for many years the subject had seemed of small academic importance. In his standard work, published by the Institute, *Ondergang. De vervolging en verdelging van het Nederlandse Jodendom 1940–1945* (*Ashes in the Wind. The Destruction of Dutch Jewry*) (London, 1968; New York, 1969, as *The Destruction of Dutch Jews*), Dr. Jacob Presser mentions Anne Frank's name just three times, including two quotations from her diary. Similarly Dr. Louis de Jong, former director of the Institute, refers to her three times only, in passing, in his monumental work *Het Koninkrijk der Nederlanden in de Tweede Wereldoorlog* (*The Kingdom of the Netherlands in the Second World War*; 12 vols., The Hague, 1969–1987). In 1957, incidentally, Dr. de Jong also published an article on Anne Frank in the *Reader's Digest* on his own authority, after he and her father had made contact.

The Institute had simply taken cognizance of the fact that there had been discussions concerning the authenticity of the published version of the diary and its relationship to the original manuscripts, no more.

However, once members of the Institute had read the manuscripts, the situation changed. It quickly became obvious that an edition of the complete diaries was needed, for historical reasons (the publication of an important source) as well as on personal and political grounds (the growing number of published slurs, particularly during the second half of the 1970s, on the diary were intended to cast doubt both on the personal integrity of the author and on the relationship between the original manuscript, the published version, and its many translations, not always identical even in content). On being approached, the Minister of Education and Science was quick to approve publication of the present edition.

The main aim of this edition has been to offer the reader the chance to compare the extant, original diary entries of Anne Frank with each other, as well as with *Het Achterhuis*, the original Dutch version of the *Diary of Anne Frank*. We have not been entirely successful in meeting the first objective: some of the persons mentioned by name in the manuscripts have asked us not to use their names; we have replaced these with initials chosen at random. Moreover, Otto Frank's second wife, Elfriede Frank-Markovits, in her position as authorized representative both of the Frank family and of the ANNE FRANK-Fonds, and as one of the persons mentioned by name in the diary, had strong objections to the inclusion of a small number of previously unpublished details. We have heeded these and similar objections by the people concerned, since the historical character of the diary remains unaffected by the loss of such negligible detail. The length of, and reason for, these deletions are set out in the appropriate notes.

We considered it important to accompany this edition with an extensive introduction giving a detailed background picture of the Frank family in Frankfurt and Amsterdam before and during the war, and as far as the only survivor, Anne's father, is concerned, in Amsterdam after the war as well. The history of those who went into hiding with the Franks, and of their protectors, has been explored to a somewhat lesser extent. We have also attempted to give detailed accounts of the events at 263, Prinsengracht during the raid by the *Sicherheitsdienst* (German Security Service, the SD) on August 4, 1944, and of the fate of those who were seized on that occasion. We have paid particular attention to the circumstances surrounding this raid as well as to the postwar investigations into the betrayal that must have led up to it—a question that has been repeatedly and widely raised both in Holland and abroad.

An examination in depth of the preparation and publication (in 1947) of *Het Achterhuis*, of the German, French and English translations, together with the relationship between these editions and Anne Frank's original manuscripts, follows. It goes without saying that we were especially concerned with the attacks on the authenticity of the diary and the consequent lawsuits and expert testimony, in particular the legal battle that raged for years around the play *The Diary of Anne Frank*, and the associated personal drama of its American author.

Finally, we have included in the introduction a summary of the detailed handwriting and technical report on the authenticity of the diary issued by the State Forensic Science Laboratory of the Ministry of Justice. The full report, which runs to 270 pages, was considered too extensive to be included in this book, and we accordingly asked its compiler, H. J. J. Hardy, for a summary of its essential findings and an explanation of the methods and techniques used. The full report is, of course, available to scholars.

In all this we have paid little attention to Anne Frank herself. The main sources for what we know of her life and of her person are her diaries. Very little other written material about her has come down to us; almost all the witnesses have died and those few to whom we were able to talk had no fresh facts or opinions to offer.

As is customary in this Institute, we submitted the text of the present work to members of the board: Professor Dr. A. F. Manning (President), Professor Dr. P. W. Klein and Professor E. J. H. Schrage. In view of the international scope of this edition, we also consulted four experts who were willing to act as an international advisory committee, namely Dr. L. Strengholt, Professor of Dutch Studies (Amsterdam), and the historians Professor Dr. K. W. Swart (London), Dr. J. Vanwelkenhuyzen (Brussels) and Professor Dr. W. Warmbrunn (Claremont, California). They have all advised on the final form of the introductory section, and Professor Strengholt has in addition taken a special editorial interest in the main text. We are most grateful to the board and to the advisory committee for their counsel and comments.

The introductory section could not have been compiled without the active support and help of scores of groups and individuals in the Netherlands and abroad. The extensive data and the quantity of previously unpublished material on which we could draw were the result of generally very positive responses to our requests. We should like to express our heartfelt thanks to all who contributed.

Our thanks are also due to our colleagues in the Institute who did a great deal of work for us, thus ensuring that the contents of the introduction and the accuracy of the reproduction of the sources are of a standard that we should have been unable to attain without their help.

So many others have helped us in one way or another that it is not possible to mention them all by name here. We should like, however, to make one exception. In 1981, when we turned to the State Forensic Science Laboratory with a request for handwriting identification and document examination to verify the the authenticity of the Anne Frank diaries, the response was immediate and positive. A number of staff members, their work coordinated by H. J. J. Hardy, M.Sc., conducted an extremely thorough and detailed investigation which resulted in the above-mentioned report. Like ourselves, they spent several years, after their "normal" duties, on research, and in so doing made a contribution of fundamental importance in establishing the final answer to the question of whether or not the manuscripts are authentic. We owe them a particularly great debt of gratitude.

THE EDITORS

The Diary of Anne Frank: The Critical Edition

". . . Originally from Frankfurt-am-Main"

HARRY PAAPE

On August 16, 1933, the following entry was made at the Amsterdam Public Registration Office: "Frank, Otto Heinrich, originally from Frankfurt-am-Main."[1]

Otto Frank was born on May 12, 1889, in Frankfurt, the second son of the marriage of Michael Frank and Alice Betty Stern. His father was the owner and director of the Bankgeschäft Michael Frank,[2] a banking concern founded in 1885 and engaged mainly in dealing in stocks and shares, bills of exchange and foreign currency. In the 1880s and 1890s, Michael Frank also acquired financial interests in the marketing of Fay's Sodener Mineral-Pastillen (medicinal throat pastilles), in a cigar store and in a travel agency.[3] With the exception of the Sodener Mineral-Pastillen, he sold all these interests before the end of the century. The subsequent change of address of the bank and of the family home reflected the Franks' increasing prosperity, but though they belonged to the liberal Jewish middle class, they could not really be called rich. Their circle of friends and acquaintances in the comparatively liberal Frankfurt of the time was made up of Jews and non-Jews alike.[4]

In 1908, Otto Frank graduated from the Lessing Gymnasium in Frankfurt and enrolled in the University of Heidelberg. After only one semester, however, he cut short his studies and went to New York with Nathan Straus, a fellow student whose family owned R. H. Macy, the big department store there. Here Otto became familiar with business practice.[5] Following his father's death in the autumn of 1909, he returned to Germany and continued his business training in Düsseldorf. In the years up to the outbreak of the First World War, he made several short trips to New York.[6]

In 1915 he joined the army and was assigned to an artillery regiment. His unit was sent to the Western Front and deployed in the vicinity of Cambrai and St.-Quentin. At the end of the war Otto was demobilized with the rank of lieutenant.[7]

On the death of her husband, Otto's mother had become the owner of the business.[8] Her oldest son, Robert, was not very interested in banking; he had studied art history for a short time, and in 1907 (he was then just twenty-one years old) he was appointed deputy manager of an art business in Frankfurt bought by his father.[9] The other sons, too, seem to have had little interest in banking. According to the short booklet entitled *Früher wohnten wir in Frankfurt* . . . ["We Used to Live in Frankfurt . . ."], both Otto and Herbert (the third son), as well as Erich Elias, the husband of their sister Helene, joined the business in about 1923 or 1924, more from necessity than by choice.[10]

The Frankfurt Chamber of Commerce gives some further details. According to its records, Erich Elias became a full partner at the beginning of 1921, Herbert resigned in the autumn of that year (the records do not say when he first joined), although in September 1923 he returned to the business. Otto is mentioned for the first time in these records in 1932.[11]

The war and the resulting lack of foreign currency, together with restrictive legislation, had a detrimental effect on the family bank. Inflation, which continued after the war and which reached giddy heights by 1923, not only made disastrous inroads into the capital of Otto's mother, who had subscribed heavily to war loans and suffered considerable losses as a result, but also had a ruinous effect on business in general. In 1923 the Weimar Republic's balance of trade became so desperate that a licensing system for dealing in foreign currency had to be introduced. An application made in September of that year by the Bank Michael Frank was only granted on appeal; the volume of trade the bank had been generating in this sector had apparently been too small.[12]

A solution to this desperate situation was obviously needed. Otto (who had more international experience than the rest of his family) went to Amsterdam and founded M. Frank & Zonen, a company whose objectives were banking and trading in foreign currency. The names of the leading partners were given as Otto Frank, Erich Elias, Herbert Frank and the Michael Frank Partnership. The company was registered at the Amsterdam Chamber of Commerce on November 22, 1923; the official registration certificate was issued on December 31 of that year.[13]

The address of the business was given as 604, Keizersgracht, which address Otto also gave as his residence.[14] The founding capital was 150,000 guilders, jointly contributed by the partners, of whom Erich Elias and Herbert Frank signed the application to the Chamber of Commerce.[15]

In May 1924 proxies were registered with the Chamber of Commerce: Jacques Heuskin, a Luxembourger born in 1876 in Belgium, whose address was also given as 604, Keizersgracht, and Johannes Kleiman, born in 1896 in Koog aan de Zaan, also resident in Amsterdam. Both men, however, had very limited powers.[16]

The Michael Frank Bank was not the only German bank to set up subsidiaries or branches in the Netherlands, a country that had remained neutral during the war, and in Amsterdam in particular, the new center of the foreign currency trade aided by the strong guilder.[17] However, the Amsterdam branches of these banks were forced to refrain from attracting Dutch money and to confine themselves to the management of German *vlucht-kapitaal* (flight capital).

The affairs of M. Frank & Zonen must have taken a disastrous turn soon afterwards—on December 15, 1924, the business went into liquidation. Otto was appointed liquidator.[18] The cause of the crash can no longer be ascertained, but it seems likely that it followed upon speculative activity, perhaps involving the French franc, a currency that was being traded with considerable losses in Amsterdam in the summer of 1924. For although Heuskin was dismissed in the summer of 1925, it seems unlikely that he was responsible for the disaster. He had had very limited authority, and moreover was only entitled to sign together with the second proxy, Kleiman, who was now given full powers. Kleiman thus enjoyed the complete confidence of the Franks, which was also reflected in the fact that the official address of the bank was then changed to 21, Rombout Hogerbeetsstraat, Amsterdam, Kleiman's residence. The application form to the Chamber of Commerce was signed by Otto Frank, whose address was this time given as Frankfurt. From the absence of any entry at the Amsterdam Public Registration Office we can take it that Otto stayed in Frankfurt from the end of 1923 until the summer of 1925, although he must have traveled to Amsterdam many times during that period—the telex service had not yet been invented, and telephone calls (still very primitive) and correspondence were too slow for the quick decisions needed in the foreign currency business.[19]

The liquidation took an unusually long time. However, no receiver was appointed, which implies that there was no bankruptcy. Since all the partners were owners of the Frankfurt bank, the creditors, who were, if not all, then mostly German citizens, must have agreed to be paid in installments. Otto notified the Chamber of Commerce of the completion of the liquidation and hence the closing of the Amsterdam business on January 30, 1929; the official entry was made two weeks later.[20]

Several inferences can be drawn. In the first place, Kleiman remained Otto's confidant and mainstay in Amsterdam until the dissolution of the business. We shall have occasion to refer to him on many other occasions—he was to play a particularly important part in the business and also in Otto's personal future.

Secondly, the Franks clearly handled the collapse of the bank in a considered, dignified and honorable manner. Obviously this was also in the best interests of the mother concern in Frankfurt, which must have gone out of its way to protect its good name. Affairs did not take a very favorable course in Frankfurt either (partly as a consequence of the Amsterdam adventure). In the summer of 1929 —shortly after the closing of the Amsterdam branch—Otto's brother-in-law Erich Elias was invited to open a Swiss agency of the Opekta-Werke, a subsidiary of the Frankfurt Pomosin-Werke, manufacturers and distributors of pectin, a gelling agent used mainly in the making of jams and jellies. He seized this opportunity and moved to Basle, followed by his wife and younger son in 1930, and by his older son in 1931.[21]

In the spring of 1925, at the age of thirty-six, Otto had married Edith Holländer, the daughter of a manufacturer from Aachen. Their first daughter, Margot Betti, was born on February 16, 1926, followed by Anneliese Marie, called Anne, on June 12, 1929.

The Great Depression, which began a few months after Erich Elias's departure, dealt fresh blows to the bank. There was another move, this time to modest rented premises—shared with another business—close to where Michael Frank had begun his business more than forty years earlier. The closure for an indefinite period of the Frankfurt Stock Exchange in the summer of 1931 and the simultaneous restrictions on dealings in foreign currency led to a further decline in activity.[22]

In 1932 the bank had another setback. In April, Otto's brother Herbert— a partner in the business since 1923 and described officially as "*der massgebliche Inhaber* [the proprietor with the controlling interest]"[23]—was suddenly arrested by income tax officials. He was accused of breaches of the 1931 *Bestimmung über den Effektenhandel mit dem Ausland* (Regulation Governing the Trade in Securities with Foreign Countries).

Toward the end of the previous year he had been approached by a stockbroker (later also referred to as a banker), who had offered him a large parcel of foreign shares as well as debentures in one or more German industrial concerns worth more than one million Reichsmarks. This man carried a passport issued by the German consulate in Luxembourg and gave an address in Karlsruhe. Although Herbert must have known that trading in foreign securities was unlawful, he accepted the offer and acted as agent. He sold the shares to various Frankfurt banks at the normal price and after deduction of the usual commission. The man who had offered him the securities appeared meanwhile to have vanished abroad. Otto told the *Frankfurter Zeitung* (from which paper we have taken the information above and below, as the court records have been destroyed) that the bank had trusted the man and had not known that the securities were of foreign origin. An appeal was lodged against the arrest.[24]

On May 14, Herbert was released.[25] The case was not heard until the following October. In a short report the *Frankfurter Zeitung* states that one Arnold Frank (no relation to the owners of the Michael Frank Bank), presumably a stockbroker, was fined 1,500 Reichsmarks; he had accepted shares to the value of nearly 130,000 Reichsmarks for sale, and by failing to report this transaction had committed a punishable offense. The main accused, Herbert Frank, did not appear in court. He had informed the public prosecutor that as a result of the delay in hearing the case he had suffered material and mental injury and as a consequence had moved abroad.[26] According to the *Frankfurter Zeitung*, the court did not fine him.[27] Having settled in Paris, Herbert Frank remained in France for nearly twenty years. During the war he was arrested and held in a camp for Jewish and non-Jewish stateless refugees in Gurs in Vichy France. He survived the war and returned to Paris, whence he moved in 1953 to St. Louis, a village on the Franco-Swiss border. In 1955 he joined his relatives in Basle.[28]

It is not quite clear what conclusions may be drawn from the fact that the court did not fine or sentence him. Herbert appears to have been thrown off balance by the whole affair. He had been—in one way or another—the victim of a swindler. Since the transaction was recorded normally in the bank's books, it would seem that he may not have fully realized that he had made himself culpable by his action. The fact that he bought the shares from a German, or at least from someone who presented himself credibly as a German, and not from a foreigner, may well have contributed to his misguided action. It is in any case regrettable that the court records have been lost.

Herbert resigned his directorship at the bank before the hearing. On October 1 his resignation was recorded at the Frankfurt *Amtsgericht* (district court) and at the Chamber of Commerce. On the same day Otto, who had previously held no responsible position in the bank, was appointed Herbert's successor.[29]

To the earlier setbacks of the bank—the difficulties during and after the First World War, the Amsterdam failure, the consequences of the 1929 Depression and of the foreign currency regulations in the summer of 1931, which proved a particularly hard blow for a bank involved to such an extent in foreign markets—there was now added a stain on the bank's name. Otto was the first to take the consequences: at the end of December he terminated the lease on his house, and when the term of notice had expired, in March 1933, he and his family moved in with his mother.[30]

The bank itself closed in the spring. The municipal elections held on March 12 brought the Nazis victory even in Frankfurt. One day later the left-wing liberal Jewish mayor was forced to resign and by the end of the month all Jewish employees of the city had been dismissed. On April 1 gangs of storm troopers (*Sturmabteilungen*, the SA) blocked the entrances to Jewish stores, businesses, lawyers' offices and medical practices.[31]

To Otto it was obvious that the bank would never revive. The events of April 1 did not make matters worse than they already were. However, the triumph of the Nazis gave him cause to worry deeply about the future of his family, and of his children in particular. After Easter, Jewish children were allotted separate benches at school, the better to distinguish them from their "Aryan" classmates, and it could only be a matter of time before all Jewish children would be segregated in special schools staffed only by Jewish teachers.[32] Otto had earlier toyed with the idea of emigrating and he now decided that the time had come. His first thought was of the Netherlands. He knew Amsterdam well and had at least one good friend there. Moreover he had heard from his brother-in-law Erich Elias that the Opekta-Werke wanted to expand the international market for pectin and were planning to open a Dutch retail agency. Thanks to the good offices of Elias, Otto was given the job of establishing a Dutch branch of Opekta.[33]

That summer he took his family from Frankfurt to Aachen, where he left his wife Edith and their two daughters with her mother. Otto himself went on to Amsterdam. In October his mother left Frankfurt too, and joined her daughter and son-in-law in Basle.[34] Robert moved—probably as early as 1933—to England, where he started an art and antiques business. He died in London in 1953, two months after the death of his mother in Switzerland.[35]

The bank had reached its end. On January 31, 1934, all its activities ceased. On September 26, 1938—a good six weeks before the *Reichskristallnacht* (Crystal Night)—the business was officially wound up and its name removed from the register.[36]

Amsterdam

In Amsterdam, Otto took up temporary accommodation as the subtenant of the second floor of a house at 24, Stadionkade.[37] He devoted himself with energy to two tasks: setting up and establishing the new business, and finding a suitable place for his family to live.

His first task was quickly accomplished. On September 15 the Nederlandsche Opekta Maatschappij N.V., in formation, established at 120, Nieuwe Zijds Voorburgwal with Otto Heinrich Frank as sole owner and director, was provisionally registered with the Amsterdam Chamber of Commerce and Industry. Under the heading "Type of Business" the entry reads: "The manufacture of, and trade in, fruit products, especially pectin." At the final registration, in July 1934, pectin alone was mentioned.[38]

It was some considerable time before that final registration could be effected. The original intention had been to open the Amsterdam business as a branch of Opekta, Cologne. However there had been a hitch: an established company, Pomosin in Utrecht (probably a subsidiary of the Pomosin-Werke in Frankfurt; in 1935 the name was changed to Pomosin-Import), had been supplying pectin to jam factories since 1928. Originally, Otto Frank had appointed the manager of this Utrecht concern, F. J. M. van Angeren, as managing director, but Van Angeren caused difficulties, so much so that, as early as August 1933, Otto Frank had decided to start an independent business under his own name, selling the product in small packets to housewives. Lacking the necessary means, he turned to his brother-in-law Erich Elias. Elias, who in the meantime had also become manager of a Swiss subsidiary of Pomosin (see p. 3), made him an interest-free loan of 15,000 guilders over ten years. Otto, for his part, had to enter into a licensing agreement with Pomosin which stipulated that he would pay 2½ percent of all profits for the right to use the Opekta trademark and that he would obtain all his pectin supplies from Opekta, Cologne. Of great importance for developments during the war was the provision that the shares of Opekta, Amsterdam would serve as security for the loan. Otto had the right to repay the debt at any time by surrendering the shares (which remained in his possession).[39]

Meanwhile, his family had been reunited. By the autumn of 1933 Otto had found a suitable apartment on the second floor of a building at 37, Merwedeplein. On August 16, the day Otto's name was entered at the Amsterdam Public Registration Office, Edith's name too was entered, although she and her children were to stay on in Aachen for another four months or so. On December 5 the

Merwedeplein, Amsterdam: Anne and a girl friend

Merwedeplein, Amsterdam. The Franks' apartment was between the dotted lines.
(© S. Finsy & Son, Amsterdam.)

move to Merwedeplein was officially registered. Two days later, the names of Margot and Anne were also registered at the new address. Their presence was not required for the registration, so this does not conflict with the recollections of the family that Edith and Margot came to Amsterdam in December 1933, but that Anne did not join them until March 1934.[40]

Otto's workforce was small at the beginning. He himself was the director. At the beginning of 1935, *mr.* A. R. W. M. Dunselman, an Amsterdam lawyer, was appointed supervisory director. Chief among the few members of the staff was Victor Gustav Kugler.

Kugler was born in 1900 in Hohenelbe, in what was then Austria-Hungary. During the First World War he served with the Austrian navy in the Adriatic.[41] In 1920 he came to Utrecht and worked for several years in a business there which sold pectin under license to the jam-making factories. He had at first been sent by this business to supervise the opening of the Amsterdam branch, but when his lack of success at this became apparent,[42] Otto took over from him. Kugler resigned from the Utrecht company to become what was more or less Otto's right-hand man.

The most pressing task for the new business was to persuade housewives, mainly in the countryside, to use pectin (which was sold either in small bottles or as a powder in little boxes or paper bags) in jam making. Various kinds of advertising material were issued (there were even several editions of an *Opekta Journal*) and advertisements were placed in the press. In 1938 an Opekta film was made and taken around regularly for showing at meetings of housewives' organizations. At the same time retail outlets, mainly pharmacists, had to be found throughout the country. At first Otto dealt with all these matters in person, but later a woman was taken on as a demonstrator at housewives' meetings, and

7

several traveling salesmen were engaged to call on the pharmacists. During the early years of the business one young woman was employed to assist in the office, together with a junior clerk.[43] After a comparatively short time she fell ill, and Otto appointed as temporary replacement someone who was to stay in his service until after the war: Hermine Santrouschitz. Hermine had been born in Vienna in 1909 and at the age of ten, after the First World War, she had been one of the thousands of—generally undernourished—Austrian children invited to stay in the Netherlands for a period to recuperate. Hermine (Miep) was adopted by a foster family in Amsterdam with whom she remained.

At first Otto gave her general routine office work, but occasionally she would accompany the demonstrator on her rounds, and she also answered questions about pectin from the public on the telephone or by letter. Gradually she took on the role of an all-rounder in the business.[44]

In the autumn of 1934 it was decided that more space was needed, and the business moved to new premises at 400, Singel.

It was not easy to boost the sales of pectin to a respectable figure. The business had been set up just too late to be able to profit from the 1933 harvest (and hence from the preserving season). By 1934, Otto was still receiving financial support, as we know from two letters of thanks he wrote to Armand (Hermann) Geiershöfer, his uncle, the owner of Albert Reinhard, the Luxembourg glove manufacturing company. As an illustration of his situation as he saw it, we can do no better than quote from one of these letters: "Though my income remains fairly modest, one must be satisfied to have found some way of earning a living and getting on."[45]

Nor did the business do particularly well during the next few years. Two other companies marketed a comparable product and competition proved arduous. In 1934 fresh impetus came in the form of an agreement with the N.V. Koninklijke Fabrieken v/h Brocades, Stheeman en Pharmacia of Meppel, which agreed, inter alia, to act as a wholesale distributor to pharmacists. In 1935, moreover, several dozen small wholesalers agreed to include pectin in their stock. For a long time the direct sale to housewives, mainly through pharmacists, accounted for only a small proportion of the turnover which, towards the outbreak of the Second World War, ran at between 48,000 and 65,000 guilders, depending largely on the results of the strawberry harvest. Before the war the net profit (after deduction of Otto's salary) exceeded 1,000 guilders per annum on just two occasions, and the initial losses incurred in 1933 had not yet been recouped by the end of 1939.[46]

An additional problem was that housewives largely confined their jam-making activities to the period following the fruit harvest. Thus while business overhead costs (apart from advertising) remained fairly constant throughout the year, revenue shrank appreciably during the "slack" season. Otto accordingly searched for a less seasonal activity into which to diversify.[47]

He found it in 1938. In the summer of 1937, Hermann van Pels, born of Dutch parents (he was also of Jewish descent) in 1890 in Gehrde, Germany, had fled with his wife and ten-year-old son from Osnabrück to the Netherlands. He was experienced in the preparation of many different herbs, and specialized in those used in sausage production.[48] On June 1, 1938, Johannes Kleiman applied for preliminary registration of the Handelsmaatschappij Pectacon N.V. in the Amsterdam Trade Registration Office. Kleiman's residence was given as the business address, and Kleiman was described as a director on the registration form. The company was stated to be concerned with the "trading in, and manufacturing

Opekta publicity truck (ca. 1936). (N.V. Nederlandsche Opekta Maatschappij.)

of, chemical and pharmaceutical products." At final registration, five months later, its activities were described as the "trading in, and manufacturing of, chemical products and provisions."[49] Otto Frank was now named as a director and Johannes Kleiman as a supervisory director, and the registered address as the premises into which Opekta had moved four years earlier. Since Kleiman had already been keeping Otto's books, he now became bookkeeper for both companies. Van Pels was taken on as herbal specialist.[50]

It is not clear whether it was Otto Frank or Kleiman who first made contact with Van Pels. It seems more likely that it was Kleiman; however, since Van Pels had been living very near the Franks since the middle of May, he might easily have met Otto before June 1.

In any case, Otto had found a way of diversifying his business. The future looked fairly bright. Goods were arriving from Hungary and Belgium, to which last country a modest export business was also being built up. It is said that following the autumn of 1939, as a result of the outbreak of war, a "marked business revival" took place. Opekta's sales figures, however, do not reflect this fact: in 1940 the turnover was again about 48,000 guilders. Still, very little was spent on advertising in 1940 and collaboration with Pectacon led to a considerable saving in overhead costs. The credit balance increased, and 6,000 guilders could be set aside as a reserve for 1941, leaving a net profit of 138 guilders.[51] At the beginning of the German occupation, Opekta employed a staff of six and Pectacon a staff of five,[52] including three or four traveling salesmen who called respectively on pharmacists (for the pectin) and on butchers (for the herbs). The office and warehouse staff worked for both companies.[53] In the summer of 1937, Miep Santrouschitz was joined in the office by young Bep Voskuijl. Kugler (who had become a naturalized Dutchman in May 1938) was instructed in the mixing of herbs by Van Pels, and he also acted as the main link between management and the warehouse staff responsible for the milling and packing of the herbs. In June 1940 he was appointed proxy for Pectacon.[54]

For several months the businesses remained untouched by the war and the occupation. The import of pectin continued normally, and the supply of herbs also posed few problems. In time, however, recourse was had to the use of substitutes. By August 1944 there was still a staff of nine, including three traveling salesmen.[55] Meanwhile, however, the occupying power had intervened drastically in the continued existence of the businesses.

German Measures and Their Consequences

The first anti-Jewish measures passed by the Nazi occupiers in the summer and autumn of 1940 did not affect the Frank family, the Jewish staff of their companies or most of their Jewish acquaintances directly. This was all to change during October of that year. Of crucial importance to Jewish businesses was the German decree of October 22, 1940, signed by the *Reichskommissar* for the Occupied Netherlands, Dr. Arthur Seyss-Inquart, and entitled *Verordnung über die Anmeldung von Unternehmen* (Decree Concerning the Registration of Companies).[56] The decree called for notification to the *Wirtschaftsprüfstelle* (Bureau of Economic Investigation) of all enterprises which "on the ninth day of May 1940 [. . .] or at a later date" were wholly or significantly (by which was meant more than 25 percent of the capital) owned by Jews, under predominantly Jewish influence, or in which at least one of the directors, legal representatives or members of the supervisory board was a Jew.

Otto and his colleagues had, like their Jewish friends and acquaintances, many of whom had also come from Germany and had lived under the Hitler regime for different lengths of time, been following developments in Germany very carefully. They realized that this decree was only the first step on the road to the complete *Entjudung* ("dejudification") of Dutch businesses as had happened with German concerns. The demonstrations outside Jewish businesses by storm troopers in Frankfurt on April 1, 1933, had been one of the first steps along a similar road.

On October 23—one day after the "Aryanization" decree—a notary in Hilversum (where Victor Kugler lived) was asked, at Otto's instigation, to register a new company, La Synthèse N.V. Kugler was given as its managing director and J. A. Gies, a municipal official in Amsterdam and for some years Miep Santrouschitz's fiancé, as supervisory director. Like Miep, Jan Gies too had become a friend of the Frank family. The paid-up shares (twenty 100-guilder shares out of a nominal capital of one hundred shares) were issued to Kugler and Gies. The business was thus wholly "Aryan," at least officially, but in practice the actual ownership of the company remained vested in Otto Frank. The company's objective was "to manufacture and trade in chemical and pharmaceutical products, foodstuffs and table luxuries, as well as to participate in similar undertakings, all in the broadest sense." On May 8, 1941, the name of the company was changed to N.V. Handelsvereniging Gies & Co. The objectives of the new business were strikingly similar to those of Pectacon but were at the same time adapted to the circumstances created by the occupying force.[57]

On November 27, 1940, both Opekta and Pectacon were officially registered with the *Wirtschaftsprüfstelle* in accordance with the decree of October 22. As far as Opekta was concerned, Otto stated that he was the sole proprietor and

Singel 400

Bilanz zum
31.12.39

Anzahl der Arbeitnehmer:

a. Art u. Nennbetrag der Beteiligung
Aard en nominale waarde van de deelname

geen

geen

geen

geen

Ich (Wir) versichern(n), obige Angaben nach besten Wissen und Gewissen vollständig und richtig gemacht zu haben.

Amsterdam, den 27 November   1940.

HANDELSMIJ PECTACON N.V.

Pectacon registration at the Wirtschaftsprüfstelle. (Netherlands State Institute for War Documentation.)

11

that he had contributed a capital of 10,000 guilders. With respect to Pectacon —which had a share capital of 10,000 guilders—he stated that only 2,000 guilders of the share capital had been taken up by himself and that the remaining shares had not been issued. On December 2 he sent an express letter with further details, together with an apology for his failure to provide them in time because of the relocation of the business.[58]

And indeed both Opekta and Pectacon had moved to a new address on December 1, 1940, an address that was later to become renowned throughout the world: 263, Prinsengracht.

In March 1941 the *Reichskommissar* issued a new decree, this time covering "the treatment of businesses subject to registration,"[59] and specifying the precise implementation of the decree of October 22, 1940. This *Wirtschaftsentjudungsverordnung* (Economic Dejudification Decree) stipulated *inter alia* that any changes in a business that might obviate the obligation to report that business as laid down in October 1940 must have (German) approval (Article 2), and that all relevant changes made between May 9, 1940, and the day that the decree came into operation (March 12, 1941) were subject to retroactive German approval (Article 3). Such approval had to be applied for within a month of the proclamation of the new decree (that is, before April 12).

We shall describe separately the quite distinct actions taken in Otto Frank's two businesses to circumvent their enforced "Aryanization" by the Germans. For purely chronological reasons, we shall look first at Pectacon.

What, they wondered in the Prinsengracht, would be the best way of responding to the new decree: to request approval for changes still to be made or to face the Germans with a *fait accompli* and request approval for changes that had already been made?

In the case of Pectacon, it was decided to take the second course. To that end a fictitious annual meeting of the board (Otto Frank) and of the supervisory board (Kleiman), ostensibly convened on February 13, decided to issue the outstanding 8,000 guilders' worth of shares. On April 4 these shares were taken up by the two founders of the business, Kleiman and the ever-obliging *mr.* Dunselman; at the same time Otto resigned from the board, Kleiman taking his place and *mr.* Dunselman following Kleiman as supervisory director. From that date, the business was completely in "Aryan" hands, except for the 2,000 guilders' worth of shares (less than the 25 percent stipulated in the decree of October 1940) which remained legally in Otto's possession. The application, as we must infer from what followed (no correspondence on the subject has been preserved), was made only just in time.

The ruse, however, did not work. From an *Ergänzungsprotokoll zum Protokoll über die 8. Planungssitzung vom 22. Juli 1941* (Supplementary minute to the minutes of the 8th Planning Session held on July 22, 1941) it appears that the Germans had convened a special meeting devoted to a review of businesses in the *Wirtschaftsgruppe Gewürze und Trockenfrüchte* (Spices and Dried Fruits Economic Section). Eighteen of the nineteen businesses in the "*Gruppe der kleinen Firmen* [Small Firms Group]" in this section were ordered to be liquidated. One of these eighteen was Pectacon.[60] A draft of the final report, dated July 8, 1942, submitted by the Deutsche Revisions- und Treuhand A.G. (German Audit and Trust Company) to the *Wirtschaftsprüfstelle*, makes it perfectly clear that the Germans had seen through the stratagem devised by Frank, Kleiman and Dunselman. Writing about the measures taken by Pectacon on February 13 and April 4, 1941, the Germans declared:

"These measures were intended to create the impression that most of the capital as well as the directorship of the business were in Aryan hands. Because the decisions taken at the annual general meeting on February 13, 1941, which according to VO 48/41 are subject to retrospective approval, were not approved and therefore have no legal validity, the General Commissioner for Finance and Economic Affairs, Division for Economic Investigation, has, on September 12, appointed *mr*. Karl Wolters as trustee of the company under VO 48/41, and has charged him with its liquidation."[61]

K. O. M. Wolters, an Amsterdam advocate and attorney, had been a member of the NSB (the Dutch Nazi Party) since 1933. During the Occupation he joined such Nazi organizations as the *Rechtsfront* (Legal Front), the *Nederlandsch-Duitsche Kultuurgemeenschap* (Dutch-German Cultural Union) and the *Economisch Front* (Economic Front), in which latter organization he held a leading position. In 1941 and 1942 he was appointed liquidator of nineteen Jewish businesses in various parts of the Netherlands.[62]

Although he was obviously a convinced and active Nazi, declarations in his dossier by Jewish owners and the staff of the Jewish firms liquidated by him show that, whenever possible, he tried to protect those he dealt with against the Germans. Thus Otto Frank and Kleiman declared after the war that, when Wolters asked them to see him in his office shortly after his appointment, he gave them "eight to ten days" to prepare for the liquidation. They used this period to wind up the company with the help of a broker and to transfer the entire stock and all the machinery to Gies & Co. Otto Frank added: "I myself owned shares in the company which I never surrendered, and hold to this day. As a result it was possible to save all the machinery, etc. Gies & Co. then set up business at our address, 263, Prinsengracht."[63] Obviously the taxable value and hence the prices given for the supplies and the machinery, as well as for the warehouse equipment, which was also transferred to Gies & Co., were kept very low. This was also the conclusion of the Deutsche Revisions- und Treuhand A.G. (whose final report has been lost), which described the writing off by about 20 percent of the book value of the machinery and the warehouse installation as "very unfavorable," and criticized Kleiman's explanation of the low proceeds from the supplies. "*Unbefriedigend*" (unsatisfactory) was the term used.[64]

On September 30, 1941, Wolters put the funds of the business at just over 22,000 guilders, nearly 17,000 guilders of which was in cash and 5,600 guilders owed by sundry debtors. This sum—the total turnover in 1939 was 40,000 guilders—was largely derived from the sale of the machinery and all of the supplies to Gies & Co. In any case, on April 15, 1942, when Wolters closed his examination of the books, the company's liquid assets stood at 17,000 guilders. Of these, 5,000 guilders were paid out to Kleiman and 3,000 guilders to Dunselman for their shares. Clearly, these sums must have been paid by Otto Frank and later returned to him by Kleiman and Dunselman. That left 9,000 guilders. After deduction of the liquidation charges there remained the sum of 7,712.83 guilders, which was deposited by Pectacon in the Nederlandse Bank on May 11, 1943. There matters were held up deliberately or otherwise: by the decrees of the *Reichskommissar* of August 8, 1941,[65] and May 21, 1942,[66] all Jewish credits had to be transferred to a bank under German supervision, namely Lippmann, Rosenthal & Co., registered at Sarphatistraat, Amsterdam, but the amount transferred by Pectacon to the Nederlandse Bank after liquidation was kept by that bank until July 23, 1947, when it was paid over to the "*Liquidatie van Verwaltung Sarphatistraat*" (LVVS) (Liquidation of the Sarphatistraat Administration), an organization founded after the war and charged, among other things, with the repayment of Jewish funds deposited with Lippmann, Rosenthal & Co.[67] The credit balance determined by the LVVS was duly paid back to Otto Frank, the rightful owner.

On May 7, 1943, Pectacon was officially wound up, but business continued as usual and at the same address in the name of Gies & Co.

Opekta's was a completely different story. From the available data it appears that for a long time no effort at all was made to save the enterprise. Not until June 1941 was a new business—obviously a successor to La Synthèse—registered with the Amsterdam Chamber of Commerce. This was a partnership trading under the name of Handelsvereniging Gebrs. Kleiman (Kleiman Bros. Trading Co.), and its registered address was Johannes Kleiman's residence. The objectives of the company were given as "trade in, and manufacture of, chemical articles, etc."[68] However, it very quickly emerged that this company did not have to act as a cover for Opekta.

At the beginning of October 1941, Otto Frank received a letter from a man called Tosin in Basle, which makes it clear that Otto's brother-in-law, Erich Elias, who had been running the Opekta agency in Switzerland since 1929, and at the time of his loan to Otto had also been manager of the Rohstoff Verkehrs A.G. (Rovag), a Swiss subsidiary of Pomosin, had lent money to Otto on behalf of that company. Otto's formal letter of August 5, 1933 to Erich Elias must therefore have been sent to confirm this arrangement.

Tosin, who had meanwhile taken over the running of Rovag, and with it the loan to Otto, now asked him to reconfirm the agreement and at the same time drew his attention to the fact that the license fee had not been paid for years.[69]

In his reply Otto pointed out that 5,000 guilders of the original debt had since been repaid. More relevant to the "Aryanization" problem, however, was his claim that his part of the agreement had, "at the request of the gentlemen in Frankfurt," been taken over by mr. Dunselman, so that Otto himself was no longer responsible.[70] He did not, however, repudiate his debt to Rovag in any way.

The sequel came two months later. On December 12 an extraordinary general meeting of the shareholders of Opekta was held in the offices of mr. Dunselman and, since he was the company's only supervisory director, as usual under his chairmanship. And as usual Otto was the only other person present (apart from a stenographer).

After stating that the allocation of the company's share capital, consisting of twenty fully paid-up 500-guilder shares, had to be reviewed, the chairman reported that a letter dated December 11, 1941, had been received from the director of the company, Otto Frank, in which Mr. Frank let it be known that he no longer wished to continue as a director of the company, and for that reason tendered his resignation.

At the suggestion of the chairman it was decided to appoint Johannes Kleiman director effective immediately; mr. Dunselman also mentioned that he had had discussions with two gentlemen from the Pomosin-Werke, "who . . . are at present in this country and have taken the steps needed to Aryanize the company, to which end they had discussions with the appropriate bodies in The Hague, as they had reported to the authorities in writing in a letter dated December 12, 1941 [. . .]."

14

The two gentlemen from Frankfurt, as the minutes also stated, added that approval of their request "can be expected with great confidence."[71]

In their letter of December 12, 1941, to the *Wirtschaftsprüfstelle*, the gentlemen from Pomosin had given a detailed account of the financial relations between Pomosin and Opekta, Amsterdam which in substance came down to the fact that the Pomosin-Werke, and not Otto Frank, were the real owners of the Opekta, Amsterdam shares (through Rovag), and this on the basis of an agreement made in 1933. Pending further investigation, the gentlemen proposed to the *Wirtschaftsprüfstelle* that they should deposit the shares held by Otto Frank with the Handelstrust West N.V. in Amsterdam, a Dutch mainstay of the Dresdner Bank, which was frequently used by the German administrators of Jewish businesses to be "Aryanized." Meanwhile the *Wirtschaftsprüfstelle* was asked to approve the appointment of Kleiman as a director.[72]

The changes in the board were immediately reported to the Chamber of Commerce.[73] The first threat to Opekta had thus been warded off, at least temporarily, because the *Wirtschaftsprüfstelle* had not yet started its "Aryanization" program. Kleiman could therefore continue the business. Not all developments, however, were entirely in Otto's favor. A claim to the business had been made by Pomosin, and Otto may well have wondered whether that claim might not be pursued after the war as well.

As the war proceeded, two further events occurred to which we shall now refer in brief.

At a *Planungssitzung* (planning session) of the *Wirtschaftsprüfstelle* held on March 12, 1942, it was decided, as part of the "Aryanization" program, to hand Opekta over to the owner/director of one of Opekta's competitors.[74]

This decision, however, was never implemented. No doubt Pomosin heard about it and appealed to the *Wirtschaftsprüfstelle* once again. The visit Anne Frank mentions in her diary entry for April 1, 1943, was probably concerned with this subject, and hence with relations between Pomosin and Opekta.

The last document that we found was a copy of a letter dated July 1, 1944, from the *Wirtschaftsprüfstelle* to Opekta, stating that the resignation of "the Jewish director Otto Frank" in December 1941 was approved, and that as a result "Jews no longer exert any personal or financial influence on this company." It followed that the company was no longer "liable to registration in terms of VO 189/1940."[75]

The fact that the business was not transferred compulsorily following its "self-Aryanization" could only mean that the Germans had implicitly recognized the claims of the Pomosin-Werke.

The "Aryanization" of Dutch business life caused Otto Frank and his associates some extremely tense moments and long periods of uncertainty, but ultimately very little damage. This was due to the shrewdness of Otto himself and of his associates Kleiman and Kugler (with the help of Jan Gies), to the not very determined *Verwalter* (administrator appointed by the Germans), and not least to Pomosin's intervention, about which we still do not know whether it was undertaken in an attempt to save Otto and his business or out of self-interest. Nor must we forget that the lawyer from Amsterdam, *mr.* Dunselman, was always ready to render advice and practical assistance, and constantly played an important supporting role in the background.

In the summer of 1942 the staff at 263, Prinsengracht consisted of Otto

Frank, Kleiman, Kugler, Van Pels, Miep Gies and Bep Voskuijl in the office section, and Bep's father, who was in charge of the warehouse. In addition there were two warehousemen, who disappeared soon afterwards and played no further part in what took place. There was also a Jewish pharmacist, Arthur Lewinsohn, who would come once or twice a week and perform various tests in the annexe at the back of the main building. When the Franks' plans for going into hiding took firm shape, he was told that the annexe was to be used for storage, and he was assigned a small room in another part of the building. He made no more appearances after about the autumn of 1942. Lewinsohn survived the war.[76]

The life of Otto Frank's family in Amsterdam proceeded along relatively peaceful paths. The apartment building which had gone up in Merwedeplein a few years before their arrival clearly suited them well; despite the wide choice of accommodation available in Amsterdam in the thirties, they made no move to leave. And the place was also large enough to accommodate Grandmother Holländer when she fled from Aachen to join them in the Netherlands in 1939 (in 1934 Edith Frank had paid several visits to her in Aachen with one or both girls).[77] Grandmother Holländer lived with the Frank family until her death in January 1942.[78] There were close bonds with other family members as well, letters were exchanged regularly, and the children were expected to send letters or cards on birthdays and other events to Switzerland. Moreover, Otto's mother Alice and brother Herbert came to Amsterdam on one or more occasions.[79]

The Franks' circle of friends grew steadily as well, and their home became a popular meeting place. Kleiman was their oldest friend; Miep and, later, Jan Gies (they married in the summer of 1941) were invited regularly. Though they seemed to have fewer social contacts with Kugler, with Herman van Pels and his wife, or with Bep, they were on the best of terms with all of them.

The dentist Dr. Friedrich Pfeffer, who later joined them in their hiding place, also belonged to their circle of acquaintances. Miep Gies first met him at the Franks' home in about 1939; Pfeffer and her own dentist shared a surgery. He was born in 1889 in Giessen in Germany, and on December 19, 1938, he was registered as a Jewish refugee in Amsterdam, where he lived with Charlotta Kaletta, a non-Jewish woman. By virtue of the notorious Nuremberg laws, intimate relations between Jews and non-Jews had been declared a criminal offense in Germany, and they feared the extension of these laws to the occupied Netherlands. Shortly after the German invasion Pfeffer therefore changed his address, at least officially. The couple made desperate but vain attempts to marry, since so-called mixed-marriage partners had a reasonable chance of being exempted from deportation. Finally Miep interceded with Otto Frank on Pfeffer's behalf, asking him to allow the dentist to join them in their hiding place. At the same time she saw to it that letters and parcels from Charlotta Kaletta—who did not know where Pfeffer had gone into hiding—reached him and that his letters reached her.[80]

In 1953, Charlotta Kaletta, under the terms of a law governing the recognition of the marriage of racially and politically persecuted persons, passed in the German Federal Republic in 1950, had her marriage to Pfeffer retroactively recorded in the Berlin *Standesamt* (Registry Office).[81]

There were other acquaintances as well. As with most German emigrants to the Netherlands, their shared past and experiences made them seek each other out, no matter how different their backgrounds or occupations.

In addition Edith Frank had made many new personal contacts in the liberal

Diese Bestätigung sorgfältig bewahren,
bei Besuchen vorzulegen und bei
Korrespondenz untenstehende Nummer angeben.   Amsterdam, den   20 JAN. 1942

Meldenummer: Name: Frank, Otto
1497a   Strasse: Merwedeplein 37
                Wohnort: Amsterdam

Diese Bestätigung sorgfältig bewahren,
Bei Besuchen vorzulegen und bei
Korrespondenz untenstehende Nummer angeben.   Amsterdam, den   20 JAN. 1942

Meldenummer: Name: Frank-Holländer, Edith
1497b   Strasse: Merwedeplein 37
                Wohnort: Amsterdam

Diese Bestätigung sorgfältig bewahren,
Bei Besuchen vorzulegen und bei
Korrespondenz untenstehende Nummer angeben.   Amsterdam, den   20 JAN. 1942

Meldenummer: Name: Frank, Margot
1497c   Strasse: Merwedeplein 37
                Wohnort: Amsterdam

Diese Bestätigung sorgfältig bewahren,
Bei Besuchen vorzulegen und bei
Korrespondenz untenstehende Nummer angeben.   Amsterdam, den   20 JAN. 1942

Meldenummer: Name: Frank, Anneliese
1497d   Strasse: Merwedeplein 37
                Wohnort: Amsterdam

Hat sich zur Bearbeitung seines Antrages auf Genehmigung zur Auswanderung
aus den besetzten niederländischen Gebieten bei uns einschreiben lassen.
Es wird darauf hingewiesen, dass auf Grund dieser Anmeldung von uns zur
Stellung des förmlichen Antrags noch besonders aufgerufen werden wird
und diesem Aufruf Folge geleistet werden muss.

JOODSCHE RAAD VOOR AMSTERDAM
AUSWANDERUNGSABTEILUNG

Nr. 2224

Name:
Naam: Frank

Vorname:
Voornaam: Frau, Sara, Sara, Sara.

Antrag überreicht am:
Aanvraag afgegeven op: 27 JAN. 1942

145592   K 287

Registration certificates issued to applicants for emigration from the occupied Netherlands by the Jewish Council and the Zentralstelle für jüdische Auswanderung.

Jewish congregation, and her two daughters, too, had each built up a circle of girl friends—a small one for Margot, and a very large one for Anne.

And so they lived in a modern suburb, on a quiet little square in the south of Amsterdam, their German past receding ever further; they felt at home in their new country and their new apartment. And the children in particular became more and more Dutch.

The Nazi threat continued to loom, of course, and increased towards the end of the thirties. What with his family connections and many friends in various countries, Otto Frank could undoubtedly have taken his family to England, the United States or Switzerland but, like so many others, he felt sure that the Nazis would respect Dutch neutrality. Moreover, and this was an important consideration for him, he had built up a new, independent life in Amsterdam. Elsewhere, he would have had to ask others for assistance for himself and his family. And so he stayed on in Amsterdam.[82]

In May 1940 the Franks were trapped by Hitler's armies. Escape was no longer possible. Pressure grew on Jews in the Netherlands. They were faced with the news of the big police roundup in the old Jewish quarter of Amsterdam on February 22 and 23, 1941. They were to suffer under the avalanche of anti-Jewish decrees that were proclaimed in 1941 and 1942, their freedom of movement being increasingly restricted.[83] Following the summer vacation of 1941 the two Frank girls had to transfer to a Jewish school, where all the teachers and pupils were Jewish and where they were completely cut off from non-Jewish children of their own age. From four stenciled forms (one for each member of the family) submitted to the Emigration Section of the Amsterdam Jewish Council, dated January 20, 1942, it appears that Otto Frank made a fresh attempt to escape the Nazis' clutches with his wife and children.[84] But from the beginning of May 1942 the future of Otto, Edith, Margot and Anne Frank was marked by a yellow star.

On June 12, Anne began to keep her diary.

Notes

Unless otherwise stated, all documents mentioned in the Notes are kept in the archives of the Netherlands State Institute for War Documentation.

[1] Amsterdam Public Registration Office, February 16, 1982.
[2] Frankfurt Chamber of Industry and Commerce, February 21, 1985. The booklet entitled *Früher wohnten wir in Frankfurt . . . Frankfurt am Main und Anne Frank* ["We Used to Live in Frankfurt . . . Frankfurt-am-Main and Anne Frank"], 1985, published by the Frankfurt History Museum, states that the bank did not become an "*offene Handelsgesellschaft* [registered partnership]" until about 1896 or 1897.
[3] *Früher . . .* , p. 13f.
[4] Ibid., p. 23.
[5] Ibid., p. 24; Elfriede Frank-Markovits, March 16, 1985.
[6] *Früher . . .* , p. 25.
[7] Ibid.
[8] According to the Frankfurt Chamber of Industry and Commerce (March 5, 1985), the owners in 1916 were: Alice Betty Frank, née Stern, "widow & 4 children."
[9] *Früher . . .* , p. 23.
[10] Ibid., p. 27.
[11] Frankfurt Chamber of Industry and Commerce, March 5, 1985.

[12] *Früher* . . . , p. 27.

[13] Amsterdam Chamber of Commerce and Industry, M. Frank & Zonen file.

[14] According to the Amsterdam Public Registration Office, Otto Frank was not registered in Amsterdam during the 1920s.

[15] See note 13.

[16] According to the Amsterdam Public Registration Office, Heuskin, too, did not register at the given address. Further information in Amsterdam Chamber of Commerce and Industry, M. Frank & Zonen file. It seems most likely that Otto was introduced to Heuskin by a relation who also lived in Luxembourg (cf. p. 8).

[17] J. Houwink ten Cate, "*Amsterdam als financieel centrum, 1914–1931* [Amsterdam as a Financial Center in 1914–1931]" in *De Florijn*, May 1984, Vol. 7, No. 5.

[18] Amsterdam Chamber of Commerce and Industry, M. Frank & Zonen file.

[19] Ibid.; as Elfriede Frank-Markovits told us on November 28, 1985, he must also have paid frequent visits to other friends and relatives abroad. These visits were said to be mainly social.

[20] See note 18.

[21] *Staatsarchiv Kanton Basel-Stadt*, October 31, 1985; *Früher* . . . , p. 65.

[22] *Früher* . . . , p. 66.

[23] *Frankfurter Zeitung*, April 23, 1932.

[24] Ibid.

[25] Ibid., May 14, 1932.

[26] Ibid., October 12, 1932.

[27] Ibid.

[28] Elfriede Frank-Markovits, November 28, 1985; *Mairie St. Louis (Haut Rhin), Bureau de l'état civil*, November 7, 1985.

[29] Frankfurt Chamber of Industry and Commerce, March 5, 1985.

[30] *Früher* . . . , p. 74.

[31] Ibid.

[32] Ibid., p. 77; *Stadtarchiv Frankfurt-am-Main*, September 28, 1984.

[33] Ibid.; also statements by Elfriede Frank-Markovits, Basle, and by Hermine (Miep) Gies-Santrouschitz, Amsterdam.

[34] *Staatsarchiv Kanton Basel-Stadt*, October 31 and November 11, 1985.

[35] Elfriede Frank-Markovits, November 28, 1985; Otto Frank to Johannes Kleiman, Amsterdam, May 24, 1953.

[36] Frankfurt Chamber of Industry and Commerce, March 5, 1985.

[37] Amsterdam Public Registration Office.

[38] Amsterdam Chamber of Commerce and Industry, N.V. Nederlandsche Opekta Maatschappij file.

[39] Utrecht Chamber of Commerce, F. J. M. van Angeren file; records of Deutsche Revisions- und Treuhand A.G. (DRT); Otto Frank to Erich Elias, August 5, 1933; records of N.V. Nederlandsche Opekta Maatschappij.

[40] *Früher* . . . , p. 77; cf. p. 189 below.

[41] Ernst Schnabel, *Anne Frank. Spur eines Kindes* (Frankfurt am Main: Fischer, 1958), p. 81. (English translation, *The Footsteps of Anne Frank* [London: Longmans Green, 1959]). We have been unable to discover the sources and notes on which Schnabel based his book. Since it contains various errors, all quotations from it should be treated with reservation.

[42] Hermine (Miep) Gies-Santrouschitz, February 19, 1985.

[43] N.V. Nederlandsche Opekta Maatschappij, Minutes 1935–1954; Hermine (Miep) Gies-Santrouschitz, February 19, 1985.

[44] See note 42.

[45] Otto Frank to Armand Geiershöfer, April 9, 1934. Records of N.V. Nederlandsche Opekta Maatschappij; Elfriede Frank-Markovits, November 28, 1985.

[46] N.V. Nederlandsche Opekta Maatschappij, Minutes 1935–1954.

[47] Ibid.

[48] Hermine (Miep) Gies-Santrouschitz, February 19, 1985.

[49] Amsterdam Chamber of Commerce and Industry, Handelsmaatschappij Pectacon N.V. file.

[50] Hermine (Miep) Gies-Santrouschitz, February 19, 1985.

[51] Otto Frank to Dr. Louis de Jong, June 15, 1957; N.V. Nederlandsche Opekta Maatschappij, Minutes 1935–1954.

[52] Records of Deutsche Revisions- und Treuhand A.G. (DRT); Opekta and Pectacon files.

[53] N.V. Nederlandsche Opekta Maatschappij, Minutes 1935–1954.

[54] Amsterdam Chamber of Commerce and Industry, Pectacon file.

[55] Hermine (Miep) Gies-Santrouschitz, February 27, 1985.

[56] *Verordnungsblatt für die besetzten niederländischen Gebiete*, VO. 189/1940, pp. 546–52.

[57] Supplement to the *Nederlandsche Staatscourant (Government Gazette)*, August 13, 1941, No. 156; J. A. Gies, December 12, 1985.

[58] Records of Deutsche Revisions- und Treuhand A.G. (DRT): Opekta and Pectacon files.

[59] *Verordnungsblatt für die besetzten niederländischen Gebiete*, VO. 48/1941, pp. 164–70.

[60] Records of *Wirtschaftsprüfstelle*, 44/2.

[61] Records of Deutsche Revisions- und Treuhand A.G. (DRT): Pectacon file.

[62] Doc. 1, *mr.* K. O. M. Wolters.

[63] Ibid.

[64] Records of Deutsche Revisions- und Treuhand A.G. (DRT): Pectacon file.

[65] *Verordnungsblatt für die besetzten niederländischen Gebiete*, VO. 148/1941, pp. 624–28.

[66] Ibid., VO. 58/1942, pp. 289–300.

[67] Summary of O. H. Frank account as of May 13, 1952, sent to Otto Frank by LVVS.

[68] Extract from the *Handelsregister (Trade Register)*, June 13, 1941. Records of N.V. Nederlandsche Opekta Maatschappij.

[69] M. Tosin (Basle) to Otto Frank, October 7, 1941. *Algemeen Rijksarchief* (General State Archives of the Netherlands), records of *Nederlands Beheers Instituut* (Board for the Administration of Enemy and Collaborators' Property).

[70] Otto Frank to M. Tosin, October 17, 1941. *Algemeen Rijksarchief* (General State Archives of the Netherlands), records of *Nederlands Beheers Instituut* (Board for the Administration of Enemy and Collaborators' Property).

[71] N.V. Nederlandsche Opekta Maatschappij, Minutes 1935–1954.

[72] Pomosin-Werke to *Wirtschaftsprüfstelle*, December 12, 1941. Records of N.V. Nederlandsche Opekta Maatschappij.

[73] Amsterdam Chamber of Commerce and Industry, Opekta file.

[74] Records of *Wirtschafsprüfstelle*, 44/3.

[75] Copy in records of Deutsche Revisions- und Treuhand A.G. (DRT): Opekta file.

[76] Hermine (Miep) Gies-Santrouschitz, April 5, 1984; Amsterdam Public Registration Office.

[77] Otto Frank to Armand (Hermann) Geiershöfer, July 9, 1934. Records of N.V. Nederlandsche Opekta Maatschappij.

[78] Amsterdam Public Registration Office; passport of Rosa Sara Holländer-Stern. Anne Frank Foundation, Amsterdam.

[79] Elfriede Frank-Markovits, November 28, 1985; Hermine (Miep) Gies-Santrouschitz, December 12, 1985.

[80] Declaration by Otto Frank, September 4, 1951 (in the possession of J. A. Gies); Hermine (Miep) Gies-Santrouschitz, April 18 and December 12, 1985.

[81] Amsterdam Public Registration Office, December 16, 1985; University of Amsterdam, Centre of Foreign Law and Private International Law, December 16, 1985.

[82] Elfriede Frank-Markovits, November 28, 1985; Hermine (Miep) Gies-Santrouschitz, December 12, 1985.

[83] For these measures, see the *Verordnungen* of the *Reichskommissar*, the *Anordnungen* of the *Generalkommissar für das Sicherheitswesen* and of the *Höhere SS- und Polizeiführer* (Commissioner-General for Security and Chief of SS and Police), Hanns Albin Rauter, and the *Joodsche Weekblad (Jewish Weekly)*, 1941–42. See also Jacob Presser, *Ashes in the Wind* (London, 1968; New York, 1969, as *The Destruction of Dutch Jews*); Louis de Jong, *Het Koninkrijk der Nederlanden in de Tweede Wereldoorlog* (The Kingdom of the Netherlands during the Second World War), especially Volumes 4–6 (The Hague: Nijhoff 1972, 1974 and 1975); and K. P. L. Berkley, *Overzicht van het ontstaan en het streven van den Joodse Raad voor Amsterdam (Survey of the Origins and Objectives of the Amsterdam Jewish Council)*, [Amsterdam], no publisher's name given [1946].

[84] Anne Frank Foundation, Amsterdam.

The Arrest

HARRY PAAPE

Friday, August 4, 1944. The great Allied offensive, which was to lead to the liberation of almost all France and Belgium within a month, had begun at the end of July. The major breakthrough had come nearly two months after the landings on the Normandy coast. Every day Radio Oranje and the BBC marveled at the astonishing advance of U. S. General Patton's tanks. The whole of occupied Western Europe was filled with joyful expectation. Otto Frank and his family had spent two years and thirty days in the so-called "Secret Annexe."

The account we are about to give of the events at 263, Prinsengracht is entirely based on reports, oral and written, by people personally involved in them. The violent emotions to which they were all exposed, and their awareness at the time they made their statements of the subsequent fate of the deported, easily account for the fact that their respective memories of August 4 differed at times, and that some of them, questioned more than once, failed to use exactly the same words when repeating their observations. In the circumstances, we can do no better than try—on the basis of their statements—to give as faithful as possible a reconstruction of the events, fully realizing that there may well have been discrepancies in the details of sequences recalled.

It was a pleasant, warm summer's day, and the doors of the warehouse in the Prinsengracht stood wide open. The two warehousemen, W. G. van Maaren and L. Hartog, were busy at their work. Between ten o'clock and half past ten a German car drew up. A uniformed German and several[1] Dutchmen in civilian clothes got out of the car and ran into the building. One of them asked Van Maaren a question. "Upstairs," Van Maaren replied, pointing with his thumb. While one of the men stayed behind in the warehouse, the German and the rest went up to the offices on the next floor.[2]

One of them opened the door to the main office. There he found Miep Gies, Bep Voskuijl and Kleiman.[3] This man, Miep reported many years later, "was holding a pistol which he pointed at us, saying: 'Just sit there quietly and don't go away.' From the noise in the corridor, I could tell there were others in the building."[4]

And Bep: "He had a long, dried-up, yellowish face [. . .] I heard Mrs. Gies say: 'Bep, we've had it.' We sat there petrified."[5] The man went out again.

Kugler, who emigrated to Canada in 1955, was officially questioned after the war about these events. Ernst Schnabel quotes a letter addressed to him by Kugler (probably written in 1957):

Suddenly a staff-sergeant of the "Green Police" and three Dutch civilians entered my office and asked me for the owner of the house. I gave them the name and address of our landlord. No, they said to me, we want the person who is in charge here. That is myself, I replied. Then, "Come along," they ordered.

The police wanted to see the storerooms in the front part of the building, and I opened the doors for them. All will be well if they don't want to see anything else, I thought. But after the sergeant had looked at everything, he went out into the corridor, ordering me again to come along. At the end of the corridor they drew their revolvers all at once and the sergeant ordered me to push aside the bookcase at the head of the corridor and to open the door behind it. I said: "But there's only a bookcase there!" At that he turned nasty, for he knew everything. He took hold of the bookcase and pulled at it; it yielded and the secret door was exposed. Perhaps the hooks had not been properly fastened. They opened the door, and I had to precede them up the steps. The policemen followed me; I could feel their pistols in my back. But since the steps were only wide enough for a single person, I was the first to enter the Franks' room. Mrs. Frank was standing at the table.[6]

Of those in hiding in the Annexe, Otto Frank was the only one left able to tell the story of the arrest after the war. Couched in the official language of the Dutch detective examining him, it read as follows:

"In the morning—it was about 10.30—I was in the Van Pels boy's room [. . .] giving him an English lesson. At the said time a civilian I did not know came into the said room. He was holding a pistol and he aimed it at us. He made us put our hands in the air and searched us for weapons. This man appeared to be a Dutch official of the German *Sicherheitsdienst* [Security Service, or SD] in Amsterdam. Then he ordered us to go downstairs. He followed us with his pistol drawn. First we entered the room of the Van Pels family where I saw Mr. and Mrs. van Pels and also Mr. Pfeffer, all of them standing with their hands up. There was a man in civilian clothes there, too, not known to me, also with a drawn pistol. Then we were all made to go down one floor to where I lived with my family. There I saw my wife and my two daughters standing with their hands up. I believe Mr. Kugler was also in our room but I am not sure. It may well have been Mr. Kleiman. At the same time I saw a man in a green uniform, not known to me, who had also drawn his pistol. This man's name, I learned later, was Silberbauer. He ordered me in a curt, barrack-room tone of voice to show him where we kept our money and jewelry. I pointed out where they were. Then he picked up a briefcase in which my daughter Anne kept her papers, including her diary notes. He shook the briefcase out onto the floor and then put our jewelry and our money into it."[7]

The German's accomplices continued to search the Annexe for money and valuables. Those who had been arrested were allowed to pack some clothes and toilet articles. One of the SD men then went downstairs to telephone for transport for the large group of prisoners. It took some time before the transport arrived.

The German, Karl Silberbauer, meanwhile walked about in the Franks' room. His eye fell on the old army footlocker belonging to Otto Frank, on which the latter's name and rank in the German army were printed. In answer to Silberbauer's question, Otto Frank confirmed that he had been a German Reserve lieutenant during the Great War.

"At once, Silberbauer's attitude changed. He even looked for a moment as if he was going to snap to attention in front of me. Then he asked why I had not reported this fact before, since I would then have been sent to the labor camp at Theresienstadt. He stopped insisting that we hurry, and told us and his subordinates to take our time."[8]

Silberbauer was obviously impressed by Otto Frank's military rank. During his examination many years later by the Austrian police, in the presence of a detective from Amsterdam, he mentioned his conversation with Otto Frank as "proof" that he had not behaved discourteously to the prisoners. Otto Frank, who had been "a German Reserve officer during the First World War, also told me," remembered Silberbauer, "that he and his family, including his daughter Anne, had spent a good two years in the hiding place. When I refused to believe him, he pointed to the marks that had been made on the doorpost, showing how much Anne had grown since they had gone into hiding."[9]

Eventually—no transport having arrived—Silberbauer went downstairs.

On the floor where the offices were something else was happening meanwhile. Quite some time after Kugler had been ordered by the SD men to show them the hiding place, they had fetched Kleiman from the front office and had questioned him in the room at the back. Then they told him to hand over the keys of the building to Miep, who was apparently not under suspicion.[10]

Kleiman made use of this opportunity to give Bep his briefcase with the request that she take it straight to a friendly pharmacist on the Leliegracht and ask him to pass it on to Mrs. Kleiman. Then he told Miep: "Make sure you stay out of this. You can't save us, so try to save what you can here." Then he returned to the back room where the SD men were waiting for him.[11]

Bep was able to walk out of the building, since no guard had been posted outside.[12]

At about twelve o'clock—Miep Gies had been left alone in the main office —her husband arrived as usual for his lunch break. Suspecting nothing (the car in which the raiders had come had left again), he walked upstairs. Miep, who had been waiting anxiously for him, had packed her bag. Through a crack in the door she handed it over to her husband and told him what was happening in a whisper. He disappeared immediately without having been spotted by anyone.[13]

A short time later Silberbauer came into Miep's office, saying: "And now it's your turn." She had heard him talking earlier in the passage and had heard one of his subordinates mention his name. And, Viennese-born herself, she had recognized his Viennese accent immediately. In an attempt "to create a favorable atmosphere that might still help to do something for the prisoners," she reacted promptly. "You're from Vienna. So am I." His tone became distinctly more friendly. He asked for her identity card, but on discovering that her name was the same as that of one of the businesses established in the building, Gies, he immediately burst out shouting that she ought to be ashamed of herself to have aided and abetted Jews. "You have betrayed your country, you deserve the worst." Miep stood quietly behind her desk. Suddenly he asked: "What am I to do with you?" He saw the house keys which Kleiman had left for her, picked them up and put them in his pocket. Miep still did not react. Silberbauer then seemed to calm down a little. He stood in front of her and looked at her for a long time. "As a personal favor, I'm going to let you stay here, but if you run away, we'll take your husband." Miep rounded on him furiously: "Keep your hands off my husband, he had nothing to do with anything." Silberbauer's mind was clearly made up, however: "Don't be stupid, child, I know he's involved." He turned on his heel and walked out of the door, calling over his shoulder: "I'll be back!"[14]

Shortly before he left the building, he stuck his head once more round Miep's door, looked in and then disappeared without saying anything.

At about one o'clock the transport finally arrived. "A closed truck," Otto Frank later described it.[15] The eight who had been in hiding, together with Kugler and Kleiman, were led down the stairs and into the truck. Jan Gies and Kleiman's brother, whom he had gone to warn, watched the scene from across the canal.[16] The truck made off towards the school building in Euterpestraat used as the headquarters of the *Aussenstelle Amsterdam des Befehlshabers der Sicherheitspolizei und des SD* (Amsterdam Bureau of the Commander of the Security Police and Security Service). No one paid any further attention to Miep Gies.

23

Those Who Stayed Behind

All was now quiet at 263, Prinsengracht. Apart from the two warehousemen, Miep was the only one left behind in the building. Silberbauer had snapped at her as he left: "I'll be back!" She could have slipped away, but concern for her husband and Kleiman's injunction to "save what you can here"[17] made her stay on. There was no question of returning to her work, of course.

During the afternoon her husband came back to find out the lie of the land. Bep, too, returned. Gradually their fear that the SD might return abated. At about five o'clock Hartog, one of the warehousemen, went home. The two women, and Van Maaren, the head warehouseman, who had been handed the front door keys by the SD and who had locked the doors, decided to have a look at what had happened in the Annexe at the back of the building.[18] The door behind the bookcase had been locked by the SD, but Miep had a duplicate key and opened it.

Fifteen years later, while being examined as a witness during the case against Stielau and Buddeberg,[19] Miep declared:

"Everything was in utter confusion [. . .]. I came across Anne Frank's diary on the floor [. . .] together with an account book with notes by Anne and a number of loose sheets of copy paper, which were also covered with Anne's handwriting. In addition Elly [= Bep] handed me something which she said had been written by Anne [. . .]. Anyway, I locked all these writings of Anne's in my office desk."[20]

On the same occasion Bep said:

"I found some of the writings left behind by Anne Frank [. . .]. The copy paper was the kind I had let Anne have from the office supplies."[21]

Another fifteen years later, in 1974, Miep made a fresh declaration. In it, she briefly confirmed her earlier statements and added:

"A week later, the furniture in the Annexe was fetched by a removal firm [sent on German orders]. I gave our senior warehouseman [Van Maaren] instructions to collect up every piece of paper, or anything else with writing on it that might still be lying about in all the mess, and to give them to me. He did so. And I stored these away too with what I had already found."[22]

In a conversation with us early in 1985, she remembered yet another detail, which she later specified in a letter: she had also taken away from the Annexe several library books, a couple of Spanish textbooks belonging to Mr. Pfeffer, Anne's dressing jacket and a shoebag embroidered by Anne with the initials "A.F."[23]

Bep, for her part, had told us on an earlier occasion that she had removed "a number of things" and had stored them with her parents. When Otto Frank came back in 1945 and she wanted to return these articles to him, "he only wanted the portable typewriter, which I had also taken to safety."[24]

According to statements by Miep and Jan Gies, neither they nor the others entered the Annexe in the period between the day of the arrest and the arrival, one or two weeks later, of the removal firm (A. Puls) used by the Germans.[25] This seems plausible. They would undoubtedly have made sure as early as August 4

24

that nothing more of any value had been left behind that ought to be put away for safekeeping and eventually returned to their rightful owners.

Still, it is obvious that their main concern was for Anne's writings; both Miep and Bep had been aware that Anne kept a diary and were unquestionably intrigued by that fact.

In 1959 Miep declared:

"At the time when she lived in Prinsengracht, Anne Frank did a lot of writing [. . .]. Once [. . .] when I went up into the Annexe and opened Anne's door, I saw her sitting at a table and writing in an account book. She was obviously startled, got up and quickly shut the book. My immediate impression was that she was embarrassed at being caught at her writing. Just then Mrs. Frank came into the room. She took the situation in straight away and said to me: 'Yes, we have a writer for a daughter.' "[26]

Bep stated on the same day:

"I knew [. . .] that quite apart from the poems and tales she wrote she must also have been keeping a diary. During that time she asked me again and again to get her a book with a lock, adding expressly that she needed it for keeping a diary. Unfortunately I was unable to grant her wish. But I frequently gave her copy paper from the office that came in various colors, for instance red, yellow, blue and white."[27]

The day after the arrest, two of the traveling salesmen came to the office, as they usually did on a Saturday morning, to hand in their reports and the orders they had taken during the past week, and to discuss plans for the next week. They had never been told anything about the people in hiding. Miep met them and gave them the news of what had happened the day before. They then came up with the idea of ransoming the arrested people, "because the SD has a really soft spot for money," as, many years later, Miep remembered one of them saying. According to Miep, he also said "that the Germans were doing badly on all fronts and so would probably be ready to cooperate if the ransom was high enough." They advised Miep to telephone Silberbauer and ask him how much money he wanted. "I'll be able to get the money together," the salesman told her.[28]

Miep telephoned Silberbauer straight away and asked to see him. "Early on Monday morning," was his reply. And early on that morning she went to Euterpestraat. Silberbauer appeared to be sharing a large office with several typists. Miep stood in front of his desk and made the gesture "money" at him. Silberbauer's only reaction was to say: "I can't do anything for you today; come back tomorrow."[29]

Next morning, Tuesday, August 8, Miep went back to Euterpestraat. Silberbauer came out to meet her and said immediately: "I'm sorry but I can't do anything for you, I'm not senior enough." When Miep responded that she didn't believe him, Silberbauer told her to go and see his superior, upstairs. When she reached the room she had been directed to, she knocked but there was no answer. Opening the door, she saw a number of SD officers sitting round a large table with a radio set on it. She just had time to take in that they were listening to an English station before she was met with loud abuse and ordered out. Silberbauer was standing in the passage downstairs. He said only: "You see?" She never went back again.[30]

Back at Prinsengracht, they carried on the business as best they could, Miep and Bep trying to take on some of Kleiman's and Kugler's work. After a few days Hartog was told by Van Maaren not to come back until further notice. If he was needed they would tell him, Van Maaren said, but he never was, and Van Maaren ran the warehouse by himself from then on.[31] Left alone with the two women, he did all he could to consolidate his position, and since the front door keys had been handed to him on Silberbauer's orders, he acted at times as if he were the head of the business.[32]

Notes

[1] The number of Dutch SD men mentioned by the various witnesses ranges from three to eight. The most probable number is four or five.

[2] Examination of W. G. van Maaren, October 6, 1964, State Criminal Investigation Department, Amsterdam. Doc. 1, K. J. Silberbauer.

[3] Hermine (Miep) Gies-Santrouschitz, February 19, 1985.

[4] Examination of Hermine (Miep) Gies-Santrouschitz, December 23, 1963, State Criminal Investigation Department, Amsterdam. Doc. 1, K. J. Silberbauer.

[5] Examination of Elisabeth (Bep) van Wijk-Voskuijl, December 13, 1963, State Criminal Investigation Department, Amsterdam. Doc. 1, K. J. Silberbauer.

[6] Schnabel, *The Footsteps of Anne Frank*, pp. 99ff. (translated by Richard and Clara Winston). The original letter has never been found. Cf. Kugler's statement in "The Reminiscences of Victor Kugler—the 'Mr. Kraler' of Anne Frank's Diary, as Told to Eda Shapiro" in *Yad Vashem Studies*, XIII, ed. by Livia Rothkirchen, Jerusalem, 1979, pp. 357–59.

[7] Examination of Otto Heinrich Frank, December 2, 1963, State Criminal Investigation Department, Amsterdam. Doc. 1, K. J. Silberbauer.

[8] Ibid. Theresienstadt was a camp in Czechoslovakia, originally described as an *Altersghetto* (Old-Age Ghetto) by the Nazis, and used as a camp for "privileged" Jews. The chances of survival in that camp were appreciably greater than in such camps as Auschwitz.

[9] Examination of Karl Silberbauer, March 4, 1964, State Criminal Investigation Department, Amsterdam. Doc. 1, K. J. Silberbauer.

[10] Hermine (Miep) Gies-Santrouschitz, April 5, 1984.

[11] Declaration made by Hermine (Miep) Gies-Santrouschitz on June 5, 1974, before A. J. Dragt, notary in Amsterdam. Anne Frank Collection, 1 d; according to her statement of April 18, 1985, this did not happen until after her husband arrived.

[12] Examination of Elisabeth (Bep) van Wijk-Voskuijl on December 13, 1963, and of Hermine (Miep) Gies-Santrouschitz on December 23, 1963, State Criminal Investigation Department, Amsterdam. Doc. 1, K. J. Silberbauer.

[13] Examination of J. A. Gies, December 23, 1963, State Criminal Investigation Department, Amsterdam. Doc. 1, K. J. Silberbauer.

[14] Examination of Hermine (Miep) Gies-Santrouschitz, January 14, 1948. Ministry of Justice, W. G. van Maaren criminal dossier; report of a conversation by Mrs. Gies on February 27 and on April 18, 1985.

[15] Examination of Otto Heinrich Frank, December 20, 1963, State Criminal Investigation Department, Amsterdam. Doc. 1, K. J. Silberbauer.

[16] J. A. Gies, April 5, 1984.

[17] See p. 23.

[18] Statements by Hermine (Miep) Gies-Santrouschitz and Elisabeth (Bep) van Wijk-Voskuijl before A. J. Dragt, notary, June 5, 1974. Anne Frank Collection; communication from Miep, February 27, 1985.

[19] See Chapter 7.

[20] Examination of Hermine (Miep) Gies-Santrouschitz, September 29, 1959, by examining magistrate Meyer. Lübeck *Landgericht* (Regional Court), Stielau/Buddeberg dossier.

[21] Examination of Elisabeth (Bep) van Wijk-Voskuijl, September 29, 1959, by examining magistrate Meyer. Lübeck *Landgericht*, Stielau/Buddeberg dossier.

[22] Statement by Hermine (Miep) Gies-Santrouschitz before A. J. Dragt, notary, June 5, 1974. Anne Frank Collection 1 d.

[23] Hermine (Miep) Gies-Santrouschitz, February 27 and April 18, 1985.

[24] Elisabeth (Bep) van Wijk-Voskuijl, February 25, 1981. She died on May 6, 1983, before we were able to talk with her for a second time.

[25] Hermine (Miep) Gies-Santrouschitz, February 27, 1985.

[26] Examination of Hermine (Miep) Gies-Santrouschitz on September 29, 1959, by examining magistrate Meyer. Lübeck *Landgericht*, Stielau/Buddeberg dossier.

[27] Examination of Elisabeth (Biep) van Wijk-Voskuijl, as above.

[28] Hermine (Miep) Gies-Santrouschitz, February 27 and April 18, 1985.

[29] Hermine (Miep) Gies-Santrouschitz, February 27, 1985; on December 23, 1963, she had previously reported her visits to Silberbauer to the State Criminal Investigation Department, Amsterdam.

[30] Hermine (Miep) Gies-Santrouschitz, April 18, 1985.

[31] Examination of L. Hartog-van Bladeren on March 18, 1948 by the Amsterdam police. Ministry of Justice, W. G. van Maaren criminal dossier.

[32] Examination of Hermine (Miep) Gies-Santrouschitz on December 23, 1963, by the State Investigation Department, Amsterdam. Doc. 1, K. J. Silberbauer.

3 The Betrayal

HARRY PAAPE

Following more than two years of pressure, worry and strain, and in particular following the last few months of growing hope and increasing confidence that liberation was just around the corner, what now prevailed at 263, Prinsengracht were desperate feelings of anguish and distress concerning the fate of those who had been taken away.

It was not long before the painful question had to be faced of how the SD could possibly have learned that Jews had been hiding in the house. How had they known about the access door, which had been so cleverly camouflaged behind the bookcase?

Of the more than 25,000 Jews who went into hiding in the Netherlands in the years 1940 to 1945 in order to escape deportation, some 8,000 to 9,000 fell into German hands.[1] The causes were various but can be grouped under four headings: organized mass raids by the Germans and their Dutch accomplices; chance; carelessness on the part of those in hiding or of their "protectors"; and betrayal. The last two causes often coincided. There were countless letters and telephone calls to the SD or the Dutch police: "Dear Sir, I have noticed that . . ." or "I have heard that . . ."

The protectors of those hidden in the Annexe realized immediately after the raid of August 4 that in this case betrayal was the only explanation, possibly as a consequence of carelessness. Kleiman—after his return in October[2]—also took this view. The SD had after all come directly to this address, and this address only. There could thus be no question of chance.[3]

Outside the small circle of protectors, no one knew that the Frank family had gone into hiding: the story that the Franks had escaped to Switzerland via Limburg had gone the rounds most successfully.[4] The Van Pels family and Mr. Pfeffer had also been able to obliterate their traces completely in 1942. Naturally, it was possible someone in the immediate neighborhood might have been made suspicious by a noise, a chink of light through one of the Annexe windows, or a shadow behind a window elsewhere in the building during the evening or at weekends, when those in hiding were able to leave their cramped quarters for a short while. It was also possible that someone had noticed the unusually large daily supply of food—enough, after all, for eight people—that came to the building. Each of these factors might have explained an SD raid after three or six months. But after more than two years? It seemed improbable. The precautionary measures and vigilance of those in hiding and of their protectors had never flagged; on the contrary, their routine, if only through long experience, had greatly improved, albeit there had been some carelessness.

No, there must have been some other explanation, those left behind believed, and after a little while their suspicions fell on the warehouseman, W. G. van Maaren.

Van Maaren had been hired after the old head warehouseman, Voskuijl

(Bep's father), had been taken to the hospital in the spring of 1943, and the new man, as Miep continued to insist many years after the war, "was a very capable storeman."[5] However, his conduct quickly began to cause annoyance and even concern for some time: petty thefts of sugar, potato flour and spices from the store had been discovered, and Van Maaren seemed to show curiosity about things that were kept from him. The protectors of those in the Annexe grew increasingly worried and tense: with every step they took, they felt that they had to reckon with the presence of the dubious Van Maaren.[6]

The inmates of the Annexe were informed of these developments. The need to be even more careful than before was impressed upon them. Anne, too, mentioned the suspicions against Van Maaren and various careless acts several times in her diary.[7]

Suspicion was increased even further when it appeared that in the evenings, before he went home, Van Maaren would set small traps in the warehouse: a pencil at the extreme edge of a table, where it could easily be knocked off; a sprinkling of potato flour on the floor in which footprints could be seen. To the protectors, this seemed to indicate that he suspected someone was hiding in the building and was trying to make sure.[8]

Then there was the even more important question of the door keys. As early as the spring of 1945, Kleiman wrote (see p. 36): "The keys of the business were [. . .] handed to v. M. on August 4 and he was informed that he was answerable for everything. He was told to expect further orders, but these never came." In a statement to the Amsterdam police in 1948, Miep Gies declared: "When one of the SD men saw the name Gies on my identity card and remembered that the name of Gies was also connected with the business, the keys were taken away from me and handed to Van Maaren."[9] In 1963 she declared in a deposition:

"Immediately after the raiders left with their loot, Van Maaren came into my office, in which I had been left alone. He told me: 'Mrs. Gies, they said that I must have the keys.' Although I did not ask, I assumed that 'they' were the SD and so I gave the keys to Van Maaren. I did not think it odd then because, in the view of the Germans at the time, I was an accomplice after all. . . . From what Van Maaren told me, I gathered that he was really to be considered the 'Verwalter [administrator].' At the time it was usual to appoint a Verwalter for every Jewish business. Since I did not then harbor any suspicion against Van Maaren, I preferred to see him appointed Verwalter rather than anyone else."[10]

Miep's husband, Jan Gies, declared on the same day that his wife had told him that she "had originally been handed the keys so that she could keep the business going, but that Silberbauer had taken them from her again and handed them to Van Maaren."[11] He himself, incidentally, "had not immediately [. . .] suspected Van Maaren" but had assumed "that our guests had probably been careless."

Van Maaren declared during his examination in 1964 that he had indeed been handed the keys by Miep when he went to the office shortly after those arrested had been taken away.[12]

When Miep Gies told us in conversation that Silberbauer had taken the keys away from her and had then handed them over to Van Maaren, we drew attention to the discrepancy between this account and her statement in 1963. She then wrote to us that Silberbauer, as far as she could remember, had taken the keys from her "with the statement that he would hand them to the senior warehouseman. For that purpose, he may well have brought in one of the SD men and asked him to convey the[se] instructions to v. M. in Dutch."[13]

And finally there was also the suspicion that Van Maaren was involved with the SD. Miep declared in 1948:

"When it looked at first as if I too would be taken away by the SD, Van Maaren boasted to me that he was on good terms with the SD and that I need not fear they would arrest me. He would go to the SD himself. When I paid a visit to Silberbauer later, his words suggested that Van Maaren had indeed been to see him to put in a good word for me."[14]

During the 1963 examination we have mentioned, she repeated Van Maaren's statement to her but no longer mentioned Silberbauer's indirect confirmation of her suspicions. Similarly, when she told us about her visits to Silberbauer a few days after the arrest, this detail was no longer mentioned—on the contrary, she emphasized that their conversations were confined to what she had stated before.[15]

These are minor details. We have nevertheless reproduced them at some length because we consider them not without bearing on our assessment of how things stood during the postwar investigations of the betrayal.

During the first two months after August 4 there was little change in the situation. Business went on as usual. Van Maaren continued to do his normal work although he sometimes behaved as if he were in charge. Miep clearly accepted this state of affairs. She looked on Van Maaren's supposed status as *Verwalter* as a means of keeping the company in business. Thus she had asked him to accompany her to the Annexe at the end of the afternoon of August 4; again, when the removal firm had arrived to clear the Annexe, she had asked him to go upstairs with them and to bring her any parts of Anne's diary he might come across.

On Kleiman's return the situation changed. He took charge of the business and Van Maaren accepted his demotion to his old status. The thefts continued, indeed the amounts that went missing increased. On one occasion—in December—goods were found to be missing from a hiding place kept secret from Van Maaren. Kleiman went to the police. A search of Van Maaren's home by detectives proved abortive. Afraid of Van Maaren's assumed links with the SD, Kleiman took no further action. Their relationship, however, became increasingly fraught. Shortly after the Liberation, Van Maaren was dismissed, having once again been caught in the act of stealing (this time pectin, salt and soda).[16]

Meanwhile the questions raised by the raid on August 4 continued increasingly to exercise Kleiman and the other protectors, and suspicions against Van Maaren grew. Very soon after the Liberation, Kleiman wrote a letter, undated and without an address but intended for the POD (*Politieke Opsporings Dienst*, the Political Criminal Investigation Department). In it he gave a detailed account of the thefts and other breaches of trust attributed to Van Maaren. The question of the keys, too, was mentioned:

"When Van Maaren had the keys and was put in charge by the SD he thought of himself as the *Verwalter* and acted as such. He borrowed money from people connected with the business and forgot to repay it. During arguments with the office staff he once claimed that he could do anything he liked and that he would not balk at anything, not even at walking over dead bodies. With my return, he was stripped of many of his illusions [. . .]. To my question whether he had known that people had been hidden away [in the building] he said that he had merely suspected it, but that the staff of one of the next-door businesses had once said something to him to that effect."

The letter ended with a question:

30

"Now that the time of the great clean-up has arrived, I must ask you whether the facts mentioned by me seem to you sufficient cause to interrogate v. M. and also the previously mentioned temporary employee[17] closely about this matter."[18]

Kleiman took the letter personally to the POD and added a verbal explanation.

His evidence was obviously insufficient. For more than two years next to nothing was done about the letter. That, too, was quite understandable. In formal terms the letter contained no complaints on which the police could have acted, and as for his and other people's suspicions of Van Maaren, Kleiman could only write: "Rightly or wrongly he was therefore considered by everyone in our business to be the traitor." Beyond that, there were only vague indications that could at best be considered indirect evidence. At the time, all public agencies engaged in the tracing and prosecuting of war criminals were flooded with work, and Kleiman's letter gave them little to go on.

Not until 1947 did things begin to move. The initiative was probably taken by Otto Frank. In July 1947, Kleiman referred, in a letter to the PRA (*Politieke Recherche Afdeling*, the Political Investigation Branch) of the Amsterdam police, to a visit Otto Frank had paid them "a few weeks ago," and enclosed a copy of the letter he had written in 1945.[19]

Slowly the wheels now began to turn. On January 12, 1948, Kleiman was finally examined by the PRA. He had nothing to add to what he had written in 1945 concerning his suspicions. About the actual arrest of those hidden in the Annexe, however, he now made a very important statement. Speaking of Silberbauer and his assistants, he declared: "They seemed to know precisely what they were doing, for they went straight to the hiding place and arrested all eight persons present there."[20] This statement implied not only that the SD knew that Jews were hidden in the building but that they also knew the location of the hiding place and also perhaps about the entrance to the Annexe, the bookcase built by Voskuijl. The conclusion must be that the traitor was someone well acquainted with all the arrangements.

Kleiman should, of course, have been asked how he had arrived at that conclusion, since he had not been present when the SD men went over the building with Kugler.

Kugler was examined two days later.

"We are absolutely certain [he declared] that there was treachery, and we suspect a man called Van Maaren who joined us in the spring of 1943. This man was always nosing around the place."[21]

To illustrate such "nosing around" he gave the example we have already mentioned above, and added another:

"In order to prevent the so-called Annexe from being discovered [. . .] we had painted over some window panes at the back of the main building with blue paint, ostensibly for the blackout. I once caught Van Maaren in the act of scraping the blue paint away. He said: 'Well, well, I've never been over there.'

"On another occasion he said to me: 'Didn't a certain Mr. Frank work in this office at one time?' He had supposedly picked this up from the firm next door."

Interesting though these statements undoubtedly were, no one thought of questioning Kugler about the precise course of events at the time of the SD raid. Nor was he confronted with Kleiman's statement about the procession to the bookcase. This must be considered a lapse on the part of the detective concerned. Moreover, many examinations by various sections of the *Bijzondere Rechtspleging* (Special Justice Administration) conducted in the first few years after the war suffered from similar shortcomings. To cope reasonably quickly with the great flood of cases under review, the Administration was forced to employ a large number of inadequately trained officials.

Miep Gies, too, who was examined the same day by the PRA, was unable to add many concrete details. She again mentioned the suspicions against Van Maaren arising from his curiosity, his questions about Otto Frank, the way he would check whether anything had been removed or shifted in the warehouse or the office at night or on weekends, the business with the keys, his relationship with the SD, his petty thefts. "When Van Maaren got his hands on the keys after the raid, it became perfectly obvious that he was extremely pleased about it," she added.[22]

For reasons unknown to us, Bep Voskuijl was not questioned on the matter. Instead, the police followed another lead. During his examination, Kleiman had stated that at about the end of June 1944 he had heard from a man called Genot that the wife of Hartog (Van Maaren's assistant) had told his (Genot's) wife that Jews were hidden at 263, Prinsengracht. Mrs. Genot was said to have retorted immediately that one had to be extremely careful with that sort of talk. The police now naturally wanted to know how much the warehouse staff had found out about the people in hiding. The protectors were, however, unable to come up with definite answers.

The Genots had meanwhile moved to Antwerp. Two months after Kleiman's examination, the couple were questioned by an Amsterdam detective. P. J. Genot declared on that occasion that his work (he was employed by CIMEX, a cleaning company owned by Kleiman and his brother) had occasionally taken him to 263, Prinsengracht and that during 1942 he had come to supect that Kleiman was keeping Jews hidden on the premises.

In the spring Genot had, at the request of Hartog's wife, who did housework for his wife, interceded to get Hartog a job with Gies & Co. In about July 1944 his wife had told him that Hartog's wife had asked her if it was right that Jews were hidden in the building where her husband worked. "That same night I told Mr. Kleiman [. . .], a brother of the above-mentioned Director Kleiman, what had happened. He, in his turn, warned his brother," she had added.

As grounds for his suspicions, Genot mentioned the help he had given in 1942 in cleaning out the Annexe, and the large quantities of bread and milk that used to be brought in after that. He added briefly that he did not think Hartog capable of betraying people. As for Van Maaren, he said: "I thought Van Maaren a very odd sort of fellow and I didn't know what to make of him. I didn't talk politics to him for safety's sake."[23]

Mrs. Genot confirmed her husband's account of her conversation with Mrs. Hartog. When the latter asked her about the Jews in hiding, she had replied: "You oughtn't talk about things like that, you ought to be very careful."[24]

A few other leads were also followed up by the police, but to no avail. The protectors believed, for instance, that they recognized some of the Dutch SD collaborators from photographs shown to them by the police. All the identified persons, however, denied that they had been present during the raid on August 4, 1944, and it was impossible to prove otherwise.

Finally, before Van Maaren himself was examined, Hartog was questioned.

As far as his suspicion that people were hidden in the building was concerned, he gave the same plausible explanation as Genot: "I occasionally noticed that a baker or a greengrocer, say, had brought a lot of bread or vegetables." He added, however, that he had never thought of Jews in this connection, "until Van Maaren [. . .] told me about fourteen days before the Jews were taken away that Jews were hidden in the building."[25]

The time factor ("fourteen days") conflicts with the statements of the Genots, an understandable discrepancy. Hartog was, however, the first witness to state unequivocally that Van Maaren knew about the presence of Jews in the building. His statement gains even greater significance in light of a remark he made at the end of his examination: "As far as the raid itself was concerned, I was struck by the fact that the detectives who raided the place were not just on the lookout for hidden Jews, but were, you might say, completely in the picture." Hartog was not asked what specific facts or remarks had led him to that conclusion.

The last to be examined was the suspect, who had, evidently in answer to questions put to him, previously lodged a written deposition.[26] In this, he had described himself as holding a position of trust in the business. He denied having had any prior knowledge that Jews were hidden in the building. As for the thefts, he tried to throw suspicion on Bep Voskuijl and her father (in fact already hospitalized by the time Van Maaren joined the company), whom he had once, he said, surprised in the building after office hours, one carrying a shopping bag and the other a parcel. The rest of the deposition also contained statements that could be considered as veiled accusations (especially against Miep Gies).

In this connection he made another allegation that should be noted. He claimed that after the arrest he had been "sent" twice to Euterpestraat (i.e., to the SD) "on the orders of Mrs. Gies":

"For some unknown reason Mrs. Gies wanted my signature [. . .] and she claimed that the key of the safe was missing; in order to get it back she had the typist Voskuijl type a letter in German which I had to sign as *Verwalter* van Maaren so as to be given the key, which was meant to be in Mr. Kugler's keeping. But at Euterpestraat this turned out not to be true, and on my return [. . .] Mrs. Gies showed me the key which she said she had found in the meantime.

"The second time I went to Euterpestraat, again on Mrs. Gies's instructions, I didn't go as *Verwalter* but as a chemist asking for [. . .] the formula for a preservative [. . .] and I was quickly given Mr. Kugler's answer."[27]

This statement cannot have been founded on fact: Kugler (like Kleiman) had been moved on the day of the arrest itself from Euterpestraat to the prison in Amstelveenseweg (see p. 49).

Van Maaren alleged in the same written deposition that when he was shown the secret entrance to the Annexe he was "dumbfounded by its technical ingenuity" and had expressed the opinion that "the SD would never have been able to find out anything about this secret door without inside information." As for the raid on August 4, 1944: "I was told that on their arrival the SD went straight upstairs to the bookcase and opened the door." He was not asked for the source of this information.

His examination on March 31, 1948, was short (the official report covered less than one page) and full of denials and explanations of his strange behavior. Thus "in the course of 1943–1944" he had "suspected that something peculiar was going on in the building, without, however, hidden Jews ever coming to mind," because the baker, the milkman and the greengrocer kept supplying so much food.

As for the business with the pencils and the potato flour, he gave a simple explanation which nobody could challenge, and which at the same time was intended to clear him of the theft charges:

"Now and then goods were also stolen from the warehouse. That is why—with Mr. Kugler's full knowledge—I placed some bottles on the floor in such a way that you'd be able to tell immediately if anyone had been on the premises after closing time. And occasionally I would also [put down] a pencil for the same reason. I can't remember anything about scattering stuff around [. . .]. I did what I did only because every so often goods were stolen and they suspected me. If I could show that people had been in the premises after hours, I would no longer be under suspicion."[28]

About the staff of the firm next door:

"It is not true that I ever spoke to the staff of the Keg company [. . .] about Jews being hidden at our place. Admittedly I did so after the Jews had been carried off."[29]

On the question of the keys:

"After the arrest, I did indeed receive the keys from Mrs. Gies, but I did not know that that was done on the orders of the SD."[30]

On his relations with the SD:

"It is absolutely untrue that I told Mrs. Gies that I was on good terms with the SD and that she need not worry about being arrested. On the contrary, I was known among my friends as a good anti-German."

He also denied "very emphatically" that he had been guilty of betraying anyone.[31]

And that was the end of the investigation. Clearly, the PRA found nothing to follow up, given the lack of concrete evidence and Van Maaren's plausible defense. The official report submitted by the PRA to the public prosecutor one day after Van Maaren's examination summed it all up in two sentences:

"The accused denies the charge of betrayal, and the circumstantial evidence is vague. Accordingly, there is no case to answer."[32]

On May 22 the public prosecutor informed the PRA that "no further steps [are] being considered."[33]

That should have been the end of the matter. Nevertheless, six months later the case was reopened and the public prosecutor at the Amsterdam Special Court of Justice granted Van Maaren a conditional discharge.[34] Van Maaren had failed to clear his name unequivocally. The only possible reason for reopening the case was that Van Maaren must have objected to the decision of May 22, on the grounds that it had done nothing to refute the allegations against him. No document to that effect has, however, been found in his file.

The discharge was conditional on Van Maaren's allowing himself to be put in the charge of the Supervisory Board for Political Offenders for a probationary period of three years. In addition, he was barred from holding public office, serving in the armed forces, passively or actively participating in elections or serving as a councillor or administrator—the usual conditions imposed on thousands of "petty" political offenders at the time.

It is not surprising that Van Maaren was not satisfied with this decision either. He appealed against it on November 30, 1948.[35]

On August 8, 1949, the appeal was heard before a district court convened under the Temporary Special Justice Act. No fresh evidence was produced. There was a brief examination only of Van Maaren, who declared: "I have appealed because I am completely innocent of the charges brought against me [. . .]. I stand by my statement to the police."[36]

The most important submission Van Maaren's lawyer made was the plea: "If the accused had felt even the smallest amount of guilt, he would not have appealed against his conditional discharge, since the restrictions imposed are so slight."[37]

Five days later the district judge delivered his verdict. He considered that treason had not been proved, and declared that there was no case against the petitioner. Van Maaren had been cleared.[38] It would be another fourteen years before the case was reopened.

This belated investigation was in response to the tracing by Simon Wiesenthal of the SD officer who had been in charge of the raid on the Annexe: the former *SS-Oberscharführer* Karl Josef Silberbauer. The name of Anne Frank had in the meantime, thanks to the worldwide distribution of her diary and the success of the play and film based on it, achieved world renown.

The State Criminal Investigation Department in Amsterdam decided to reopen its files, and the ensuing investigation was much more thorough than that of 1947–48. New witnesses—including, of course, Silberbauer himself—were heard in addition to those who had been heard before. Kleiman had meanwhile died (in 1959), as had Hartog; Kugler had emigrated to Canada in 1955. Van Maaren was once again the central figure in the investigation.

A warehouseman by the name of J. J. de Kok, who had worked for a few months in 1943 as Van Maaren's assistant, had been traced. He confirmed that Van Maaren had been stealing even then. Moreover, he described Van Maaren's pilfering in great detail, and his testimony was the more credible because he frankly admitted that he himself had been involved, that he had sold part of the loot on the black market and had been paid for these activities by Van Maaren. But he also added: "As far as Van Maaren was concerned, I never saw any sign that he was at all interested in National Socialism or even sympathized with the occupying power."[39]

Otto Frank was questioned again on December 2, 1963. He could not—and this is not surprising—contribute anything new to the investigation and declared only that he and his protectors had become "increasingly convinced that [. . .] Van Maaren was the only likely suspect."[40]

Bep Voskuijl, too, had nothing new to add to her deposition of 1948. As far as she could remember, the first thefts had occurred in the winter of 1944. As to her personal view of Van Maaren, she said only that she had been "terribly afraid of the man at the time and considered him capable of anything. On one occasion, he even told me that he would walk over corpses."[41]

The most important reasons for Miep Gies's suspicions and mistrust have already been mentioned. She too was "unable [. . .] to name any facts and/or circumstances that would make it clear beyond doubt that he was the man who betrayed the hiding place of the eight Jewish persons to the SD," she stated during her examination in December 23.[42]

There was a strange discrepancy between her declaration on this occasion concerning her handing over the keys to Van Maaren and her deposition in 1948 (see p. 29), and also her husband's statement to the State Criminal Investigation Department on the same day.[43]

Apparently in response to a question about Van Maaren's 1948 declaration (see p. 33) about his visits to the SD, Miep Gies attested:

"What you're asking me now is if I sent the aforesaid Van Maaren to the SD in Euterpestraat after the people in hiding had been arrested. I believe I even did so twice. Once it concerned a particular key, and another time a particular recipe of which Mr. Kugler knew the composition. I still remember well that in this connection I asked the aforesaid Bep to type out a letter I had drafted in German [. . .] which I had Van Maaren sign as 'Verwalter.' I did this in order to stop the Germans from appointing someone else as our Verwalter. Whether the two errands were successful I am no longer able to say today."

To which she added:

"You ask me further if the aforesaid Van Maaren also had connections with the SD. Although I cannot prove it, I assume that was indeed the case. For when I came back from the fruitless call I made on Silberbauer, in a mood of dejection, Van Maaren said to me: 'I know people who can make inquiries for you.' He did not tell me who or what these people were or if they had any connection with the SD, but he gave me the clear impression that in one way or another he had some influence with the Germans. How much of that was boasting on his part, I cannot judge."[44]

On the one hand there is her reaction to the statement by Van Maaren with which she had suddenly been confronted, and which—in view of her answer to the question put to her—was probably read out in part or in full to her; on the other hand there is her report about Van Maaren's contacts with the SD, which now appear in a different context than when she spoke about them in 1948: at that time Van Maaren was supposed to have said something similar to her, but in connection with her fear of being arrested (see p. 30).

At the end of her 1963 deposition she also stated emphatically:

"The disagreeable behavior of the aforesaid Van Maaren, and my talks after the Liberation with Messrs. Kleiman and Kugler, were enough to fill me with growing doubts about Van Maaren, although I am not really in a position to provide you with the sort of facts and details you would need to substantiate my suspicions."[45]

The State Criminal Investigation Department followed up other leads too, just as the Amsterdam police had done in 1948. Thus they questioned two former Dutch SD men who were supposed to have accompanied Silberbauer during his raid on 263, Prinsengracht, and who were allegedly identified in photographs after the war by one or more of the Franks' protectors. These enquiries, too, led nowhere: both men declared that they could not remember the raid. Other leads proved equally abortive. The conclusion could only be that the evidence to hand was based partly on false and partly on inadequate information.[46]

They also interrogated Willi Lages, former head of the *Aussenstelle Amsterdam des Befehlshabers der Sicherheitspolizei und des SD* (Amsterdam Bureau of the Commander of the Security Police and Security Service), still a prisoner in Breda. Although he was able to provide some information about Silberbauer, as well as about Silberbauer's Amsterdam chief, Julius Dettmann, who committed suicide shortly after the end of the war, none of it cast any fresh light on the betrayal.[47]

More important was Silberbauer's own testimony. After he had been traced by Simon Wiesenthal in 1963, he submitted a *Bericht* (written report) in August of that year to a senior Austrian police officer attached to the Ministry of the Interior. He was examined on November 25, and on March 4, 1964, he was questioned once again by the senior police officer in the presence of a detective from the Netherlands State Criminal Investigation Department. The results were recorded in a *Niederschrift* (deposition) in question and answer form.[48]

From all these depositions and documents the following picture emerges. On August 4, 1944, at about noon (here Silberbauer must have been mistaken either in the date or in the time) Silberbauer took a telephone call from Dettmann, who told him that he had just received a telephone message to the effect that a number (during the examination in March the figure was given as eight) of Jews were in hiding at 263, Prinsengracht. Silberbauer did not know whether the person who had supplied the information was a Dutchman or a German. Dettmann, he said, also instructed Abraham Kaper, the head of the group of Dutchmen employed by IVB4 to track down Jews in hiding,[49] to detail eight of his men to accompany Silberbauer.

When they arrived at the Prinsengracht, he and his men (Kaper himself was not with them) went to the warehouse.

"There was a firm's warehouse on the ground floor, where we met a worker who, when asked by the D[utch] C[a]r[a]b[iniers] where the Jews were hidden, gestured with a finger up the stairs."[50]

Silberbauer gave a detailed account of what happened next:

"We then went up to the office on the next floor, where we found one of the two heads of the company. The Crb[s]. immediately questioned this man, telling him to his face that there were Jews hidden in the building and that they had been denounced. Since the man could see it was pointless to deny this fact, he led us up a staircase to a small room one floor up. On entering the latter we could see a dresser or set of shelves against the end wall. To the right of it was a window. The head of the firm pointed to the piece of furniture. This was then pushed to one side and another staircase was revealed which led to the top story. I drew my pistol and went up the stairs with the Crb[s]."[51]

Later—in his examination in March 1964—Silberbauer had this to add about Kugler:

"The head of the firm [. . .] immediately became terribly nervous and went quite red in the face. Without any coercion [. . .], not one pistol was drawn, the man immediately got up and led us to the Frank family's hiding place [. . .]. He also opened the hidden door of his own free will."[52]

He was brief on the subject of his contacts with Miep: he could remember nothing of a "Viennese or Austrian woman" in connection with the arrest. Miep's story about her attempt to ransom the prisoners he considered, in the light of his official position, to be "sheer fabrication."[53]

The visits to Euterpestraat by Van Maaren, whom he failed, however, to recognize from a photograph shown to him, did not strike him as impossible, but he could not remember anything about them.[54]

Clearly, although Silberbauer's testimony contained a number of concrete data concerning the course of the raid, it added very little to the question of the actual betrayal. And he rightly added that, when Van Maaren had pointed upstairs in response to his question, he could well have been pointing the way to the head of the company. In any case, on the basis of this exchange with Van Maaren it was not possible to conclude that Van Maaren knew whether—and where—Jews were hidden in the building.

It was not until November 1964 that Van Maaren was examined again. He admitted the thefts although he tried to minimize them. The footprints in the warehouse, he claimed, together with Kugler's evasive reaction when his attention had been drawn to them, had indeed aroused his suspicions, as had the ample supply of provisions. He denied having scraped the paint off the window that overlooked the back of the building, but admitted that he had seen the house at the back when he (and Kugler) had been on the roof to repair a leak; however, he denied that he knew that Jews were hidden there.[55]

During the SD raid, he contended, one SD man had asked him "where the office was." The keys, he insisted, were handed to him by Miep Gies. "She did it of her own accord, I didn't make her." He denied that Silberbauer had appointed him *Verwalter*. He repeated his earlier claim that he had visited the SD at Miep's request, adding this time that he had recognized Kugler's handwriting on the letter which he brought back with him from his second visit.

Once again the investigator failed to realize that this could not have been possible, since Kugler had been taken away from Euterpestraat by then.

Van Maaren also declared that he had noticed "a sort of air of secrecy in the building before the arrests, which I was never able to explain properly."

Confronted with Miep's statement about his connections with the SD, he asserted that if he had ever said anything like that to her he had certainly not meant that he had direct contacts with the SD, but rather that he had contacts with the Resistance movement in his district. In this connection he mentioned the name of a man who, according to him, "had played an important part in the Resistance," and who allegedly "did have SD contacts." However, when the Criminal Investigation Department came to check this story, they found that the man had left for an unknown destination in Germany "quite some time after the war."[56]

Van Maaren also stated during his examination that he had kept his son in hiding in his own house, and he continued to insist with great emphasis that he had had absolutely nothing to do with the betrayal.

On that matter, he tried to direct suspicion (much as he had previously tried to incriminate Miep Gies) toward the owner of a business in the immediate vicinity, who, when Van Maaren had once gone there to pick up a bag of salt, had begun to chat with him and, alluding to Opekta, had asked him: "Have you got anything hidden there?"

"I told him [Van Maaren said during his examination] that I knew absolutely nothing about it, whereupon he told me: 'They'd better take care, because they go out in the evenings and visit the pharmacist in Leliegracht.' When I asked him who went out, he didn't give me a straight answer but said: 'Come, come.' Then I told him it must have been my boss, who occasionally worked late."[57]

In view of the fact that all those in hiding had agreed not to venture out at any time and also because Anne would certainly have reported such "outings" in her diary, it is most unlikely that one or more of the eight people in the Annexe should have been seen in the street. However, the State Criminal Investigation Department rightly decided to inquire into the matter further. And indeed it turned out that the man in question had been an NSB member and had, moreover, been urged "repeatedly" by his block warden, a brother of the Abraham Kaper mentioned before, to "show greater initiative." The man had, however, died in 1950, and the two Kaper brothers had died as well.[58]

At the same time the State Criminal Investigation Department carried out a detailed inquiry into Van Maaren's past, personal circumstances and connections. It appeared that from 1925 to 1930 he had owned a cigar store, which he sold in 1930. During the first two years of the war he had run a small laundry delivery service but was declared bankrupt at the beginning of 1943 "as a consequence of indiscriminate withdrawals of money." The business, the detectives concluded, had been a "last resort." Both before and at the beginning of the war Van Maaren had been supported by *Liefdadigheid naar Vermogen* (Charity according to Ability), a private charity for which he had also worked as a warehouseman. Here, too, he was found to be "a dishonest person, since from time to time he would purloin goods from the store." In the autumn of 1940, when all private charities were closed down and replaced by the Nazis with *Winterhulp Nederland* (Winter Aid Netherlands), Van Maaren refused on principle to take aid from that body, as the detectives were told by a former committee member of *Liefdadigheid naar Vermogen*.

In 1964 this lady could still remember the Van Maaren family very well, because she had had a great deal of contact with them. She described Van Maaren as "a dishonest man who was too big for his boots. His wife was much more intelligent than he was" but "very cantankerous and hard on her husband and her children." There was, it seemed, "quite a lot of tension in that family." The small laundry delivery service had apparently been started when, as a result of Van Maaren's refusal to accept aid from *Winterhulp Nederland*, the family was in dire financial straits.[59]

The inquiries carried out by the State Criminal Investigation Department in Van Maaren's neighborhood also produced valuable information. According to the official report, the investigators questioned members of the Resistance "closest to" the above-mentioned Resistance leader who had left for Germany, including a retired detective sergeant of the Amsterdam municipal police. All of them said that they knew Van Maaren, and all agreed that he was "financially untrustworthy, which explains why nobody in the neighborhood thought very highly of him." However it had never occurred to any of them that he might have had contacts during the war with "people who had served the enemy or the enemy's henchmen." It was known, too, that during the war Van Maaren had "repeatedly visited his neighbor," the above-mentioned Resistance leader; he certainly "must have known about that man's activities." There had never been any hint of treachery. They therefore did not believe that Van Maaren betrayed those in hiding in the Prinsengracht.[60]

Another of Van Maaren's neighbors, however, alleged that Van Maaren not only received substantial aid from *Winterhulp Nederland* but had "on his own admission" also been a purchasing agent for the German army. On one occasion he is alleged to have told this witness that the flowers in his apartment had been sent as a present "from the Germans" on the occasion of his wife's birthday, which happened to be on the same day as Hitler's. Having already concluded that the contacts between this witness and Van Maaren were "very minimal" and that Van Maaren had denied "again and again" that he had been a purchasing agent for the *Wehrmacht*, the detectives came to the further conclusion that Van Maaren's bankruptcy and his work at Opekta were "adequate refutations" of the testimony of this witness.[61]

The Van Maaren file was closed by the State Criminal Investigation Department on November 4, 1964. Two days later it was sent to the public prosecutor. In an accompanying letter signed by the two detectives concerned, we can read "that the inquiry did not lead to any concrete results."[62]

Van Maaren was left alone from that time on. He died in 1971, at the age of seventy-six, at his home in Amsterdam.

There would be—apart from the odd notice in the daily or weekly press wholly or partly based on interviews with those involved—quite a few more occasions to make the surviving protectors wonder about the events of August 4, 1944, and the question of the betrayal.

In 1974 the mayor and aldermen of the city of Amsterdam received a letter from Toronto, Canada, alleging that *The Diary of Anne Frank* had not been written by Anne Frank but was concocted after the war by the American journalist and playwright, Meyer Levin.[63] Seeing that similar reports had been published previously, the municipal council decided to conduct an official investigation into the authenticity of the diary and the authorship of Anne Frank while some of the witnesses were still alive.

Thus it came about that on June 5, 1974, Miep and Bep handed depositions to the Amsterdam notary A. J. Dragt. They confined their comments to what they had learned about the diary during the period of hiding and to their contacts with Anne in this connection, and also to the discovery of the written material on the afternoon of August 4, 1944. Both declared that on this last occasion Jan Gies and Van Maaren had also been present. In her account of the events during that afternoon, Miep declared:

"At about five o'clock in the afternoon, my husband, called 'Henk' in the published diary, appeared in the office and Elli [= Bep] came back as well. The older of the two workmen also came upstairs. He had been handed the keys of the building by the 'Green' police; they had been taken from me [. . .] and [. . .] after the younger warehouseman had left [. . .] and the older had locked the front door, the four of us returned to the Annexe."[64]

Needless to say, Bep, who had been away all afternoon after leaving with Kleiman's briefcase, knew nothing about the keys.[65]

In our account of the arrests we did not follow Silberbauer, his men and Kugler to the Annexe, but merely referred to Silberbauer's own account of this episode (see p. 37). According to the list of contents of the file covering the investigation begun in 1963, that file contained two letters from Kugler dated 1963. These two letters, however, could no longer be found when we ourselves examined the file.

Even earlier, Kugler had given his account of what happened to Ernst Schnabel, whose book was published in 1958.[66] More than twenty years later Kugler told his story again to the Canadian journalist Eda Shapiro.[67]

Her report of Kugler's account is somewhat more detailed than the one we find in Schnabel's book. Thus we read that Kugler claimed the policemen asked to be shown all the rooms in the building, whereupon he also took them to the office in which Kleiman, Miep and Bep worked, opening "all the bookcases and cabinets." "Outwardly I showed great calm, but inwardly I was terrified. I wondered why these men were here. Had they found out that I had been taking pictures for the Dutch underground; or were they searching for the secret hiding place? Had we been betrayed?"

When they came to the storeroom on the second floor (Silberbauer's aides having remained behind in the passage), Kugler continued, Silberbauer said: "Now, let's look for secret weapons." Kugler then volunteered to open all the boxes, cases and bags. When they eventually went back into the passage, Kugler saw that one of the bookcases had been pushed aside, apparently, as he told Eda Shapiro, by the three Dutchmen. He watched them working away at the bookcase that concealed the door to the Annexe. "Again and again they tried to move it but failed." In the end, however, they discovered the hook that held the bookcase in place.[68]

When we review all the available evidence relating to the progress of Kugler and the SD men through the building, we feel more than justified in querying the version given by Kugler to both Schnabel and Shapiro. In 1948, Kleiman had stated that they had gone "directly to the hiding place"; Van Maaren had said "straight to the bookcase." Neither had, it is true, been an eyewitness. In addition, there is also an account by Bep to which we have not yet referred. During her examination in 1963 she stated that when Kleiman returned to the office during the raid he said "that they'd had it, because with five pistols pointing at him, Mr. Kugler had been forced to reveal the hiding place."[69] This story was emphatically denied by Miep when she spoke to us. It remains a fact, however, that the statement was made by Bep to the policeman who had been questioning her.

Finally Silberbauer's own full account of the events seems to us highly plausible. The SD had known in advance that Jews were hidden in the building. That is why they asked Van Maaren—though he denied this later—about Jews straight away. His gesture would then have meant: "The Jews are upstairs." There was no reason why the SD men should not have immediately told Kugler to show them the hiding place. Silberbauer's account of the scene in Kugler's office tallies with everything we know about the behavior of policemen in such situations: to surprise the person concerned with a question that goes straight to the point and to give him the impression that "we know everything."

That Kugler played a less than heroic role in this scene is something one can scarcely hold against him. The situation in which he found himself, quite without warning, must undoubtedly have appeared to him one of extreme danger. He had no experience as a fighter in the Resistance and for that reason, we must assume, had not planned for the kind of situation with which he was suddenly faced. He must have been ashamed later that he submitted so easily. Perhaps Bep's statement about the five pistols was based on information given by Kugler himself with the aim of making his original account, probably to Kleiman ("straight to the hiding place"), sound less feeble. The accounts he gave to Schnabel and Shapiro many years later must be seen in the same light. One can readily understand this attempt by Kugler to present himself as a braver man than he actually was.

In light of the foregoing, it is clear that the question of the betrayal is no longer one of legal culpability: on the basis of the evidence produced during the investigations in 1948 and 1963–64 it was a foregone conclusion that Van Maaren would be allowed to go free. We have set out our objections to some aspects of the 1948 investigation. On that occasion there was an obvious lack of expertise and resourcefulness, as well as alertness to the gaps and inconsistencies in the evidence taken. Moreover, at a time when so many potential witnesses were still alive, the case was allowed to turn into too much of a "Van Maaren investigation" instead of taking the form of a broad inquiry into the betrayal at 263, Prinsengracht. Had it been that, then there might well have been conclusions—positive or negative—to the effect that someone other than Van Maaren might have been the betrayer. The subsequent investigations—in 1963–64—were indeed much more extensive but were doomed to failure because of the lapse of time since the event.

Though we have dwelled at length on the evidence produced by the protectors, their original statements were little more than justifications of their suspicions and gave the detectives few concrete facts to go on.

The detectives involved in the 1963–64 investigation showed more imagination and tenacity than their predecessors in 1948; their chief, the then head of the State Criminal Investigation Department in Amsterdam, took a great interest in the matter. Their investigation can be faulted in only a few (not entirely unimportant) details. However, when they too realized that they had reached a dead end, they exaggerated the importance of some of the conclusions they presented in a report to the public prosecutor. In particular, they considered Van Maaren's refusal to accept aid from *Winterhulp Nederland*; his being unacquainted with the people hiding in the Annexe "so that the factor of a personal grudge must be excluded"; and the fact that he did not seem to have received any financial reward for his alleged betrayal, as so many "factors [. . .] that must be considered to exonerate him."[70]

This brings us to a number of aspects of Van Maaren's character. Life had not been kind to him, what with the failure of his cigar store, his many years of unemployment, his bankruptcy (at that time certainly still considered a black mark against a man), his petty thefts, first from *Liefdadigheid naar Vermogen* and later at the Prinsengracht, his marriage to a woman intellectually superior to him and given—one may assume—to repeated recriminations. He must have felt galled by his failures, his lack of success and his isolation. The files contain not a single positive comment on Van Maaren's personality. He compensated to some extent by misrepresenting himself as bigger, better and more important than he really was—a not unusual reaction. He was a braggart. Even his contacts with the SD, of which he boasted to Miep, can be explained in this way.

How would this type of person have felt about the situation at 263, Prinsengracht, where he quickly discovered that the rest of the staff treated him as an outsider and that "something" was going on in the building of which all the others were aware while he was left in ignorance?

The flour, the pencil and the bottles, the scraping of the blue paint from the window and the frequent displays of curiosity are an indication: he wanted and needed to confirm his suspicions. That confirmation may perhaps have come the morning he found a briefcase in the storeroom which he—after having examined its contents, of course—handed to Kugler, who was not quick enough to react convincingly, showing too much surprise. The briefcase turned out to belong to

Van Pels, who had left it in the storeroom the night before. Characteristic of the importance that everyone, Kugler included, attached to this incident is the fact that the State Criminal Investigation Department in its report about two letters Kugler wrote in 1963–64 (and which we did not see) paid exclusive attention to the briefcase incident.[71]

We, for our part, feel certain that Van Maaren knew that Jews were hidden in the back of the building. He may perhaps have known the names of some of them as well—of Van Pels, to start with, and also of Otto Frank. After all, he surprised Kugler with the question (or statement): "Didn't a certain Mr. Frank work in this office at one time?"—a piece of information he was supposed to have received from a member of the staff of the firm next door.[72]

However secondary, the question of the keys must also play a role in our conclusions. Miep has given partly conflicting testimony about the way in which Van Maaren gained possession of the keys: in 1948 she claimed "the keys were taken away from me and handed to Van Maaren"; in 1963 (presumably after she was confronted with Van Maaren's 1948 statement to the Amsterdam police: "After the arrest, I did indeed receive the keys from Mrs. Gies, but I did not know that that was done on the orders of the SD") she claimed that she had handed the keys to Van Maaren at his own request.[73] This last statement, as we have already said,[74] conflicts with Jan Gies's testimony given that same day, in which he said that Silberbauer took the keys from her. In her declaration of 1974 and her later statements to us she insisted on the accuracy of her 1948 version and of her husband's statement in 1963.[75] There is no doubt that she herself had thought of bestowing the title of *Verwalter* (administrator) on Van Maaren. She obviously believed that this would help ensure the survival of the business; for the same reason she also sent Van Maaren to the SD with an otherwise pointless letter she made him sign as *Verwalter*. In April 1985, incidentally, she wrote to us saying that she could no longer recall this event.[76]

In 1948 she declared that when Van Maaren was handed the keys "it became perfectly obvious that he was extremely pleased about it."[77] In 1985, however, she wrote to us that Van Maaren had come up to her during the afternoon of August 4 "to apologize for the fact that he had had to accept the keys from Silberbauer and that he was therefore in charge. He clearly did not feel happy about it."[78] Even earlier, in April 1984, she had told us that she had been convinced for a long time that Van Maaren was not guilty of the betrayal.[79]

For all her respect for Van Maaren ("a very capable storeman"), for all the confidence she had in him (the keys; *Verwalter*; the request to accompany her to the Annexe that same afternoon; the later request, in the presence of the removal men, to look out for Anne's papers), Miep Gies was nevertheless one of those who, in 1948, gave the most incriminating testimony against Van Maaren.

We believe that this contradiction can only be explained by the fact that both Kleiman and Kugler, who himself had the closest contact with Van Maaren, had not discussed the odd behavior of the warehouseman at any great length with the female office staff before the raid, so that Miep and Bep knew very little about, for instance, the thefts. Bep's assumption that the thefts had only started in the winter after the raid seems to bear out this view.

The following picture of events after the raid thus emerges: until Kleiman's return, Van Maaren enjoyed Miep's confidence to at least some extent, and only after Kleiman's return did the question of the betrayal become one of central importance. In particular, Kleiman must have put together several pieces of the puzzle; perhaps (unlike Miep and Bep) he also knew about Van Maaren's past —after all, he had taken him on as a warehouseman and must have made some inquiries. Under his—and also Kugler's—influence, Miep and Bep thus became convinced that Van Maaren must have been the betrayer. Thus it was Kleiman who, shortly after the Liberation, wrote his first letter to the POD (see p. 30), who in 1947 persuaded Otto Frank—certainly not a vengeful man (see p. 45)— to go to the PRA, and who then wrote his second letter, this time to the PRA. For him Van Maaren's guilt must have been beyond doubt from the very outset.

Nor was he the only one to have a poor opinion of Van Maaren. The workers in the firm next door as well as Van Maaren's own neighbors all considered him to be an obnoxious fellow. But of his treachery there was no proof.

We, too, continue to have doubts. A possible vindication of Van Maaren may be a statement Lages made during his examination on January 3, 1964. We have only the Dutch version, as incorporated in the report by the State Criminal Investigation Department officer:

"Then you ask me whether it makes sense that having received a telephone call giving away the hiding place of one or more people, we should have immediately gone to the building in question and arrested those concerned. My reply to you is that it makes little sense to me, unless the tip came from someone who was well known to us as an informer [. . .] and whose reports had always been based on the truth."[80]

Only Dettmann, who committed suicide shortly after the war, could have provided the answer. In any case, Van Maaren's history and character make it most unlikely that he should have been more than an occasional informer.

All we can say with any conviction is that Van Maaren must have known that Jews were hidden in the building, where they were, as well as how to get there: he must have put two and two together—his general observations, the statements made to him, his "discovery" (both from the roof and also when he scraped off the paint on the back window) of the house at the back, and the position of the bookcase. We can, however, again draw no conclusions from this about his alleged treachery.

There are, as we have said, scores of other possible explanations of the raid. Perhaps Van Maaren was only an indirect link. He was a loudmouth and a boaster, and he undoubtedly mentioned his suspicions and growing knowledge of what was going on in the building to others—to Hartog, and to the warehouseman of the firm next door. There was Hartog's wife's indiscretion. There were others who must have known or suspected something: the merchant in chemical supplies a few buildings up the street, the tradespeople who took provisions to 263, Prinsengracht. How good were they at keeping their own counsel? There is a story about an NSB man who lived in the Westermarkt, diagonally behind 263, Prinsengracht, and who made inquiries of his neighbors about what was going on in the building[81]—he died in 1943, but how many others in the block knew too much and did not keep quiet? There is a letter from a man who, when he was eight years old, climbed into the back of the warehouse one evening with a friend to see what they could find. They were frightened by the flushing of a lavatory in the building above them, and ran away. He never told anyone about this incident, as he informed us by letter in 1981 when confessing to his minor break-in.[82]

How many kept what they knew to themselves? How fast did the rumors grow, the stories in the neighborhood about what was happening at the back of 263, Prinsengracht? It took a good two years before someone picked up the telephone and called the SD. That this someone was Van Maaren does not strike us as an impossibility. To what length could not frustration and rancor drive a man? That it could have been someone else, however, is, we feel, at least as likely. It is no longer possible to reconstruct exactly what happened.

Silberbauer

We referred earlier to the fact that the leader of the group of men who carried out the raid of August 4, 1944, *SS-Oberscharführer* Karl Josef Silberbauer, was traced by Simon Wiesenthal in 1963, eighteen years after the war. The reason it took so long to trace him was due in part to Otto Frank's behavior. He had lost his wife and two daughters but he was not seeking vengeance or retribution. Thus soon after the end of the war, when he realized that Silberbauer's name was known to his former protectors, he asked them not to make this name public. In Austria, he argued, there were many Silberbauers, and any one of them might be mistaken for the SD man in charge of the raiding party. He asked them, instead, to refer to the man as Silberthaler, a name he believed was not to be found in Austria.[83]

In the letter Kleiman wrote shortly after the Liberation, and also in the testimony the other protectors gave during the examination of 1948, the name "Silberbauer" was indeed mentioned, but Schnabel, in his short book published in 1958, referred to the man as Silberthaler.

Simon Wiesenthal, too, started by looking for a Silberthaler. According to an article by Jules Huf, Vienna correspondent of a Dutch paper, it took Wiesenthal two years to look into the past of the fourteen Austrians by that name. When it appeared that the name did not fit any of them, he turned his attention to an internal SD telephone directory kept in the Netherlands State Institute for War Documentation, in which the name of Silberbauer did appear. Through this lead he attained his object.[84]

Silberbauer was born in Vienna in 1911. From 1931 to 1935 he served in the Austrian army; next he joined the Vienna *Schutzpolizei* (the regular, uniformed police). In 1939 he reported for service with the SS; he had not been a member of the Nazi Party. In 1941 he served in the *Staatspolizei* (i.e., the Gestapo) in his native Vienna.[85] In November 1943 he was transferred to the *Sicherheitsdienst* (the SD, the Security Service of the SS) in The Hague, where he was assigned a position in Division IVB4 of the Amsterdam *Aussenstelle* (outpost). In October 1944 he was involved in a serious traffic accident on the road from Amsterdam to The Hague. Following stays in the hospital in both Amsterdam and Groningen he returned to Vienna in April 1945. After the war, according to his statements to Jules Huf, he was imprisoned for fourteen months "because communists complained that I had ill-treated them in 1938." In 1954 he was able to resume his career in the Vienna police force. On October 4, 1963, he was obliged to surrender his revolver and was placed on the non-active list pending a fresh investigation into his activities in the Netherlands.[86]

As soon as the press found out where he lived, he was quick to concede that he was indeed the one who had arrested the people in hiding in the Annexe. That in itself, however, was not sufficient to bring him to trial.

The press fell as one on the news of Silberbauer's identification and immediately also reported that he had named "the warehouseman" as the informer.[87]

The investigation by the Viennese authorities, who were working in close collaboration with the Amsterdam police, did not produce enough evidence to start proceedings against Silberbauer. On June 3, 1964, the Dutch daily newspapers reported that the judicial investigation had been dropped. Disciplinary proceedings against Silberbauer (who was still suspended) were, however, continued. A month later the disciplinary commission concluded that, though Silberbauer had not mentioned the raid of August 4, 1944, when applying for a post in the Vienna police after the war, he had not concealed his wartime role. The commission accordingly decided to lift his suspension. The police authority appealed against this decision.[88] Three months later the disciplinary commission of the Austrian Ministry of Internal Affairs dismissed that appeal. A declaration by Otto Frank that Silberbauer had obviously acted on instructions and that he had behaved correctly during the raid had, as the Austrian newspaper *Volksblatt* reported, been a crucial factor in this decision.[89] Silberbauer returned to his old job.

Notes

[1] L. de Jong, *Het Koningrijk der Nederlanden in de Tweede Wereldoorlog*, Vol. 7 (The Hague: Nijhoff, 1978), p. 441.

[2] See p. 49.

[3] See Silberbauer's statement, p. 37.

[4] *Anne Frank's Diary*; Schnabel, *The Footsteps of Anne Frank* (London: Longmans Green, 1959), p. 99.

[5] Examination of Hermine (Miep) Gies-Santrouschitz by the State Criminal Investigation Department, Amsterdam, December 23, 1963. Doc. 1, K. J. Silberbauer.

[6] Examination of Hermine (Miep) Gies-Santrouschitz, ibid.; examination of Elisabeth (Bep) van Wijk-Voskuijl, December 13, 1963, ibid.; examination of J. Kleiman by Amsterdam police, January 12, 1948. Ministry of Justice, W. G. van Maaren dossier.

[7] Entries on September 16 and October 17, 1943, and on April 15, 18, 21 and 25, 1944.

[8] Examination of J. Kleiman by Amsterdam police, January 12, 1948. Ministry of Justice, W. G. van Maaren dossier.

[9] Examination of Hermine (Miep) Gies-Santrouschitz by Amsterdam police, January 14, 1948. Ministry of Justice, W. G. van Maaren dossier.

[10] Examination of Hermine (Miep) Gies-Santrouschitz by the State Criminal Investigation Department, Amsterdam, December 23, 1963. Doc. 1, K. J. Silberbauer.

[11] Examination of J. A. (Jan) Gies by the State Criminal Investigation Department, Amsterdam, December 23, 1963. Doc. 1, K. J. Silberbauer.

[12] Examination of W. G. van Maaren by the State Criminal Investigation Department, Amsterdam, October 6, 1964. Doc. 1, K. J. Silberbauer.

[13] Hermine (Miep) Gies-Santrouschitz, February 27, 1985; Mr. and Mrs. Gies, April 18, 1985.

[14] Examination of Hermine (Miep) Gies-Santrouschitz by Amsterdam police, January 14, 1948. Ministry of Justice, W. G. van Maaren dossier.

[15] Hermine (Miep) Gies-Santrouschitz, February 27 and April 18, 1985.

[16] J. Kleiman, [1945]. Ministry of Justice, W. G. van Maaren dossier; examination of W. G. van Maaren by the State Criminal Investigation Department, Amsterdam, October 6, 1964. Doc. 1, K. J. Silberbauer.

[17] The warehouseman L. Hartog, to whom we shall refer again.

[18] As in note 16.

[19] N.V. Nederlandsche Opekta Maatschappij (signed by J. Kleiman), July 16, 1947, to PRA, Amsterdam. Ministry of Justice, W. G. van Maaren dossier.

[20] Examination of J. Kleiman by Amsterdam police, January 12, 1948. Ministry of Justice, W. G. van Maaren dossier.

[21] Examination of V. G. Kugler by Amsterdam police, January 14, 1948. Ministry of Justice, W. G. van Maaren dossier.

[22] Examination of Hermine (Miep) Gies-Santrouschitz by Amsterdam police, January 14, 1948. Ministry of Justice, W. G. van Maaren dossier.

[23] Examination of P. J. Genot by Amsterdam police, March 10, 1948. Ministry of Justice, W. G. van Maaren dossier.

[24] Examination of A. Genot-van Wijk by Amsterdam police, March 10, 1948. Ministry of Justice, W. G. van Maaren dossier.

[25] Examination of L. Hartog by Amsterdam police, March 20, 1948. Ministry of Justice, W. G. van Maaren dossier.

[26] W. G. van Maaren on February 2, 1948, to Political Investigation Branch, Amsterdam police. Ministry of Justice, W. G. van Maaren dossier.

[27] Ibid.

[28] Examination of W. G. van Maaren by Amsterdam police, March 31, 1948. Ministry of Justice, W. G. van Maaren dossier.

[29] Ibid.

[30] Ibid.

[31] Ibid.

[32] Interim Report, April 1, 1948, of PRA, Amsterdam. Ministry of Justice, W. G. van Maaren dossier.

[33] Ministry of Justice, W. G. van Maaren dossier.

[34] Public Prosecutor of the Amsterdam Special Court of Justice to the Chief Commissioner, Amsterdam police, November 15, 1948. Ministry of Justice, W. G. van Maaren dossier.

[35] Ministry of Justice, W. G. van Maaren dossier.

[36] Ibid.

[37] Ibid.

[38] Ibid.

[39] Examination of J. J. de Kok by the State Criminal Investigation Department, Amsterdam, November 26, 1963. Doc. 1, K. J. Silberbauer.

[40] Examination of Otto Frank by the State Criminal Investigation Department, Amsterdam, December 2, 1963. Doc. 1, K. J. Silberbauer.

[41] Examination of Elisabeth (Bep) van Wijk-Voskuijl by the State Criminal Investigation Department, Amsterdam, December 13, 1963. Doc. 1, K. J. Silberbauer.

[42] Examination of Hermine (Miep) Gies-Santrouschitz by the State Criminal Investigation Department, Amsterdam, December 23, 1963. Doc. 1, K. J. Silberbauer.

[43] Examination of J. A. (Jan) Gies by the State Criminal Investigation Department, Amsterdam, December 23, 1963. Doc. 1, K. J. Silberbauer. Cf. p. 29.

[44] As in note 42.

[45] Ibid.

[46] State Criminal Investigation Department, Amsterdam. Doc. 1, K. J. Silberbauer.

[47] Examination of W. P. F. Lages by the State Criminal Investigation Department, Amsterdam, December 6, 1963. Doc. 1, K. J. Silberbauer.

[48] The documents in question are dated August 21, 1963, November 25, 1963, and March 4, 1964. Doc. 1, K. J. Silberbauer.

[49] Examination of K. J. Silberbauer by Polizeirat Dr. Wiesinger, March 4, 1964. Doc. 1, K. J. Silberbauer. The reference here is to Abraham Kaper, a former detective attached to the Amsterdam police who was sentenced to death for war crimes in 1948 and executed in 1949.

[50] Statement by K. J. Silberbauer, August 21, 1963. Doc. 1, K. J. Silberbauer.

[51] Ibid.

[52] Examination of K. J. Silberbauer by Polizeirat Dr. Wiesinger, March 4, 1964. Doc. 1, K. J. Silberbauer.

[53] Deposition of K. J. Silberbauer, November 25, 1963. Doc. 1, K. J. Silberbauer.

[54] As in note 52.

[55] Examination of W. G. van Maaren by the State Criminal Investigation Department, Amsterdam, October 6, 1964. Doc. 1, K. J. Silberbauer.

[56] Report of the State Criminal Investigation Department, Amsterdam, 1964, pp. 34–35, Doc. 1, K. J. Silberbauer.

[57] As in note 55.

[58] Report of the State Criminal Investigation Department, Amsterdam, 1964, pp. 36–37, Doc. 1, K. J. Silberbauer.

[59] Ibid., p. 34.

[60] Ibid., p. 35.

[61] Ibid., pp. 35–36.

[62] State Criminal Investigation Department, Amsterdam, to the public prosecutor, Amsterdam District Court, November 6, 1964. Doc. 1, K. J. Silberbauer.

63 Eric Pedersen to Amsterdam Municipality, January 1974, Anne Frank Collection, 1 a.

64 Statement by Hermine (Miep) Gies-Santrouschitz before notary A. J. Dragt, June 5, 1974, Anne Frank Collection, 1 d.

65 Statement by Elisabeth (Bep) van Wijk-Voskuijl before notary A. J. Dragt, June 5, 1974, Anne Frank Collection, 1 d.

66 Schnabel, *The Footsteps of Anne Frank*, p. 104; *cf.* p. 21.

67 *Yad Vashem Studies*, XIII (1979), pp. 353–83.

68 Ibid., p. 358.

69 Examination of Elisabeth (Bep) van Wijk-Voskuijl by the State Criminal Investigation Department, Amsterdam, December 13, 1963. Doc. 1, K. J. Silberbauer.

70 State Criminal Investigation Department, Amsterdam, to public prosecutor, Amsterdam District Court, November 6, 1964. Doc. 1, K. J. Silberbauer.

71 Report by the Criminal Investigation Department, Amsterdam, 1964, p. 21. Doc. 1, K. J. Silberbauer.

72 See p. 31.

73 Examination of W. G. van Maaren by Amsterdam police, March 31, 1948. Ministry of Justice, W. G. van Maaren dossier; *cf.* pp. 23 and 29.

74 See p. 29.

75 See p. 29.

76 Letter from Mr. and Mrs. Gies, April 18, 1985.

77 See p. 32.

78 As in note 76.

79 Hermine (Miep) Gies-Santrouschitz, April 5, 1984.

80 Examination of W. P. F. Lages by the State Criminal Investigation Department, Amsterdam, January 3, 1964. Doc. 1, K. J. Silberbauer.

81 Telephone call from Mrs. N. N. (who does not wish to have her name published), February 6, 1981.

82 Telephone call from H. Weinberg, Schiedam, October 13, 1981. He also informed us in writing that the boys must have broken in on March 25, 1943, one of the dates mentioned in Anne's diary.

83 Hermine (Miep) Gies-Santrouschitz, April 5, 1984.

84 *Nieuws van de Dag*, November 20, 1963; all national newspapers gave a great deal of coverage to Silberbauer in their editions of November 20 and 21.

85 Berlin Document Center, Berlin.

86 Draft of article by Jules Huf, a Dutch journalist resident in Vienna, November 1963.

87 Various Dutch daily newspapers, November 21, 1963.

88 *Algemeen Handelsblad* and *De Telegraaf*, July 2, 1964.

89 *Volksblatt* (Vienna), October 16, 1964.

HARRY PAAPE

The prisoners were driven straight from the Prinsengracht to the Amsterdam headquarters of the SD, which had been established in two requisitioned school buildings in Euterpestraat. Since about the end of 1943, the Jewish Section (*Judenreferat* IVB4) had been located in a building directly across the street with its main entrance in Adama van Scheltemaplein. This building also housed the notorious *Zentralstelle für jüdische Auswanderung* (Central Office for Jewish Emigration). Almost from the start the people of Amsterdam referred to these German administrative centers not by their titles nor by the name of the school, but simply as "the Euterpestraat." The address, and the scenes played out there during the Occupation, had so sinister a reputation that Euterpestraat was renamed shortly after the war in memory of Gerrit van der Veen, a leading Resistance fighter who was killed in 1944 by a German firing squad. On November 26, 1944, the main building was badly damaged during a British air raid and the building in Adama van Scheltemaplein was largely destroyed.[1]

Once they had reached their destination, the protectors were separated from the hiders. Kleiman and Kugler were taken that same day to detention in the prison in Amstelveenseweg. On September 7—just over a month later—they were transferred to Weteringschans prison. They were not brought before a court, any more than were many other Dutchmen arrested for rendering help to Jews. Four days later both men were sent to the *Polizeiliches Durchgangslager Amersfoort* (Amersfoort police transit camp), bound for *Arbeitseinsatz* (labor service) in Germany.[2] After a few days Kleiman (who had been suffering from a stomach complaint for some time) had a gastric hemorrhage which rendered him unfit for any form of work. Thanks to the intervention of the Netherlands Red Cross, he and several other camp inmates were released on September 18. "*Entlassen Heimatort* [Released to home address]," we can read in one of the camp registers.[3] For several weeks he was not well enough to leave his home, but by about the end of October he had recovered sufficiently to take charge at Prinsengracht again. On November 6 he registered at the Chamber of Commerce as acting director of Gies & Company. After the war he became a director of Pectacon once more. He continued to serve in this capacity until his death in 1959.[4]

Kugler was to have been transported from Amersfoort to a German labor camp during the night of September 17 in the company of another 1,100 men, but as a consequence of the landings near Arnhem and the beginning of Operation Market Garden, their transport was canceled. On September 26 the 1,100 were taken to Zwolle under German guard to dig antitank trenches and build other defense works. On December 30, Kugler and a large number of others were taken to Wageningen to carry out trench work there, again under German guard. Almost three months later, on March 28, 1945, some six hundred of them left Wageningen under guard to be marched towards Germany. In the little town of Zevenaar, close to the German border, the column was attacked by British Spitfires. Kugler took advantage of the ensuing confusion and escaped into a field. He hid with a farmer in the neighborhood for a few days, then headed west on a bicycle. By about the middle of April he was back in his home in Hilversum, where he lay low until the Liberation a few weeks later.[5] After the Liberation he returned to his old job, but in 1955 he emigrated to Canada; he died in Toronto in 1981.

The eight Jewish prisoners were transferred the day after their arrest to Weteringschans prison. On August 8 they were sent from there to Westerbork, the *Judendurchgangslager* (Jewish transit camp), to which virtually every Jew in the Netherlands who failed to keep out of German hands was taken before starting the journey "to the East" (the extermination camps in Poland). They remained in Westerbork for the whole of August. We know little about what happened to them there. Ernst Schnabel quotes an eyewitness report that Anne and Peter were always together and that Anne looked radiant and happy.[6]

On September 3 the Frank and Van Pels families and Friedrich Pfeffer were transported from Westerbork to Auschwitz, arriving at the station in the small Polish town on the night of September 5–6. They were part of a group of 1,019 people from Westerbork: 498 men, 442 women and 79 children. Their "selection" took place on the platform. Those who were in any way capable of walking were marched from the station to Auschwitz-Birkenau extermination camp. Two hundred and fifty-eight men and 212 women were admitted, having first had a number tattooed on their arms; the remaining 549 persons—among them all the children under the age of fifteen—were gassed that same day, September 6.[7] Among them was Van Pels.[8] Pfeffer was the next of the little group of eight to lose his life (the group, incidentally, had been separated immediately upon arrival in Auschwitz; the women were sent to *Frauenblock* [women's block] 29,[9] but no further details are known about the men). Pfeffer died on December 20, 1944, but in Neuengamme concentration camp,[10] not in Auschwitz. According to the *Hefte von Auschwitz* (Auschwitz Notebooks), there was no direct transfer of male prisoners from Auschwitz to Neuengamme during the period from September 6 to December 20. It is probable that Pfeffer was transferred from Auschwitz to the Sachsenhausen concentration camp on October 29 and from there to Neuengamme. Alternatively, he may have been on a transport from Auschwitz to Buchenwald on October 28.[11]

In Auschwitz, the approaching end of Nazi rule meanwhile gradually made itself felt. By October only a few large transports were still arriving: on October 20 and 24 two transports from Theresienstadt brought 1,500 and 1,715 prisoners respectively, of whom more than 1,800 were gassed on the day of their arrival; on October 28 a transport arrived from Bolzano, Italy, and 137 men and an unknown number of women and children were gassed. Sometimes the exterminations were aimed at special groups. Thus on October 20 the *Hefte von Auschwitz* reported the gassing of "1,000 boys aged 12 to 18"; that same day 1,000 adult men from the camp suffered the same fate. The next day, too, the gas chambers were working to full capacity: they again consumed almost 2,000 people. On other days, the *Hefte* mention "only" a few, or a few dozen, victims.

On November 2, *Reichsführer-SS* Heinrich Himmler ordered the gassings stopped and the eradication of all traces of the mass murders. Nevertheless on November 3 several hundred more people—only the number of the men, 481, is known—from a large transport from Czechoslovakia were gassed. The murders continued, albeit by other means and on a smaller scale. According to the *Hefte von Auschwitz*, the last gassing took place on November 28 (five women). On November 25 the SS had begun dismantling the crematoria. One day later Himmler ordered the destruction of all the crematoria in Auschwitz.

Ausgangs Transporte
nach dem Osten.

innen	Frauen	Kinder	Total	Bemer-kungen TRANSPORT Nº		Datum 1943:	Männer	Frauen	Kinder	Total	Bemer-kungen TRANSP. Nº
			33581								
			726	37		Juli 20	824	996	389	2209	69
			709	38		Aug 24	391	503	107	1001	70
			826	39		" 31	365	481	157	1003	71
			811	40		Sept. 7	371	454	164	989	72
			927	41		Sept 14	416	476	112	1004	73
			1157	42		" 21	445	465	69	979	74
			750	43		Okt. 19	495	425	87	1007	75
			748	44		Nov. 16	395	440	161	996	76
			516	45		1944 Januar 25	391	435	122	948	77
			659	46		Februar 8	340	454	221	1015	78
			890	47		März 3	353	316	63	732	79
			1184	48		März 23	387	169	43	599	80
			1108	49		April 5	106	112	22	240	81
			45615			Mei 19	199	220	34	453	82
						Sept. 3	498	442	79	1019	83
979	630	92	1101	50							
863	634	108	1105	51							
790	620	95	1105	52							
738	520	98	464	53							
403	720	127	1250	54							
414	662	179	1255	55							
710	1063	247	2020	56							
418	642	144	1204	57							
416	592	158	1166	58							
444	632	128	1204	59							
414	510	263	1187	60							
534	756	156	1446	61							
908	1084	519	2511	62							
954	1369	539	2862	63							
944	1347	513	3066	64							
612	1348	1055	3015	65							
	2	3	5								
863	1104	430	2397	66							
797	1057	363	2417	67							
732	911	345	1988	68							

The train in which the eight inmates of the Annexe were deported was the last
to leave Westerbork for Auschwitz. The Westerbork "transport book" lists 83
"eastward-bound" trains; 64 went to Auschwitz and 19 to Sobibor. (Netherlands
State Institute for War Documentation.)

Conditions at Auschwitz-Birkenau, and especially in the *Frauenlager* (women's camp), may be gleaned from a laconic report in the *Hefte von Auschwitz*: "From December 1–27, 1944, 2,093 female prisoners died in the women's camp."

The mother of Margot and Anne was not yet among those. She was to be, however, the next victim after Pfeffer from among those arrested in Amsterdam on August 4: she died in Auschwitz-Birkenau on January 6, 1945.[12]

On the approach of the Red Army, which had started its winter offensive on January 12, the SS dragged tens of thousands of prisoners away with them from the Auschwitz complex. Large groups were made to cover scores of kilometers a day during week-long "evacuation expeditions," better known as "death marches," in the biting cold. Those of the exhausted prisoners, poorly clad and shod and severely debilitated, who could not keep up with the column were shot at the side of the road by the SS escort. And thousands of those, too, who were carried off in railroad trucks, many of them open, to unknown destinations (the escorting SS men were simply looking for other concentration camps farther to the west with room to take a few hundreds or thousands more prisoners), perished "somewhere in Europe" of hunger, thirst or exhaustion, or from an SS bullet.

On January 20 the remaining SS men left Auschwitz, but the following day other SS units turned up in the camp; they continued to erase the traces of their crimes, and in passing shot another few dozen prisoners. Then they moved on again. During the night of January 25 the last crematorium was blown up. By the time the Russians arrived in the camp on January 27 all the SS men had fled.[13]

Mrs. van Pels and a group of eight other women had been transferred from Auschwitz to Belsen on November 24. On February 6, 1945, she was sent from Belsen to Buchenwald and on April 9 to Theresienstadt. She was probably dragged on farther still, although the Dutch Red Cross has no additional information about her and simply states that she died "between April 9 and May 8, 1945, in Germany or in Czechoslovakia."[14]

Her son Peter could not have survived her for very long. On January 16, when the liberation of Auschwitz was imminent, he was taken away by the SS guards on one of their "death marches." He survived the journey but according to the Red Cross died on May 5, 1945, in Mauthausen concentration camp in Austria, three days before that camp's liberation.[15]

Anne and Margot stayed in Auschwitz for less than two months. From the end of October there were a great many transports from the *Frauenlager* to other concentration camps. Three of these transports—on October 28 and on November 1 and 2 respectively—went to Bergen-Belsen.[16] The names of the transportees have not been preserved. If an entry in the *Hefte von Auschwitz* about one of the prisoners taken from Auschwitz to Bergen-Belsen on November 1 ("the artist Lin Jaldati, [whose real name was Carolina Rebecca Rebling-Brilleslijper] who met Anne and Margot Frank in Bergen-Belsen")[17] means that she met both girls on her arrival in the new camp, they must have been on the October 28 transport. Of the latter the *Hefte von Auschwitz*[18] had this to say: "From the transit camp of the *Frauenlager* Auschwitz II [Auschwitz-Birkenau] 1,308 female Jewish prisoners were transferred to Bergen-Belsen concentration camp." This was confirmed to us by Lin Jaldati's sister, who arrived in Bergen-Belsen with the November 1 transport. She told us that Anne and Margot (whom she had previously met in both Westerbork and Auschwitz) ran up to them shortly after she and her sister had arrived.[19]

Bergen-Belsen[20] was originally one of the "better" concentration camps in the Third Reich. It was planned as an *Aufenthaltslager* (transit camp) for Jews

52

earmarked for exchange against Germans held in territories not under Nazi control, or otherwise potentially useful to German interests. This explains why the camp was also referred to as an *Austauschlager* (exchange camp) and why the name Bergen-Belsen had an auspicious ring for many Jews: those in Westerbork in particular felt priviledged if they managed to escape the transports to Auschwitz and were put down for transport to Bergen-Belsen. There always seemed to be the possibility of an exchange to Palestine from there. Altogether the camp accommodated 125,000 Jews, of whom some 50,000 perished, the great majority during the last months before and the first few weeks after the Liberation. Of the 3,750 Dutch prisoners who ended up in Bergen-Belsen, 1,700 lost their lives.[21]

The camp was situated on a bare, barren stretch of the Lüneburgerheide (Lüneburg Heath). The Dutch lawyer Abel Herzberg, who was transported from Westerbork to Bergen-Belsen in 1944, described it as follows:

"The earth in the camp is barren, mud or ice in the winter, and in the summer, sand and dust and gravel. There are no worms in the soil, no butterflies in the air, no dragonflies. No sparrow comes in search of seed, no bird alights on any pole or perch to sing."[22]

And yet Bergen-Belsen was a relatively good camp, even though hunger made itself felt very quickly. There was relatively little ill-treatment and no killing. True, most of the barracks were so badly built that the wind swept through them, the roofs leaked so badly that the beds were often unfit for use and puddles of water stood on the floor, but there was no daily threat of death. People could cling to the hope of an exchange, of emigration to Palestine.

In the autumn of 1944 the two mustering grounds in the *Sternlager* (the "star camp," one of the worst sections in Bergen-Belsen) were used for putting up more barracks, built with wood taken from a concentration camp for Jews in the vicinity of Cracow, some fifty kilometers from Auschwitz. The barracks were described as "in the worst possible condition and crawling with lice."[23]

At the end of October and the beginning of November 1944, when the transports from Auschwitz-Birkenau arrived—a total of 3,659 "sick but potentially curable women" who "after several days' journey in overcrowded cattle trucks reached BB in utter exhaustion"—the new barracks were not yet ready, and the women had to make do with tents. "In the cold and wet of autumn they had to sleep—on a thin layer of straw—in tents completely crammed with people and with neither light nor toilet facilities."

This picture is borne out by one of the women who arrived on these transports: "It was almost impossible to squeeze through the crowds of people in order to get to the tent entrance if you needed to visit the open latrine in front of the tent."[24]

Margot and Anne Frank must have encountered these conditions on arrival at Bergen-Belsen, presumably on October 30, having left Auschwitz on October 28. Their stay in the tent camp came to a dramatic close just over a week later, when a violent storm raged over the heath on November 7 and swept many of the tents away.[25]

For hours the women stood in the hail and the streaming rain, thin blankets over their shoulders; then they were driven with blows into the kitchen tent, and had to spend the night there. Next morning they were put in the shoe workshop to wait while the *Sternlager* hospital, the old age home and two more barracks were cleared within an hour to make room for the women."[26]

Bergen-Belsen at the time of the arrival of British troops. (Netherlands State Institute of War Documentation.)

It took another few weeks before the situation finally settled down; the "Auschwitz women" all ended up in the former *Sternlager*. Margot and Anne were among them.

We know a great deal about conditions at Bergen-Belsen from war correspondents; the pictures taken by allied press photographers when British troops liberated the camp appeared in newspapers and journals all over the world and provided millions of people with their first glimpse of the horrors of German concentration camps.

During the winter months overcrowding in the camp grew even worse. The wretched housing conditions in many parts of the camp allowed the elements full play. The supply of food broke down. In the growing chaos and with the imminent risk of infection, the SS were unable to keep even a semblance of order and concentrated on just one task: preventing escape. Hunger, cold, rain and snow and the lack of even the most elementary hygienic measures contributed to the spread of infectious diseases among the weakened prisoners. An acute shortage of doctors and the almost complete lack of drugs ensured that even the simplest cases could no longer be cured.[27]

As the winter drew to an end, a typhus epidemic laid claim to tens of thousands of victims. Weakened and exhausted as they were, Margot and Anne, too, fell victim to it. We do not know exactly when they died, since there was no longer any question of administration at the camp. After the war the Dutch Red Cross went to a great deal of trouble to try to determine the date of death of all Dutch victims. In many cases they failed and had to confine themselves to estimates and probabilities.

54

In Margot and Anne's case, the date arrived at in this way was March 31.[28] There are, however, some indications that they both died a few weeks earlier, possibly at the end of February or the beginning of March. After the war a number of prisoners—all of them women—made statements that Margot had died a few days before Anne.[29]

After the Liberation

Otto Frank was the only one of the eight who had been in hiding in the Annexe to survive the deportation. He was among the prisoners who were left behind in Auschwitz and was liberated by the advancing Russian armies on January 27, 1945. He began his long journey home to the Netherlands on March 5, and while on the train he met a companion in distress, Elfriede Geiringer-Markovits.

She had fled to the Netherlands from Vienna with her husband and two children in March 1940, and the family had made their home in the same Amsterdam square as the Frank family.[30]

During the war, she remembered, she had met Anne (who knew her daughter) on one occasion. "I was at the dressmaker's when a young girl walked in alone. She only tried on one dress."[31] She was surprised by Anne's self-possession, which contrasted sharply with the much more diffident manner of her own daughter, a girl of the same age.

With her husband, son and daughter she had been deported to Auschwitz from Westerbork on May 19, 1944.[32] Her husband and son had perished.[33] At one of the stops made by the train taking them away from Auschwitz, her daughter came to tell her: "I've just seen Anne Frank's father." And so Otto and Elfriede met. The train took them to Odessa, in the south of the Soviet Union on the Black Sea, where they arrived on April 25, leaving again on May 21 on the *Monoway*, a New Zealand ship. The ship took them to Marseilles, where they arrived on May 27, and there their ways parted. Otto reached Amsterdam on June 3, over four months after his liberation.[34] Elfriede took a few weeks longer over the last part of her journey. They met up again some time later, and were married in November 1953.[35] In February 1954 the Amsterdam Public Registration Office recorded that Elfriede had moved to Basle. Otto Frank, who had acquired Dutch nationality in 1949,[36] himself moved to Basle, where his mother and sister lived, as early as 1952. He went back to Amsterdam regularly for a few days at a time every year until 1955.

On his return to Amsterdam after the war Otto continued to look after the affairs of his companies, which remained established in the Prinsengracht for some considerable time. On September 17, 1944, the Dutch government in exile in London had decided that the regulations concerning the removal of Jews from business life "must be deemed never to have been promulgated."[37] As a result, Pectacon could be resurrected immediately after the Liberation, with Otto Frank and Kleiman as directors and Kugler as their proxy. Both Otto and Kugler retired on February 1, 1955; Kleiman stayed in office until his death in January 1959. Like Pectacon, Gies & Co. also survived. Kleiman retired as acting director in the summer of 1945; Kugler stayed on as director. In 1948, Otto Frank and Jan Gies were made supervisory directors. In 1955 all three of them retired and the business was sold.[38]

As far as Opekta was concerned, Otto Frank was faced with considerable problems. The exchange of letters with Tosin in 1941 and the letter from Pomosin to the *Wirtschaftsprüfstelle* were to affect the implementation of a statutory order promulgated in 1944 by the Dutch government in London concerning the property of the nationals of enemy powers.[39] As a stateless person of German origin, Otto was subject in principle to this decision. However, in his case the Nederlands Beheers Instituut (NBI)* decided in 1947 that he was no longer "an enemy national in the sense of the Order concerning enemy property."[40] He was accordingly allowed to resume his directorship of Opekta, at Kleiman's side.[41]

However, no amount of argument by Otto or Tosin helped to convince the NBI that the loan granted to Otto by Erich Elias in 1933 and taken over by Tosin in 1941 was a "friendly arrangement" of a personal kind.[42] According to the NBI, Otto's debt had been transferred, not to Tosin personally, but via Opekta-Switzerland to the firm of Rovag and hence ultimately to Pomosin-Frankfurt; it was therefore due to be repaid to the NBI under the terms of the order concerning enemy property. The affair dragged on for a long time, the Amsterdam Tax Inspectorate also becoming involved. In the end, Otto obtained permission from the NBI to repay the loan in installments. Because of his own claims on the LVVS (see p. 13) and the relatively poor results of Opekta during the first postwar years, the sums he had to remit were small.[43]

The matter was finally resolved by a decision of the Minister of Internal Affairs on September 4, 1950: Opekta-Switzerland would be removed from the list of enemy nationals by virtue of an agreement between the Netherlands and Switzerland in February 1950 concerning settlement of conflicting claims to German property. Three weeks later the NBI drew the necessary conclusions.[44] On January 23 it had already transferred the amounts paid in by Otto (5,000 guilders) to the Nederlandse Bank, on behalf of the Swiss company.[45] Further repayments of his old debt caused Otto few worries: by 1952, Opekta was producing exceptionally favorable results.[46]

Otto remained a director for some time following his move to Switzerland. In 1953, all financial difficulties having been overcome, he retired. That same year Opekta, at Otto's urgings, bought the premises at 263, Prinsengracht, which, as the minutes of the general meeting of shareholders on April 27, 1953, noted, were "of special interest to Mr. Frank." It was laid down that Otto "or a foundation appointed by him" would take the premises over in due course and that no financial disadvantages would accrue to Opekta. Some time later, however, it looked as if the property would be under serious threat from the demolition of the next-door premises. It was therefore sold in 1954 to a broker, who a year later sold it to an Amsterdam clothing company. The latter donated the building in 1957 to the recently established Anne Frank Foundation.

Opekta continued to be run by Kleiman as managing director and Dunselman as supervisory director. Kleiman continued in office until his death in 1959; Dunselman retired on January 1, 1975.[47] Miep and Bep had both resigned in 1947; Miep in order to devote herself to her family, and Bep because she was expecting a baby.[48]

Otto Frank, who had been living in Basle since 1952 and in the small suburb of Birsfelden since 1962, died in Birsfelden on August 19, 1980.

---

*The body charged with the administration of enemy property in the Netherlands, of the property of members of the NSB (the Dutch Nazi Party), and of the property of deported Dutch citizens who had not returned.

56

Notes

[1] A. Korthals Altes, *Luchtgevaar. Luchtaanvallen op Nederland 1940–1945 (Danger from the Air. Air Attacks on the Netherlands 1940–1945)* (Amsterdam; Sijthoff, 1984), pp. 268–71.

[2] Netherlands Red Cross form filled in by Kleiman on October 14, 1945; "The Reminiscences of Victor Kugler, the 'Mr. Kraler' of Anne Frank's Diary," as told to Eda Shapiro, in *Yad Vashem Studies* XIII (1979), pp. 365 and 372.

[3] Kugler to CADSU (Centraal Afwikkelingsbureau Duitse Schade Uitkeringen [Central Office for the Reparation of German Damages]), January 23, 1963; letter [1945] by Kleiman, intended for the POD, Amsterdam; report by the Netherlands Red Cross Information Bureau; the records of *Polizeiliches Durchgangslager Amersfoort* (Amersfoort police transit camp).

[4] Amsterdam Chamber of Commerce and Industry, files of Gies & Co. and Pectacon.

[5] Kugler to CADSU, January 23, 1963; *Yad Vashem Studies* XIII, pp. 372–82.

[6] Schnabel, *The Footsteps of Anne Frank*, p. 127.

[7] *Hefte von Auschwitz*, 1964, No. 8, p. 63.

[8] Netherlands Red Cross, dossier 103586.

[9] Schnabel, *The Footsteps of Anne Frank*, p. 131.

[10] Netherlands Red Cross, dossier 7500.

[11] *Hefte von Auschwitz*, 1964, No. 8, pp. 63–90.

[12] Netherlands Red Cross, dossier 117265.

[13] For these data we have relied, first, on the *Hefte von Auschwitz* mentioned earlier, and on De Jong, *Het Koninkrijk . . .* , Vol. 10b. For general literature on the extermination of the Jews and the use of poison gas by the Nazis (against other groups as well), the reader is referred to Raoul Hilberg, *The Destruction of the European Jews*, revised and definitive edition, 3 vols. (New York: Holmes and Meier, 1985); *Nationalsozialistische Massentötungen durch Giftgas (National Socialist Mass Murder by Poison Gas)*, published by Eugen Kogon, Hermann Langbein, Adalbert Rückerl et al. (Frankfurt am Main: Fischer, 1983); Ino Arndt/Wolfgang Scheffler, "*Organisierter Massenmord an Juden in national-sozialistischen Vernichtigungslagern. Ein Beitrag zur Richtigstellung apologetischer Literatur* [Organized Mass Murder of Jews in National Socialist Extermination Camps. A Contribution to the Correction of Apologetic Literature]" in *Vierteljahrshefte für Zeitgeschichte*, Vol. 24 (1976), No. 2., pp. 105–35.

[14] Netherlands Red Cross, dossier 103586.

[15] Kleiman to the Netherlands Red Cross on October 14, 1945; Netherlands Red Cross, dossier 135177.

[16] *Hefte von Auschwitz*, 1964, No. 8, pp. 82–83.

[17] Ibid., p. 83.

[18] Ibid., p. 82.

[19] Mrs. M. Brandes-Brilleslijper, November 8, 1985.

[20] For the history of this camp, see Eberhard Kolb, *Bergen-Belsen, Geschichte des "Aufenthaltslagers" 1943–1945 (Bergen-Belsen. History of the "Transit Camp" 1943–1945)* (Hanover: Verlag für Literatur und Zeitgeschehen, 1962), and L. de Jong, *Het Koninkrijk . . .* , particularly Vols. 6 (1975), 7 (1976) and 8 (1978).

[21] L. de Jong, *Het Koninkrijk . . .* , Vol. 8, pp. 117 and 888.

[22] A. J. Herzberg, *Amor Fati. Zeven opstellen over Bergen-Belsen (Amor Fati. Seven Essays on Bergen-Belsen)* (Amsterdam: Moussault, 1946), p. 45.

[23] Kolb, *Bergen-Belsen*, p. 115.

[24] Ibid., p. 116.

[25] Ibid.

[26] Ibid.

[27] Ibid., *passim*.

[28] Netherlands Red Cross, dossiers 117267 and 117266.

[29] Among others the Brilleslijper sisters (see p. 52).

[30] Amsterdam Public Registration Office.

[31] *The Times*, London, April 16, 1977.

[32] Westerbork Records.

[33] Amsterdam Public Registration Office.

[34] Otto Frank to the Netherlands Red Cross Information Bureau, May 22, 1950.

[35] Elfriede Frank-Markovits, November 28, 1985.

[36] *Staatsblad (Government Gazette)* J 518, November 30, 1949.

[37] Decision Implementing the Order Governing Occupation Regulations, September 17, 1944, E 93.

[38] Amsterdam Chamber of Commerce and Industry, Gies & Co. dossier.

[39] Decision on Enemy Property, October 20, 1944, E 133.

[40] Nederlands Beheers Instituut, February 7, 1947. General State Archives, NBI Archives, Opekta dossier.

[41] N.V. Nederlandsche Opekta Maatschappij, Minutes 1935–1954, meeting April 10, 1947.

[42] Otto Frank to NBI, October 7, 1946. General State Archives, NBI Archives, Opekta dossier.

[43] General State Archives, NBI Archives, Opekta dossier.

[44] Decision of the Nederlands Beheers Instituut, September 25, 1950. General State Archives, NBI Archives, Opekta dossier.

[45] NBI to Nederlandse Bank, January 23, 1951. General State Archives, NBI Archives, Opekta dossier.

[46] N.V. Nederlandsche Opekta Maatschappij, Minutes 1935–1954, meeting April 27, 1953.

[47] Amsterdam Chamber of Commerce and Industry, N.V. Nederlandsche Opekta Maatschappij dossier.

[48] Hermine (Miep) Gies-Santrouschitz, December 12, 1985.

5   The Diaries, *Het Achterhuis* and the Translations

GERROLD VAN DER STROOM

Anne Frank was thirteen years old on June 12, 1942. Among her presents was an album of the type used to collect autographs, nearly square in shape, with a red and white checked cover. She was to use it as her diary. On her birthday she wrote on the front page: "I hope I shall be able to confide in you completely, as I have never been able to do in anyone before, and I hope that you will be a great support and comfort to me." This album, to which we shall be referring as "Diary 1,"[1] covers the period from June 12 to December 5, 1942, although Anne Frank made some additions to it in 1943 and 1944 when she also used up some of the pages she had previously left blank.

"Daddy has tracked down another new diary for me" was the first sentence Anne wrote in the next diary that has come down to us. This one, to which we shall be referring as "Diary 2," was an exercise book,[2] begun on December 22, 1943, more than one year after the last entry in Diary 1. It seems unlikely that Anne should have failed to keep a diary during this interval,[3] and we must take it that this portion (made up, perhaps, of more than one part) has been lost. Diary 2 continues until April 17, 1944.

In 1943 and at the beginning of 1944 she also wrote *Verhaaltjes en gebeurtenissen uit het Achterhuis (Tales and Events from the House Behind)*, many of which have been published in English translation as *Tales from the House Behind* (The World's Work [1913] Ltd., 1962), and later as *Tales from the Secret Annex* (New York: Doubleday & Company, Inc., 1983). The account book in which these tales were written down, and to which we shall be referring as *Tales*, has also come down to us.[4]

On the first page of the last diary, "Diary 3"—another exercise book[5]—we read: "Diary of Anne Frank. from 17 April 1944 to." No end date is given. Anne Frank wrote in this volume for the last time on August 1, 1944.

A good four months earlier, on March 28, 1944, Gerrit Bolkestein, Minister of Education, Art and Science in the Dutch government in London, had delivered the following address to the Dutch nation on Radio Oranje:

"History cannot be written on the basis of official decisions and documents alone. If our descendants are to understand fully what we as a nation have had to endure and overcome during these years, then what we really need are ordinary documents—a diary, letters from a worker in Germany, a collection of sermons given by a parson or a priest. Not until we succeed in bringing together vast quantities of this simple, everyday material will the picture of our struggle for freedom be painted in its full depth and glory."

To that end, a "national center"—the later Netherlands State Institute for War Documentation—would be set up "in which all the historical material covering these years will be collected, edited and published—a center that will publish source material and papers, in Dutch and in the other leading languages."

Anne's list of name changes.

"Of course, they all made a rush at my diary immediately," Anne Frank wrote a day after this broadcast. And she continued: "Just imagine how interesting it would be if I were to publish a romance of the 'Secret Annexe.' The title alone would be enough to make people think it was a detective story."

A week later she wrote:

I must work, so as not to be a fool, to get on, to become a journalist, because that's what I want! I know that I *can* write, a couple of my stories are good, my descriptions of the "Secret Annexe" are humorous, there's a lot in my diary that speaks, but—whether I have real talent remains to be seen. [...] I can shake off everything if I write; my sorrows disappear, my courage is reborn. But, and that is the great question, will I ever be able to write anything great [...]?"

On May 11, 1944, she confided to her diary:

12 juni 1942

Dagboek I

Losse vellen

Het Achterhuis

1942

5 december 1942

1943

22 december 1943

2

29 maart 1944
17 april 1944

1944

3

1 augustus 1944

versie a

versie b

versie c

Diagrammatic representation of the successive versions of Anne Frank's diaries.

You've known for a long time that my greatest wish is to become a journalist someday and later on a famous writer. Whether these leanings towards greatness (or insanity?) will ever materialize remains to be seen, but I certainly have the subjects in my mind. In any case, I want to publish a book entitled *Het Achterhuis* after the war. Whether I shall succeed or not, I cannot say, but my diary will be a great help.

And then, after "a great deal of reflection," she wrote on May 20 that she had started on *Het Achterhuis*. "In my head it's already as good as finished, although it won't go as quickly as that really, if it ever comes off at all."

She rewrote her first diaries on sheets of copy paper, to which we shall be referring as the "loose sheets."[6] Thus a second version in her handwriting came about. She changed, rearranged, sometimes combined entries of various dates, expanded and abbreviated. In addition she drew up a list of name changes: "Anne [Frank]" became "Anne Robin," "v. Pels" became "v. Daan, "Pfeffer" became

"Dussel," "Kleiman" became "Koophuis," "Kugler" became "Kraler," "Bep" became "Elly" and so on. She no doubt compiled this list with an eye to the eventual publication of her diary. All the vicissitudes of life in the Annexe in 1943 were described by her on the loose sheets, and there can be no doubt that at the time she must still have been in possession of the relevant part (or perhaps the relevant parts) of her first version. That version was therefore not lost until later. But her second version, also, has not come down to us in full. The last entry on the loose sheets records the events of March 29, 1944. Anne must have reached this point in her rewriting at the beginning of August 1944. It was on August 4 that the *Sicherheitsdienst* raided the Annexe.

On the afternoon of that fatal day, after the eight hidden Jews, together with Kleiman and Kugler, had been taken away, Miep Gies was left alone in the office while the two warehousemen were below. Wisely, Bep Voskuijl stayed away for the first few hours. She and Jan Gies came back at about five o'clock. With Miep and Van Maaren they then went up to the Annexe. According to Miep:

"They'd gone through all the cupboards. On the floor lay books, papers and whatever else was of no importance to the 'Green Police.' At one point we found some loose pieces of paper, an old account book and the exercise books which we had given to Anne when the checked diary was running out of space for her notes. We took the diary, the account book, the exercise books and all the loose pages away with us. But we didn't dare stay up there too long because we were afraid that the 'Green Police' might come back."[7]

Miep locked the diaries and the loose sheets away in her office desk.

One or more weeks later the Annexe was cleared by the removal firm of Abraham Puls on German instructions. On that occasion Miep told Van Maaren to go and collect any pieces of paper covered with writing that might come to light during this operation and give them to her. This he did, and she locked away those sheets, too, in her desk.[8]

Otto Frank returned, via Odessa and Marseilles, to Amsterdam on June 3, 1945.[9] He went straight from the station to the home of Miep and Jan Gies, and he stayed with them for the next few years. He already knew then that his wife was dead, but hope still lingered for his two daughters. At the time, Miep had Anne's writings and papers under lock and key in her desk. At the end of July or the beginning of August, when the fate of Margot and Anne became known, Miep handed Anne's writings over to Otto Frank.[10] He took them with him to his private office and stayed away "for a few hours."[11]

When Otto Frank had read his younger daughter's album, exercise books, account book and loose sheets, he began to make a copy of them on the typewriter in his room in the Gieses' home. As he later explained, at the time he only copied "the essentials" for the benefit of relatives and friends. He omitted whatever he felt would prove of no interest to them, together with passages that might offend living persons, or remarks about Anne's mother that "didn't concern anyone else."[12] The rest he translated into German and sent to his mother, who knew no Dutch, in Basle, Switzerland.[13] According to Otto Frank, this first copy was lost.[14] However the Frank family still have in their possession a copy of Diary I that was probably typed later.

Next, Otto Frank typed out another copy, based on Anne's loose sheets, i.e., on her own second—and final—version. For this typescript (to which we shall be referring as "Typescript I") Otto Frank also selected from the album and the exercise books—that is, from the first version—those items which again struck him as "essential."[15] Seeing that it was not granted to Anne to rewrite her experiences in the Annexe after March 29, 1944, on the loose sheets, Otto Frank had no option but to use the first version for that period. Finally he added four "events" Anne had recorded in her *Tales*, that is, in the account book.

Typescript I has been preserved and is in the possession of the Frank family. The family placed it at the disposal of the Netherlands State Institute for War Documentation for the duration of the investigation into the authenticity of the diaries.[16]

On examining Typescript I, we see that it was indeed compiled from the loose sheets, supplemented with some items from the first version and some from the *Tales*. By far the largest number of pages are composed of pieces of paper pasted together; they contain passages from the second version, or—to a lesser extent—from the first. Clearly, Otto Frank typed out those items in the two versions he wanted to use, cut some out and then joined them up.

Now, while it is true that Anne's second version was his guide in this, he did not copy it blindly, which is not surprising in view of his scruples when preparing the first copy, now lost. Thus he omitted an entry about the home of one of Anne's girl friends (a "bear garden") and also a passage attacking the Van Pels family; again, he left out a number of remarks his dead daughter had made about his dead wife. At the same time he omitted some rather duller entries: a report about Anne's Ping-Pong club, for instance, which was indeed of little interest.

Typescript I was thus compiled by Otto Frank from the extant writings of his daughter. For the sake of propriety, the good name of third parties, and in order to maintain interest, he felt he had here and there to omit certain passages. However, he copied the sections from his daughter's manuscripts that he did use with great accuracy. Typescript I contains only very occasional alterations to the manuscripts. Let us give a few examples: he changed the slightly wrong word "*pogromen* [pogroms]" into the quite wrong "*progrooms*," "North America" into "U.S.A." and "*overbriefadres* [forwarding address]" into "*overbrengadres* [redelivery address]." One may wonder whether any of these changes were improvements.

Apparently Otto Frank did not feel altogether sure of his ground; thus he handed Typescript I to his old friend Albert Cauvern, the husband of his former secretary Isa Cauvern.[17] In 1945, Cauvern was a dramatist working for VARA (the workers' broadcasting channel). Frank asked him to "revise" the manuscript, or, as he put it many years later, "to check it for grammatical errors and to remove Germanisms, that is, to correct expressions my daughter had borrowed from the German language and which were therefore bad Dutch."[18] And Cauvern did as he was asked.[19]

Typescript I does indeed show numerous changes and improvements with respect to punctuation, spelling *("broschjes* [brooch]" became "*broche*," "*nog* [yet]" became "*noch* [nor]"), word order ("*kennen geleerd* [get acquainted with]" became "*leeren kennen* [get to know]") and terminology ("*Onze 4-familie* [our family of four]" became "*Ons gezin van vier* [the four of us]"). Then there were changes of proper names, generally in agreement with Anne's list. Finally there were some amplifications: "it is even more difficult to stand alone with character and soul" became "it's even harder to stand on your own feet as a conscious, living being. Because if you do, then it's twice as difficult to steer a right path through the sea of problems." Deleted, on the other hand, were such entries as: "Frits Pfeffer. He lives with a much younger, very nice Christian woman to whom he is probably not married, but that makes no difference." The following passage was inserted on the last page:

Anne's Diary ended here.
On 4th August, the "Grüne Polizei" made a raid on the "Secret Annexe" . . .
In March, 1945, two months before the liberation of our country, Anne died in the concentration camp at Bergen-Belsen.

This passage had been added by Cauvern.[20]

The alterations are in pencil and in ink and they are by more than one hand. Cauvern was evidently not alone in making corrections, but we can no longer tell who was responsible for the rest. Moreover, when he was shown Typescript I thirty-six years later, Cauvern considered it "most unlikely" that that was the typescript to which he had made corrections, "because this typescript [I] contains errors which I [Cauvern] would certainly have corrected. Furthermore, the words that were added are not in my hand."[21] This can only mean that there must have been another "first" typescript which has not come down to us.

In the late 1950s the German magazine *Der Spiegel* alleged that Cauvern had made a number of deletions from Anne Frank's text.[22] Even earlier, another German magazine, *Welt am Sonntag*, had written to him about this. His reply was that "at the time" he "made only the most essential corrections (typing errors and lapses in idiom, grammar and punctuation).[23] And he continues: "As for me, I have not deleted a single passage." This is plausible in view of the fact that Typescript I was in any case Otto Frank's abbreviated version of Anne's manuscript, and there was no reason for Cauvern to have cut it further. The typescript produced by Otto Frank and corrected and altered by others was retyped into a fair copy by Isa Cauvern, probably at the beginning of 1946.[24] The resulting new typescript we shall refer to as Typescript II. This too has come down to us and is in the possession of the Frank family, who put it at the disposal of the Netherlands State Institute for War Documentation for the duration of the investigation.[25]

As we said earlier, Otto Frank's first wish was that a wider circle should read the "essential" parts of his daughter's diary. To that end he had copies of Typescript II made for friends and close acquaintances, "that is, for people who I [Otto Frank] believe would be interested in these notes, from which much that concerns our fate emerges."[26]

Dr. Kurt Baschwitz, lecturer in, and later professor of, journalism and mass psychology at Amsterdam, was one who saw the typescript. Baschwitz had emigrated in 1933 from Hitler's Germany to the Netherlands and had met Otto Frank in Amsterdam. The two families were on regular visiting terms. Baschwitz, too, went into hiding during the war. Later, one of his daughters spent some time abroad, and on February 10, 1946, her father wrote to her:

I have just been reading the diary of Anne Frank, the younger daughter of our friend Frank. You must have known her. They were, as you know, in hiding for 2 years. The girl, 14 and then 15 years old, kept a diary which got past the Germans as if by a miracle. It is the most moving document about that time I know, and a literary masterpiece as well. It reveals the inner experiences of a maturing girl, her impressions in close confinement with her father—whom she loved dearly, her mother—with whom she clashed, her sister—whom she discovered to be a friend, with the other family that shared their hiding place, and with their son, with whom she began to fall in love. I think it ought to appear in print.[27]

Prinses Elizabeth van York. Door de B.B.C. is doorgegeven, dat
zij nog niet meerderjarig verklaard is, zoals bij prinsessen
anders vaak het geval is. We hebben ons al afgevraagd, aan
welke Prins deze schoonheid zal worden uitgehuwelijkt, konden
echter geen geschikte vinden; misschien kán haar zuster, Prinses Margaret Rose, Kroonprins Boudewijn van België krijgen?
Hier komen we van de ene misère in de andere, nauwelijks zijn
nu de buitendeuren versterkt, of de magazijnman komt weer op
de proppen. Naar alle waarschijnlijkheid heeft hij aardappel-
meel gestolen en wil nu Elli de schuld in de schoenen schuiven.
Het Achterhuis is begrijpelijkerwijs weer in rep en roer, Elli
is buiten zichzelf van woede.
Ik wil bij "De Prins" aanvragen, of ze een sprookje van me plaat-
sen, natuurlijk onder een pseudoniem.
Tot de volgende keer, darling.
                              Je Anne.

                    ~~Dinsdag~~, 25 April 1944,.

Lieve Kitty,
Sinds 10 dagen spreekt Dussel niet met van Daan en dat alleen,
omdat wij na de inbraak een heleboel nieuwe veiligheidsmaatre-
gelen genomen hebben, waarmee hij zich niet verenigen kan.
Hij beweert dat van Daan hem afgeblaft heeft."Alles gaat hier
ook achter mijn om" zei hij tegen mij,"ik zal er wel met je vader
over spreken." Hij mag nu ook Zaterdagmiddags en Zondags niet
meer beneden op kantoor zitten, maar hij deed het toch, van Daan
was woedend en vader ging naar beneden om met hem te praten.
Natuurlijk had hij weer het een of andere smoesje, maar dat
ging deze keer zelfs bij vader niet op.Vader spreekt nu ook zo
weinig mogelijk met hem, omdat hij hem beledigd heeft.Op welke
manier weten wij geen van allen, maar het zal wel erg zijn.
Ik heb een leuk verhaal geschreven, het heet Blurry de Wereld-
ontdekker en het is zeer in de smaak gevallen van mijn 3 toe-
hoorders.
Ik ben nog steeds verkouden en heb zowel Margot als vader en
moeder aangestoken. Als Peter het maar niet krijgt, hij moest
een zoen hebben en noemde mij zijn "Eldorado" Kan niet eens,
gekke jongen! toch liet is hij toch!
                              haar blz.118

                    Donderdag, 27 April 1944.

Lieve Kitty,
Vanochtend had mevrouw een slecht humeur; niets dan klagen!
Eerst over de verkoudheid, dat zij geen dropjes krijgt, dat
veel neussnuiten niet om uit te houden is. Dan, dat de zon
niet schijnt, dat de invasie niet komt, dat we niet uit het raam
kunnen kijken enz.enz. Wij moesten vreselijk om haar lachen
en het was nog niet zo erg of ze lachte mee.
Op het ogenblik lees ik:Keizer Karel V, door een hoogleraar
van de Universiteit te Göttingen geschreven; deze man heeft
40 jaar aan dit boek gewerkt. In 5 dagen las ik 50 bladzijden,
meer is niet mogelijk. Het boek bevat 598 blz.,nu kun je uit-
rekenen hoe lang ik hierover zal doen en dan nog het tweede deel!
maar...H zeer interessant!
Waar een schoolmeisje in één dag al niet van hoort, neem mij
nu eens. Eerst vertaalde ik van het Hollands in het Engels
een stuk van Nelsons laatste slag. Daarna nam ik het vervolg
van de Noorse oorlog door (1700-1721) , van Peter de Grote,
Karel XII, Augustus de Sterke, Stanislaus Lescinsky, Mazeppa,
van Görz, Brandenburg, Voor- Pommeren, Achter - Pommeren en
Denemarken plus de gebruikelijke jaartallen.
Vervolgens belandde ik in Brazilië, las van de Bahia-tabak, de

A page from Typescript II.

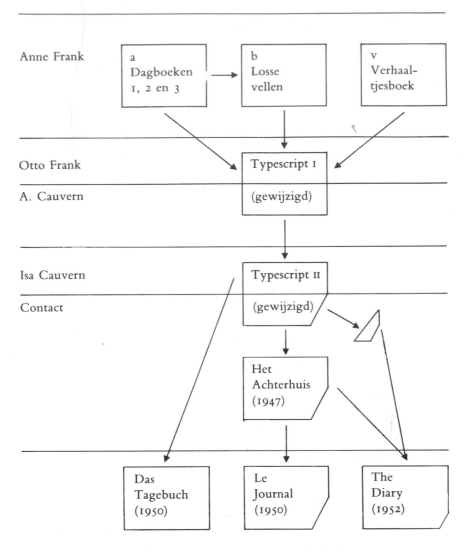

That idea turned out to be not quite as simple as it looked.

Otto Frank had read parts of his daughter's manuscript to his friend Dr. Werner Cahn, who had escaped from Germany to the Netherlands in 1934 and was later active in the Dutch publishing world. It made a "great impression" on Cahn and his wife, and Cahn said that he would try to find a publisher. Otto Frank himself had not thought of publishing the diary at that juncture. As it was, both Em. Querido's Uitgeverij, the Amsterdam publishers, and the Fischer Verlag in Germany turned him down.[28]

Cahn then obtained a copy of Typescript II. He was by this time working as copy editor for the ENSIE–Encyclopedia,[29] whose editor was the well-known Dutch historian, Dr. Jan Romein. Cahn also knew Dr. Romein's wife, Dr. Annie Romein-Verschoor, all three of them being involved in "the left-wing intellectual journal,"[30] *De Nieuwe Stem*. Its editorial board at the time consisted of N. A. Donkersloot, J. P. B. de Josselin de Jong, H. J. Pos, H. M. van Randwijk, Jan Romein and O. Noordenbos.

Cahn was anxious to hear Annie Romein's opinion of Anne Frank's writings and gave her his copy of Typecript II.[31] Evidently she recognized its importance and seems, in her turn, to have looked for a publisher. Among others she, too, tried Querido, "but the certainty prevailed there at the time that interest in anything to do with the war was stone cold dead."[32] In all probability she also offered the manuscript to De Republiek der Letteren, another publishing house, but they, too, failed to appreciate its significance.[33] The publishers De Bezige Bij and J. M. Meulenhoff were apparently also approached, but this can no longer be confirmed.[34]

Dr. O. Noordenbos, at the time reader for the publishers H. Meulenhoff (not to be confused with J. M. Meulenhoff), then advised publication of the diary. But because of "the very intimate nature of the diary and the sexual revelations in it," Meulenhoff rejected it.[35]

It looked as if it was going to be impossible to find a publisher for the book.

Years later Jan Romein commented, in a film produced by Jan Vrijman, that Otto Frank had come to see his wife with "a typed manuscript" (probably Type-script II) and had asked her to help him find a publisher.[36] Otto had probably been introduced or recommended by Cahn. Finding a publisher for Anne's writings was proving to be no easy task. In the end Annie Romein was able, as we have said, to do very little. Jan Romein read the manuscript and was so deeply impressed that he wrote an article about it. The article was published on April 3, 1946, in *Het Parool*:

A Child's Voice

By chance a diary written during the war years has come into my possession. The Netherlands State Institute for War Documentation already holds some two hundred similar diaries, but I should be very much surprised if there were another as lucid, as intelligent, and at the same time as natural. This one made me forget the present and its many calls to duty for a whole evening as I read it from beginning to end.

When I had finished it was nighttime, and I was astonished to find that the lights still worked, that we still had bread and tea, that I could hear no airplanes droning overhead and no pounding of army boots in the street—I had been so engrossed in my reading, so carried away back to that unreal world, now almost a year behind us.

It is written by a Jewish girl who was thirteen years old when she went into hiding with her parents and an older sister and began this diary, and it ends one wretched day more than two years later when the Gestapo discovered the family. One month before the Liberation she died in one of the worst German concentration camps, not yet sixteen.

How she died, I do not wish to ask; it was probably in much the same way as has been described in so many camp reminiscences, for instance in the recently published pamphlet "*Tusschen leven en dood in Auschwitz* [Between Life and Death in Auschwitz]," although that was a different camp.

The way she died is in any case not important. What matters far more is that her young life was willfully cut short by a system whose witless barbarity we swore never to forget or to forgive while it still raged, but which, now that it belongs to the past, we are already busily, if not forgiving, then forgetting, which ultimately comes to the same thing.

To me, however, this apparently inconsequential diary by a child, this "de profundis" stammered out in a child's voice, embodies all the hideousness of fascism, more so than all the evidence at Nuremberg put together. To me the fate of this Jewish girl epitomizes the worst crime perpetrated by everlastingly abominable minds. For the worst crime is not the destruction of life and culture as such—these could also fall victim to a culture-creating revolution—but the throttling of the sources of culture, the destruction of life and talent for the mere sake of mindless destructiveness.

If all the signs do not deceive me, this girl would have become a talented writer had she remained alive. Having arrived here at the age of four from Germany, she was able within ten years to write enviably pure and simple Dutch, and showed an insight into the

67

failings of human nature—her own not excepted—so infallible that it would have astonished one in an adult, let alone in a child. At the same time she also highlighted the infinite possibilities of human nature, reflected in humor, tenderness and love, which are perhaps even more astonishing, and from which one might perhaps shrink, especially when they are applied to very intimate matters, were it not that rejection and acceptance remain so profoundly childlike.

That this girl could have been abducted and murdered proves to me that we have lost the fight against human bestiality. And for the same reason we shall lose it again, in whatever form inhumanity may reach out to us, if we are unable to put something positive in its place. The promise that we shall never forget or forgive is not enough. It is not even enough to keep that promise. Passive and negative rejection is too little, it is as nothing. Active and positive "total" democracy—politically, socially, economically and culturally —is the only solution; the building of a society in which talent is no longer destroyed, repressed and oppressed, but discovered, nurtured and assisted, wherever it may appear. And with all our good intentions, we are still as far from that democracy as we were before the war.

J. Romein

This article caused a stir. Various publishers approached Jan Romein, who referred them to Cahn. One was Uitgeverij Contact in Amsterdam. "I remember very clearly," said K. Lekkerkerker, then an editorial consultant at Contact, "coming into the office one morning with Jan Romein's article about Anne Frank. It must have been April 4, 1946, for the article had been published in *Het Parool* the day before."[37] He gave it to F. E. A. Batten, another editorial consultant at Contact, and asked him to bring it to the attention of the managing director, G. P. de Neve. According to Lekkerkerker, De Neve too must have been impressed by Romein's article[38] and Batten then contacted Cahn. Batten's enthusiasm persuaded Cahn to submit the typescript for consideration.[39] Thus Typescript II found its way to Contact.

Batten advised publication, but De Neve had reservations.[40] The precise nature of these remains unclear, but it is probable that he entertained scruples about certain passages concerning Anne's sexual development. Thus we know that Otto Frank wrote in 1978 to C. Blom, former financial director of Contact, that he knew "that [Contact] had not wanted, among other things, to publish letters referring to sexual topics (menstruation)."[41] Blom told him in his reply that he had raised the matter with Batten:

"He [Batten] told me about the events leading up to the publication of the diary by Contact in great detail. After all, he had played a leading part in it. He also said on the subject that he remembered De Neve telling him that he had suggested to you that certain passages be omitted."[42]

Frank's reaction to this letter was:

"Naturally, after so many years, I no longer remember the precise sequence of events, but I do remember Mr. de Neve telling me that religious advisers had objected to the printing of certain passages (e.g., about menstruation). The proof that I myself did not object to these passages is that they are included in the German and other translations."[43]

In other words, the copy which De Neve saw—Typescript II—which had been compiled by Otto Frank, contained passages that De Neve thought unsuitable or indecorous and accordingly left out. This agrees with what Batten wrote to the Amsterdam historian Dr. Richter Roegholt in 1979:

"I know [. . .] that passages about Anne Frank's mother and Anne's account of her own development into adulthood were deleted from the text offered to Contact on option. These passages were still in the text handed to me by Werner Kahn, who at the time represented Mr. Frank in matters concerning the publication of Anne's book."[44]

To this we should add that all omissions and changes had to be agreed to by Otto Frank, as Anne's heir. And this is indeed what happened, for in 1949 he declared:

"The text was edited at the request of the publishing house. Some unimportant changes were made with my agreement. In addition some passages were left out, again with my agreement. These were entries by my daughter which it was felt might cause offense to the readers. Thus, for instance, the penultimate paragraph of the Dutch version of the entry on January 5, 1944, was a slight abbreviation of the typescript and the original version, in that the story of the two girls touching each other's breasts was omitted; that passage, however, was included in the German edition without objection."[45]

Miep and Jan Gies also

"knew that there were passages referring to Anne's sexuality which were left out by G. P. de Neve. They appear at greater length in the German and English translations. De Neve was a very devout Roman Catholic, and discussed these passages in the diary with his priest."[46]

His partner Blom, however, denied that De Neve was a Roman Catholic, and he may well have been right: G. P. de Neve is not registered in the Roman Catholic Public Registration Office in Amsterdam, while the Municipal Public Registration Office states that he is of "no denomination."[47] But De Neve did discuss possible deletions with people in his own publishing house. His then secretary Elly Hildering still remembers "very clearly a conversation between Batten, De Neve and [H. J.] Scheepmaker in De Neve's office," in which she worked,

"about making deletions. These concerned offensive remarks about Anne's mother as well as a passage about Anne's menstruation that had to be taken out. The three of them agreed on that. Another reason for the omission of certain passages may have been that the book had to fit into the so-called Prologue series published by Contact. It may be that it had to be shortened for that purpose."[48]

The copy of Typescript II which is now in the hands of the Frank family is without doubt the same copy as was submitted to Contact at the time; Lekkerkerker recognized a note in it as being by his own hand.[49] It also contains instructions attributed to Batten by various sources.[50] At the time both men were working for Contact.

In the summer of that year De Nieuwe Stem, founded in 1946, published five "Fragments from the Diary of Anne Frank."[51] It seems most likely that Werner Cahn contributed the copy; De Nieuwe Stem ceased publication in 1968 and its only surviving founder, Dr. O. Noordenbos, said when referring to the journal's first few years: "We also printed passages from the diary of Anne Frank. [. . .] Her father had given it to a friend of mine."[52] That friend was Cahn.[53] Thus the first publication of Anne Frank's writings had taken place. And work was in progress on the book.

Like Typescript I, Typescript II was also amended. Typing errors were corrected and the manuscript style altered to agree with the "house rules"[54] of Contact, rules such as "Do not use abbreviations in fiction." The resulting changes were added to the typescript. Thus next to "Minjh." and "Mevr." we find the instruction—in all probability made by Batten—"write mevrouw/mijnheer out in full!" And the abbreviated forms "'t [the]" and "m'n [my]" become "het" and "mijn," and so on.

Nor was it left at that. Changes were also made in the choice of words. Thus "specerijkamer, tussenkamer, voorkamer [spice room, middle room, front room]" were combined into "pakhuisruimten [storerooms]"; "twee dagen [two days]" became "een paar dagen [a few days]," "Woensdag [Wednesday]" became "Verleden week [last week]"; "strijdpunten [controversial points]" became "twistpunten [points at issue]"; and in "wanhopig en ongelukkig [desperate and unhappy]" the "wanhopig en" was deleted. Altogether there were several dozen such changes in pencil and ink.

In addition, some lines had been pasted over: "ik vaar op eigen kompas [I steer by my own compass]" became "ik schipper alleen" (translated as "I am my own skipper") (which had been used in the original version of the uncorrected Typescript I), "ingredienten [ingredients]" became "toebehoorselen [components]," and "kwam mevrouw die bij de radio had geluisterd, naar boven [the lady (i.e., Mevrouw van Pels) who had been listening to the radio came upstairs]" was changed to "kwam mevrouw, die beneden in het prive-kantoor naar de radio had geluisterd, naar boven [the lady who had been listening to the radio in the private office below came upstairs]." Similarly, the entry "Albert Dussel" was amplified with "wiens vrouw gelukkig in het buitenland verblijft [whose wife is fortunately abroad]." The sentence in Typescript I saying that Dussel was living with a "much younger, very nice Christian woman" was simply crossed out. The change in Typescript II from "zijn Lotje [his Lottie]" into "Lotje, zijn vrouw [Lottie, his wife]" was along the same lines.

In addition to these editorial changes, the typescript was also shortened; twenty-five passages were crossed out in pencil. We should mention in this connection an undated and unsigned note on Contact letter paper under the head of "Proposed deletions."[55] It suggested twenty-six deletions, of which eighteen were in fact made in the typescript. In addition a further seven passages not mentioned in the note were cut. Most of the deleted passages deal with "innocent" matters: a book by Jo van Ammers-Küller, the comedies of Karl Theodor Körner, French irregular verbs, St. Nicholas Day poems, washing of hair, Anne hurting her little toe, the vacuum cleaner being broken, the planning of a Sunday, Franz Liszt, and so on. The size of the cuts varies from two lines (of verse) to a complete "Tale" ("Kitty") or entire diary entries. At the same time—as witnesses remember—two references to menstruation were omitted, together with the reference to two girls touching each other's breasts. These three passages figure on the Contact list.

It is clear that the deletions in Typescript II were made by Contact. Otto Frank obviously saw no reason for omitting the relevant passages from his Typescript I, and for that reason they also appear in Typescript II, i.e., in the typescript handed to Contact. They were probably cut by Contact in order to make the book fit into their Prologue series. The deletion of several other passages was above all the result of the view—held especially by De Neve—that they offended against propriety. Otto Frank concurred.[56] It is by no means unusual for a publisher to make changes, and that is what happened at Contact. As a result the reader was left with a literary work by Anne Frank rather than with an auto-biographical document *sensu strictu*.

The manuscript was now ready. Lekkerkerker took one more look at it and wrote on the title page: "ready for compositor, K[ees] L[ekkerkerker]." And so, in an edition of 1,500 copies,[57] with a preface by Annie Romein-Verschoor and an extract from Jan Romein's article "A Child's Voice" on the jacket, Anne Frank's *Het Achterhuis. Dagboekbrieven van 12 juni 1942–1 augustus 1944* was published as part of the Prologue series in the summer of 1947. "BOOK," Otto Frank wrote in his own diary on June 25, 1947.[58]

He had carried out his daughter's wish, and *Het Achterhuis* was its fulfill-ment.

Het Achterhuis attracted unanimously favorable reviews. We shall quote briefly from some.

Anne Frank had "written a diary in which her intellectual development from the age of thirteen to fifteen is movingly expressed."[59] The "precocity" of "this richly talented child" was remarkable[60]; "the intelligence, the honesty, the insight with which she observed herself and her surroundings and the talent with which she was able to depict what she saw was astonishing."[61] *Het Ach-terhuis* was also judged to be of value educationally: "parents and teachers are most strongly advised to read this book."[62] The book was "a miracle,"[63] "uniquely tragic"[64] and "transcends the misery so recently [in 1947] behind us."[65] Anne Frank would "undoubtedly" have developed into a gifted writer,[66] though the raising of that question was also described as "pointless and full of pain."[67] *Het Achterhuis* was not only "a war document of admirable conciseness," but also "a human document of great clarity and honesty"[68]; her "moral testament" was a "moving" human document,[69] though *Het Achterhuis*—"one of the most poignant" books in Occupation literature—"is by no means a war document as such"—but "purely and simply the diary of an adolescent girl,"[70] a girl who had become "the symbol of those who shared her fate, those murdered by the Germans."[71]

In 1946, meanwhile, a German translation of Typescript II had been made.[72] This translation was originally intended for Anne's grandmother in Basle,[73] who, after all, could not read Dutch, the translation previously done by Otto Frank of the earliest (lost) copy being apparently inadequate.

The journalist Anneliese Schutz, an acquaintance of Otto Frank, offered her services for the new translation. She came from Berlin, had also escaped to the Netherlands, and before the war she had taught Margot literature and had also known Anne.[74] Otto Frank accepted her offer and she set to work. It was probably while the translation was still in preparation that it was decided to find a German publisher,[75] but nothing came of that for the time being. Four copies of the German translation have come down to us, all in the possession of the Frank family. They differ no more than marginally from one another. The Netherlands State Institute for War Documentation has had charge of them for the duration of the inves-tigation.

Anneliese Schutz did not prove to be the most suitable translator for Anne's work. "She was," Otto Frank admitted later, "too old for the job, many of her expressions were pedantic and not in a youthful enough style. In addition she [. . .] misunderstood many Dutch expressions." We can give a number of examples of this.[76] "*De hele rataplan* [the whole bag of tricks]" became "*das ganze Rattennest* [the whole rats' nest]," when the Dutch "*rataplan*" has nothing at all to do with rats; "*het mag misschien onbenullig lijken* [it may seem fatuous]" becomes "*es mag unverständlich sein* [it may seem incomprehensible]"; "*mijn gewiekste antwoorden* [my telling replies]" becomes "*meine beschwingte Antworten* [my bewinged replies]," Schutz presumably having looked up "*gewiekt*" in the dictionary instead of the preceding entry, "*gewiekst*."

Nevertheless Otto Frank felt that "Frau Schutz's translation could by and large be called faithful and in the spirit of the original."[77] According to Werner Cahn, the translation

"although correct, did not always reflect the style of the young Anne Frank. That is, in any case, a particularly difficult thing to do. But this may well be the reason why well-intentioned German literary circles occasionally expressed doubts about the authenticity of the diary."[78]

Since Anneliese Schutz translated a copy of the complete Typescript II, her translation is more comprehensive than the Dutch edition, which was based on a shortened version of Typescript II. Thus in the German edition one does indeed find references to Körner's comedies, to French irregular verbs, the tale "Kitty" (not deleted until later), the vacuum cleaner, the touching of each other's breasts, the passages about menstruation, and so on. On the other hand, in Schutz's version, too, the St. Nicholas Day poems and the reference to Jo van Ammers-Küller have been omitted; they were probably thought to be incomprehensible to non-Dutch readers.

In fact, the translation made further concessions to the non-Dutch reader. Thus it failed to show that those in the Annexe spoke to each other in Dutch, and only now and then in German. The sentence "Because Pim wrote most of his poetry in German, Margot had to translate it" was left out, and so were the words "in German" in the translation of "Mrs. van Pels came back and began to curse in German [. . .]." Similarly the phrase "'*t Kan verkeren*" (roughly: "it's a long lane that has no turning") was thought—no doubt rightly so—to have no exact German equivalent. The sentence in which Anne mentions this motto of Bredero was accordingly not translated.

In addition some changes were made of a more "political" nature. The explanation that to those listening to the radio in the Annexe "there were no forbidden stations with the proviso that it was understood that only exceptionally could one listen to German stations, for instance to hear classical music and the like," was omitted from the German version. The Dutch sentence "he ended up looking like a giant and he was the worst fascist there was" was shortened in German to "watching him grow into an invincible giant." The Dutch: "And indeed, there is no greater hostility than exists between Germans and Jews," became in German: "And there is no greater hostility in the world than between *these* Germans and Jews!" This change was agreed to by Otto Frank and Anneliese Schutz on the grounds that it reflected what Anne had actually wanted to say, since Anne,

who despite the great tribulations she had suffered as a result of the persecution of the Jews and which she felt so acutely despite her youth, by no means measured all Germans by the same yardstick. For, as she knew so well, even in those days we had many good friends among the Germans.[79]

72

The rule that people in the Annexe were required "to speak softly at all times, in any civilized language, therefore not in German," became in translation: "*Alle Kultursprachen . . . aber leise*!!! [All civilized languages . . . but softly!!!]." According to Otto Frank, this change was made by the German publisher.[80] However, since it occurs in all four copies Otto must have been mistaken on this point. In addition "heroism in the war or when confronting the Germans" became in the German translation "heroism in the war and in the struggle against oppression."

Finally, we have the curious addition to the translation of phrases that add nothing to our understanding of Anne's text. The sentence: "He actually got Miep to bring him a banned book" was expanded in the German translation to "He got Miep—who of course had not the slightest suspicion—to bring him a banned book," and the statement "she forgot all about the soup so the peas were burned to a cinder and utterly refused to leave the pan" is amplified in the German with: "What a pity I can't tell Kepler about that . . . Theory of heredity!" Nowhere in the Anne Frank manuscripts is there any reference to the theory of heredity; in addition we have here the confusion of the astronomer Kepler with the geneticist Mendel, who based his laws of heredity on experiments with peas.

In short, in her translation of the Dutch version into German, Anneliese Schutz made mistakes, amplified—with or without consulting Otto Frank—and omitted references to the everyday speech of the Germans in hiding in the Netherlands lest German readers took offense.

That she did this last because, according to *Der Spiegel*, she believed that "a book intended after all for sale in Germany [. . .] cannot abuse the Germans"[81] makes it likely that even while the translation was being undertaken it was planned to publish Anne's writings in German. In view of the negative attitude of Dutch publishers this need not surprise us.

Nevertheless it was not until 1950—by which time the Dutch edition was already in its sixth impression—that a German publisher, the Lambert Schneider Verlag in Heidelberg, agreed to add Anneliese Schutz's translation of Typescript II to its list. It appeared under the title *Das Tagebuch der Anne Frank*. The edition ran to about 4,500 copies.[82] It sold moderately well.

In 1955 a German paperback edition was published under license by Fischer Bücherei. This edition was to prove immensely successful. It differed slightly from the Lambert Schneider edition, in that from the first impression it included the two "Tales" "Kitty" and "Kathy," whereas these were only included in the tenth, Lambert Schneider edition, published in 1974. Lambert Schneider therefore must have taken them from the Fischer edition. How Fischer came by the texts of "Kitty" and "Kathy" in the middle of the 1950s can no longer be established.[83]

In 1950, Calmann-Lévy published the first French translation under the title of *Journal de Anne Frank*. The translators from the Dutch were T. Caren and Suzanne Lombard. Since the Dutch and French editions consisted of the same diary entries, Caren and Lombard probably based their translation directly on *Het Achterhuis*.

The English edition, on the other hand, had a more complicated history.

In November 1950, Vallentine, Mitchell & Co. Ltd. of London asked Mrs. B. M. Mooyaart-Doubleday to translate *Het Achterhuis*, and even before her translation was ready, Doubleday & Company, Inc., of New York had bought the U.S. rights.[84]

In July 1951, Otto Frank called on the offices of Vallentine, Mitchell & Co. and handed them

the text of those passages in the original Dutch typescript [= Typescript II] which were not printed in the Dutch edition because they were either too long, or were likely to offend Dutch Puritan or Catholic susceptibilities. [...] We think the English edition definitely ought to contain them, and wonder whether you would be so good as to translate them for us.

Thus wrote Vallentine, Mitchell to Mrs. Mooyaart.[85] A month later she sent her translation of the extra passages to Vallentine, Mitchell. "So your long labour is really completed," the latter replied. "Today [August 17, 1951], the last batch went on to America. Everyone feels, who has read it, that it is going to be a wonderful book. Some passages go on moving me so deeply, though I've read them four or five times now."

As far as the later sections were concerned, the publishers wrote that "nearly all of it will go in."[86]

In 1952, *The Diary of a Young Girl* by Anne Frank appeared in England as well as in the United States, where it had previously been rejected by some ten publishers.[87] Both editions contained seven passages more than the Dutch, among them the letters of August 3, 1943, and April 15, 1944, about the mutual touching of breasts, menstruation and Franz Liszt. In addition we find the sentence "The Germans have a means of making people talk" inserted in the letter of May 22, 1944. No Dutch equivalent can be found in the typescripts that have come down to us or in the extant manuscripts. The origin of this phrase therefore remains obscure.[88]

The Netherlands, West Germany, France, Britain and the United States were followed by East Germany, Switzerland, Italy, Denmark, Sweden, Norway, Finland, Iceland, Spain, Argentina, Mexico, Uruguay, Portugal, Brazil, Greece, Turkey, Hungary, Poland, Rumania, the Soviet Union, Czechoslovakia, Yugoslavia, Japan, Israel, India, South Korea, Thailand, Nationalist China,[89] South Africa, Indonesia and Bulgaria.[90]

Anne Frank had posthumously captured the world.

Her triumphal progress has since taken on unprecedented proportions. Between fifteen and sixteen million copies of the book have been sold so far. In 1955 it was turned into a play in the United States and in 1957 a film was made. Both film and play were international successes. These achievements stimulated the sale of the book in the Netherlands; *Het Achterhuis* had not been reprinted since 1950, but in 1955 three editions rolled off the presses; there were three more in 1956 and nine in 1957. This renewed Dutch interest thus came about "via an international detour."[91] In 1957, too, the Anne Frank Foundation was established for the purpose of "maintaining the premises at 263, Prinsengracht, Amsterdam, and especially the attached Annexe, as well as implementing the ideals bequeathed to the world in the Diary of Anne Frank."[92] Almost half a million people visit the Annexe every year. Schools and streets have been named after Anne Frank throughout the world. For countless people she has become a symbol of the six million Jews murdered by the Nazis, but as Ed van Thijn, Mayor of Amsterdam, put it, in an address in English:

not a symbol in an abstract sense, far away from reality: no, she is a symbol because she reflects reality, because she was just a girl of fourteen, fifteen years old.

She made the incomprehensible story of the Second World War comprehensible.

She brought abstract statistics down to a human level; and everybody understands that the story of the Second World War is the story of six million individual human tragedies, six million dramatic personal life stories at least.[93]

Notes

[1] For a full account see pp. 122ff.

[2] For a full account see pp. 122 and 144ff.

[3] *Cf.* the phrase "*another new* diary" (our italics).

[4] Portions were published in: Anne Frank, *Weet je nog? Verhalen en sprookjes* (Amsterdam/Antwerp; Contact, 1949); Anne Frank, *Verhalen rondom het achterhuis* (Amsterdam/Antwerp; Contact, 1960); *Het korte leven van Anne Frank* (Amsterdam; Contact, 1970); and *Weerklank van Anne Frank* (Amsterdam; Contact, 1970). Complete edition: Anne Frank, *Verhaaltjes, en gebeurtenissen uit het achterhuis*. With a preface by Joke Kniesmeyer (Amsterdam: Bert Bakker, 1982).

[5] For a full account, see pp. 122 and 158ff.

[6] For a full account, see pp. 122 and 158ff.

[7] Statement by Hermine (Miep) Gies-Santrouschitz before A. J. Dragt, notary, June 5, 1974, Anne Frank Collection 1 d.

[8] Ibid.

[9] Otto Frank to the Information Bureau of the Netherlands Red Cross, May 22, 1950.

[10] Mr. and Mrs. Gies, February 18, 1981.

[11] Ibid.

[12] Examination of Otto Frank, July 16, 1959. Lübeck *Landgericht*, Stielau/Buddeberg dossier.

[13] Mr. and Mrs. Gies, February 18, 1981.

[14] Examination of Otto Frank, p. 43.

[15] Ibid., p. 42.

[16] The Netherlands State Institute for War Documentation holds a photocopy.

[17] Examination of Otto Frank, p. 43.

[18] Ibid.

[19] Ibid.; A. Cauvern, January 23, 1981.

[20] A. Cauvern, January 23, 1981.

[21] Ibid.

[22] *Der Spiegel*, April 1, 1959.

[23] A. Cauvern to *Welt am Sonntag*, January 8, 1959.

[24] Examination of Otto Frank, p. 43.

[25] The Netherlands State Institute for War Documentation holds a photocopy.

[26] Examination of Otto Frank, p. 43.

[27] Kurt Baschwitz to his daughter, now Mrs. R. Bloklander-Baschwitz, February 10, 1946.

[28] Werner Cahn, March 12, 1981.

[29] The *Eerste Nederlandse Systematisch Ingerichte Encyclopaedie*.

[30] Max van Weezel and Anet Bleich, *Ga dan zelf naar Siberie* (Amsterdam, SUA, 1978), p. 106.

[31] Werner Cahn, March 12, 1981.

[32] Annie Romein-Verschoor, *Omzien in verwondering. Herinneringen van Annie Romein-Verschoor*, Vol. 2 (Amsterdam; De Arbeiderspers, 1971), p. 109.

[33] Ger Harmsen, *Daan Goulooze. Uit het leven van een communist* (Utrecht: Ambo, 1967), p. 154; Ger Harmsen, October 25, 1981.

[34] Geert Lubberhuizen, February 16, 1982; Meulenhoff Nederland BV, February 3, 1981.

[35] R. Meulenhoff, February 20, 1981. According to R. Meulenhoff, this took place "just before the September 1944 railroad strike." His memory must, however, have misled him on this point.

[36] *Het wonder van Anne Frank*, a film by Jan Vrijman, shown by the AVRO on August 30, 1959. According to Jan Romein, Otto Frank approached Annie Romein "at the end of March 1946." In view of Cahn's account of the time Annie Romein spent trying to find a publisher for the book on the one hand, and the date of Jan Romein's article (April 3, 1946) on the other, Jan Romein must have been mistaken.

[37] K. Lekkerkerker, February 14, 1981.

[38] Ibid.

[39] Werner Cahn, March 12, 1981.
[40] Mrs. A. Batten, January 5, 1981.
[41] Otto Frank to C. Blom, August 6, 1978.
[42] C. Blom to Otto Frank, October 26, 1978.
[43] Otto Frank to C. Blom, November 13, 1978.
[44] F. E. A. Batten to R. F. Roegholt, September 23, 1979.
[45] Examination of Otto Frank, p. 44.
[46] Mr. and Mrs. Gies, February 18, 1981.
[47] C. Blom, May 1, 1985; Stichting R.K. Bevolkingsregister Amsterdam, September 10, 1985.
[48] Mrs. E. Hildering, February 16, 1981.
[49] K. Lekkerkerker, February 14, 1981.
[50] Mrs. A. Batten, January 5, 1981, and K. Lekkerkerker, February 14, 1981.
[51] *De Nieuwe Stem* 1 (1946/6), pp. 432–42.
[52] *Trouw*, March 5, 1968.
[53] Mrs. Cahn, November 13, 1984.
[54] The Netherlands State Institute for War Documentation holds a photocopy of these "house rules." The original is held by the Foeken family, Amsterdam.
[55] The Netherlands State Institute for War Documentation holds a photocopy of this note. The original is held by the Frank family.
[56] See pp. 68–69.
[57] G. P. de Neve in *Het wonder van Anne Frank*, a film by Jan Vrijman, shown by the AVRO on August 30, 1959.
[58] This diary is held by the Frank family and has been put at the disposal of the Netherlands State Institute for War Documentation for the duration of the investigation.
[59] Jaap Meijer, "*Vermoorde jeugd. Naar aanleiding van een dagboek*," in *Nieuw Israelitisch Weekblad*, August 1, 1947.
[60] Dirk Coster, "*Ontroerend, feilloos relaas van een Joods meisje*," in *Elseviers Weekblad*, January 24, 1948.
[61] J. v[an] S[chaik-Willing]: "*Het Achterhuis. Dagboek van Anne Frank*," in *De Groene Amsterdammer*, August 16, 1947.
[62] B. Andreas, "*Het Achterhuis door Anne Frank*," in *De Vlam*, November 8, 1947.
[63] J. Presser, "*De kindermoord van Amsterdam*," in *De Vrije Katheder*, August 16, 1947.
[64] J. v[an] S[chaik-Willing], "*Het Achterhuis*," in *De Groene Amsterdammer*, August 16, 1947.
[65] H[ermien] v[an] V[oorst], "*Achter geblindeerde ramen*," in *Je Maintiendrai*, July 18, 1947.
[66] Ibid., and B. Andreas, "*Het Achterhuis door Anne Frank*," in *De Vlam*, November 8, 1947.
[67] Jaap Meijer, "*Vermoorde jeugd*," in *Nieuw Israelitisch Weekblad*, August 1, 1947.
[68] C. T. R., "*Over echte dagboeken gesproken*," in *De Nederlander*, September 24, 1947.
[69] Anna Blaman [= J. P. Vrugt], "*Oorlogsdocument en document humain*," in *NRC*, September 8, 1947.
[70] B. Andreas, "*Het Achterhuis door Anne Frank*," in *De Vlam*, November 8, 1947.
[71] J. v[an] S[chaik-Willing], "*Het Achterhuis*," in *De Groene Amsterdammer*, August 16, 1947.
[72] Examination of Otto Frank, p. 44. Otto Frank to Mrs. Xenia von Bahder, May 16, 1958.
[73] Werner Cahn, March 12, 1981; Mrs. L. van Collem-Randerath, April 10 and May 26, 1981.
[74] Otto Frank to Mrs. Xenia von Bahder, May 16, 1958.
[75] Mrs. L. van Collem-Randerath, April 10 and May 26, 1981.
[76] Otto Frank to Mrs. Xenia von Bahder, May 16, 1958. We were provided with the examples by Mrs. von Bahder, Kleinrinderfeld, German Federal Republic.
[77] Examination of Otto Frank, p. 44.
[78] Werner Cahn, March 12, 1981.
[79] Examination of Otto Frank, p. 45.
[80] Otto Frank to Mrs. Xenia von Bahder, May 16, 1958.
[81] *Der Spiegel*, April 1, 1959.
[82] Otto Frank to Mrs. Xenia von Bahder, May 16, 1958.
[83] Verlag Lambert Schneider, March 6, 1985, and Fischer Taschenbuch Verlag, March 18, 1985.
[84] Mrs. B. M. Mooyaart-Doubleday, March 12, 1981.
[85] Vallentine, Mitchell & Co. Ltd. to Mrs. B. M. Mooyaart-Doubleday, July 26, 1951.
[86] Vallentine, Mitchell & Co. Ltd. to Mrs. B. M. Mooyaart-Doubleday, August 17, 1951.
[87] Otto Frank to L. de Jong, June 15, 1957.
[88] Vallentine, Mitchell & Co. Ltd., February 13, 1985, and Mrs. B. M. Mooyaart-Doubleday, February 20, 1985.

[89] According to *Weerklank*, Amsterdam, Contact, 1970. M. Hanemaayer, *Anne Frank bibliografie* (Amsterdam: no publisher, 1968), differs slightly.

[90] ANNE FRANK-Fonds, March 16, 1985.

[91] See A. G. H. Anbeek van der Meijden, "*De Tweede Wereldoorlog in de Nederlandse roman*," in David Barnouw, Madelon de Keizer and Gerrold van der Stroom (eds.), *1940–1945: Onverwerkt verleden?* (Utrecht: HES, 1985), pp. 78f.

[92] Constitution, Art. 2, Para 1.

[93] Address given at the presentation of the Anne Frank literature prize, September 5, 1985.

6

The Play

DAVID BARNOUW

In June 1952 the English translation of *Het Achterhuis* was published in the United States by Doubleday & Co. under the title of *Anne Frank: The Diary of a Young Girl*. It carried a preface by Eleanor Roosevelt, the widow of the President who had died in 1945. The American journalist and novelist Meyer Levin reviewed the book the same month in the *New York Times Book Review*.[1] "Anne Frank's voice becomes the voice of six million vanished souls," wrote Levin, and he ended his review with: "Surely she will be widely loved, for this wise and wonderful young girl brings back a poignant delight in the infinite human spirit."

Levin had eulogized Anne Frank's diary even earlier in a review of John Hersey's novel *The Wall* in the *Congress Weekly*,[2] journal of the American Jewish Congress. Here he had explained that he had read the French translation during a working visit to France and that he had contacted Otto Frank there and then. "Her father informed me that the book had been rejected by a whole series of eminent American publishers [. . .]. Finally, one American publisher offered to bring out the Journal if a British publisher could be found to share translation and typesetting costs."

Shortly after his article in the *New York Times Book Review*, the *National Jewish Post*[3] published another review by Levin. In this he argued forcefully that a play and a film ought to be made of the book.

Anne Frank's diary was to come to dominate a large part of his life and the book he later wrote on the subject was aptly called *The Obsession*.[4] In September 1952 a radio program written by him was broadcast under the title of "Anne Frank; The Diary of a Young Girl." But Levin wanted more. He himself wanted to write the play he had championed.

Otto Frank had sent him a cable on March 31, 1952, appointing Levin his literary agent in the United States for the express purpose of bringing about a dramatized version, but he later gave in to Levin's insistence that Levin himself should write the play. In July 1952, at Levin's suggestion, Otto Frank approached the producer Cheryl Crawford, who agreed to stage the play Levin was writing providing it was good enough. However when Levin's version was ready in October of that year, she turned it down, after, according to Levin, having had it read by her friend, the playwright Lillian Hellman.[5] Levin stuck by his play and suggested Kermit Bloomgarden as producer in place of Cheryl Crawford. Bloomgarden had made his name with productions of Arthur Miller's *Death of a Salesman* and *A View from the Bridge*. If Bloomgarden also rejected the play, then he, Levin, would give up.

Cheryl Crawford, who still had the production rights, agreed, but Bloomgarden, too, rejected Levin's version after having read it. Levin refused to admit defeat and to break the deadlock signed a contract with Otto Frank on November 21, 1952.[6]

The main thrust of the contract was that Levin was entitled to submit his play to fourteen named producers, one of whom would have to agree in writing

From left to right: Johannes Kleiman, Elfriede Frank-Markovits, Frances Goodrich, Albert Hackett, Otto Frank and Garson Kanin. (Anne Frank Foundation.)

within a month to produce the play. A standard contract to this effect was drawn up. If Levin failed, then he would have to stand down for good, make no further use of his script, and Otto Frank would be entitled to find another playwright. The rest of the agreement covered a number of technical details, and the last clause specified that Levin would no longer act as Frank's literary agent.

Four days later two further clauses were added[7]; the second of these provided for the possible staging of a Hebrew version of Levin's script in Israel.

None of the named producers reacted positively, and again Levin refused to accept his brainchild for what it was. In April 1953, Cheryl Crawford withdrew, weary of all the efforts to put on the play; on October 1, Otto Frank granted Kermit Bloomgarden the production rights.[8]

Bloomgarden took up a suggestion made by Lillian Hellman and at the end of 1953 asked Albert Hackett and his wife Frances Goodrich to produce a dramatized version of the diary.[9] Both were working as scriptwriters at MGM but were given leave to write the play. They started in December, although the contract between themselves and Bloomgarden was not signed until February 23, 1954.

In a letter to Dr. Louis de Jong, then director of the Netherlands State Institute for War Documentation, they later explained how difficult it had been to turn the diary into a play. In particular, having all eight people in hiding visibly "present" throughout the play caused complications. No less than eight versions were needed before the Hacketts, Bloomgarden, the director Garson Kanin and Otto Frank were satisfied with the result.[10]

Following two weeks of previews in Philadelphia, the New York premiere took place on October 5, 1955. The play was an overwhelming success, reviews ranging from good to very good.[11] Actors, the director and the Hacketts won various awards, including the Pulitzer Prize for drama.

In Europe, interest in the play grew and it seemed only right that the winner of the 1955 Pulitzer Prize should be represented in the spring of the next year at the Paris drama festival, following a tradition that had been established several years earlier. In 1956, however, that tradition was broken: *The Diary of Anne Frank* was not performed in Paris. According to *De Telegraaf*,[12] the reason was pressure from the U.S. State Department, which was afraid that delicate Franco-German relations might be prejudiced by the staging of the play.

The play had its European premiere at the end of August 1956 at Gothenburg in Sweden, and on October 1 that year the German-language version was staged in West Berlin, Dresden, Düsseldorf, Hamburg, Karlsruhe, Constance, Vienna and Zurich. "Anne Frank's Diary conquers Germany," proclaimed a headline in *Trouw*.[13] The newspapers reported very mixed reactions: at the end of the performance there would be complete silence for a long time and the audience would leave the theater quietly and "with feelings of shame"[14]; or there would be prolonged applause, longer than for any other play. In many of the countries where the diary of Anne Frank was well known, seats for the Hacketts' play sold out long in advance. And so it was in the Netherlands, where the play was first staged on November 27, 1956.

Meyer Levin had meanwhile not sat idly by, determined as he was to see his version produced instead of the Hacketts' "Broadway hit." At the end of 1956 he took his case against Otto Frank and Kermit Bloomgarden to the Supreme Court of the State of New York.[15] Levin contended that he had been chosen to write the play and that he was the victim of fraud and breach of contract. In addition, his rights concerning Israel had been jeopardized, and he further claimed that the Hacketts had made use of his material and his ideas. He sued for damages totaling $200,000. He based his charge of breach of contract on the claim that he had in fact signed the contract of November 21, 1952, under coercion and that his prior verbal arrangement with Otto Frank must take precedence.

Otto Frank submitted that Levin was wrong on all counts and that the claim for damages should therefore be dismissed.[16] Moreover, he asked the court to declare that Meyer Levin had lost his rights concerning Israel because he had taken no steps toward implementing his plans.

On January 7, 1958, Judge Coleman dismissed Levin's claims for fraud and breach of contract. In his opinion published later in the *New York Law Journal*,[17] Judge Coleman wrote that in his view the 1952 contract between Otto Frank and Levin must stand, in part because Levin had made no attempt to abrogate it.

Levin's other allegation—namely, that the Hacketts had made use of his material and his ideas—had been put by the judge to a jury. A few days later, after a retirement of ten hours,[18] the jury had found for Levin and awarded him the $50,000 damages he had claimed on this count, to be paid jointly by Otto Frank and Kermit Bloomgarden.

The New York State Supreme Court, however, set aside the jury's verdict, and Judge Coleman explained why the jury had been wrong. It could not be established that plagiarism had been committed since Levin and the Hacketts had drawn on the same source, the diary of Anne Frank, so that similarities were unavoidable. The jury, wrote Coleman, had also failed to make clear how they had arrived at the figure of $50,000. However, he stated that Levin still had the right to stage his version in Israel, Otto Frank's objections notwithstanding.

A new lawsuit seemed inevitable, and the royalties that Levin had had frozen in expectation of a verdict in his favor remained blocked, despite attempts by Otto Frank to have the attachment lifted.

One year later Coleman, in a further opinion in the *New York Law Journal*,[19] explained that the case was not simply a matter of the jury assessing damages without guidance. Experts would have to be consulted on the artistic relationship between the Levin and the Hackett versions and on the artistic merits of both. Their conclusion would then have to be quantified.

Coleman added that, though it was true that the parties had done their utmost to reach an agreement, negotiations had obviously reached an impasse. To find a way out, Levin now proposed that a committee of "wise members" of the American Jewish community be set up to work out a compromise.[20] This was done, the committee consisting of Rabbi Joachim Prinz, the president of the American Jewish Congress, and two other leading Jews. Through their good offices a settlement was agreed before the New York State Supreme Court on October 26, 1959.[21]

Meyer Levin, Otto Frank, Kermit Bloomgarden and their lawyers signed the settlement. Otto Frank agreed to pay $15,000 to Meyer Levin, who in turn agreed to drop his claim to royalties and to assign all author's rights in his dramatization in whatever language, Hebrew included, in his radio script and in whatever else he may have written concerning Anne Frank's diary, to Otto Frank. The assignment of author's rights was signed before a lawyer that same day. Part of the settlement involved the following joint declaration.

Mr. Levin's adaptation of The Diary, and his role in connection with it, should no longer be a subject of public or private controversy. [. . .] Mr. Levin takes this opportunity to state that he believes that both Otto Frank and Kermit Bloomgarden are honorable men, and that nothing Mr. Levin has ever said should be construed to the contrary.

Both Mr. Frank and Mr. Bloomgarden take this opportunity to state that nothing they have ever said was intended to be a reflection upon Mr. Levin's talent or capacity as an author or playwright.

All parties regret that the Hacketts received unfortunate publicity as a by-product of the dispute.[22]

Fourteen years later, in his book *The Obsession*, Meyer Levin argued that the committee he himself had approved had not been fair, that the settlement, just like the first contract, had been nothing but "lawyers' work," that "thought control"[23] had been imposed and that he, Levin, had signed against his will. Hence he did not feel morally bound by the agreement. He went on to relate how before long he had begun to besiege rabbis, fellow writers and others with requests to help him stage his version of the play. His chance came at the end of 1966 when an army theatrical company staged his version in Tel Aviv as the opening production at the new "Soldiers' House."[24] Levin had wisely kept quiet about the fact that he no longer held the rights in his play: "So I let Peter [the director in Tel Aviv] assume that I still held production rights in Israel."[25]

The New York firm of lawyers representing Otto Frank insisted that the production be closed down,[26] and to Levin's intense displeasure performances came to an end.

What was the real story behind all this?

Levin's own explanation in *The Obsession* amounts to the following: because he had come to the United States from Eastern Europe, the U.S. Jewish establishment, including Lillian Hellman, Otto Frank and their lawyers, all of whom were of German origin, had discriminated against him. As a Zionist socialist Jew he had, moreover, fallen victim to a Stalinist, anti-Zionist plot in the United States. All in all, he had been subjected to a form of McCarthyite persecution in reverse. In January 1974 one of Otto Frank's lawyers protested to the publishers of *The Obsession*: "He has accused Mr. Frank, Mr. Bloomgarden, and my firm of being all kinds of things from anti-Semitic to being parts or pawns of a Communist conspiracy."[27]

Lillian Hellman, the longtime companion of the detective story writer Dashiell Hammett, imprisoned in 1951 for his alleged Communist sympathies, who herself had refused to give evidence against others to McCarthy's Un-American Activities Committee, was Levin's chief bête noire. She had been the first to reject his version, influencing Cheryl Crawford, and she was part of a high-powered literary clique, "more apt today to be thought of as a Mafia."[28] It was this clique, according to Levin, which had made it impossible for him to put on his play.

But above all, as the last pages of *The Obsession* make clear, Levin felt that his play was not being produced because it was "too Jewish." As proof he cited an ex-employee of Doubleday who had spoken to Otto Frank about Levin's version. "He [Otto Frank] said they [Hellman and Bloomgarden] told him your play couldn't be done because it was too Jewish."[29]

What Levin means by "too Jewish" is Orthodox Jewish. Nowhere in the diary itself, however, either in the published or the hitherto unpublished sections, is there anything to justify an Orthodox Jewish approach. Indeed a significant scene in the diary takes place on November 3, 1943, when Otto Frank proposes to give Anne a New Testament as a Hanukkah present, to Margot's dismay (see p. 412).

The rejection of Levin's version gave Otto Frank small comfort. Even after the "illegal" production in Israel, Levin continued "to renew a battle that had been going on for almost 15 years . . . a battle which was settled in 1959 and was thought to be over."[30]

An unforeseeable side effect of the court case in New York was the misuse to which it was put many years later. Pamphlets and other publications appeared with allegations that, following the decision of the jury in New York, Otto Frank had had to pay $50,000 to the Jewish writer Meyer Levin in connection with the writing of the diary. That this award had been set aside, that the case concerned a play and not the diary itself, and that Otto Frank finally paid $15,000 for Levin's rights in the *play*, was ignored in these distorted accounts of events that had never taken place.

Notes

[1] *New York Times Book Review*, June 15, 1952.
[2] *Congress Weekly*, November 13, 1950.
[3] *National Jewish Post*, June 30, 1952.
[4] Meyer Levin, *The Obsession* (New York: Simon & Schuster, 1973).

[5] Ibid., p. 70.

[6] Contract between Otto Frank and Meyer Levin, November 21, 1952. Paul, Weiss, Rifkind, Wharton & Garrison, lawyers, New York: Frank/Levin file.

[7] Ibid., November 25, 1952.

[8] E. N. Costikyan (Otto Frank's lawyer) to L. Shimkin of Simon & Schuster, January 17, 1974. Paul, Weiss, Rifkind, Wharton & Garrison, lawyers, New York: Frank/Levin file.

[9] Statement by Mr. and Mrs. Hackett in an article entitled "Diary of 'The Diary of Anne Frank' " in the New York *Times*, September 30, 1956.

[10] The Hacketts to L. de Jong, May 27, 1957. At the time, De Jong was writing an article on Anne Frank for the *Reader's Digest*.

[11] For a survey of U.S. press reviews see *De Tijd* of October 6, 1955.

[12] *De Telegraaf*, May 12, 1956.

[13] *Trouw*, October 12, 1956.

[14] *Algemeen Handelsblad*, October 2, 1956.

[15] Meyer Levin, Plaintiff, against Otto Frank and Kermit Bloomgarden, Defendants. Verified Complaint. Paul, Weiss, Rifkind, Wharton & Garrison, lawyers, New York. Frank/Levin file.

[16] Ibid., Amended Answer. December 7, 1956. Paul, Weiss, Rifkind, Wharton & Garrison, lawyers, New York, Frank/Levin file.

[17] *New York Law Journal*, February 28, 1958.

[18] *Het Vrije Volk*, January 9, 1958.

[19] *New York Law Journal*, February 27, 1959.

[20] As under note 8.

[21] Meyer Levin, Plaintiff, against Otto Frank and Kermit Bloomgarden, Defendants. Stipulation. October 26, 1959. Paul, Weiss, Rifkind, Wharton & Garrison, lawyers, New York. Frank/Levin file.

[22] Ibid., annex.

[23] *The Obsession*, p. 215.

[24] The New York *Times*, November 27, 1966.

[25] *The Obsession*, p. 262.

[26] The New York *Times*, December 11, 1966.

[27] As under note 8.

[28] *The Obsession*, p. 64.

[29] Ibid., p. 310.

[30] As under note 8.

7

Attacks on the Authenticity of the Diary

DAVID BARNOUW

The earliest attacks on the authenticity of Anne Frank's diary we could discover in print come in two articles published in November 1957 in the Swedish paper *Fria Ord*[1] under the heading of "*Judisk Psyke—En studie kring Anne Frank och Meyer Levin* [Jewish Psyche—A Study Around Anne Frank and Meyer Levin]." Their author was Harald Nielsen, a Danish literary critic. Basing himself on a brief factual report in *De Telegraaf* of April 11, 1957, Nielsen alleged that the diary owed its final form to Meyer Levin. In support of this opinion, he produced such spurious arguments as the claim that Anne and Peter were not Jewish names. He went on to delve into the Jewish background of Meyer Levin's writing. He concluded his articles with the comment that Levin's reminiscences, published in 1951 in a book entitled *In Search*,[2] had the advantage of undisputed authenticity.

In March 1958 the Norwegian paper *Folg og Land*, the organ of the former SS Viking Division, referred to Meyer Levin's lawsuit and went on to allege that Anne Frank's diary was very probably a forgery.[3] One month later, part of this article was published in translation in the *Europa Korrespondenz*[4] in Vienna, and another month later it appeared in *Reichsruf, Wochenzeitung für das nationale Deutschland*,[5] the weekly journal of the extreme right-wing *Deutsche Reichspartei*,[6] founded in 1950.

It is not clear whether Otto Frank himself or any of his publishers ever saw these or other attacks on the diary; in any case no legal action was taken by any of them.

This was not the case with Lothar Stielau, a high school teacher of English at the Lübeck *Oberschule zum Dom*. Stielau, who was born in 1908, had joined the NSDAP (Nazi Party) and the SA (storm troopers) in 1932 and had been a Hitler Youth leader. Ten years after the war he joined the *Deutsche Reichspartei* and in 1957 he became district chairman of the party in Lübeck.[7] On October 10, 1958, he wrote a review of the play *Tom Sawyers grosses Abenteuer (The Adventures of Tom Sawyer)* for the *Zeitschrift der Vereinigung ehemaliger Schüler und der Freunde der Oberschule zum Dom e.V. Lübeck* (Journal of the Association of Former Students and Friends of the Lübeck *Oberschule zum Dom*), which contained the following passage:

The forged diaries of Eva Braun, of the Queen of England and the hardly more authentic one of Anne Frank may have earned several millions for the profiteers from Germany's defeat, but they have also raised our own hackles quite a bit.[8]

One month later Fischer Verlag had its attention drawn to Stielau's article by the *Zentralrat der Juden in Deutschland* (Central Council of German Jews) and a week later Otto Frank, who had come to the publishing house for a meeting, heard about it as well.[9]

The Ministry of Culture in the federal state of Schleswig-Holstein then decided to determine whether Stielau, who had clearly "caused offense," had also breached his professional obligation of political neutrality. On December 5, Stielau was given the opportunity to explain the passage objected to in front of a senior official. At this interview he conceded that there was no doubt that Anne Frank had kept a diary, but went on to allege that none of the published versions of any of the diaries was anything like the original. He referred to the earlier article in the *Reichsruf* and said that he should have used the word *verfälscht* instead of *fälschen* (while *fälschen* signifies that something is entirely fake, *verfälschen* refers to an original to which greater or smaller alterations have been made). For the rest he insisted that he had been punctilious in the performance of his pedagogic duties.[10]

That was also the view of Heinrich Buddeberg, chairman of the *Deutsche Reichspartei* in Schleswig-Holstein, who wrote a letter to the *Lübecker Nachrichten*, published on January 6, 1959, in which he described Stielau as a political victim of the Social Democrats who, with others, had been pressing for Stielau's suspension. And he, too, came up with the distorted account of the Meyer Levin story, quoting this time from the *Deutsch-Amerikanische Bürger-Zeitung* of October 2, 1958.[11]

Buddeberg, born in 1893, was a farmer at Woltersdorf über Büchen in Schleswig-Holstein. Unlike Stielau, he refused during the preliminary examination to say anything about his political past other than that from 1933 to 1945 he had been *Kreisbauernführer* (District Farmers' Leader), which had earned him two years' internment.[12]

On the day Buddeberg's letter was published, the first official steps were taken to have Stielau disciplined. He was alleged to have neglected his duties and to be unworthy of the respect and confidence to which the teaching profession is entitled. As a teacher, he had propagated political attitudes in conflict with his educational duties. The Ministry of Culture ordered his temporary suspension.[13]

In January 1959, Dr. A. Flesch, a Frankfurt advocate acting for Otto Frank, and a few days later for the two publishing houses as well, laid criminal charges against Stielau and Buddeberg before the public prosecutor of the Lübeck *Landgericht*. The charges included libel, slander, insult, defamation of the memory of a dead person and anti-Semitic utterances. Dr. Flesch stated in his indictment that the manuscripts written by Anne Frank were in Amsterdam and that their authenticity could be checked. He next explained the difference between the actual diary and the Hacketts' dramatization, and emphasized that what Stielau had done was to impugn the authenticity of the diary itself and not that of the play.[14]

The public prosecutor's office reacted very quickly: within two days of the complaint being lodged it confirmed receipt and inquired when Otto Frank had first become aware of Stielau's article.[15]

That same month, too, the Federal Minister of Justice in Bonn asked the Schleswig-Holstein Minister of Justice to keep him informed because of the special interest of the case.[16] The preliminary examination could begin.

In April the public prosecutor set out at the end of a long preamble the reason why it was necessary to determine the authenticity of the diary by court action, namely:

"Given the delicate nature of the attitude of foreign countries towards Germany and her people due to their National Socialist past, a judicial inquiry is the only way of arriving at a satisfactory conclusion."[17]

If there were a conviction the court would have to take into account the accused's inner attitude *("innere Einstellung")* toward Jews, toward the persecution of the Jews and toward Anne Frank. Moreover, Stielau's attitude as a teacher would also be a factor.

The public prosecutor further noted that an inquiry into the authenticity of the diary would prove extraordinarily difficult, and referred to a recent article in *Der Spiegel*.[18] The magazine, which had focused attention on Cauvern (see Chapter 5), quoted the latter as saying: "At the beginning I made a good many changes." It also claimed that the well-known clergyman J. J. Buskes had served as a spiritual guide to Otto Frank, who had granted him "censorship rights." The impression that the translation was inadequate was confirmed by a number of obvious inconsistencies in it. The article ended with the following statement by Baschwitz: "I believe that the solution of this case lies in the speedy publication of a word-for-word edition of the diary."

Stielau's first appearance before the examining magistrate, on June 18, was entirely devoted to establishing his background, past and political views. He declared that, because he had considered communism a grave threat, he had joined the NSDAP before the war, but "I was never particularly interested in questions of race, the Jewish question included." After the war he had looked for a party that suited him, one that was "unreservedly pro-German," and had ended up in the *Deutsche Reichspartei*.

Seven days later, when the examination was resumed, Stielau made the astonishing allegation that in his article he had not been referring to the published version of the diary, *Das Tagebuch der Anne Frank*, but to the play. The examining magistrate pointed out that this was something he had failed to mention to the Ministry of Culture.

Stielau wisely refused to be drawn, although he had to admit that at the time he himself had neither read the play nor seen a performance of it. He referred, however, to a number of articles in the press that had given him cause to doubt the authenticity of the diary.[19]

It was not until April 25 of the next year that Stielau was examined again. He now refused to discuss the statements of other witnesses or the expert opinion that had meanwhile been prepared (see p. 87), and stuck by his earlier declaration that in 1958 he had been referring to the play.[20] Otto Frank had been interviewed two weeks after the examination, on July 2, 1959, of one of Stielau's colleagues about the *Journal of the Association of Former Students*.[21] Frank stated on what date he had first been told about Stielau's article and then explained what his daughter had written originally, that those writings had been handed to him by Miep after the war, and what he had done with them after that. According to him, Cauvern had merely corrected Germanisms and grammatical errors, and that was all there was to the claim by *Der Spiegel* that Cauvern had "made a good many changes." Otto Frank had himself given information to *Der Spiegel* but was not very happy with the way his words had been reported.

The next day, during his continued examination, Otto Frank denied that any pressure had been put on him "by the clergy." He did not know the Reverend J. J. Buskes personally. He was in favor of an official investigation into the authenticity of Anne's writings; an expert was free to study all the relevant documents in Basle. The dispute with Meyer Levin was also brought up. Finally, Otto Frank agreed to appear as a witness in Lübeck if that proved necessary; all he wanted was to help remove any doubts about the authenticity of his daughter's diary.[22]

On September 29, Bep Voskuijl and Miep and Jan Gies were heard. Each of them gave a separate account of events in the Annexe at 263, Prinsengracht, declared they had known about Anne keeping a diary, and mentioned the discovery of the diaries and the loose sheets and their return to Otto Frank.[23]

For an expert opinion on the authenticity of the diary, the examining magistrate turned to the *Institut für Zeitgeschichte* in Munich. The Institute, however, advised that the case called for philological and graphological rather than historical expertise. Moreover, since no member of the Institute was proficient in the Dutch language they could do no more than recommend two professors of Dutch studies, one in Münster and the other in Berlin.[24]

It was decided to look closer to home, and at the end of September 1959, Dr. Annemarie Hübner of Hamburg University declared herself willing to prepare an expert assessment of *Das Tagebuch der Anne Frank*. She would investigate whether there had been crucial changes between the so-called Typescript II (see p. 64) and the German edition, and what the omissions and additions amounted to. In addition she would try to determine whether the German could be considered a "true" and "faithful" translation of the original.

The Hamburg handwriting expert Minna Becker, for her part, was asked to determine whether the diaries in the possession of Otto Frank and the loose sheets had been written by the same person who had written a letter on December 13, 1940, and two postcards on July 25, 1941, and July 5, 1942, all of which had been signed "Anne."

After formal instruction on October 13, 1959, Dr. Hübner, Mrs. Becker and Dorothea Ockelmann—who had been added by the examining magistrate to the panel of experts at a later stage—traveled to Basle to make their investigations on the spot. Mrs. Becker and Mrs. Ockelmann concluded in their report, dated March 7, 1960, and running to 131 pages, that all the written entries in Diaries 1, 2 and 3, including the pages that had been pasted in, the loose sheets and all improvements and additions were "identical" with the specimen handwriting of Anne Frank. They did not mention that a pasted-in letter from Otto Frank, a card from "Jacque" and a birthday card from Ruth Cauvern had been included in Diary 1.

The examining magistrate also asked them to determine which had been written first—Diaries 1, 2 and 3 or the loose sheets? Mrs. Becker and Mrs. Ockelmann both concluded that the loose sheets had not been written before Diaries 1, 2 and 3.[25]

A month later Dr. Hübner handed in her report to the examining magistrate.[26] Although it had not been part of her brief, she had perforce looked first of all into the relationship between the manuscripts and Typescript II. Her conclusion:

The text of the printed manuscript [= Typescript II] must be considered authentic by virtue of its substance, the ideas expressed in it and its form.[27]
  The translation must be considered to correspond [to the original] and on the whole to be factually correct. There are mistakes in translation and these are to be deprecated, but most of them can be considered minor faults which are immaterial to an understanding of the total context.[28]

Dr. Hübner concluded that "the text published in German translation as *Das Tagebuch der Anne Frank* may be considered true to its sources in substance and ideas."[29]

Stielau was defended by Professor Dr. Noack and by Dr. Noack, both from Kiel. In May 1960, they submitted their objections to Dr. Hübner's opinion to the examining magistrate in writing. They questioned Dr. Hübner's qualifications, arguing that her academic status ("*Dozent ohne Lehrauftrag*," literally "lecturer without a teaching assignment") was not such as to entitle her to give an expert opinion in the field of "comparative philology." Her opinion was therefore dismissed by them as "worthless."[30] This argument appeared to impress the public prosecutor, who communicated it to the Schleswig-Holstein Minister of Justice and added that it seemed advisable, even during the preliminary investigation, to appoint an *Obergutachter* ("senior assessor").[31]

One month later the public prosecutor commented on Dr. Hübner's actual findings. There were two central questions, namely, whether *Das Tagebuch der Anne Frank* was authentic in "documentary" respects (which seemed unlikely in view of the changes) and whether it was authentic in literary respects. The second question could not be answered by Dr. Hübner because she lacked the qualifications to do so.[32]

In July 1960, Professor Dr. Friedrich Sieburg, a well-known publicist and a contributor to the *Frankfurter Allgemeine Zeitung*, was formally asked to be the senior assessor and to prepare an expert opinion, though the precise terms of his brief were not made clear.[33]

Stielau's lawyers had other strings to their bow. In a letter to the examining magistrate they complained that the preliminary investigation had started from the wrong premise, since the article to which the plaintiff objected had referred to the play, not to the book. Moreover, Stielau had been shocked by the fact that adaptations not faithful to the text had been used to make money, and also by the fact that the U.S. edition had contained a photograph, not of Anne, but of one of the actresses who had played her. Further, Noack and Noack submitted that Albert Hackett, and to a lesser extent his wife, had been Communist fellow travelers since 1937; their source for this information was a series of reports by the California Un-American Activities Committee. In the circumstances, it was not at all surprising that Stielau had not wanted to see the play.[34]

Although Noack and Noack had argued earlier that Dr. Hübner's opinion was "worthless" they felt free to make use of it. After all, she had discovered differences between the original "document" and the translation, and Noack and Noack concluded that the translation was no longer "a document": "A document must be authentic word for word, or else it is not a document."[35]

On October 30, 1960, Sieburg concluded his expert opinion, and Noack and Noack turned their attention to it in December that year. They argued, with justification, that it was difficult to come to grips with the expert opinion since it had not been addressed to any specific question: "It is impossible to tell from the opinion which question the expert is actually trying to answer, nor is it known which question he should have answered."[36]

Sieburg had confined himself in his report to the content and the importance of *Das Tagebuch der Anne Frank;* he did not consider it his task to review the manuscripts or the quality of the translation, not least because he had no Dutch. He did nevertheless refer to Diaries 1, 2 and 3, the loose sheets and the "Tales," though his comments were clearly based on Dr. Hübner's opinion, a fact he failed to mention. Sieburg seemed to think that, in view of the large number of loose sheets (which he had never seen), it must have been necessary to make a selection from them. However this selection in no way affected the picture that Anne Frank had drawn of her life.

An important part of Sieburg's evidence concerned the absurdity of forging the diary of a completely unknown person. Moreover the diary contains references to events, for instance the persecution of the Jewish people, which had been confirmed from thousands of historical sources.

Noack and Noack dismissed this expert opinion, too, as completely "worthless," and returned to the changes discovered by Dr. Hübner, the better to prove that the diary "lacked youthfulness and had been schematized and systematized."[37]

In fact, Mrs. Becker's and Mrs. Ockelmann's conclusion that everything in the diary was by Anne's hand was not correct, in view of the pasted-in letter, the postcard and the birthday card, none of which had been written by her. The reader is referred to the report of the State Forensic Science Laboratory.

There are also several objections to Dr. Hübner's conclusion that the German translation must be judged by its substance and the ideas expressed. There is no doubt that the translator made Anne "more adult" than she was and omitted items from the translation that the German public might have found "embarrassing."

The purpose of Sieburg's expert opinion remains unclear. His contribution is no more than an essay on the importance of *Das Tagebuch der Anne Frank*.

A few weeks after Noack and Noack's last letter, the public prosecutor was ready to present his case against Stielau and Buddeberg. The indictment was characterized by its thoroughness. It contained a summary of what the accused had done, what the witnesses had stated, and of the evidence three of the expert witnesses had submitted. Next it went into why Stielau's belated assertion that he had been referring to the play and not to the diary was unacceptable. Stielau's wording, the comparison with the two other diaries, the framework within which the remark had been made, Stielau's statement to the official in the Ministry of Culture, the newspaper articles he had quoted, none of which dealt with the play, together with the fact that Stielau was not even familiar with the dramatization of the diary—all served to rebut the submissions of the defense.

Stielau and Buddeberg had furthermore been guilty of "*üble Nachrede*" (libel: Article 186 of the German Penal Code) by denying the authenticity of the diary, and of "*Beleidigung*" (defamation: Article 185) by using the term "profiteers from Germany's defeat." These offenses were punishable with a fine or a maximum prison sentence of two years. The public prosecutor asked for the case to be heard before the *Landgericht* (regional court) in Lübeck.[38]

In their objection Stielau's lawyers repeated that their client had been referring to the play and not to the book. For an opinion of the play they asked the court to call Hans Gomperts, drama critic of *Het Parool*, who, according to *Der Spiegel* of October 10, 1956, had described the dramatic adaptation as "Kitsch sailing under false colors."[39] Now, Gomperts had admittedly used these words in his review of the U.S. premiere of the play, but he reversed that opinion in his review of the Dutch premiere.[40]

In June the Third Criminal Division of the Lübeck *Landgericht* concluded that Stielau and Buddeberg had a case to answer.[41]

In the end, on October 17, 1961, three years after Stielau had published his article, the whole case simply petered out. Before it had a chance to come to court, Stielau's and Buddeberg's lawyers on the one hand, and Otto Frank's and the publishers' lawyers on the other, had arrived at a settlement. All that the court had left to do was to assess costs. The settlement was put in writing:

Stielau and Buddeberg declared that the preliminary investigation had convinced them that Stielau had had no grounds for claiming that the diary was a forgery—the expert opinions and the evidence of witnesses had persuaded them of the contrary. They expressed regret for their statements, which they had made with no attempt at verification. Stielau also withdrew the phrase "profiteers from Germany's defeat" with expressions of regret.

Stielau and Buddeberg declared further that they had meant no offense to either Otto Frank or the publishers, or to sully the memory of Anne Frank. Otto Frank and the publishers, for their part, acknowledged that preliminary examination had revealed no anti-Semitic tendencies on the part of the defendants.

The defendants agreed to the publication of the terms of this settlement, and Otto Frank and the publishers declared that they would drop criminal proceedings. Stielau agreed to contribute DM 1,000 to the legal costs.[42]

From newspaper reports about the case[43] and statements made later by Otto Frank it appeared that the presiding judge had pressed them to reach a settlement. He had argued that if the injured party declared itself satisfied with a public apology by the offender this was to be preferred to a judicial sentence. Moreover, according to the judge, the continuation of the case would have raised domestic and foreign issues which, although not directly, or at most marginally, connected with it, could have invited unwelcome repercussions.

This was a nebulous argument but one that was given more concrete form perhaps by a letter from Otto Frank to Heinz Roth (see p. 93) in which we read that his lawyer had told Otto Frank on October 17 that, had the case been continued, the defendant would have received a very light sentence. The judge was afraid that he would then have been accused by a large section of the press of being too lenient in his treatment of Nazis. Because he, Otto Frank, was not concerned with revenge but only with the authenticity of the diary, he had agreed to the settlement.[44]

The question of the high costs of the preliminary examination was also settled in a somewhat unsatisfactory manner. Stielau offered to contribute DM 1,000, but Buddeberg refused to pay anything, and the bench agreed that he need not. The remaining sum, DM 10,000, would be paid by the state.[45]

On the day after the hearing, *Vrij Nederland* quoted approvingly a headline from the West German *Bildzeitung*: "High school teacher libels Anne Frank [. . .] but judge lets him off."[46]

Otto Frank may have been satisfied at the time, but later he regretted the settlement. "Had I but known that there would be people who would consider a settlement in this case as insufficient proof [of the authenticity of the diary], I should certainly not have dropped the case."[47]

The fact that the bench had established the authenticity of Anne Frank's diary did not put an end to the allegations.

In January 1959, even before the Stielau case, the Vienna *Europa Korrespondenz* had published an article with the title "*Der Anne Frank-Skandal. Ein Beitrag zur Wahrheit* [The Anne Frank Scandal. A Contribution to the Truth]," in which Dr. Louis de Jong, until 1979 director of the Netherlands State Institute for War Documentation, was alleged to have been the real author of the diary.

The father came back to Amsterdam after the war, learned about the alleged diary, did not want to publish it, but was practically forced to do so by his friends. The Dutch journalist Louis de Jong, now director of the Netherlands State Institute for War Documentation, was crucially involved in the diary, and from the publications it is clear that De Jong is the author of the book.[48]

In October 1957, De Jong had admittedly written an article on Anne Frank which had appeared in the *Reader's Digest*, and later in foreign editions of that magazine, but there is nothing to indicate that De Jong ever had anything to do with the publication of *Het Achterhuis*.

In the course of the next few decades the authenticity of the diary was to be challenged in various journals and writings.

Thus, in the summer of 1967, Teressa Hendry took aim at the diary's authenticity in the *American Mercury*. She claimed that its real author had been Meyer Levin and went on to quote in English what was allegedly a summary of the *Fria Ord* articles published in the *Economic Council Letter* on April 15, 1959:

History has many examples of myths that live a longer and richer life than the truth, and may become more effective than truth.

The Western World has for some years been aware of a Jewish girl through the medium of what purports to be her personally written story, "Anne Frank's Diary." Any informed literary inspection of this book would have shown it to have been impossible as the work of a teenager.

A noteworthy decision of the New York Supreme Court confirms this point of view, in that the well known American Jewish writer, Meyer Levin, has been awarded $50,000 to be paid him by the father of Anne Frank as an honorarium for Levin's work on the "Anne Frank Diary."

Mr. Frank, in Switzerland, has promised to pay to his race-kin, Meyer Levin, not less than $50,000 because he had used the dialogue of Author Levin just as it was and "implanted" it in the diary as being his daughter's intellectual work.[49]

However, neither the judgment of the court nor the sum mentioned appeared in the two *Fria Ord* articles.

The *American Mercury* article is typical of the way in which right-wing extremists have challenged and continue to challenge the authenticity of the diary: they like to refer to earlier publications and to quote from them in such a way as to suggest that what has merely been alleged is "really true." Several years later the article in the *Economic Council Letter* was used again, in a pamphlet called *Did Six Million Really Die? The Truth at Last*.[50] Its author was Richard Harwood, a pseudonym of Richard Verrall of the extreme-right-wing British National Front.[51] German and Dutch translations of the pamphlet were published in 1975 and 1976 respectively.

Teressa Hendry had used a question mark at the end of the title of her article: "Was Anne Frank's Diary a Hoax?"; Harwood, however, wrote unequivocally: "Best-seller a hoax." His article ended with: "Here, then, is just one more fraud in a whole series of frauds in support of the 'Holocaust' legend and the saga of the Six Million."[52]

In 1975, David Irving, the extreme-right-wing British historian, had this to say in the Introduction to his book *Hitler und seine Feldherren* (Hitler and His Generals):

Many forgeries are on record, as for instance that of the "Diary of Anne Frank" (in this case a civil lawsuit brought by a New York scriptwriter has proved that he wrote it in collaboration with the girl's father).[53]

91

Otto Frank protested successfully to the publishers, and the passage was omitted when the book was reprinted. However, because a large number of copies of the first impression had been sold, Otto Frank also asked for damages to be paid to the Anne Frank Foundation in Amsterdam; this too was done.[54]

That same year Richard Harwood's publishers brought out a book by an American, A. R. Butz, called *The Hoax of the Twentieth Century*, a mainly demographic study in which the author denied the "Final Solution." He went at length into the existing literature, the better to suggest that he was a serious scholar. Here again Anne Frank's diary played a part, albeit a subsidiary one:

The question of the authenticity of the diary is not considered important enough to examine here; I will only remark that I have looked it over and don't believe it. For example, already on page 2 one is reading an essay on why a 13 year old girl would start a diary, and then page 3 gives a short history of the Frank family and then quickly reviews the specific anti-Jewish measures that followed the German occupation in 1940. The rest of the book is in the same historical spirit.[55]

The first book of any size to be devoted exclusively to the so-called unmasking of the diary appeared in 1978. *Anne Frank Diary—A Hoax?* was written by Ditlieb Felderer[56] from Sweden, whose own publishing house, Bible Researcher, had also published such books as *Zionism The Hidden Tyranny*.

Felderer conceded that there was no truth in the story that Meyer Levin had written the diary but used a different line of attack, as witness some of his chapter headings: "Drug Addict at Tender Age" ("proven" by the fact that Anne wrote on September 16, 1943, that she swallowed valerian pills every day); "Anne's Character—Not Even a Nice Girl"; "Teenage Sex"; "Sexual Extravaganza" (Anne's entries about her growing love for Peter are styled by Felderer "the first child porno"). Felderer went on to "unmask" the diary as "a forgery, a monstrous travesty."[57]

In the United States people were not yet ready to drop the Meyer Levin myth; on May 1, 1978, Teressa Hendry's article was reprinted in the Washington weekly *The Spotlight*.[58]

That year also saw the foundation of the Institute for Historical Review in Torrance, California, by Willis Carto, director of the Noontide Press, a man closely involved in the *American Mercury* and the Liberty Lobby, publishers of *The Spotlight*.[59] The Institute championed the so-called revisionist approach to history, and to the history of the Second World War in particular. Now, there had been a trend among a small group of American historians ever since the First World War to take a special interest both in the question of war guilt and in why the United States had become involved.[60] This trend resurfaced after the Second World War. It included serious historians, who, for example, reexamined the causes of, and responsibility for, the outbreak of the war, as well as a number of persons who wrote of Nazi Germany in nothing but positive terms, minimizing Nazi war crimes. This second group took on itself the title of "revisionists." The group's "revisions" were so many denials of the persecution of the Jews and the existence of the gas chambers.

The Institute for Historical Review tried to act as an umbrella organization for all these separately operating "revisionists" by distributing "revisionist" and blatantly Nazi literature and, from 1979 onward, by organizing an annual Revisionist Conference at which European "revisionists" were also welcome. The first issue of the quarterly *Journal of Historical Review*, devoted in the main to the lectures delivered at the annual conferences, appeared in 1980.

The obvious purpose of all these activities was to provide anti-Semitism and neo-Nazism with an ostensibly scientific foundation.[61]

In Germany, too, there were fresh stirrings. In 1976, Anne Frank's diary was again the subject of a court case, heard this time by the *Landgericht* in Frankfurt following the activities of Heinz Roth, an architect from Odenhausen, north of the city.

In 1975, Roth, whose own publishing house issued neo-Nazi brochures, began to distribute pamphlets with such titles as *Anne Franks Tagebuch—eine Fälschung (Anne Frank's Diary—A Forgery)* and *Anne Franks Tagebuch—der grosse Schwindel (Anne Frank's Diary—The Big Fraud)*. Quoting Irving and Harwood, he referred again to the old story that Otto Frank had written the diary with the help of a New York playwright. In December 1975 a quotation from one of his pamphlets appeared in the *"Leserbriefe"* (readers' letters column) of the Austrian periodical *Neue Ordnung*. When Otto Frank heard about this, he made a request to the editor of *Neue Ordnung* that a letter by himself be published in the same column setting out the successful outcome of his protests against David Irving's Introduction, and stating that the Lübeck *Landgericht* had established the authenticity of the diary.[62] We do not know whether or not this letter was in fact published.

Otto Frank sent a copy of his letter to Heinz Roth, who continued to maintain in the ensuing correspondence that he was concerned with the *"reine historische Wahrheit* [pure historical truth]," and continued to refuse to enter into Otto Frank's detailed arguments.[63]

Roth's activities had not escaped the notice of the German Department of Justice, and after a preliminary legal investigation had been ordered against a distributor of one of Roth's pamphlets, the Bochum public prosecutor inquired of Otto Frank in February 1976 if he had already laid criminal charges. The public prosecutor wanted to know when Frank had first heard about the pamphlet in question; this because of the statute of limitations.[64] Otto Frank replied a few weeks later; he had first heard about the pamphlet in September 1975 and although he had been indignant he had taken no steps because of his age and his health. He enclosed photocopies of his correspondence with Wappen Verlag, the publishers of *Neue Ordnung* (who had not replied), and with Roth, and added that the latter was "stubborn and intractable." This was written by Otto Frank following a performance of the Anne Frank play on February 3, 1976, in Hamburg at which Roth's pamphlet had been distributed, and he asked if it would be possible to proceed not only against the distributor of Roth's pamphlet but also against Roth himself.[65] On July 16, 1976, following the publication of one of Roth's later pamphlets, *Das Tagebuch der Anne Frank—Wahrheit oder Fälschung? (The Diary of Anne Frank—Truth or Forgery?)*, Otto Frank applied for an injunction to restrain Roth from using certain expressions in the future.

From the information available, we gather that the Frankfurt *Landgericht* decided on July 22, 1978, that Heinz Roth would incur a maximum fine of DM 500,000 or a maximum prison sentence of six months if he repeated any of the following statements in public:

a) "Anne Frank's diary—a forgery."
b) "This world-famous best-seller is a forgery."

93

c) "Millions of schoolchildren have been forced and are still being forced to read this fake . . . —and now it turns out that it is the product of a New York scriptwriter in collaboration with the girl's father!"

d) "This fraud was exposed for the first time not just recently but over a decade ago!"[66]

From its deliberations it appears that the bench considered the expert opinions given at the preliminary examination in Lübeck and the statements of the various witnesses carried sufficient weight to refute Roth's allegations. Roth's lawyers had also submitted an expert opinion, which was to play an important part over the years in attacks on the authenticity of the diary. It took the form of a study by Robert Faurisson, to which we shall now turn our attention.

Faurisson, of the Department of Literature at the University of Lyons, produced his expert opinion, written in German, in 1978. It was published two years later in France under the title of *Le Journal d'Anne Frank est-il authentique? (The Diary of Anne Frank—Is It Authentic?).*[67] In 1985 a Dutch translation was published in Belgium under the title of *Het Dagboek van Anne Frank—een vervalsing (The Diary of Anne Frank—a Forgery)*, this time without the question mark.[68] For the purposes of his investigation, Faurisson had examined the published diary in the French translation, compared the Dutch edition with the German, spoken to Otto Frank in Basle and gone into the circumstances of those who had been in hiding and of their arrest in August 1944.

It goes without saying that a life in hiding carried countless risks; the possibility of discovery was ever present, and many thousands of those who hid from the Germans did indeed fall into enemy hands as a result of betrayal, accident or their own carelessness.

From the diary it appears that the inhabitants of the Annexe, too, had to brave many dangers, not least the chance that they might make too much noise and be overheard. Faurisson, however, did not examine the overall picture of life in hiding in any depth, or concern himself greatly in this context with the fact that the Frank family and their fellow fugitives were in the end arrested. On the contrary, he used his findings only in order to demonstrate that it must have been impossible to hide in the Annexe and that therefore the diary could not have been written by Anne Frank.

A typical example of his approach is the way in which he examined the problem of noise as presented in *Het Achterhuis*:

Let us take the case of noise. The people in hiding, we are told, are not allowed to make the slightest noise, to the extent that if they cough they are made quickly to take some codeine. The "enemies" might hear them. The walls are so "thin" (March 25, 1943). The "enemies" are very numerous: Lewin, who "knows the whole building well" (October 1, 1942), the men in the warehouse, the clients, the tradesmen, the postman, the *charwoman*, Slagter the *nightwatchman*, the sanitary department, the bookkeeper, the police flushing people out of their homes, neighbors near and far, the owner of the building, etc. It is therefore improbable, even inconceivable, that Mrs. van Daan should have been in the habit of using *the vacuum cleaner* daily at 12:30 (August 5, 1943). Vacuum cleaners at that time were exceptionally noisy. I must ask: "Is this credible?" My question is not just a formality. It is not rhetorical. Its purpose is not to astonish. My question is simply a question. An answer will have to be found. That question could be followed by forty others concerning noise. The use of an *alarm clock*, for instance, needs explanation (August 4, 1943). The noisy *carpentry* must be explained: dismantling wooden stairs, turning a door into a movable cupboard (August 21, 1942), making a wooden candlestick (December 7, 1942). Peter chops wood in the loft in front of the open window (February 23, 1944). There is mention of making "a few little cupboards for the walls and other odds and ends" with wood from the attic (July 11, 1942). There is even talk of building a little compartment in the attic as a place to work in (July 13, 1943). There is the almost constant noise of the *radio*, the *slamming of doors*, the *incessant shouting* (December 6, 1943), the *rows*, the *crying*, the *clamor*, the "*noise . . . enough to waken the dead*" (November 9, 1942), "*a great din and disturbance followed* [. . .] I was doubled up with *laughter*" (May 10, 1944). The episode described on September 2, 1942, cannot be reconciled with the need for keeping quiet and for discretion. We see the people in hiding sitting at table. They *chatter gaily*. Suddenly there is *a piercing whistle* and they hear Peter's voice *calling* down the chimney saying that he isn't coming down anyway. Mr. van Daan springs to his feet, his napkin falls to the floor and scarlet in the face he *shouts*: "I've had enough of this." He goes up to the attic and then we hear *a good deal of resistance and stamping*. The episode recorded on December 10, 1942, was of the same type. We see Mrs. van Daan being attended to by the dentist, Dussel. With his scraper he touches a bad tooth. Mrs. van Daan utters "incoherent cries." She tries to pull the thing out of her mouth. The dentist stands with hands against his sides calmly watching the little comedy. The rest of the audience "*roared with laughter*." Anne is not in the least anxious about the screams and the roars of laughter. Instead she says: "It was rotten of us, because I for one am quite sure that I should have screamed even louder."[69]

Given the above extract, we have no need to subject all the examples mentioned by Faurisson to review. We shall make use of just three examples in order to highlight Faurisson's method.

A comparison with the diary will show that to prove his point Faurisson relates his chosen examples in part only. Thus the fact that Mrs. van Daan should have used the vacuum cleaner daily at twelve-thirty (August 5, 1943) is indeed mentioned by Anne on that date, but the sentence before reveals: "The warehousemen have gone home now."

On December 6, 1943, Anne refers to "resounding . . . laughter" (the "incessant shouting" is our translation of Faurisson's "*cris interminables*" whereas the French translation of *Het Achterhuis* has "*éclats de rire interminables*"). Again Faurisson fails to mention that Anne sets this scene on a Sunday evening (December 5).

On November 9, 1942, Anne recorded that a sack of brown beans had burst open and that "the noise was enough to wake the dead." Faurisson omits to quote the next sentence: "(Thank God there were no strangers in the house.)"

In the spring of 1977, Faurisson called on Otto Frank, and in the presence of Frank's wife asked a number of questions concerning his time in hiding and the way *Het Achterhuis* had come to be written. Faurisson's account of this conversation gives the impression that Otto Frank was entangled in all sorts of contradictions: "The interview turned out to be grueling for Anne Frank's father."[70] Eighteen months later Otto Frank, in a written commentary on Faurisson's study and in particular on Faurisson's report of their conversation, challenged most of what Faurisson had put into his mouth.[71]

A few items examined by Faurisson have already been discussed. They concern the background of *Het Achterhuis*, the disparities between *Het Achterhuis* and the translations, particularly the German, and the course of events surrounding the arrest of the Frank family.

One point will suffice to clarify Faurisson's work method. In his story of the arrest he mentions a witness "who, I believe, is well informed and of good faith and at the same time has a good memory. [. . .] I have promised to keep his name secret. [. . .] The name and address of this witness [. . .] have been noted in a sealed envelope."[72] A photograph of this sealed envelope is printed as an appendix to Faurisson's "investigation," albeit only in the French version of 1980; the publisher of the Dutch version had the sense to leave out this piece of evidence.

In the same year that the French edition of Faurisson's study appeared, his new book, *Mémoire en défense*, was published in Paris.[73] In it he denied, not for the first time, the existence of the gas chambers and defended himself against those who accused him of falsifying history. The introduction by Noam Chomsky, the distinguished U.S. linguistic philosopher and well-known opponent of United States policy in Vietnam, caused a sensation. Chomsky declared that he would defend freedom of speech everywhere and at all times, even if Faurisson were an anti-Semite or a fanatical Nazi apologist.

In 1981, Faurisson was called before a French judge in order to substantiate his statement on the radio and in various publications that the gas chambers had never existed. He received a three-month suspended prison sentence and was ordered to pay fines and damages for defamation, incitement to discrimination, race hatred and racial violence.[74] The sentence was confirmed on appeal.[75]

And it was Faurisson's study that was presented as expert evidence during Roth's appeal to the Frankfurt *Oberlandesgericht* (Higher Regional Court) against his sentence. Roth continued to insist that his doubts concerning the authenticity of the diary were justified. He based that claim on the *Der Spiegel* article of April 1959 and also on statements by Harwood, Butz and Faurisson. The court, however, did not seem very impressed and found that Roth had been unable to substantiate his allegations. His appeal was rejected on July 5, 1979; after having taken all the submissions into consideration, the court concluded:

"From the foregoing we must concur with the *Landgericht* that the accused has not succeeded in establishing the truth of his allegations, and that he has failed to submit any evidence that would result in a different conclusion. As a consequence the plaintiff is entitled to demand that he cease from making these claims and from propagating them in future."[76]

Although Roth had died in November 1978,[77] the *Bundesgerichtshof* (the Federal High Court) referred the case back to the Frankfurt *Oberlandesgericht* on December 6, 1980. In the view of the *Bundesgerichtshof* the case concerned not only the good name of Otto Frank but also the not unimportant role of "proprietary interests," by which the court was probably referring to royalties, although no specific mention of them was made. Otto Frank died on August 19, 1980, so that the question now involved his heirs. The *Bundesgerichtshof* took the view that the court had confined itself to the question of whether Meyer Levin and Otto Frank had jointly written the diary, a claim that had proved to be false. Roth had not, however, been given enough opportunity to prove his allegations that the diary was a "*Fälschung* [forgery]"; he was to be given that opportunity during the review of the case.[78] The fact that the accused had been dead for two years was plainly irrelevant.

While the case against Roth came to a rather unsatisfactory conclusion, two other cases actually ended in aquittals. In July 1978, E. Schönborn, chairman of the extreme-right-wing *Kampfbund Deutscher Soldaten* (Combat League of German

Soldiers), distributed pamphlets outside the Anne Frank Schools in Frankfurt and Nuremberg claiming, *inter alia*, that the diary of Anne Frank was "a forgery and the product of a Jewish anti-German atrocity propaganda campaign intended to support the lie about the six million gassed Jews and to finance the state of Israel." So read the report in *De Volkskrant*.[79]

According to the same daily newspaper, the prosecution asked for a ten-month suspended sentence, but the judge held that Schönborn, too, had the right of free speech. Schönborn, the judge went on to say, had acted within the law inasmuch as he had not denied human rights to any Jews. He was therefore acquitted. The judge, according to *De Volkskrant*, did not exonerate Schönborn, he had simply held that a sentence for defamation must be consequent upon charges being laid by those personally affected.[80]

The second case was heard in Stuttgart. Here a former Hitler Youth leader called Werner Kuhnt, who after the war became editor-in-chief of the extreme-right-wing monthly *Deutsche Stimme*, was charged with *Volksverhetzung* (incitement of the people) and defaming the memory of a dead person. Kuhnt had stated in the issue of October 1979 that Anne Frank's diary was "a forgery" and "a fraud," that it had not been written by Anne and that it was the result of "collaboration between a New York scriptwriter and the girl's father." In June 1980, Kuhnt was acquitted by the Stuttgart *Amtsgericht* (district court). The public prosecutor entered an appeal.[81]

On October 27, 1980, the appeal was heard before the Stuttgart *Landgericht* (regional court), which found that the charge of inciting the people could not be substantiated, that there had been no evidence of anti-Semitism and that Kuhnt had in no way insulted human dignity. As far as the misleading statement in Kuhnt's article was concerned, the bench found that Otto Frank should have lodged a complaint, which he had failed to do. The appeal was therefore dismissed and Kuhnt acquitted.[82]

At the end of February and the beginning of March 1976 it came to the notice of the police in Hamburg that pamphlets had been handed out after performances of the play there. The pamphlets were headed "Best-Seller—a Fraud" and repeated the old Meyer Levin allegation. The pamphlet was, in fact, a reprint of two pages from the German translation of Harwood's *Did Six Million Really Die? The Truth at Last*, and had been distributed, it appeared, by Ernst Römer, born in 1904. On January 13, 1977, almost a year later, Römer was fined DM 1,500 for defamation by the Hamburg *Amtsgericht*. He appealed, and his case was heard on August 21, 1978, before the Hamburg *Landgericht*. During the hearing the journalist Edgar Geiss, born in 1929, distributed pamphlets in the courtroom alleging in effect that the diary was "a fraud."

Geiss was also taken to court, and in April of the following year the *Amtsgericht* sentenced him to one year in prison for defamation. His sentence was more severe than Römer's because he had several previous convictions.

Geiss, too, appealed, and three months later the *Landgericht* decided to hear the cases of Römer and Geiss jointly.

The *Bundeskriminalamt* (the BKA, or Federal Criminal Investigation Bureau) in Wiesbaden was charged with preparing an expert opinion on whether it was possible "by an examination of paper and writing material to establish that the writings attributed to Anne Frank were produced during the years 1941 to 1944."

The investigation—in the spring of 1980—was therefore restricted by this limited brief. The BKA came to the conclusion that the types of paper used, including the covers of Diaries 1, 2 and 3, as well as the types of ink found in the three diaries and on the loose sheets, were all manufactured before 1950–51 (and could thus have been used during the stated period). On the other hand:

Some of the corrections made subsequently on the loose pages were [. . .] written in black, green and blue ballpen ink. Ballpen ink of this type has only been on the market since 1951.[83]

The BKA report ran to a mere four pages. The precise location of the corrections on the loose sheets and their nature and extent are not mentioned, nor is the number of such corrections.

In itself this was a less than sensational report and did not touch upon the authenticity of the diary as such. That was not, however, the view of *Der Spiegel*, which on October 6, 1980, published a long article with the following introductory paragraph printed in bold type:

Proved by a *Bundeskriminalamt* report: "The Diary of Anne Frank" was edited at a later date. Further doubt is therefore cast on the authenticity of that document.[84]

It was a suggestive article in other respects too. Without asking when the writing in ballpoint had been made on the loose sheets, what the nature of these corrections was or whether they had been incorporated in the published texts, the author of the article, instead of referring to *Korrecturen* (corrections) as the BKA had done, wrote of "additions to the original that up till now had always been considered to be in the same hand as the rest of the text."

In support of the phrase "up till now had always been considered," the reader was referred to Minna Becker's mistaken 1960 opinion (see p. 87). *Der Spiegel* added: "Now if the handwriting of the original entries matched that of the additions, then there must have been an impostor at work," which, the magazine generously conceded, "cannot be seriously maintained even now in view of the controversial nature of graphological evidence."

It is only towards the end of the article that *Der Spiegel* quotes briefly from the BKA report and uses the term "*Korrekturen*"; before that, however, the reader had been told that the published diary had been subjected to countless "*Manipulationen* [manipulations]."

True, *Der Spiegel* also pointed out that those who had cast doubt on the authenticity of the diary had done so for the purpose of establishing "the truth about the persecution of the Jews," in the manner, as the magazine remarked critically, of "one of the pamphlet distributors at the Römer trial who wanted to put a stop to the 'gas chamber fraud.' "

David Irving, too, was portrayed critically, as was the "oft-repeated legend" that Otto Frank had incorporated quotations from a film script (what was meant, of course, was from the text of a play) into the diary.

The article aroused great interest both in Germany and abroad. *Der Spiegel*'s message seemed clear: there was something wrong. Members of the Anne Frank Foundation let it be known in the Dutch press that, at the request of Otto Frank, Kleiman had made minor corrections to the manuscript after the war but that these had simply been clarifications.[85]

We have just called the *Spiegel* article suggestive. The magazine had, however, been indirectly encouraged to take this line by the failure of the *Bundeskriminalamt* to publish the concrete data on which it had based its findings, thus rendering any kind of verification impossible.

We asked the *Bundeskriminalamt* to put these data at our disposal. The reply was that no such data were in their possession.

On December 20, 1985, at our request, the BKA then used the State Forensic Science Laboratory of the Netherlands Ministry of Justice in Rijswijk in an attempt to give concrete expression to the findings of their report.

They were in part successful. The reader is referred to Chapter VI of the State Forensic Science Laboratory's report, which also discusses the relevance of the ballpoint writing to the authenticity of the diary.

The BKA was unable to indicate where just one alleged correction in green ballpoint ink was to be found.

Notes

[1] *Fria Ord*, November 9 and 11, 1957. Lübeck *Landgericht*, Stielau/Buddeberg dossier.

[2] Meyer Levin, *In Search* (London-Paris: Constellation Books, 1951).

[3] *Folg og Land*, March 1, 1958. Lübeck *Landgericht*, Stielau/Buddeberg dossier.

[4] *Europa Korrespondenz*, April 1958. Lübeck *Landgericht*, Stielau/Buddeberg dossier.

[5] *Reichsruf. Wochenzeitung für das nationale Deutschland* [Weekly of National Germany] May 17, 1958. Lübeck *Landgericht*, Stielau/Buddeberg dossier.

[6] P. R. A. van Iddekinge and A. H. Paape, *Ze zijn er nog* (Amsterdam: De Bezige Bij, 1970), p. 148.

[7] Examination of Stielau, June 18, 1958. Lübeck *Landgericht*, Stielau/Buddeberg dossier.

[8] *Zeitschrift der Vereinigung ehemaliger Schüler und der Freunde der Oberschule zum Dom, e.V.*, Lübeck, October 10, 1958. Lübeck *Landgericht*, Stielau/Buddeberg dossier.

[9] Examination of Otto Frank, July 16, 1959. Lübeck *Landgericht*, Stielau/Buddeberg dossier.

[10] Record of interview, December 5, 1985. Lübeck *Landgericht*, Stielau/Buddeberg dossier.

[11] *Lübecker Nachrichten*, January 6, 1959. Lübeck *Landgericht*, Stielau/Buddeberg dossier.

[12] Examination of Buddeberg, July 7, 1959. Lübeck *Landgericht*, Stielau/Buddeberg dossier.

[13] Dr. A. Flesch, Otto Frank's lawyer, to public prosecutor at the Lübeck *Landgericht*, January 14, 1959. Stielau/Buddeberg dossier.

[14] Ibid.

[15] Letter from public prosecutor, Lübeck *Landgericht*, to Flesch, January 16, 1959. Lübeck *Landgericht*, Stielau/Buddeberg dossier.

[16] Letter from Federal Minister of Justice to Schleswig-Holstein Minister of Justice, January 29, 1959. Lübeck *Landgericht*, Stielau/Buddeberg dossier.

[17] Memorandum by Lübeck public prosecutor, April 1959, p. 11. Lübeck *Landgericht*, Stielau/Buddeberg dossier.

[18] *Der Spiegel*, April 1, 1959, pp. 51–55.

[19] Examination of Stielau, June 18 and 25, 1959. Lübeck *Landgericht*, Stielau/Buddeberg dossier.

[20] Ibid., April 25, 1960.

[21] Examination of Erich Heim, July 2, 1959. Lübeck *Landgericht*, Stielau/Buddeberg dossier.

[22] Examination of Otto Frank, July 16 and 17, 1959. Lübeck *Landgericht*, Stielau/Buddeberg dossier.

[23] Examination of Bep Voskuijl, September 29, 1959; examination of Miep Gies, September 29, 1959 and examination of Jan Gies, September 29, 1959. Lübeck *Landgericht*, Stielau/Buddeberg dossier.

[24] *Institut für Zeitgeschichte* to examining magistrate, July 1, 1959. Lübeck *Landgericht*, Stielau/Buddeberg dossier.

[25] Expert handwriting opinion in proceedings for defamation against: 1. *Studienrat* Stielau from Lübeck; and 2. farmer Buddeberg from Woltersdorf. Lübeck *Landgericht*, Stielau/Buddeberg dossier.

[26] Memorandum by examining magistrate, April 14, 1960. Lübeck *Landgericht*, Stielau/Buddeberg dossier.

[27] Expert opinion in the preliminary examination of 1. *Studienrat* Lothar Stielau; and 2. farmer Heinrich Buddeberg, p. 29. Lübeck *Landgericht*, Stielau/Buddeberg dossier.

[28] Ibid., p. 34.

[29] Ibid.

[30] Noack and Noack to examining magistrate, December 12, 1960. Lübeck *Landgericht*, Stielau/Buddeberg dossier.

[31] Lübeck public prosecutor to Schleswig-Holstein Minister of Justice, June 14, 1960. Lübeck *Landgericht*, Stielau/Buddeberg dossier.

[32] Ibid., July 3, 1960.

[33] Expert opinion in criminal proceedings against *Studienrat* Stielau, p. 1. Lübeck *Landgericht*, Stielau/Buddeberg dossier.

[34] Noack and Noack to examining magistrate, July 29, 1960. Lübeck *Landgericht*, Stielau/Buddeberg dossier.

[35] Ibid.

[36] Ibid. December 12, 1960.

[37] Ibid., p. 6.

[38] Indictment, Lübeck public prosecutor, Lübeck *Landgericht*, Stielau/Buddeberg dossier.

[39] Noack and Noack to examining magistrate, February 20, 1961. Lübeck *Landgericht*, Stielau/Buddeberg dossier.

[40] *Het Parool*, November 28, 1956.

[41] Decision of Third Criminal Division of Lübeck *Landgericht*, June 1, 1961. Lübeck *Landgericht*, Stielau/Buddeberg dossier.

[42] Report of open session of Third Criminal Division of Lübeck *Landgericht*, October 17, 1961. Lübeck *Landgericht*, Stielau/Buddeberg dossier.

[43] *Het Vaderland*, October 8, 1961, and *Vrij Nederland*, October 28, 1961.

[44] Otto Frank to Heinz Roth, January 21, 1976. Frankfurt *Landgericht*, Roth dossier.

[45] Lübeck public prosecutor to Schleswig-Holstein Minister of Justice, October 17, 1961. Lübeck *Landgericht*, Stielau/Buddeberg dossier.

[46] *Vrij Nederland*, October 28, 1961.

[47] Otto Frank to Heinz Roth, January 21, 1976. Frankfurt *Landgericht*, Roth dossier.

[48] *Europa Korrespondenz*, January 1959. Lübeck *Landgericht*, Stielau/Buddeberg dossier.

[49] From the Summer 1967 issue of the *American Mercury*, in Ditlieb Felderer, *Anne Frank Diary—A Hoax?* (Taby [Sweden]: Bible Researcher, 1978).

[50] Richard Harwood, *Did Six Million Really Die? The Truth at Last* (Richmond [Surrey]: Historical Review Press, 1974), p. 19.

[51] Jan Barnes, "Revisionism and the Right," in *Contemporary Affairs Briefing*, Vol. 1, No. 1 (January 1982), p. 7.

[52] Harwood, op. cit., p. 19.

[53] David Irving, *Hitler und seine Feldherren* (Frankfurt-am-Main, Berlin, Vienna: Ullstein Verlag, 1975), p. III.

[54] Otto Frank to David Irving, October 23, 1979.

[55] A. R. Butz, *The Hoax of the Twentieth Century* (Richmond [Surrey]: Historical Review Press, 1975), p. 37.

[56] Under the slightly altered title of *Anne Frank's Diary—A Hoax*, Felderer's book was reprinted by the Institute for Historical Review, Torrance, California.

[57] Felderer, op. cit., p. 29.

[58] *The Spotlight*, May 1, 1978.

[59] Colin Holmes, "Historical Revisionism in Britain: the Politics of History," in *Trends in Historical Revisionism* (London: Centre for Contemporary Studies, 1985).

[60] M. C. Brands, "*Revisionistische bewegingen in de Amerikaanse historiografie*," in *Theoretische Geschiedenis*, 2 (1977), pp. 77–92.

[61] Vera Ebels-Dolanová, ed., *The Extreme Right in Europe and the United States* (Amsterdam: Anne Frank Foundation, 1975).

[62] Otto Frank to Wappen Verlag, December 17, 1975. Hamburg *Landgericht*, Römer-Geiss dossier.

[63] Correspondence between Otto Frank and Heinz Roth, January 18 and 25, 1975, and January 8, 15, 21 and 26, 1976. Frankfurt *Landgericht*, Roth dossier.

[64] Bochum public prosecutor to Otto Frank, February 20, 1976. Frankfurt *Landgericht*, Roth dossier.

[65] Otto Frank to Bochum public prosecutor, March 3, 1976. Frankfurt *Landgericht*, Roth dossier.

[66] Verdict of Frankfurt *Landgericht*, March 22, 1978. Frankfurt *Landgericht*, Roth dossier.

[67] In Serge Thion, *Vérité historique ou vérité politique?* (Paris: La Vieille Taupe, 1980). For a more moderate version, see Hervé le Goff, *Les grands truquages de l'histoire* (Paris; Jacques Grancher, 1983), pp. 13–40.

[68] Robert Faurisson, *Het Dagboek van Anne Frank—een vervalsing* (Antwerp: Vrij Historisch Onderzoek, 1985).

[69] Ibid., pp. 9–10

[70] Ibid., p.18.

[71] Reply to the document submitted by Professor Faurisson on July 4, 1978, and Comments on the motion to receive evidence by the Counsel for the defense, dated November 1978. Frankfurt *Landgericht*, Roth dossier.

[72] Faurisson, op. cit., p. 58.
[73] Robert Faurisson, *Mémoire en défense. Contre ceux qui m'accusent de falsifier l'Histoire. La question des chambres à gaz* (Paris: La Vieille Taupe, 1980).
[74] *Le Monde*, July 18, 1981.
[75] *Le Monde*, April 28, 1983.
[76] Verdict of Frankfurt *Oberlandesgericht*, July 5, 1979, p. 14. Frankfurt *Oberlandesgericht*, Roth dossier.
[77] Christiaan Raabe (notary) to Netherlands State Institute for War Documentation, April 24, 1985.
[78] Press communiqué of the *Bundesgericht*, December 16, 1980. *Bundesgesgerichtshof*, Roth dossier.
[79] *De Volkskrant*, March 23, 1979.
[80] Ibid.
[81] Verdict of Stuttgart *Landgericht*, October 27, 1980. Stuttgart *Landgericht*, Roth dossier.
[82] Ibid.
[83] Opinion of Federal Criminal Investigation Bureau, May 28, 1980. Hamburg *Landgericht*, Römer/Geiss dossier.
[84] *Der Spiegel*, October 6, 1980.
[85] *Het Algemeen Dagblad, De Telegraaf, Trouw*, October 7, 1980.

Document Examination and Handwriting Identification of the Text Known as the Diary of Anne Frank: Summary of Findings

H. J. J. HARDY, M.Sc.

The findings of the State Forensic Science Laboratory, which was charged with the above analysis by the Netherlands State Institute for War Documentation, are published in a report of more than 250 pages, which is for the most part devoted to handwriting identification.

Because of the length and the detailed technical language used, the full report is not suitable for inclusion in this publication of the complete texts of the diary of Anne Frank. The following summary has been compiled, however, in order to convey to the interested lay reader some idea of the most important findings.

Introduction

An investigation into the authenticity of the text known as the diary of Anne Frank has many facets. The State Forensic Science Laboratory has concerned itself with two of these: handwriting identification and document examination.

Besides the diary, the Netherlands State Institute for War Documentation also provided the Laboratory with a number of handwriting samples for comparison purposes, the State Institute submitting that the handwriting was that of Anne Frank.

If the diary is authentic, then it was written in the period from 1942 to 1944. The materials used—the ink, paper, glue, etc.—will therefore have been manufactured before or during that period; to discover whether or not they were, the document examiner must compare them with a representative collection of reference material from the same period.

The handwriting expert faces a similar problem. He too must, on the basis of an adequate collection of reference material, form a picture of the kind of handwriting produced at the alleged time by someone whose age, education and so on agree as closely as possible with those of the supposed writer of the diary. He must, moreover, bear in mind the development of his or her handwriting with time, and judge whether or not handwriting analysis is applicable.

However, document examination and handwriting identification differ essentially in one respect. The former hinges on the discovery of possible anachronisms; to that end it investigates, for instance, whether the paper includes whiteners, not used in paper manufacture before about 1952. If such materials are absent and if no other anachronisms can be found, then forgery becomes increasingly unlikely.

The document examiner may not always be able to specify a precise date. However, if in a hypothetical case it is possible to determine that, for instance, a certain type of ink was only manufactured between 1942 and 1945, then the use of such ink would be a factor in weighing up the authenticity of a document allegedly produced at that time. The handwriting expert, on the other hand, is concerned with the identification of the writer of a given text rather than with dates. If he can show agreement between two handwriting samples, then he may, within the bounds of his technical powers, of course, conclude that the two samples came from the same hand. Needless to say, if the document examination should reveal the existence of anachronisms, then any further research by the handwriting expert becomes pointless.

Document examination and handwriting identification are highly specialized skills. Moreover, the term "handwriting identification" is used as a collective name for a number of analytical techniques, each of which calls for special knowledge. Several departments of the State Forensic Science Laboratory have therefore been involved in our investigation.

In the light of the above, Section I of the report deals with the results of the document examination.

Sections II to VI inclusive are devoted to handwriting identification. This comprises:

II. An explanatory study of the handwriting of young people and the changes that take place in it.
III. A more detailed examination of the so-called standards of comparison, or standards for short.
IV. A justification of the comparative methods used.
V. The handwriting identification of the diary.
VI. The handwriting identification of the corrections found in the diary.

Our handwriting identification has been based on purely technical considerations. Thus the relationship between handwriting and personality traits has been ignored. That relationship—which in the case under investigation might well have been influenced by the age and the exceptional life situation of the alleged writer of the diary—falls into the province of graphology or grapho-analysis.

I The Results of the Document Examination

The findings of the various examiners, as recorded in their reports, can be summarized as follows:

The document examination has, where possible, borne on the paper, the glue and the fiber used in the manufacture of the diaries and the standards of comparison. In addition, the ink and pencil deposits of the written text have been examined.

The glue and fibers used in the binding of the diaries were analyzed by infrared spectrometry. The spectra of the glue used in the diaries were found to agree with those of bone glue (parts 1 and 2) and of nitrocellulose glue (part 3). These types of glue were in common use during the supposed period of manufacture. After about 1950 they were generally displaced by synthetic glue (polyvinyl acetate).

A fiber analysis was made of the material used to cover the diary, part 1, and of the thread used in the binding of the sections in parts 1, 2 and 3. In the first case, cotton and viscose (rayon) fibers were found. The bindings consisted of cotton fiber (parts 1 and 3) and flax (linen) fiber (part 2). These fibers were in common use during the supposed period of manufacture.

The samples of the paper used in the diaries, parts 1, 2 and 3, and in the loose sheets were analyzed as to their sizing, glues and fibers. The sizing was examined by X-ray fluorescence. The elementary composition obtained by this method agreed fully with that obtained from the analysis of six random samples of reference material manufactured during the period from 1939 up to, and inclusive of, 1942.

The glues were examined by qualitative chemical analysis. The main substance found was starch paste.

The possible presence of so-called whiteners was first examined under ultraviolet light. No fluorescent phenomena were observed. Upon further analysis, using thin-layer chromatography, the presence of whiteners could be positively excluded.

The fiber of the paper samples was found by TNO, the Delft fiber institute, to consist in the main of coniferous cellulose, straw cellulose and ground wood pulp.

These findings all served to show that no anachronism whatsoever existed between the supposed and the actual period of manufacture.

The standards of comparison could not, because of partial destruction, be subjected to all the methods of analysis mentioned above. All the tests that could be made failed to reveal any anachronism.

The ink deposits found on the standards of comparison, on the diaries and on the loose sheets, consist, in the main, of gray-blue fountain pen ink in which iron was clearly present. At the time, iron-gallotannate ink was in general use. Only after 1950 were inks with no, or a much lower, iron content introduced.

Besides the gray-blue fountain pen ink, the diaries and loose sheets also contained
—thin red ink,
—green and red pencil,
—black pencil.
The writing used for the pagination will be considered separately below.

The results of the document examination can be summed up as follows:

None of the tests produced any indication that the diaries, the loose sheets and the items submitted for comparison, together with the ink deposits found in them, are of later date than the supposed period of origin.

II An Explanatory Study of the Handwriting of Young People and the Changes That Take Place in It

As we have pointed out, the handwriting expert requires a frame of reference if he is to form a picture of the writing practices of contemporaries. And it is virtually a fact of nature that the handwriting of young people undergoes changes, gradual or otherwise, during the period between their first learning to write and the final stabilization of their hand. In the case under consideration, the frame of reference is the writing found in four albums of the type used for collecting autographs and other contributions from friends. These belonged to former classmates of Anne Frank, and hence contain handwriting specimens from people whose age and school education are comparable to hers. The collection comprises the writing of seventy-eight persons, among them eleven who made an entry in one of the albums on more than one date. When compared with the reference group, the writing skill reflected in Anne Frank's handwriting samples was admittedly found to be high, but not exceptionally so. Nor was the use of two types of handwriting—handprinting (a disconnected style of writing in which each letter is written separately) and cursive writing (writing in which the letters are for the most part joined together)—a rare phenomenon. This characteristic of the Anne Frank handwriting samples was present in at least 15 percent of all the writers in the group.

The reference material, moreover, served to determine whether or not the methods of analysis used were generally applicable to the writing of young people. It appeared that in any one of the items examined the handwriting characteristics were highly consistent and well within the natural variation. This was also true of handwriting produced on different dates, although after long enough intervals changes did occur. This fact confirms the experts' expectation that changes in the handwriting of young people must be considered a natural phenomenon.

The technical literature covering what were sometimes very extensive investigations shows that the development of children's handwriting passes through various phases. Although different authors describe these phases in different words, their conclusion is nevertheless clear: increased writing skill is associated with further stabilization and development of individuality in the writing. Among the works consulted were:

De Ajuriaguerra, J., et al., *L'Ecriture de l'enfant*, I, 3rd ed. (Paris: Delachaux et Niestlé, 1979).
Bracken, H. von, "*Die Konstanz der Handschrift-Eigenart bei Kindern der ersten vier Schuljahre,*" in *Nederlands Tijdschrift voor Psychologie*, 1934, I, 541–54.
Gallmeier, M., "*Über die Entwicklung der Schülerschrift.*" Dissertation, Munich, 1934.
Gramm, D., "*Schrift und Geläufigkeitsstufen im Grundschulalter,*" in *Schule und Psychologie*, 1957, 4, 70–76.
Lockowandt, O., "*Die Kinderhandschrift—ihre diagnostischen Möglichkeiten und Grenzen,*" in *Zeitschrift für Menschenkunde*, 1970, 301–26.
Lockowandt, O., and C. H. Keller, "*Beitrag zur Stabilität der Kinderhandschrift,*" in *Psychologische Beiträge*, 1975, 17, 273–82.

III A More Detailed Examination of the Standards Offered for Comparison

A total of twenty-four documents that, according to the Netherlands State Institute for War Documentation, contain writings by Anne Frank was made available to the team of experts. Some of these documents also contain writings by one or other family member(s). Anne Frank's own writing is almost invariably accompanied by the name "Anne," "Anne Frank" or by similar indications.

The standards of comparison submitted included both cursive writing and handprinting. Twenty-two of the documents were original; the other two were good-quality photocopies. The standards date from the period 1936–42. Apart from those in the possession of the Frank family, the handwriting samples came from acquaintances, friends and classmates of Anne Frank.

Several such comparative standards are illustrated in this section namely:

III-1: A letter dated July 30, 1941.
III-2: A New Year card sent at the end of 1941 to the Kugler family. *The arrow*

on the address has been added by the investigator (see the section on post-marks).

III-3 a,b,c: A letter probably written in the spring of 1942.

III-4 a,b,c: Fragment from a letter from the Frank family to "Berndt Elias." Reproduced are the parts written by Anne Frank (4 a) and the front and back of the envelope (4 b,c). The name and address of the sender (4 c) are in Anne Frank's hand.

III-5: Fragment from a letter in handprinting, probably written in the summer of 1941.

III-6: A short poem in handprinting from an autograph album belonging to Jacqueline van Maarsen, dated March 23, 1942.

III-7: A postcard addressed to "Leni Elias," dated July 5, 1942. A short fragment in handprinting on the top left is by Anne Frank. The rest of the writing is by other members of the Frank family. The reverse side, written by Otto Frank, is also shown. *The arrows on this photograph have been added by the investigator* (see the section on postmarks).

The magnification or reduction of the figures can be determined from the accompanying graduated scale. The figures convey some idea not only of the diversity of the source material but also of the range of Anne Frank's hand-writing.

When comparing handwritings it is always advisable to look critically at the standards. Normally, standards obtained on request are compared with collected standards in order to establish whether they are uniform. In the analysis of historical documents, however, standards on request are very often not available or produced only much later than the document under investigation. In our case, too, other means were needed to investigate the authenticity of the collected standards more closely.

The following conclusions, some of which can be checked with the help of our illustrations, justify the examiners' confidence that the collected standards were indeed written by Anne Frank:

—The collected standards from one and the same period, though obtained from a variety of sources, show a high measure of uniformity. Apart from items in the possession of the Frank family, they also come from acquaintances, friends and classmates.

—In content the texts have a natural feel to them. They agree with the age of the supposed writer. Whenever several hands can be distinguished on one document—for instance, contributions by other members of the Frank family—the impression of naturalness is even stronger.

—Anne Frank's writing reflects the natural development of a young person. Her later hand is considerably more proficient than that used in her writings prior to 1940. Moreover, the later samples show fewer drastic changes.

—The technical examination of the documents casts no doubt on the authenticity of the paper and ink.

—The authenticity of the collected standards is corroborated further by analysis of the postage paid, the postmarks and the censorship marks. A number of items bear these marks and it appears that the postage paid conformed to the requirements of the time. This finding gains in importance from the fact

30-7-1941.

Lieve Omi,

Ik ben nu in Beekbergen, het is hier erg fijn, alleen jammer dat het zulk slecht weer is. Hoe is het met jullie is het fijn in Sils-Maria? Als je terug schrijft doe het dan naar Amsterdam want ik blijf hier niet zo lang, en anders zouden ze de post moeten nasturen, en dat is onnodig werk. Hier is een klein kindje, hij heet Reymond, Sanne en ik zijn de hele dag met hem aan het spelen. Hij is 1½ jaar oud. Hoe lang blijven jullie weg, en is Sils nog altijd zo mooi? Hier is het een erg ouderwets*) huis maar toch gezellig.**) Sanne en ik hebben een eigen kamertje. Ik lees veel, jammer dat we niet naar buiten kunnen gaan. 's Nachts slapen wij hier veel rustiger dan in Amsterdam wij worden helemaal niet gestoord. Nu ga ik weer met Ray spelen want hij roept al. Krijg ik gauw bericht van jullie, en veel zoentjes.

van

Anne.

ouderwets = altmodisch*) gezellig = gemütlich**)

III-1. *Standard of Anne Frank.*

107

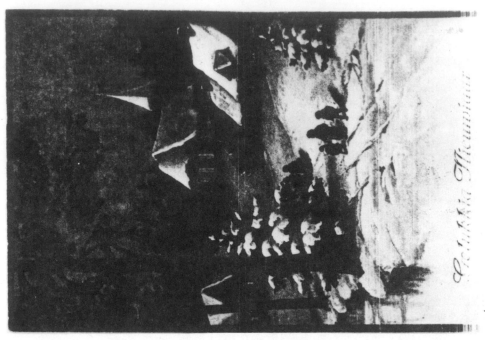

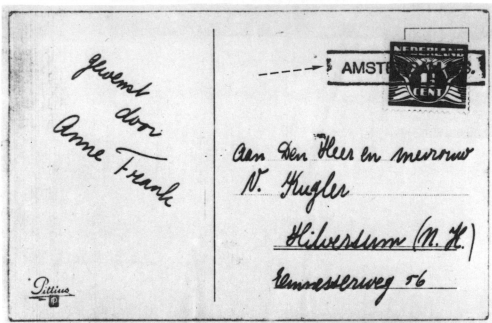

III-2. *Standard of Anne Frank.*

that during the period from 1940 to 1945 some postage stamps were withdrawn or overprinted. The use of postage stamps for other than actual posting purposes could therefore have been readily detected. The postmarks make a natural impression. They display the kind of deformations that arise with normal usage. The use of simplified postmarks lacking date and time on Christmas and New Year cards (see, for instance, figure III-2) also corresponds with actual routine during that period.

The inks in use at the time, slow to dry, often produced smudges, as may indeed be found on figure III-2, indicated by an arrow. Moreover, postmarks still wet when they come in contact with other postal items may be expected to leave traces on the latter. Such traces are found on a number of the original items available (see the arrow on III-7; the original censorship marks and smudges are in red ink).

All the indications are, therefore, that the postal items concerned were indeed dispatched on or about the dates given on them.

This is corroborated by the characteristics of postal items sent abroad during the Occupation, and subject to special censorship provisions. Thus the standards addressed to Switzerland (see, for instance, III-4 b, c and III-7):

—was stamped by the censors of Frankfurt-am-Main, as shown by the letter "e" underneath the eagle symbol. Post from the occupied Netherlands destined for Switzerland was as a rule censored at that office.
—bore small rectangular postmarks incorporating special numbers used by the censors
—contained handwritten numbers added by the censors. Thus the figure "8" has a formation not generally used in the Netherlands but fairly common in Germany (see III-4 b, lower left corner).
—was resealed with a gummed label bearing the censor's mark once they had been opened by him. On III-4 c the square censor's mark beneath the label is still partly visible.

Although these details themselves indicate that the postal items concerned were actually posted, their importance is increased even further when we realize that much of this information only became known long after the Second World War, thanks largely to the work of philatelists. An authoritative publication on the subject is K. H. Reimer's *Zensurpost aus dem III. Reich*, etc. (*Censored Post from the Third Reich*, etc.). As far as we have been able to discover, this publication first appeared in 1966.

In addition, the red and black ink marks found on several items indicate that these items came into contact with other postal material.

In sum, these findings taken together justify the conclusion that the documents concerned were actually sent, and indeed at about the dates indicated.

I believe that this conclusion, although applicable in principle to the documents themselves only, also helps to increase our confidence in the authenticity of the handwriting used in these documents, and does so to a marked degree.

The results of the examination of postmarks and postage stamps and also the other arguments mentioned above clearly indicate that the collected standards, which the Netherlands State Institute for War Documentation holds to have been written by Anne Frank, is genuine.

mijn rug, maar het is gelukkig
weer over.
Jullie moeten mij ook weer
eens schrijven, ik vind het zo
leuk om een brief voor mij
helemaal alleen te krijgen.
Gauw laten wij ons in een
winkel fotograferen, ik denk
dat jullie dan wel weer een
foto zullen krijgen.
Ik zie er nu heel anders
uit, want mijn haar is afgeknipt en ik heb krulletjes
in, maar dat zullen jullie
op de foto wel zien, als ze
er niet uit gewaaid zijn.
Vanavond is Margot uit, maar

III-3 a. *Standard of Anne Frank.*

3591 3

I

Lieve Omi;

Ik heb je erg lang niet geschreven maar dat komt ook
omdat wij zoveel huiswerk
hebben, en dan heb ik haast
geen tijd over.

Met Pasen hebben wij rappor-
ten gekregen, met Wiskunde
ben ik 3 punten vooruit
gegaan, maar met Nederlands,
Duits en Frans 3 punten
achteruit (samen natuurlijk.)
Hoe gaat het met jullie?
Vandaag is het voor het
eerst eens echt zomerweer.
De vacantie is Dinsdag al-
weer voorbij, het gaat wel

111

II.

¹⁹ te gauw. Deze brief is wel
²⁰ aan Omi gericht, maar is
²¹ natuurlijk ook voor de hele
²² familie.
²³ Het schaatenrijden is nu weer
²⁴ afgelopen niet waar Bernd?
²⁵ Ik ben nu helemaal uit
de oefening, want ik heb het
in lange tijd niet meer gedaan.
Op het Lyceum is het verder
wel leuk, we hebben 12 meisjes
³⁰ en 18 jongens in de klas. In
het begin liepen we veel niet
de jongens maar het haalt nu
³³ wel weer wat af, gelukkig, want
ze worden echt vervelend.

III-3 b. *Standard of Anne Frank.*

112

35 Met Hanneli zit ik weer in
dezelfde klas, haar zusje is
erg schattig en kan al los
lopen.

39 Sanne is niet bij ons op
40 school, maar ik zie haar nog
vaak, zij is net als ik, dol
op Moortje. Zo heet onze poes
die we sinds een half jaar
hebben. Het is een vrouwtje
45 en ik loop gauw op holletjes,
kindertjes, maar zij op het
ogenblik op het dak veel
mannetjes ontmoet.
  Hier gaat het verder wel goed.
50 Vader had spit of rheumatiek

113

1 Club van school, maar zij
2 moet jammer genoeg vroeg
3 thuis zijn, anders heb ik het
4 rijk alleen.
5 Nu ga ik weg, daag allemaal,
6 ik hoop dat ik gauw bericht
7 krijg.

Anne.

III-3 c. *Standard of Anne Frank*.

Lieve Bernd,

Welgefeliciteerd met ji verjaardag (zo be-
gint een verjaardagsbrief altijd) en nog
vele jaren. Hopelijk zijn jullie allemaal
gezond. net als wij.

Wij hebben 5 dagen Pinksterbacantie
gehad, het was erg fijn, en ik ben erg
bezet met mijn dagen. 'S avonds kom ik
niet voor 10 uur thuis, maar meestal
wordt ik wel door een jongen thuisgebracht.
Hoe gaat het met dat meisje? waarvan
ji die foto gestuurd hebt? Schrijf daar
eens over, deelde dingen interesseren
mij veel. Margot heeft ook een vriend
maar hij is nog jonger dan de mijne.
Het epistel is niet erg lang uitgevallen
maar ik heb ook geen tijd, daar ik met
vader naar een filmvoorstelling bij
kennissen ga. De groeten aan allemaal.
Schrijf eens aan mij terug
Anne

III-4 a. *Standard of Anne Frank.*

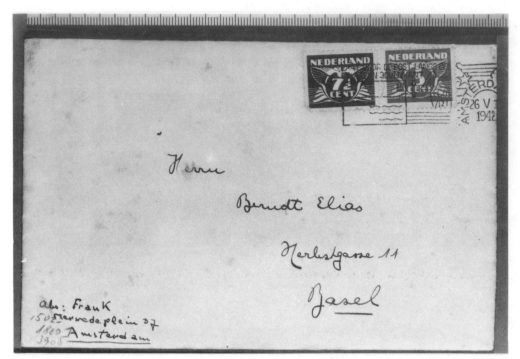

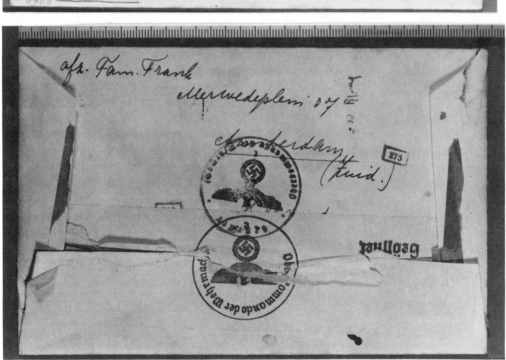

III-4 b/c. *Front and back of envelope of letter III-4 a.*

²⁴Op school doen we niet veel 'smorgens tekenen we ᵐ¹·
²⁵een beetje en 'smiddlags zitten we in de tuin
²⁶vliegen te vangen of bloemen te plukken.
²⁷Nu moet ik eindigen want het wordt te warm om
²⁸verder te schrijven. Veel groeten en zoentjes aan
allemaal van jullie

Anne.

ᵐ¹·
tuin=garten.

III-5. *Fragment of a letter by Anne Frank.*

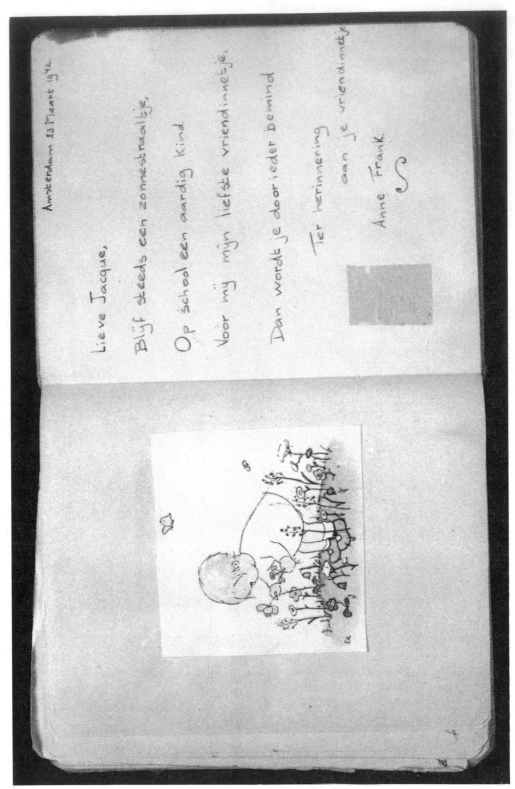

Amsterdam 23 Maart 1942.

Lieve Jacque,

Blijf steeds een zonnestraaltje,

Op school een aardig Kind.

Voor mij mijn liefste vriendinnetje,

Dan wordt je door ieder bemind

Ter herinnering

aan je vriendinnetje

Anne Frank.

III-6. *Standard of Anne Frank in an autograph album.*

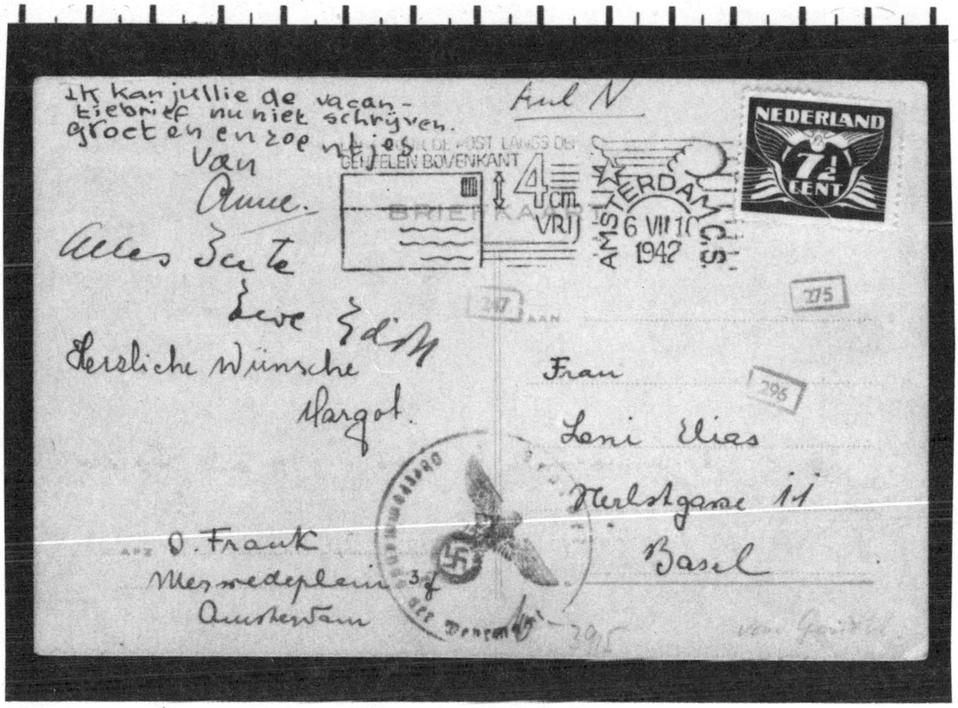

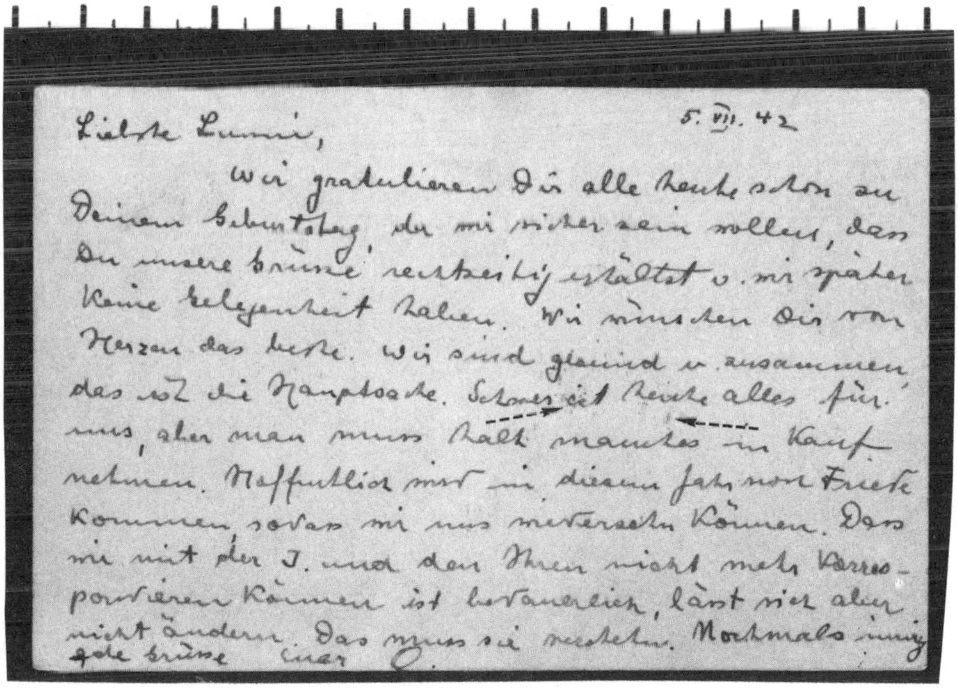

III-7. *Postcard with a short message from Anne Frank.*

Handwriting is a complex product but can be examined and described by a number of established methods. It is broken down by analysts into a series of characteristics which fall into a number of categories. The State Forensic Science Laboratory distinguishes four main groups:

Microcharacteristics represent writing movements within self-contained units.

Writing is a form of movement, and handwriting is the record of these movements by means of, for instance, ink deposits on paper. The writing movement of the hand can be resolved into a component in the plane of the writing, and another vertical to the plane of the writing. This second component (by physical standards), wrongly called writing pressure, may lead to a widening or narrowing of the writing trace, and may also affect its color intensity and depth.

Let us look first at the *movement component in the plane of the writing*, responsible for the overall form of the handwriting.

Analysis of this component generally yields a verbal description of certain properties of the handwriting.

Thus the ovals of the letters "a," "d," "g," and "o" can, in our case, be characterized as narrow or pointed and sharp. This description can be applied both to the material to be analyzed and also to the standards.

Microcharacteristics make it possible to break down the terms "narrow," "pointed" and "sharp" even further, and to express the results more objectively, describing not only the quality itself but also the way in which it comes about. Other parts of the oval formation are subjected to analysis and comparison next. In short, the analysis is applied to the entire oval and not to any specific part of it. The study of microcharacteristics is not an innovation but the extension and refinement of established methods of analysis.

Here we shall be giving a simplified account of microcharacteristics; for a fuller account, the reader is referred to H. J. J. Hardy et al., "*Handschriftvergelijkend onderzoek: een fysisch model en de toepassing ervan* [Comparative Handwriting Analysis: A Physical Model and Its Application]" in A. J. W. M. Thomassen et al., *Studies over de schrijfmotoriek (Studies of Motor Aspects of Handwriting)* (Lisse: Swets & Zeitlinger, 1985).

The analysis of microcharacteristics is based on the study of the movements involved in the act of writing. Thus the movement needed to produce a letter seems to be a combination of partial movements, caused by muscle-joint systems, especially in the hand and the wrist. When provided with appropriate information by the brain, each separate muscle-joint system is responsible for a small part of the movement. Moreover, the temporary collaboration of several systems may produce a partial movement. The process of engaging or partly disengaging muscle-joint systems can be partly reconstructed from the written letter, because it is associated with more or less marked changes in the angle or curvature of the writing trace. The points in which such changes occur are called *interaction points*. A series of successive interaction points make up a *microcharacteristic*.

Figures V-1-5 a-1 and a-2 (see p. 129) illustrate how interaction points are determined. If the original movement in the upper loop were continued, then the writing trace would have proceeded in the direction of the arrow. In fact, however,

120

following on the activation of a muscle-joint system, the original line is bent at point 1: the point of the nib has been forced into a different direction. Point 1 is an interaction point. Without entering into the scientific details, we may put it that interaction points occur where:

—a curved writing trace makes way for a straight one;
—a straight line makes way for a curve;
—the direction of movement is reversed, i.e., a movement to the left makes way for a movement to the right, etc.;
—a curved part of a line makes way for a part with a clearly different curvature; interaction points belonging to this category are sometimes more difficult to identify.

In example V-1-5 a-1, a-2, point 2 is a reversal point, while point 4 marks the beginning of a straight line.

The analysis of a microcharacteristic rests on the localization of the most prominent interaction points and helps to describe the original writing movement.

When comparing microcharacteristics, we ask whether the position of a particular interaction point agrees. In practice, of course, the analyst is faced with a natural variation in handwriting. Two versions of one and the same letter of any length produced by the same writer are rarely identical. The handwriting expert will have to take this variation into account; the theoretical model tells him how. In a report, however, the comparative process and the permissible variation are difficult to describe, which explains the frequent use of so-called *visual equivalents*. We speak of "visual equivalents" when the position of a series of interaction points, for instance in a curved letter, looks practically identical to the naked eye. That series is often based on just part of a letter or of a combination of letters. A detailed application of the principle of visual equivalents is shown in figures V-1-5 a-1 and a-2. The explanation will be found in section V-1.

The movement component vertical to the writing plan can, depending on the writing instrument, result in changes in the thickness of the line and the intensity of material deposits and to changes in the depth of the writing trace. The variation in these magnitudes can also serve as a measure of the variation in writing pressure. Because factors other than writing pressure can also influence these magnitudes, more general descriptions are often preferred. Thus a distinction is often made between the up and down strokes of a letter, though differences within either are often less obvious. Sometimes attention must be paid to the *tendencies* reflected in an entire piece of writing rather than to changes within, say, a single letter.

Besides microcharacteristics, handwriting experts also compare general, individual and spatial features.

General characteristics, to which I also refer as derived characteristics, describe the general appearance of the handwriting. This category includes the slant of the writing, the relative dimensions and lengths of the various areas of a letter, the method of joining letters, the roundness, etc., together with variations in these magnitudes.

Individual characteristics reflect marked deviations from the norm by one or more elements. Thus the descender of a letter may be significantly shorter than that usually formed by a large group of other writers. Individual characteristics often prove extremely useful in handwriting comparisons.

Neither the general nor the individual characteristics are completely independent of microcharacteristics. Thus the comparison of microcharacteristics partly includes the comparison of general and individual characteristics.

Spacing characteristics cover, *inter alia*, the distance between words, lines, left and right margins and also variations in these elements.

V The Identification of the Handwriting in the Diary

What has hitherto been referred to as the diary in fact consists of the following:

1. An autograph album with unlined paper and a red/white checked cover, which will be called the diary, part 1. The pages measure 14.3 × 16.6 cm.
2. An exercise book with lined paper, a black cover and black cloth binding, to be referred to as the diary, part 2. The pages measure 16.4 × 20.7 cm.
3. An exercise book with lined paper and a green/gold speckled cover with a black cloth binding, to be called the diary, part 3. The pages measure 16.4 × 20.7 cm.
4. Three folders containing loose sheets of unlined paper, often covered with writing on both sides; we shall call these the loose sheets. On average a complete sheet measures 21.4 × 27.5 cm.

In view of the fact that in the nature of things the handwriting of young people undergoes changes, comparisons should preferably be based on standards produced at about the same time or on dates as close together as possible. This is what was done with part 1 of the diary and the standards. The remaining parts and the loose sheets were then checked against the standards, reference being made to the results of the previous comparisons. Before describing the results, I must make a few remarks about related matters.

In Section IV of the report, we are told on what characteristics the comparisons of handwriting is based. With longer texts, we also consider characteristics reflecting content and use of language. As a rule, the handwriting expert is not a specialist in these fields and although he can arrive at some general conclusions he must remember that these can play no more than a subsidiary role in his final opinion.

V-I THE RESULTS OF THE IDENTIFICATION OF THE HANDWRITING IN THE DIARY, PART I

Part 1 of the diary covers the period from June 12 up to and including December 5, 1942, with some additions made at a later date. The pages are numbered 1 to 122 inclusive.

Sometimes a line number is given, suggesting that these numbers may have been added during an earlier handwriting examination, so as to facilitate the

122

search for handwriting characteristics. Between pages 28 and 29 a number of sheets have been torn out. In addition two pages following page 77 have been stuck together with brown tape.

Figures V-1-1 to 4 inclusive as well as V-2-7 and 8 will give the reader an idea of the general appearance of the handwriting in the diary, part 1.

The whole makes a most spontaneous impression: the contents, the pasting in and the writing on loose pages and sheets, some of which are lined, the inclusion of photographs, of a postcard and of a letter, and the use of two types of handwriting, together with the presence of variations within either type. The words seem to have been penned fluently and confidently.

A number of mirror-image ink impressions also corroborates the natural use of the document as a diary. If an entry ends halfway down one page while the next entry is written one or more days later, it may be assumed that the diary was closed in the interval. As a result, writing that is still wet will have produced a mirror image on the opposite page. Conversely, from the presence of such mirror images it can be inferred that the diary was closed, which again points to its natural use. Figures V-2-3 and V-3-1 taken from parts 2 and 3 of the diary are examples of impressions produced in this way (I have indicated the corresponding items with arrows). A number of mirror images can also be found in the diary, part 1.

Part 1 of the diary contains two types of script in the main, one joined and sloping (also known as cursive handwriting), and the other known as handprinting. Both types of script, which sometimes merge smoothly, were compared with standards of Anne Frank on the basis of the characteristics mentioned in Section IV.

The reader can gain an idea of the comparative method if he examines figures V-1-5 to V-1-14 inclusive in conjunction with the description that follows. It must be stressed that though the figures are representative they do not provide a complete picture.

Let us look first of all at the *spacing arrangements*. When using either the cursive hand or the printed script in the diary, part 1, the writer has left a narrow left-hand and a broader, less regular, right-hand margin. The space between the words is regular. In the cursive writing, few breaks occur within individual words. The printed script is almost entirely unjoined. Both types of script run almost horizontally (possibly with the help of a ruled guide); fluctuations around an imaginary base line are small. The standards (see the illustrations to Section III) display the same spacing arrangement.

This is also true of the *general characteristics*. The examples shown may be called regular forms with small variations in the angle between the ascending or descending strokes and the imaginary base line. There is also close correspondence in the proportions of the length of the upper and lower loops and the middle zone (letters "m" and "n"). The joins present in the cursive writing and the largely unconnected letters of the handprinting have already been mentioned.

Figures V-1-5 to 7 inclusive show the localization of interaction points as well as the principle of visual equivalence.

On figures V-1-5 a-1 and a-2 several conspicuous interaction points have been marked. They can be localized by extrapolation. If the point of the pen had followed the original path, then it would have described the broken line at point 1. However, at point 1, the actual writing deviates from the extrapolated trajec-

123

hem ...., dat hij gevraagd heeft. Toch vind
ik hem een eng jong, want hij is

3 erg grappig.

4 Emiel Bonewit is de aanbidder van
5 ███ maar het kan ███ niet
erg veel schelen. Hij is nogal saai.

7 Bob Cohen was ook verliefd op mij, maar
nu kan ik hem niet meer uitstaan
9 het is een huichelachtig, langdradig,
huilerig, gek, vervelend jongetje, die
11 zich ontzettend veel verbeeld.
12 Max van de Velde is een boerenjongen
13 uit Medemblik, maar wel geschikt
14 naar Margot zeggen.
15 Herman Koopman is ook erg schunnig
net als Jopie de Beer, die een erge flirt en

V-1-1. *Cursive writing on page 24 of diary, part 1.*

meisjesgek is. Leo Blom is de boezemvriend

van Jopie de Beus ~~Leo Blom~~ maar wordt door schun-

nigheid ook aangestoken.

4 Albert de Mesquita is een jongen die van

de 6e Montessorischool af komt en een

6 klas overgeslagen heeft, hij is erg knap.

Leo Slager, komt van dezelfde school maar

8 niet zo knap.

9 Ru Stoppelman is een klein, gek jongetje

10 uit Almelo, die pas later op school is

11 gekomen.

12 * .... haat alles wat niet mag

???????????????????????????? *Dunk bedoelde ik toen*
maar wilde dat niet
schrijven, als er eens
iemand het boek zou
vinden 1943. nietwaar?

Jacques Kocernoot zit achter ons met ~~~~

* .... bij mij lachen om niets (* .... in ik.)

---

*At the request of the person concerned, the name has been omitted.

zijn familie te maken, en dan vertelt hij er van 62
iedereen wat bij. Miep en Jan zijn net van
vacantie terug, en ik kan Miep nu steeds
weer aankijken. Ik heb zo'n zin om met
iemand te corresponderen, en dat zal ik
dan in het vervolg maar met mijn dagboek
doen. Ik schrijf dus nu in brief vorm, wat fijtelijk
op hetzelfde neerkomt.
Lieve Jettje, (zal ik maar zeggen,)
Mijn lieve vriendin, ik zal je in het vervolg en
ook nu nog veel te vertellen hebben. Ik ben
met brei werk begonnen een trui uit van die
witte wol. Maar ik mag er niet te veel aan
breien anders is hij te gauw af. Ik heb nu ook
een lichtje boven mijn bed gekregen. Daag ik
moet aardappels schillen voor het rottigste
mens van de wereld, een beetje overdreven,
maar ook maar een beetje. Groeten allemaal
en zoenen van

Anne Frank

21 Sept. 1942.
Dezelfde dag.

Ik heb van avond nog tijd beste Emmy, daarom
zal ik jou nog maar gauw een paar regeltjes
schrijven, van middag heb ik een tamelijk schaap-
achtige brief aan Jettje geschreven, want ik was
nog geen minuut bezig toen ik voor, "mevrouw
mama" aardappelen moest schillen, dat zegt ze
dan op zo'n kommando-toon, en als ik dan

V-1-3. *Handprinting on page 62 of diary, part 1.*

126

27 Sept. 1942.

Beste Conny,

V-1-4. *Cursive writing and handprinting on page 72 of the diary, part 1.*

tory. In accordance with the theory set out in Section IV, a new muscle-joint system was introduced at point 1, pushing the pen in a different direction. We call point 1 an *interaction point*. Much the same happened around point 3. At point 4, the originally curved path becomes a straight line. Such changes can be attributed to the inactivation of a muscle-joint system. Point 2, finally, is a reversal point: the movement to the right makes way for a movement to the left, while the upstroke turns into a downstroke at practically the same point. We refer to a series of successive interaction points as a *microcharacteristic*. A microcharacteristic thus describes the original act of writing. Moreover, the examples we have given also include other interaction points, which we have not marked on the illustration for the sake of greater clarity.

The *comparison of microcharacteristics* involves a search for so-called *visual equivalents*. We investigate whether a characteristic to be investigated matches a characteristic of the standards of comparison so well that the respective interaction points can no longer be distinguished from each other. *In practice, that means that both samples exhibit a corresponding curvature in essential subsections.* This principle is illustrated in detail on figures V-1-5 to 7 inclusive: on the left is the standard and on the right the visual equivalents from the questioned writing. Though the illustrations are enlarged, visual equivalents can often be determined without magnification. This was done in figures V-1-8 to 14 inclusive. The illustrations are photocopies of the previously mentioned standards and of pages from the diary, part 1. Interaction points have not been marked.

Wherever possible we have also shown *how variations in the handwriting have been treated for purposes of comparison*. We have also included some extreme variations of the characteristic concerned. Three variations of the letter "t" in the standards of comparison have been marked t 1, t 2 and t 3 respectively. The visual equivalents in the questioned handwriting have been marked similarly.

The result is the series of similarities described below which, in addition to the characteristics described above, also reflect a correspondence in the curvature of essential elements.

A: Cursive Writing

—We have illustrated three types of *ascender* in figures V-1-5 a, b and 6 a. Variant 5 b has a very pointed top, partly accentuated by the straight course of the downstroke (2 to 3). In 6 a we have a much shorter variant.
—We have included two types of *descender*. V-1-7 a shows a long straight downstroke which only begins to deviate close to the lowest point (1). A sharp transition marks the final upstroke of the letter, the curvature of which is largely determined by the position of the interaction points 2 and 3. In 7 b we see a wider bottom loop, with a different curvature over the interval 2 to 3.
—Ovals occur, *inter alia*, in the letters "a," "d," "g" and "o." A typical oval is shown on figure V-1-6 b. Because of the quick rise of the movement after the reversal point 3, and the slight curvature over the intervals 2 to 3 and 3 to 4, the ovals have a characteristically narrow and pointed appearance.
—Large variations are found in the *base of the letters "h" and "k."* On figures V-1-8 to 14 inclusive these are indicated as *h 1* and *h 2*, and *k 1* and *k 2*. In

128

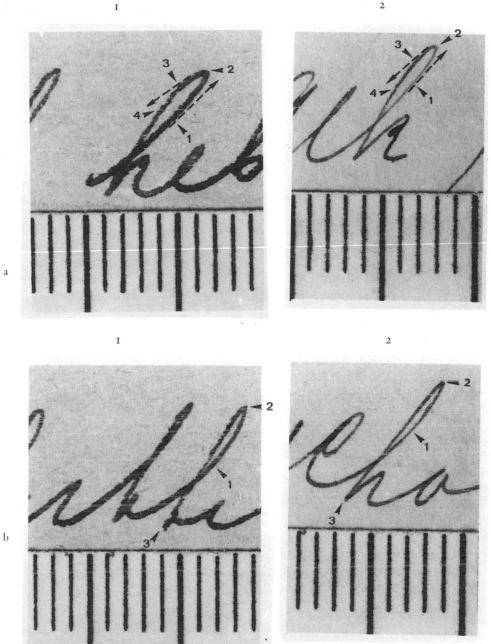

V-1-5. a-1, top left: *ascender (asc) found in the standards of Anne Frank (cf.* figure V-1-9; asc 1) *with several marked interaction points.*

These are points where changes in the direction of the writing movement originate. They can be inferred from deviations of the writing trace.

a-2, top right: *visually equivalent ascender found in diary, part 1 (cf.* figure V-1-11; asc 1).

Visual equivalence implies that the position of the interaction points or the curvature is practically identical.

b-1 and b-2: *visual equivalents of another ascender.*

b-1 from the standards of Anne Frank (*cf.* figure V-1-9; asc 2).

b-2 from the diary, part 1 (*cf.* figure V-1-12; asc 2).

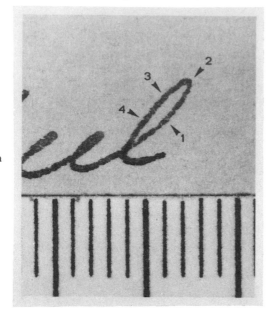

a

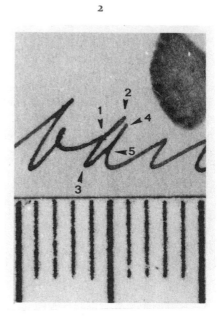

b

V-1-6. *Visually equivalent ascenders* (asc) *and one oval* (ovl) *with interaction points.*
a-1 from the standards of Anne Frank (*cf.* figure V-1-9; asc 3).
a-2 from the diary, part 1 (*cf.* figure V-1-12; asc 3).
b-1 from the standards of Anne Frank (*cf.* figure V-1-8; ovl).
b-2 from the diary, part 1 (*cf.* figure V-1-12; ovl).

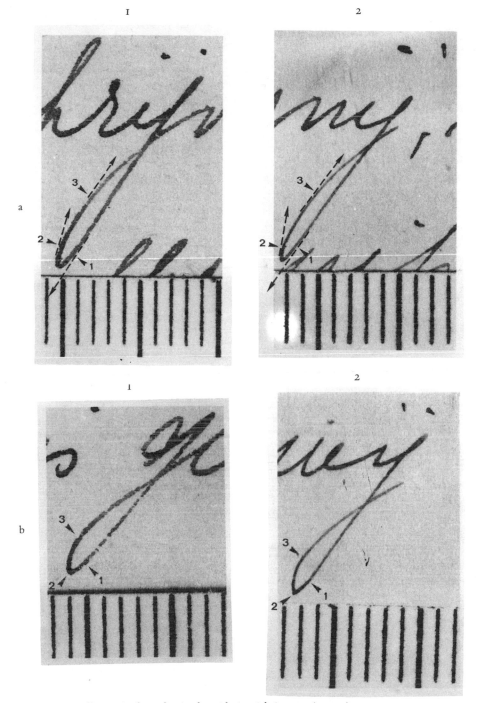

V-1-7. *Visually equivalent descenders* (des) *with interaction points.*
a-1 from the standards of Anne Frank (*cf.* figure V-1-8; des 1).
a-2 from the diary, part 1 (*cf.* figure V-1-11; des 1).
b-1 from the standards of Anne Frank (*cf.* figure V-1-8; des 2).
b-2 from the diary, part 1 (*cf.* figure V-1-12; des 2).

h 1 and k 1 we see very narrow bases; k 2 and h 2, by contrast, have relatively broad bases.

—*The letter "t,"* too, ends in a variety of formations. The equivalents indicated on the figures all have the same main part. The variant *t 3* has a relatively elongated final movement or cross-stroke. In *t 2* the cross-stroke is missing; the letter ends with a short rising movement. In *t 1*, the distance from the foot of the letter to the cross-stroke is very short.

—On figures V-1-8 to 14 inclusive we find five variations in the *method of joining letters (jt 1* to *jt 5* inclusive). Usually the joins are elongated and curved, but in *jt 1* and *jt 2* they are very short and have lost their curvature; as a result the letters i-s and t-s combine to make a single character, a so-called personal ligature. In *jt 3* the curvature, though present, is very restricted; in *jt 4* the curvature is absent and the join is not shortened; in *jt 5* the join is curved and long. Because it is exceptionally long, the loop of the letter "g" in *jt 5* extends above the base line.

—The *base* of the *letter "ij"* (the Dutch form of "y") is related to *jt 5*. The second top protrudes markedly above the first, thanks to the elongated join between them.

—The *letter "f"* reflects a different movement. This, incidentally, is in full accord with the descenders in systems of letter design in use at the time. Two variations are shown: *f 1* and *f 2*. In both cases, the loop ends in a swaying movement which is more pronounced in *f 1* than it is in *f 2*.

—The *letter "e"* has unusually large dimensions in the variant marked *e 1*. Not only is it almost twice as large as the variant *e 2*, it is also considerably higher than other letters in the middle zone ("m," "n," ovals, etc.).

—Equivalents are also shown for the letters "p" *(p)*, "s" *(s 1* and *s 2)* and "r" *(r 1* and *r 2)* in which the "hook" is more or less central; for the letter "z" *(z)* which has a dipping cross-stroke at the top and an arched foot, and for the elongated tails *(ts)*.

—Similarly, we have included equivalents for the capital letters *"B," "J," "L," "M"* and *"V."*

We have said nothing yet about *changes in pen pressure*. In the case of fountain pens, the description of pressure changes with the help of the usual parameters —line thickness, intensity of ink deposits and possible depth of grooves—comes up against practical difficulties. However, the angle of the nib and the backflow of the ink influence these parameters in much the same way as the effects of writing pressure. No more than an overall description of the course of the pen pressure is possible in this brief review.

No significant differences in pressure could be discovered in the specimens submitted for analysis and the standards. As a rule, the upstrokes of the upper loops show less pen pressure than the downstrokes. The lower loops may, however, occasionally give the opposite impression.

The middle zone, in which movements from left to right are given some weight, usually reflects greater pressure than do the ascenders and descenders.

The comparison of the microcharacteristics automatically involves a comparison of the *individual characteristics*, which may deviate from the norm in one or more respects. Whether, and to what extent, they do can only be determined by recourse to a very large quantity of representative reference material. Now, in the case of Anne Frank's writing, the available reference material can only be called "representative" in part. It follows that the term "individual" must therefore be treated with some reserve.

Among the reference material the following elements have been considered to be more or less individual:

—narrow, pointed ovals;
—the combination of slightly and generously formed feet in the letters "h" and "k";
—some joins *(jt 1* and *jt 2);*
—the extremely large "e" variant;
—the shape of some letters "d," in which the ascender is hardly longer than the oval.

B: *The Handprinting*

Figures V-1-13 and 14 show a number of corresponding microcharacteristics in the printed handwriting:

—In addition to the characteristics to be described in greater detail below, the figures show visual equivalents for the descenders *(des 1* and *2),* the small letters "n," "r" *(r 1* and *r 2),* "s," "t," "z" and the capital letters "*D*" and "*J.*"
—There are two variants of the letter "a": a narrow, flattened form *(a 1)* and a small oval form *(a 2).* The same two forms also occur in the letter "d."
—The variant *e 1* of the letter "e" is curved and has an unconnected cross-stroke. In the more familiar variant *e 2,* the cross-stroke is joined to the rest of the letter.
—Interruptions in the movement are also found in the variant *v 1* of the letter "v"; *v 2* is formed by a continuous movement.
—Although less detectable on photocopies and photographs of the standards of comparison, the capital "M" is made up of four unconnected strokes. On figure V-1-14 illustrating the printed writing in question, this construction can be seen more clearly.

The pen pressure is very largely uniform. Variations in pressure are present to a limited extent only.

The comparison of the *general and the spacing characteristics* has already been discussed.

With due reservations, the last four microcharacteristics described above can be considered as *individual,* particularly the combined occurrence of two main forms.

The method of comparison illustrated by our examples was extended to all characteristics that could be distinguished in both the cursive hand and the handprinting. It established the full correspondence of all comparable

—microcharacteristics;
—general characteristics;
—spacing characteristics;
—individual characteristics.

mijn rug, maar het is gelukkig weer over.

Jullie moeten mij ook weer eens schrijven, ik vind het zo leuk om een brief voor mij helemaal alleen te krijgen.

Gauw laten wij ons in een winkel fotograferen, ik denk dat jullie dan wel weer een foto zullen krijgen.

Ik wil er nu heel anders uit, want mijn haar is afgeknipt en ik heb krulletjes in, maar dat zullen jullie op de foto wel zien, als ze er niet uit gewaaid zijn. Vanavond is Margot uit, maar

V-1-8. *A page from the standards of Anne Frank.* The signs des 1, jt 1 . . . etc., refer to corresponding signs in figures V-1-11 or V-1-12.
Like signs mark visual equivalents or corresponding characteristics.

Lieve Omi,

Ik heb je erg lang niet geschreven maar dat komt ook
omdat wij zoveel huiswerk
hebben, en dan heb ik haast
geen tijd over.

Met Pasen hebben wij rappor-
ten gekregen, met Wiskunde
ben ik 3 punten vooruit
gegaan, maar met Nederlands,
Duits en Frans 3 punten
achteruit (samen natuurlijk)
Hoe gaat het met jullie?
Vandaag is het voor het
eerst eens echt zomerweer.
De vakantie is Dinsdag al-
weer voorbij, het gaat wel

te gauw. Deze brief is wel
aan Omu gericht, maar is   ◀- - - - - - - f1
natuurlijk ook voor de hele
familie.
Het schaatenrijden is nu weer
afgelopen niet waar Bernd?   ◀- - - B
Ik ben nu helemaal uit   - - - - bv1
de oefening, want ik heb het
in lange tijd niet meer gedaan.
Op het Lyceum is het verder
wel leuk we hebben 12 meisjes
en 18 jongens in de klas. In
het begin liepen we veel met   t3
de jongens maar het haalt nu
wel weer wat af, gelukkig, want   ◀- - - - bv2
ze worden echt vervelend.

V-1-9. *A page from the standards of Anne Frank.* The signs asc 1, t 1 ... etc., refer to corresponding signs in figures V-1-11 or V-1-12.
Like signs mark visual equivalents or corresponding characteristics.

35 Met Hanneli zit ik weer in
dezelfde klas, haar zusje is
erg schattig en kan al los
lopen.

e2 ——————————————→
39 Sanne is niet bij ons op   vb5
40 school, maar ik zie haar nog
vaak, zij is net als ik, dol
op Maartje. Zo heel onze poes   k2
die we sinds een half jaar   p
hebben. Het is een vrouwtje
45 en ik loop gauw op hollen.   t1
kinderlijk, maar zij op het
ogenblik op het dak wel heel   bv3
mannetjes ontmoet.   t2
Hier gaat het verder wel goed.
V ——→ 55 Vader had spit of rheumatiek

137

'Club van School, maar zij
moet jammer genoeg vroeg
3 thuis zijn, anders heb ik het
rijk alleen.
5 Nu ga ik weg, dáág allemaal,
6 ik hoop dat ik gauw bericht
7 krijg.
Anne.

V-1-10. *A page from the standards of Anne Frank.* The signs s 1, h 2 ... etc., refer to corresponding signs in figures V-1-11 or V-1-12.
Like signs mark visual equivalents or corresponding characteristics.

i hem grond, dat hij gezanikt heeft. Toch vind
ik hem een eng jog, want hij is
3 erg grappig.
4 Emiel Bonewit is de aanbidder van
5 ▬▬▬ maar het kan ▬▬ niet
erg veel schelen. Hij is nogal saai.
7 Rob Cohen was ook verliefd op mij, maar
nu kan ik hem niet meer uitstaan
het is 'n huichelachtig, leugenachtig,
taktig, gek, vervelend jongetje, die
zich ontzaglend veel verbeeld.
nellak van de Velde is een haringjongen
uit Medemblik, maar wel geschikt
han Margot Heffen.
Herman Koopman is ook erg schunnig
net als Jopie de Beer, die een erge flirt is

V-1-11. A page from the diary, part 1, with visually equivalent characteristics.

139

menschelijk is. Leo Blom is de boezemvriend

van ~~Leo Blom~~ (Jopie de Beer) maar wordt door schuw-

nigheid ook aangestoken.

Albert de Mesquita is een jongen die van

de 6e Montessorischool af komt en een

klas overgeslagen heeft, hij is erg knap.

Leo Slager, komt van dezelfde school maar

niet zo knap.

Ru Stoppelmon is een klein, gek jongetje

uit Almelo, die pas later op school is

gekomen.

* dat alles wat niet mag

???????????????????????????????? [illegible annotation] dat ik een
heleboel
te lezen
door ... het boek zou.
April 1943.

Jacques Kocernoot zit achter ons, met

* bij wij lachen om hem. * [illegible]

ov2

k2

*At the request of the person concerned, the name has been omitted.

140

If we had to draw a conclusion from these findings, we would first have to determine to what extent such correspondences suffice to identify a particular writer. There are two ways of assessing the significance of characteristics:

—An estimate based on the determination of how often particular characteristics occur in a sample chosen at random. In the present case, the representativity of that sample, namely, short poems from the autograph albums of contemporaries, is of disputable value.
—A theoretical estimate. This is based on the fact that a comprehensive combination of corresponding features guarantees the individuality of that combination.

Now in the case under consideration we can speak of a very large combination of similarities, the more so as agreements exist both in the cursive writing and in the handprinting. Further corroboration is the fact that the writing to be compared is easily distinguished from that of an (incidentally) small group of classmates and contemporaries.

All these findings impose the following conclusion:

the writing in the autograph album referred to as the diary, part 1, with the exception of:
—the items, corrections, additions, etc., to be discussed below, all dated after December 5, 1942, together with undated corrections and completions except for those entered on page 30 in blue ink,
—writing obviously by another hand, for instance, on the pasted-in envelopes and their contents and the page and line numbering

is with a probability bordering on certainty by the hand of the author of the standards of comparison, Anne Frank.

The State Forensic Science Laboratory invariably gives the results of a handwriting comparison in degrees of probability, the phrase "with a probability bordering on certainty" expressing the highest degree of correspondence. This formulation is used when the items to be compared correspond in respect of a large number of both prominent and also significant features.

A lower degree of correspondence is attended by a lower degree of probability. In decreasing order, the designations "most probable," "probable," "very possible" and "possible" are used. In the case of apparent differences, the various degrees of probability are used in a negative sense.

Degrees of probability are widely used in handwriting reports (*cf.* L. Michel, *Gerichtliche Schriftvergleichung* [Berlin: W. de Gruyter, 1982]). Some experts extend the range of degrees of probability with the qualification "certain."

The difference between these experts and the others is more one of principle than of practical significance. It does not reflect any differences in expertise, nor does the use of the term "probable" rather than "certain" suggest the least doubt in the rightness of the conclusion. The two categories of experts simply differ on whether or not certain conclusions can ever be justified on scientific grounds.

The appendix to the extensive report by the State Forensic Science Laboratory, which explains the method of comparison used, stresses to what great

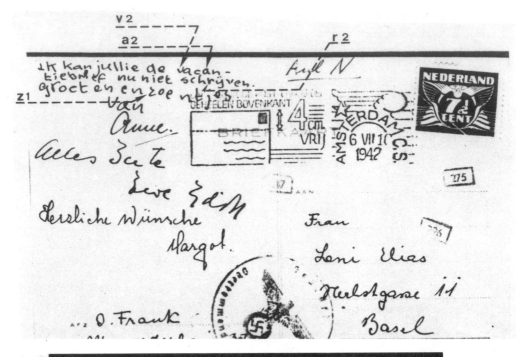

Ik kan jullie de vacan-
tiebrief nu niet schrijven.
Groeten en zoen v

van

Anne.

Alles Gute

Liebe Edith

Herzliche Wünsche
Margot.

Frau
Leni Elias
Herbstgasse 11
Basel

afz. O. Frank

NEDERLAND
7½ CENT

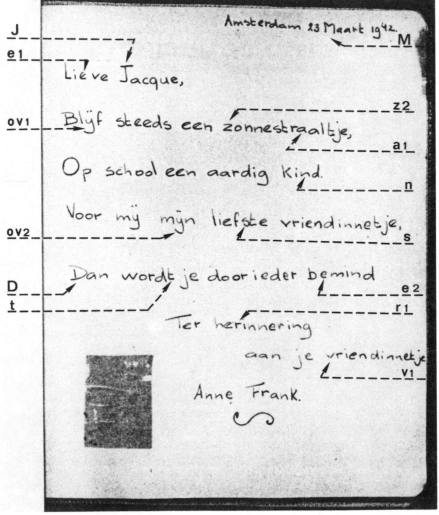

Amsterdam 23 Maart 1942.

Lieve Jacque,

Blijf steeds een zonnestraaltje,

Op school een aardig kind.

Voor mij mijn liefste vriendinnetje,

Dan wordt je door ieder bemind

Ter herinnering

aan je vriendinnetje

Anne Frank.

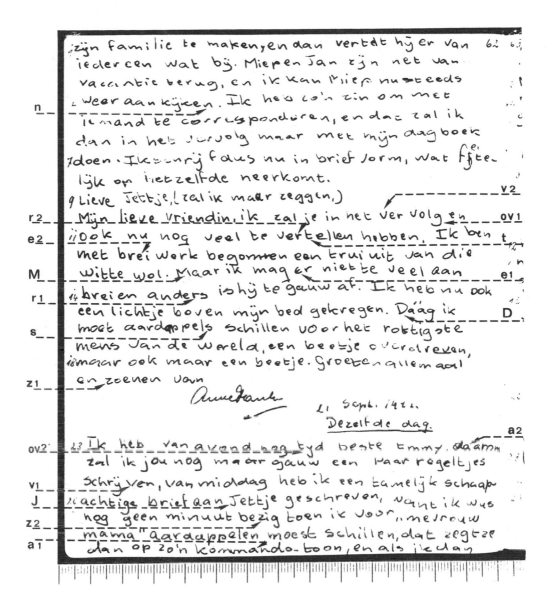

◄V-1-13. *Fragments of Anne Frank's handprinting.* The signs refer to corresponding signs in figure V-1-14. Like signs mark visual equivalents or corresponding characteristics.

extent the comparison of handwriting is based on statistical considerations. Thus the decision whether or not particular sets of characteristics correspond, as well as the determination of their significance, are inherently beset with statistical uncertainties, however minimal.

Next, any conclusions must take certain skills and qualities of the writer into account. In our case, this means making allowances, among other things, for such changes in handwriting as can be expected from a growing young person, and comparing these changes with those found in a reference group. Both the reference group, considered as a random sample, and also the comparison of individual characteristics with those of the group, constitute a source of fundamental uncertainty. While the latter may be small, it cannot be absolutely defined.

When a conclusion is based on theoretically uncertain elements, then the conclusion itself must be theoretically uncertain. It should be mentioned that this uncertainty can be ignored for all practical purposes. However, in the absence of an accurate evaluation, it is best to speak of degrees of probability.

V-2   THE RESULTS OF THE IDENTIFICATION OF THE HANDWRITING IN THE DIARY, PART 2

With the exception of a few later additions, the last entry in part 1 of the diary is dated December 5, 1942. Part 2 of the diary starts on December 22, 1943, and ends on April 17, 1944. In addition to the actual diary entries, this exercise book also contains a story entitled "Cady's Life." The relevant pages are numbered 1 to 203 and 1 to 37 respectively. It was impossible to determine who wrote these figures.

Figures V-2-1, 2 and 3 give a representative picture of the handwriting used in the diary, part 2.

The layout, presentation and handwriting make a quieter and more regular impression than part 1 of the diary, perhaps because of the use of lined paper. With three exceptions, no further pages, photographs, etc., have been pasted in. At page 191 a sheet of paper written in pencil has been pasted in: it reports a break-in. The handwriting differs clearly from the rest of the text.

Among the subjects described in letter form (letters to Kitty), the author's relationships with the other people in hiding take pride of place. These descriptions—like those of the author's changes of mood—have a natural feel to them. The natural use to which part 2 was put is also borne out by the presence of mirror-image ink deposits (see arrows on figure V-2-3), whose origin has already been explained.

On average 3 to 3½ pages were written every day. The text seems to have been penned with fluency. Most of the writing is cursive, though handprinting occurs in a few places.

The cursive writing and handprinting in the diary, part 2, were compared with those used in part 1 and also with the standards of Anne Frank.

A comparison of the *microcharacteristics* revealed a number of corresponding features. On figure V-2-4 the visual equivalents of a number of characteristics illustrated earlier (figures V-1-8 to 12) have been marked. This shows that a relatively small amount of material (one page) contains a great number of corresponding features. However, several characteristics reflect an apparent shift in

mogen wij weer eens die lucht ruiken?
Geloof me, Kitty, als je 1½ jaar zo opgesloten
zit, dan kan het je, op sommige dagen, wel
eens teveel worden. Of het rechtvaardig of
ondankbaar is, het gevoel laat zich niet weg-
staan.
Ook weer eens fietsen, dansen, fluiten en weet-ik-
wat-nog-meer, dat zou ik wel willen omar-
men; als ik eerst maar weer eens vrij ben!
Ik denk zelf wel eens, zou iemand me hierin
begrijpen, zou iemand over de ondankbaarheid
heenkijken, heenkijken over Jood of niet Jood,
alleen maar in me zien de bakvis, die zo'n
behoefte heeft naar uitgelaten pret? Ik weet het
niet en ik zou er ook niet, met niemand over
kunnen spreken, want ik weet dat ik dan
ja huilen. Huilen kan zo'n verlichting brengen,
als je maar bij iemand kunt huilen en ondanks
alles, ondanks theorieën en moeiten, mis ik
elke dag en elk uur, de moeder, die me begrijpt.
En daarom ook, denk ik bij alles wat ik doe
en wat ik schrijf, dat ik later voor mijn kin-
deren wil zijn, de mams, die ik me voorstel.
De mams, die niet alles zo ernstig opvat, wat
zo gezegd wordt, en wel ernstig opvat, wat
van me komt. Ik merk, ik kan het niet

V-2-1. *Cursive writing on page 4 of the diary, part 2.*

145

V-2-2. *Cursive writing on pages 28 and 29 of the diary, part 2.*

V-2-3. *Cursive writing and handprinting on pages 130 and 131 of the diary, part 2.* The arrows point to mirror-image ink impressions which were produced when the diary was closed.

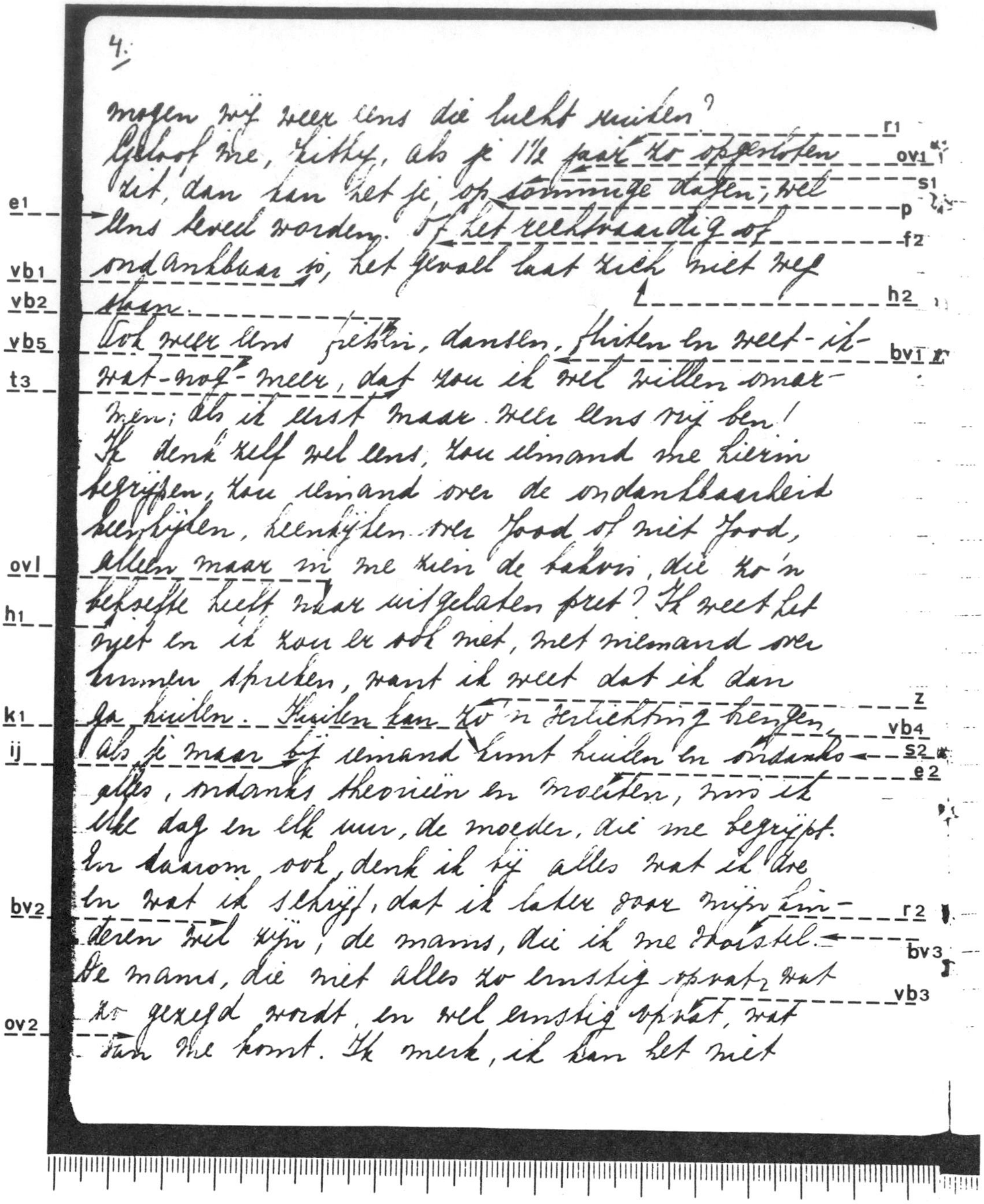

4.

[Handwritten diary text in Dutch, with margin annotation codes: e1, vb1, vb2, vb5, t3, ovl, h1, k1, ij, bv2, ov2 (left margin); r1, ov1, s1, p, f2, h2, bv1, z, vb4, s2, e2, r2, bv3, vb3 (right margin)]

mogen wij weer eens die lucht ruiken?
Geloof me, Kitty, als je 1½ jaar zo opgesloten
zit, dan kan het je, op sommige dagen, wel
eens teveel worden. Of het rechtvaardig of
ondankbaar is, het gevoel laat zich niet weg-
denken.
Ook wel eens fietsen, dansen, fluiten en weet-ik-
wat-nog-meer, dat zou ik wel willen, maar
wennen; als ik eerst maar weer eens vrij ben!
Ik denk zelf wel eens, zou iemand me hierin
begrijpen, zou iemand over de ondankbaarheid
heenkijken, heenkijken over Jood of niet Jood,
alleen maar in me zien de bakvis, die zo'n
behoefte heeft naar uitgelaten pret? Ik weet het
niet en ik zou er ook niet, met niemand over
kunnen spreken, want ik weet dat ik dan
ja huilen. Huilen kan zo'n verlichting brengen,
Als je maar bij iemand kunt huilen en ondanks
alles, ondanks theorieën en moeiten, mis ik
elke dag en elk uur, de moeder, die me begrijpt.
En daarom ook, denk ik bij alles wat ik doe
en wat ik schrijf, dat ik later voor mijn kin-
deren wil zijn, de mams, die ik me voorstel.
De mams, die niet alles zo ernstig opvat, wat
er gezegd wordt, en wel ernstig opvat, wat
van me komt. Ik merk, ik kan het niet

V-2-4. Page 4 of the diary, part 2. The marked characteristics are visual equivalents of corresponding characteristics shown on figures V-1-8 to V-1-12 (inclusive).

148

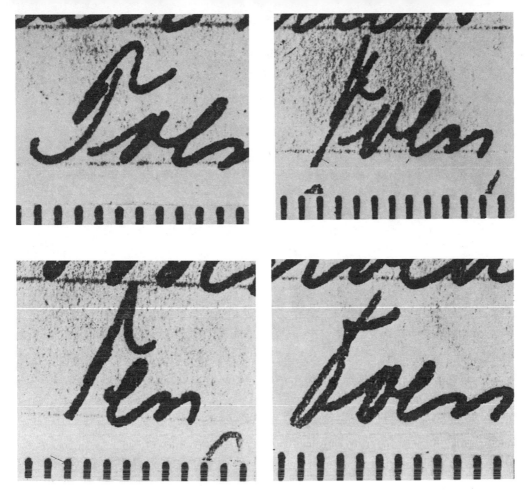

March 10, 1944   March 19, 1944

V-2-5. *Shaping of the letter "T" in the diary, part 2, on various dates.*

statistical weight. This remark needs some amplification. In the comparative analysis on part 1, we mentioned two variants of the foot of the letter "h": a narrow and slight foot *(h 1)* and a more generous one *(h 2)*. Both variants also occur in part 2, although with a different relative frequency than is found in the compared item: *h 1* occurs very much less frequently than *h 2* in part 2. The frequency distribution has shifted toward *h 2*. Another example is afforded by the "t" variants. The forms of *t 1* and *t 2* described earlier do admittedly occur in part 2, but less often than variant *t 3*. Thus variant *t 2* appears on figure V-2-2 (right-hand page), on line 14 from the top. As far as the other microcharacteristics are concerned, part 2 contains new variants in addition to some known from part 1, while omitting others. The interested reader can form an idea of this process by examining the relevant illustrations.

Change is inherent in the writing of young people, as we know from the literature. In the course of part 2 itself, moreover, some characteristics experience a partial, sometimes subtle change. Figure V-2-5 shows a number of variants of the letter "T," with the appropriate dates.

A comparison of part 2 with part 1 and with the standards of Anne Frank shows that, with due allowance for the shift in statistical weight and except for certain

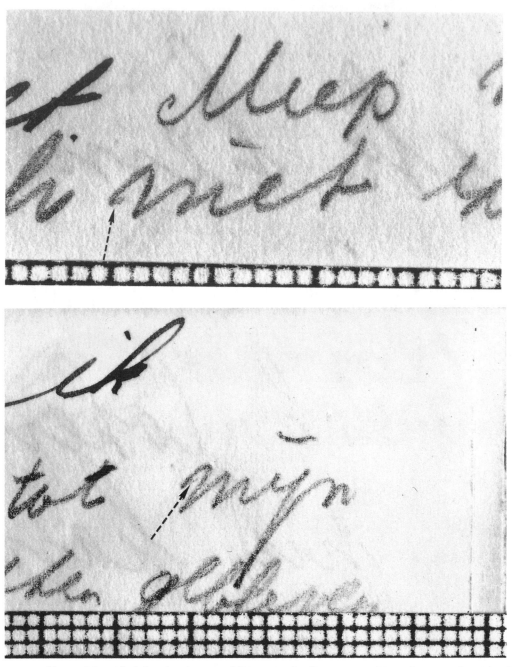

V-2-6. *Magnified details of some additions in the diary, part 1.* Note the entry flourish of the letter "m."

V-2-7. *Pages 91 and 92 (pasted in) of the diary, part 1.* The text at the bottom of page 91 is discussed on page 91 b (see figure V-2-8).

V-2-8, V-2-8 a. *Commentary on page 91 b of the diary, part 1, following on page 91* (see V-2-7). The commentary is dated January 22, 1944, and contains characteristics typical of that period, for instance the letters "w" (*w*orden) and "m" (*m*aar) with entry flourish.

V-2-8 b. *Magnified detail of a similar commentary on page 95 a of the diary, part 1. It, too, contains characteristics typical of the handwriting in 1944.*

characteristics to be discussed below, there is agreement in respect of all comparable

—microcharacteristics, including the pen pressure;
—general or derived characteristics;
—spacing characteristics;
—individual characteristics.

The diary, part 2, contains a number of forms without equivalents in the main text of part 1 or the standards of Anne Frank. Examples are the letters "v" and "w" at the beginning of words and the entry flourishes at the beginning of the capital letters "B," "M," "N," "V" and "W," and of the lower-case letters "m," "n," "v" and "w."

It can be shown that these differences need not be considered as essential. Briefly, the arguments for this view are as follows:

—The entry flourishes of the letters "m" and "n" are temporary features—they disappear again in the later course of part 2.
—Some additions to part 1 dated 1943 show rudimentary flourishes (see figure V-2-6). The flourishes in part 2 must be considered the culmination of this development.
—Part 1 contains two additions dated 1944. The writing in these not only has marked similarities with that found in part 2 (in which we also find the flourishes and the new shapes of the letters "v" and "w"), but also follows naturally as a commentary on the appropriate passages in part 1. Figures V-2-7 and 8 a and b depict pages 91, 91 a and 91 b of part 1. The text at the bottom of page 91 is the subject of a comment on page 91 b. The general impression of the handwriting on page 91 b is also found on page 95 a. Figure V-2-8 shows a detail from that page.

Similar conclusions and arguments apply to the handwriting.

The overall conclusion is that:

—the handwriting in the exercise book with the hard black cover and black binding referred to as the diary, part 2, with the exception of:
  ●the additions, corrections, etc., to be discussed below,
  ●the penciled passage evidently by a different writer pasted in on page 191

and

—the handwriting (discussed earlier) in the diary, part 1, and the standards of comparison of Anne Frank

are by the same hand with a probability bordering on certainty.

It was not possible to investigate the pagination for lack of adequate comparative material.

For a more detailed explanation of probability formulations, the reader is referred to Section V-1.

153

V-3-1. *Cursive writing on pages 75 and 76 of the diary, part 3.* The arrows point to mirror-image ink impressions which were produced when the diary was closed.

154

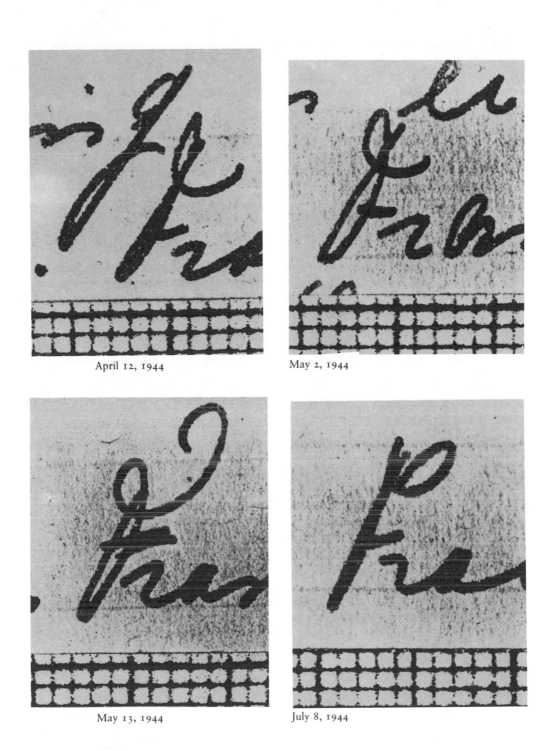

April 12, 1944

May 2, 1944

May 13, 1944

July 8, 1944

V-3-2. *Shaping of the letter "F" in the diary, part 3, on various dates.*

155

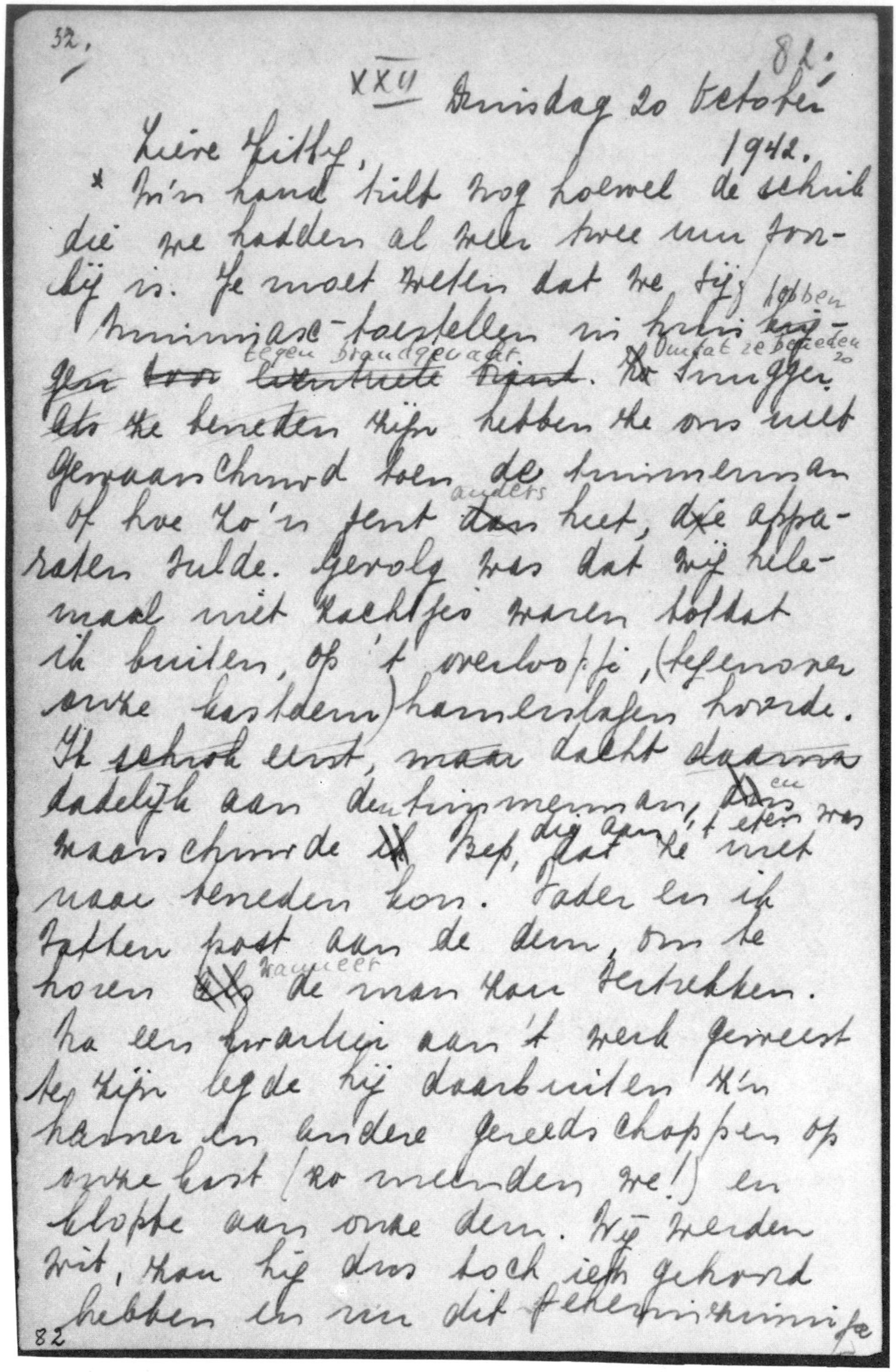
32,
XXII Dinsdag 20 October 1942. 82.
Lieve Kitty,
Mijn hand trilt nog hoewel de schrik die we hadden al weer twee uur voorbij is. Je moet weten dat we bij hebben brandblusch-toestellen in huis tegen brandgevaar. Omdat ze beneden zijn hebben ze ons niet gewaarschuwd toen de timmerman of hoe zo'n vent anders heet, die apparaten vulde. Gevolg was dat wij helemaal niet stil waren totdat ik buiten, op 't overloopje, (tegenover onze kastdeur) hamerslagen hoorde. Ik schrok eerst, maar dacht dadelijk aan den timmerman, en waarschuwde Bep, die aan 't eten was, dat ze niet naar beneden kon. Vader en ik zetten post aan de deur, om te horen wanneer de man zou vertrekken. Na een kwartiertje aan 't werk geweest te zijn legde hij daarbuiten z'n hamer en andere gereedschappen op onze kast (zo meenden we!) en klopte aan onze deur. Wij werden wit, zou hij dus toch iets gehoord hebben en nu dit geheimzinnige
82

V-4-1. *Cursive writing with corrections as found on the loose sheets numbered 82 and 80 (lower left).*

Grapje dan / nu blein kal hij wel niets
anders krijgen en / bom is al genoeg,
tijd ik hier niet erg op z'n plaats.
Behen is hem met de brige die nog
moet gaan, haast elke dag gaan er volle
treinen met krijgers weg. Onderweg
als ze op een klein stationnetje stop-
pen kappen ze wel een spieken
uit en proberen te onder te duiken;
't is toch altijd dan een klein percentage
die dat lukt dat misschien.
Ik ben nog niet klaar met m'n
herinnang. Heb je wel eens van
Gijzelaars gehoord? Dat voeren ze
nu als nieuwste straf-maatregel toe
reboteurs in. 't Is het meest ziekelijke
dat je je voor kunt stellen. Verschil-
lige, vooraanstaande burgers worden gevangen gezet, om te wachten op
hun terugkeer. Als iemand
saboteert en de dader wordt niet
gevonden, hebben de officiele heren dood-
gewoon een stuk of 5 Gijzelaars
tegen de muur. Ook staan er
doodsberichten van deze mensen
in de krant. In een voodslottig
ongeval wordt deze misdaad

80

The diary, part 3, which begins on April 17, 1944, corresponds very clearly both in layout and the general impression made by the writing to that of the diary, part 2. The number of "spontaneous" manifestations (pasting in of loose pages and of photographs) has decreased further, as has the number of passages in handprinting.

The last entry in part 3 is dated August 1, 1944. Each entry is, on average, 3 to 3½ pages long.

Once again, it proved impossible to determine who added the pagination 1 to 128 (on top) and 325 to 450 (at the bottom).

The written material, which is in letter form (to "Kitty"), seems once again to have been penned with great ease. It contains observations of day-to-day life in the Annexe and its immediate vicinity and of the military and political situation together with personal reflections. The changes of mood reflected in the text make a natural impression. This is also true of the passages in which the writer discusses her relationship with "Peter" and with her father. Finally, the various mirror-image ink deposits found reflect the "natural" use of the diary, part 3. Figure V-3-1 gives examples.

The handwriting itself, apart from some changes in movement in the capital letters "D," "H," "F" and "T," presents a very stable picture (figure V-3-2 shows the changes in the letter "F").

The similarity of the handwriting characteristics in parts 2 and 3 respectively is obvious. The interested reader can form some idea of this correspondence by comparing some of our reproductions of passages from part 3 with those from part 2. All comparable micro-, general, spacing and individual characteristics were found to correspond. The comparison of part 3 with part 1 and the standard of Anne Frank therefore yielded the same results as for part 2.

The conclusion, accordingly, is once again that

—the handwriting found in the exercise book with the stiff green/gold speckled cover with a black binding, referred to as the diary, part 3, with the exception of the additions and corrections to be discussed later

and

—the handwriting found in the diary, part 1, and the standard of Anne Frank

are by the same hand with a probability bordering on certainty.

For a more detailed account of the application of degrees of probability the reader is referred to Section V-1. As regards the pagination, the same remarks apply as have been made earlier.

V-4   THE RESULTS OF THE IDENTIFICATION OF THE HANDWRITING ON THE LOOSE SHEETS

These sheets are held in three folders. The separate, unlined sheets are slightly smaller than A4 format (21 × 29.7 cm). If such sheets are folded double, with the fold parallel to the shorter side, each gives rise to four pages. They contain various paginations: the numbers on the lower left go up to 324. Pages 280–81 of the manuscript are photocopies. It is impossible to determine who added the various paginations. The loose sheets are colored salmon-pink, rose-pink, ivory and blue.

Ink has been spilled on page 1, forming as a result a blot that has soaked through as far as page 13, decreasing gradually in size. Some of the words covered by the blot have been rewritten.

The contents of the text, once again in the form of letters, have clear parallels in passages from parts 1, 2 and 3.

Two passages in part 2 (dated March 29, 1944) and part 3 (dated May 20, 1944) point to the existence of these loose sheets, inasmuch as their writer mentions that she is writing a novel, *Het Achterhuis*. This "rewriting of the diary" is reflected in a more remote tone and less obvious emotional involvement. It also explains the relatively large number of corrections and sentence reconstructions, particularly during the initial phase.

The precise starting date as well as the date the rest was written is not fully known. If we take May 20, 1944, as the starting date (on the basis of the comment in part 3), and August 1, 1944, as the date of the last entry, then the average daily entry would run to from 4 to 5 pages a day. These must have been written in addition to the entries in the diary, part 3.

The presence of corrections, etc., in the initial phase has resulted in pages with an irregular appearance. Later, regularity is, however, restored. Figure V-4-1 conveys some idea of the look of the script and of the corrections.

Because changes in handwriting characteristics with time in part 3 are paralleled by changes in the loose sheets, the latter, which were written at the same time, can be dated more closely. It appears that the writer worked more intensely on the loose sheets, particularly during the period between July 15 and August 1, 1944. During that period, 162 pages were completed, or about 11 pages a day. During that period, too—apart from July 15 and August 1, 1944—no work was done on part 3 of the diary. This fact, and also the variation of the characteristics with time, points to a "natural" use of the material.

A comparison of the handwriting characteristics of the loose sheets and the diary, parts 2 and 3, shows that all comparable micro-, general, spacing and individual characteristics are in clear correspondence—as our illustrations exemplify. Thanks to this very close relationship, the same conclusions apply to the comparison of the loose sheets with the diary, part 1, and to the standard of Anne Frank as have been set out for parts 2 and 3.

This leads to the following general conclusion:

—the handwriting on the loose sheets, with the exception of the additions, corrections, etc., to be discussed later, the first date and the various paginations

together with

—the previously described handwriting in parts 2 and 3

and

—the previously described handwriting in the diary, part 1, and the standards of Anne Frank are by the same hand with a probability bordering on certainty.

For a more detailed explanation of the terminology used to express probability, the reader is referred to Section V-1.

VI   The Identification of the Corrections, etc.

Following the publication of an article in *Der Spiegel*, No. 41, 1980 (pp. 121–22), the State Forensic Science Laboratory at the request of the Netherlands State Institute for War Documentation paid particular attention to the possible inclusion in the diary of entries written with a ballpoint pen. To that end, all the handwriting, with the exception of the photocopied loose sheet, was examined closely by the document examiner. The only ballpoint writing was found on two loose scraps of paper included among the loose sheets. Figures VI-1-1 and 3 show the way in which these scraps of paper had been inserted in the relevant plastic folders. As far as the factual contents of the diary are concerned, the ballpoint writings have no significance whatsoever. Moreover, the handwriting on the scraps of paper and in the diary differ strikingly.*

The page numbers of the loose sheets differ internally as well as from one another but have not been subjected to analysis for lack of adequate comparative material. This also applies to the pagination of part 3.

It might, however, be pointed out that the page numbers found on the bottom left of the loose sheets, running up to number 324, are continued in part 3, also on the bottom left.

The handwriting characteristics of the pagination in both cases show a clear correspondence. On pages 62f, Gerrold van der Stroom has already pointed out that Otto Frank, when making a copy of the loose sheets, used supplementary material from, among others, part 3. It seems not unlikely that the consecutive page numbers were added for the purposes of the copy. In that case, the pagination would not have been in Anne Frank's hand.

The page numbers at the top are all written in pencil.

Those at the bottom are in black ink, with some penciled additions, for instance the numbers 86a to 86g.

In no more than six places do we find corrections and additions to the page numbers in black, which, considered morphologically, display the characteristics of ballpoint writing. Number 309a is a striking example. When analyzed chemically, however, the ink behaved differently from a series of reference ballpoint inks, including samples from an earlier date.

However, even if further investigation had brought to light a ballpoint with a similar chemical reaction, this discovery would not have detracted from the authenticity of the diary, for all we have here is the addition of page

*The Hamburg psychologist and court-appointed handwriting expert, Hans Ockelmann, stated in a letter to the ANNE FRANK-Fonds dated September 27, 1987, that his mother, Mrs. Dorothea Ockelmann, wrote the ballpoint texts in question when she collaborated with Mrs. Minna Becker in investigating the diaries (see p. 87).

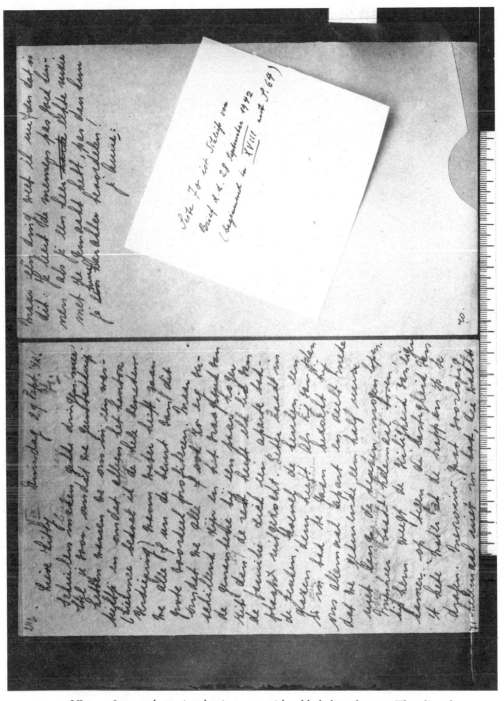

VI-1-1. *Loose sheets in plastic cover with added slip of paper.* The slip of paper bears ballpoint writing which differs markedly from the writing used in the diary itself.

VI-1-2. *Magnified reproductions of the slips of paper with ballpoint writing shown in figures VI-1-1 and VI-1-3.*

162

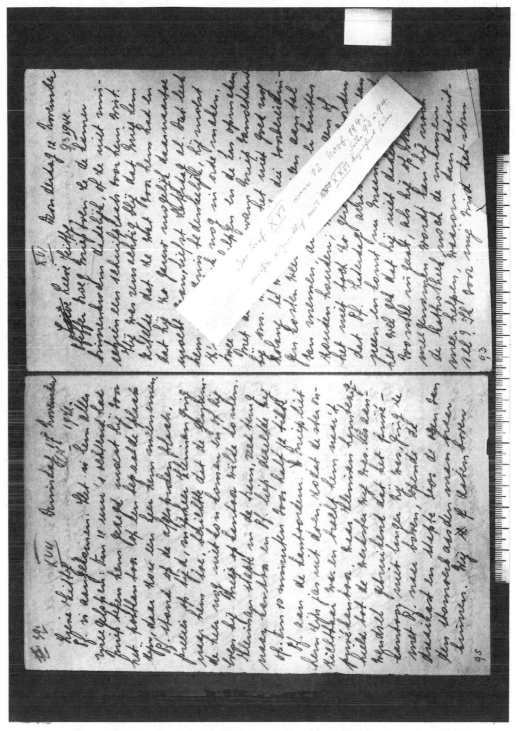

VI-1-3. *Loose sheets in plastic cover with added slip of paper.* The slip of paper
bears ballpoint writing which differs markedly from the writing used in the diary
itself.

163

numbers for which there are indications that they were not written by Anne Frank.

What we have referred to under the collective name of "corrections" consists, in fact, of a series of amendments to writing and spelling mistakes which includes deletions, amendments to faulty sentence construction, the rewriting or substitution of words or sentences, and amplification by the addition of sentences or passages of text.

The corrections are relatively insignificant in scale with respect to the main text, although on the loose sheets in particular the use of a different-colored ink is quite conspicuous. However, anyone attempting to present as authentic an edition of the diary of Anne Frank as possible must determine which corrections were actually by her hand. In that sense, the more comprehensive corrections are of greater importance than, for example, the deletion of a single letter. Similarly, textual corrections running to several sentences may be attributed to an individual by the handwriting expert, where a single deletion may not.

During the analysis of the corrections, an attempt was made to discover possible links with other corrections, so that the need for analyzing isolated corrections was reduced. Such links may take the form of the use of the same writing implement, the color of the ink deposit, the occurrence of corrections on a single page, and so on. The links can also be of a textual kind.

For comparison of the corrections, etc., the experts often used the main text found in the immediate vicinity of the correction. Since the corrections might have been added later, however, and indeed could have been in a different type of handwriting, it was also necessary to make use of writings of a different date. The relationship between the material submitted for comparison and the standards of Anne Frank has been discussed earlier.

The result of the investigation can be summarized briefly.

In only a very few cases did the handwriting used for comparison and the corrections prove to be by different hands. These corrections, attributed to a different writer, vary from a single letter to three words, and amount to a total of twenty-six examples.

They are scattered through the loose sheets from pages 104 to 311. In seven cases, they are amendments of faulty sentence construction; in the other cases they cannot be considered absolutely necessary.

The comparisons showed that these corrections, *considered as a whole*, were made by Otto Frank with a probability bordering on certainty.

The initial date on page 1 also differs from the material used for comparison. It was not possible to identify the writer.

With the exception of the deletions, which will be discussed separately, and the corrections consisting of a single symbol, all the other changes, additions and so on in parts 1, 2 and 3 and the loose sheets show no essential differences from the material used for comparison. Where writings of some length could be compared, the correspondence was qualitatively good. The degree of probability with which the writer could be identified ranged from "possible" to "with a probability bordering on certainty." In some cases the qualification "possible" meant no more than the absence of essential differences, for instance in short, unconnected words. Additions consisting of several sentences could be identified to a very large degree.

In places where a deletion is attended by an attributable correction, the characteristics of the deletion, such as the slope and the number of deletion strokes, can be inferred. Many deletions not accompanied by associated corrections show similar characteristics. Corrections consisting of a single symbol also correspond with forms used elsewhere in the text. The significance of these brief expressions was, however, considered to be such as not to justify a probability statement.

Afterword

The role of Otto Frank in the preparation of the Dutch edition of the diary of Anne Frank and the subsequent translations has been discussed at length in Chapter 5. Highly personal motives were involved: his strong attachment to his dead daughter; his awareness that with publication he would be putting into effect Anne's dearest wish—to become a famous writer one day; and his feelings of respect, first and foremost towards his dead wife, but also towards those others about whom Anne had made less than pleasant remarks. He also agreed in the end to the corrections and abridgments that the publishing house had introduced for a variety of reasons.

All this may seem natural and understandable in one who aspired merely to publish the essence *("das Wesentliche")* of the literary bequest, the *document humaine*, of his daughter, in what appeared to him a fit and proper manner. However, the sentence inserted on his authority at the conclusion of the Dutch edition of the *Diary*: "With the exception of a few sections of little interest to the reader, the original text has been retained," must be seen as something more than an obvious understatement.

Otto Frank stuck to this conviction to his death: "the essence" had been published and that was the end of the matter. No amount of argument could make him change his mind.

As a result, over the long years during which the diary went on to play an increasingly important role in the view of millions of people who came to look on it as a historical document rather than as a work of literature, he did not make it easier to ward off attacks on the book.

The report of the State Forensic Science Laboratory has convincingly demonstrated that both versions of the diary of Anne Frank were written by her in the years 1942 to 1944. The allegations that the diary was the work of someone else (after the war or otherwise) are thus conclusively refuted.

With this publication of the two versions of Anne's manuscript and the possibility it offers of comparing these with the published text, and also on the basis of the events described in Chapter 5 of this book, we feel justified in claiming—despite corrections and omissions—that *The Diary of Anne Frank* does indeed contain "the essence" of Anne's writings, and that there are no grounds on which the term "forgery" can be applied to the work of the editors or publishers of the book.

As far as we are concerned, there is not the slightest reason to doubt either the authenticity of the manuscripts or the intrinsic quality of *The Diary of Anne Frank*.

The content of the complete texts of Anne Frank's diary portrays her no differently than did that of the first version published in 1947, except for conveying a more rounded, a more detailed picture both of her development from a thirteen-year-old into a fifteen-year-old girl, and of her inner life and her progress as a writer.

Anne Frank has stayed the person she was, despite our investigation, despite our full publication of her diaries. We believe that with this publication we have provided a conclusive answer to all the questions raised over the years. Her diary as a historical document is now open to all. In making it so, we have enjoyed the support of the Netherlands Minister of Education and Science, Dr. A. Pais, who in 1981 concluded his answer to a question in the Dutch parliament by stressing another, equally important, element: "I also emphatically regard the publication of the Diary as an act of homage to Anne Frank and to the more than one million other Jewish children who were murdered in the Second World War."

On the Presentation of the Text

GERROLD VAN DER STROOM

An authoritative edition of the diaries of Anne Frank must satisfy the following demands:

- the available texts must be included as fully as possible and presented in their context;
- the three versions to be differentiated must be so presented that both the comparison of each with the others and the separate reading of each version may be as simple as possible;
- the published texts must faithfully reproduce the spelling, punctuation, sentence structure and so on of the originals and of the original translation into English by Mrs. B. M. Mooyaart-Doubleday.
- any deletions, additions or changes to the original manuscripts, whatsoever, however and wherever they were made, must be indicated and explained;
- all these provisions notwithstanding, the texts should be so arranged as to enable the reader to proceed without lengthy commentaries or an unwieldy apparatus of footnotes.

In order to satisfy these conditions as best we could, we began by making the following arrangement of the text.

Scheme

As we have explained, Anne Frank wrote two versions of her diary, the second being based on the first. In addition she also wrote *Verhaaltjes en gebeurtenissen uit het Achterhuis (Tales from the Secret Annex)*, referred to in short as the *Tales*.[1] It was on the basis of these manuscripts that the first Dutch publication of her diaries, *Het Achterhuis*, was brought out in 1947.

The texts of the two versions of the diary and that of the English translation of *Het Achterhuis* are presented in this edition in such a way that each can be read on its own and at the same time compared with the other two versions.

We have adopted the following procedure: in general, the three texts have been printed one under the other, page by page.

a) The first version (as written in "Diaries 1, 2 and 3") appears at the top of the page. It is indicated by the letter **a** in the left margin:
b) Under that is the second version (written on the "loose sheets") and indicated by the letter **b**.
c) Finally there is the translation by B. M. Mooyaart-Doubleday of *The Diary of Anne Frank*, published as *Anne Frank: The Diary of a Young Girl* in the 1952 U.S. edition of *Het Achterhuis* (which was published in 1947), and indicated by the letter **c**.

If the reader wishes to follow only what Anne Frank wrote in her first draft, he should read version **a** and ignore versions **b** and **c**. He will then be reading the book horizontally, so to speak. Versions **b** and **c** can be read in the same way.

Section **c** includes a few scenes from the *Tales from the Secret Annex*. These items have been marked with the letter **T** instead of **a** or **b**. Anne Frank also recorded some events in the "Secret Annexe" in both her diaries as well as in the *Tales*.

When comparing two versions of, say, a poem the reader can place them side by side. Such line-by-line comparisons are not generally possible in the case of texts written in prose: the lines are either not of the same length or the versions differ too greatly from each other. It might be possible to compare the different versions paragraph by paragraph, but two or more paragraphs from one version may be combined into one in another version, so that long gaps appear on the relevant pages.

In this edition, each of the three versions has been divided into rounded-off events or "scenes." The corresponding passages of the three versions are printed one above the other. This simplifies comparisons. The beginning or end of a "scene" often coincides with the beginning or end of a diary "letter," a paragraph, a concluding dash or something similar in the original, but that is not always the case. We have accordingly based our divisions on content rather than on the actual limits to be found in the original text. The reader should bear in mind that our method of dividing the text is meant to serve a practical purpose, that is, the production of a (typographically) presentable text.

Anne Frank often describes an event at much greater length in one version than in another. This can mean that, in the description of a particular "scene," version **a**, for instance, does not continue over onto the next page while version **b** does. It can also happen that a particular event is only described in one or two versions. In the place of text, in that case, the reader will find a line of six dots in the other version(s).

The text of every version is printed in its original sequence and has not been rearranged in chronological order. Since, however, we are dealing with a diary, the sequence of the diary letters is largely a chronological one in any case. Sometimes Anne Frank later added a few lines of commentary to earlier letters, and dated these as well. These lines make direct reference to the contents of the diary letter concerned, and it would therefore be wrong to separate them from the letter.

Moreover, some events mentioned in one version under one date may be dated differently in another version. Since the different versions of a "scene" must be read together for comparison, the relevant extracts from one version have been taken out of their context in these cases and placed with the corresponding passages of the other version(s). Whenever this has been done the passages of text concerned have been marked off by long brackets. These passages will, of course, also appear under their original date, that is, they will appear twice. When reading one version at a time (horizontal reading), the passages between long brackets should be ignored.

Transcription, Deletions and Additions

In this edition, the text of Anne Frank's diaries has been published "diplomatically," as have those parts of *Tales from the Secret Annex* which have been included in the published *Diary of Anne Frank*.

By "diplomatic" publication we mean that the text has been presented as it appears in the last extant version of the manuscript.[2] In other words, we have not been given pause by different letter formations, mistakes have been retained, crossed-out passages have been omitted, and so on. The resulting text is a faithful reproduction of the final version of the manuscript. In general, our aim with this method of presentation has been to keep footnotes and other symbols out of the main text.

There have had to be, nevertheless, some exceptions to this rule. Page endings in the original have been marked in the present version with the sign |. The sign is repeated in the left margin, followed by the relevant page number. This arrangement makes it possible to establish where any of the passages transposed in this edition—and marked off by long brackets—came from originally.

Secondly, we have added asterisks referring the reader to notes at the bottom of the page conveying historical information about the events Anne describes in her diaries, or informing the reader that a particular event is also described in the *Tales*. These notes also explain why some words or passages in the original text have been left out. (What few asterisks Anne Frank herself used in her diaries have been ringed in our text.)

Thirdly, there are numerical superscripts which refer to the "Deletions and Additions," appended as a separate section of the text.

The conversion of Anne's handwriting into print—the transcription—presented few problems. It has generally proved possible to decipher even those words that have been crossed out, what has been added, in what way and with what writing implement. As a result, the origins of the text can be reconstructed version by version. All the linguistically significant signs used in the manuscript are thus accounted for. What do we mean by that? An example will make it clear. Anne Frank often added an extra downstroke to the letters "m," "n" and "r." Thus a letter intended to be an "n" often turned into an "m." In most cases Anne Frank corrected this mistake by crossing out the additional stroke. Now, the extra stroke has no linguistic significance, so that we have ignored it in this edition— neither the existence of the downstroke nor its (possible) deletion has been indicated.

Traditionally, deletions, additions and so on are marked by various sign systems;[3] in this edition we have used the following:

Explanations of the Signs Used in "Deletions and Additions"

<a>	*a* added on the line
≤a≥	*a* added between the lines
[−a]	*a* crossed out
[−a]<b>	*a* crossed out and *b* added on the line
[−a]≤b≥	*a* crossed out and *b* added between the lines
[a+]<b>	*b* written over *a*
...	illegible (one dot for each indecipherable letter or sign)
<u>≤a≥</u>	*a* added in upper margin
<u>≤a≥</u>	*a* added in lower margin
a↔b	inversion of *a* and *b* to *b* followed by *a*
a→b	*a* changed to *b*

Notes referring to punctuation marks have been spelled out in full and printed in *italics*. Asterisks which occur in the original manuscripts or in *The Diary of Anne Frank* have been ringed ⊛ in the text.

170

In addition the following signs have been used:

a?	*a* is uncertain
a *ip*	*a* in pencil
a *igp*	*a* in green pencil
a *irp*	*a* in red pencil
a *iri*	*a* in red ink
OF	according to the State Forensic Science Laboratory by the hand of Otto Frank with a probability bordering on certainty (see page 164).

Different Types of Handwriting

Anne Frank used handprinting as well as cursive writing, particularly in "Diary 1." The cursive writing later became dominant. She used both scripts interchangeably for no discernible functional reason (see page 123).[4] Nevertheless the difference has been indicated in this edition: cursive writing is printed in roman letters; handprinting in italics. It seemed pointless to continue this distinction into the appendix; it has therefore been omitted from it.

Underlinings

Words underlined in the original have also been underlined in this edition, even if only a fragment of the intended underlining stroke was put to paper. This happened particularly with the signature "Anne Frank" at the end of the diary letters.

Paragraph Indications

The beginning of a paragraph is indicated by the indentation of the first line, even if that was not done in the original. Had this system not been used, the beginning of a new paragraph would not have been identifiable when the last line of the previous paragraph was complete.

Accents

Anne Frank usually put both accents in the word "*één* [one]" over the second "e." This peculiarity has been ignored in this edition.

Ampersand Signs

Instead of the ampersand sign (&), Anne Frank used either a sign that looked very much like the Greek letter alpha α, for instance in "Gies α Co." or a short horizontal serpentine stroke. In this edition, these signs have been replaced by an ampersand.

Notes

[1] All tales are published in Anne Frank's *Verhaaltjes en gebeurtenissen uit het Achterhuis* (Amsterdam: Bert Bakker, 1982); portions of this work were first translated by Michel Mok and H. H. B. Mosberg as *Tales from the House Behind* (Tadworth, Surrey: The World's Work Ltd., 1962). Full translation by Ralph Manheim and Michel Mok (*Anne Frank's Tales from the Secret Annex*) published by Doubleday & Co., Inc. (New York, 1983).

[2] See W. G. Hellinga, "*Principes linguistiques d'édition de textes*" in *Lingua* 3 (1952–1953), pp. 295–308.

[3] See P. J. Verkruysse, "*Over diplomatisch editeren van handschriften en het gebruik daarbij van diacritische tekens* [On the Diplomatic Editing of Handwritings with the Help of Diacritic Signs]" in *Spektator* 3 (1973–1974), pp. 325–46.

[4] See, for instance, p. 288, where Anne Frank used cursive writing but then went on to note in printed letters: "Oh, I completely forgot that I used to write in print all the time, I was so immersed in what I was doing."

Translator's Note

ARNOLD J. POMERANS

Because so many English-speaking readers are familiar with the original translation of Anne Frank's diary by Mrs. B. M. Mooyaart-Doubleday (first published in 1952), it was the wish of the U.S. publisher that this original translation be used for version **c** of the present work. The edition used is that published by Doubleday & Co., Inc., New York, in 1967 under the title *Anne Frank: The Diary of a Young Girl*, with the Epilogue taken from the edition published by Vallentine, Mitchell & Co., Ltd., London, 1952.

The use of Mrs. Mooyaart-Doubleday's translation for version **c** has, of course, meant using it as well for the English version of **a** or **b**—including all her wording, paragraphing, punctuation, and methods of writing figures, times, and dates—wherever **a** or **b** in Dutch are the same as Dutch **c**.

In other words, the present translator's brief has been to make a new translation of only those parts of the original diary (versions **a** and **b**) that have not been published before.

This brief has been faithfully executed except in cases of apparent misinterpretations and omissions in the original translation. These have been indicated by the use of brackets in version **c**.

Also, where Mrs. Mooyaart-Doubleday introduced emphasis by the use of italics in her published translation (version **c**), and versions **a** or **b** agree with **c** but Anne Frank did not herself indicate such emphasis (by her own underlining), the words concerned have been underlined with a wavy line in versions **a** or **b**.

The original translation included some footnotes written for the English edition and reproduced here in version **c**. In addition, footnotes from the present Dutch book will be found in versions **a** or **b**. There are also superscribed numerals in the text referring the reader to the "Deletions and Additions" section at the end of the book. Finally, the present translator has added a few footnotes of his own to versions **a** and **b**, marked with the initials "A. J. P."

Most of the entries in the "Deletions and Additions" appended to the main text are minor Dutch grammatical or spelling corrections. Only those reflected in the English translation have been numbered in the text. The corresponding numbers have been ringed in the appendix. The Dutch alterations have, however, been retained in the appendix to demonstrate the nonsubstantial nature of most of the alterations and deletions.

The translator has attempted to mark slight differences in the Dutch versions of the diary (other than changes in word order) by slight differences in the English translation. Few of these add anything to the text; they simply signpost changes. However, some differences which recur have been ignored, for instance Anne Frank's use of " *'t*" for "*het*" (the definitive article), "*ij*" for "*y*" or the repeated substitution in the Dutch published edition of "*onderduiken* [go underground]" for Anne Frank's "*schuilen* [go into hiding]."

Finally, many of the titles of books referred to by Anne Frank have been translated into English so as to give the reader an idea of the reading matter available to her. This is not, of course, meant to suggest that Anne read these books in English.

The Diaries of Anne Frank

Gorgeous photograph isn't it!!!![1]

I hope I shall be able to confide in you completely, as I have never been able to do in anyone before, and I hope that you will be a great support and comfort to me.

Anne Frank. 12 June 1942.

I have had a lot of support from you so far, and also from our beloved club to whom I now write regularly, I think this way of keeping my diary is much nicer and now I can hardly wait for when I have time to write in you

28 Sept. 1942.
AnneFrank.

I am, Oh, so glad that I took you along.

———

2   The 7 or 12 beautiful features (not mine mind you!) should come here, then I can fill in which ones I have, and which ones I don't!

28 Sept. 1942. *(drawn up by myself.)*

   1. blue eyes, black hair. (no.)
   2. dimples in cheeks (yes.)
   3. dimple in chin (yes.)
   4. widow's peak (no.)
   5. white skin (yes.)
   6. straight teeth (no.)
   7. small mouth (no.)
   8. curly eyelashes (no.)
   9. straight nose (yes.) {at least so far.}
   10. nice clothes (sometimes.) {not nearly enough in my opinion.}
   11. nice fingernails (sometimes.)
   12. intelligent (sometimes.)

3   Sunday 14 June 1942.

I think the next few pages will all have the same (page) date, because I still have a lot to tell you.

   I'll start with the moment I got you, or rather saw you lying on my birthday table, (because the buying, when I was there as well, doesn't count.)

   On Friday, June 12th, I woke up at six o'clock, and no wonder; it was my birthday. But I was not allowed to get up at that hour, and so I still had to control[6] my curiosity
|4 until | a quarter to seven. Then I could bear it no longer, and went to the dining room,

. . . . . .

Sunday, 14 June 1942

   On Friday, June 12th, I woke up at six o'clock and no wonder; it was my birthday. But of course I was not allowed to get up at that hour, so I had to control my curiosity until a quarter to seven. Then I could bear it no longer, and went to the dining room,

177

a

where I received a warm welcome from Moortje (the cat).

    I closed the communicating doors of course. Soon after seven I[1] went to Mummy and Daddy and then to the sitting room to undo my presents, the first to greet me was <u>you</u>, possibly the nicest of all. Then on the table[2] there were a bunch of roses, a plant, and

| 5   some peonies, and more arrived | during the day.

    From Mummy and Daddy I got a blue blouse, Variety, which is the latest party game for adults, something like Monopoly, a bottle of grape juice, which to my mind tasted a bit like wine, and which has now begun to ferment so that I can't drink it any more[3] and I may have been right, since wine is made from grapes after all; then a puzzle; a bottle of peek-aroma* "with acorns" (I got that later, I mean "the acorns"; a jar of ointment; a 2½ guilder banknote; a token for 2 books; a book from Katze, the Camera Obscura, but

| 6   Margot has got that already, so | I swapped it; a plate of home-made biscuits (baked by me, of course, for I'm very keen on baking biscuits at the moment)[5]; a little dish of molasses candy, but it is horribly sticky; a bowl of "truffles," from Daddy; a little plate of Marie biscuits; a letter from Grandma, right on time, but that was an accident, of course; and a home-made strawberry tart from Mummy[6]

---

*A brand of substitute coffee based on chicory. A.J.P.

a   11

    Aunt Helene brought me a puzzle; aunt Stephanie a lovely little brooch; aunt Leny a marvelous book Daisy's mountain holiday, and a bracelet from Anneke with a kiss; Mr. Wronker a box of Droste and a game; Mrs. Ledermann a roll of acid drops; Mrs. Pfeffer a roll of acid drops; Mr. van Maarsen a bunch of sweet peas; Peter van Pels a bar of milk chocolate, Mrs. Pfeffer and Mr. Wronker flowers as well and so I was thoroughly spoiled.

Then Hanneli called for me and we went to school. During recess, I treated everyone to sweet biscuits; and then back to our lessons.

a   12

    Now I must stop next time I'll have so much to write in you again, I mean to tell you, bye-bye, we're going to be great pals.

b   . . . . . .

c

where I received a warm welcome from Moortje (the cat).

    Soon after seven I went to Mummy and Daddy and then to the sitting room to undo my presents. The first to greet me was *you*, possibly the nicest of all. Then on the table there were a bunch of roses, a plant, and some peonies, and more arrived during the day.

    I got masses of things from Mummy and Daddy, and was thoroughly spoiled by various friends. Among other things I was given *Camera Obscura*, a party game, lots of sweets, chocolates, a puzzle, a brooch, *Tales and Legends of the Netherlands* by Joseph Cohen, *Daisy's Mountain Holiday* (a terrific book), and some money. Now I can buy *The Myths of Greece and Rome*—grand!

    Then Lies called for me and we went to school. During recess I treated everyone to sweet biscuits, and then we had to go back to our lessons.

    Now I must stop. Bye-bye, we're going to be great pals!

178

a   16

> Monday 15 June 1942.
>
> I had my party on Sunday afternoon, my school friends thoroughly enjoyed Rin-tin-tin I was given a little brooch by G.; Leny also gave me a brooch; E. S. a bookmark; J., Nanny van Praag and Eefje, a book called "good morning milkman"; Henny and Betty also gave me a book "Lydia's troubles."

a | 15

> Mummy always wants to know who I'm going to marry, but I don't think | she'll ever guess that it's Peter, because I managed without blushing or flickering an eyelid, to get that idea right out of their minds. I am fonder of Peter than I have ever been of anyone else, and I keep telling myself that it's only to hide his feelings that Peter goes round with all those girls; he also probably thinks that Hello and I are in love, which is quite untrue, because he is just a friend or as Mummy puts it one of my beaux.

  | 7

Then I came home at five o'clock, | because I had gone to gymnastics, (although I am not allowed to do it because my arms and legs go out of joint) and I chose volleyball for my classmates as my birthday game. Later they all danced in a circle around me and sang "happy birthday to you". When I got home Sanne Ledermann was already there, and I'd brought Ilse Wagner, Hanneli Goslar and Jacqueline van Maarsen along with me from gymnastics, because they are in my class.

  | 8

Hanneli and Sanne used to be my | two best friends, and people who saw us together always said there they go Anne, Hanne and Sanne. I only got to know Jacqueline van Maarsen at the Jewish Secondary School and she is now[1] my best friend. Ilse is Hanneli's best friend, and Sanne goes to a different school, where she has her friends.

b   . . . . . .

c

Monday, 15 June, 1942

I had my birthday party on Sunday afternoon. We showed a film *The Lighthouse Keeper* with Rin-Tin-Tin, which my school friends thoroughly enjoyed. We had a lovely time. There were lots of girls and boys. Mummy always wants to know whom I'm going to marry. Little does she guess that it's Peter Wessel; one day I managed, without blushing or flickering an eyelid, to get that idea right out of her mind. For years Lies Goosens and Sanne Houtman have been my best friends. Since then, I've got to know Jopie de Waal at the Jewish Secondary School. We are together a lot and she is now my best girl friend. Lies is more friendly with another girl, and Sanne goes to a different school, where she has made new friends.

179

20.6.42

1   It's an odd idea for someone like me, to keep a diary; not only because I have never done so before, but because it seems to me that neither I—nor for that matter anyone else—will be interested in the unbosomings of a thirteen-year-old schoolgirl. Still, what does that matter? I want to write[3] but more than that, I want to bring out all kinds of things that lie buried deep in my heart. There is a saying that paper is more patient than man[4]"; it came back to me[5] on one of my slightly melancholy days while I sat chin in hand, feeling too bored and limp even to make up my mind whether to go out, or stay at home. Yes there is no doubt that paper is patient and as I don't intend to show this cardboard-covered notebook, bearing the proud name of diary to anyone, unless I find a real friend,

| 2 | boy or girl, probably nobody cares.[11]

And now I touch the root of the matter the reason why I started a diary;[12] it is that I have no such real friend.

Let me put it more clearly, since no one will believe that a girl of 13 feels herself quite alone in the world, nor is it so.[13] I have darling parents and a sister of sixteen.[14] I know about thirty people whom one might call friends, I have strings of boy friends, anxious to[16] catch a glimpse of me and who, failing[17] that, peep at me through mirrors in

Saturday, 20 June, 1942

I haven't written for a few days, because I wanted first of all to think about my diary. It's an odd idea for someone like me to keep a diary; not only because I have never done so before, but because it seems to me that neither I—nor for that matter anyone else—will be interested in the unbosomings of a thirteen-year-old schoolgirl. Still, what does that matter? I want to write, but more than that, I want to bring out all kinds of things that lie buried deep in my heart.

There is a saying that "paper is more patient than man"; it came back to me on one of my slightly melancholy days, while I sat chin in hand, feeling too bored and limp even to make up my mind whether to go out or stay at home. Yes, there is no doubt that paper is patient and as I don't intend to show this cardboard-covered notebook, bearing the proud name of "diary," to anyone, unless I find a real friend, boy or girl, probably nobody cares. And now I come to the root of the matter, the reason for my starting a diary: it is that I have no such real friend.

Let me put it more clearly, since no one will believe that a girl of thirteen feels herself quite alone in the world, nor is it so. I have darling parents and a sister of sixteen. I know about thirty people whom one might call friends—I have strings of boy friends, anxious to catch a glimpse of me and who, failing that, peep at me through mirrors in class. I have class. I have relations, darling aunts and a good home, no I don't seem to lack anything, save "the" friend. But it's the same with all my friends, just fun and joking, nothing more. I can never bring myself to talk of anything outside the common round[1] or we don't seem to be able to get any closer, that is the root of the trouble. Perhaps I lack confidence, but anyway, there it is, a stubborn fact and I | don't seem to be able to do anything about it. Hence, this diary. In order to enhance in my mind's eye the picture of the friend for whom I have waited so long I don't want to set down a series of bald facts in a diary like most people do, but I want this diary, itself to be my friend, and I shall call my friend Kitty.

| 3

relations, aunts and uncles, who are darlings too, a good home, no—I don't seem to lack anything, [save "the" friend]. But it's the same with all my friends, just fun and joking, nothing more. I can never bring myself to talk of anything outside the common round. We don't seem to be able to get any closer, that is the root of the trouble. Perhaps I lack confidence, but anyway, there it is, a stubborn fact and I don't seem to be able to do anything about it.

Hence, this diary. In order to enhance in my mind's eye the picture of the friend for whom I have waited so long, I don't want to set down a series of bald facts in a diary like most people do, but I want this diary itself to be my friend, and I shall call my friend

a   26

> how idiotic <u>My own story</u> you don't forget that sort of thing
> I was born on 12 June 1929 in Frankfurt a/M. I lived in Frankfurt until I was 4,
> then my father Otto, Heinrich Frank went to Holland to look for a post that was
> in June. He found something, and his wife Edith Frank-Holländer moved to Holland
> in September. Margot and I went to Aachen, to our grandmother Rosa Holländer-
> Stern, Margot went on to Holland in December, and I followed in Feb-

| 27

> ruary, and was put on Margot's | table as a birthday present.

a   49

> On 9 May 1940 war broke out here in the Netherlands, the Germans marched their
> army in and within 5 days they had conquered the Netherlands. They have been at
> war with England since September 1939. Now they have the Netherlands, Belgium,
> France (almost the whole of it) Poland, Norway, Denmark, Jugo-Slavia, Greece,
> Rumania, Bulgaria, Hungary is an ally of Germany.

| 50

>   Now that the Germans rule the roost here | we are in real trouble, first there
> was rationing and everything had to be bought with coupons, then during the two
> years they have been here, there have been all sorts of Jewish laws.

b

No one will grasp what I'm talking about if I begin my letters to Kitty just out of the blue
so[1] I'll start by sketching in brief the story of my life[2], much as I don't like to. My father,
the dearest darling of a father I have ever seen, was thirty-six when he married my mother
who was then twenty-five. My sister Margot, was born in 1926 in Frankfort-on-main in
Germany. I followed on June 12, 1929 and, as we are Jewish we emigrated to Holland
in 1933, where my father was appointed Managing Director of the Netherlands Opekta
Co., which manufactures jam. The rest of our family who were left in Germany felt

| 4

the full impact of Hitler's anti-Jewish laws, so life was filled with | anxiety. In 1938 after
the Pogroms, my two uncles (my mother's brothers) escaped to North America, my old
grandmother came to us, she was then seventy-three. After May 1940 good times rapidly
fled, first the war, then the capitulation, followed by the German invasion which is when
the sufferings of us Jews really began. Anti-Jewish decrees followed each other in quick

c

Kitty. No one will grasp what I'm talking about if I begin my letters to Kitty just out of
the blue, so, albeit unwillingly, I will start by sketching in brief the story of my life.

    My father was thirty-six when he married my mother, who was then twenty-five. My
sister Margot was born in 1926 in Frankfort-on-Main, I followed on June 12, 1929, and,
as we are Jewish, we emigrated to Holland in 1933, where my father was appointed
Managing Director of Travies N.V. This firm is in close relationship with the firm of Kolen
& Co. in the same building, of which my father is a partner.

    The rest of our family, however, felt the full impact of Hitler's anti-Jewish laws, so
life was filled with anxiety. In 1938 after the pogroms, my two uncles (my mother's
brothers) escaped to the U.S.A. My old grandmother came to us, she was then seventy-
three. After May 1940 good times rapidly fled: first the war, then the capitulation, followed
by the arrival of the Germans, which is when the sufferings of us Jews really began. Anti-
Jewish decrees followed each other in quick succession. Jews must wear a yellow star,*

---

*To distinguish them from others, all Jews were forced by the Germans to wear, prominently displayed,
a yellow six-pointed star.

a

Jews must wear a yellow star; Jews must hand in their bicycles; Jews are banned from trams and are forbidden to use any car, even a private one; Jews are only allowed to do their shopping between three and five o'clock, and then only in shops which bear the placard Jewish Shop; Jews may only use Jewish barbers; Jews must be indoors from eight o'clock in the evening until 6 o'clock in the morning; Jews are forbidden to visit Theaters, cinemas and other places of entertainment; Jews may not go to swimming baths, nor to tennis, hockey or other sports grounds; Jews may not go rowing; Jews may not take part in public sports. Jews must not sit in their own or their friends' gardens after 8 o'clock in the evening; Jews may not visit Christians; Jews must go to Jewish schools, and many more restrictions of a similar kind, so we could not do this and we were forbidden to do that. But life went on in spite of it all. Jacque used to say to me: "You're scared to do anything because

| 51   it | may be forbidden.

a   28

In the summer of 1941 Granny Hollaender fell very ill, (she was staying with us by then) she had to have an operation and my birthday didn't mean much. It didn't in the summer of 1940 either, for the fighting in the Netherlands was just over then.

Granny died this winter 1941–1942. And no one will ever know how much she is in _my_ thoughts and how much I love her still.

The celebration of this 1942 birthday was to make up for everything then, and granny's little light shone over it.

b

succession and our freedom was strictly limited. Yet things were still bearable[1], despite the star, separate schools, curfew[2], etc. etc.[3]

Granny died in [4]January 1942, Margot and I transferred to the Jewish Secondary

c

Jews must hand in their bicycles, Jews are banned from trams and are forbidden to drive, Jews are only allowed to do their shopping between three and five o'clock and then only in shops which bear the placard "Jewish shop." Jews must be indoors by eight o'clock and cannot even sit in their own gardens after that hour. Jews are forbidden to visit theaters, cinemas, and other places of entertainment. Jews may not take part in public sports. Swimming baths, tennis courts, hockey fields, and other sports grounds are all prohibited to them. Jews may not visit Christians. Jews must go to Jewish schools, and many more restrictions of a similar kind.

So we could not do this and were forbidden to do that. But life went on in spite of it all. Jopie used to say to me, "You're scared to do anything, because it may be forbidden." Our freedom was strictly limited. Yet things were still bearable.

Granny died in January 1942; no one will ever know how much she is present in my thoughts and how much I love her still.

183

a   27   Soon afterwards I joined the 6ᵗʰ grade of the Kindergarten of the Montessori School. I stayed there until I was 6, then I went up into the first form. I found myself in 1B with Mr. van Gelder, I stayed with him into the 4ᵗʰ form, then Mr. van Gelder left and Miss Gadron took over, after one year in the 5ᵗʰ with Miss Gadron, I ended up in 6C with Mrs. Kuperus the headmistress, at the end of the school year we had to say good-by, we both wept, it was very sad. But after the vacation I was back with Mrs. Kuperus, I was supposed to stay with her into the 7ᵗʰ year, but it didn't turn out that way since I was accepted at the Jewish Secondary School where Margot was going too. My reports surprised everyone, but perhaps they are not yet good enough to go up.

b | 5   School in ¹Oct. 1941, She into the 4ᵗʰ, I into the 1ˢᵗ form.² | ³So far everything is all right with the four of us and here I come to the present day and to the solemn inauguration of my diary.

Amsterdam

20 June 1942.   <u>Anne Frank.</u>

c   In 1934 I went to school at the Montessori Kindergarten and continued there. It was at the end of the school year, I was in form 6B, when I had to say good-by to Mrs. K. We both wept, it was very sad. In 1941 I went, with my sister Margot, to the Jewish Secondary School, she into the fourth form and I into the first.

So far everything is all right with the four of us and here I come to the present day.

184

a

| 9

Five of us have formed a club called "the little Bear, minus 2" or t.l.B − 2 for short. That was because we thought the little Bear had 5 stars, but we were wrong | there, because it has seven stars, just like the great Bear; minus 2 therefore means that Sanne is the leader and Jacque is the secretary and that we (Ilse Hanneli and I) are left to make up the club. It's a ping-pong club.

b 6

20 June 1942
Saturday[1]

Dear Kitty,

I'll start straight away. It is so peaceful at the moment, Mummy and Daddy are out and Margot has gone to play ping-pong with some young people at her friend Trees's. I've been playing ping-pong a lot myself lately, so much that five of us girls have started a club. The club is called the little bear minus 2; it is a very silly name but then it's based on a mistake. We wanted to have a very special name for our club[3] and to compare our 5 members to stars. We all thought the great bear[4] had 7 stars and the little bear 5, but on closer enquiry it turned out that both have 7. Hence the minus 2. Ilse Wagner has a ping-pong set and the Wagners' large dining room is always at our disposal, Susanne Ledermann is our[6] president[7], Jacqueline van Maarsen the secretary,[9] Elizabeth Goslar, Ilse and I are the other members[10]. We 5[14] ping-pongers[15] are very partial to an ice cream, especially in summer, when one gets warm at the game, so we usually finish up with a

| 7

visit | to the nearest ice cream shop, Oasis or Delphi[18],* where Jews are allowed. We've quite given up scrounging for extra pocket money. Oasis[19] is usually[20] full and among our large circle of friends we always manage to find some kindhearted gentleman or boy friend, who presents us with more ice cream than we could devour in a week.

*Delphi was a tea-room at 1, Daniel Willinkplein, and Oasis a tea-room and ice cream parlor at 1, Geleenstraat (1942 Amsterdam Telephone Directory).

c

Saturday, 20 June, 1942

Dear Kitty,

I'll start straight away. It is so peaceful at the moment, Mummy and Daddy are out and Margot has gone to play ping-pong with some friends.

I've been playing ping-pong a lot myself lately. We ping-pongers are very partial to an ice cream, especially in summer, when one gets warm at the game, so we usually finish up with a visit to the nearest ice-cream shop, Delphi or Oasis, where Jews are allowed. We've given up scrounging for extra pocket money. Oasis is usually full and among our large circle of friends we always manage to find some kindhearted gentleman or boy friend, who presents us with more ice cream than we could devour in a week.

I was given a lovely book on the occasion namely Tales and Legends of the Netherlands by Joseph Cohen, but unfortunately they gave me the second part, and so I swapped the Camera Obscura for Tales and Legends of the Netherlands part 1, including a book from

| 10 Mummy, for it is very expensive. | I got 6 beautiful carnations from Hello. Hello is a second cousin or a first cousin once removed of Wilma de Jonge, and Wilma de Jonge is a girl who takes our tram and who seemed very nice at first and actually is quite nice, but she talks all day long about nothing but boys and that gets a bit tiresome.

Hello has a girl friend Ursula or Ursul for short.

But I am his real girl friend odd isn't it!

| 11 Everyone thinks I'm in love with Hello, but that is absolutely untrue. | Aunt Helene brought me a puzzle; aunt Stephanie a lovely little brooch; aunt Leny a marvelous book Daisy's mountain holiday[3], and a bracelet from Anneke[4] with a kiss; Mr. Wronker a box of Droste and a game; Mrs. Ledermann a roll of acid drops; Mrs. Pfeffer a roll of acid drops; Mr. van Maarsen a bunch of sweet peas;

Peter van Pels a bar of milk chocolate, Mrs Pfeffer and Mr. Wronker flowers as well and so I was thoroughly spoiled. This afternoon I also got something from the children

| 12 in my | class. Yesterday evening we showed a film "The lighthouse keeper", with Rin-tin-tin,[5] and we're going to have it this afternoon again, lovely !!!!

I shall still get the Myths of Greece and Rome with my own money. Another book from Mr. Kohnke and at Blankevoort's a box for storing Variety. Now I must stop next time I'll have so much to write in you again, that is to tell you, bye-bye, we're going to be great pals.

13 [6]Daisy's mountain holiday is really a very beautiful book; I was deeply moved by the story about the girl who was so rich and yet so good and who died at the end, but that was inevitable and precisely what makes it so beautiful.

This morning in my bath I was thinking how wonderful it would be if I had a dog like Rin-tin-tin. I would call him Rin-tin-tin too and he'd be at school all the time with the caretaker or if the weather was good in the bicycle shed. I have made a rough sketch

| 14 of my underground palace, | as I call it to myself. I hope that this wish of mine will be fulfilled one day, but there would have to be a miracle then, since it doesn't usually happen that food and money and things like that are supplied all the time and that you can set sail even to America or that you can just disappear under the ground and then live there, it's <u>too</u> beautiful to be true. Mummy always wants to know who I'm going to marry,

| 15 but I don't think | she'll ever guess that it's Peter, because I managed without blushing or flickering an eyelid, to get that idea right out of their minds. I am fonder of Peter than I have ever been of anyone else, and I keep telling myself that it's only to hide his feelings that Peter goes round with all those girls; he also probably thinks that Hello and I are in love, which is quite untrue, because he is just a friend or as Mummy puts it one of my beaux.

. . . . . .

. . . . . .

Monday 15 June 1942.

I had my party on Sunday afternoon, my school friends thoroughly enjoyed Rin-tin-tin I
was given a little brooch by G.;* Leny also gave me a brooch; E.S. a bookmark; J., Nanny
van Praag and Eefje, a book called "good morning milkman"²; Henny and Betty also gave
me a book "Lydia's troubles."³ I shall now say a few things about our class and our

| 17   school, beginning with the pupils. | The pupils in class 1L II.

1.) Betty Bloemendaal, looks rather poor, but that's what she is I think, she lives in
Jan Klasenstraat in West [Amsterdam] and none of us knows where that is. She is very
clever at school, but that's because she works so hard, since her cleverness isn't all it seems.
She is a fairly quiet girl.

2.) Jacqueline van Maarsen, considered to be my best friend, but I've never had a
real friend, I thought at first that Jacque would be one, but it turned out badly.

18   She's always having little secrets and going off with other girls such as J.R.

3.) D.Q., is a very nervous girl, who always forgets⁴ things and gets one detention
after another. She is very kind-hearted particularly towards G.Z.

4.) E.S., is a girl whose dreadful tittle-tattle is beyond a joke. When she asks you
something she's always fingering your hair or fiddling with your buttons.

| 19   They say that E. can't stand me, but I | can manage to put up with that all right since
I don't think she's all that likeable either.

5.) Henny Mets, is a nice, cheerful girl, except that she talks much too loudly, and
is very babyish when she plays in the street. It's a great pity about Henny's friend Beppy⁵,
who has a really poisonous effect on her, since she's a horribly mean and dirty-minded
girl.

6.) J.R., you could write whole chapters about her. J. is a swanky, whispery, nasty,
| 20   boastful, underhand, hypocritical | girl. She has got right round Jacque which is a real
pity.

J. cries at the slightest little thing, is really petty, and on top of everything else horribly
affected.

Miss J. always has to be right. She is very rich and has a wardrobe full of gorgeous
dresses, but they're much too old for her. She thinks she's very beautiful, but she is just
the opposite. She has a perky but cheeky (chutzpahish) expression. J. and I can't stand
each other.

21   7.) Ilse Wagner is a nice, cheerful girl, but she is very fussy and can go on and on
about something for hours e.g. when she has wet feet, first she decides to come back to
my place and then she wants to go home. Then instead of going home and putting on dry
stockings, she comes with me but never stops going on about it. Ilse is very fond of me,
she is very clever but lazy.

8.) Hanneli Goslar is a bit of a strange girl, she is shy on the whole and very cheeky
at home, but quite unassuming with other people.

| 22   She blabs everything you tell | her to her mother.

But she has an open mind and I respect her a lot particularly recently. continued next
time.

---

b   . . . . . .

---

c   . . . . . .

---

*At the request of a number of those involved, their names have been replaced in this book with
initials chosen at random.

Hanneli or Lies as she is called at school, did something silly again to Ilse and Jacque, I don't really know what to think of it.

9.) Nannie v. Praag-Sigaar, is a funny little, sensible girl, I think she is very nice. She is fairly clever as well, there isn't much one can say about Nannie van Praag-Sigaar.

10.) Eefje de Jong, is a wonderful girl I think. She is only just twelve years old, but is quite a lady. She acts as if I am a baby.

23 Eefje is also very helpful, and so I like her a lot.

11.) G.Z. is probably the most beautiful girl in our class she has a darling face, but is pretty stupid at school, so that I really think that she'll be kept down, which is something I don't tell her of course. To my great astonishment G. wasn't kept down after all.

12.) And finally of our 12 girls there is me, sitting next to G.Z.

There is a lot, as well as very little to say about the boys.

Maurice Coster is one of my many admirers, but is rather boring. Sallie Springer is

| 24 terribly mean, and rumor has it | that he's gone all the way with a girl. Still, I think he's great because he's very funny.

Emiel Bonewit is G.Z.'s admirer but that doesn't mean much to G. He is a bit dull.[6]

Rob Cohen was also in love with me, but now I can't stand him any more he is a hypocritical, lying, whining, crazy, boring little boy, who thinks he's the cat's whiskers.

Max van de Velde is a country boy from Medemblik, but very eligible as Margot would put it.

Herman Koopman has also got a filthy mind just like Jopie de Beer who is a terrible

| 25 flirt and | mad about girls. Leo Blom is Jopie de Beer[7]'s bosom friend but is also infected with dirty-mindedness.

Albert de Mesquita comes from the 6th grade of the Montessori School and has skipped a class, he is very clever.

Leo Slager, comes from the same school but is not so clever.

Ru Stoppelmon is a small, funny little boy from Almelo, who joined the school later.

C.N. does everything he's not allowed ????????????????????????? What I meant was he spoke German but I didn't want to write that down in case somebody found the book. 1943 the "Secret Annexe"[8]

| 26 Jacques Kocernoot sits behind us with A. and we laugh ourselves sick (G. and I.) |

Harry Schaap, is the decentest boy in our class, he is really nice.

Werner Joseph (ditto, ditto) but too quiet because of the times we live in so he appears dull.

Sam Salomon is just a brat from the slums, a bit of riffraff (Admirer![10])

Appie Riem is slightly orthodox but she's a nasty piece of work too.

. . . . . .

. . . . . .

how idiotic <u>My own story</u> you don't forget that sort of thing[1]

I was born on 12 June 1929 in Frankfurt a/M. I lived in Frankfurt until I was 4, then my father Otto, Heinrich Frank went to Holland to look for a post that was in June. He found something, and his wife Edith Frank-Holländer moved to Holland in September. Margot and I went to Aachen, to our grandmother Rosa Holländer-Stern, Margot went | 27 on to Holland in December, and I followed in February,* and was put on Margot's | table as a birthday present.

Soon afterwards I joined the 6th grade of the Kindergarten of the Montessori School. I stayed there until I was 6, then I went up into the first form. I found myself in 1B with Mr. van Gelder, I stayed with him into the 4th form, then Mr. van Gelder left and Miss Gadron took over, after one year in the 5th with Miss Gadron, I ended up in 6C under Mrs. Kuperus the headmistress, at the end of the school year we had to say good-by, we both wept, it was very sad. But after the vacation I was back with Mrs. Kuperus, I was supposed to stay with her into the 7th year, but it didn't turn out that way since I was accepted at the Jewish Secondary School where Margot was going too. My reports sur- | 28 prised everyone, but perhaps they are not yet good enough to go up. | In the summer of 1941[3] Granny Hollaender[4] fell very ill, (she was staying with us by then) she had to have an operation and my birthday didn't mean much. It didn't in the summer of 1940 either, for the fighting in the Netherlands was just over then.

Granny died this winter 1941–1942. And no one will ever know how much she is in <u>my</u> thoughts and how much I love her still.

The celebration of this 1942 birthday was to make up for everything then, and granny's little light shone over it.

Friday 19 June 1942.

This morning I was at home, I slept a long, long time, then Hanneli came and we had a bit of a gossip. Jacque has suddenly become very taken with Ilse and behaves very childishly and stupidly towards me, the more I know her the less I like her

<u>Anne</u>

---

*In November 1985, Mrs. Elfriede Frank Markovits, Otto Frank's widow, stated that it was her recollection, and that of the family, that Anne arrived in Amsterdam in March 1934. See p. 7. A.J.P.

---
b   . . . . . .

---
c   . . . . . .

This is June 1939.
It is the only photograph of granny Hol-
länder. I still think of her so often and wish
she still kept the peace at home.
Margot and I had just got out of the water
and I still remember how terribly cold I was,
that's why I put on my bathrobe, granny
sitting there at the back so sweetly and
peacefully. Just as she was wont to do.
                                    Anne Frank.
                            28 Sept. 1942.

This is in 1940, Margot and I again. I
console myself with the thought that on
the photograph above taken in 1939
Margot was not all that well-developed
either. She was 13 at the time, the same
age I am now or even a little older. So
she's got no cause to look down on me.
                                    Anne Frank.
                            28 Sept. 1942.

I started with Margot's photograph and fin-
ish with my own. This is January 1942. This
photograph is horrible, and I look abso-
lutely nothing like it.

Grandma is in Switzerland she is a very dear and
clever woman, who gets on well with all her acquain-
tances friends and relatives and would do anything
for them. She now lives with Daddy's sister, aunt
Leni and Stephan and Bernd. Grandma has always
been very kind to me too. She is now in 1942 76
years old and we hope that we shall find her in good
health again after the war.
AnneFrank.

b   . . . . . .

c   . . . . . .

190

On 11 May 1939 I got this marvelous letter from Daddy, it will be a support to me all my life, unless like Margot I leave it lying about somewhere, just as Margot has done at home.

12.v.39*

My dear little Anne,
When you were still very small, Grandma used to call you:
"Little woman." And that you have remained, you flattering little kitten.
You know we often have secrets from each other. It's true, things haven't always gone as smoothly for you as they did for your sister, though in general your sense of humor and your amiability allow you to sail through so much so easily. I have often told you that you must educate yourself. We have agreed the "controls" with each other and you yourself are doing a great deal to swallow the "buts." And yet you like to spoil yourself and like even more to be spoiled by others.
All that isn't bad, if deep in your little heart you remain as lovable as you always have been. I have told you that as a child I, too, often rushed into things without thinking twice and made many mistakes. But the main thing is to reflect a little bit and then to find one's way back to the right path.
You are not obstinate and so, after a few tears, the laughter is soon back again.
"Enjoy what there is"—as Mummy says.
May this happy laughter stay with you, the laughter with which you enhance your, our and other people's lives.

Your
Pim

AnneFrank 28 Sept 1942

32 I got this letter from Daddy in 1939, and I think it is very beautiful, and it really is, but Daddy isn't always like that. I used to think he was but I've been proved wrong[2]
Jacque thought this was a declaration of love by some boy and I didn't try to enlighten her. I have never had any declarations of love in writing, but tomorrow is another day, as the saying is, and anyway I've had them verbally, and often too.
28 Sept. 1942. Daddy is being such a darling now, he understands me so completely, and I would love to have a heart-to-heart talk with him one day without my immediately bursting into tears, but that seems to be because of my age. I'd love to be able to go on writing all the time, but it becomes much too tedious AnneFrank.

---

*Otto Frank's letter was written in German. A.J.P.

33 *This is the only letter I had from Jacqueline van Maarsen, I asked her often enough for a photograph and she said she would look one out for me, but now on 28 Sept. 1942 it is too late, as anyone who reads this will know, for we've been in hiding now for quite some time. Anne Frank.*

{This is the only written token of Jacque's friendship, apart from my poor autograph album. She is being very nice again at the moment, and I hope things will stay like that.}

| 34 | I now think quite differently about the things I wrote down earlier but I can't rip pages out of my diary and I hope I shan't be told off later for what an ugly handwriting I had then, since it isn't true. It was only because I didn't feel like it, and found it so hard to write in my diary.

All I want to do is to apologize and to explain things.

28 Sept. 1942.
Anne Frank

If I have added anything, or shall add anything, to what I have written, it is only to change it for the better or to look at things from my new standpoint.

28 Sept. 1942.
Anne Frank.

35 This is the printed notice of little Ruth Cauvern's birth.

36 Tuesday 30² June 1942.
I still have to give an account of the whole week.

x On Friday 26 June, Jacque and G. came over in the afternoon, it was very nice and we made some biscuits.

x On Saturday 27 June I went to synagogue in the morning and in the afternoon I was invited to Hello Silberberg's at half past three; there was another boy called Fredie Weiss³ there and it was quite pleasant. We went to oasis and bought an ice cream for 12 cents, then Wilma came, and they wanted to stand us another ice cream but Wilma and I didn't want to, but they bought us each one for 12 [cents] anyway, but we didn't accept it, so Fredie and Hello had 2 more 12-cent ice creams.

x On Sunday 28 June, Jacque and I wanted to go to Alfred Bloch's in the afternoon to see a film, but it didn't come off because Hanneli and Sanne had gone there first. Jacque

. . . . . .

. . . . . .

Met blijdschap laten

Isa Cauvern-Monas

en

Ab Cauvern

weten, dat

RUTH

haar intrede in 't Konijnenhol heeft gedaan

Laren, Oude Kerkweg 25 (tijdelijk St. Jansziekenhuis)
27 September 1941

Translation: Isa Cauvern-Monas and Ab Cauvern are happy to announce that RUTH has made her entry into the Rabbit Warren
Laren, Oude Kerkweg 25 (temporarily at St. John's Hospital)
27 September 1941

b

I expect you will be rather surprised at the fact that I ([1]the youngest member of the club) should[2] talk of boy friends at my age. Alas, or in some cases[3] not alas[5], one simply can't seem to avoid it at our school. As soon as a boy asks if he may bicycle home with me and we start a conversation, 9 out of 10 times I can be sure that he will fall head over heels in love immediately and simply won't allow me out of his sight. After a while it cools down of course, especially as I | take little notice of ardent looks and pedal blithely on.

| 8

If it gets so far that they begin about asking Father, I swerve slightly on my bicycle, my satchel falls, the young man is bound to get off and hand it to me, by which time I have introduced a new topic of conversation. These are the most innocent types; you get some who blow kisses or try to get hold of your arm, but then they are definitely knocking at the wrong door. I get off my bicycle and[19] refuse to go further in their company, or I pretend to be insulted and tell them in no uncertain terms to clear off.

There, the foundation[21] of our friendship is laid, till tomorrow

Yours, Anne

c

I expect you will be rather surprised at the fact that I should talk of boy friends at my age. Alas, one simply can't seem to avoid it at our school. As soon as a boy asks if he may bicycle home with me and we get into conversation, nine out of ten times I can be sure that he will fall head over heels in love immediately and simply won't allow me out of his sight. After a while it cools down of course, especially as I take little notice of ardent looks and pedal blithely on.

If it gets so far that they begin about "asking Father" I swerve slightly on my bicycle, my satchel falls, the young man is bound to get off and hand it to me, by which time I have introduced a new topic of conversation.

These are the most innocent types; you get some who blow kisses or try to get hold of your arm, but then they are definitely knocking at the wrong door. I get off my bicycle and refuse to go further in their company, or I pretend to be insulted and tell them in no uncertain terms to clear off.

There, the foundation of our friendship is laid, till tomorrow!

Yours, Anne

194

a   . . . . . .

b   9

21 June 1942.
Sunday.

Dear Kitty,

Our whole 1 L II is trembling, the reason is of course that the teachers' meeting is to be held soon.[1] There is much speculation as to who will move up and who will stay put, G.Z., my neighbor and I, are highly amused at C.N. and Jacques Kokernoot, the two boys behind us. They won't have a florin left for the holidays, it will all be gone on betting. "You'll move up," "shan't," "shall," from morning till night. Even[3] G.'s pleas for silence and my angry outbursts don't calm them. According to me, a quarter of the class should stay where they are; there are some absolute cuckoos, but teachers are the most biggest freaks on earth, so perhaps they will be freakish in the right way for once.

| 10   I am not afraid about my girl friends and myself,[5] some holiday tasks and reexaminations and we'll squeeze[6] through somehow, though I am not too certain | about my math. Still, we can but wait patiently. Till then, we cheer each other along.[9] [10]

c

Sunday, 21 June, 1942

Dear Kitty,

Our whole class B1 is trembling, the reason is that the teachers' meeting is to be held soon. There is much speculation as to who will move up and who will stay put. Miep de Jong and I are highly amused at Wim and Jacques, the two boys behind us. They won't have a florin left for the holidays, it will all be gone on betting. "You'll move up," "Shan't," "Shall," from morning till night. Even Miep pleads for silence and my angry outbursts don't calm them.

According to me, a quarter of the class should stay where they are; there are some absolute cuckoos, but teachers are the greatest freaks on earth, so perhaps they will be freakish in the *right* way for once.

I'm not afraid about my girl friends and myself, we'll squeeze through somehow, though I'm not too certain about my math. Still we can but wait patiently. Till then, we cheer each other along.

195

a

. . . . . .

b

I get along quite well with all my teachers, 9 in all, 7 masters and 2 mistresses.[1] Mr. Keesing, the old man who teaches math, was very annoyed with me for a long time because I chatter so much, so I had to write a composition with "a chatterbox" as the subject. A chatterbox, whatever could one write?[5] However, deciding I would puzzle that out later, I wrote it in my notebook and tried to keep quiet.[7]

That evening when I'd finished my other homework, my eyes fell on the title in my notebook.[9] [10]I pondered, while chewing the end of my fountain pen, that anyone can scribble some nonsense in large letters with the words well spaced, but the difficulty | was to find a proof beyond doubt of the necessity of talking. I thought and thought and then, suddenly having an idea, filled my three allotted sides and felt completely satisfied. My arguments were that talking is a feminine characteristic and that I would do my best to keep it under control, but I should never be cured, for my mother talked as much as I, probably more, and what can one do about inherited qualities?

| 11

c

I get along quite well with all my teachers, nine in all, seven masters and two mistresses. Mr. Keptor, the old math master, was very annoyed with me for a long time because I chatter so much. So I had to write a composition with "A Chatterbox" as the subject. A chatterbox! Whatever could one write? However, deciding I would puzzle that out later, I wrote it in my notebook, and tried to keep quiet.

That evening, when I'd finished my other homework, my eyes fell on the title in my notebook. I pondered, while chewing the end of my fountain pen, that anyone can scribble some nonsense in large letters with the words well spaced but the difficulty was to prove beyond doubt the necessity of talking. I thought and thought and then, suddenly having an idea, filled my three allotted sides and felt completely satisfied. My arguments were that talking is a feminine characteristic and that I would do my best to keep it under control, but I should never be cured, for my mother talked as much as I, probably more, and what can one do about inherited qualities?

196

b

     Mr. Keesing had to[1] laugh at my arguments but when I carried on holding forth in the next lesson, another composition followed. This time it was "Incurable Chatterbox," I handed this in and Keesing made no complaints for two whole lessons. But in the third lesson it was too much for him again. "Anne Frank, as punishment for talking, will do a composition entitled 'Quack, quack quack, says Mrs. Natterbeak.' " Shouts of laughter from the class. I had to laugh too, although I felt that my inventiveness on this subject was exhausted. I had to think of something else, something entirely original. I was in luck, as my friend Susanne writes good poetry and offered to help by doing the composition from beginning to end in verse. I jumped for joy. Keesing wanted to make a fool of me with this absurd theme, I would get my own back and make him the laughingstock of the whole class. The poem was finished and was perfect! It was about a mother duck and a father swan who had 3 baby ducklings. The baby ducklings were bitten to death by Father because they quacked too much. Luckily Keesing saw the joke, he read the poem out loud to the class, with comments, and also to various other classes. Since then I am allowed to talk, never get extra work, in fact Keesing always jokes about it.

Yours, Anne

| 12 (margin note)

c

     Mr. Keptor had to laugh at my arguments, but when I continued to hold forth in the next lesson, another composition followed. This time it was "Incurable Chatterbox," I handed this in and Keptor made no complaints for two whole lessons. But in the third lesson it was too much for him again. "Anne, as punishment for talking, will do a composition entitled 'Quack, quack, quack, says Mrs. Natterbeak.' " Shouts of laughter from the class. I had to laugh too, although I felt that my inventiveness on this subject was exhausted. I had to think of something else, something entirely original. I was in luck, as my friend Sanne writes good poetry and offered to help by doing the whole composition in verse. I jumped for joy. Keptor wanted to make a fool of me with this absurd theme, I would get my own back and make him the laughingstock of the whole class. The poem was finished and was perfect. It was about a mother duck and a father swan who had three baby ducklings. The baby ducklings were bitten to death by Father because they chattered too much. Luckily Keptor saw the joke, he read the poem out loud to the class, with comments, and also to various other classes.

     Since then I am allowed to talk, never get extra work, in fact Keptor always jokes about it.

Yours, Anne

197

· · · · · ·

13

Wednesday 24 June 1942.

Dear Kitty,

It is boiling hot, we are all positively melting and in this heat I have to go on foot everywhere. Now I can fully appreciate how nice a tram is, but that is a forbidden luxury for Jews. Shanks's pony is good enough for us. I had to visit the dentist in the Jan Luikenstraat in the lunch hour yesterday, it is a long way from our school in the Stad-stimmertuinen, I nearly fell asleep in school that afternoon. Luckily, the dentist's assistant was very kind and gave me a drink[4]—she's a good sort. We are allowed to go on the ferry and that is about all, there is a little boat from the Jozef Israëlskade, where the man took us at once when we asked him.* It is not the Dutch people's fault that we are having such a miserable time. I do wish I didn't have to go to school, as my bicycle was stolen in the Easter holidays[14] and Daddy has given Mummy's to some Christian acquaintances for

| 14 safekeeping. But thank goodness, the holidays are almost here, | one more week and the agony is over. Something amusing happened yesterday, I was passing the bicycle sheds when someone called out to me. I looked around and there was the nice-looking boy I met on the previous evening, at Wilma's home. He came shyly towards me and introduced himself as Hello Silberberg. I was rather surprised and wondered what he wanted, but I didn't have to wait long, he asked if I would allow him to accompany me to school. "As

*From the 1920s a ferry point between Jozef Israëlskade and Amstelkade, facing the Apollo Hall, was used by foot passengers to cross the Amstel Canal.

Wednesday, 24 June, 1942

Dear Kitty,

It is boiling hot, we are all positively melting, and in this heat I have to walk every-where. Now I can fully appreciate how nice a tram is; but that is a forbidden luxury for Jews—shank's mare is good enough for us. I had to visit the dentist in the Jan Luykenstraat in the lunch hour yesterday. It is a long way from our school in the Stadstimmertuinen; I nearly fell asleep in school that afternoon. Luckily, the dentist's assistant was very kind and gave me a drink—she's a good sort.

We are allowed on the ferry and that is about all. There is a little boat from the Josef aelskade, the man there took us at once when we asked him. It is not the Dutch people's fault that we are having such a miserable time.

I do wish I didn't have to go to school, as my bicycle was stolen in the Easter holidays and Daddy has given Mummy's to a Christian family for safekeeping. But thank goodness, the holidays are nearly here, one more week and the agony is over. Something amusing happened yesterday, I was passing the bicycle sheds when someone called out to me. I looked around and there was the nice-looking boy I met on the previous evening, at my girl friend Eva's home. He came shyly towards me and introduced himself as Harry Goldberg. I was rather surprised and wondered what he wanted, but I didn't have to wait

slept here on Saturday night. | x Monday 29 June was a fairly quiet day. In the morning I went as usual to Hanneli's and we did some shopping together; in the afternoon Jacque went to Hanneli's and I was bored stiff. Hello was to have come in the evening, but he

you are going my way in any case,⁹ I will," I replied and so we went together. Hello is sixteen and can tell all kinds of amusing stories, he was waiting for me again this morning and I expect he will from now on.

Anne.

Wednesday 1 July 1942.

Dear Kitty,

I have not had a moment to write to you until today. I was ⁸with friends all day on Thursday. On Friday we had visitors, and so it went on until today.

Hello and I have got to know each other well in a week, and he has told me a lot about his life, he comes from Gelsenkirchen and came to Holland alone and is living with his grandparents. His parents are in Belgium but he has no chance of getting there himself. Hello had a girl friend called Ursula, I know her too, a very soft, dull creature, now that he has met me he realizes that he was just daydreaming in Ursul's presence. I seem to act as a stimulant to keep him awake, you see we all have our uses and queer ones too at times!

long. He asked if I would allow him to accompany me to school. "As you're going my way in any case, I will," I replied and so we went together. Harry is sixteen and can tell all kinds of amusing stories. He was waiting for me again this morning and I expect he will from now on.

Yours, Anne

Tuesday, 30 June, 1942

Dear Kitty,

I've not had a moment to write to you until today. I was with friends all day on Thursday. On Friday we had visitors and so it went on until today. Harry and I have got to know each other well in a week, and he has told me a lot about his life; he came to Holland alone, and is living with his grandparents. His parents are in Belgium.

Harry had a girl friend called Fanny, I know her too, a very soft, dull creature. Now that he has met me, he realizes that he was just daydreaming in Fanny's presence. I seem to act as a stimulant to keep him awake. You see we all have our uses, and queer ones too at times!

Jopie slept here on Saturday night, but she went to Lies on Sunday and I was bored

a

rang up at six[7] P.M., I went to the telephone, and he said:

"Helmuth Silberberg here please may I speak to Anne."

"Yes, Hello, Anne speaking"

"Hullo Anne, how are you?"

"Very well, thank you!"

"I'm terribly sorry I can't come this evening, but I would like to just speak to you, is it all right if I come in ten minutes?"

"Yes, that's fine, good-by!!!!"

"good-by, I'll be with you soon"

Receiver down, I quickly changed into another frock, and tidied up my hair a bit.

| 38   Then I stood nervously at the window watching for him. At last I saw <u>him</u> coming. | It was a wonder I didn't dash down at once, instead I waited patiently until he rang. Then I went down, and as soon as I opened the door he burst out talking. "Anne, my grandmother thinks you are too young to go out regularly with me, and that I should go to the Löwenbachs, but perhaps you know that I'm not going out with Ursul any more!"

"No, I don't, have you quarreled?"

b

. . . . . .

c ·

stiff. Harry was to have come in the evening, but he rang up at 6 P.M., I went to the telephone, he said, "Harry Goldberg here, please may I speak to Anne?" "Yes, Harry, Anne speaking."

"Hullo, Anne, how are you?"

"Very well, thank you."

"I'm terribly sorry I can't come this evening, but I would like to just speak to you; is it all right if I come in ten minutes?"

"Yes, that's fine, good-by!"

"Good-by, I'll be with you soon."

Receiver down.

I quickly changed into another frock and smartened up my hair a bit. Then I stood nervously at the window watching for him. At last I saw *him* coming. It was a wonder I didn't dash down at once; instead I waited patiently until he rang. Then I went down and he positively burst in when I opened the door. "Anne, my grandmother thinks you are too young to go out regularly with me, and that I should go to the Leurs, but perhaps you know that I am not going out with Fanny any more!"

"No, why is that, have you quarreled?"

"No, not at all I told Ursul that we didn't get on well together, so it was better for us not to go out together any more, but she was always welcome in our home, and I hoped I should be in hers. You see, I thought Ursul had been going out with another boy and treated her accordingly. But that was quite untrue. And now my uncle says I should apologize to Ursul, but of course I didn't want to do that so I finished the whole affair, that was just one of the many reasons. |

39

My grandmother would rather I went with Ursul than you, but that's not what I think or what I plan to do, old people have such terribly old-fashioned ideas at times, but I just can't fall into line. I need my grandparents, but in a sense they need me too. From now on I shall be free on Wednesday evenings. Officially I go to wood-carving lessons to please my grandparents, in actual fact I go to a meeting of the Zionist party. I'm not supposed to because my grandparents are very much against Zionism, I am by no means a fanatic, but I have a leaning that way and find it interesting.

But lately it has become such a mess there that I am going to quit, so next Wednesday will be my last time. Then I shall be able to see you on Wednesday evening, Saturday evening, Saturday afternoon, Sunday afternoon and perhaps more."

"But your grandparents are against it, you can't do it behind their backs."

40

"Love finds a way."

. . . . . .

"No, not at all. I told Fanny that we didn't get on well together, so it was better for us not to go out together any more, but she was always welcome in our home, and I hope I should be in hers. You see, I thought Fanny had been going out with another boy and treated her accordingly. But that was quite untrue. And now my uncle says I should apologize to Fanny, but of course I didn't want to do that so I finished the whole affair. That was just one of the many reasons. My grandmother would rather I went with Fanny than you, but I shan't; old people have such terribly old-fashioned ideas at times, but I just can't fall into line. I need my grandparents, but in a sense they need me too. From now on I shall be free on Wednesday evenings. Officially I go to wood-carving lessons to please my grandparents, in actual fact I go to a meeting of the Zionist Movement. I'm not supposed to, because my grandparents are very much against the Zionists. I'm by no means a fanatic, but I have a leaning that way and find it interesting. But lately it has become such a mess there that I'm going to quit, so next Wednesday will be my last time. Then I shall be able to see you on Wednesday evening, Saturday afternoon, Sunday afternoon, and perhaps more."

"But your grandparents are against it, you can't do it behind their backs!"

"Love finds a way."

Then we passed Blankevoort's bookshop,* and there stood Peter Schiff with two other boys; it's the first time he has greeted me for ages, I was really pleased. Hello and I walked on and on and suddenly we were walking behind Daddy and Mummy, by pure chance since they were coming back from the Katzes' at this odd hour.

And then I stopped outside the house a little while talking to Hello then the Sulmans came by with Jantje, who was tagging along again of course, and the end of it all was that I should meet Hello at 5 minutes past eight in front of his house on Thursday evening.

On Monday night I also met Mr. van Pels, who treated Jacque, Lies, Ilse and me to an ice cream, then we went to oasis where we met Mr. Bernhardt, who also bought me an ice cream.

*Blankevoort's Subscription Library was at 62, Zuider Amstellaan, now Rooseveltlaan (1942 Amsterdam Telephone Directory).

a 15 [because he is just a friend or as Mummy puts it one of my beaux.]

b | 16 On Monday night Hello visited us to meet Daddy and Mummy, I had bought a cream cake, sweets, tea and fancy biscuits, quite a spread, but | neither Hello nor I felt like sitting stiffly side by side indefinitely, so we went for a walk and it was already ten[2] past eight when he brought me home. Daddy was very cross, and thought it was very wrong of me to be[6] home so late and I had to promise to be in at ten to 8 in future. Next Saturday[7] I've been invited to his house. My girl friend Jacque teases me the whole time about Hello; I'm honestly not in love, oh, no, I can surely have boy friends,[9] no one thinks anything of that.

c Then we passed the bookshop on the corner, and there stood Peter Wessel with two other boys; he said "Hullo"—it's the first time he has spoken to me for ages, I was really pleased.

Harry and I walked on and on and the end of it all was that I should meet him at five minutes to seven in the front of his house next evening.

Yours, Anne

Friday, 3 July, 1942

Dear Kitty,

Harry visited us yesterday to meet my parents, I had bought a cream cake, sweets, tea, and fancy biscuits, quite a spread, but neither Harry nor I felt like sitting stiffly side by side indefinitely, so we went for a walk, and it was already ten past eight when he brought me home. Daddy was very cross, and thought it was very wrong of me because it is dangerous for Jews to be out after eight o'clock, and I had to promise to be in by ten to eight in future.

Tomorrow I've been invited to his house. My girl friend Jopie teases me the whole time about Harry. I'm honestly not in love, oh, no, I can surely have boy friends—no one thinks anything of that—but one boy friend, or beau, as Mother calls him, seems to be quite different.

a | 41   Hello went | to see Wilma one evening and she told me that she asked him, who do you like best Ursul or Anne, he said; "it's nothing to do with you." But when he left (they hadn't chatted together any more the whole evening) he said: now listen it's Anne, so long, and don't tell a soul." And like a flash he was gone. It's easy to see that Hello is in love with me, rather fun for a change.

Margot would say Hello is a decent lad, and I agree, but he is more than that. Mummy is full of praise, a good-looking boy, a well-behaved, nice boy; I'm glad that the whole family approve of him, except for my girl friends, whom he thinks very childish, *and there*

| 42   *he is right, except for Ilse whom I consider* | *not only childish, but no longer very nice either!!!!¹ Anne Frank.*

b   18
┌──┐
                                              Sunday morning 5 July 1942.
Dearest Kitty,
    Our examination results were announced in the Jewish Theater last Friday, I couldn't have hoped for better, my report is not at all bad, I had one unsatisfactory, a 5 for algebra, and the rest were all sevens or eights, and two sixes. They were certainly pleased at home, although over the question of marks my parents are quite different from most, they don't care a bit whether my reports are good or bad as long as I am well and happy, and not too cheeky, then the rest will come by itself.
└──┘

c   Harry went to see Eva one evening and she told me that she asked him, "Who do you like best, Fanny or Anne?" He said, "It's nothing to do with you!" But when he left (they hadn't chatted together any more the whole evening), "Now listen, it's Anne, so long, and don't tell a soul." And like a flash he was gone.

It's easy to see that Harry is in love with me, rather fun for a change. Margot would say, "Harry is a decent lad." I agree, but he is more than that. Mummy is full of praise: a good-looking boy, a well-behaved, nice boy. I'm glad that the whole family approves of him. He likes them too, but he thinks my girl friends are very childish, and he's quite right.

Yours, Anne

                                              Sunday morning, 5 July, 1942
Dear Kitty,
    Our examination results were announced in the Jewish Theater last Friday. I couldn't have hoped for better. My report is not at all bad, I had one *vix satis* [unsatisfactory], a five for algebra, two sixes, and the rest were all sevens or eights. They were certainly pleased at home, although over the question of marks my parents are quite different from most. They don't care a bit whether my reports are good or bad as long as I'm well and happy, and not too cheeky: then the rest will come by itself. I am just the opposite.

203

. . . . . .

b

> I am just the opposite. I don't want to do badly; I should really have stayed in the 7th form in the Montessori School, but was accepted for the Jewish Secondary, but when all the Jewish children had to go to Jewish schools, Mr. Elte took Lies Goslar and me conditionally after a bit of persuasion. Lies also went up but after a tough re-examination in geometry.
>
> 19
>
> My sister Margot has her report too, brilliant as usual. She would move up cum laude if that existed at school, she is so brainy!

b

¹Daddy has been at home a lot lately, as there is nothing for him to do at business, it must be rotten to feel so superfluous. Mr. Kleiman has taken over Opekta and Mr. Kugler Gies and Co, which deals in (substitute) spices and was only founded in 1941. When we walked across our little square together a few days ago Daddy began to talk of us going into | 17 hiding, he is very worried that it will be very | difficult for us to live completely cut off from the world. I asked him why on earth he was beginning to talk of that already "Yes Anne," he said "you know that we have been taking food, clothes, furniture to other people for more than a year now, we don't want our belongings to be seized by the Germans, but we most certainly don't want to fall into their clutches⁹ ourselves. So we shall disappear of our own accord and not wait until they come and fetch us."

"But Daddy, when would it be?"

he spoke so seriously that I grew very anxious.

c

I don't want to be a bad pupil; I should really have stayed in the seventh form in the Montessori School, but was accepted for the Jewish Secondary. When all the Jewish children had to go to Jewish schools, the headmaster took Lies and me conditionally after a bit of persuasion. He relied on us to do our best and I don't want to let him down. My sister Margot has her report too, brilliant as usual. She would move up with *cum laude* [move up *cum laude*] if that existed at school, she is so brainy. Daddy has been at home a lot lately, as there is nothing for him to do at business; it must be rotten to feel so superfluous. Mr. Koophuis has taken over Travies and Mr. Kraler the firm Kolen & Co. When we walked across our little square together a few days ago, Daddy began to talk of us going into hiding. I asked him why on earth he was beginning to talk of that already. "Yes, Anne," he said, "you know that we have been taking food, clothes, furniture to other people for more than a year now. We don't want our belongings to be seized by the Germans, but we certainly don't want to fall into their clutches ourselves. So we shall disappear of our own accord and not wait until they come and fetch us."

"But, Daddy, when would it be?" He spoke so seriously that I grew very anxious.

204

. . . . . .

"Don't you worry about it, we shall arrange everything. Make the most of your carefree young life while you can."

That was all. Oh, may the fulfillment of these somber words remain far distant yet.

Yours, Anne

18

Sunday morning 5 July 1942.

Dearest Kitty,

Our examination results were announced in the Jewish Theater last Friday, I couldn't have hoped for better, my report is not at all bad, I had one unsatisfactory, a 5 for algebra, and the rest were all sevens[2], [3]two eights[4], and two sixes.[5] They were certainly pleased at home, although over the question of marks my parents are quite different from most[6], they don't care a bit whether my reports[8] are good or bad as long as I am well and happy, and not too cheeky, then the rest will come by itself. I am just the opposite. I don't want to do badly; I should really have stayed in the 7th form in the Montessori School, but was accepted for the Jewish Secondary, but when all the Jewish children had to go to Jewish schools, Mr. Elte took Lies Goslar and me conditionally after a bit of persuasion[17]. Lies also went up, but after a tough re-examination in geometry. Poor Lies, she can never work

19 properly[18] at home; her little sister plays in her tiny[20] room all day, | a spoilt baby nearly 2 years old. If Gabi doesn't get her way she starts yelling and if Lies doesn't bother with her then Mrs. Goslar starts yelling. Lies can't possibly work properly like that and the hundreds of extra lessons she's getting won't be of much use to her.

[25]And the kind of household the Goslars run;[26] of the five rooms on Zuider Amstellaan one is rented out, Mrs. Goslar's parents live in the porch next to it but[28] eat with the family, then there is a maid, the baby, the always absent-minded and absent Mr. Goslar, and the always nervous and irritable Mrs. Goslar, who is expecting again. Lies with her two left hands is as good as lost in this bear garden.

My sister Margot has her report too, brilliant as usual. She would move up cum laude
20 if that existed at school, she is so brainy! | There goes the doorbell, Hello's here, I'll stop

yours, Anne

"Don't you worry about it, we shall arrange everything. Make the most of your carefree young life while you can." That was all. Oh, may the fulfillment of these somber words remain far distant yet!

Yours, Anne

205

Wednesday 8 July 1942.

I still have a whole lot to write in my diary, on Sunday Hello came over to our place, on Saturday we went out with Fredie Weiss, and over to oasis of course. On Sunday morning Hello and I lay on our balcony in the sun, on Sunday afternoon[1] he was going to come back, but at about 3 o'clock a policeman arrived and called from the door downstairs, Miss Margot Frank, Mummy went down and the policeman gave her a card which said that Margot Frank has to report to the S.S.*

Wednesday 8 July 1942.

Dear Kitty,

Years seem to have passed[5] between Sunday and now, so much has happened, it is as if the whole world had turned upside down, but I am still alive, Kitty, and that is the main thing, Daddy says.

Yes, I'm still alive indeed, but don't ask where or how. You wouldn't understand a word, so I will begin by telling you what happened on Sunday afternoon.

At three o'clock (Hello had just gone, but was coming back later) someone rang the front doorbell, I was lying lazily reading a book on the veranda in the sunshine so I didn't hear it[14]. A bit later, Margot appeared at the kitchen door looking very excited. "The S.S. have sent a call-up notice for Daddy," she whispered "Mummy has gone to see Mr. van Pels[16] already."*

---

*On Saturday 4 July 1942 the *Zentralstelle für jüdische Auswanderung* [Central Office for Jewish Emigration] issued the first few thousand call-up notices to Jews. Most of those called up were German Jews and their number included many boys and girls aged from fifteen to eighteen, who had to leave without their parents. The call-up notices were sent by registered post and delivered by the Post Office one day later. (L. de Jong, *Het Koninkrijk der Nederlanden in de Tweede Wereldoorlog.* Vol. 6 [1975: The Hague, Nijhoff], p. 5.)

Wednesday, 8 July, 1942

Dear Kitty,

Years seem to have passed between Sunday and now. So much has happened, it is just as if the whole world had turned upside down. But I am still alive, Kitty, and that is the main thing, Daddy says.

Yes, I'm still alive, indeed, but don't ask where or how. You wouldn't understand a word, so I will begin by telling you what happened on Sunday afternoon.

At three o'clock (Harry had just gone, but was coming back later) someone rang the front doorbell. I was lying lazily reading a book on the veranda in the sunshine, so I didn't hear it. A bit later, Margot appeared at the kitchen door looking very excited. "The S.S. have sent a call-up notice for Daddy," she whispered. "Mummy has gone to see Mr. Van Daan already." (Van Daan is a friend who works with Daddy in the business.) It was a

Mummy was terribly upset and went straight to Mr. van Pels he came straight back to us and I was told that Daddy had been called up. The door was locked and no one was allowed to come into our house any more. Daddy and Mummy had long ago taken measures, and Mummy assured me that Margot would not have to go and that all of us would be leaving next day. Of course I started to cry terribly and there was an awful to-do in our house. Daddy and Mummy had taken a whole lot of things out of the house already, but when it comes to the point one is bound to miss so much.

| 22

It was a great shock to me, a call-up; everyone knows what that means, I picture concentration camps and lonely cells | —should we let him be doomed to this? "Of course ¹he won't go," declared Margot while we waited together "Mummy has gone to the v.P.s to ask whether we should move into our hiding place tomorrow. The v.P.s are going with us, there will be 7 of us in all." Silence. We couldn't talk any more, thinking about Daddy, who, little knowing what was going on, was visiting in the Joodse invalide;* waiting for Mummy, the heat and suspense all made us very overawed and silent.

Suddenly the bell rang again. "That is Hello," I said. "Don't open the door." Margot held me back, but it was not necessary as we heard Mummy and Mr. v.P. downstairs, talking to Hello, then they came in and closed the door behind them. Each time the bell went Margot or I had to creep softly down to see if it was Daddy, not opening the door to anyone else.

---

*The Joodse Invalide provided shelter for needy and elderly Jews. It was on the corner of Weesperstraat and Nieuwe Achtergracht.

great shock to me, a call-up; everyone knows what that means. I picture concentration camps and lonely cells— should we allow him to be doomed to this? "Of course he won't go," declared Margot, while we waited together. "Mummy has gone to the Van Daans to discuss whether we should move into our hiding place tomorrow. The Van Daans are going with us, so we shall be seven in all." Silence. We couldn't talk any more, thinking about Daddy, who, little knowing what was going on, was visiting some old people in the Joodse Invalide; waiting for Mummy, the heat and suspense, all made us very overawed and silent.

Suddenly the bell rang again. "That is Harry," I said. "Don't open the door." Margot held me back, but it was not necessary as we heard Mummy and Mr. Van Daan downstairs, talking to Harry, then they came in and closed the door behind them. Each time the bell went, Margot or I had to creep softly down to see if it was Daddy, not opening the door to anyone else.

Margot and I were sent | out of the room, v.P. wanted to talk to Mummy alone. (V.P. is an acquaintance and a partner in Daddy's business) When we were alone together in our bedroom, Margot told me that the call-up did not concern Daddy but her. I was more frightened than ever and began to cry. Margot is 16, would they really take girls of that age away alone? But thank goodness she won't go, Mummy said so herself, that must be what Daddy meant when he talked about us going into hiding.

Into hiding, where would we go, in a town or the country, in a house or a cottage, when, how, where? . . . . These were many questions I could not ask but I couldn't get them out of my mind. Margot and I began to pack some of our most vital belongings into a school satchel, the first thing I put in was this diary, then hair curlers, handkerchiefs, schoolbooks, a comb, old letters, I put in the craziest things with the idea that we were

going into hiding, but I'm not sorry, memories | mean more to me than dresses.

At five o'clock Daddy finally arrived, and we phoned Mr. Kleiman to ask if he could come round in the evening. V.P. went and fetched Miep. Miep came and took some shoes, dresses, coats, underwear, and stockings away in a bag, promising that she would return in the evening. Then silence fell on the house; not one of us felt like eating anything, it was still hot and everything was very strange. We let our large upstairs room to a certain Mr. Goldschmidt, a divorced man in his thirties, who appeared to have nothing to do on this particular evening, we simply could not get rid of him without being rude[23], he hung around until ten o'clock.

Margot and I were sent out of the room. Van Daan wanted to talk to Mummy alone. When we were alone together in our bedroom, Margot told me that the call-up was not for Daddy, but for her. I was more frightened than ever and began to cry. Margot is sixteen; would they really take girls of that age away alone? But thank goodness she won't go, Mummy said so herself; that must be what Daddy meant when he talked about us going into hiding.

Into hiding—where would we go, in a town or the country, in a house or a cottage, when, how, where . . . ?

These were questions I was not allowed to ask, but I couldn't get them out of my mind. Margot and I began to pack some of our most vital belongings into a school satchel, The first thing I put in was this diary, then hair curlers, handkerchiefs, schoolbooks, a comb, old letters; I put in the craziest things with the idea that we were going into hiding. But I'm not sorry, memories mean more to me than dresses.

At five o'clock Daddy finally arrived, and we phoned Mr. Koophuis to ask if he could come around in the evening. Van Daan went and fetched Miep. Miep has been in the business with Daddy since 1933 and has become a close friend, likewise her brand-new husband, Henk. Miep came and took some shoes, dresses, coats, underwear, and stockings away in her bag, promising to return in the evening. Then silence fell on the house; not one of us felt like eating anything, it was still hot and everything was very strange. We let our large upstairs room to a certain Mr. Goudsmit, a divorced man in his thirties, who appeared to have nothing to do on this particular evening; we simply could not get rid of him without being rude; he hung about until ten o'clock. At eleven o'clock Miep and

208

a

Miep Gies and her husband Jan arrived at about 11 o'clock in the evening to take some more things away. Next day we left the house by a quarter to eight I had a (combinashion) on then two vests and two pairs of pants then a dress and a skirt then a wool cardigan and a coat, it was pouring and so I put on a headscarf, and Mummy and | I each carried a satchel under our arm. Margot went too with a satchel on her bicycle, and we all made for the office.

| 43

b

[1]At eleven o'clock Miep and Jan Gies arrived, Miep has been in the business with Daddy since 1933 and has become a close friend, likewise her brand-new husband, Jan. Once again shoes, stockings, books and underclothes disappeared into Miep's bag and Jan's deep pockets; and at eleven-thirty they too disappeared.

| 25

I was dog-tired and although I knew it would be | my last night in my own bed, I fell asleep immediately and didn't wake up until Mummy called me at 5.30 the next morning. [7]Luckily it was not so hot as Sunday; [8]warm rain fell steadily all day. We put on heaps of clothes as if we were going to the North Pole, the sole reason being to take clothes with us. No Jew in our situation would have dreamed of going out with a suitcase full of clothing. I had on two vests, three pairs of pants, a dress, on top of that a skirt, jacket, summer coat, two pairs of stockings, lace-up shoes, woolly cap, scarf, and still much more[9]; I was nearly stifled before we started, but no one inquired about that. Margot filled her satchel with schoolbooks, fetched her bicycle and rode off behind Miep into the unknown as far as I was concerned. You see I still didn't know where our secret hiding place was to be.

26

At 7.30 the door closed behind us, Moortje, my little cat, was the only creature to whom I said farewell. She would have a good home with the neighbors. This was all written in a letter addressed[16] to Mr. Goldsmith

c

Henk Van Santen arrived. Once again, shoes, stockings, books, and underclothes disappeared into Miep's bag and Henk's deep pockets; and at eleven-thirty they too disappeared. I was dog-tired and although I knew that it would be my last night in my own bed, I fell asleep immediately and didn't wake up until Mummy called me at five-thirty the next morning. Luckily it was not so hot as Sunday; warm rain fell steadily all day. We put on heaps of clothes as if we were going to the North Pole, the sole reason being to take clothes with us. No Jew in our situation would have dreamed of going out with a suitcase full of clothing. I had on two vests, three pairs of pants, a dress, on top of that a skirt, jacket, summer coat, two pairs of stockings, lace-up shoes, woolly cap, scarf, and still more; I was nearly stifled before we started, but no one inquired about that.

Margot filled her satchel with schoolbooks, fetched her bicycle, and rode off behind Miep into the unknown, as far as I was concerned. You see I still didn't know where our secret hiding place was to be. At seven-thirty the door closed behind us. Moortje, my little cat, was the only creature to whom I said farewell. She would have a good home with the neighbors. This was all written in a letter addressed to Mr. Goudsmit.

b

The stripped beds, the breakfast things lying on the table, a pound of meat in the kitchen for the cat, all giving the impression that we had left helter-skelter. But we didn't care about impressions, we only wanted to get away, only escape and arrive safely, nothing else.

Continued tomorrow.

Yours, Anne

Thursday 9 July 1942.

27   Dear Kitty,
So we walked through the pouring rain, Daddy, Mummy and I, each with a school satchel and shopping bag filled to the brim with all kinds of things thrown together anyhow. We got sympathetic looks from people on their way to work. You could see by their faces how sorry they were they couldn't offer us a lift, the gaudy yellow star spoke for itself.[13]

c

There was one pound of meat in the kitchen for the cat, breakfast things lying on the table, stripped beds, all giving the impression that we had left helter-skelter. But we didn't care about impressions, we only wanted to get away, only escape and arrive safely, nothing else. Continued tomorrow.

Yours, Anne

Thursday, 9 July, 1942

Dear Kitty,
So we walked in the pouring rain, Daddy, Mummy, and I, each with a school satchel and shopping bag filled to the brim with all kinds of things thrown together anyhow.

We got sympathetic looks from people on their way to work. You could see by their faces how sorry they were they couldn't offer us a lift; the gaudy yellow star spoke for itself.

Daddy and Mummy now told me lots of things. We would be going to Daddy's office and over it a floor had been made ready for us. The van Pels family would also be coming, so that there would be seven of us, the van Pels cat would be coming along too, which meant we'd have a bit of variety.

We arrived safely at the office and went straight upstairs there was first a W.C. and then a small bathroom with a new basin, next door to that was a small room with two divans, that was Margot's and my room. It had three built-in cupboards, next door to it was another room, Daddy's and Mummy's, there were two divans there as well and two small tables and a smoker's table, and a small set of bookshelves and another built-in cupboard, there were 150 cans of vegetables and all sorts of other supplies, then we came to a small corridor with another two doors, one went to the passage that led downstairs to Daddy's office. And the other led to our small bathroom, then a very steep staircase led upstairs to the large kitchen-living room for the van Pels family and a little room for Peter and then there was an attic with a loft.

Only when we were on the road did Mummy and Daddy begin to tell me bits and pieces about the plan. For months as many of our goods and chattels and our necessities of life as possible had been sent away, and they were sufficiently ready for us to have gone into hiding of our own accord on July 16. The plan had had to be speeded up 10 days because of this call-up, so our quarters would not be so well organized but we had to make the best of it.

28   The hiding place itself would be in the building where Daddy had his office. It will be hard for outsiders to understand, but I shall explain that later on. Daddy didn't have many people working for him, Mr. Kugler, Kleiman and Miep, and Bep Voskuyl, a twenty-three-year-old[7] typist, who all knew of our arrival. Mr. Voskuyl, Bep's father, who had not been told and two men worked in the warehouse.

Only when we were on the road did Mummy and Daddy begin to tell me bits and pieces about the plan. For months as many of our goods and chattels and necessities of life as possible had been sent away and they were sufficiently ready for us to have gone into hiding of our own accord on July 16. The plan had had to be speeded up ten days because of the call-up, so our quarters would not be so well organized, but we had to make the best of it. The hiding place itself would be in the building where Daddy has his office. It will be hard for outsiders to understand, but I shall explain that later on. Daddy didn't have many people working for him: Mr. Kraler, Koophuis, Miep, and Elli Vossen, a twenty-three-year-old typist who all knew of our arrival. Mr. Vossen, Elli's father, and two boys [men] worked in the warehouse; they had not been told.

a | ......

---

b

I will describe the building, there is a large warehouse on the ground floor which is[1] used as a store and that is subdivided into various little compartments, such as the milling room, where cinnamon, clove and substitute pepper were ground up, the stockroom and the veranda,[2] The front door to the house is next to the warehouse door, and inside the front door is a second doorway which leads to a staircase. There is another door at the top of the stairs with a frosted glass window in it, which has "Office" written in black | 29   letters across it. This is the large main office, very big, very light, and very full. | Bep, Miep and Mr. Kleiman work there in the daytime, a small dark room containing the safe, a wardrobe and a large cupboard, leads to a small, stuffy, dark director's office. Mr. Kugler and Mr. v.P. used to sit here, now it is only Mr. Kugler. One can reach Kugler's office from the passage, but only via a glass [6]door which can be opened from the inside but not easily from the outside from Kugler's office a long passage goes past the coal store, up four steps and leads to the showroom of the whole building, the private office. Dark, dignified furniture[10] linoleum and carpets on the floor, radio, smart lamp, everything first-class, next door there is a roomy kitchen with a hot-water faucet and a gas stove and next door the w.c. That is the first floor.

---

c

I will describe the building: there is a large warehouse on the ground floor which is used as a store. The front door to the house is next to the warehouse door, and inside the front door is a second doorway which leads to a staircase (A). There is another door at the top of the stairs, with a frosted glass window in it, which has "Office" written in black letters across it. That is the large main office, very big, very light, and very full. Elli, Miep, and Mr. Koophuis work there in the daytime. A small dark room containing the safe, a wardrobe, and a large cupboard leads to a small somewhat dark second office. Mr. Kraler and Mr. Van Daan used to sit here, now it is only Mr. Kraler. One can reach Kraler's office from the passage, but only via a glass door which can be opened from the inside, but not easily from the outside.

From Kraler's office a long passage goes past the coal store, up four steps and leads to the showroom of the whole building: the private office. Dark, dignified furniture, linoleum and carpets on the floor, radio, smart lamp, everything first-class. Next door there is a roomy kitchen with a hot-water faucet and a gas stove. Next door the W.C. That is the first floor.

212

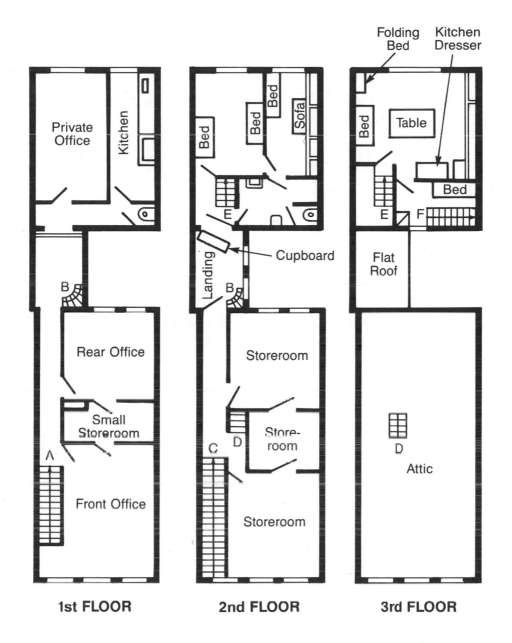

1st FLOOR **2nd FLOOR** **3rd FLOOR**

213

b

| 30   A wooden staircase leads from the downstairs passage to the next floor.[1] There is a small landing at the top. There is a door to the right and left of the landing, the left one leading | to the front of the house, with spice room, corridor room, a front room, and to the attics. One of those really steep Dutch staircases runs from the side to the other door opening on to the street.

To the right of the landing lies our "Secret Annexe." No one would ever guess that there would be so many rooms hidden behind that plain door painted gray. There's a little step in front of the door and then you are inside. There is a steep staircase immediately opposite the entrance. On the left a tiny passage brings you into a room, this room was to become the Frank family's bed-sitting-room, next door an even smaller room, study and bedroom for the two young ladies of the family. On the right a little room without windows, containing the washbasin and small w.c. compartment, with another door leading to Margot's and my room. If you go up the next flight of stairs and open the door,

| 31   you are simply amazed that there could be such a big light room | in such an old house by the canal. There is a stove in This[19] room (thanks to the fact that it was used before as Kugler's laboratory) and a sink. This is now the kitchen as well as bedroom for the v.P. couple, besides being general living room, dining room and scullery. A tiny little corridor room will become Peter v.P.'s apartment. Then just as on the lower landing there is a large attic. So there you are I have introduced you to the whole of our beautiful "Secret Annexe!"

yours, Anne

c

A wooden staircase leads from the downstairs passage to the next floor (B). There is a small landing at the top. There is a door at each end of the landing, the left one leading to a storeroom at the front of the house and to the attics. One of those really steep Dutch staircases runs from the side to the other door opening on to the street (C).

The right-hand door leads to our "Secret Annexe." No one would ever guess that there would be so many rooms hidden behind that plain gray door. There's a little step in front of the door and then you are inside.

There is a steep staircase immediately opposite the entrance (E). On the left a tiny passage brings you into a room which was to become the Frank family's bed-sitting-room, next door a smaller room, study and bedroom for the two young ladies of the family. On the right a little room without windows containing the washbasin and a small W.C. compartment, with another door leading to Margot's and my room. If you go up the next flight of stairs and open the door, you are simply amazed that there could be such a big light room in such an old house by the canal. There is a gas stove in this room (thanks to the fact that it was used as a laboratory) and a sink. This is now the kitchen [as well as bedroom] for the Van Daan couple, besides being general living room, dining room, and scullery.

A tiny little corridor room will become Peter Van Daan's apartment. Then, just as on the lower landing, there is a large attic. So there you are, I've introduced you to the whole of our beautiful "Secret Annexe."

Yours, Anne

a

. . . . . .

b   32

Friday 10 July 1942.

Dear Kitty,

I expect I have thoroughly bored you with my long-winded descriptions of our dwelling. But still I think you should know where I've landed up; how I've landed up is something you will gather only too well from all the letters that follow.

But first to continue my story—you see, I've not finished yet—when we arrived at 263, Prinsengracht, Miep led us quickly through the long passage, up the wooden stairs, straight to the "Secret Annexe." She closed the door behind us and we were alone[7] Margot was already waiting for us, having arrived much more quickly on her bicycle. Our living room and all the other rooms were chock-full of rubbish, indescribably so, all the cardboard boxes which had been sent to the office in the previous months lay piled on the floor and the beds; the little room was filled to the ceiling with bedclothes,[13]

33   We had to start clearing up[14] immediately, if we wished to sleep in decent beds that night. Mummy and Margot were not in a fit state to take part; they were tired and lay down on their unmade beds, they were wretched, [21]and lots more besides, but the two "clearers-up" of the family, Daddy and myself, wanted to start at once.

The whole day long we unpacked boxes, filled cupboards, hammered and tidied, until we were dead beat. We sank into clean beds that night. We hadn't had a bit of anything warm the whole day but we didn't care, Mummy and Margot were too tired and keyed up to eat and Daddy and I were too busy.

c

Friday, 10 July, 1942

Dear Kitty,

I expect I have thoroughly bored you with my long-winded descriptions of our dwelling. But still I think you should know where we've [I've] landed [up].

But to continue my story—you see, I've not finished yet—when we arrived at the Prinsengracht, Miep took us quickly upstairs and into the "Secret Annexe." She closed the door behind us and we were alone. Margot was already waiting for us, having come much faster on her bicycle. Our living room and all the other rooms were chock-full of rubbish, indescribably so. All the cardboard boxes which had been sent to the office in the previous months lay piled on the floor and the beds. The little room was filled to the ceiling with bedclothes. We had to start clearing up immediately, if we wished to sleep in decent beds that night. Mummy and Margot were not in a fit state to take part; they were tired and lay down on their [unmade] beds, they were miserable, and lots more besides. But the two "clearers-up" of the family—Daddy and myself—wanted to start at once.

The whole day long we unpacked boxes, filled cupboards, hammered and tidied, until we were dead beat. We sank into clean beds that night. We hadn't had a bit of anything warm the whole day, but we didn't care; Mummy and Margot were too tired and keyed up to eat, and Daddy and I were too busy.

215

b

On Tuesday morning we went on where we had left off the day before, Bep and Miep collected our rations for us, Daddy improved the poor blackout, we scrubbed the kitchen floor, and were on the go the whole day long

| 34 once more. I hardly had time to think about the great[2] change in my life | until Wednesday; then I had a chance, for the first time since our[5] arrival, to tell you[6] all about it[7], and at the same time to realize myself what had happened to me, and what was still going to happen.

Yours, Anne

35

Saturday 11 July 1942.

Dear Kitty,

[9]Daddy, Mummy and Margot can't get used to the sound of the Westertoren clock* yet, which tells us the time every quarter of an hour. I can. I loved it from the start, and especially in the night it's like a faithful friend. I expect you will be interested to hear what it feels like to hide; well, all I can say is that I don't know myself yet. I don't think I shall ever feel really at home in this house but that does not mean that I loathe it here, it is more like being on vacation in a very peculiar boardinghouse. Rather a mad way of looking at being in hiding perhaps but that is how it strikes me. The "Secret Annexe" is an ideal hiding place, although it leans to one side and is damp, you'd never find such a comfortable hiding place anywhere in Amsterdam, no perhaps not even in the whole of Holland.

*See photograph on p. 532. A.J.P.

c

On Tuesday morning we went on where we left off the day before. Elli and Miep collected our rations for us, Daddy improved the poor blackout, we scrubbed the kitchen floor, and were on the go the whole day long again. I hardly had time to think about the great change in my life until Wednesday. Then I had a chance, for the first time since our arrival, to tell you all about it, and at the same time to realize myself what had actually happened to me and what was still going to happen.

Yours, Anne

Saturday, 11 July, 1942

Dear Kitty,

Daddy, Mummy, and Margot can't get used to the sound of the Westertoren clock yet, which tells us the time every quarter of an hour. I can. I loved it from the start, and especially in the night it's like a faithful friend. I expect you will be interested to hear what it feels like to "disappear"; well, all I can say is that I don't know myself yet. I don't think I shall ever feel really at home in this house, but that does not mean that I loathe it here, it is more like being on vacation in a very peculiar boardinghouse. Rather a mad idea [mad way of looking at being in hiding], perhaps, but that is how it strikes me. The "Secret Annexe" is an ideal hiding place. Although it leans to one side and is damp, you'd never find such a comfortable hiding place anywhere in Amsterdam, no, perhaps not even in the whole of Holland.

b 36 Our little room looked very bare at first with nothing on the walls; but thanks to Daddy who had brought my picture postcards and film-star collection on beforehand, and with the aid of paste pot and brush I have transformed the walls into one gigantic picture. This makes it look much more cheerful, and when the v.Ps. come we'll get some wood from the attic and make a few little cupboards for the walls and other odds and ends to make it look more lively. Margot and Mummy are a little bit better now, Mummy felt well enough to cook some soup for the first time yesterday, but then forgot all about it, while she was downstairs talking, so the peas were burnt to a cinder and utterly refused to leave the pan. Mr. Kleiman has brought me "the young people's annual." The four of us went to the private office yesterday evening and turned on the radio, I was so terribly

37 frightened that someone might hear it that I simply begged Daddy | to come upstairs with me; Mummy understood how I felt and came too. We are very nervous in other ways too that the neighbors might hear us or see something going on. We made curtains straight away on the first day, really one can hardly call them curtains they are only loose, draughty strips of material, all different shapes, quality and pattern, which Daddy and I sewed together in a most unprofessional way; these works of art are fixed in position with drawing pins not to come down until we emerge from here[15][16]

c Our little room looked very bare at first with nothing on the walls; but thanks to Daddy who had brought my film-star collection and picture postcards on beforehand, and with the aid of paste pot and brush, I have transformed the walls into one gigantic picture. This makes it look much more cheerful, and, when the Van Daans come, we'll get some wood from the attic, and make a few little cupboards for the walls and other odds and ends to make it look more lively.

Margot and Mummy are a little bit better now. Mummy felt well enough to cook some soup for the first time yesterday, but then forgot all about it, while she was downstairs talking, so the peas were burned to a cinder and utterly refused to leave the pan. Mr. Koophuis has brought me a book called *Young People's Annual.* The four of us went to the private office yesterday evening and turned on the radio. I was so terribly frightened that someone might hear it that I simply begged Daddy to come upstairs with me. Mummy understood how I felt and came too. We are very nervous in other ways, too, that the neighbors might hear us or see something going on. We made curtains straight away on the first day. Really one can hardly call them curtains, they are just light, loose strips of material, all different shapes, quality, and pattern, which Daddy and I sewed together in a most unprofessional way. These works of art are fixed in position with drawing pins, not to come down until we emerge from here.

217

b   To the right of us is the local branch of the Keg company from Zaandam, and on the left a furniture workshop, so those people are not there after working hours, but even so, sounds could travel through the walls. We have forbidden Margot to cough at night[2], although she has a bad cold, and make her swallow large doses of codeine.

38   I am looking forward to Tuesday when the v.P.s arrive; it will be much more fun and not so quiet. It is the silence that frightens me so in the evenings and at night. I wish like anything[4] that one of our protectors could sleep here at night.

Yesterday we had a lot of work, we had to stone two baskets of cherries for the office, Mr. Kugler wants to preserve them. We are turning the cherry boxes into little bookshelves. We have to whisper and tread lightly during the day, otherwise the people in the warehouse might hear us.

Someone is calling me
yours, Anne

c   There are some large business premises on the right of us, and on the left a furniture workshop; there is no one there after working hours but even so, sounds could travel through the walls. We have forbidden Margot to cough at night, although she has a bad cold, and make her swallow large doses of codeine. I am looking for[ward to] Tuesday when the Van Daans arrive; it will be much more fun and not so quiet. It is the silence that frightens me so in the evenings and at night. I wish like anything that one of our protectors could sleep here at night. I can't tell you how oppressive it is *never* to be able to go outdoors, also I'm very afraid that we shall be discovered and be shot. That is not exactly a pleasant prospect. We have to whisper and tread lightly during the day, otherwise the people in the warehouse might hear us.

Someone is calling me.

Yours, Anne

a   . . . . . .

b   39

Friday 14 August 1942.

Dearest Kitty,

I have deserted you for a whole month, but honestly, there is so little news here that I can't find amusing things to tell you every day. The v.Ps. arrived on July 13. We thought they were coming on the 14th, but between 13 and 16[2] July the Germans called up people right and left[3] which created more and more unrest, so they played for safety, better a day too early than a day too late. At nine-thirty in the morning (we were still having breakfast) Peter arrived, the v.P.s' son, not sixteen yet, rather soft, shy, gawky youth; can't expect much from his company. Mr. and Mrs. v.P. arrived half an hour later; and to our great amusement she had a large pottie in her hat box. "I don't feel at home anywhere without my chamber," she declared, so it was the first thing to find its permanent resting place under her divan. Mr. v.P. did not bring his but carried a folding tea table under his arm. From the day they arrived we all had meals cozily together | and after three days it was just as if we 7[6] were one large family. Naturally the v.P.s were able to tell us a lot about the extra week they had lingered in the inhabited world. Among other things we were very interested to hear what had happened to our house and to Mr. Goldsmith.

| 40

c

Friday, 14 August, 1942

Dear Kitty,

I have deserted you for a whole month, but honestly, there is so little news here that I can't find amusing things to tell you every day. The Van Daans arrived on July 13. We thought they were coming on the fourteenth, but between the thirteenth and sixteenth of July the Germans called up people right and left which created more and more unrest, so they played for safety, better a day too early than a day too late. At nine-thirty in the morning (we were still having breakfast) Peter arrived, the Van Daans' son, not sixteen yet, a rather soft, shy, gawky youth; can't expect much from his company. He brought his cat (Mouschi) with him. Mr. and Mrs. Van Daan arrived half an hour later, and to our great amusement she had a large pottie in her hat box. "I don't feel at home anywhere without my chamber," she declared, so it was the first thing to find its permanent resting place under her divan. Mr. Van Daan did not bring his, but carried a folding tea table under his arm.

From the day they arrived we all had meals cozily together and after three days it was just as if we were one large family. Naturally the Van Daans were able to tell us a lot about the extra week they had spent in the inhabited world. Among other things we were very interested to hear what had happened to our house and to Mr. Goudsmit. Mr.

b   Mr. v. P. told us.

"Mr. Goldsmith phoned at nine o'clock on Monday morning and asked if I could come around. I went immediately and found G. in a state of great agitation. He let me read a letter that the Franks had left behind and wanted to take the cat to the neighbors as indicated in the letter, which pleased me. Mr. G. was afraid that the house would be searched so we went through all the rooms, tidied up a bit and cleared the table. Suddenly

c   Van Daan told us:

"Mr. Goudsmit phoned at nine o'clock on Monday morning and asked if I could come around. I went immediately and found G. in a state of great agitation. He let me read a letter that the Franks had left behind and wanted to take the cat to the neighbors as indicated in the letter, which pleased me. Mr. G. was afraid that the house would be searched so we went through all the rooms, tidied up a bit, and cleared away the breakfast things. Suddenly I discovered a writing pad on Mrs. Frank's desk with an address in

220

a   44   [Mr. van Pels repeated the story about Daddy being friends with an army captain
who had helped him to get away to Belgium, the story is now on everyone's lips
and we are greatly amused.]

b

| 41   I discovered a writing pad on Mrs. Frank's desk with an address in Maastricht* written
on it. Although I knew that this was done on purpose, I pretended to be very surprised
and | shocked and urged Mr. G. to tear up this unfortunate little piece of paper without
delay. I went on pretending that I knew nothing of your disappearance all the time, but
after seeing the paper I got a brain wave. "Mr. G"—I said—"it suddenly dawns on me
what this address may refer to. It all comes back to me very clearly, a high-ranking officer
was in the office about six[1] months ago, he appeared to be very friendly with Mr. F. and
offered to help him, should the need arise. He was indeed stationed in Maastricht. I think
he must have kept his word and somehow or other managed to take Mr. F. along with
him to Belgium and then on to Switzerland. I should tell this to any friends who may
inquire, don't of course mention Maastricht."

   With these words I left the house. Most of your friends know already, because I have
| 42   been told myself several times by different people." | We were highly amused at the story
and, when Mr. v.P. gave us further details laughed still more at the way people can let
their imagination run away with them.

   One family from the Merwedeplein had seen all four of us pass on bicycles very early
in the morning and another lady knew quite definitely that we were fetched by a military
car in the middle of the night.

Yours, Anne

*A city near the Belgian border. A.J.P.

c   Maastricht written on it. Although I knew that this was done on purpose, I pretended to
be very surprised and shocked and urged Mr. G. to tear up this unfortunate little piece
of paper without delay.

   "I went on pretending that I knew nothing of your disappearance all the time, but
after seeing the paper, I got a brain wave. 'Mr. Goudsmit'—I said—'it suddenly dawns
on me what this address may refer to. Now it all comes back to me, a high-ranking officer
was in the office about six months ago, he appeared to be very friendly with Mr. Frank
and offered to help him, should the need arise. He was stationed in Maastricht. I think
he must have kept his word and somehow or other managed to get them into Belgium
and then on to Switzerland. I should tell this to any friends who may inquire. Don't, of
course, mention Maastricht.'

   "With these words I left the house. Most of your friends know already, because I've
been told myself several times by different people."

   We were highly amused at the story and, when Mr. Van Daan gave us further details,
laughed still more at the way people can let their imagination run away with them. One
family had seen the pair [all four] of us pass on bicycles very early in the morning and
another lady knew quite definitely that we were fetched by a military car in the middle
of the night.

Yours, Anne

221

It's not really all that bad here, for we can cook for ourselves, and downstairs in Daddy's office we can listen to the radio.

| 44   I can write all the names and everything | openly in my diary now. Mr. Kleiman and Miep and also Bep Voskuyl have helped us so much, we have already had rhubarb, strawberries and cherries, and I don't think we'll be bored here just yet.

Mr. van Pels repeated the story about Daddy being friends with an army captain who had helped him to get away to Belgium, the story is now on everyone's lips and we are greatly amused. We have things to read as well and we are going to buy all sorts of games.

Of course we are not allowed to look out of the window at all or to go outside. Also we have to do everything softly in case they hear us below.

Now I shall stop because I still have a lot to do.

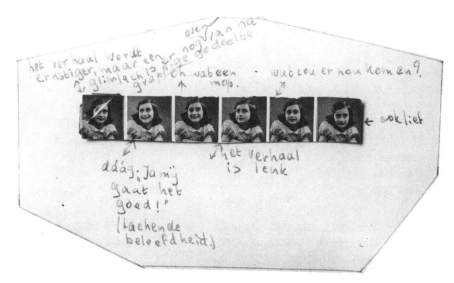

Captions (clockwise from top left):
Things are getting more serious, but there's still a smile left over from the funny bits.
Oh, what a joke.
Whatever next?
Nice one, as well.
That's a funny story.
Hello. "Yes I'm fine!" (smiling politely.)

To the whole club* in general.

Dearest Kitty,

When I am frightened at night, I get into Daddy's bed, he doesn't mind at all. One night the shooting went on so long that I bundled together all the bedthings and lay down on the floor next to his bed like a dog. 'Bye, Kitty Franken and friend François³ from Anne Frank.

Dearest Pop,

When there is a storm or if I can't sleep, I can get in with Pim, he doesn't mind. Greetings to Kees ter Heul, 'bye, Pop, or Emilie ter Heul-Helmer, from Anne Frank.

Dearest Phien,

If I have to go to the w.c. at night, I wait till Daddy has to go too we often meet in the bathroom at night, Greetings to Bobbel Breed-Philippiene Breed-Greve, from Anne Frank.

Dearest Marjan,

Daddy is a treasure⁴!!!! Marjan van Hoven and Jaap ter Duin from Anne Frank

Dearest Conny,

Most of the time Mummy is not nice, I'm much fonder of pim, greetings to Ru Duyff— Connie Duyff-Ralandt, from Anne Frank.

Dearest Lou,

Greetings to Kaki Kruivers—Lou Kruivers, de Poll from Annef rank.

Dearest Jetje and Emmy,

I only write to you once a month and Jacqueline isn't included.

Sunday 12 July 1942

A month ago today they were all being so nice to me because it was my birthday, but I have the feeling that I'm getting more estranged from Mummy and Margot, I worked very hard today, and everyone praised me to the skies but 5 minutes later they were getting at me again.

You can easily see the difference in how she treats Margot and how she treats me, for instance Margot has broken the vacuum cleaner which has meant we've had no light the whole day. Mummy said: "But Margot, it's easy to see⁶ you aren't used to work, or else you'd have known you don't jerk a vacuum cleaner out at the socket."**

⁸Margot said something or other and that was the end of the matter.

But this afternoon when I wanted to copy something out from Mummy's shopping list, because Mummy's writing is so illegible, she didn't want me to and I got another stiff

dressing down on the spot, with the whole family | joining in.

I don't fit in with them and that's something I've been feeling very much, especially lately. They get so soppy with each other that I would rather be on my own. And then they say how nice it is for the four of us to be together, ⁹and that we get on so well, but it never occurs to them for one moment that I mightn't feel like that at all.

---

*Mirjam Pressler, the German translator of the present work, has pointed out in the German edition (S. Fischer Verlag, 1988) that the names mentioned here by Anne Frank come from a series of Dutch books for young girls named after the heroine, Joop ter Heul. This series, also referred to in the diaries, concerns a club founded by Joop ter Heul and her girlfriends, including one by the name of Kitty Francken. The author, Cissy van Marxfeldt (1893–1948) describes their schooldays, marriage, motherhood and marital problems in four volumes. A.J.P.

**In German. A.J.P.

$$\frac{}{b}\ \ \ldots\ldots$$

$$\frac{}{c}\ \ \ldots\ldots$$

224

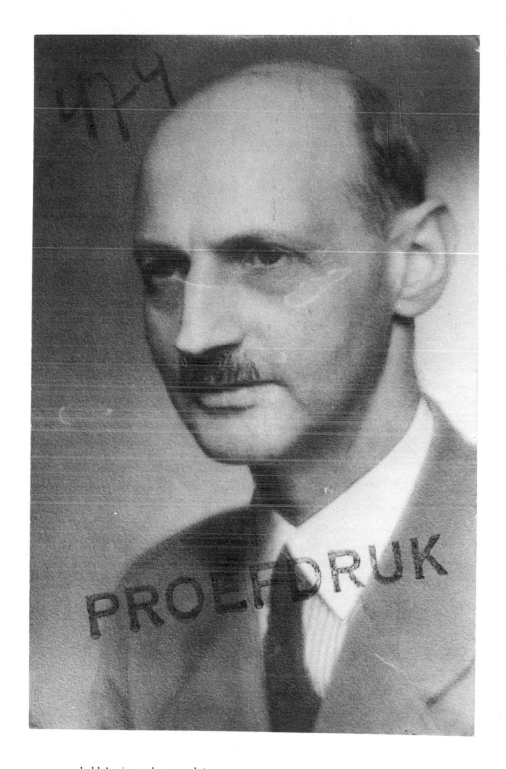

daddy's nicest photograph.[1]

45   1939.[2]

225

Daddy's the only one who understands me occasionally, but generally he sides with Mummy and Margot. And I can't stand it when strangers are there and they tell them how much I cried or how sensible I <u>am</u>, it's awful, and then they sometimes speak about Moortje and I can't bear that, for that's my softest and weakest point. I miss Moortje every moment of the day and no one knows how often I think of her; whenever I think of her I get tears in my | eyes. Moortje is such a darling and I love her so much, I dream up all sorts of plans in which she comes back again because she's such a darling and I can trust her with everything.

| 49

Daddy says you could fill a whole diary just saying how fantastic the Dutch are, he means a book of course, but I'll stop now, good-by.

<u>Anne.</u>

Thursday July 1942.

I may have already written, but I'm not sure, that we are now in hiding at 263, Prinsengracht with the van Pels family lots of things are happening in the city right now, but let me start from the beginning. On 9 May 1940 war broke out here in the Netherlands, the Germans marched their army in and within 5 days they had conquered the Netherlands. They have been at war with England since September 1939. *Now they have the Netherlands, Belgium, France (almost the whole of it) Poland, Norway, Denmark, Jugo-Slavia, Greece, Rumania, Bulgaria, Hungary is an ally of Germany.*

| 50

Now that the Germans rule the roost here | we are in real trouble, first there was rationing and everything had to be bought with coupons, then during the two years they have been here, there have been all sorts of Jewish laws. Jews must wear a yellow star; Jews must hand in their bicycles; Jews are banned from trams and are forbidden to use any car, even a private one; Jews are only allowed to do their shopping between three and five o'clock, and then only in shops which bear the placard Jewish Shop; Jews may only use Jewish barbers; Jews must be indoors from eight o'clock in the evening until 6 o'clock in the morning; Jews are forbidden to visit Theaters, cinemas and other places of entertainment; Jews may not go to swimming baths, nor to tennis, hockey or other sports grounds; Jews may not go rowing; Jews may not take part in public sports. Jews must not sit in their own or their friends' gardens after 8 o'clock in the evening; Jews may not visit Christians; Jews must go to Jewish schools, and many more restrictions of a similar kind, so we could not do this and were forbidden to do that. But life went on in spite of

| 51

it all. Jacque used to say to me: "You're scared to do anything because it | may be forbidden. I always dream such nice dreams here, but the reality is that we have to stick it here until the war is over, we are not allowed to go out and we can only be visited by Miep Gies-Santroschits, Jan Gies her husband, Bep Voskuyl, Mr. Voskuyl, Mr. Kugler, Mr. Kleymann and Mrs. Kleyman, but she doesn't come because she thinks it's too risky. I can't write down everything that goes on inside me and that I'm accused of, because it's so bad.

. . . . . .

. . . . . .

Dear diary, I hope no one will ever read you except my dear sweet husband, and you know very well who that is, although I sometimes have my doubts about my love, and my dream boy is Frits van Althoven. I don't believe I have ever written anything in here about Peter Schiff and that is really scandalous or shkandalous as Mrs. van Pels would say, for he is my one and only.

AnneFrank Anne} {Peter

In the meantime she's been here already!oooooooo you get what I mean!!!!

52 Anne. 28 Sept. 1942
1 August 1942

So far I have put almost nothing in my diary other than thoughts and have never got round to nice stories I might read out aloud one day. But from now on I shan't be so sentimental or a bit less and keep closer to reality.

Here we are then, it all starts early in the morning, we get up at 7 and line up for the bathroom, then we go upstairs to have breakfast, then comes the washing up and some sort of household chore or other. And so it goes until evening in the evening we usually do an hour of exercises, and I practice hard at my dancing steps. It's very cozy here in our small room but I feel anything but at home. The fact that we can never go outside bothers me more than I can say, and then I'm really afraid that we'll be discovered and shot, not a very nice prospect, needless to say. Then there is the fact that Mr. v. Pels

| 53 *is mad about Margot but hates me, he keeps trying to get me in | to trouble now, but he doesn't manage too well, because Daddy and Mummy are always on my side. Like last night, for instance, when we had cold meat and eel. I didn't have any meat of course, just eel. Now there was only a very little bread, but Margot and I still had a small slice and then Mr. v. Pels said Margot, put the meat on your bread now and have some cheese afterwards. I made a mental note of this and put a small piece of cheese on my bread for that's all we had, and then Margot and I ate our sandwiches. When Margot had finished, she didn't want the cheese any more and I asked if I could have it, Daddy laughed and gave it to me, for he said if Margot can have it then so can you. Mr. v. Pels looked down his nose and then he said: "No, the cheese is only for children who eat meat."*

"Yes but Anne has had eel," Margot said quickly.[4]

"Yes but a lot more people don't eat eel, and everyone eats meat!"

54 Then I said, yes but Mr. v.P you're always looking for some excuse so that I get nothing or something like it and then I got down from the table.

. . . . . .

. . . . . .

Anne looking "thoughtful," "proud," "smiling in her sleep" and "sweet."

Another example:

We had barley soup which I don't like and anyway it was very hot and I never eat much then. Now I had to eat something of course but there was meat in it and I didn't want that, so I gave it to Mummy, no said Mummy you must eat it up and she gave it back to me. So Mr. v.P. said I couldn't have any seasoning.[2] Margot had some fat not even 1 millimeter thick on her meat, she cut it off and Mr. v.P. said nothing. Then the barley was too much for me and I couldn't finish it, so I left it on the plate; Mr. v.P. said quickly that I couldn't have any yogurt, but Mummy wouldn't have that and so I got the most.

V.P. was highly indignant and suddenly they started churning out wonderful stories about Peter, who was so good with his food.

Daddy and Mummy ignored it all.

55 . . . .

We had agreed to have tea in the morning, Peter doesn't like tea; but once when we had cocoa and I pulled a face I really got it in the neck from everybody. Peter doesn't like it when we have tea, but Mrs. v.P. slips him cocoa then on the quiet. That's really mean because nobody takes any notice if we don't like something.

. . . . .

    so something happens every day, but I
    am too lazy and too tired to
    write everything down.

'bye AnneFrank.

Friday 14 Aug. 1942.

There is little change in our life here. Today Peter had his hair washed, but that's nothing special, Mr. v. Pels and I usually manage to upset each other, and tonight we laughed ourselves sick. Mummy always treats me just like a baby, which I can't bear. Otherwise things are going better.

Tonight Miep is going to see Mr. Goldsmit our tenant, to fetch some more clothes,

| 56   *I hope she'll come back with | nice things. Daddy gives me regular lessons now, but it's shocking how much I've forgotten already. I've heard meanwhile that Hanneli and Jacque (at least I think it was them) were in our house to look at my diary, they wanted to get hold of Daddy's mysterious letter of course. In the evening we do office work, but it so happens that I have nothing to do tonight.*

Things are getting very mysterious round here now, Mr. Kugler was afraid they might come to look for hidden bicycles, and that's why he wanted to have the door to our hiding place camouflaged, now it's been done so as to look like an ordinary bookcase, when in fact it is a door, for the bookcase with all its books swings on hinges so you can open it like a door, <u>notwithstanding</u> (what a grand word, eh?) that it looks as if it's fixed to the wall.

57   *If we want to go downstairs, that is to the office, we have to bend down first and then jump.*

Enough for today, my arm can't move any more, '<u>bye</u>.

Anne Frank

a 56

Things are getting very mysterious round here now, Mr. Kugler was afraid they might come to look for hidden bicycles, and that's why he wanted to have the door to our hiding place camouflaged, now it's been done so as to look like an ordinary bookcase, when in fact it is a door, for the bookcase with all its books swings on hinges so you can open it like a door, notwithstanding (what a grand word, eh?) that it looks as if it's fixed to the wall.

If we want to go downstairs now, that is to the office, we have to bend down first and then jump.

b 43

Friday 21 August 1942.

Dearest Kitty,

The entrance to our hiding place has now been properly concealed. Mr. Kugler thought it would be better to put a cupboard in front of our door (because a lot of houses are being searched for hidden bicycles.)³ but of course it had to be a movable cupboard that can open like a door.

Mr. Voskuyl made the whole thing; but first the walls of the corridor had to be papered. (We had already let Mr. Voskuyl into the secret and he can't do enough to help). If we want to go downstairs we have to first bend down and then jump,⁵. The first 3 days we were all going about with masses of lumps on our foreheads because we all knocked ourselves against the low doorway. So Peter has made it as soft as possible by nailing a cloth filled with wood wool against the top of the door. Let's see if that helps! I am not working much at present,⁷ I'm giving myself holidays until September. Then Daddy is going to give me lessons, but first we must buy all the schoolbooks again.

c

Friday, 21 August, 1942

Dear Kitty,

The entrance to our hiding place has now been properly concealed. Mr. Kraler thought it would be better to put a cupboard in front of our door (because a lot of houses are being searched for hidden bicycles), but of course it had to be a movable cupboard that can open like a door.

Mr. Vossen made the whole thing. We had already let him into the secret and he can't do enough to help. If we want to go downstairs, we have to first bend down and then jump, because the step has gone. The first three days we were all going about with masses of lumps on our foreheads, because we all knocked ourselves against the low doorway. Now we have nailed a cloth filled with wood wool against the top of the door. Let's see if that helps!

I'm not working much at present; I'm giving myself holidays until September. Then Daddy is going to give me lessons; it's shocking how much I've forgotten already.

230

a | 55 | There is little change in our life here. Today Peter had his hair washed, but that's nothing special. Mr. v. Pels and I usually manage to upset each other, and tonight we laughed ourselves sick. Mummy always treats me just like a baby, which I can't bear. Otherwise things are going better.

| 56 | Tonight Miep is going to see Mr. Goldsmit our tenant, to fetch some more clothes, I hope she'll come back with | nice things. Daddy gives me regular lessons now, but it's shocking how much I've forgotten already.

b | 44 | Miep and Jan have been to see G. to fetch some more of our clothes, but all the wardrobes were empty. G. said that he couldn't make out how we had managed to eat[1] in the end since there had been only one plate and one cup left in the house. Isn't that awful? Goodness knows what he's done with our stuff, it was mean of him not to give anything to Miep. It can't be that he's afraid to hand our things over to some stranger because he knows Miep very well. We were really indignant but there's nothing we can do about it.

It is lovely weather and in spite of everything we make the most we can of it by lying on a camp bed in the attic.

I still don't like Peter any better, he is so boring he flops lazily on his bed half the time, does a bit of carpentry and then goes back for another snooze. What a fool!

Yours, Anne.

c There is little change in our life here. Mr. Van Daan and I usually manage to upset each other, it's just the opposite with Margot whom he likes very much. Mummy sometimes treats me just like a baby, which I can't bear. Otherwise things are going better. I still don't like Peter any more [better], he is so boring; he flops lazily on his bed half the time, does a bit of carpentry, and then goes back for another snooze. What a fool!

It is lovely weather and in spite of everything we make the most we can of it by lying on a camp bed in the attic, where the sun shines through an open window.

Yours, Anne

231

Miep and Jan went to see Mr. Goldsmith, as you know he is our tenant, and asked if they could look over the apartment to see whether they could rescue anything for us. Goldsmith said that we had carted everything away and that he couldn't understand how we had managed to eat, since there was only one plate left. So he[2] must have carted everything away in our house. He tried as well to make them believe that Mrs. Goslar had come for the cigarettes and Mrs. Lefkowitz for the baby linen for Kohnke, but that he had had to

| 58 *turn them both away empty-handed. I think he has sold some | of it and given the rest to Ulla Cohen because he got married recently and we think to Ulla Cohen.*

Now Mr. Kleiman has gone to see Mr. Lefkowitz to ask him to come with him to see Goldsmith, but Lefkowitz wanted to speak to Goslar about it first, and I don't know whether Goslar will agree. What they want is to get Goldsmith to tell Kleiman where our things are, and Mr. Dunselman has our power of attorney so they can always use that.

It's really very mean of Goldsmith to steal our stuff, and then to lie about it as well. Apart from that there's nothing special, except that Mr. and Mrs. v. Pels have had a

| 59 *furious quarrel and Mr. v.P. yelled | so much that they must surely have been able to hear him houses away.*

Dear Kitty,

Mr. and Mrs. v.P. have had a terrific quarrel, I've never seen anything quite like it before. Mummy and Daddy would never dream of shouting at each other. The cause was so trivial that the whole thing was a pure waste of breath,[1] but still, everyone to his own liking.

Naturally it is very unpleasant for Peter, who has to stand by, but then no one takes him seriously, he is so frightfully touchy and lazy. Yesterday he was badly upset as he found that his tongue was blue instead of red; this unusual phenomenon of nature disappeared just as quickly as it had come. Today he is going about with a thick scarf on, as he has a stiff neck, in addition "M'lord" complains of lumbago. Pains around the heart, kidneys and lungs are not unusual either, he is a real[5] hypochondriac (that's the word for such people, isn't it?)

Dear Kitty,

Mr. and Mrs. Van Daan have had a terrific quarrel, I've never seen anything quite like it before. Mummy and Daddy would never dream of shouting at each other. The cause was so trivial that the whole thing was a pure waste of breath. But, still, everyone to his own liking.

Naturally it is very unpleasant for Peter, who has to stand by. No one takes him seriously, he is so frightfully touchy and lazy. Yesterday he was badly upset because he found that his tongue was blue instead of red; this unusual phenomenon of nature disappeared just as quickly as it had come. Today he is going about with a scarf on, as he has a stiff neck; in addition "M'lord" complains of lumbago. Pains around the heart, kidneys, and lungs are not unusual either, he is a real hypochondria [hypochondriac] (that's the word for such people, isn't it?)!

232

Mummy gave me another frightful sermon this morning; I can't bear them, our ideas are diametrically opposed. Daddy is a darling, although he can sometimes be angry with me[1] for five minutes on end.

'Bye. Anne Frank.

21[2] September
1942.

I do a lot of work, although I say so myself.
I haven't written anything for ages, but no doubt I'll make up for it. Mr. v. Pels is all sugar to me nowadays, I take it quietly as my due. We die laughing about Peter one day he has lumbago, next day he has a blue tongue and itches and so on.

46 It is not all honey between Mummy and Mrs. v.P., there is plenty of cause for unpleasantness, to give a small example I will tell you that Mrs. v.P.[6] has taken all three of her sheets out of the common linen cupboard, she takes it for granted that Mummy's sheets will do for all of us. It will be a nasty surprise for her when she finds that Mummy has followed her good example.

Also[11] she is thoroughly piqued that her dinner service and not ours is in use. She is always trying to find out where we have actually put our plates; they are in a cardboard box behind a lot of Opekta advertising stuff in the attic. Our plates are ungettatable as long as we are here, and a good thing too!

I always have bad luck; I smashed one of Mrs. v.P.'s soup plates into a thousand pieces yesterday.

47 "Oh," She angrily, "couldn't you be careful for once, that's the only one I've got left." Please bear in mind, dear Kitty, that the two ladies here speak terrible Dutch. (I daren't say anything about the gentlemen, because they would be very offended.)[15], if you could hear their bickerings you would burst out laughing; we don't pay any attention to it any more, it's no good correcting them either. when I write about Mummy or Mrs. v.P. I shan't repeat their actual words but put them in proper Dutch.

It is not all honey between Mummy and Mrs. Van Daan; there is plenty of cause for unpleasantness. To give a small example, I will tell you that Mrs. Van Daan has taken all three of her sheets out of the common linen cupboard. She takes it for granted that Mummy's sheets will do for all of us. It will be a nasty surprise for her when she finds that Mummy has followed her good example.

Also, she is thoroughly piqued that her dinner service and not ours is in use. She is always trying to find out where we have actually put our plates; they are closer than she thinks, they are in a cardboard box behind a lot of junk in the attic. Our plates are ungettatable at [ungettatable] as long as we are here, and a good thing too. I always have bad luck; I smashed one of Mrs. Van Daan's soup plates into a thousand pieces yesterday. "Oh!" she cried angrily. "Couldn't you be careful for once—that's the last one I've got." Mr. Van Daan is all sugar to me nowadays. Long may it last. Mummy gave me another frightful sermon this morning; I can't bear them. Our ideas are completely opposite. Daddy is a darling, although he can sometimes be angry with me for five minutes on end. Last

233

There was a big drama just now. Peter and Margot are allowed to read practically any book, but Mr. Kleiman brought along a book about the last war that was very outspoken. So Peter and Margot were not allowed to read it. Immediately Peter just had to have it so he got hold of it, whereupon Mrs. v.P. went to Mummy (she didn't know that Peter was reading the

| 60 *book) and told her | she thought it very strange that Margot was allowed to read any book she wanted to.*

Last week we had a little interruption in our monotonous life, it was over a book about women, and Peter. First I must tell you that Margot and Peter are allowed to read nearly all the books that Mr. Kleiman lends us, but the grownups held back this particular book on the subject of women. Peter's curiosity was aroused at once. what was it the two of them were not

| 48 allowed to read in this book? He got hold of the book on the sly | while his mother was downstairs talking and disappeared with his missive to the attic. All went well for two days, his mother knew what he was doing but didn't tell tales, until Mr. v.P. found out. He was very angry, took the book away and thought that that would finish the whole business.[9] However he had not allowed for his son's curiosity, which waxed rather than waned because of his father's attitude.

Peter, determined to finish it, thought of a way to get hold of this [13]enthralling book. In the meantime Mrs. v.P. had asked Mummy what she thought about it all, Mummy thought this particular book was not suitable for Margot, but she saw no harm in letting her read most others.

week we had a little interruption in our monotonous life; it was over a book about women—and Peter. First I must tell you that Margot and Peter are allowed to read nearly all the books that Mr. Koophuis lends us, but the grownups held back this particular book on the subject of women. Peter's curiosity was aroused at once. What was it the two of them were not allowed to read in this book? He got hold of the book on the sly, while his mother was downstairs talking, and disappeared with his booty to the attic. All went well for a few days. His mother knew what he was doing, but didn't tell tales, until Father found out. He was very angry, took the book away, and thought that that would finish the whole business. However, he had not allowed for his son's curiosity, which waxed rather than waned because of his father's attitude. Peter, determined to finish it, thought of a way to get hold of this enthralling book. In the meantime, Mrs. Van Daan had asked Mummy what she thought about it all. Mummy thought this particular book was not suitable for Margot, but she saw no harm in letting her read most books.

Mummy said of course that Margot was very sensible in such matters (much too sensible for me), but that even so she wasn't allowed to read the Trilogy. In the evening Peter came downstairs with "the" book and he and his mother talked about it half the evening, and then Mrs. van Pels said that really she didn't see much wrong with it. But Mr. v.P. wouldn't have it and snatched the book away, 'then Peter was furious and said either he had the book or he would refuse to learn any more English. That made Mr. van Pels furious and Piet rushed upstairs. Before supper Mr. v.P. called to Peter come and eat! But nothing happened. Some more calling, then he called I'm not coming I'm going to sleep on the camp bed in the attic. After that Mr. v.P. brought the bed downstairs and then said you can have 10 more minutes to think about it and after that it'll be too late and you'll have to sleep in the attic on your own. Peter said that was fine, but at table we all said that if Peter slept upstairs he might catch cold. It wouldn't hurt if he got no food.

| 49

"There is a great difference, Mrs. v.P.," said Mummy "between Margot and Peter. In the first place Margot is a girl and girls are always more grownup than boys, secondly Margot has read quite a lot of serious books and does not go in search of things that are no longer forbidden her, and thirdly, Margot is far more developed and intel | ligent, shown by the fact of her being in the 4th form at school." Mrs. v.P. agreed, but still thought it wrong in principle to let children read books which were written for grownups.

In the meantime Peter had found a time of the day when no one bothered about him or the book: seven-thirty in the evening—then everyone was in the private office listening to the radio. That was when he took his treasure to the attic again. He should have been downstairs again by eight-thirty, but because the book was so thrilling he forgot the time and was just coming downstairs as his father came into the room. You can imagine the consequences, with a slap and a snatch the book lay on the table and Peter was in the attic. That's how matters stood as we sat down to table. Peter stayed upstairs—no one bothered about him, and he had to go to bed without any supper. We went on with the

"There is a great difference, Mrs. Van Daan," said Mummy, "between Margot and Peter. In the first place Margot is a girl and girls are always more grownup than boys, secondly, Margot has read quite a lot of serious books, and does not go in search of things that are forbidden her, and thirdly, Margot is far more developed and intelligent, shown by the fact of her being in the fourth form at school." Mrs. Van Daan agreed, but still thought it was wrong in principle to let children read books which were written for grownups.

In the meantime Peter had found a time of the day when no one bothered about him or the book: seven-thirty in the evening—then everyone was in the private office listening to the radio. That was when he took his treasure to the attic again. He should have been downstairs again by eight-thirty, but because the book was so thrilling he forgot the time and was just coming downstairs as his father came into the room. You can imagine the consequences! With a slap and a snatch, the book lay on the table and Peter was in the attic. That's how matters stood as we sat down to table. Peter stayed upstairs—no one bothered about him, and he had to go to bed without any supper.

235

Suddenly we heard whistling. We were startled, because we didn't know where it came from at first, and then a voice called out very loud,—I'm not coming down anyway! Mr. v.P. sprang to his feet scarlet in the face but Daddy went with him, and then they brought him downstairs. The next day he said that he wouldn't come down again unless he was given the book. But he had to anyway. And now Mrs. van Pels says he's quite right. What an idiot of a woman!!!!

| 50   meal chattering gaily when suddenly we heard a piercing whistle; we all stopped eating and looked with | pale changed faces from one to another. Then we heard Peter's voice calling down the chimney, "I say, I'm not coming down anyway."

Mr. v.P. sprang to his feet, napkin falling to the floor, and scarlet in the face he shouted, "I've had enough of this."

Daddy took his arm, afraid of what might happen, and the two men went together to the attic; after a good deal of resistance and stamping Peter ended up in his room with the door closed and we went on eating. Mrs. v.P. wanted to leave one slice of bread for the dear boy but his father stood firm "if he doesn't apologize soon he will have to sleep in the attic." Loud protests from the rest of us as we thought missing supper was quite enough punishment, besides Peter might catch cold and we couldn't call a doctor.

Peter did not apologize; he was already in the attic, v.P. did nothing more about it, but I noticed the next morning that Peter's bed had been used, Peter was back in the attic
| 51   at seven o'clock, but Daddy managed with a few friendly | words to persuade him to come down again. Sour faces and obstinate silences for three days, and everything went smoothly once more.

yours, Anne

We went on with the meal, chattering gaily, when suddenly we heard a piercing whistle; we all stopped eating and looked with pale changed faces from one to another. Then we heard Peter's voice, calling down the chimney, "I say, I'm not coming down anyway." Mr. Van Daan sprang to his feet, his napkin fell to the floor, and scarlet in the face he shouted, "I've had enough of this." Daddy took his arm, afraid of what might happen, and the two men went together to the attic. After a good deal of resistance and stamping, Peter landed up in his room with the door closed and we went on eating. Mrs. Van Daan wanted to save one slice of bread for the dear boy, but his father stood firm. "If he doesn't apologize soon, he will have to sleep in the attic." Loud protests from the rest of us, as we thought missing supper was quite enough punishment. Besides, Peter might catch cold and we couldn't call a doctor.

Peter did not apologize; he was already in the attic. Mr. Van Daan did nothing more about it, but I noticed the next morning that Peter's bed had been slept in. Peter was back in the attic at seven o'clock, but Daddy managed with a few friendly words to persuade him to come down again. Sour faces and obstinate silences for three days and then everything went smoothly once more.

Yours, Anne

And this afternoon she simply took all our sheets and pillowcases, except for two, out of the cupboard. All our towels are already in use. Now she wants to make sure that all our sheets get torn to shreds by being washed and used, while her ladyship keeps her own nice and neat for after the war. But Daddy won't leave it at that. Yesterday it was Yom Kippur,* and there can't be many people who will have kept it as quietly as we did. Bep told us that Betty Bloemendal from my class has been packed off to Poland, too, it's horrible isn't it, and we are so well off here. There is talk that Mr. Pfeffer will be coming to join us, so we shall be able to save him as well. The war still goes on, and we get almost | 62 *no butter now on our bread. I'm busy with Daddy at the moment working out | his family tree, and as we go along he tells me little bits about everyone. Miep and Jan have just come back from their vacation, and now I can see a lot of Miep again. I would just love to correspond with somebody, so that is what I intend to do in future with my diary. I shall write it from now on in letter form, which actually comes to the same thing.*

Dear Jettje, (I shall simply say,)

My dear friend, both in the future as well as now I shall have a lot to tell you. I have started knitting a sweater out of white wool. But I mustn't knit too much otherwise it'll be finished too soon. I now have a little light above my bed. 'Bye I've got to go and peel potatoes for the most rotten person in the world, that's a bit exaggerated, but only a little bit. Regards to everyone and kisses from

Anne Frank 21 Sept. 1942.

---

*Yom Kippur, or the Day of Atonement, is the most important day in the Jewish calendar. It is a fast day and a day of repentance.

. . . . . .

. . . . . .

The same day

I have some time left tonight dearest Emmy, and so I shall drop you a few lines, this afternoon I wrote a fairly sheepish letter to Jettje, but I had hardly sat down for a minute when I had to peel potatoes for "her ladyship my mama," she says it in such commanding | 63 *tones, and if I | don't hop to it then she shouts "loos," that is German but I don't know exactly how you spell it. Just as in "Joop ter Heul." Incidentally, have you read "Joop ter Heul"? How are things with Janeau? Are you all right, you two, or do you still squabble every day and make up in the evenings, that is the best bit of all for sure. I listen to the radio every Saturday night, there is a variety program then from Germany, but it's been getting duller all the time, ever since the first night, when the program was called "In Love, Engaged, Married," in German of course, but I shan't talk too much about German, because you get furious at that, which I understand perfectly well. Tonight I was working in the office again, and whoops tore a delivery note right through the middle, I haven't said anything about it, but I think they'll have to make out a new one. Mr. Kleiman went yet again to see Mr. Goldschmith after he hadn't been at home twice, he left his telephone number, then Goldschmith rang him up and he went to the Joodse Invalide where Goldschmith works. Goldschmith said that he had told people there was nothing left in the house, because otherwise everyone would have wanted to take something* | 64 *| he's packed away most of our things in chests and suitcases now and put them in the box room, he gave a little bit to the Jewish Council, well if it's only a little bit, I couldn't care less, but Mummy thinks that he's probably embezzled it all, but I think that one shouldn't be so suspicious, and kind Daddy of course agrees with me. Today Peter changed his room, the store cupboard is now in the attic and where it was are floorboards with a little space on which you can put things, I suggested that he put his table there, with a nice cloth and hang the little cupboard against the wall where the table is now, then it will look quite cozy, though I wouldn't like to sleep there. Madame is off on a new tack,*

b . . . . . .

c . . . .

the latest is that she doesn't want to wash up the pans, if there is a fragment left instead of putting it into a glass dish she leaves it in the pan to go bad. That's stupid of course. Then, when Margot has lots of pans to scrub in the afternoon, Madame says oh Margotchen, Margotchen, you do have a lot to do, but it's all put¹ on, and Margot sometimes | 65 has seven dirty pans, when she should have just one or at most | two, now I must stop, dearest Emmy regards to Georgette from

.Anne Frank

I am busy with Daddy at the moment working out | his family tree, and as we go along he tells me little bits about everyone.

Monday 21 Sept. 1942.

Dear Kitty,

Today I'm going to tell you our general news. A small light has been fitted above my divan with a bit of string I shall be able to pull when there is shooting. I can't use it at the moment, because our window is always slightly ajar.

The male v.P. division has built a very convenient, varnished store cupboard with real fly screens. This magnificent object used to stand in Peter's room but has been moved to the attic for better ventilation. Mrs. v.P. is unbearable. I get nothing but "blow ups" from her for my continuous chatter. But I don't take any notice of what she says! Now and then we have news of other Jews, unfortunately things are going badly for them. For instance a girl I know from my class has been carried off with her family.

Monday, 21 September, 1942

Dear Kitty,

Today I'm going to tell you our general news.

Mrs. Van Daan is unbearable. I get nothing but "blow ups" from her for my continuous chatter. She is always pestering us in some way or other. This is the latest: she doesn't want to wash up the pans if there is a fragment left, instead of putting it into a glass dish, as we've always done until now, she leaves it in the pan to go bad.

After the next meal Margot sometimes has about seven pans to wash up and then Madame says: "Well, well, Margot, you have got a lot to do!"

I'm busy with Daddy working out his family tree: as we go along he tells me little bits about everyone—it's terribly interesting.

239

a

Dear Kitty,
Yesterday I wrote to Emmy and Jettje, but I prefer writing to you, you know that don't
you and I hope the feeling is mutual. Last night we were talking about the fact that in a

b

| 53

Mr. Kleiman
brings a few special books for me every other week | I'm thrilled with the Joop ter Heul
series. I've enjoyed the whole of Cissy van Marxveldt very much, and I've read "een
Zomerzotheid" 4 times and I still laugh about some of the ludicrous situations that arise.

Term time has begun again, I am working hard at my French and manage to pump
in 5 irregular verbs per day, Peter sighs and groans over his English. Some schoolbooks
have just arrived, we have a good stock of exercise books, pencils, rubbers and labels, as
I brought these with me. I sometimes listen to the Dutch news from London, heard Prince
Bernhard recently, he said that they are expecting a baby about next January.* I think it
is lovely; the others don't understand why I'm so keen on the Royal Family.

——

I was being discussed and they decided that I'm still rather silly, which had the effect of
making me work extra hard the next day, I certainly don't want to still be in the first
form when I'm fourteen or fifteen.

---

*Princess Margriet was born in Ottawa on January 19, 1943.

c

Mr. Koophuis brings a few special books
for me every other week. I'm thrilled with the *Joop ter Heul* series. I've enjoyed the whole
of Cissy van Marxveldt very much. And I've read *Een Zomerzotheid* four times and I still
laugh about some of the ludicrous situations that arise.

Term time has begun again, I'm working hard at my French and manage to pump in
five irregular verbs per day. Peter sighs and groans over his English. A few schoolbooks
have just arrived; we have a good stock of exercise books, pencils, rubbers, and labels,
as I brought these with me. I sometimes listen to the Dutch news from London, heard
Prince Bernhard recently. He said that Princess Juliana is [they are] expecting a baby about
next January. I think it is lovely; it surprises the others that I should be so keen on the
Royal Family.

I was being discussed and they decided that I'm not completely stupid after all, which
had the effect of making me work extra hard the next day. I certainly don't want to still
be in the first form when I'm fourteen or fifteen.

240

a

way I'm still rather silly, which had the effect that little Anne set to work extra hard the next day, today I spent all morning swotting French irregular verbs, good of me isn't it, but then I certainly don't want to still be in the first form when I'm 14 or 15. Yesterday we also mentioned that I'm hardly allowed to read anything, Mummy is reading "Heren, vrouwen, knechten" [Men, women, servants] now, don't laugh at me, I don't remember the precise title, but that's another book I'm not allowed, because I must first be more developed, like my talented sister, we also talked about psychology, and philosophy and other deep subjects. Tomorrow I think I'll write my farewell letter to Jacqueline, it should have been done 2½ months ago. It has turned terribly cold here already, and I have just woken up to the disturbing fact that I have only one long-sleeved dress² and 3 cardigans here, I am still busy knitting the white thing, but that will get dirty so quickly. All my sweaters are at the Brokses' but perhaps Miep will ask if she could store them for me, in | 66 *which case we'll get them back, of course. How are | you all? I think it's such a shame*

b 54

Also the fact that I'm hardly allowed to read anything was mentioned;¹

Mummy is reading "Heren, knechten en vrouwen," which I'm not allowed (Margot is!). First I must be more developed, like my talented sister. Then we talked about my ignorance ³of philosophy, psychology and⁴ physiology, about which I admittedly know nothing,⁷ perhaps by next year I shall be wiser! (I looked up these difficult words quickly in *Koenen*!)⁹* I have just woken up to the disturbing fact that I have one long-sleeved dress and 3 cardigans for the winter; I've received permission from Daddy to knit a jumper of white sheep's wool, it's not very nice wool but as long as it provides warmth that's all that matters. We have some clothes deposited with friends (including the Brokses)¹² but unfortunately we shall not see them until after the war, that is if they are still there then.

*The Dutch dictionary *Koenen, Endepols, Bezoen.* A.J.P.

c

Also the fact that I'm hardly allowed to read any decent books was mentioned. Mummy is reading *Heeren, Vrouwen en Knechten* now, which I'm not allowed (Margot is). First I must be more developed, like my talented sister. Then we talk [talked] about my ignorance of philosophy and psychology [and physiology], about which I know nothing. Perhaps by next year I shall be wiser! (I looked up these difficult words quickly in *Koenen.*)

I have just woken up to the disturbing fact that I have one long-sleeved dress and three cardigans for the winter. I've received permission from Daddy to knit a jumper of white sheep's wool; it's not very nice wool, but as long as it's warm that's all that matters. We have some clothes deposited with friends, but unfortunately we shall not see them until after the war, that is if they are still there then.

241

a

that I never get a reply. Yesterday I was writing to Emmy about Mrs. v.P., when in she came, slap, I closed the book. Hey, Anne, can't I just have a look?

I'm afraid not. Just the last page, then? No, I'm sorry. Naturally it scared me out of my wits because there was a less than agreeable description of her. I have finished Joop ter Heul so quickly that I shan't be getting any new books before Saturday, When I've read the last two as well I shall ask Kleiman if I can't have "Kees de Jongen" by Theo Thijssen, do you know that one? I wish you could just come and have a look at our house here, although it's not at all bad you'd kill yourself laughing. Now my fountain pen (I mean Mummy's fountain pen) has run dry and I don't like writing in pencil, and so an embrasse (sentimental isn't it, I got it from darling Jettje) from

Anne Frank

b

| 55

I had just written something about Mrs. v.P. when in she came, slap, I closed the book. "Hey, Anne, | can't I just have a look?"

"I'm afraid not."

"Just the last page, then?"

"No, I'm sorry."

Naturally it gave me a frightful shock, because there was an unflattering description of her on this particular page.

Yours, Anne

c

I had just written something about Mrs. Van Daan when in she came. Slap! I closed the book. "Hey, Anne, can't I just have a look?"

"I'm afraid not."

"Just the last page then?"

"No, I'm sorry."

Naturally it gave me a frightful shock, because there was an unflattering description of her on this particular page.

Yours, Anne

242

This is the promised fare-well letter
25-Sept. 1942.

Dear Jacqueline,
I am writing this letter in order to bid you good-by, that will probably surprise you, but fate has decreed that I must leave (as you will of course have heard a long time ago) with my family, for reasons you will know.

    When you telephoned me on Sunday afternoon I couldn't say anything, for my mother had told me not to, the whole house was upside down and the front door was locked. | 67 Hello was due to come, but we didn't | answer the door. I can't write to everyone and that's why I'm just writing to you. I'm taking it that you won't talk to anybody about this letter nor from whom you got it. I would be so grateful if you would be really nice and keep up a secret correspondence with me. <u>All inquiries to Mrs. Gies!!!!</u> I hope we'll meet again[2] soon, but it probably won't be before the end of the war. If Lies or anyone else asks you if you've heard anything from me say absolutely nothing, otherwise you'll get us and Mrs. Gies into mortal trouble, so I hope you'll be really careful. Later, of course, you'll be able to tell people that you had a farewell letter from me. Well then Jackie I hope things go well with you, that I hear from you soon and that we'll meet again soon.

    Your *"best"* friend   <u>Anne</u>
    P.S. I hope that we'll[3] always stay <u>"best"</u> friends until we meet again.

                         'bye.

Second letter.
25 Sept. 1942.

Dear Jackie,
I was very glad to get your letter, if no Germans have been to our apartment so far, please could you go round to Mr. Goldschmith and pick up some of our books and papers and games you can have them or look after them for me, or else you could take them to Mrs. Gies. I forgot to tell you in my last letter that you must not keep these letters from me, | 68 because <u>no one must</u> find them. So cut them up into | tiny pieces, just like we did that time with the letter from Mummy's box. Please do it. How are you all, I mustn't write about myself of course. I think of you so often. How is Ilse is she still around. I've heard from Mrs. Gies that Lies is still here. We're not bored and we have company, I mustn't write anything more about our life until later, although it is weird but interesting. This letter mustn't get too long be seeing you and a little kiss from

                                   Anne

25 Sept. 1942.

Dearest Pop,
Just a short scribble, you haven't heard from me for a long time have you, but things are still all right. How is Kees? When will it be, he is a really good boy friend isn't he, but I don't really have to ask you, since you obviously[4] think that anyway of your intended. I

243

must just tell you about our "Dreher-drama." You probably know that Mr. Dreher is the old, deaf gentleman whom Pim always used to visit. Today he telephoned to speak to Mr. Kugler and was simply told that Miep would be coming round to see him, Miep put down the phone and then Mrs. Dreher telephoned three times and Miep had to imitate Bep's voice because she had said the first time that Miep had gone out with Mr. Kugler. When Miep tells stories like that you kill yourself laughing. I can still sit for hours just looking at Miep. Today the weather is so damp and chilly that I've put on long stockings for the first time, at home I would never have had to do that. Yesterday evening I visited the van

---

b 56

Friday 25 September 1942.

Dear Kitty,

Daddy has an old acquaintance, Mr. Dreher, a man in his 70s, very hard of hearing, sick and poor and in addition he has a troublesome appendage a woman 27 years younger than he is, also poor, her arms and legs loaded with real and imitation bracelets and rings, left over from the good old days. This Mr. Dreher used to give Daddy quite a bit of trouble and I always admired Daddy for the angelic patience with which he spoke to this pathetic old man on the telephone. When we were still at home, Mummy told Daddy to put a gramophone next to the telephone, a gramophone that would say every 3 minutes, yes Mr. Dreher . . . . . no Mr. Dreher, since the old man didn't understand Daddy's lengthy answers in any case. Today Mr. Dreher telephoned the office and asked[12] Mr. Kugler whether he wouldn't come along to see him, Mr. Kugler didn't feel like it and said[13] he would send Miep. Miep put down the phone. Mrs. Dreher then telephoned | three times but because Miep was supposed to be away the whole afternoon she had to imitate Bep's voice on the telephone[15]. Downstairs (in the office) as well as upstairs there was horrible mirth and every time the telephone rings now Bep says:[17] "There's Mrs. Dreher!" Whereupon Miep bursts out laughing all over again and giggles very impolitely when she has to answer people. You know what, you won't see carryings-on like ours[19] anywhere else in the whole world, the directors and the office girls have the greatest fun together!

| 57

---

c   . . . . . .

244

Pels again, it is always great | fun there. Yesterday I got two slices of buttered bread with thick treacle, and a glass of fizzy lemonade. We talked about Peter, I told them how Peter keeps stroking my cheek and that I wished he wouldn't as I don't like being pawed by boys. Then they told me that Peter must like me very much and couldn't I get fond of him too, and I thought oh dear, and said, no I can't. Then they asked a whole lot of questions about my friends, but I didn't let on about Peter [Schiff], I might just as well have said Fritz or Sallie. Then I said that I thought Peter rather awkward but that it was probably shyness, as many boys who haven't had much to do with girls are like that

In the evenings I sometimes go to the v.P.s to have a chat. Then we have a moth biscuit with syrup (the biscuit tin is kept in the wardrobe which is full of mothballs) and have fun. Just now the talk was about Peter. I told them that Peter often stroked my cheek and that I didn't like it. In a typical way parents have they asked if I couldn't get fond of Peter, because he certainly liked me very much, I thought | "Oh dear" and said "Oh no;" Imagine it!

Friday, 25 September 1942

Dear Kitty,

Yesterday evening I went upstairs and "visited" the Van Daans. I do so occasionally to have a chat. Sometimes it can be quite fun. Then we have some moth biscuits (the biscuit tin is kept in the wardrobe which is full of moth balls) and drink lemonade. We talked about Peter. I told them how Peter often strokes my cheek and that I wished he wouldn't as I don't like being pawed by boys.

In a typical way parents have, they asked if I couldn't get fond of Peter, because he certainly liked me very much. I thought "Oh dear!" and said: "Oh, no!" Imagine it!

I did say that I thought Peter rather awkward, but that it was probably shyness, as many boys who haven't had much to do with girls are like that.

245

a

Well Pop I can smell the typewriter and my fingers are tingling Best regards to Betty and her boy friend.

Anne Frank.

26 Sept. 1942.

Dearest Marianne,

I have been writing to each of you in turn but the series ends with you. This morning I again spent the whole morning doing French. I am giving Pim Dutch lessons now as well, he made a few blunders e.g. een kikker klotst met zijn ogen [a frog laps with his eyes] instead of de golven klotsen [the waves lap], that is nothing but a Germanism, and een dievegge [a female thief] instead of dievegge and een schitterende (instead of een schitterend) overwinning [a glorious victory], when the verb schitteren is used in e.g. de zon schitterde in het water [the sun shone on the water].

b

Pim (that is Daddy's nickname) wants Dutch lessons, and I think that's a very good way of repaying him for his help with French and other subjects. But the howlers he makes are incredible,[1] one of them is "de kikker klotst met zijn ogen" [the frog laps with his eyes] instead of "de golven klotsten tegen de pier," [the waves lapped against the pier] that is the purest Germanism.

c   . . . . . .

246

a

| 70

Here they're busy plotting again. Broks the representative of Opekta as you know, in whose house all our things are stored, keeps asking about us and harping on the subject, so they're going to try and write a letter. They're going to write to a man | in South Zeeland who is supplied by Opekta every year asking him if he has received the goods this year and doing it in such a way that he has to put a tick on a form and send it straight back as usual in the enclosed envelope, but Daddy will write the address on the envelope so that it will get here with Daddy's handwriting on it. Then Mr. Kleiman will open the envelope, take out the man's letter and get Daddy to write a letter which he will then put inside. And so they will have a letter sent by us from Belgium and smuggled across the border. They specially chose South Zeeland, because no one is allowed to go there, so neither Broks nor anyone else will be able to go there either. A clever plan! That's what I think too.

b

| 59

I must say that the Refuge Committee of the "Secret Annexe" (male section) is very ingenious. I'll tell you what they've done now to get news of us through to Mr. Broks, Opekta's representative and a friend who has surreptitiously hidden some of our things for us! They typed a letter to a shopkeeper in South Zeeland, who does business indirectly[3] with Opekta, in such a way that he has to fill in the enclosed reply and send it back in the envelope supplied. Daddy addressed the envelope to the office. When this envelope[6] arrives from Zeeland, the enclosed letter is taken out, and is | replaced by a message in Daddy's handwriting as a sign of life. Like this, Broks won't become suspicious when he reads the note. They specially chose Zeeland because it is so close to Belgium and [the letter] could have easily been smuggled over the border and[7] in addition no one is allowed into Zeeland without a special permit. An ordinary representative like Broks is sure not to get such a permit.

Yours, Anne

c

I must say that the Refuge Committee of the "Secret Annexe" (male section) is very ingenious. I'll tell you what they've done now to get news of us through to Mr. Van Dijk, Travies' chief representative and a friend who has surreptitiously hidden some of our things for us! They typed a letter to a chemist in South Zeeland, who does business with our firm, in such a way that he has to send the enclosed reply back in an addressed envelope. Daddy addressed the envelope to the office. When this envelope arrives from Zeeland, the enclosed letter is taken out, and is replaced by a message in Daddy's handwriting as a sign of life. Like this, Van Dijk won't become suspicious when he reads the note. They specially chose Zeeland because it is so close to Belgium and the letter could have easily been smuggled over the border, in addition no one is allowed into Zeeland without a special permit[; so if they thought we were there, he couldn't try and look us up*].

Yours, Anne

---

*The words following the semi-colon at the end of this letter do not appear in any Dutch version of the diary. A.J.P.

247

Daddy played up once again last night, he was feeling queasy, wanted to sleep and tumbled into bed, there his feet felt cold so I put my bed socks on them. Five minutes later they were lying by his bed again. Then he didn't like the light and put his head under the blankets. When the light was switched off he reappeared very gingerly, it was too comical. Then when the rest of us were talking about Peter's calling Margot "tante" [aunt], a voice from the deep suddenly emerged from Daddy, whom we had thought fast asleep, "Kaffee," by which he meant "Kaffeetante" [coffee addict]. Madame has a cold and is very catty, Mummy and I kept on pinching each other at table. Mrs. Kleiman is upstairs now, that makes a pleasant change. Musschie (the cat) gets nicer all the time and more friendly towards me, but I am still a little afraid of him. Today we got three small baskets of little plums, very tasty, although I haven't | 71 *tried | them myself yet. Today Mr. Kleiman brought Joop-van Dil-ter Heul, and Joop and her boys, he's a nice man, he produces everything exactly on time. Tonight I am going to listen to the radio, it was broken, but it's working again now, in much better condition. More next time 'bye Marian, regards to Jaap.*

Anne

P.S. How are you two getting on and how is Gabi's singing. When is the little one due, it can't be long now. Is your mother all right, and how is your bank-papa. I hope all of you are well. In my letters I always forget to ask, because I always have so much to write about ourselves and our life here. 'Bye now.

Anne.

26. Sept. 1942.

Dear Kitty,

For once I shall write to you out of turn, because I can well imagine how you must be feeling. It is disagreeable of course, but Kit I think you'll have to find someone else; of course you'll think me heartless, for I know how sincerely you love Henk and I had never expected that of Henk either, but you have a great advantage Kitty, that is that you can discuss everything with your mum, I can't and though I am very close to Pim still a woman is different. But let's drop that now and leave it at that, because I don't know whether you mind my bothering you with it, but if you don't mind you can safely write everything about him to me, for as you know I shall never mention it to anybody.

72   Yesterday I watched Mummy rummaging about in the cupboard and take out all our ten cent and twenty-five cent pieces, Daddy said I could have them all back again and that makes me feel good. I can't tell you everything that happens here for if I did I would use up all my paper in a single day, and I have to be economical with it. Just now the "old nanny goat" came moaning to me again because I have removed Margo's things from the pigeonhole in my little cupboard, well yes I don't want to have to look at a filthy lamp and an even filthier fountain-pen case, [. . .],* she says scathingly that it's Margo's cupboard and that she can put what she wants in it, but I'll soon tell Margo where she gets off.

---

*At the request of the Frank family an unkind expression has been deleted.

. . . . . .

. . . . . .

a   There I am going on about myself again, but that person always turns up at the most intimate moments. Now all my nice feelings have vanished again, 'bye Kit, regards to everyone from me your

Anne Frank.
27 Sept. 1942.

Dearest Conny,
How are you and Nanny, poor soul you are so lonely, yes but here's a fine prospect, you can stay with me, I was with your mother the whole morning, and she agrees, I hope that this diversion is to your liking, so come as quickly as possible. Today I had a so-called "discussion" with Mummy, but the boring thing was that I burst into tears straight away, I can't help it, Daddy is always so nice to me, and he understands me so much better too. Oh, I can't stand Mummy at such times, and I am a stranger as far as she is concerned as well, for you see, she doesn't even know how I think about the most ordinary things.

|73 *We were talking about servants, | that you should call them the "household help," and will most definitely have to after the war, but I had hardly brought out the words when she said that I'm always carrying on about "later" and that just like Peter I make myself out to be a grand lady, but that is absolutely not true, and surely I can build castles in the air, that's not so bad, one doesn't have to take everything so seriously. Daddy at least defends me, without him I would honestly be almost unable to stand it here.*

b   60

Sunday 27 September 1942.

Dear Kitty,

Just had a big bust-up with Mummy for the umpteenth time, we simply don't get on together these days, and Margot and I don't hit it off any too well either. As a rule we don't go in for such outbursts as this in our family. Still, it's by no means always pleasant for me. Margot's and Mummy's natures are completely strange to me. I can understand my friends better than my own mother—too bad, isn't it!

We often discuss postwar problems, e.g. that one should not talk disparagingly of servants, but I don't find that as bad as making a distinction between *mevrouw* and *juffrouw* in married women.*[6]

Juffrouw used to be the title of married and unmarried women of the "genteel" classes. A.J.P.

c

Sunday, 27 September, 1942

Dear Kitty,

Just had a big bust-up with Mummy for the umpteenth time; we simply don't get on together these days and Margot and I don't hit it off any too well either. As a rule we don't go in for such outbursts as this in our family. Still, it's by no means always pleasant for me. Margot's and Mummy's natures are completely strange to me. I can understand my friends better than my own mother—too bad!

We often discuss postwar problems, for example, how one ought to address servants [for example, that one should not talk disparagingly of servants, but I don't find that as bad as making a distinction between *mevrouw* and *juffrouw* in married women].

249

Mrs. v.P. had another tantrum yesterday because everything was wrong first of all Mummy had taken a clean towel, she hadn't realized that madam had hung the towels up in the attic, because she thinks it's so squalid to hang them up in the room, something new again.

Then the vegetables had to be taken out of the pan because otherwise she'd have to wash it up in the evening, and she wanted Margot to wash it up now at lunchtime. But that's ridiculous because in the evening the vegetables will have to be heated up again in the pan anyway.

Then she took her glass saucers away, and now we only use ours. Hers are too good, but we are free to smash ours.

At table I didn't want to have any vegetables, so Mrs. v.P. claimed I couldn't have any potatoes either, but that didn't bother me because I knew Mummy would let me have some anyway. Whereupon Mummy immediately served me with potatoes before anybody else. Mr. v.P. also said that I would have to eat some vegetables, but I didn't.

| 61   Mrs. v.P. had another tantrum for the umpteenth time[1], she is really terribly moody. She keeps hiding[2] more of her private belongings. Mummy ought to answer each v.P. | "disappearance" with a Frank "disappearance." How some people do adore bringing up other people's children in addition to their own, the v.P.s for instance. Margot doesn't need it, she is such a goody-goody, perfection itself, but I seem to have enough mischief in me for the two of us put together. You should hear us at mealtimes, with reprimands and cheeky[8] answers flying to and fro. Mummy and Daddy always defend me stoutly. I'd have to give up if it weren't for them. Although they do tell me that I mustn't talk so much, that I must be more retiring and not poke my nose into everything, still I[11] seem doomed to failure and if Daddy wasn't so patient I'd be afraid I was going to turn out to be a terrific disappointment to my parents[13] and they are pretty lenient with me.

62   If I take a small helping of some vegetable I detest and make up with[14] potatoes, the v.P.s, and Mevrouw in particular, can't get over it, that any child should be so spoiled.

"Come along Anne have a few more vegetables," she says straight away."

Mrs. Van Daan had another tantrum [for the umpteenth time]. She is terribly moody. She keeps hiding more of her private belongings. Mummy ought to answer each Van Daan "disappearance" with a Frank "disappearance." How some people do adore bringing up other people's children in addition to their own. The Van Daans are that kind. Margot doesn't need it, she is such a goody-goody, perfection itself, but I seem to have enough mischief in me for the two of us put together. You should hear us at mealtimes, with reprimands and cheeky answers flying to and fro. Mummy and Daddy always defend me stoutly. I'd have to give up if it weren't for them. Although they do tell me that I mustn't talk so much, that I must be more retiring and not poke my nose into everything, still I seem doomed to failure. If Daddy wasn't so patient, I'd be afraid I was going to turn out to be a terrific disappointment to my parents and they are pretty lenient with me.

If I take a small helping of some vegetable I detest and make up with potatoes, the Van Daans, and Mevrouw in particular, can't get over it, that any child should be so spoiled.

"Come along, Anne, have a few more vegetables," she says straight away.

Then
Mrs. v.P. chimed in and said that she didn't think that was good manners, and that if I
were her child I would certainly have had to eat the vegetables, and that I was badly
brought up. Daddy then said he thought that Anne was very well brought up, since she
doesn't answer back, and he added "vise versa" which means that others copy the kind
of example you set. That was of course aimed at madam, because she can't have beans
at night or any kind of cabbage at all, otherwise she gets "wind."

74   *But I could say that as well. She's a fool isn't she. Regards to your parents and come*
as quickly as possible to your waiting-in-anticipation

AnneFrank

"No thank you Mrs. v.P.", I answer. "I have plenty of potatoes."

"Vegetables are good for you, your mother says so too. Have a few more," she says, pressing them on me until Daddy comes to my rescue.

⁴Then we have from Mrs. v.P.—"You ought to have been in our home, we were properly brought up. It's absurd that Anne's so frightfully spoiled. I wouldn't put up with it if Anne were my daughter."

These are always her first and last words "If Anne were my daughter," thank heavens I'm not! But to come back to this "upbringing" business, there was a deadly silence after Mrs. v.P. had finished speaking so eloquently⁸ yesterday⁹. Then Daddy said, "I think Anne is extremely well brought | up; she has learned one thing anyway, and that is to make no reply to your long sermons. As to the vegetables, look at your own plate." Mrs. v.P. was beaten, well and truly beaten, she had taken a minute helping of vegetables herself. But she is not spoiled! Oh, no, too many vegetables in the evening are bad¹⁶ for her bowels. Why on earth doesn't she keep her mouth shut about me, then she wouldn't need to make such feeble excuses. It's gorgeous the way Mrs. v.P. blushes, I don't, and that is just what she hates.

Yours, Anne¹⁷

"No, thank you, Mrs. Van Daan," I answer, "I have plenty of potatoes."

"Vegetables are good for you, your mother says so too. Have a few more," she says, pressing them on me until Daddy comes to my rescue.

Then we have from Mrs. Van Daan—"You ought to have been in our home, we were properly brought up. It's absurd that Anne's so frightfully spoiled. I wouldn't put up with it if Anne were my daughter."

These are always her first and last words "if Anne were my daughter." Thank heavens I'm not!

But to come back to this "upbringing" business. There was a deadly silence after Mrs. Van Daan had finished speaking yesterday. Then Daddy said, "I think Anne is extremely well brought up; she has learned one thing anyway, and that is to make no reply to your long sermons. As to the vegetables, look at your own plate." Mrs. Van Daan was beaten, well and truly beaten. She had taken a minute helping of vegetables herself. But *she* is not spoiled! Oh, no, too many vegetables in the evening make her constipated. Why on earth doesn't she keep her mouth shut about me, then she wouldn't need to make such feeble excuses. It's gorgeous the way Mrs. Van Daan blushes. I don't, and that is just what she hates.

Yours, Anne

251

27 Sept. 1942.

Dearest Pien,
haven't written to you for a long time, but I am fairly busy. Please don't think that I'm
cross with you, because that's absolutely not true.

64

Monday 28 Sept. 1942

Dear Kitty,
[1]the letter I wrote yesterday was nowhere near finished when I had to break off, hence
this sequel.[2] [3]and straight away I have to report another argument[4]

64

Monday 28 Sept. 1942

Dear Kitty,
I had to stop yesterday long before I'd finished. I just must tell you about another quarrel,
but before I start on that, something else. Why do grownups quarrel so easily, so much,
and over the most idiotic things? Up till now I thought that only children squabbled and
that that wore off as you grew up. Of course, there is sometimes a real reason for a
quarrel, but this is just plain bickering. I suppose I should be used to it. But I can't nor
do I think I shall as long as I am the subject of nearly every discussion (they use the word
"discussion" instead of quarrel, quite wrongly, of course, but then these Germans[10] know
no better than that!).

Monday, 28 September, 1942.

Dear Kitty,
   I had to stop yesterday, long before I'd finished. I just must tell you about another
quarrel, but before I start on that, something else.
   Why do grownups quarrel so easily, so much, and over the most idiotic things? Up
till now I thought that only children squabbled and that that wore off as you grew up.
Of course, there is sometimes a real reason for a quarrel, but this is just plain bickering.
I suppose I should get used to it. But I can't nor do I think I shall, as long as I am the
subject of nearly every discussion (they use the word "discussion" instead of quarrel).

a   . . . . . .

b

| 65   Nothing I repeat nothing about me is right; my general appearance, my character, my manners are discussed from A to Z. I'm expected (by order) to simply swallow all the harsh | words and shouts in silence and I am not used to this. In fact, I can't! I'm not going to take all these insults lying down, I'll show them that Anne Frank wasn't born yesterday. Then they'll be surprised and perhaps they'll keep their mouths shut when I let them see that I am going to start educating them. Shall I take up that attitude? Plain barbarism! I'm simply amazed again and again over their awful manners and especially . . . . stupidity, (Mrs. v.P.'s!) but as soon as I get used to this and it won't be long, then I'll give them some of their own back, and no half measures. Then they'll change their tune! Am I really so bad-mannered, conceited, headstrong, pushing, stupid, lazy, etc., etc., as they all say? Oh, of course not. I have my faults, just like everyone else,

| 66   I know that, but they thoroughly exaggerate everything! | Kitty, if only you knew how I sometimes boil under so many gibes and jeers and I don't know how long I shall be able to stifle my rage. I shall just blow up one day.

c

Nothing, I repeat, nothing about me is right; my general appearance, my character, my manners are discussed from A to Z. I'm expected (by order) to simply swallow all the harsh words and shouts in silence and I am not used to this. In fact, I can't! I'm not going to take all these insults lying down, I'll show them that Anne Frank wasn't born yesterday. Then they'll be surprised and perhaps they'll keep their mouths shut when I let them see that I am going to start educating them. Shall I take up that attitude? Plain barbarism! I'm simply amazed again and again over their awful manners and especially . . . stupidity (Mrs. Van Daan's), but as soon as I get used to this—and it won't be long—then I'll give them some of their own back, and no half measures. Then they'll change their tune!

Am I really so bad-mannered, conceited, headstrong, pushing, stupid, lazy, etc., etc., as they all say? Oh, of course not. I have my faults, just like everyone else, I know that, but they thoroughly exaggerate everything.

Kitty, if only you knew how I sometimes boil under so many gibes and jeers. And I don't know how long I shall be able to stifle my rage. I shall just blow up one day.

253

I must tell you about a drama that took place a few weeks ago, which will give you a clear picture of our relations here.

One Sunday morning we were sitting at breakfast, and we were talking about how modest Daddy is and then Mrs. v.P. said:

"I too have an unassuming nature, more so than my husband!"

Mr. v.P: "I don't wish to be modest," and to me: "Take my advice, Anne, don't be too unassuming, it will never get you anywhere!" with which Mummy agreed.

Still, no more of this, I've bored you long enough with all these quarrels. But I simply must add one highly interesting discussion at table: Somehow or other, we got on the subject of Pim's extreme modesty. Even the most stupid people have to admit this modesty about Daddy. Suddenly Mrs. v.P. says, "I too, have an unassuming nature, more so than my husband!"

Did you ever! This sentence in itself shows quite clearly how thoroughly forward and pushing she is! Mr. v.P. thought he ought to give an explanation regarding the reference to himself. "I don't wish to be modest³—in my experience | it does not pay." Then to me: "Take my advice, Anne, don't be too unassuming, it doesn't get you anywhere"; Mummy agreed with this too.

| 67

Still, no more of this, I've bored you long enough with all these quarrels. But I simply must tell you of one highly interesting discussion at table. Somehow or other, we got on to the subject of Pim's (Daddy's nickname) extreme modesty. Even the most stupid people have to admit this about Daddy. Suddenly Mrs. Van Daan says, "I too, have an unassuming nature, more so than my husband."

Did you ever! This sentence in itself shows quite clearly how thoroughly forward and pushing she is! Mr. Van Daan thought he ought to give an explanation regarding the reference to himself. "I don't wish to be modest—in my experience it does not pay." Then to me: "Take my advice, Anne, don't be too unassuming, it doesn't get you anywhere."

Mrs. v.P.: "What a stupid thing to say to Anne, that outlook on life is just too silly!"

Mummy: "I myself also think that you don't get much further with it, just look, my husband and Margot and Peter are exceptionally modest while Anne, your husband, and I are not modest at all. We are not immodest, but we are not modest either."

Mrs. v.P.: "Oh, no, on the contrary, I am very modest, how can you say that I am immodest?"

Mummy: "I haven't said that you are immodest, but you aren't all that modest either."

But Mrs. van Pels had to add, as always, her ideas on the subject. Her next remark was addressed to Mummy and Daddy: "You have a strange outlook on life. Fancy saying such a thing to Anne; it was very different when I was young, but then it must still be so except in your modern home!" This was a direct hit at the way Mummy brings up her daughters.

Mrs. v.P. was scarlet by this time. Mummy calm and cool as a cucumber. People who blush get so hot and excited, it is a great handicap in such a situation. | Mummy, still entirely unruffled, but anxious to close the conversation as soon as possible, thought for a second and then said: "I find, too, Mrs. v.P., that one gets on better in life if one is not overmodest. My husband, now, and Margot, and Peter are exceptionally modest, whereas your husband, Anne, you and I, though not exactly the opposite, don't allow ourselves to be completely pushed to one side." Mrs. v.P.: "But, Mrs. Frank, I don't understand you; I'm so very modest and retiring, how can you think of calling me anything else?" Mummy: "I did not say you were exactly forward, but no one could say you had a retiring disposition."

Mummy agreed with this too. But Mrs. Van Daan had to add, as always, her ideas on the subject. Her next remark was addressed to Mummy and Daddy. "You have a strange outlook on life. Fancy saying such a thing to Anne; it was very different when I was young. And I feel sure that it still is, except in your modern home." This was a direct hit at the way Mummy brings up her daughters.

Mrs. Van Daan was scarlet by this time. Mummy calm and cool as a cucumber. People who blush get so hot and excited, it is quite a handicap in such a situation. Mummy, still entirely unruffled, but anxious to close the conversation as soon as possible, thought for a second and then said: "I find, too, Mrs. Van Daan, that one gets on better in life if one is not overmodest. My husband, now, and Margot, and Peter are exceptionally modest, whereas your husband, Anne, you, and I, though not exactly the opposite, don't allow ourselves to be completely pushed to one side." Mrs. Van Daan: "But, Mrs. Frank, I don't understand you; I'm so very modest and retiring, how can you think of calling me anything else?" Mummy: "I did not say you were exactly forward, but no one could say you had a retiring disposition."

Mrs. v.P.: How am I pushing then, if I didn't look after myself, I'd soon starve to death!"

Mummy laughed, and so they went on. I got so involved, that I found myself shaking my head at one point. She got even more furious then, of course, and delivered another sermon at me, which made me burst out laughing.

75 *She is an idiot, and he's a bit of one too but much nicer, and their son is very nice but dull. Well Pien here you have another little bit of gossip, but better that than some long and boring tale. Regards to your family and Kaki from me. As ever, your*

AnneFrank

Mrs. v.P.: "Let us get this matter cleared up once and for all. I'd like to know in what way I am pushing? I know one thing, if I didn't look after myself I'd soon be starving."

69   This absurd remark in self-defense just made Mummy rock with laughter. That irritated Mrs. v.P., who added a string of German-Dutch, Dutch-German expressions, until she became completely tongue-tied; then she rose from her chair and was about to leave the room. Suddenly her eye fell on me. You should have seen her, unfortunately at the very moment that she turned round, I was shaking my head sorrowfully—not on purpose, but quite involuntarily, for I had been following the whole conversation so closely, Mrs. v.P. turned round and began to reel off a lot of harsh German, common, and ill-mannered, just like a coarse, red-faced fishwife—it was a marvelous sight. If I could draw, I'd have

| 70 liked to catch her like this, it was a scream, such a stupid, foolish little person! | Anyhow, I've learned one thing now. You only really get to know people when you've had a jolly good row with them, then and then only can you judge their true characters!

Yours, Anne.

    Mrs. Van Daan: "Let us get this matter cleared up, once and for all. I'd like to know in what way I am pushing? I know one thing, if I didn't look after myself, I'd soon be starving."

    This absurd remark in self-defense just made Mummy rock with laughter. That irritated Mrs. Van Daan, who added a string of German-Dutch, Dutch-German expressions, until she became completely tongue-tied; then she rose from her chair and was about to leave the room.

    Suddenly her eye fell on me. You should have seen her. Unfortunately, at the very moment that she turned round, I was shaking my head sorrowfully—not on purpose, but quite involuntarily, for I had been following the whole conversation so closely.

    Mrs. Van Daan turned round and began to reel off a lot of harsh German, common, and ill-mannered, just like a coarse, red-faced fishwife—it was a marvelous sight. If I could draw, I'd have liked to catch her like this; it was a scream, such a stupid, foolish little person!

    Anyhow, I've learned one thing now. You only really get to know people when you've had a jolly good row with them. Then and then only can you judge their true characters!

Yours, Anne

Tuesday 29 Sept. '42.

Dear Kitty,

Extraordinary[1] things can happen to people who go into hiding.[2] Just imagine, as there is no bath, we use a washtub and because there is hot water only in the office (by which I always[4] mean the whole of the lower floor) all 7 of us take it in turns to make use of this great luxury. But because we are all so different and some are more modest than others, each member of the family has found his own place for carrying out the performance. Peter uses the kitchen in spite of its glass door. When he is going to have a bath he goes to each one of us in turn and tells us that we must not walk past the kitchen for half an hour. He seems to think this is sufficient.[12] Mr. v.P. goes right upstairs; to him it is worth the bother of carrying hot water all that way, so as to have the seclusion of

| 72   his own room. Mrs. v.P. simply doesn't bathe at all at present, she is waiting to see | which is the best place. Daddy has his bath in the private office, Mummy behind a fire guard in the kitchen, Margot and I have chosen the front office for our scrub.[13] The curtains there are drawn on Saturday afternoons, so we wash ourselves in semi-darkness while the one awaiting her turn[20] peers out of the window through a chink in the curtain and gazes in wonder at[21] all the funny people outside.

Tuesday, 29 September, 1942

Dear Kitty,

Extraordinary things can happen to people who go into hiding. Just imagine, as there is no bath, we use a washtub and because there is hot water in the office (by which I always mean the whole of the lower floor) all seven of us take it in turns to make use of this great luxury.

But because we are all so different and some are more modest than others, each member of the family has found his own place for carrying out the performance. Peter uses the kitchen in spite of its glass door. When he is going to have a bath, he goes to each one of us in turn and tells us that we must not walk past the kitchen for half an hour. He seems to think this is sufficient. Mr. Van Daan goes right upstairs; to him it is worth the bother of carrying hot water all that way, so as to have the seclusion of his own room. Mrs. Van Daan simply doesn't bathe at all at present; she is waiting to see which is the best place. Daddy has his bath in the private office, Mummy behind a fire guard in the kitchen; Margot and I have chosen the front office for our scrub. The curtains there are drawn on Saturday afternoons, so we wash ourselves in semidarkness [while the one awaiting her turn peers out of the window through a chink in the curtain and gazes in wonder at all the funny people outside].

27 Sept. 1942.

Dear Pop,
Another little scribble, today I took a really peculiar bath, like this, first I carry a small
washtub downstairs to the large W.C., then I take it to the water heater, run hot water
into the tub in the office kitchen, and then I go and put my feet in it, meanwhile sitting
on the W.C. and start to wash myself, but of course it all splashes everywhere and later
when I'm clean, I have to wipe everything up with the dirty mop. At home I would never
have believed that one day I'd be taking a bath in a w.c., but it isn't all that bad, for it
could still happen that I might have to live in a w.c. one day, then I'd have a little bookshelf
made and a little table and use the w.c. as a chair, but there wouldn't be anywhere to
sleep, I'd have to be able to push everything out of the way and that couldn't be done.
There is a light as well and you can also black the place out. Well Pop the family has
arrived, with the cat, and now I am being distracted, because I want to go and look.
Kindest regards to Kees, and love from

Anne Frank

28 Sept. 1942.

Dearest Kit,
We can't use the W.C. this afternoon which is most unpleasant, but there's nothing we
can do about it, worse things could happen. The workmen came to change the pipes in
the office W.C. and they are afraid that the pipes might break, so they're having to come
| 76   upstairs, which is pretty awkward, but Kleiman said he didn't have the key | *with him,*
so they're going to have to come back tomorrow, and then we'll have to clear out the
bathroom and the w.c., but we hope this won't happen. The rack which we use as our
door which I think I told you about some time ago will probably have to be taken away
in that case, but I don't know if that can be done.

However, I don't like this place any longer, and since last week I've been on the
lookout for more comfortable quarters. Peter gave me an idea and that was to try the
large office w.c. There I can sit down, have the light on, lock the door, pour⁶ my own
bath water away, and I'm safe from prying eyes. I tried my beautiful bathroom on Sunday
| 73   for the first time and although it sounds mad, I think it is the best | place of all. ⁹On
Wednesday the plumber was at work downstairs to move the drains and water pipes from
the office w.c. to the passage. This change is a precaution against frozen pipes in case we
should have a cold winter. The plumber's visit was far from pleasant for us, not only were
we unable to draw water the whole day, but we could not go to the w.c. either.

However, I don't like this place any longer, and since last week I've been on the
lookout for more comfortable quarters. Peter gave me an idea and that was to try the
large office W.C. There I can sit down, have the light on, lock the door, pour my own
bath water away, and I'm safe from prying eyes.
I tried my beautiful bathroom on Sunday for the first time and although it sounds
mad, I think it is the best place of all. Last week the plumber was at work downstairs to
move the drains and water pipes from the office W.C. to the passage. This change is a
precaution against frozen pipes, in case we should have a cold winter. The plumber's visit
was far from pleasant for us. Not only were we unable to draw water the whole day, but
we could not go to the W.C. either.

a   . . . . . .

b

           Now it is rather indecent to tell you what we did to overcome this difficulty, however, I'm not such a prude that I can't talk about these things. The day we arrived here, Daddy and I improvised a pottie for ourselves; not having a better receptacle, we sacrificed a glass preserving jar for this purpose. During the plumber's visit, nature's offerings were deposited in these jars in the sitting room throughout the | day, I don't think this was anything like as bad as having to sit still and not talk the whole day. You can't imagine what a trial that was for "Miss Quack-Quack." I have to whisper on ordinary days;[3] but not being able to speak or move was ten × worse.

       After being flattened by three days of continuous sitting, my bottom was very stiff and painful. Some exercises at bedtime helped.

Yours, Anne

| 74

c

           Now it is rather indecent to tell you what we did to overcome this difficulty; however, I'm not such a prude that I can't talk about these things.

       The day we arrived here, Daddy and I improvised a pottie for ourselves; not having a better receptacle, we sacrificed a glass preserving jar for this purpose. During the plumber's visit, nature's offerings were deposited in these jars in the sitting room during the day, I don't think this was nearly as bad as having to sit still and not talk the whole day. You can't imagine what a trial that was for "Miss Quack-Quack." I have to whisper on ordinary days; but not being able to speak or move was ten times worse. After being flattened by three days of continuous sitting, my bottom was very stiff and painful. Some exercises at bedtime helped.

Yours, Anne

259

The Broks family want to let out a room, *well it can only be our room, and that's pretty mean of them because they'll be getting double rent then for a single room. We're so afraid that they'll throw our stuff out.*[1] *This morning we worked really hard making potato cholent* and the whole orphanage as we call it had to help with peeling potatoes and putting them through the grating machine, I rubbed them just like apples over the little thingummy with holes, it makes it much finer that way, but it's a terrible job, and you need a lot of strength and it takes much longer of course than putting it through the machine. Margot and I got in the same bed together last evening, it was a frightful squash, but that was just the fun of it, she asked if she could read my diary sometime, I said yes at least bits of it, and then I asked if I could read hers, and then we got on to the subject of the future and then I asked her what she wanted to be, but she wouldn't say and made a great secret of it, but I gathered something about teaching, I'm not sure if I'm right of course but I think that's the direction she's going in. I really shouldn't be so curious. This morning I was lying on Peter's bed, having chased him off at first, he was furious with me, not that I cared very much, he might be a bit more friendly with me for once; after all I did give him an apple yesterday as consolation for his desperate love which I am conceited enough to imagine exists. I asked |* Margot *if she thought I was very ugly, she said that I was quite attractive and that I had nice eyes, rather vague don't you think? Till next time then, with greetings to your parakeet other half from*

| 77

Anne Frank

---

*A stew cooked in the oven overnight and normally intended to meet the need for a hot dish on the Jewish Sabbath. A.J.P.

28 Sept. 1942.

Dearest Pien,

I use a preserving glass as a potty, it's in the bathroom during the day but I am horribly afraid that they might want to use it as a preserving glass again, but just smelling it should be more than enough for them. At night I manage it all by feeling and I put it right round my "vagina" and a little bit further round it works all right. Not too long and not too nice a letter is it, well, another time, last time I didn't do you too badly. Regards to your sweetheart, from your friend,

Anne Frank.

28 Sept. 1942.

Dearest Loutje,

Peter goes to the storeroom in the evenings to empty the slop buckets, on Monday nights someone often rings the doorbell and then we jump out of our skins. Someone also telephones after office hours once in a while. I could easily write on every page "Pim is a darling!!!! Mummy isn't!!!!"[6] *The first I mean just as much as the second, nasty of me isn't it!!!! It's really interesting I think to have an impressive "something" like that on every page. How is Kaki, I have finished the "Joop ter Heul" books, and just like you I thought the last book was the nicest. I am not sitting properly, as you might have noticed from my handwriting, and so good bye my girl, jour**

Anne Frank.

---

*Anne wrote "good bye my girl, jour" in the original. A.J.P.

. . . . . .

. . . . . .

260

a 80

Dearest Conny,

Yesterday I couldn't write to you because it was Mrs. v.P.'s birthday, it was very enjoyable, and in the afternoon I drank five cups of tea. Mrs. v.P. was given chrysanthemums by the staff and roses by us. Mr. v.P. presented her with red carnations, very pretty. For lunch we had cauliflower with tongue and potatoes, with tomato soup as a delicious gravy. Then in the afternoon the whole office came upstairs including Mr. Voskuyl we had apple tarts and coffee (except for me who had tea). In the evening we laughed ourselves silly at table because I put Mrs. Dreher's fur collar round Daddy's head which made him look so divine you could have died laughing, Mr. van Pels tried it on too and he looked even sillier, particularly when he put Margot's spectacles on his nose as well. He looked just like a little old German lady, and no one would have been able to recognize Mr. v. Pels inside. It wasn't such fun in the evening, since we were all without exception very tired. Mrs. v.P. had baked a delicious plum cake.

This morning we were glad that the plumber didn't come, because his son who was in Germany and had returned, was having to go back again because he had received another call-up. Mr. Levinsohn came instead, he had to boil up test samples for Mr. Kugler. It wasn't very pleasant, because this person, just like the plumber, knows the whole house, so we had to be as quiet as mice.

b 75

Thursday 1 Oct. 1942.

Dearest Kitty,

I got a terrible shock yesterday, suddenly at 8 o'clock there was a loud ring; of course, I thought that someone had come, you'll guess who I mean. But I calmed down a bit when everyone said it must be some urchins or perhaps the postman.

The days are becoming very quiet here. Levinsohn, a small Jewish chemist and dispenser, works for Mr. Kugler in the kitchen. He knows the whole house very well and therefore we are always afraid that he'll take it into his head to have a peep in the old laboratory. We are as quiet as baby mice.[4] Who, 3 months ago, would have guessed that quicksilver Anne would have to sit still for hours—and what's more, could?

c

Thursday, 1 October, 1942

Dear Kitty,

I got a terrible shock yesterday. Suddenly at eight o'clock the bell rang loudly. Of course, I thought that someone had come: you'll guess who I mean. But I calmed down a bit when everyone said it must be some urchins or perhaps the postman.

The days are becoming very quiet here. Lewin, a small Jewish chemist and dispenser, works for Mr. Kraler in the kitchen. He knows the whole building well and therefore we are always afraid that he'll take it into his head to have a peep in the old laboratory. We are as quiet as [baby] mice. Who, three months ago, would ever have guessed that quicksilver Anne would have to sit still for hours—and, what's more, could?

| 81 *I am working hard at my French irregular verbs, and also at the vocabulary of "La | belle Nivernaise." Miep came later and went upstairs, Daddy and I who had been sitting downstairs followed her up. I went and lay down next to Mr. v. Pels, it was lovely and warm and when Miep had gone again I started to write to you. Miep and Jan are coming to sleep here this Friday or next, we'll take Daddy's bed into our room then and the two of them can sleep there. Miep is bringing two woolen blankets and we can also get a fluffy blanket and an eiderdown and pillows from Mr. Fuchs's suitcase upstairs so they can't possibly be too cold. We'll wheel my little divan into the next-door room, and Margot will sleep on the camp bed. Mrs. van Pels and I have non-stop quarrels because she's always trying to stroke Daddy's hair, and I happen to be jealous as you know, so I can't stand that, particularly as she puts on such airs, Mummy doesn't behave like that with Mr. v.P., I've said that to Mrs. v.P.'s face.*

76   The 29th was Mrs. van Pels's birthday. Although there were no big celebrations we managed a little party in her honor with a specially nice meal and she received some small presents and flowers. Red carnations from her husband; that seems to be a family tradition.

To pause for a moment on the subject of Mrs. v.P., I must tell you that her attempts to flirt with Daddy are a source of continual irritation for me. She strokes his face and hair, pulls her skirt right up and makes so-called witty remarks, trying in this way to attract Pim's attention. Pim, thank goodness, doesn't find her either attractive or funny and so he plays ball.

Now and then Peter comes out of his shell and can be quite funny. We have one thing in common, from which everyone usually gets a lot of amusement: we both love dressing up. He appeared in one of Mrs. v.P.'s very narrow dresses and I in his suit we topped it all off with a hat and a cap. The grownups were doubled up with laughter and we enjoyed ourselves as much as they did.

The twenty-ninth was Mrs. Van Daan's birthday. Although it could not be celebrated in a big way, we managed a little party in her honor, with a specially nice meal, and she received some small presents and flowers. Red carnations from her husband; that seems to be a family tradition. To pause for a moment on the subject of Mrs. Van Daan, I must tell you that her attempts to flirt with Daddy are a source of continual irritation for me. She strokes his face and hair, pulls her skirt right up, and makes so-called witty remarks, trying in this way to attract Pim's attention. Pim, thank goodness, doesn't find her either attractive or funny, so he doesn't play ball. [I happen to be jealous, as you know, so I can't stand that.] Mummy doesn't behave like that with Mr. Van Daan, I've said that to Mrs. Van Daan's face.

Now and then Peter comes out of his shell and can be quite funny. We have one thing in common, from which everyone usually gets a lot of amusement: we both love dressing up. He appeared in one of Mrs. Van Daan's very narrow dresses and I put on his suit. He wore a hat and I a cap. The grownups were doubled up with laughter and we enjoyed ourselves as much as they did.

262

Bep's friend Bertus has to go to Germany too. Bep is very down,* which is understandable.

I have a terrible pain in my index finger (on my left hand luckily) and can't do any ironing right now, luckily!

Mr. v. Pels would rather I sat next to him at table, because Margot no longer eats as much as he would like, well changes like that suit me too. There's a little black pussy cat that keeps running about in the garden reminding me of my¹ moortje, oh, the darling. Mummy always has some comment or other to make, especially at table, so the change | 82 is nice for that reason too, now | Margot will bear the brunt of it, or rather she won't since Mummy doesn't make such sarcastic comments to her, model child that she is! I keep teasing her all the time about being a model child which she can't stand, perhaps she'll give it up, it's high time.

When anyone is downstairs we all have to go up to the attic with our jam-preserving glasses or potties, since we can't use the w.c. That's enough for today now, 'bye Con, regards to your dear husband from

Anne Frank

*The word "down" is in English. A.J.P.

20 Oct. 1942.
Tuesday.

Dearest Kitty,

We've now received the skirts. But how ridiculous they are, just listen, mine is miles too long and very tight, and the material is a bit like jute, which they use to make potato sacks. The seams split the moment I put it on. The snap fasteners were loose by the time the skirts got here, and wherever there was any sewing there were long threads and holes in the seam. This kind of thing which the shops would never have dared to sell in the olden days now costs 7.75 florins. I had a skirt at home that I wore for three years and is still good and it cost 1.95 florins. Margot has a similar object also made from jute, with pleats. Much too wide on top and much too tight around the hips and the seams all lumpy and it cost 24 florins. It's just ludicrous.

Bep has bought new skirts for Margot and me at Bijenkorf's. The material is tatty¹, just like sacking, and they cost 24 florins and 7.75 florins respectively. What a difference | 77 compared with before the war! | Another nice thing I have been keeping up my sleeve, Bep has written to some secretarial school or other and ordered a correspondence course in shorthand for Margot, Peter and me. You wait and see what perfect experts we shall be by next year. In any case it's extremely important to be able to write in a code.

To end this mishmash of news, here is a particularly witty joke told by Mr. v.P. What goes tick 999 times and tack once? A millipede with a club foot!

'bye yours, Anne

Elli has bought new skirts for Margot and me at Bijenkorf's. The material is rotten, just like sacking, and they cost 24.00 florins and 7.50 florins respectively. What a difference compared with before the war!

Another nice thing I've been keeping up my sleeve. Elli has written to some secretarial school or other and ordered a correspondence course in shorthand for Margot, Peter, and me. You wait and see what perfect experts we shall be by next year. In any case it's extremely important to be able to write in a code.

Yours, Anne

1 *30 sept.**

1942

This morning we were able to go downstairs again after breakfast as usual. The plumber wasn't coming, because his son had received a call-up notice for Germany and had to leave straight away. I went downstairs to work. At about half past twelve Mr. Levinsohn came, he had to be in the kitchen boiling things with Mr. Kugler. More nuisance, because Mr. Levinsohn knows the building just as well if not better than the plumber. So the family had to be as quiet as mice and Mr. Levinsohn argued about something with Mr. Kugler in his booming voice, and if Mr. Kugler left the kitchen for just 5 minutes he started shouting after him: "Mr. Kugler!!!! Mr. Kugler!!!!"

The poor man didn't have a minute's peace. No sooner had he finally seen the back of Mr. Levinsohn at half past two, than Mr. Kugler had to go downstairs again to see the accountant whose nose was buried in the books.

A big change at table, where I am sitting next to Mr. van Pels and Margot next to Mummy, this is because Margot was having a bad effect on Mr. v.P.'s appetite so now I 2 have to act as substitute. The menu | was not very tempting, at least for me, whereas Mr. v.P. ate 3 large platefuls and according to him could have eaten a 4th one as well.

1 October 1942. Today the three dangerous people have joined forces, i.e. Levinsohn, the charwoman and Mr. Broks. Mr. Levinsohn now refers to himself as Mijnheer Muller on the telephone because he is not allowed to telephone Christians.

So the family was upstairs again this morning. The menu consisted of hash, only without the fun bits as Peter calls them.

6 Oct. 1942.

Bokkie Pepertje Sokkie Tokkie Pepertje—Pokkie Pepertje Pokkie

Today we finally got a bit of peace again, if you can call it that seeing that Levinsohn is still coming in the afternoon. In the morning I did some French and History with Daddy, but not without interruptions from Kugler and Kleiman. Kleiman has something really horrible Hemorites they are veins in your bowels, if you go to the w.c. or break wind that presses against the blood vessels and they burst so that the blood runs out and people 3 often get their trousers full of blood | in the street. The operation for it is really nasty, the bowels have to be taken out of the body and for 8 days you cannot go to the w.c. so you get a really fat stomach of course. Kleiman has already had one operation like that and doesn't want another one at all, but perhaps he will manage with some ointment. This

---

*These pages (1 to 5 inclusive) were stuck in by Anne with brown adhesive tape at the beginning of Diary 1.

b . . . . . .

c . . . . . .

afternoon Miep came with last May's list of outstanding debts, Daddy and I dealt with it before supper. Tonight, the sales ledger has to be brought completely up to date as well, but I think Daddy will do it, he won't finish of course because the list of debts has to be totted up too.

Miep has had a spot of bother again there were house searches at her parents' (foster parents) and one room was sealed off, because the man was keeping his son-in-law's things in the room now there are a lot of other things in there as well it's really annoying. Every night people are being picked up without warning and that is awful particularly for old

| 4

and sick people, they treat them just like slaves in the olden days. The poor old | people are taken outside at night and then they have to walk for instance as far as Adama v. Scheltemaplein in a whole procession with children and everything then when they arrive at Adama v. Scheltemaplein they are sent to Ferdinand Bolstraat and from there back again to A. v. Scheltemaplein and that's how they plague these poor people. Also they throw water over them if they scream. How lucky we are to be here. Miep has also been to see Helene she runs a rest home and is trying to get a special exemption so that she doesn't have to leave. Mr. Rozendaal, the deaf man from the Tokita has also been picked up because he took the J off his identity card. Mr. Huisburg is in Westerborg too but can stay on there for the time being and work for the Jewish Council. Mr. Holland the sports commentator [with] his son and wife are also gone just like Mr. de Vries from the Noorder Amstellaan sports club. Mrs. Bunjes had a baby on 1 October Joke, Regina a lovely name. Mr. Bunjes has been sacked from Cineac because one evening he cut a film a bit short in

| 5

order to catch the last tram, but they | really did it because he is a quarter Jew, but doesn't count as one. Tonight we laughed and laughed at what were really nothing but feeble jokes. Margot looks as if she has just escaped from a slum and I don't look much better because yesterday our hair was washed.

I eat an enormous amount, so much that everyone is astounded even greens though not so much in the evenings. This afternoon and tonight again we had kale but without any sausage, tonight I didn't eat it. This afternoon I had a nap again after a long time without and before that, instead of reading I dressed up my little doll from Mrs. Eichwald's cradle it looks very nice and fixed the bear, the only bit of jewelry I have left (that sounds sad doesn't it) so that it looks as if he's crawling. I finished The Kingford School but I don't think it's nearly as nice as the other books by Cissy van Marxveldt there is nothing gripping in it.

3 Oct. 1942.

Dearest Marianne,

It's been a few days again since I last wrote, but a lot of really bad things have happened in the meantime. Yesterday they went on at me because I lay on the bed beside Mr. v. Pels. At your age, for shame!, and suchlike expressions. Silly of course. I would never want to sleep with Mr. v. Pels in the general sense of the word I mean of course. This morning Miep told us that last night they were dragging Jews from house after house again in South Amsterdam.* Horrible. God knows which of our acquaintances are left. A crippled old woman was sitting on Miep's doorstep because she couldn't walk and so the scoundrels went to fetch a car, meanwhile the poor person had to wait out in the cold (she wasn't allowed to go indoors) and there was terrible shooting. You just can't imagine how awful it all is, I am only so glad that we are here. There was another dust-up yesterday and Mummy kicked up a frightful row, she told Daddy just what she thought of me and had an awful fit of tears so, of course, off I went too, and I'd got such a frightful headache anyway. Finally I told Daddy that I'm much more fond of "him" than Mummy, to which

| 83

he replied that I'd get | over that. But I don't believe it. I simply can't stand Mummy, and I have to force myself not to snap at her all the time and to stay calm with her, I could easily slap her face, I don't know how it is that I have taken such a terrible dislike to her. Daddy said that I should sometimes volunteer to help Mummy, when she doesn't feel well or has a headache; but I shan't since I don't like her and I don't feel like it. I would

---

*On Friday and Saturday, October 2 and 3, 1942, there were large-scale raids in Amsterdam and nearly 5,000 Jews were seized.

| 81

⌐ I am working hard at my French irregular verbs, and also at the vocabulary of "La ⌐
⌐ | belle Nivernaise." ⌐

. . . . . .

Saturday, 3 October, 1942

Dear Kitty,

There was another dust-up yesterday, Mummy kicked up a frightful row and told Daddy just what she thought of me. Then she had an awful fit of tears so, of course, off I went too; and I'd got such an awful headache anyway. Finally I told Daddy that I'm much more fond of him than Mummy, to which he replied that I'd get over that. But I don't believe it. I have to simply force myself to stay calm with her. Daddy wishes that I would sometimes volunteer to help Mummy, when she doesn't feel well or has a headache; but I shan't. I am working hard at my French and am now reading *La Belle Nivernaise.*

Yours, Anne

certainly do it for Daddy, I noticed that when he was ill. Also it's easy for me to picture Mummy dying one day, but Daddy dying one day seems inconceivable to me. It may be very mean of me, but that's how I feel. I hope that Mummy won't ever[1] read "this" or any of the other things.

Peter has something wrong with his foot again, that softy, and it's easy to see that he is in love. Yesterday I cut out the coupons, that's quite a nice little job. Peeling potatoes is something else I often do these days, but I dread shelling peas. Today I have to read things in the prayer book, I have no idea why Mummy wants to force me to do that, but I'll do it to oblige her and above all for Pim.

Mummy has just said that if we ever get back home and are allowed to stay, we shall probably take in the Goslar baby, I think that's terrific; but I don't think we would ever let go of her again in that case. I have such a lovely book, it's called "Eva's youth." The Eva in it thought that children grow like apples on a tree and that the stork plucks them off when they are ripe and carries them to their mothers. But her girl friend's cat had kittens and they came out of the cat, then she thought that the cat lays eggs like a chicken, and then goes and sits on the brood, and that mothers who are having a baby go upstairs a few days earlier, lay an egg and sit on it, when the baby comes the mothers are still a

| 84 *bit weak from all the squatting. Eva wanted | to have a baby too and so she took a woolen shawl, laid it on the ground so that the egg could drop into it and then squatted down and began to push. She tried clucking but no egg came out. In the end after all that long squatting something did come out of her though not an egg, a little sausage. Oh, Eva was so ashamed. And the maid thought she was sick. Funny isn't it. I take my leave with this dear Marianne, next time more from*

Anne Frank.

P.S. Regards to Jaap. I like you. You do get my meaning don't you?

4 Oct. 1942.
Sunday.

Dearest Kitty,

Today's the kind of lazy day again that I detest. This morning I was in the tub-bath, it was very cozy and I make myself very comfortable there. This morning I put on the radio for a bit. Göring was cursing the Jews something awful!!!! Last night I listened to the radio with Peter it was good fun for the first time in weeks, the jokes were as follows:

{{[8] A photographer wanted to photograph a tall slender lady, but it didn't come out, the photograph was just one long black stripe. Still, the lady was happy with it and said that her husband, who was in the Scouts, was happy too. A few days later the lady came back and asked if the photographer could come round to photograph her again one night. The photographer came and realized what was wanted and began to take off his clothes, whereupon the lady ran away.}}}}[9] Daddy is still in a bad mood today, but that will pass. I lay with Margot on the divan and we read "The Assault" it's quite amusing, but doesn't touch "Joop ter Heul" in fact most of the words are the same in both that is only natural with the same writer.

. . . . . .

. . , . , ,

As a matter of fact Cissij van Marxveld is | first class. I shall definitely let my children read her. In "Eva's youth" there are also bits about unknown women selling their bodies in back streets, and they ask a packet of money for it. I'd die of shame if anything like that happened to me. Also it says that Eva has a monthly period, oh, I'm so longing to have it too, then at least I'd be grown up. Daddy is grumbling again, and threatens to take my diary away, oh insuperable horror. I'm going to have to hide it in future, 'bye (have fun)

AnneFrank

5 Oct. 1942.
<u>Monday</u>

Dearest Pop,

I'm just going to gossip with you for 5 minutes before my hair is washed. "Silence!" was the order of the day once again today. The plumber, Levinsohn (without Susi, the dog) and the charwoman were the three black perils. My white sweater has already become a slipover because it is finished apart from the sleeves. Mrs. v.P. is being as the Jordaaners* put it like a bear with a sore head again, but we are gradually getting used to that. This afternoon we all nearly had to go in our pants because we couldn't go to the w.c. ///³ I get those yellow things in my panties all the time like male seed I imagine, weird but I daren't ask ///⁵ 'bye I can't go on because the water is boiling.

Anne Frank

7 Oct. 1942.
<u>Wednesday.</u>

Dearest Phien,

No one is downstairs this morning luckily so we can be down here. I did a little French but Margot needed the dictionary and then I started on History. Today we baked spiced

gingerbread for Friday when Miep and Jan are coming, I think | that's marvelous, Bep wants to come too one day. My new dream is Switzerland, maybe I'll draw the 8 new dresses here, but I'm not sure yet because my talent for drawing isn't that great, and I'm afraid I'll spoil them, which means that my dream won't have such a nice effect any more. Mummy and I are on better terms again, while Daddy was very touchy yesterday, but we shan't blame him for that. I have now fixed up a dressing case, but it's not nearly as nice as my Swiss one. And I'd really like to have the film. Piet's big toenail is festering, he walks about at night now with a big sock round it, he looks fit to scream. Last night he looked like a baker's boy in his pajama pants and bare chest, then the lumpy foot and a towel over his shoulder and a nailbrush it was a real scream. Daddy was just coming out of the w.c. in his shirt and underpants, he was walking like old Dreher again, you would have died laughing. My back is beginning to hurt so until next time darling Phien.

AnneFrank.

---

*People from the Jordaan, a district of Amsterdam. A.J.P.

b   . . . . . .

c   . . . . . .

7. Oct. 1942.
Wednesday.

Dearest Conny,
Last night I was still hungry for a sandwich and we talked about there being no butter
on the table, downstairs we were picturing them upstairs eating bread and butter, but of
course we couldn't say so. I went upstairs and cut some bread. They were cross because
they said that I would have to eat some kale as well, but I said that as the youngest I was
entitled to at least one favor. Everyone ought to be able to have his say in an argument,
still I couldn't just come out with yes but Mrs. v.P. only ate enough for a bird since I
didn't want to sound impertinent. I fetched the butter as cool as cucumber, but then Mr.
v.P. rounded on me, I was to go downstairs at once and let them see what I'd been up

[85b]   *to and he | was furious with me. I went downstairs as cool as a cucumber while upstairs*
Mrs. v.P. managed to calm Mr. v.P. down a bit, when I got downstairs it wasn't much
better because Daddy began to shout as well, which made me die of shame of course,
because they could hear every word upstairs. But it was all over quickly and the upshot
was that I had behaved stupidly, this morning or rather last night everything was forgotten
again. For breakfast I had bread without butter while the rest had butter on theirs. Miep
came, but luckily she didn't have much to tell, for what she does tell is mostly not very
nice. Bep had brought a box with the clothes Corry had finished, only the skirt wasn't
ready, but of course we can't ask because of course Miep doesn't know about it.

AnneFrank.

87a   Now I imagine that . . . .
I go to Switzerland and take everything along including the furniture and the money.
We get there Daddy and I sleep in 1 room while the boys' study becomes my own little
room where I sit and receive visitors. As a surprise they have bought furniture for it a
teatable, desk, armchairs and divan, the usual. After a few days Daddy gives me 150
florins converted of course but I shall simply call them florins and says that I must use
them to buy things just for me everything I need, I could spend it straightaway and after
that I would be getting 1 florin every week to buy anything I wanted. I go out with Bernd
and buy:[5]

89a			
	3 summer vests	@ ƒ 0.50	= ƒ 1.50
	3 " panties	@ ƒ 0.50	= ƒ 1.50
	3 winter vests	@ ƒ 0.75[1]	= ƒ 2.25
	3 " panties	@ ƒ 0.75	= ƒ 2.25
	2 petticoats	@ ƒ 0.50	= ƒ 1.00
	2 bras (smallest size)	@ ƒ 0.50	= ƒ 1.00
	5 pajamas	@ ƒ 1.00	= ƒ 5.00
	1 summer dress	@ ƒ 2.50	= ƒ 2.50
	1 winter "	@ ƒ 3.–	= ƒ 3.–
	2 bed jackets	@ ƒ 0.75	= ƒ 1.50
	1 small cushion	@ ƒ 1.–	= ƒ 1.–
	1 pair summer slippers[2]	@ ƒ 1.–	= ƒ 1.–
	1 " winter "	@ ƒ 1.50	= ƒ 1.50
	1 " summer shoes (school)	@ ƒ 1.50	= ƒ 1.50
	1 " " " (good)[3]	@ ƒ 2.00	= ƒ 2.00
	1 " winter shoes (school)	@ ƒ 2.50	= ƒ 2.50
	1 " " " (good)	@ ƒ 3.–	= ƒ 3.–
	2 aprons	@ ƒ 0.50	= ƒ 1.–
	25 handkerchiefs	@ ƒ 0.05	= ƒ 1.25.
	4 pairs silk stockings	@ ƒ 0.75	= ƒ 3.–
	4 " knee "	@ ƒ 0.50	= ƒ 2.–
	4 " socks	@ ƒ 0.25	= ƒ 1.–
	2 " thick "	@ ƒ 1.00[4]	= ƒ 2.–

89b		
	3 skeins white wool (skating trousers, cap)	ƒ 1.50
	3 " blue wool (sweater, skirt.)	ff 1.50
	3 " colored wool (cap, scarf,)	ff 1.50
	5 scarves,[6] belts, collars, buttons	ƒ 1.25

$$\underline{ƒ\ 50.}{}^{7}$$

[1]2 *school dresses* (summer.)	@ ƒ 2.– = ƒ 4.–	*Phien.*
2 ″ ″ (winter.)	@ ƒ 3.75 = ƒ 7.50	*Con.*
2 good ″ (summer.)	@ ƒ 2.50 = ƒ 5.–	
2 good ″ (winter.)	@ ƒ 4.–[2] = ƒ 8.–	(*Em.*)
		(*Jet.*)
1 summer skirt	@ ƒ 100 = ƒ 1.–	
1 good winter skirt	@ ƒ 300 = ƒ 300	(*Lou.*)
1 school ″ ″	@ ƒ 2.– = ƒ 2.–	
1 raincoat	@ ƒ 5.– = ƒ 5.–	
1 summer coat	@ ƒ 7.50 = ƒ 7.50	
1 winter coat	@ ƒ 10.– = ƒ 10.–	
2 hats	@ ƒ 2.– = ƒ[3] 4.00[4]	
2 caps	@ ƒ 050 – ƒ 1.–	
	–58. –[5]	

91a

2 *bags* @ ƒ 2.– = ƒ 4.–   108. –[6]
1 *skating dress* = ƒ 2.50
1 *pair skates + shoes* = ƒ 10.–
1 *case with (powder, cold cream, foundation cream, cleansing cream, sun lotion, cotton,*
a little tin of bandages, rouge, lipstick, eyebrow pencil, bath salts, talcum powder, eau de
cologne, soap, powder puff) @ ƒ 5.–
1 *manicure set and nail polish* @ ƒ 2.50
1 *belt and bag* = ƒ1.–
            = ƒ 25.[7]
            ƒ 133.[8]
4 *thin sweaters* @ ƒ 1.50 = ƒ 1.50
4 *blouses* @ ƒ 1.– = ƒ 1.–
various items @ ƒ 10.– *and books*
Small presents ƒ 4.50.

91b   22 January 1944.
       I just want to
       note that toothpaste
       etc. is still being supplied
       to us!
                 AnneFrank.

. . . . . .

. . . . . .

a

Anne.

18 Oct. 1942
Sunday.

In these photographs I was 11 years old.

Captions (clockwise from top left):
Sorry to hear that
all ears
nostrils flared
childishly bashful

---

a 97b

> Miep told us about a man who escaped from Westerbork, things are terrible there, and if it's so bad there what can it be like in Poland? People get hardly anything to eat let alone drink, for they have water for only 1 hour a day and 1 w.c. and 1 washstand for a few 1000 people. They all sleep mixed up together men and women and the latter + children often have their hair cut off so that everyone can recognize them if they escape.
>
> AnneFrank.

---

b 78

Friday 9 October 1942.

Dear Kitty,

I've only got dismal and depressing news[1] for you today. Our many Jewish friends are being rounded up by the dozen. These people are treated by the Gestapo without a shred of decency, being loaded into cattle trucks and sent to Westerbork, the big Jewish camp in Drente. Westerborg sounds terrible, only 1 washstand for thousands of people, 1 w.c. and there is no separate sleeping accommodation. Men, women and children all sleep together.[6] One hears of frightful immorality because of this,[7] and a lot of the women and even girls who stay there any length of time are expecting babies.

It is almost impossible to escape, the people in the camp are all branded as inmates by their shorn heads and many also by their Jewish appearance.

---

c

Friday, 9 October, 1942

Dear Kitty,

I've only got dismal and depressing news for you today. Our many Jewish friends are being taken away by the dozen. These people are treated by the Gestapo without a shred of decency, being loaded into cattle trucks and sent to Westerbork, the big Jewish camp in Drente. Westerbork sounds terrible: only one washing cubicle for a hundred people and not nearly enough lavatories. There is no separate accommodation. Men, women, and children all sleep together. One hears of frightful immorality because of this; and a lot of the women, and even girls, who stay there any length of time are expecting babies.

It is impossible to escape; most of the people in the camp are branded as inmates by their shaven heads and many also by their Jewish appearance.

a   82

This morning Miep told us that last night they were dragging Jews from house after house again in South Amsterdam. Horrible. God knows which of our acquaintances are left. A crippled old woman was sitting on Miep's doorstep because she couldn't walk and so the scoundrels went to fetch a car, meanwhile the poor person had to wait out in the cold (she wasn't allowed to go indoors) and there was terrible shooting. You just can't imagine how awful it all is, I am only so glad that we are here.

b

| 79

If it is as bad as this in Holland, whatever will it be like in the distant and barbarous regions[4] | they are sent to? We assume that most of them are murdered.[5] The English radio speaks of their being gassed;* perhaps that is the quickest way to die.

I feel terribly upset. I couldn't tear myself away while Miep told these dreadful stories, and she herself was just as badly wound up for that matter. Just recently[11] for instance a poor old crippled Jewess was sitting on her doorstep, she had been told to wait there by the Gestapo who had gone to fetch a car to take her away. The poor old thing was terrified by the guns and the shooting at English planes overhead and by the glaring beams of the searchlights. But Miep did not dare to take her in, no one would have done that. The German gentlemen strike without the slightest mercy.

*In June 1942 the British press and the BBC began to refer to the gassings in Poland. Thus the 6 P.M. news on the BBC Home Service on July 9, 1942, included the following item: "Jews are regularly killed by machinegun fire, hand grenades—and even poisoned by gas." (BBC Written Archives Centre, Reading.)

c

If it is as bad as this in Holland whatever will it be like in the distant and barbarous regions they are sent to? We assume that most of them are murdered. The English radio speaks of their being gassed.

Perhaps that is the quickest way to die. I feel terribly upset. I couldn't tear myself away while Miep told these dreadful stories; and she herself was equally wound up for that matter. Just recently for instance, a poor old crippled Jewess was sitting on her doorstep; she had been told to wait there by the Gestapo, who had gone to fetch a car to take her away. The poor old thing was terrified by the guns that were shooting at English planes overhead, and by the glaring beams of the searchlights. But Miep did not dare take her in; no one would undergo such a risk. The Germans strike without the slightest mercy.

a   81

Bep's friend Bertus has to go to Germany too, Bep is very down, which is understandable.

a   94

Another 15 hostages have been shot isn't that dreadful? These people have done absolutely nothing, but are kept as guarantees against possible sabotage. They are all prominent citizens and the papers said it was for sabotage but of course no one can prove that. Now if somebody does something e.g. shooting a German or causing an explosion and he isn't found out then about 5 prominent citizens, who

| 95

have had absolutely nothing to do with it | are shot dead. They do that of course because they think that if someone does commit sabotage then his compatriots must suffer for it and that is really awful.

b

Bep too is very quiet[1], her boy friend[2] has got to go to Germany. Each time[3] she's afraid that the airmen who[4] fly over our homes will let their bombs, often weighing 1 million kilos, fall on Bertus's head.

80

Jokes such as he's not likely to get[7] 1 million and it only takes 1 bomb are in rather bad taste. Bertus is certainly not the only one who has to go, trainloads of boys leave [10]daily. If they stop at a small station en route sometimes some of them manage to slip out on the quiet and escape, perhaps a few manage it.[15]

This, however, is not the end of my bad news. Have you ever heard of hostages? That's the latest thing in penalties for sabotage. Can you imagine anything so dreadful? Prominent citizens—innocent people—are thrown into prison to await their fate. If the saboteur can't be traced the Green police[20] simply put about five hostages against the wall.

| 81

Announcements of their deaths appear in the papers frequently. These outrages | are described as[21] "fatal accidents."[22] Nice people the Germans and to think that I am really one of them too![23] But no, Hitler took away our nationality long ago, in fact Germans and Jews are the greatest enemies in the world.

yours, Anne

c

Elli too is very quiet: her boy friend has got to go to Germany. She is afraid that the airmen who fly over our homes will drop their bombs, often weighing a million kilos, on Dirk's head. Jokes such as "he's not likely to get a million" and "it only takes one bomb" are in rather bad taste. Dirk is certainly not the only one who has to go: trainloads of boys leave daily. If they stop at a small station en route, sometimes some of them manage to get out unnoticed and escape; perhaps a few manage it. This, however, is not the end of my bad news. Have you ever heard of hostages? That's the latest thing in penalties for sabotage. Can you imagine anything so dreadful?

Prominent citizens—innocent people—are thrown into prison to await their fate. If the saboteur can't be traced, the Gestapo simply put about five hostages against the wall. Announcements of their deaths appear in the papers frequently. These outrages are described as "fatal accidents." Nice people, the Germans! To think that I was once one of them too! No, Hitler took away our nationality long ago. In fact, Germans and Jews are the greatest enemies in the world.

Yours, Anne

274

10 Oct. 1942.
Saturday.

Dearest Marianne,

It's a disgrace, isn't it, that you haven't heard from me for so long, and yet so much has happened that I simply haven't had the time to write. Yesterday afternoon Miep went to see Mrs. Stoppelman who is hiding in Bussum with Mrs. van der Horst, Miep went there to look her up. On her return she came straight to us from the station, for she and Jan are to sleep here tonight. First we all ate carrots, potatoes and soup with 2 meatballs each. We were still at the table and Mrs. v.P. was in the middle of washing up, when suddenly ping the light went out, we got a terrible fright of course and Daddy called from below, is the light out? Yes, we called back. And I ran downstairs | to fetch candles. The illumination was festive and of course we thought that the men wouldn't be going back to the warehouse any more. But it was only a quarter past seven and the men went all the same. After 5 minutes our house was bathed in light again. The short had been caused by Daddy's desk lamp. At half past 8 we went upstairs which they had meanwhile aired and had coffee with ginger cake and Marie biscuits. The children had lemon juice. At 10 o'clock we all had to go to the bathroom and soon we were all in bed. The men went with Jan to listen to the radio and the women sat with Miep upstairs, meanwhile Lord* Peter had already gone to bed and was reading there. At half past 10 they all finally made a move and went to bed. At 11 o'clock the lights went out. Margot and I had been in bed reading from 10 to 11, which we are allowed to do on special occasions. This morning I was up early, and Jan was already dressed he had to leave at half past 8, so he was already upstairs having his breakfast at 8 o'clock. Miep was busy getting dressed. And was still in her slip when I came in. Miep also has exactly the same kind of woolen pants for her bicycle as I wear. Margot and I then went to get dressed so we were upstairs much earlier than usual. After a cozy breakfast Miep went downstairs. It was pouring, and she was glad not to have to cycle to the office. Miep offered to take me along one evening to take a bath at her place, and to bring me back home the next evening. But that is much too dangerous for someone could easily see me. After breakfast I first went with Daddy to make the beds, and then I learned 5 French irregular verbs, hard-working, eh? Margot and Peter were reading in our room, | and Musschi was sitting with Margot on the divan, after my French irregularity I also went in and read some of "And the woods sing for ever," it's a very beautiful book, but most unusual, I've almost finished it now. Musschi is lying down with Mummy again now, just like a kitten, I have completely covered her over and she looks sweet. Daddy did my hair just now with the curling tongs, lovely, isn't it! Mr. Kleiman has brought 2 of his daughter's books, Else's jobs and Riek the scamp, I know one of them already, and the other seems very childish to me. Mr. Kleiman's daughter is always referred to as that here, which I think is awfully formal. Mr. Kleiman pretends to her that the books he brings are for Bep's younger sisters, and he said that I'm 16 or 15. On the one hand I wish it were true but on the other hand I don't. 'Bye dearest Marjan love to Jaap from me, and remembering our "secret oo.

AnneFrank

*The word "Lord" is in English. A.J.P.

. . . . . .

. . . . . .

10 Oct. 1942.
Saturday

Dearest Kitty,

My vagina is getting wider all the time, but I could also be imagining it. When I'm on the w.c. I sometimes look then I can see quite definitely that the urine comes out of a little hole in the vagina, but above it there is something else, there is a hole in that too, but I don't know what for. Pim is sweet again,² I always feel in the 7th heaven when he cuddles me. Madame was having a bath but she took the tub down to the kitchen, frightfully odd that seems to me. Now I shall take my leave, I have to go to the w.c. 'Bye. Hoping that we shall be able to continue our peculiar conversation, I send my regards to you and all those dear to you. 'Bye.

AnneFrank.

Wednesday. 14 Oct. 1942.

Dearest Pop,

I simply can't get round to writing to you. I'm terribly busy. Yesterday I first translated a chapter out of "La belle Nivernaise," and made notes of new words. I did a perfectly foul³ math problem and then another 3 pp. of French grammar. Today French Grammar and history. I flatly refuse to do these foul⁴ math problems every day. Daddy agrees that they're horrible. I'm almost better at them than he is, though neither of us is much good and we have to fetch Margot all the time. I'm also busy doing shorthand I think it's marvelous I am the furthest on of the three of us. Bep is ordering the lessons for us and each of us will get a shorthand book, Margot has one already. Tonight I dreamed about P.S. again and he was the same as always. I just wish he would come and hide with us here too. Perhaps the poor boy is already dead in Poland. I just hope he wouldn't let me down. Mummy is her usual again. Last night I did office work. Miep has a terrible cold and so she can't come, Jan neither. We've suggested she should come and stay in bed here, then we can look after her, but she doesn't want to. Madame called me an egotist again today, how stupid!!!! That rotten woman has no character, she just puts it on from time to time, and then she can really be nice. On Monday I washed Mummy's hair and yesterday Mrs. v.P.'s she has such lovely shampoo that I can still smell it on me and my hands. Pim is a darling. He has clipped his little mouse-mustache back a bit again, it was quite a sight, now he's only letting the mustache grow sideways. A letter came today from Erich, Herbi is with them in Switzerland and they are also expecting Paul, Erich's brother. I wish Pim

| 90 *and I could go there as well, it's quite a dream, isn't it!!!! | Darling Poppety, until I hope no longer than 5 days' time, then I'll be back with you in my thoughts!*

Anne Frank.

. . . . . .

Friday, 16 October, 1942

Dear Kitty,

I'm terribly busy. I've just translated a chapter out of *La Belle Nivernaise* and made notes of new words. Then a perfectly foul math problem and three pages of French grammar. I flatly refuse to do these math problems every day. Daddy agrees that they're vile. I'm almost better at them than he is, though neither of us are much good and we often have to fetch Margot. I'm the furthest on of the three of us in shorthand.

14 Oct. 1942.
<u>Wednesday.</u>

Dear Phien,
I haven't written for a long time have I, but then I don't want to keep on spoiling your
honeymoon with my chatter, or doesn't it bother you? Has Bob started work again? And
are you showing any signs of fertilization, I hope so, but it's not all that easy. Goslar's
baby must finally have arrived by now too. Pity we can't see it, when Miep is better again,
she's sure to go there and have a look at it. 'Bye darling Phien, love to your better half,
longing to see you.

AnneFrank.

a   84   I lay with Margot on the divan and we read "The Assault" it's quite amusing, but
doesn't touch "Joop ter Heul" in fact most of the words are the same in both that
| 85   is only natural with the same writer. As a matter of fact Cissij van Marxveld is |
first class. I shall definitely let my children read her.

b   . . . . . .

c   Yesterday I finished *The Assault*. It's quite amusing, but doesn't touch *Joop ter Heul*.
As a matter of fact, I think Cissy van Marxveldt is a first-rate writer. I shall definitely let
my children read her books.

a 96 Mummy, Margot and I are as thick as thieves again. It's really much better. I get into Margot's bed now almost every evening we have spoken about Margot's wanting to be a maternity nurse, I think it's a nice profession, but I would much rather be with toddlers than with babies, but then I would also like to be there one day when someone is having a baby, for then it'll probably seem much less weird to me.

a 76 Margot and I got in the same bed together last evening, it was a frightful squash, but that was just the fun of it, she asked if she could read my diary sometime, I said yes at least bits of it, and then I asked if I could read hers, and then we got on to the subject of the future and then I asked her what she wanted to be, but she wouldn't say and made a great secret of it, but I gathered something about teaching, I'm not sure if I'm right of course but I think that's the direction she's going in. I really shouldn't be so curious. This morning I was lying on Peter's bed, having chased him off at first, he was furious with me, not that I cared very much, he might be a bit more friendly with me for once; after all I did give him an apple yesterday as consolation for his desperate love which I am conceited enough to imagine exists.

| 77 I asked | Margot if she thought I was very ugly, she said that I was quite attractive and that I had nice eyes, rather vague don't you think? Till next time then, with greetings to your parakeet other half from

Anne Frank

b . . . . . .

c   Mummy, Margot, and I are as thick as thieves again. It's really much better. Margot and I got in the same bed together last evening; it was a frightful squash, but that was just the fun of it. She asked if she could read my diary. I said "Yes—at least, bits of it"; and then I asked if I could read hers [and she said "Yes."*] Then we got on to the subject of the future. I asked her what she wanted to be. But she wouldn't say and made a great secret of it. I gathered something about teaching; I'm not sure if I'm right, but I think so. Really, I shouldn't be so curious!

This morning I was lying on Peter's bed, having chased him off at first. He was furious with me, not that I cared very much. He might be a bit more friendly with me for once; after all I did give him an apple yesterday.

I asked Margot if she thought I was very ugly. She said that I was quite attractive and that I had nice eyes. Rather vague, don't you think?

Till next time,

Yours, Anne

---

*The words "and she said 'Yes'" do not appear in any Dutch version of the diary. A.J.P.

a

Dearest Conny,

Yesterday we had another terrible fright. The carpenter was working in front of our cupboard, he had to fill the fire extinguishers and do some repairs to the door leading to the front of the house. We hadn't been warned and were calling blithely to one another all through the house. Suddenly after lunch, Bep had just decided to go downstairs, I heard some hammering and I said psst upstairs, but we thought it was Mummy who was just coming down the attic stairs, but it was Bep on the stairs I heard it again, and the others did too, that's when we realized the carpenter was there. Daddy and I went to the door to listen, but it went on about a quarter of an hour, and Mr. Carpenter hadn't budged. Bep couldn't go downstairs of course because then this man would have seen through our camouflage. Suddenly we heard terrible rattling, at our door. We thought it

| 91   *had to be the carpenter wanting to come and have a | look here. It was absolutely terrifying. Then whistling and thumping all the time. I was horribly frightened and thought our*

---

b   82

Dear Kitty,

My hand still shakes although it's two hours since we had the shock. I should explain that there are five fire extinguishers in the house. Downstairs they are such geniuses that they didn't warn us when the carpenter,[7] or whatever the fellow is called,[8] was coming to fill them. The result was that we weren't making any attempt to be silent until I heard hammering outside on the landing opposite our cupboard door. I [9]thought of the carpenter at once and warned Bep, who was having a meal with us[14] that she shouldn't go downstairs. Daddy and I posted ourselves at the door, so as to hear when the man left. After he'd been working for a quarter of an hour, he laid his hammer and tools down on top of our cupboard (as we thought!) and knocked at our door. We turned absolutely white. Perhaps he had heard something after all and wanted to investigate our secret den. It seemed like it.

---

c

Dear Kitty,

My hand still shakes, although it's two hours since we had the shock. I should explain that there are five fire extinguishers in the house. We knew that someone was coming to fill them, but no one had warned us when the carpenter, or whatever you call him, was coming.

The result was that we weren't making any attempt to keep quiet, until I heard hammering outside on the landing opposite our cupboard door. I thought of the carpenter at once and warned Elli, who was having a meal with us, that she shouldn't go downstairs. Daddy and I posted ourselves at the door so as to hear when the man left. After he'd been working for a quarter of an hour, he laid his hammer and tools down on top of our cupboard (as we thought) and knocked at our door. We turned absolutely white. Perhaps he had heard something after all and wanted to investigate our secret den. It seemed like it.

279

*last hour had come. In my mind I saw us all in a concentration camp or up against a wall. Finally we heard Kleiman call something and we breathed again. An hour later my knees were still trembling and my hands were still shaking. Kleiman hadn't been able to get the door off the hook so had not been able to warn us. In the meantime the carpenter had gone downstairs so he had wanted to fetch Bep, but he couldn't get the door open again. What a fright we had, I can tell you! [2]Daddy and I spoke to each other in French yesterday and nearly died laughing. We have done the first written shorthand lesson of the "Self-development" course, it's going very nicely and quickly. Next week I'll be getting a shorthand book. 'Bye, my darling.***

AnneFrank.

---

*"My darling" is in English. A.J.P.

The knocking, pulling, pushing, and[7] wrenching went on. I nearly fainted at the thought that this utter stranger might discover our beautiful secret hiding place. And just as I thought my last hour was[4] at hand, we heard Mr. Kleiman's voice say "open the door, it's only me." We opened it immediately. What had happened? The hook that holds the cupboard had got jammed, that was why no one had been able to warn us about the carpenter, the man had now gone downstairs and Kleiman wanted to fetch Bep, but couldn't open the cupboard again. It was a great relief to me, I can tell you. In my imagination the man who I thought was trying to get in had been growing and growing in size until in the end he appeared to be a giant and the greatest fascist that ever walked the earth. Well! Well! Luckily everything was okay this time.

The knocking, pulling, pushing, and wrenching went on. I nearly fainted at the thought that this utter stranger might discover our beautiful secret hiding place. And just as I thought my last hour was at hand, I heard Mr. Koophuis say, "Open the door, it's only me." We opened it immediately. The hook that holds the cupboard, which can be undone by people who know the secret, had got jammed. That was why no one had been able to warn us about the carpenter. The man had now gone downstairs and Koophuis wanted to fetch Elli, but couldn't open the cupboard again. It was a great relief to me, I can tell you. In my imagination the man who I thought was trying to get in had been growing and growing in size until in the end he appeared to be a giant and the greatest fascist that ever walked the earth.

Well! Well! Luckily everything was okay this time.

280

15 Oct. 1942.
Thursday.

Dearest Emmy,
Just a little scribble in between whiles, although a month isn't up yet. This morning we
had to stay upstairs again, because of the charwoman, tiresome person! We had potatoes
done in the ovenproof dish but they were still raw, with applesauce and stewed pears.
Yesterday we read in the paper what things you can't get any more,[1] e.g. toothpaste, eau
de cologne, antiques, [2]rouge and powder, leather gloves, porcelain, tiles, fur and other
things like that. Emmy, I still have office work and French to do because I didn't do much
during the day so until next time from AnneFrank.

92

16 Oct. 1942.
Friday.

Dearest Jet,
If Emmy can get a scribble in between whiles then you can't be treated like a poor cousin,
so how are you? There was a little bit of a fright again, I hope everything's okay. Everything
here is still as it was, luckily. Today I made a list of French irregular verbs. It's a fiddly
and boring job but I'd really like to finish it. I haven't done any shorthand yet maybe this
evening, but it's Friday so it's critical. Mummy is in a rotten mood again. We've heard
that the Kohnke family has gone into hiding, good luck to them. I am now reading Körner,
he writes very well. Until next time then Jettie-love from

AnneFrank

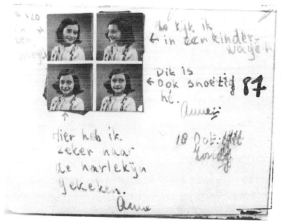

18 Oct. 1942
Sunday

Dear Marianne,
Yesterday there was no time for writ-
ing again. In the first place because I
wanted to finish the list of French ir-
regular verbs and in the second be-
cause I had other work as well. I have
had another 2 books from Kleiman,
the Arcadia. That deals with a voyage
to Spits | bergen and The Purge, they

| 93

captions (clockwise from top left):

> *[illegible]*
> *That's how I look in a pram*
> *Gorgeous as well, isn't it? Anne.*
> *18 October 1942 Sunday*
> *I must have been watching the clown here.*
> > *Anne*

. . . . . .

. . . . . .

281

both seem very good. He also brought me The Rebels. That's by Ammersküller.[1] *The one who wrote Men, Women, Slaves. I am allowed to read that as well now, great! Then I've read a whole pile of romantic plays by Körner, I think he's a fine writer. E.g. Hedwig, der Vetter aus Brehen, Hans Heilings Felsen, Der Grüne* [3]*Domino, Die Gouvernante, Der Vierjährige Posten, Die Sühne, Der Kampf met dem Drachen, Der Nachtwächter and so on. Daddy wants me to read Hebbel now as well and other books by other well-known German writers. I can read German relatively easily now. Only I mostly whisper it instead of reading it to myself. But that will pass no doubt.*

This is a photograph of me as I wish I looked all the time. Then I might still have a chance of getting to Holywood. But at present, I'm afraid, I usually look quite different.

Anne Frank.
10 Oct. 1942
Sunday.

Yesterday I put up some more film stars in my room, but this time with photo corners, so that I can take them down again. Bep went into town yesterday and bought skirts for Margot and me. But they're going to have to be changed, since they don't fit at all.

. . . . . .

. . . . . .

a

[addition
93b]

I've managed to catch up at school by having private tuition and know enough French and German to keep up, anyway I know a good bit of Swiss German as well. I'm in the second class of the high school with nice boys and girls and I soon ferreted out Kitty amongst them a nice girl 14 years old we've become great friends I am good friends with the boys as well.

Bernd is busy teaching me figure skating and I am going to be his partner because his partner happens to be away,[3] we make a lovely pair and everyone is mad about us we sent five photographs to the office 1[4] Anne doing a turn 2[5] Anne arm in arm with Bernd left foot forwards 3[6] Anne waltzing with Bernd 4[7] Anne with Berd doing the swan 5[8] Anne from the left, Bernd from the right blowing a kiss to each other. There will be a film later

93a

for Holland and Switzerland, my girl friends in both Holland and Switzerland think it's great. It's in three parts.

1st part. Anne on skates.

First you see her entering from one side while her partner enters from the other side with a blue skating dress trimmed with white fur with zipped pockets and a zipper and a belt with a bag.

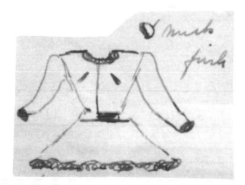

Then they do the swan together and Anne does a tremendous leap in the air. Later they waltz and joke about the lessons.

2nd part. Anne making a visit and at school. Busy at the tea table in the small room with Kitty and two boys including Bernd then at school surrounded by a noisy crowd of children and all sorts of silly scenes e.g. in bed with Daddy and at table.

3rd part. Anne's wardrobe the 8 new dresses skating dress which is a present a white one and shoes.

b   . . . . . .

c   . . . . . .

Bertus Bep's boy friend is leaving on wednesday together with a whole lot of other Dutch people. Nowadays they send nearly all of them to work in Germany. Men as well as women. This morning we all went on the scales again,

Margot now weighs	120	*pounds*	
Mummy	"	124	"
Daddy	"	141	"
Anne	"	87	"
Peter	"	134	*pounds*
Mrs. v.P.	"	106	"
Mr. v.P.	"	150	"

In the three months I have been here I have gained 17 pounds, an enormous amount isn't it! This morning I started to sort out a card index file from the office that had fallen over and was in a complete mess. It nearly drove me mad, and I asked Margot and Peter if they wanted to help me, but they were too lazy. So I put it away again, I'm not so stupid as to do it all by myself. I'm about to go downstairs with my knitting or a book and listen to the radio. I should also have a bath, but I don't feel like it at all, perhaps there won't be enough time left for it.

Mrs. v.P. asked Mr. Kleiman to get all sorts of toilet articles including a small tube of fancy face cream,* which she didn't like, but Mummy did and so they decided to share it. A few days later Mrs. v.P. discovered that the cream was marvelous, and made in the olden days and now all at once she wants to save it, but Mummy isn't stupid. Mrs. v.P. | 94 *doesn't know of course that Margot | and I are also allowed to use it. But we don't care We'll go on doing it anyway. Well Marjan regards to your (bed or marriage) partner from*

Anne Frank

---

*The word "cream" is in English. A.J.P.

20 Oct. 1942.
Tuesday.

Dearest Kitty,

We've now received the skirts. But how ridiculous they are, just listen, mine is miles too long and very tight, and the material is a bit like jute, which they use to make potato sacks. The seams split the moment I put it on. The snap fasteners were loose by the time the skirts got here, and wherever there was any sewing there were long threads and holes in the seam. This kind of thing which the shops would never have dared to sell in the olden days now costs 7.75 florins. I had a skirt at home that I wore for three years and is still good and it cost 1.95 florins. Margot has a similar object also made from jute, with pleats. Much too wide on top and much too tight around the hips and the seams all lumpy and it cost 24 florins. It's just ludicrous. Another 15 hostages have been shot isn't that dreadful?[3] These people have done absolutely nothing, but are kept as guarantees against possible sabotage. They are all prominent citizens and the papers said it was for sabotage but of course no one can prove that.* Now if somebody does something e.g. shooting a

---

*On 16 October 1942 the papers reported that fifteen hostages had been shot by the Germans in response to a number of acts of sabotage in Twente Province. (L. de Jong, *Het Koninkrijk der Nederlanden in de Tweede Wereldoorlog*, Vol. 6, p. 79.)

$$\frac{\quad\quad}{b}\quad\ldots\ldots$$
$$\frac{\quad\quad}{c}\quad\ldots\ldots$$

285

| 95   *German or causing an explosion and he isn't found out then about 5 prominent citizens, who have had absolutely nothing to do with it | are shot dead. They do that of course because they think that if someone does commit sabotage then his compatriots must suffer for it and that is really awful. And in France all men between the ages of 18 and 50 have to report for labor service and that's going to happen here very soon as well. Rosel and Wronker have been sent to Poland.*

    Today first the charwoman was here, and she had hardly left when Daatselaar arrived and when he had gone Levinsohn came back, no one could go to the w.c. Bep has brought the shorthand book. Yesterday I had to draw up the list of outstanding debts again for Miep, but it isn't finished yet.

    There's been a big row here. Mr. Westerman telephoned and said that if Mr. Kugler doesn't stop his laboratory tests now then Hijbroek and he will get their supplies elsewhere. Now if Westerman and Heibroek withdraw then the firm of Gies & Co. is finished. So Kugler's going to have to start selling but he doesn't want to accept that. Mr. v.P. and Pim were so angry that both of them slept badly. Kugler is really being silly. Now he wants to employ a girl but obviously he can't for our sake and for his own as well. "The Rebels" is a first-class book. It's about the Coornvelt family who had 14 children, 2 of whom died of smallpox and 4 from convulsions. The other 8 were Nicolaas the oldest who also has convulsions, then Keejetje who got married to Willem Wijsman and has 4 children Willem, Lize, Agatha, Constance. Constance has a child of her own. Then comes Henrik who is a parson and then Koosje who keeps house for Henrik the widower,[6] Koosje

| 95b   *has smallpox. Then comes David who is a Prof. and who is married to[8] | Aleida and whose children are Clara and Louis. Then comes Saartje who is married to a retired officer and also has 4 children Sophie, Betsy, Cateau, Coba. Then there is a cousin from Paris in the book as well, Marie Elisabeth Sylvain, who is one of the first to join the women's eman- cipation movement, that's the fight there was so that women could study too,[9] if they wanted and have the same rights as men. For in the old days if a woman didn't get married she ended up as a simple old drudge working for one of her brothers in his house. I forgot two children Naatje who is not married and who keeps house for Abraham and Abraham who has 12 children including two that were there before he got married.*

| 95a   *Perhaps I'll ask Bep if she can go and see sometime if Perrij's still sell diaries, or else I'll have to use an exercise book, | because my diary is getting full, what a pity![11] Luckily I can stretch it a bit by sticking in pages. Now enough of this interminable epistle 'bye my darling from*

                                                        AnneFrank

b   . . . . . .

c   . . . . . .

P.S. I forgot to tell you the important news that I shall probably be having my period soon. I noticed that because I keep having a kind of sticky seed in my panties and Mummy has told me about it. I can hardly wait it seems so important to me, it's only a pity that I shan't be able to wear sanitary towels because you can't get them any more, and the little plugs Mummy wears can only be worn by women who have had a baby. Well farewell my child

AnneFrank

I shall never be able to write such things again!

AnneFrank
22 Jan. 1944

96

22 Oct. 1942.
Thursday

Dearest Poppie,

2 days without writing again it's a real disgrace. Rosel and Wronker have been brought back, we don't know why but it's very lucky for them. Miep is going to find out tomorrow. I'm making good progress with my shorthand, perhaps I'll write you something in short-hand by and by. Daddy has asked Bep to buy me a potty luckily. Mummy, Margot and I are as thick as thieves again. It's really much better. I get into Margot's bed now almost every evening we have spoken about Margot's wanting to be a maternity nurse, I think it's a nice profession, but I would much rather be with toddlers than with babies but then I would also like to be there one day when someone is having a baby, for then it'll probably seem much less weird to me. Margot and I both have terrible colds, but that will no doubt pass. Bertus and his 2 brothers and a sister-in-law have gone to Germany, it was a great big drama, but it's too long to write about. Mr. v.Pels has told a few nice jokes, I'll put them down here.

Who goes tick 999 times and tack once?
A millipede with a club foot.

Who is black, sits on the roof, has two feet and can whistle?
The chimney sweep's apprentice.

(Daddy)

A hotel had walls made of lath and plaster just like ours so you could hear everything through them. On one occasion there was a couple on the one side and | a gentleman on the other. The male half of the couple kept slapping the female half on her bottom saying: "Oh what a lovely little botty, whose is that wonderful little botty?" Then the man on the other side called out: "Surely you can find out whose damned ass that is!"

| 96a

They are good, aren't they! Dearest Pop there's not much more news, and I always find that when I read through the letters there is nothing very amusing in them and so 'bye, I hope I'll get a reply before long.

AnneFrank.

b   . . . . . .

c   . . . . . .

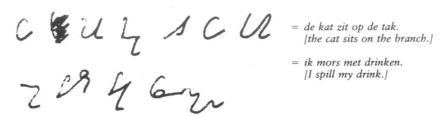

= de kat zit op de tak.
[the cat sits on the branch.]

= ik mors met drinken.
[I spill my drink.]

26 Oct. 1942.
Monday

[96b]   Friday and Saturday I stayed in bed, I had a cold and didn't feel very well.

—

Dearest Phienny,
Daddy has asked Mr. Kleiman for a diary and Bep for a potty. *Oh, I completely forgot that I used to write in print all the time, I was so immersed in what I was doing. They've warned us that Levinsohn will probably be downstairs for a whole month on end. We've rearranged the cupboards because the linen gets wet in the cupboard against the wall, it's so damp in there, ³now I have 3 shelves, it's great. A new offensive has started in Africa,*
| 97b   *we can only hope that the English don't make any fresh blunders.* | *and that the war will soon be over. Mr. Kugler has brought us 12 Panoramas again, now we have something to read. Miep went to see Mrs. Stoppelman the poor woman can't stand it in her hiding place with homesickness and hunger. In the little greengrocer's where she always does her shopping, Bep came across an ex-"Tokita" girl with her 3-year-old child. I asked straight away, is she married then, which she wasn't of course, and people think it must be Tozendael's umpteenth child. Shocking, what a man.*
    Miep told us about a man who escaped from Westerbork, things are terrible there, and if it's so bad there what can it be like in Poland? People get hardly anything to eat let alone drink, for they have water for only 1 hour a day and 1 w.c. and 1 washstand for a few 1000 people. They all sleep mixed up together men and women and the latter + children often have their hair cut off so that everyone can recognize them if they escape.
                                                                                  Anne Frank.

Mr.: "Fräulein es blitst!" ["Miss, it's snowing down south!"]
Miss: "Zieht mann arg?" ["Is it very bad?"]
Mr.: "Nein, nur den Unterrock!" ["No, it's only your slip!"]
        — . — . — . —

28 Oct. 1942.
Wednesday.

97a   Dearest. Lou.
How are you? Everything has upset me again this morning, so I wasn't able to finish a single thing properly. I have learned something new again brothel and cocotte, I have got a separate little book for them but it's kept with the letters, otherwise nothing special
                                                                                  AnneFrank

b   . . . . . .

c   . . . . . .

a 86 Yesterday afternoon Miep went to see Mrs. Stoppelman who is in hiding in Bussum with Mrs. van der Horst, Miep went there to look her up. On her return she came straight to us from the station, for she and Jan are to sleep here tonight. First we all ate carrots, potatoes and soup with 2 meatballs each. We were still at the table and Mrs. v.P. was in the middle of washing up, when suddenly ping the light went out, we got a terrible fright of course and Daddy called from below, is the light

87 out? Yes, we called back. And I ran downstairs | to fetch candles. The illumination was festive and of course we thought that the men wouldn't be going back to the warehouse any more. But it was only a quarter past seven and the men went all the same. After 5 minutes our house was bathed in light again. The short had been caused by Daddy's desk lamp.

a 87 This morning I was up early, and Jan was already dressed he had to leave at half past 8 and so he was already upstairs having his breakfast at 8 o'clock. Miep was busy getting dressed. And was still in her slip when I came in. Miep also has exactly the same kind of woolen pants for her bicycle as I wear. Margot and I then went to get dressed so we were upstairs much earlier than usual. After a cozy breakfast Miep went downstairs. It was pouring, and she was glad not to have to cycle to the office.

b 84 Meanwhile we had great fun on Monday. Miep and Jan stayed here overnight. ¹Margot and I went in Mummy and Daddy's room for the night so that the Gieses could have our room. The celebratory dinner² tasted³ divine, there was one small interruption.⁴ Daddy's⁵ lamp blew a fuse, and all of a sudden we were sitting in darkness. What was to be done? There was some fuse wire in the house, but the fuse box is right at the back of the dark storeroom—not such a nice chore after dark. Still the men ventured forth and after ten minutes we were able to put the candles away again.⁷ Next week Bep is coming to stay for a night.

Yours, Anne

c Meanwhile we had great fun on Monday. Miep and Henk spent the night here. Margot and I went in Mummy and Daddy's room for the night, so that the Van Santens could have our room. The meal tasted divine. There was one small interruption. Daddy's lamp blew a fuse, and all of a sudden we were sitting in darkness. What was to be done? There was some fuse wire in the house, but the fuse box is right at the very back of the dark storeroom—not such a nice job after dark. Still the men ventured forth and after ten minutes we were able to put the candles away again.

I got up early this morning. Henk had to leave at half past eight. After a cozy breakfast Miep went downstairs. It was pouring and she was glad not to have to cycle to the office. Next week Elli is coming to stay for a night.

Yours, Anne

289

a 85 ⌐ In "Eva's youth" there are also bits about unknown women selling their bodies ⌐
in back streets, and they ask a packet of money for it. I'd die of shame if anything
like that happened to me. Also it says that Eva has a monthly period, oh, I'm so
longing to have it too, then at least I'd be grown up. ⌐

b 85

Thursday 29
October 1942.

Dearest Kitty,

I am awfully worried, Daddy is ill. He has a high temperature and a red rash, it looks
like measles. Think of it; we can't even call the doctor![2] Mummy is letting him[3] have a
good sweat. Perhaps that will send his temperature down. This morning Miep told us that
all the furniture has been removed from the v.P.s' home in Zuider Amstellaan. We haven't
told Mrs. v.P. yet. She's "all nerves" already, and we don't feel like listening to another
moan over all the lovely china and beautiful chairs that she left at home. We had to leave
almost all our nice things behind, so what's the good of grumbling about it now? I'm
allowed to read more grown-up books lately. I'm now reading Eva's youth by Nico van

| 86 Suchtelen, I can't see much difference between this and the | schoolgirl love stories. Daddy
has brought the plays of Goethe and Schiller from the big bookcase. He is going to read
to me every evening. We've started with Don Carlos.

Following Daddy's good example,[19] Mummy has pressed her prayer book into my
hand. For decency's sake I read some of the prayers in German, they are certainly beautiful,
but they don't convey much to me. Why does she force me to be pious, just to oblige her?

c

Thursday, 29 October, 1942.

Dear Kitty,

I am awfully worried, Daddy is ill. He has a high temperature and a red rash, it looks
like measles. Think of it, we can't even call a doctor! Mummy is letting him have a good
sweat. Perhaps that will send his temperature down.

This morning Miep told us all that all the furniture has been removed from the Van
Daans' home. We haven't told Mrs. Van Daan yet. She's such a bundle of nerves already,
and we don't feel like listening to another moan over all the lovely china and beautiful
chairs that she left at home. *We* had to leave almost all our nice things behind; so what's
the good of grumbling about it now?

I'm allowed to read more grown-up books lately. I'm now reading *Eva's Youth* by
Nico van Suchtelen. I can't see much difference between this and the schoolgirl love stories.
It is true there are bits about women selling themselves to unknown men in back streets.
They ask a packet of money for it. I'd die of shame if anything like that happened to me.
Also it says that Eva has a monthly period. Oh, I'm so longing to have it too; it seems so
important.

Daddy has brought the plays of Goethe and Schiller from the big cupboard. He is
going to read to me every evening. We've started with *Don Carlos*.

Following Daddy's good example, Mummy has pressed her prayer book into my
hand. For decency's sake I read some of the prayers in German; they are certainly beautiful
but they don't convey much to me. Why does she force me to be pious, just to oblige her?

290

2 Nov. 1942.
<u>Monday.</u>

Dearest Marianne,
Friday night Bep came to our place, it was very cozy, but she didn't sleep well because she had had some wine. Other than that there's nothing special. Yesterday I had a bad headache and went to bed early. Tonight winter has come. Margot is being tiresome again. Yesterday we lit the fire for the first time and today the whole room is full of smoke. Until the next time

AnneFrank.

97

2 Nov. 1942.
<u>Monday.</u>

Dearest Kitty,
I don't think I've told you, but the Goslar's had a dead baby, that's awful, and poor Hanneli, how busy she's going to be. This morning Miep came to tell us that the van Pels home has been cleared out, but Mrs. v.P. was in such a bad mood that we haven't told her yet. Sunday I had a bath, this time in the kitchen, but it was still early and no one could see me behind the fire guard. I peeped out for a little while into the street through a chink in the office curtains, it's a strange feeling, it looks just as if the people outside are mad. I am now doing Algebra as well but I like Geometry much better. Shorthand is going well, I shall scribble in a trivial little sentence in passing.

de man keek naar den hond
[the man looked at the dog]

Things are going well, but now I have to practice and I don't feel like it. Daddy has just said that he doesn't feel in a good mood. His eyes look so sad again—poor soul. I can't drag myself away from a book called "The Knock at the Door" by Ina Boudier-Bakker. The story of the family is exceptionally well written. But what it says about war, writers, or the emancipation of women is not so well done, but then quite honestly I'm not awfully interested. Bertus has written to Bep from Berlin, so far things have been pretty fair. I simply can't wait to ask Mr. Kleiman for the new diary well so long

AnneFrank

Tomorrow we are going to light the fire for the first time. I expect we shall be suffocated with smoke; the chimney hasn't been swept for ages, let's hope the thing draws!

<u>yours,</u> Anne

Tomorrow we are going to light the fire for the first time. I expect we shall be suffocated with smoke. The chimney hasn't been swept for ages, let's hope the thing draws.

Yours, Anne

5 Nov. 1942.
<u>*Thursday.*</u>

Dearest Pop,

We've been lucky and got 270 pounds of dried peas and beans, but some of it is for the staff. We have country ration cards now instead of town ration cards because there's a saving of 7 guilders. Country cards only cost 33 guilders and if we sell the bread coupons from them as well then they're only 20 guilders. Mr. v.P. has almost no money left now, luckily Pim's all right, Mr. Siemans (that's our baker) can get milk sugar now and that's why he's supplying us with bread again without coupons at the normal price. Kleiman has been to see Goldschmidt again but he won't release our things, and anyway he says | *[98b]* *he's given almost everything away to the Welfare, but we don't |* *believe it, and he says Mrs. Levie will bear him out but Miep is going to see Pfeffer and get him to ask Mrs. Levie herself. Mr. Voskuijl often has something to eat with us now at lunchtime. The office closes these days at about 5 o'clock but the warehouse stays open a little longer. I have almost finished "The Knock on the Door," but it has to go back on Friday. Yesterday I fixed up my film stars a bit, but it isn't finished yet. The English have at last had a few successes in Africa and Stalingrad is still holding out too, so the gentlemen here are very cheerful and this morning we had coffee and tea. There is nothing else special. Peter's birthday is on Sunday the 8th November, and the Kleimans are coming for the occasion. Regards to Kees from*

AnneFrank

98

7 Nov. 1942.
<u>*Saturday.*</u>

Dearest Phien,

It really has been a long time now since I wrote to you. I've been reading a lot during the past week and working little, that's the way of the world and no doubt one gets on like that. Tomorrow is Peter's birthday but I'll probably be writing about that. Lately Mummy and I have been getting on better together, but <u>never</u> confide. Margot is more catty than ever and Daddy has got something he is keeping to himself, but he remains the same darling. Levinsohn still bothers us each day. On Thursday night I was downstairs with Daddy drawing up the debtors' lists in Kugler's office it was very creepy down there, and I was glad when the work was finished. Mrs. v.P. saw a ghost downstairs but it was only a piece of plaster that had fallen off the wall. Daddy took a tin can out of Kugler's office and is now trying to see if it's watertight, if it is I am going to have it as a potty, but Mr. v.P. still has to put a handle on it, it can have a lid as well, so it will be just the job, I only hope it doesn't leak. I am longing for a little Moor more than ever and I can hardly wait to have him or 1 of his kittens. I still feel lonely here all the time and not wanted and I dream a lot about the underground vault but then reality looks so gray again so I'm all at sixes and sevens. The stove has been lit for a few days now, and the whole room is full of smoke, I like central heating so much better and I'm not alone in that. I can only describe Margot as a little wretch who gets on my nerves horribly day | 99 *and |* *night. Regards to everybody from*

Anne.

b . . . . . .

c . . . . . .

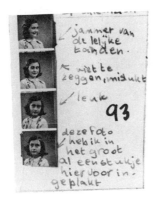

pity about the ugly teeth

obviously a flop

nice

I stuck the same photograph in befo[...]

Vrijdag en Zaterdag heb ik 26 Oct. 1942
in bed gelegen, ik was verkouden en niet erg lekker.

Beste Thierry,

Papa heeft mijnk 4 kleinreren van
en dagboek gevraagd en naar ben p. Hè, ik had helemaal vergeten, dat ik anders
altijd blokschrift schreef, zo was
ik in gedachten. Ze hebben ons
voorspeld dat [...] Lerinsohn wel
een maand achter elkaar beneden zal zijn. De kasten zijn om-
geruimd, want in de kast aan
de muur wordt het wasgoed
nat, zo vochtig is het, nu heb
ik 3 planken ter beschikking,
dat is geweldig. In Afrika is
een nieuw offensief begonnen,
we zullen nu maar hopen dat
de Engelsen geen nieuwe blund[...]
maken.

specimen writing (See entry for 26 O[...]

293

b 86a

Saturday 30 Oct. 1943.[1]

Dear Kitty,

Mummy is frightfully irritable and that always seems to herald unpleasantness for me. Is it just chance that Daddy and Mummy never rebuke Margot and that they always drop on me for everything? Yesterday evening, for instance: Margot was reading a book with lovely drawings in it, she got up and went upstairs, put the book down ready to go on with it later. I wasn't doing anything, so picked up the book and started looking at the pictures. Margot came back, saw "her" book in my hands, wrinkled her forehead and asked for it back angrily. Just because I wanted to look a little further on, Margot got more and more angry. Then Mummy[2] joined in: "Give the book to Margot; she was reading it," she said. Daddy came into the room. He didn't even know what it was all about, but saw the injured look on Margot's face and promptly dropped on me: I'd like

| 86b

to know what you'd say if Margot ever started looking at one of your books!" | I gave way at once, laid the book down and left the room—"offended" as they thought. It so happened I was neither offended nor cross, just miserable. It wasn't right of Daddy to judge without knowing what the squabble was about. I would have given Margot the book myself, and much more quickly too, if Mummy and Daddy hadn't interfered and taken Margot's part at once as though she were the victim of some great injustice.

c

Saturday, 7 November, 1942

Dear Kitty,

Mummy is frightfully irritable and that always seems to herald unpleasantness for me. Is it just chance that Daddy and Mummy never rebuke Margot and that they always drop on me for everything? Yesterday evening, for instance: Margot was reading a book with lovely drawings in it, she got up and went upstairs, put the book down ready to go on with it later. I wasn't doing anything, so picked up the book and started looking at the pictures. Margot came back, saw "her" book in my hands, wrinkled her forehead and asked for the book back. Just because I wanted to look a little further on, Margot got more and more angry. Then Mummy joined in: "Give the book to Margot; she was reading it," she said. Daddy came into the room. He didn't even know what it was all about, but saw the injured look on Margot's face and promptly dropped on me: "I'd like to see what you'd say if Margot ever started looking at one of your books!" I gave way at once, laid the book down and left the room—offended as they thought. It so happened I was neither offended nor cross, just miserable. It wasn't right of Daddy to judge without knowing what the squabble was about. I would have given Margot the book myself, and much more quickly too, if Mummy and Daddy hadn't interfered. They took Margot's part at once as though she were the victim of some great injustice.

......

It's obvious that Mummy would stick up[1] for Margot, she and Margot always do back each other up, I'm so used to that that I'm utterly indifferent to both Mummy's jawing[7] and Margot's moods. I love them, but only because they are Mummy and Margot, as human beings they can both go hang[10]. With Daddy it's different, if he holds Margot | 86c up as an example, approves of what she does, praises and | caresses[13] her, then something gnaws at me inside because I adore Daddy, he is the one I look up to. I don't love anyone in the world but him. He doesn't notice that he treats Margot differently from me: now Margot is just the prettiest, sweetest, most beautiful girl in the world. But all the same I feel I have some right to be taken seriously too; I have always been the dunce, the ne'er-do-well of the family, I've always had to pay double for my deeds; first with the scolding and then again because of the way my feelings are hurt. Now I'm not satisfied with this apparent favoritism any more. I want something from Daddy that he is not able to give.

I'm not jealous of Margot, never have been. I don't envy her her good looks or her beauty. It is only that I long for Daddy's real love: not only as his child but for me— | 86d Anne, myself. | I cling to Daddy because each day I look upon Mummy with more contempt and because it is only through him that I am able to retain the remnant of family feeling. [23]Daddy doesn't understand that I need to give vent to my feelings over Mummy sometimes. He doesn't want to talk about it; he simply avoids anything which might lead to remarks about Mummy's failings. Just the same, Mummy and her failings are something I find

It's obvious that Mummy would stick up for Margot; she and Margot always do back each other up. I'm so used to that that I'm utterly indifferent to both Mummy's jawing and Margot's moods.

I love them; but only because they are Mummy and Margot. With Daddy it's different. If he holds Margot up as an example, approves of what she does, praises and caresses her, then something gnaws at me inside, because I adore Daddy. He is the one I look up to. I don't love anyone in the world but him. He doesn't notice that he treats Margot differently from me. Now Margot is just the prettiest, sweetest, most beautiful girl in the world. But all the same I feel I have some right to be taken seriously too. I have always been the dunce, the ne'er-do-well of the family, I've always had to pay double for my deeds, first with the scolding and then again because of the way my feelings are hurt. Now I'm not satisfied with this apparent favoritism any more. I want something from Daddy that he is not able to give me.

I'm not jealous of Margot, never have been. I don't envy her her good looks or her beauty. It is only that I long for Daddy's real love; not only as his child but for me— Anne, myself.

I cling to Daddy because it is only through him that I am able to retain the remnant of family feeling. Daddy doesn't understand that I need to give vent to my feelings over Mummy sometimes. He doesn't want to talk about it; he simply avoids anything which might lead to remarks about Mummy's failings. Just the same, Mummy and her failings

b

harder to bear than anything else. I don't know how to keep it all to myself. I can't always be drawing attention to her untidiness, her sarcasm, and her lack of sweetness, neither can I believe that I'm always in the wrong.

We are exact opposites in everything; so naturally we are bound to run up against each other. I don't pronounce judgment on Mummy's character for that is something I can't judge. I only look at her as a mother, and she just doesn't succeed in being that to me;[2] I have to be my own mother. I've drawn myself apart[3] from them all, I am my own | 86e   skipper and later on I shall see where I come to land. | All this comes about particularly because I have in my mind's eye an image of what a perfect mother and wife should be; and in her whom I must call "Mother" I find no trace of that image.

I am always making resolutions not to notice Mummy's bad example. I want to see only the good side of her and to seek in myself what I cannot find in her. But it doesn't work;[12] and the worst of it is that neither Daddy nor Mummy understands this gap in my life, and I blame them for it. I wonder if anyone can ever succeed in making their children absolutely content? Sometimes I believe that[18] God wants to try me both now and later on; I must become good through my own efforts, without examples and without good advice, then later on I shall be all the stronger?

c

are something I find harder to bear than anything else. I don't know how to keep it all to myself. I can't always be drawing attention to her untidiness, her sarcasm, and her lack of sweetness, neither can I believe that I'm always in the wrong.

We are exact opposites in everything; so naturally we are bound to run up against each other. I don't pronounce judgment on Mummy's character, for that is something I can't judge. I only look at her as a mother, and she just doesn't succeed in being that to me; I have to be my own mother. I've drawn myself apart from them all; I am my own skipper and later on I shall see where I come to land. All this comes about particularly because I have in my mind's eye an image of what a perfect mother and wife should be; and in her whom I must call "Mother" I find no trace of that image.

I am always making resolutions not to notice Mummy's bad example. I want to see only the good side of her and to seek in myself what I cannot find in her. But it doesn't work; and the worst of it is that neither Daddy nor Mummy understands this gap in my life, and I blame them for it. I wonder if anyone can ever succeed in making their children absolutely content.

Sometimes I believe that God wants to try me, both now and later on; I must become good through my own efforts, without examples and without good advice. Then later on I shall be all the stronger.

b

| 86f

Who besides me will ever read these letters? From whom but myself shall I get[1] | comfort? As I need comforting often, I frequently feel weak, and dissatisfied with myself; my shortcomings are too great. I know this, and every day I try to improve myself again and again.

[2]My treatment varies so much; one day Anne is so sensible and is allowed to know everything; and the next day I hear that Anne is just a silly little goat who doesn't know anything at all and imagines that she has learned a wonderful lot from books! I'm not a baby or a spoiled darling any more, to be laughed at, whatever she does. I have my own views, plans and ideas, though I can't put them into words yet.

Oh so many things bubble up inside me, as I lie in bed[10], having to put up[13] with people I'm fed up with, who always misinterpret my intentions.[14] That's why recently I've always come back to my diary. That is where I start and finish, because Kitty is always

| 86g

patient, | I'll promise her that I shall persevere, in spite of everything, and find my own way through it all, and swallow my tears. I only wish I could see the results already or occasionally receive encouragement from someone who loves[21] me.

Don't condemn me; remember rather that sometimes I too can reach the bursting point.

yours, Anne

c

Who besides me will ever read these letters? From whom but myself shall I get comfort? As I need comforting often, I frequently feel weak, and dissatisfied with myself; my shortcomings are too great. I know this, and every day I try to improve myself, again and again.

My treatment varies so much. One day Anne is so sensible and is allowed to know everything; and the next day I hear that Anne is just a silly little goat who doesn't know anything at all and imagines that she's learned a wonderful lot from books. I'm not a baby or a spoiled darling any more, to be laughed at, whatever she does. I have my own views, plans, and ideas, though I can't put them into words yet. Oh, so many things bubble up inside me as I lie in bed having to put up with people I'm fed up with, who always misinterpret my intentions. That's why in the end I always come back to my diary. That is where I start and finish, because Kitty is always patient. I'll promise her that I shall persevere, in spite of everything, and find my own way through it all, and swallow my tears. I only wish I could see the results already or occasionally receive encouragement from someone who loves me.

Don't condemn me; remember rather that sometimes I too can reach the bursting point.

Yours, Anne

13 *Nov. 1942.*
Friday.

Dearest Jetty,

Yesterday morning Miep came to tell us that she had been to see Dr. Pfeffer. He had naturally jumped at the suggestion that he should go into hiding. But he literally implored Miep to put it off for a week because he was in the middle of 2 dental operations, he is still owed money by van der Hoeden (that is the dentist for whom he works clandestinely) and he still has to bring the card index up to date for van der Hoeden, or else he won't be able to make head or tail of it. But we felt that would be much too risky, for he could well say to van der Hoeden, look, I'm going into hiding a week on Thursday. Then van der Hoeden might tell someone else and then Pfeffer would be bombarded with questions. And secondly people might notice the Jew Pfeffer going over every day to Miep and Jan's carrying his things, and if anything should happen to Miep and Jan then we'd be at risk ourselves. And so we said that if Pfeffer says today that he must have more time and won't be able to come by Saturday, then he needn't come at all, since supposing he was picked up today or tomorrow in the street or at home, or maybe even at the practice, he wouldn't be able to say I've still got to bring my card index up to date and I'm still owed some money. Miep is going to talk to him again and he'll have to make up his mind today whether he's coming tomorrow. If so, he'll have to be at the Post Office at 10 o'clock

| 100

tomorrow morning and pretend he's writing a | postcard to his father in Germany, then Mr. Kleiman will happen to bump into him and will get him to follow him about 10 yards behind. Then when Kleiman goes into the office Pfeffer can come in as well, it won't seem odd because Levinsohn and Kahn and a lot of other Jews call here at the office every day. I'll stop now, nothing else special has happened here. Politics are going well. Morocco and Algiers, Casa Blanca and Oran have surrendered, now for Tunis. My white sweater is finished I was given the zip fastener by Mrs. v. Pels, and it looks really smart. Regards to your mum from

AnneFrank.

FOUND LOOSE IN THE OTHER DIARY.

Dearest Kitty,
5 *Dec. 1942.*

Last night it was wonderful, first we lit candles and then we went upstairs, the place was strewn with flowers, from Pim for Mummy, from Mr. v. Pels and Mr. Pf. for Mummy, from Mr. v. Pels for Mrs. v. Pels and from Pim and Mr. Pf. for Mrs. v.P. Mummy also got a pack of cigarettes and 1 bar of choclate. Margot and I each got a lovely sewing box, Piet and the two of us had fudge, and M. and I 1 bar choc. and 1 silver dish. I also got a lock for my diary. Today I was in a bad state again, I could have cried all morning, and Pim too can turn on one so, but he is a darling all the same

'bye from AnneFrank.

. . . . . .

. . . . . .

a 99b

10 Nov. 1942.
<u>Tuesday.</u>

Dearest Conny,

I haven't given you my report yet about Sunday, it was really a very important day too. In the morning the stove was lit by 7 o'clock, so no one could sleep any more and all the females of the house were very angry. At 8 o'clock I went upstairs and looked at the presents with Peter. There was a board game from the office staff, a little lighter set, mirror, shaving brush, tie, toffees, a tin of pea soup from his parents and a razor with a styptic pencil from us. At half past twelve we went downstairs and happened to hear on the radio that English and American troops had landed in Tunis, Algeria, Casablanca and Oran. That was a surprise. In the afternoon the Kleimans came and they had also heard

b 87

Monday 9 Nov. 1942.

Dear Kitty,

Yesterday was Peter's birthday, he was sixteen. He had some nice presents, e.g. a board game, a razor and a lighter. Not that he smokes much; it's really just for show. The biggest surprise came from Mr. v.P., when at 1 o'clock he announced that the British had landed in Tunis, Algiers, Casablanca and Oran. This is the beginning of the end, everyone was saying, but Churchil, the British Prime Minister, who had probably heard the same thing in England, said: "This is not the end. It is not even the beginning of the end. But it is, perhaps, the end of the beginning."* Do you see the difference? There is certainly reason for optimism, Stalingrad, the Russian place which they have already been defending for 3 months, still hasn't fallen into German hands.

*On 10 November 1942 Churchill gave a speech and used these words on the occasion of the Lord Mayor's Day luncheon in London (*The End of the Beginning, War Speeches by the Rt. Hon. Winston S. Churchill, C.H., M.P., 1942,* compiled by Charles Eade [London: Cassell and Company Ltd., 1943], p. 214.)

c

Monday, 9 November, 1942

Dear Kitty,

Yesterday was Peter's birthday, he was sixteen. He had some nice presents. Among other things a game of Monopoly [a board game], a razor, and a lighter. Not that he smokes much; it's really just for show.

The biggest surprise came from Mr. Van Daan when, at one o'clock, he announced that the British had landed in Tunis, Algiers, Casablanca, and Oran. "This is the beginning of the end," everyone was saying, but Churchill, the British Prime Minister, who had probably heard the same thing in England, said: "This is not the end. It is not even the beginning of the end. But it is, perhaps, the end of the beginning." Do you see the difference? There is certainly reason for optimism. Stalingrad, the Russian town which they've already been defending for three months, still hasn't fallen into German hands.

| the great news. In the evening Hitler delivered a speech saying nothing. On Monday we treated the office staff in honor of the birthday. Sleep well and regards to Nanny from your loving

AnneFrank

But to return to affairs in our secret den, I must tell you something about our food supply. (As you know we have some real greedy pigs on the top floor!) We get our bread from a very nice baker a friend of Kleiman. We don't get so much as we used to at home, naturally. But it's sufficient. Ration cards have also been bought illegally. Their price is going up all the time; it has now gone up from twenty-seven florins to thirty-three. And all that for a little slip of printed paper!

But to return to affairs in our secret den. I must tell you something about our food supply. As you know, we have some real greedy pigs on the top floor. We get our bread from a nice baker, a friend of Koophuis. We don't get so much as we used to at home, naturally. But it's sufficient. [Four*] ration cards have also been bought illegally. Their price is going up all the time; it has now gone up from twenty-seven florins to thirty-three. And all that for a little slip of printed paper!

*The word "Four" does not appear in any Dutch version of the diary. A.J.P.

. . . . . .

In order to have something in the house that will keep, apart from our hundred tins, we have bought 270 pounds of dried peas and beans. They are not all for us[1], [3]some are for the office people.[4] They are in sacks which[5] hang on hooks in our little passage ([6]inside the hidden door[7]). Owing to the weight of the contents a few stitches in the sacks burst[9] open.[10] [11] [12] [13]

| 89   We decided to put our winter store[14] in the attic then and Peter was given the job of dragging it all up there. He had managed to get 5 of the 6 sacks upstairs intact, and he was just busy pulling up number 6, when the bottom seam of the sack split and a shower—no a positive hailstorm of brown beans came pouring down and rattled down the stairs. There were about fifty pounds in the sack and the noise was enough to waken the dead.[22] Downstairs they[23] thought the old house with all its contents was coming down on them. It gave Peter a moment's fright, but he was soon roaring with laughter, especially when he saw me standing at the bottom of the stairs like a little island in the middle of a sea of beans! I was entirely surrounded up to my ankles in beans. Quickly we started to pick them up. But beans are so slippery and small that they seemed to roll into all the possible and impossible[29] corners and holes.[30] Now, every time anyone goes upstairs they bend down once or twice in order to be able to present Mrs. v.P. with a handful of beans.

| 90   [33]I'd almost forgotten to mention | that Daddy is quite better again.

yours, Anne

P.S. The news has just come over the radio that Algiers has fallen. Morocco, Casablanca and Oran have been in British hands for several days. Now we're waiting for Tunis.

yours, Anne[34]

In order to have something in the house that will keep, apart from our 150 tins of vegetables, we have bought 270 pounds of dried peas and beans. They are not all for us, some are for the office people. They are in sacks which hang on hooks in our little passage (inside the hidden door). Owing to the weight of the contents, a few stitches in the sacks burst open. So we decided it would be better to put our winter store in the attic and Peter was given the job of dragging it all up there.

He had managed to get five of the six sacks upstairs intact, and he was just busy pulling up number six, when the bottom seam of the sack split and a shower—no, a positive hailstorm of brown beans came pouring down and rattled down the stairs. There were about fifty pounds in the sack and the noise was enough to waken the dead. Downstairs they thought the old house with all its contents was coming down on them. (Thank God there were no strangers in the house.) It gave Peter a moment's fright. But he was soon roaring with laughter, especially when he saw me standing at the bottom of the stairs, like a little island in the middle of a sea of beans! I was entirely surrounded up to my ankles in beans. Quickly we started to pick them up. But beans are so slippery and small that they seemed to roll into all the possible and impossible corners and holes. Now, every time anyone goes downstairs they bend down once or twice, in order to be able to present Mrs. Van Daan with a handful of beans.

I'd almost forgotten to mention that Daddy is quite better again.

Yours, Anne

P.S. The news has just come over the radio that Algiers has fallen. Morocco, Casablanca, and Oran have been in British hands for several days. Now we're waiting for Tunis.

20. 6. 42

Het is voor iemand als ik, een heel eigenaardige gewaarwording om een dagboek te schrijven. Niet alleen dat ik nog nooit geschreven heb, maar het komt me zo voor dat later noch ik, noch een ander anders in de ontboezemingen van een dertienjarig schoolmeisje belang zal stellen. Maar ja, eigenlijk komt dat er niet op aan, ik heb zin om het te ~~schrijven~~ schrijven en nog veel meer om m'n hart over allerlei dingen eens grondig en helemaal te luchten., "Papier is geduldiger dan ~~mensen~~", dit gezegde schoot me te binnen toen ik op een van m'n licht – melancholieke dagen, verveeld met m'n ~~handen onder~~ hoofd op m'n ~~handen~~ zat en van lamlendigheid niet wist of ik uit moest gaan, dan wel thuis blijven, en zo uiteindelijk op dezelfde plek bleef zitten piekeren. Ja inderdaad, papier is geduldig, en daar ik niet van plan ben, dat gecartonneerde schrift, wat de weidse naam "dagboek" draagt, ooit aan iemand te laten lezen, tenzij ik nog eens ooit in m'n leven een vriend of vriendin krijg, die

Page 1 of the loose sheets

10 Nov. 1942.
<u>Tuesday night.</u>

Dearest Emmy,
Today we were properly taken by surprise again, for we had been saying once more that we really ought to take in another person and fate pointed to Mr. Pfeffer, for he doesn't have much family. We have already spoken to Kugler about it and he will think it over for one more night, but the decision is as good as taken. How surprised the man will be, but I'll be able to tell you all about it when he arrives in our hiding place. We shall ask him to bring what he can to fill holes in teeth, for he is a dentist, and I think he will be sleeping in my room.
Farewell

AnneFrank.

Tuesday 10 November
1942.

Dear Kitty,
Great news—we want to take in an 8th person.
    Yes, really, we have always thought that there was quite enough room and food for one more. We were only afraid of giving Kugler and Kleiman more trouble. But now that the appalling stories we hear about Jews are getting even worse Daddy[3] got hold of two agents who had to decide and they thought it was an excellent plan. It is just as dangerous for 7 as for 8 they said, and quite rightly. When this was settled we ran through our circle of friends, trying to think of a single person who would fit in well with our "family." It wasn't difficult to hit on[8] someone. After Daddy had refused all members of the v.P. family, we chose[10] a dentist called Fritz Pfeffer. He lives with a much younger, nice Christian | woman, to whom he is probably not married, but that doesn't matter.[14] He is known to be[15] quiet and refined[16] and so far as we and Mr. v.P. can judge from a superficial acquaintance both families think he is a congenial person.

| 92

Tuesday, 10 November, 1942

Dear Kitty,
    Great news—we want to take in an eighth person. Yes, really! We've always thought that there was quite enough room and food for one more. We were only afraid of giving Koophuis and Kraler more trouble. But now that the appalling stories we hear about Jews are getting even worse, Daddy got hold of the two people who had to decide, and they thought it was an excellent plan. "It is just as dangerous for seven as for eight," they said, and quite rightly. When this was settled, we ran through our circle of friends, trying to think of a single person who would fit in well with our "family." It wasn't difficult to hit on someone. After Daddy had refused all members of the Van Daan family, we chose a dentist called Albert Dussel, whose wife was fortunate enough to be out of the country when war broke out. He is known to be quiet, and so far as we and Mr. Van Daan can judge from a superficial acquaintance, both families think he is a congenial person.

a

[Edith Frank-Holländer]

102   *Saturday 22 January 1944.*
It was stupid of me to have left all these lovely pages blank, but perhaps it'll be all to the good if I am now able to put down my thoughts in general about what I have written.

When I look over my diary today, 1½ years on, I cannot believe that I was ever such an innocent young thing. I cannot help but realize that no matter how much I should like to, I can never be like that again. I still understand those moods, those remarks about Margot, Mummy and Daddy so well that I might have written them yesterday, but I no longer understand how I could write so freely about other things.

I really blush with shame when I read the pages dealing with subjects that I'd much better have left to the imagination. I put it all down so bluntly! But enough of that.

b

Miep knows him too, so she will be able to make arrangements for him to join us. If he comes, he will have to sleep in my room instead of Margot, who will use the camp bed.

yours, Anne

c

Miep knows him too, so she will be able to make arrangements for him to join us. If he comes, he will have to sleep in my room instead of Margot, who will use the camp bed.

Yours, Anne

a 103

What I also understand so well is my longing for Moortje. I have been longing, often consciously but much more often unconsciously, for trust, love and caresses all the time I've been here. This longing is sometimes stronger and sometimes weaker, but it's always there

Anne Frank.

117 *Anne's note reads: a page of shorthand*

Attitudes to the war in the "Secret Annexe."

Mr. v. Pels.

It is the opinion of us all that this honorable gentleman has a great deal of insight into politics. But he does warn us that we shall have to stay here until the end of '43. That's a terribly long time, though we'll make it. But who can guarantee that this war, which has brought nobody anything but injury and grief, will be over by then? And who can guarantee that nothing will happen to us and our helpers in the meantime? Absolutely no one!² And that's why we live under pressure every day. Pressure from expectation and hope, but also from fear if we hear any sounds outside, or if there is shooting anywhere, or new "proclamations" are published in the papers, since it could happen any day that some of our helpers might have to come into hiding here themselves.

Hiding has become quite an everyday word. How many people must there be in hiding; not many comparatively speaking, of course, but no doubt we shall still be absolutely amazed later on at how many good people there are in the Netherlands who have taken in Jews as well as Christians on the run, with or without money. And it is also incredible the number of people one hears about who have a false identity card.

Mrs. v. Pels. When this beautiful lady (in her opinion only) heard that it is not as difficult as it used to be to get a false identity card, she immediately suggested we have one made for each of us. As if Daddy and Mr. v. Pels were made of money.

As Mrs. van Pels talks the biggest nonsense non-stop, Putti often blows up. But anyone would, since first Kerli says: "I'll have myself baptized later" and the next day it's: "I always wanted to go to Jerusalem, because I only feel at home among Jews!⁵

= = = = = = = = = = = = = =
=   =   =   =   =   =   =

[118a]   *Pim Is a great optimist, but he always finds a reason to be because*

Mr. Pfeffer invents everything at random and if anyone contradicts his highness, he is sent away with a flea in his ear. I think it was laid down in Mr. Fritz Pfeffer's home that what he says goes; but that is certainly not the case as far as Anne Frank is concerned.

What other members of the "Secret Annexe" think about the war is of no interest, these four are the only ones who count in matters of politics, actually only two but Madam van Pels and Pfeffer include themselves.

b   . . . . . .

c   . . . . . .

2 May 1943.
<u>Sunday.</u>

If I just think of how we live here, I usually come to the conclusion that it is a paradise compared with how other Jews who are not in hiding must be living. Even so, later on, when everything is normal again, I shall be amazed to think that we, who were so spick and span at home, should have sunk, as one can indeed call it, to such a low level. By this I mean that our manners have declined. For instance, ever since we have been here we have had one oilcloth on our table which, owing to so much use, is not one of the cleanest. Admittedly I often try to clean it with a dirty dishcloth, which is more hole than cloth and which was new before we went into hiding long ago, the table doesn't do us much credit either, in spite of hard scrubbing. The van Pelses have been sleeping on the same flannelette sheet the whole winter, one can't wash it here because the soap powder we get on the ration isn't sufficient, and besides it's not good enough. Daddy goes about in frayed trousers and his tie is beginning to show signs of wear too. Mummy's corsets have split today and are too old to be repaired, while Margot goes about in a brassiere two sizes too small for her.

Mummy and Margot have managed the whole winter with 3 vests between them, and mine are so small that they don't even come to my tummy. Certainly, these are all things which can be overcome. But still, I sometimes wonder with a shock, how are we, now going about in worn-out things, from my pants down to Daddy's shaving brush, ever going to get back to our prewar standards?

122   here I had a mouth without teeth and am therefore hideously ugly.

A	B	c	D	E	F	G	H	I	J	K	L	M	N	O	P	Q	R	S	T	U	V	W	X	Y	Z
3	5	4	1	2	6	8	7	9	11	12	10	14	13	16	18	15	17	20	19	21	22	24	23	25	26

b

c

Entrance to the "Secret Annexe." (Anne Frank Foundation.)

13 Nov. 1942.
Friday.

Dearest Jetty,

Yesterday morning Miep came to tell us that she had been to see Dr. Pfeffer. He had naturally jumped at the suggestion that he should go into hiding. But he literally implored Miep to put it off for a week because he was in the middle of 2 dental operations, he is still owed money by van der Hoeden (that is the dentist for whom he works clandestinely) and he still has to bring the card index up to date for van der Hoeden, or else he won't be able to make head or tail of it. But we felt that would be much too risky, for he could well say to van der Hoeden, look, I'm going into hiding a week on Thursday. Then van der Hoeden might tell someone else and then Pfeffer would be bombarded with questions. And secondly people might notice the Jew Pfeffer going over every day to Miep and Jan's carrying his things, and if

Thursday 12 November
1942.

Dear Kitty,

Pfeffer asked Miep the moment she entered the room if she didn't perhaps know of a hiding place for him. He was awfully pleased when Miep told him that she had one for him and that he should go there as soon as possible, preferably Saturday. He thought that this was rather doubtful, since he had to bring his card index up to date first, see to a couple of clients and settle his accounts. Miep came to us with this news this morning. We thought it was unwise of him to put it off any longer. All these preparations cost us explanations to a number of people whom we would rather keep out of it, Miep will ask if he can't manage to come on Saturday after all. Pfeffer said no, and now he is coming

Thursday, 12 November, 1942

Dear Kitty,

Dussel was awfully pleased when Miep told him that she had got a hiding place for him. She urged him to come as soon as possible. Preferably Saturday. He thought that this was rather doubtful, since he had to bring his card index up to date first, see to a couple of patients, and settle his accounts. Miep came to us with this news this morning. We thought it was unwise of him to put it off. All these preparations entail explanations to a number of people, whom we would rather keep out of it. Miep is going to ask if he can't manage to come on Saturday after all.

Dussel said no; now he is coming on Monday. I must say I think it's pretty crazy that

anything should happen to Miep and Jan then we'd be at risk ourselves. And so we said that if Pfeffer says today that he must have more time and won't be able to come by Saturday, then he needn't come at all, since supposing he was picked up today or tomorrow in the street or at home, or maybe even at the practice, he wouldn't be able to say I've still got to bring my card index up to date and I'm still owed some money. Miep is going to talk to him again and he'll have to make up his mind today whether he's coming tomorrow.

| 100   If so, he'll have to be at the Post Office at 10 o'clock tomorrow morning and pretend he's writing a | postcard to his father in Germany, then Mr. Kleiman will happen to bump into him and will get him to follow him about 10 yards behind. Then when Kleiman goes into the office Pfeffer can come in as well, it won't seem odd because Levinsohn and Kahn and a lot of other Jews call here at the office every day.

| 94   on Monday I must say I think it's pretty crazy that he doesn't jump at the proposal, whatever it is, if he were to get picked up outside would he still be able to do his card index and go on seeing to his patients, why delay then? I think it's stupid | of Daddy to have given in. No other news——

yours, Anne

95   Tuesday 17 November
1942.

Dear Kitty,

Pf. has arrived. All went well: Miep had told him that he must be at a special place in front of the Post Office at 11 o'clock in the morning, where a man would meet him. Pf. was standing at the rendezvous dead on time. Mr. Kleiman went up to him and told him that the said gentleman could not come, but asked whether he would go to Miep at the office directly. Kleiman got into a tram and went back to the office, while Pf. walked in the same direction.

he doesn't jump at the proposal—whatever it is. If he were to get picked up outside, would he still be able to do his card index, settle his finances, and see to his patients? Why delay then? I think it's stupid of Daddy to have given in. No other news——

Yours, Anne

Tuesday, 17 November, 1942.

Dear Kitty,

Dussel has arrived. All went well. Miep had told him that he must be at a special place in front of the Post Office at eleven o'clock, where a man would meet him. Dussel was standing at the rendezvous dead on time. Mr. Koophuis, who knows Dussel too, went up to him and told him that the said gentleman could not come, but asked whether he would just go to Miep at the office. Koophuis got into a tram and went back to the office, while Dussel walked in the same direction. At twenty past eleven Dussel tapped at the

b

| 96

| 97

At 20 past eleven Pf. tapped at the office door. Miep helped him off with his coat, so that the yellow star would not be seen, and took him to the private office, where Kleiman engaged him in conversation until the charwoman had gone. Using the trick that the private office was needed for something, she went upstairs with Pf., opened the swinging cupboard and stepped inside before the eyes of the dumfounded Pfeffer. The 7 of us were sitting around the table | upstairs waiting with coffee and cognac to greet the³ newcomer. Miep showed him into our sitting room first. He recognized our furniture at once, and had not the remotest idea that we were there, above his head. When Miep told him, he nearly passed out with surprise. But luckily Miep didn't give him much time and went with him straight upstairs. Pf. sank into a chair, speechless, and looked at us all for a while, as if he really had to take it all in first. After a while he stuttered: But . . . aber, sind you not in Belgiumthen? Ist der Militär nicht come, das Auto, the escape is sie nicht successful? We explained the escape is everything to him, that we had spread the story about the soldiers and the car on purpose to put people, and especially the Germans, on the wrong track should they try to find us. Pf. was again struck dumb by such ingenuity, and, when he had explored further our superpractical exquisite little "Secret Annexe," he could do nothing all day long but gaze about him in astonishment.

c

office door. Miep helped him off with his coat, so that the yellow star would not be seen, and took him to the private office, where Koophuis engaged him in conversation until the charwoman had gone. Then Miep went upstairs with Dussel under the pretext that the private office was needed for something, opened the swinging cupboard, and stepped inside before the eyes of the dumfounded Dussel.

We all sat around the table upstairs, waiting with coffee and cognac to greet the newcomer. Miep showed him into our sitting room first. He recognized our furniture at once, and had not the remotest idea that we were there, above his head. When Miep told him he nearly passed out with surprise. But luckily Miep didn't give him much time and took him straight upstairs.

Dussel sank into a chair, speechless, and looked at us all for a while, as if he had to really take it all in first. After a while he stuttered "But . . . aber, sind you not in Belgium then? Ist der Militar [Militär] nicht come, das Auto, the escape is sie nicht successful?"

We explained everything to him, that we had spread the story about the soldiers and the car on purpose to put people, and especially the Germans, on the wrong track, should they try to find us.

Dussel was again struck dumb by such ingenuity and, when he had explored further our superpractical exquisite little "Secret Annexe," he could do nothing but gaze about him in astonishment.

311

b

                                          We all had lunch together. Then he had a little nap and joined us for tea, tidied up his things a bit, (Miep had brought them beforehand) and began to feel more at home. Especially when he received the following typed "Secret Annexe Rules" (v.P. product)[1].

     <u>Prospectus and guide</u> to the "Secret Annexe." Special institution as temporary residence for Jews and suchlike.

     <u>Open all the year round.</u> Beautiful, quiet, wooded surroundings, in the heart of Amsterdam. No residential neighbors. Can be reached by trams 13 and 17 also by car or bicycle. In special cases also on foot if the German authorities prevent the use of transport.

     Distance from the Mint: 5 minutes. Distance from South Amsterdam: 45 minutes. | 98 | Furnished and unfurnished apartments and rooms always available with or without board. Board and lodging free. <u>Special, fat-free diet.</u>

c

     We all had lunch together. Then he had a little nap and joined us for tea, tidied up his things a bit (Miep had brought them beforehand), and began to feel more at home. Especially when he received the following typed "Secret Annexe Rules" (Van Daan product).

PROSPECTUS AND GUIDE TO THE "SECRET ANNEXE"

     Special institution as temporary residence for Jews and suchlike.

Open all the year round. Beautiful, quiet, free from woodland surroundings,* in the heart of Amsterdam. [No residential neighbors.] Can be reached by trams 13 and 17, also by car or bicycle. In special cases also on foot, if the Germans prevent the use of transport.

Board and lodging: Free.

Special fat-free diet.

---

*The original Dutch edition had the word "*bosvrije* [unwooded]" here, although Anne Frank wrote "*bosrijke* [wooded]" in her diary (see **b** above). A.J.P.

Running water in the bathroom (alas, no bath) and down various inside and outside walls. Wonderful fireplaces. Ample storage room for all types of goods. 2 large modern safes. Own radio center.

direct communication with London, New York, Tel Aviv and numerous other stations.

This appliance is only for residents' use after 6 o'clock in evening. No stations are forbidden on the understanding that German stations are only listened to in special cases, such as classical music, etc. The radio news service works continuously in 3 shifts. In the | 99 morning at 7 o'clock, in the afternoon at 1 o'clock, in the evening at 6 o'clock. | Rest hours: 10 o'clock in the evening until 7.30 in the morning. 10.15 on Sundays. Residents may rest during the day, conditions permitting, as the directors indicate. For reasons of public security rest hours must be strictly observed!!!! Free time: that spent outside the house suspended until further notice.

Use of Language: Speak softly at all times, by order! All civilized languages are permitted, therefore no German! Reading and relaxation: No German books may be read, with the exception of scientific and classical works, everything else is allowed. Physical exercise: daily. Singing: only softly and after 6 o'clock in the evening.

films: by arrangement.

Lessons: One written shorthand lesson per week. English, French, Mathematics, and History at all times.

Running water in the bathroom (alas, no bath) and down various inside and outside walls. *Ample storage room* for all types of goods.

Own radio center, direct communication with London, New York, Tel Aviv, and numerous other stations. This appliance is only for residents' use after six o'clock in the evening. No stations are forbidden, on the understanding that German stations are only listened to in special cases, such as classical music and the like.

Rest hours: 10 o'clock in the evening until 7:30 in the morning. 10:15 on Sundays. Residents may rest during the day, conditions permitting, as the directors indicate. For reasons of public security rest hours must be strictly observed ! !

Holidays (outside the home): postponed indefinitely.

Use of language: Speak softly at all times, by order! All civilized languages are permitted, therefore no German!

[*Physical exercise:* daily.]

Lessons: One written shorthand lesson per week. English, French, Mathematics, and History at all times.

313

...

b

100   Payment by lessons in return, e.g. in Dutch.
It is strictly forbidden to listen to German news bulletins (no matter from where trans-mitted) or to repeat them.

Small pets—special department, good treatment available (vermin excepted, for which permit must be. . . . . .

——

Payment by arrangement.

——

Mealtimes: Breakfast, every day except Sundays and Bank Holidays, 9 a.m. Sundays and Bank Holidays 11.30 a.m. approximately.

——

Lunch, not very big.
1.15 p.m.—1.45 p.m.

——

Dinner, cold and/or hot, no fixed time (depending on the news broadcast).

——

101   Corrections:
The residents kindly ask to be corrected should any of them make mistakes when speaking or pronouncing the Dutch language; this would certainly benefit all residents.
Duties:
Residents must always be ready to help with office work.
Baths: The washtub is available for all residents from 9 a.m. on Sundays. The W.C., kitchen, private office or main office, according to desire, are available.
Alcoholic beverages only on doctor's prescription. End.

yours, Anne

c

Small Pets—Special Department (permit is necessary): Good treatment available (vermin excepted).
Mealtimes: breakfast, every day except Sundays and Bank Holidays, 9 A.M. Sundays and Bank Holidays, 11:30 A.M. approximately.
Lunch: (not very big): 1:15 P.M. to 1:45 P.M.
Dinner: cold and/or hot: no fixed time (depending on the news broadcast).
Duties: Residents must always be ready to help with office work.
Baths: The washtub is available for all residents from 9 A.M. on Sundays. The W.C., kitchen, private office or main office, whichever preferred, are available.
Alcoholic Beverages: only with doctor's prescription.

END
Yours, Anne

. . . . . .

Thursday 19 Nov. 1942.

Dear Kitty,

Pf. is a very nice man, just as we had all imagined. Of course he thought it was all right to share my little room; quite honestly I'm not so keen that a stranger should use my things, but one must be prepared to make some sacrifices for a good cause, so I shall make my little offering with a good will; if we can save any of our acquaintances then everything else is of secondary importance, says Daddy, and he's absolutely right. The first day that Pf. was here he immediately asked me a whole lot of questions: When does the charwoman come? When can one use the bathroom? When is one allowed to use the lavatory? You may laugh but these things are not so simple in a hiding place. During the day we mustn't

make any noise that might be heard downstairs and if there is some stranger— | such as the charwoman for example—then we have to be extra careful. I explained all this carefully to Pf. But one thing that amazed me is that he finds it very hard to take things in. He asks everything twice over and still doesn't seem to remember.

Perhaps that will wear off in time, and it's only that he's thoroughly upset by the sudden change. Apart from that, all goes well, Pf. has told us a lot about the outside world, which we have missed for so long now. He had very sad news, countless friends and acquaintances have gone to a terrible end. Evening after evening the green and gray

Thursday, 19 November, 1942

Dear Kitty,

Dussel is a very nice man, just as we had all imagined. Of course he thought it was all right to share my little room.

Quite honestly I'm not so keen that a stranger should make use of my things, but one must be prepared to make some sacrifices for a good cause, so I shall make my little offering with a good will. "If we can save someone, then everything else is of secondary importance," says Daddy, and he's absolutely right.

The first day that Dussel was here, he immediately asked me all sorts of questions: When does the charwoman come? When can one use the bathroom? When is one allowed to use the lavatory? You may laugh, but these things are not so simple in a hiding place. During the day we mustn't make any noise that might be heard downstairs; and if there is some stranger—such as the charwoman for example—then we have to be extra careful. I explained all this carefully to Dussel. But one thing amazed me: he is very slow on the uptake. He asks everything twice over and still doesn't seem to remember. Perhaps that will wear off in time, and it's only that he's thoroughly upset by the sudden change.

Apart from that, all goes well. Dussel has told us a lot about the outside world, which we have missed for so long now. He had very sad news. Countless friends and acquaintances have gone to a terrible fate. Evening after evening the green and gray army lorries trundle

315

. . . . . .

b

army lorries trundle past and ring at every front door to inquire if there are any Jews living in the house, if there are, then the whole family has to go at once. If they don't find any they go on to the next house. No one has a chance of evading them, unless one goes into hiding.² Often they go round with lists, and only ring when they know they can get

| 104   a good haul. Sometimes they let them off for a ransom | —so much per head. It seems like the slave hunts of olden times. But it's certainly no joke; it's much too tragic for that, in the evenings when it's dark, I often see rows of good, innocent⁶ people accompanied by crying children, walking on and on, in the charge of a couple of these chaps, bullied and knocked about until they almost drop. Nobody is spared, old people, children, babies, expectant mothers, the sick each and all join in the march of death.

How fortunate we are here, so well cared for and undisturbed. We wouldn't have to worry about all this misery were it not that we are so anxious about all those dear to us whom we can no longer help. I feel wicked sleeping in a warm bed, while my dearest friends have been knocked down or have fallen into a gutter somewhere out in the cold night.

| 105   I get frightened when I think | of close friends who have now been delivered into the hands of the cruelest brutes the world has ever seen.⁹ And all because they are Jews.

yours, Anne

c

past. The Germans ring at every front door to inquire if there are any Jews living in the house. If there are, then the whole family has to go at once. If they don't find any, they go on to the next house. No one has a chance of evading them unless one goes into hiding. Often they go around with lists, and only ring when they know they can get a good haul. Sometimes they let them off for cash—so much per head. It seems like the slave hunts of olden times. But it's certainly no joke; it's much too tragic for that. In the evenings when it's dark, I often see rows of good, innocent people accompanied by crying children, walking on and on, in [the] charge of a couple of these chaps, bullied and knocked about until they almost drop. No one is spared—old people, babies, expectant mothers, the sick— each and all join in the march of death.

How fortunate we are here, so well cared for and undisturbed. We wouldn't have to worry about all this misery were it not that we are so anxious about all those dear to us whom we can no longer help.

I feel wicked sleeping in a warm bed, while my dearest friends have been knocked down or have fallen into a gutter somewhere out in the cold night. I get frightened when I think of close friends who have now been delivered into the hands of the cruelest brutes that walk the earth. And all because they are Jews!

Yours, Anne

316

a

. . . . . .

b 106

Friday 20 Nov. 1942.

Dear Kitty,

Not one of us really knows how to react. The news about the Jews had not really penetrated through to us until now, and we thought it best to remain as cheerful[1] as possible. On the few occasions[2] when Miep lets out something that has happened to a friend Mummy and Mrs. v.P. always begin to cry, so Miep thinks it better not to tell us any more. But Pf. was immediately plied with questions from all sides and the stories he told us were so gruesome and dreadful that one can't get them out of one's mind. Yet we shall still have our jokes and tease each other when these horrors have faded a bit in our minds; it won't do us any good or help those outside to go on being as gloomy as we are at the moment | 107 and what would be the object | of making our "Secret Annexe" a "Secret Annexe of Gloom"? Must I keep thinking about those other people whatever I am doing and if I want to laugh about something, should I stop myself quickly and feel ashamed that I am cheerful? Ought I then to cry the whole day long? No, that I can't do and, besides, in time this gloom will wear off.

c

Friday, 20 November 1942

Dear Kitty,

None of us really knows how to take it all. The news about the Jews had not really penetrated through to us until now, and we thought it best to remain as cheerful as possible. Every now and then, when Miep lets out something about what has happened to a friend, Mummy and Mrs. Van Daan always begin to cry, so Miep thinks it better not to tell us any more. But Dussel was immediately plied with questions from all sides, and the stories he told us were so gruesome and dreadful that one can't get them out of one's mind.

Yet we shall still have our jokes and tease each other, when these horrors have faded a bit in our minds. It won't do us any good, or help those outside, to go on being as gloomy as we are at the moment. And what would be the object of making our "Secret Annexe" into a "Secret Annexe of Gloom"? Must I keep thinking about those other people, whatever I am doing? And if I want to laugh about something, should I stop myself quickly and feel ashamed that I am cheerful? Ought I then to cry the whole day long? No, that I can't do. Besides, in time this gloom will wear off.

317

a   . . . . . .

b   Added to this misery there is another, but of a personal kind; and it pales into
insignificance beside all the wretchedness just told. Still, I can't refrain from telling you
that lately I have begun to feel deserted, I am surrounded by too great a void. I never used
to feel like this, my fun and amusements, my girl friends, completely filled my thoughts.
Now I either think about unhappy things, or about myself. And at long last I have made
the discovery that Daddy, although he's such a darling, still cannot take the place of my
| 108   entire little world of bygone days.[2] | Mummy and Margot have long since ceased to count
in my feelings. But why do I bother you with such foolish things? I'm very ungrateful,
Kitty; I know that. But it often makes my head swim if I am jumped on too much, and
then on top of that have to think about all those other miseries!

yours, Anne

c   Added to this misery there is another, but of a purely personal kind; and it pales into
insignificance beside all the wretchedness I've just told you about. Still, I can't refrain from
telling you that lately I have begun to feel deserted. I am surrounded by too great a void.
I never used to feel like this, my fun and amusements, and my girl friends, completely
filled my thoughts. Now I either think about unhappy things, or about myself. And at
long last I have made the discovery that Daddy, although he's such a darling, still cannot
take the place of my entire little world of bygone days. But why do I bother you with
such foolish things? I'm very ungrateful, Kitty; I know that. But it often makes my head
swim if I'm jumped upon too much, and then on top of that have to think about all those
other miseries!

Yours, Anne

318

b 109   Saturday 28 Nov. 1942.

Dear Kitty,

We have used too much electricity, more than our ration, result: exaggerated economy
and the prospect of having it cut off,* no light for a fortnight; a pleasant thought, that,
but who knows perhaps it won't happen after all! It's too dark to read in the afternoons
after 4 or half past, we pass the time in all sorts of crazy ways: asking riddles, physical
training in the dark, talking English and French, criticizing books, but it all begins to pall
in the end. Yesterday evening I discovered something new: to peer through a powerful
pair of field glasses into the lighted rooms of the houses at the back. In the daytime we
can't allow even as much as a centimeter's chink to appear between our curtains, but it
can't do any harm after dark. I never knew before that neighbors could be such interesting
people, at any rate ours are, I found one couple having a meal, one family was in the act
of taking a home movie, and the dentist over the way was just attending to an old lady,
| 110 | who was awfully scared.

It was always said about Mr. Pf., that he could get on wonderfully with children and
that he loved them all. Now he shows himself in his true colors; a stodgy, old-fashioned

---

*The rationing bylaws of 1941 restricted the use of gas and electricity. If the ration was exceeded,
the consequence could be temporary suspension of services.

c   Saturday, 28 November, 1942

Dear Kitty,

We have used too much electricity, more than our ration. Result: the utmost economy
and the prospect of having it cut off. No light for a fortnight; a pleasant thought, that,
but who knows, perhaps it won't happen after all! It's too dark to read in the afternoons
after four or half past. We pass the time in all sorts of crazy ways: asking riddles, physical
training in the dark, talking English and French, criticizing books. But it all begins to pall
in the end. Yesterday evening I discovered something new: to peer through a powerful
pair of field glasses into the lighted rooms of the houses at the back. In the daytime we
can't allow even as much as a centimeter's chink to appear between our curtains, but it
can't do any harm after dark. I never knew before that neighbors could be such interesting
people. At any rate, ours are. I found one couple having a meal, one family was in the
act of taking a home movie; and the dentist opposite was just attending to an old lady,
who was awfully scared.

It was always said about Mr. Dussel that he could get on wonderfully with children
and that he loved them all. Now he shows himself in his true colors; a stodgy old-fashioned

b

disciplinarian and preacher of long, drawn-out sermons on manners. As I have the unusual good fortune (!) to share my bedroom, alas, a small one, with his lordship and as I am generally considered to be the most badly behaved of the three young people, I have a lot to put up with and have to sham deafness in order to escape the much too often repeated tickings-off and warnings. All this wouldn't be too bad if he wasn't such a frightful sneak and he didn't pick on Mummy of all people to speak to every time. When I've already just had a dose from him, Mummy goes over it all again, so I get a gale aft as well as fore, then if I'm really lucky, I'm called on to give an account of myself to Mrs. v.P. and

| 111   then I get a | veritable hurricane!

      Honestly you needn't think it's easy to be the "badly brought-up" central figure of a hypercritical family in hiding. When I lie in bed at night and think over the many sins and shortcomings attributed to me I get so confused by the masses of things that ought to be looked into that I either laugh or cry: it depends what sort of mood I am in. And then I fall asleep with a stupid feeling of wishing to be different from what I am or from what I want to be; or perhaps to behave differently from the way I want to behave, or do behave. Oh, heavens above, now I'm getting you in a muddle too. Forgive me, but I don't like crossing things out, and in these days of paper shortage we're not allowed to throw paper away. Therefore I can only advise you not to read the above sentence again, and certainly not to try to understand it, because you won't succeed anyhow!

yours, Anne

c

disciplinarian, and preacher of long, drawn-out sermons on manners.

      As I have the unusual good fortune (!) to share my bedroom—alas, a small one— with His Lordship, and as I'm generally considered to be the most badly behaved of the three young people, I have a lot to put up with and have to pretend to be deaf in order to escape the old, much-repeated tickings-off and warnings. All this wouldn't be too bad, if he wasn't such a frightful sneak and he didn't pick on Mummy of all people to sneak to every time. When I've already just had a dose from him, Mummy goes over it all again, so I get a gale aft as well as fore. Then, if I'm really lucky, I'm called on to give an account of myself to Mrs. Van Daan and then I get a veritable hurricane!

      Honestly, you needn't think it's easy to be the "badly brought-up" central figure of a hypercritical family in hiding. When I lie in bed at night and think over the many sins and shortcomings attributed to me, I get so confused by it all that I either laugh or cry: it depends what sort of mood I am in.

      Then I fall asleep with a stupid feeling of wishing to be different from what I am or from what I want to be; perhaps to behave differently from the way I want to behave, or do behave. Oh, heavens above, now I'm getting you in a muddle too. Forgive me, but I don't like crossing things out, and in these days of paper shortage we are not allowed to throw paper away. Therefore I can only advise you not to read the last sentence again, and certainly not to try to understand it, because you won't succeed anyhow!

Yours, Anne

320

FOUND LOOSE IN THE OTHER DIARY.

5 Dec. 1942.

Dearest Kitty,

Last night it was wonderful, first we lit candles and then we went upstairs, the place was strewn with flowers, from Pim for Mummy, from Mr. v. Pels and Mr. Pf. for Mummy, from Mr. v. Pels for Mrs. v. Pels and from Pim and Mr. Pf. for Mrs. v.P. Mummy also got a pack of cigarettes and 1 bar of choclate. Margot and I each got a lovely sewing box, Piet and the two of us had fudge, and M. and I 1 bar choc. and 1 silver dish. I also got a lock for my diary.

Monday 7[1] Dec. 1942.

Dear Kitty,

Chanuka* and St. Nicholas Day came almost together this year—just one day's difference. We didn't make much fuss about Chanuka: we just gave each other a few trifles and then we had the candle. Because of the shortage of candles, we only had them alight for 10 minutes, but it is all right as long as you have the song.** Mr. v.P. has made a wooden candlestick so that too was all properly arranged. Saturday, the evening of St. Nicholas Day, was much more fun. Bep and Miep had made us very inquisitive by whispering all the time with Daddy while we were eating so naturally we guessed that something was on. And so it was. At 8 o'clock we all filed down the wooden staircase, through the passage in pitch-darkness (it made me shudder and wish that I was safely upstairs again) into the little middle room, there, as there are no windows, we were able to turn on a light. When that | was done Daddy opened the big cupboard. "Oh! how lovely," we all cried. A large basket decorated with Santa Claus paper stood in the corner and on top there was a mask of Black Peter.

| 113

*Chanuka is the eight-day Jewish festival of lights, celebrated during November/December.
**Probably the Chanuka hymn *Ma'oz Zur* (Heb.: "O Fortress, Rock [of my Salvation]").A.J.P.

Monday, 7 December, 1942

Dear Kitty,

Chanuka and St. Nicholas Day came almost together this year—just one day's difference. We didn't make much fuss about Chanuka: we just gave each other a few little presents and then we had the candles. Because of the shortage of candles we only had them alight for ten minutes, but it is all right as long as you have the song. Mr. Van Daan has made a wooden candlestick, so that too was all properly arranged.

Saturday, the evening of St. Nicholas Day, was much more fun. Miep and Elli had made us very inquisitive by whispering all the time with Daddy, so naturally we guessed that something was on.

And so it was. At eight o'clock we all filed down the wooden staircase through the passage in pitch-darkness (it made me shudder and wish that I was safely upstairs again) into the little dark room. There, as there are no windows, we were able to turn on a light. When that was done, Daddy opened the big cupboard. "Oh! how lovely," we all cried. A large basket decorated with St. Nicholas paper stood in the corner and on top there was a mask of Black Peter.

a ......

b We quickly took the basket upstairs with us. There was a nice little present for everyone with a suitable poem attached. You probably know all about St. Nicholas poems, so I won't write them all down, but both Mummy's and Mrs. v.P.'s were most appropriate:
Bide your time
That's simply said
Like this rhyme.
But it's fraught
With bitter thought
Crown of thorn,
That's hard to bear,
But must be borne.
Santa chose as his reward
A lovely calendar and card
114 Wrap them well, Piet my boy
So Mrs. F. will beam with joy.

c We quickly took the basket upstairs with us. There was a nice little present for everyone, with a suitable poem attached. I got a doll, whose skirt is a bag for odds and ends;

322

a
. . . . . .

b —

What a hustle and a bustle
Every day and everywhere
Could that be the reason why
Everyone's so fond of her?
Nor is that an idle boast
For she cooks the finest roast.
When for once she takes a rest
What is it that she likes best?
Knitting! Knitting! Knitting!
For that reason Santa dear,
Do look kindly on her face
And present the lady here
With a first-rate needle case.

A Jan Gies product.
I got a doll whose skirt is a bag for odds and ends. Daddy got book ends and so on. In any case it was a nice idea and as none of us had ever celebrated St. Nicholas, it was a good way of starting.

yours, Anne.

P.S. Of course we also had something for downstairs, stuff left over from the good old days, and Miep and Bep can always do with some money as well.

Today we heard that the ashtray for v.P., the photo-frame for Pf. and the book ends for Daddy were all made by Mr. Voskuyl himself. How anyone is able to make things so well with his hands is a mystery to me!

yours, Anne.

c Daddy got book ends, and so on. In any case it was a nice idea and as none of us had ever celebrated St. Nicholas, it was a good way of starting.

Yours, Anne

b 116

Dear Kitty,

Mr. v.P. used to be in the meat, sausage, and spice business. It was because of his spicy skills that he was taken on in Daddy's business, but now he is showing the sausagy side of himself, which for us is by no means disagreeable. We had ordered a lot of meat (under the counter, of course) for preserving in case we should come on hard times. He proposed making frying sausages, Gelderland sausages and sausage spread. It was fun to watch, first the way the pieces of meat went through the mincer, 2 or 3 times, then how all the accompanying ingredients were mixed with the minced meat, and then how the intestine was filled by means of a spout to make the sausages. We fried the sausage meat and ate it with sauerkraut for supper that evening, but the Gelderland sausages, which were meant for preserving, had to be thoroughly dried first, so we hung them over a stick tied to the ceiling with string.⁴ Everyone who came into the room began to laugh when they caught a glimpse of the row of sausages on show; they looked | terribly funny!

| 117

The room was in a glorious mess: Mr. v.P. was wearing one of his wife's aprons swathed round his substantial person (he looked fatter than he is!) and was busy with the meat, hands smothered in blood, red face and the messy apron made him look like a butcher. Mrs. v.P. was trying to do everything at once: learning Dutch from a book, stirring the soup, watching the meat being done, sighing and complaining about her injured rib. That's what happens to elderly ladies (!) who do such idiotic exercises to reduce their large behinds!

c

Thursday, 10 December, 1942

Dear Kitty,

Mr. Van Daan used to be in the meat, sausage, and spice business. It was because of his knowledge of this trade that he was taken on in Daddy's business. Now he is showing the sausagy side of himself, which, for us, is by no means disagreeable.

We had ordered a lot of meat (under the counter, of course) for preserving in case we should come upon hard times. It was fun to watch, first the way the pieces of meat went through the mincer, two or three times, then how all the accompanying ingredients were mixed with the minced meat, and then how the intestine was filled by means of a spout, to make the sausages. We fried the sausage meat and ate it with sauerkraut for supper that evening, but the Gelderland sausages had to be thoroughly dried first, so we hung them over a stick tied to the ceiling with string. Everyone who came into the room began to laugh when they caught a glimpse of the row of sausages on show. They looked terribly funny!

The room was in a glorious mess. Mr. Van Daan was wearing one of his wife's aprons swathed round his substantial person (he looked fatter than he is!) and was busy with the meat. Hands smothered in blood, red face, and the soiled apron, made him look like a butcher. Mrs. Van Daan was trying to do everything at once, learning Dutch from a book, stirring the soup, watching the meat being done, sighing and complaining about her injured rib. That's what happens to elderly ladies (!) who do such idiotic exercises to reduce their large behinds!

......

Pf. had inflammation in one eye and was bathing it with camomile tea by the fire. Pim, who was sitting on a chair in a beam of sunlight that shone through the window, kept being pushed from one side to the other. In addition, I think his rheumatism was bothering him, because he sat rather hunched up with a miserable look on his face, watching Mr. v.P. at work. He looked exactly like some shriveled-up old man from an old-age home. Peter was doing acrobatics round the room with his cat | (called Muschi). Mummy, Margot and I were doing the potato peeling; and of course all of us were doing everything wrong because we were so busy watching Mr. v.P.*

| 118

Pf. has opened his dental practice. For the fun of it I must just tell you about his first patient. Mummy was ironing and Mrs. v.P., who was the first to face the ordeal, went and sat on a chair in the middle of the room. Pf. began to unpack his case in an important way, asked for some³ eau de cologne as a disinfectant and vaseline to take the place of wax. Pf. looked in Mrs. v.P.'s mouth and found two teeth which, when touched, just made her crumple up as if she was going to pass out, all the while uttering incoherent cries of pain. After a lengthy examination (in Mrs. v.P.'s case, lasting in actual fact no

---

* Anne Frank has also described these events in her *Verhaaltjesboek (Tales)* under the title of "*Worstdag* [Sausage Day]."

Dussel had inflammation in one eye and was bathing it with camomile tea by the fire. Pim, who was sitting on a chair in a beam of sunlight that shone through the window, kept being pushed from one side to the other. In addition, I think his rheumatism was bothering him, because he sat rather hunched up with a miserable look on his face, watching Mr. Van Daan at work. He looked exactly like some shriveled-up old man from an old people's home. Peter was doing acrobatics round the room with his cat. Mummy, Margot, and I were peeling potatoes; and, of course, all of us were doing everything wrong because we were so busy watching Mr. Van Daan.

Dussel has opened his dental practice. For the fun of it, I must just tell you about his first patient. Mummy was ironing; and Mrs. Van Daan was the first to face the ordeal. She went and sat on a chair in the middle of the room. Dussel began to unpack his case in an awfully important way, asked for some eau de cologne as a disinfectant and vaseline to take the place of wax.

He looked in Mrs. Van Daan's mouth and found two teeth which, when touched, just made her crumple up as if she was going to pass out, uttering incoherent cries of pain. After a lengthy examination (in Mrs. Van Daan's case, lasting in actual fact no more

b

| 119   more than 2 minutes) Pf. began to scrape away at one of the holes, but, no fear—it was out of the question—the patient flung her arms and legs about wildly in all directions until at a given moment Pf. let go of the scraper— | which remained stuck in Mrs. v.P.'s tooth. Then the fat was really in the fire! She cried (as far as it was possible, with such an instrument in one's mouth), tried to pull the thing out of her mouth, and only succeeded in pushing it further in. Mr. Pf. stood with his hands against his sides calmly watching the little comedy. The rest of the audience lost all control and roared with laughter; it was rotten of us, because I for one am quite sure that I should have screamed even louder. After much turning, kicking, screaming and calling out, she got the instrument free at last and Mr. Pf. went on with his work as if nothing had happened! This he did so quickly that Mrs. v.P. didn't have time to start any fresh tricks. But he'd never had so much help in all his life before; two assistants are pretty useful, v.P. and I performed our duties well. The whole scene looked like a picture from the Middle Ages, entitled "a quack at work. In the meantime, however, the patient hadn't much patience; she had to keep an eye on "her" soup and "her" meal. One thing is certain, Mrs. v.P. won't be in such a hurry to allow herself to be treated again!*

yours, Anne[3]

---

*Anne Frank has also described these events in her *Verhaaltjesboek (Tales)* under the title of "*De tandarts* [The Dentist]."

c

than two minutes) Dussel began to scrape away at one of the holes. But, no fear—it was out of the question—the patient flung her arms and legs about wildly in all directions until at one point Dussel let go of the scraper—that remained stuck in Mrs. Van Daan's tooth.

Then the fat was really in the fire! She cried (as far as it was possible with such an instrument in one's mouth), tried to pull the thing out of her mouth, and only succeeded in pushing it further in. Mr. Dussel stood with his hands against his sides calmly watching the little comedy. The rest of the audience lost all control and roared with laughter. It was rotten of us, because I for one am quite sure that I should have screamed even louder. After much turning, kicking, screaming, and calling out, she got the instrument free at last and Mr. Dussel went on with his work, as if nothing had happened!

This he did so quickly that Mrs. Van Daan didn't have time to start any fresh tricks. But he'd never had so much help in all his life before. Two assistants are pretty useful: Van Daan and I performed our duties well. The whole scene looked like a picture from the Middle Ages entitled "A Quack at Work." In the meantime, however, the patient hadn't much patience; she had to keep an eye on "her" soup and "her" meal. One thing is certain, Mrs. Van Daan won't be in such a hurry to allow herself to be treated again!

Yours, Anne

326

b   120

Dear Kitty,

I'm sitting cozily in the main office, looking outside through a slit in the curtains. It is dusk but still just light enough to write to you.

It is a very queer sight, as I watch the people walking by; it looks just as if they are all in a terrible hurry and tripping over their own toes.[3] With cyclists, now one simply can't keep pace with their speeds. I[4] can't even see what sort of person is riding on the machine. The people in this neighborhood don't look so very attractive now. The children especially are so dirty you wouldn't want to touch them with a barge pole, real slum kids with running noses; I can hardly understand a word they say. Yesterday afternoon Margot and I were having a bath here and I said, "Supposing we were to take the children who are walking past one by one, hoist them up with a fishing rod, give them each a bath,

| 121   wash and | mend their clothes, and then let them go again, then". . . . Margot replied, "by tomorrow they would look just as filthy and ragged as before." But I'm just talking

c

Sunday, 13 December, 1942

Dear Kitty,

I'm sitting cozily in the main office, looking outside through a slit in the curtain. It is dusk but still just light enough to write to you.

It is a very queer sight, as I watch the people walking by; it looks just as if they are all in a terrible hurry and nearly trip over their own toes. With cyclists, now, one simply can't keep pace with their speed. I can't even see what sort of person is riding on the machine.

The people in this neighborhood don't look very attractive. The children especially are so dirty you wouldn't want to touch them with a barge pole. Real slum kids with running noses. I can hardly understand a word they say.

Yesterday afternoon Margot and I were having a bath here and I said, "Supposing we were to take the children who are walking past, one by one, hoist them up with a fishing rod, give them each a bath, wash and mend their clothes, and then let them go again, then . . ." Margot interrupted me, "By tomorrow they would look just as filthy and ragged as before."

. . . . . .

nonsense; besides, there are other things to see—cars, boats, and rain. I like particularly the screech of the trams as they go by.

There is no more variety in our thoughts than there is for ourselves, everything goes round and round like a roundabout—from Jews to food and from food to politics. By the way, talking of Jews, I saw 2 Jews through the curtain yesterday, I could hardly believe my eyes; it was a horrible feeling, just as if I had betrayed them and was now watching them in their misery.

There is a houseboat immediately opposite, where a bargeman lives with his family. He has a small yapping dog. We only know the little dog by his bark and his tail, which | 122   we can see when he runs round the deck. Ugh! Now it's started to rain and | most of[7] the people are hidden under umbrellas, I see nothing but raincoats and occasionally the back of someone's hat. Really[8] I don't need to see more. I'm gradually getting to know all the women outside by sight, blown out with potatoes wearing a red or green coat, trodden-down heels and with a bag under their arms, with grim or kind faces—depending on their husbands' dispositions

yours, Anne

But I'm just talking nonsense; besides, there are other things to see—cars, boats, and rain. I like particularly the screech of the trams as they go by.

There is no more variety in our thoughts than there is for ourselves. They go round and round like a roundabout—from Jews to food and from food to politics. By the way, talking of Jews, I saw two Jews through the curtain yesterday. I could hardly believe my eyes; it was a horrible feeling, just as if I'd betrayed them and was now watching them in their misery. There is a houseboat immediately opposite, where a bargeman lives with his family. He has a small yapping dog. We only know the little dog by his bark and his tail, which we can see when he runs round the deck. Ugh! Now it's started to rain and most of the people are hidden under umbrellas. I see nothing but raincoats and occasionally the back of someone's hat. Really I don't need to see more. I'm gradually getting to know all the women at a glance, blown out with potatoes, wearing a red or a green coat, trodden-down heels and with a bag under their arms. Their faces either look grim or kind—depending on their husbands' dispositions.

Yours, Anne

Tuesday
22 Dec. 1942.

Dear Kitty,

The "Secret Annexe" has heard the joyful news that each person will receive an extra ¼ pound of butter for Christmas. It says ½ pound in the newspapers but that's only for the lucky mortals who get their ration books from the government and not for Jews who have gone into hiding, who can only afford to buy 4 illegal ration books, instead of 8.

We are all going to bake something with our butter, I made some biscuits and two cakes this morning. Everyone is very busy upstairs and Mummy has told me not to go there to work or read until the household jobs are done. Mrs. v.P. is in bed with her bruised front rib, complains the whole day long, allows herself to be given fresh dressings all the time, and isn't satisfied with anything. I shall be glad when she's back on her two short legs again and tidies up her own things, because I must say this for her; she's exceptionally industrious and tidy, all the while she is healthy in mind and body. | She is cheerful too. Just as if I didn't hear enough sh-sh during the day, for making "too much" noise, my gentleman bedroom companion now repeatedly calls out sh to me at night too.

| 124

Tuesday, 22 December, 1942

Dear Kitty,

The "Secret Annexe" has heard the joyful news that each person will receive an extra quarter of a pound of butter for Christmas. It says half a pound in the newspapers, but that's only for the lucky mortals who get their ration books from the government, not for Jews who have gone into hiding, who can only afford to buy four illegal ration books, instead of eight.

We are all going to bake something with our butter, I made some biscuits and two cakes this morning. Everyone is very busy upstairs and Mummy has told me I must not go there to work or read, until the household jobs are done.

Mrs. Van Daan is in bed with her bruised rib, complains the whole day long, allows herself to be given fresh dressings all the time, and isn't satisfied with anything. I shall be glad when she's on her feet again and tidies up her own things, because I must say this for her; she's exceptionally industrious and tidy, all the while she is healthy in mind and body. She is cheerful too.

Just as if I didn't hear enough "ssh-ssh" during the day, for making too much noise, my gentleman bedroom companion now repeatedly calls out "ssh-ssh" to me at night too.

. . . . . .

According to him, I am not even allowed to turn over; I refuse to take the slightest notice of him, and shall go sh back at him the next time.

He gets more tiresome and selfish by the day, I didn't see a single one of the generously promised biscuits after the first week. He makes me furious, on Sundays especially when he turns the light on early to do his 10 minutes of[2] exercises.[4]

It seems hours, while I, poor tormented creature, feel the chairs—which are placed at the head of my bed to lengthen it—slide backwards and forwards continuously under my sleepy head. When he has ended with a couple of violent arm-waving exercises to loosen his muscles, his lordship begins his toilet. | His pants are hanging up, to and fro he must go then to collect them, his tie is lying on the table, so once more he pushes and bumps past the chairs to get it. But I won't bore you any longer on the subject of old men, it won't make things any better and all my plans of revenge (such as disconnecting the lamp, shutting the door, hiding his clothes) must be abandoned in order to keep the peace, more's the pity. Oh, I'm becoming so sensible! One must apply one's reason to everything here, learning to obey, to hold your tongue, to help, to be good, to give in, and I don't know what else! I'm afraid I shall use up all my brains too quickly, and I haven't got so very many. Then I shall not have any left for when the war is over.

yours, Anne

| 125

According to him, I am not even allowed to turn over! I refuse to take the slightest notice of him, and shall go "ssh-ssh" back at him the next time.

He makes me furious, on Sundays especially, when he turns the light on early to do his exercises. It seems to take simply hours, while I, poor tormented creature, feel the chairs, which are placed at the head of my bed to lengthen it, slide backwards and forwards continually under my sleepy head. When he has ended with a couple of violent arm-waving exercises to loosen his muscles, His Lordship begins his toilet. His pants are hanging up, so to and fro he must go to collect them. But he forgets his tie, which is lying on the table. Therefore once more he pushes and bumps past the chairs to get it.

But I won't bore you any longer on the subject of old men. It won't make things any better and all my plans of revenge (such as disconnecting the lamp, shutting the door, hiding his clothes) must be abandoned in order to keep the peace. Oh, I'm becoming so sensible! One must apply one's reason to everything here, learning to obey, to hold your tongue, to help, to be good, to give in, and I don't know what else. I'm afraid I shall use up all my brains too quickly, and I haven't got so very many. Then I shall not have any left for when the war is over.

Yours, Anne

Everything has upset me again this morning, so I wasn't able to finish a single thing properly.

Wednesday 13 Jan. 1943.[1]

Dear Kitty,

We have a new job, namely filling packets with gravy (in powder form). The gravy is a product of Gies and Co; Mr. Kugler cannot find any fillers and if we do it the cost is much lower in any case. It's the kind of work they do in prisons, it's terribly boring and makes you giddy and giggly. It is terrible outside, day and night more of those poor miserable people are being dragged off, with nothing but a rucksack and a little money. On the way they are deprived even of these possessions. Families are torn apart, men, women and children all being split up. Children coming home from school find that their parents have disappeared. Women return from shopping to find their homes shut up and their families gone. The Dutch people are anxious too, their sons are being sent to Germany.

| 127   Everyone is afraid. | And every night hundreds of planes fly over Holland and go to German towns where the earth is plowed under by their bombs and every hour hundreds, even thousands of people are killed in Russia and Africa. No one is able to keep out of it, the whole globe is waging war and although it is going better for the Allies, the end is not yet in sight.

Wednesday, 13 January, 1943

Dear Kitty,

Everything has upset me again this morning, so I wasn't able to finish a single thing properly.

It is terrible outside. Day and night more of those poor miserable people are being dragged off, with nothing but a rucksack and a little money. On the way they are deprived even of these possessions. Families are torn apart, the men, women, and children all being separated. Children coming home from school find that their parents have disappeared. Women return from shopping to find their homes shut up and their families gone.

The Dutch people are anxious too, their sons are being sent to Germany. Everyone is afraid.

And every night hundreds of planes fly over Holland and go to German towns, where the earth is plowed up by their bombs, and every hour hundreds and thousands of people are killed in Russia and Africa. No one is able to keep out of it, the whole globe is waging war and although it is going better for the Allies, the end is not yet in sight.

331

a · · · · · ·

b
And as for us, we are fortunate. Yes, we are luckier than millions of people. It is quiet and safe here, and we are, so to speak, living on capital. We are even so egoistic as to talk about "after the war," brighten up over the thought of having new clothes and new shoes, whereas we really ought to save every penny, to help other people, and save what is left from the wreckage after the war. The children here run about in just a thin blouse and clogs; no coat, no hat, no stockings, and no one helps them. Their tummies are empty; they chew an old carrot to stay the pangs, go from their cold homes out into the cold street and, when they get to school, find themselves in an even colder classroom. | 128 Yes, it has even got so bad in Holland that countless children | stop the passers-by and beg for a piece of bread. I could go on for hours about all the suffering the war has brought, but then I would only make myself more dejected. There is nothing we can do, but wait as calmly we can till the misery comes to an end. Jews and Christians wait, the whole earth waits; and there are many who wait for death.

yours, Anne

c
And as for us, we are fortunate. Yes, we are luckier than millions of people. It is quiet and safe here, and we are, so to speak, living on capital. We are even so selfish as to talk about "after the war," brighten up at the thought of having new clothes and new shoes, whereas we really ought to save every penny, to help other people, and save what is left from the wreckage after the war.

The children here run about in just a thin blouse and clogs; no coat, no hat, no stockings, and no one helps them. Their tummies are empty; they chew an old carrot to stay the pangs, go from their cold homes out into the cold street and, when they get to school, find themselves in an even colder classroom. Yes, it has even got so bad in Holland that countless children stop the passers-by and beg for a piece of bread. I could go on for hours about all the suffering the war has brought, but then I would only make myself more dejected. There is nothing we can do but wait as calmly as we can till the misery comes to an end. Jews and Christians wait, the whole earth waits; and there are many who wait for death.

Yours, Anne

332

b   128a

Saturday 30 Jan.
1943.

Dear Kitty,

I'm boiling with rage, and yet I mustn't show it, I'd like to stamp my feet, scream, give Mummy a good shaking, cry, and I don't know what else, because of the horrible words, mocking looks, and accusations which are leveled at me every day, and find their mark, like shafts from a tightly strung bow, and which are just as hard to draw from my body. I would like to shout to Mummy, Margot, v.P., Pf.—and Daddy too—Leave me in peace, let me sleep one night at least without my pillow being wet with tears, my eyes burning and my head pounding.⁶ Let me go, away from it all, preferably away from the world!" But I can't do that, they mustn't know my despair; I can't let them see the wounds which

| 128b   they have caused, I couldn't stand their sympathy and their kindhearted jokes, | it would only make me want to scream all the more.

If I talk, everyone thinks I am showing off; when I'm silent they think I'm ridiculous; rude if I answer, sly if I get a good idea, lazy if I'm tired, selfish if I eat a mouthful

---

c

Saturday, 30 January, 1943

Dear Kitty,

I'm boiling with rage, and yet I mustn't show it. I'd like to stamp my feet, scream, give Mummy a good shaking, cry, and I don't know what else, because of the horrible words, mocking looks, and accusations which are leveled at me repeatedly every day, and find their mark, like shafts from a tightly strung bow, and which are just as hard to draw from my body.

I would like to shout to [Mummy], Margot, Van Daan, Dussel— and Daddy too— "Leave me in peace, let me sleep one night at least without my pillow being wet with tears, my eyes burning and my head throbbing. Let me get away from it all, preferably away from the world!" But I can't do that, they mustn't know my despair, I can't let them see the wounds which they have caused, I couldn't bear their sympathy and their kindhearted jokes, it would only make me want to scream all the more. If I talk, everyone thinks I'm showing off; when I'm silent they think I'm ridiculous; rude if I answer, sly if I get a good idea, lazy if I'm tired, selfish if I eat a mouthful more than I should, stupid,

b

| 128c

more than I should, stupid, cowardly, crafty, etc., etc. The whole day long I hear nothing else but that I'm an insufferable baby, and although I laugh about it and pretend not to take any notice, I do mind. I would like to ask God to give me a different nature, so that I didn't put everyone's back up. But that can't be done. I've got the nature that has been given to me and I'm sure it can't be bad. I do my very best to please everybody, far more than they'd ever guess. I try to laugh it all off, because I don't want to let them see my trouble. More than once after a whole string of undeserved rebukes, I have flared up at Mummy: I don't care | what you say anyhow. Leave me alone: I'm a hopeless case anyway." Naturally I was then told I was rude and virtually ignored for two days; and then, all at once, it was quite forgotten, and I was treated like everyone else again. It is impossible for me to be all sugar one day and spit venom the next, I'd rather choose the golden mean (which is not so golden), keep my thoughts to myself, and try for once to be just as disdainful to them as they are to me. Oh, if only I could

yours, Anne

c

cowardly, crafty, etc., etc. The whole day long I hear nothing else but that I am an insufferable baby, and although I laugh about it and pretend not to take any notice, I *do* mind. I would like to ask God to give me a different nature, so that I didn't put everyone's back up. But that can't be done. I've got the nature that has been given to me and I'm sure it can't be bad. I do my very best to please everybody, far more than they'd ever guess. I try to laugh it all off, because I don't want to let them see my trouble. More than once, after a whole string of undeserved rebukes, I have flared up at Mummy: "I don't care what you say anyhow. Leave me alone: I'm a hopeless case anyway." Naturally, I was then told I was rude and was virtually ignored for two days; and then, all at once, it was quite forgotten, and I was treated like everyone else again. It is impossible for me to be all sugar one day and spit venom the next. I'd rather choose the golden mean (which is not so golden), keep my thoughts to myself, and try for *once* to be just as disdainful to them as they are to me. Oh, if only I could!

Yours, Anne

a   . . . . . .

b   129   Friday 5 Feb. 1943.[1] [2]

Dear Kitty,

Although I haven't written anything about our rows for a long time there still isn't any change. The discord, long accepted by us, struck Mr. Pf. as a calamity at first. But he's getting used to it now and tries not to think about it. Margot and Peter aren't a bit what you would call "young," they are both so staid and quiet. I show up terribly against them and am always hearing "You don't find Margot and Peter doing that[4]—why don't you just once follow your dear sister's example? I simply loathe it. I might tell you I don't want to be in the least like Margot. She is much too soft and passive for my liking, and allows everyone to talk her around, and gives in about everything. I want to be a stronger character! But I keep such ideas to myself: they would tease me terribly if I came along

130   with this as an explanation of my attitude. The atmosphere at table is usually strained, | though luckily[7] the outburst is sometimes checked by the soup eaters. The soup eaters are the people from downstairs who come in to get a cup of soup. This afternoon Mr. v.P. was talking about Margot eating so little again. "I suppose you do it to keep slim," he added, teasing her. Mummy, who always defends Margot said loudly: "I can't bear your stupid chatter any longer." Mrs. v.P. turned scarlet, Mr. v.P. looked straight in front of him and said nothing.

c   Friday, 5 February, 1943

Dear Kitty,

Although I haven't written anything about our rows for a long time, there still isn't any change. The discord, long accepted by us, struck Mr. Dussel as a calamity at first. But he is getting used to it now and tries not to think about it. Margot and Peter aren't a bit what you would call "young," they are both so staid and quiet. I show up terribly against them and am always hearing, "You don't find Margot and Peter doing that—why don't you follow their example?" I simply loathe it. I might tell you I don't want to be in the least like Margot. She is much too soft and passive for my liking, and allows everyone to talk her around, and gives in about everything. I want to be a stronger character! But I keep such ideas to myself: they would only laugh at me, if I came along with this as an explanation of my attitude. The atmosphere at table is usually strained, though luckily the outbursts are sometimes checked by "the soup eaters"! The "soup eaters" are the people from the office who come in and are served with a cup of soup. This afternoon Mr. Van Daan was talking about Margot eating so little again. "I suppose you do it to keep slim," he added, teasing her. Mummy, who always defends Margot, said loudly: "I can't bear your stupid chatter any longer." Mr. [Mrs.] Van Daan turned scarlet, [Mr. Van Daan] looked straight in front of him, and said nothing.

335

a

. . . . . .

b   We often laugh about things, too, just recently Mrs. v.P. came out with some perfect nonsense. She was recalling the past, how well she and her father got on together and what a flirt she was. "And do you know," she went on "if a man gets a bit aggressive, my father used to say, then you must say to him, 'Mr. So and So, remember I am a lady!' and he will know what you mean." We thought that was a good joke and burst out laughing. Peter too although usually so quiet, sometimes gives cause for mirth.[3]

| 131   He has an unfortunate passion for | foreign words, although he does not always know their meaning. One afternoon we couldn't go to the lavatory because there were visitors in the office; however, Peter had to pay an urgent call, so he didn't pull the plug. He put a notice up on the lavatory door to warn us against the less than pleasant smell, with "S.V.P. gas" on it. Of course he meant to put "Beware of gas"; but he thought the other looked more genteel. He hadn't got the faintest notion it meant if you please.

                                                              yours, Anne

c   We often laugh about things; just recently Mrs. Van Daan came out with some perfect nonsense. She was recalling the past, how well she and her father got on together and what a flirt she was. "And do you know," she went on, "if a man gets a bit aggressive, my father used to say, then you must say to him, 'Mr. So and So, remember I am a lady!' and he will know what you mean." We thought that was a good joke and burst out laughing. Peter too, although usually so quiet, sometimes gives cause for mirth. He is blessed with a passion for foreign words, although he does not always know their meaning. One afternoon we couldn't go to the lavatory because there were visitors in the office; however, Peter had to pay an urgent call. So he didn't pull the plug. He put a notice up on the lavatory door to warn us, with "S.V.P. gas" on it. Of course he meant to put "Beware of gas"; but he thought the other looked more genteel. He hadn't got the faintest notion it meant "if you please."

                                                              Yours, Anne

a . . . . . .

b 132

Sat . 27 Feb. 1943.

Dear Kitty,

Pim is expecting the invasion any day. Churchil has had pneumonia, but is improving slowly. The freedom-loving Gandi of India is holding his umpteenth fast.* Mrs. v.P. claims to be fatalistic. And who is the most scared when the guns go off? No one else but Gusti. Jan brought a copy of the bishop's letter to churchgoers for us to read; it was very fine and inspiring. "Do not rest, people of the Netherlands, everyone is fighting with his own[4] weapons to free the country, the people and their religion. Give help, be generous and do not dismay!" is what they cry from the pulpit, just like that.** Will it help? It won't help the people of our religion. You'd never guess what has happened to us now! The owner

---

*In his struggle against the British government, Gandhi repeatedly used the hunger strike weapon, something the German-controlled press in the Netherlands naturally played up for all it was worth. (See, for instance, *De Telegraaf* of February 23 and 25, 1943.)

**On Sunday, February 21, 1943, a message was read from the pulpits of all Catholic churches, and probably of most Protestant churches, protesting against the rounding up of young people and against the persecution of the Jews. (L. de Jong: *Het Koninkrijk der Nederlanden in de Tweede Wereldoorlog*, Part 6, pp. 631ff.)

c

Saturday, 27 February, 1943

Dear Kitty,

Pim is expecting the invasion any day. Churchill has had pneumonia, but is improving slowly. The freedom-loving Gandhi of India is holding his umpteenth fast. Mrs. Van Daan claims to be fatalistic. But who is the most scared when the guns go off? No one else but Petronella.

Henk brought a copy of the bishop's letter to churchgoers for us to read. It was very fine and inspiring. "Do not rest, people of the Netherlands, everyone is fighting with his own weapons to free the country, the people, and their religion." "Give help, be generous, and do not dismay!" is what they cry from the pulpit, just like that. Will it help? It won't help the people of our religion.

a 97a

I have learned something new again, brothel and cocotte, I have got a separate little book for them but it's kept with the letters

a 98

Lately Mummy and I have been getting on better together but <u>never</u> confide. Margot is more catty than ever, and Daddy has got something he is keeping to himself, but he remains the same darling.

b

| 133

of these premises has sold the house without informing Kugler and Kleiman.* One morning the new owner arrived with an architect to have a look at the house; luckily, Mr. Kleiman was present and showed the gentlemen everything except our little "Secret Annexe," | he professed to have forgotten the key of the communicating door. The new owner didn't question any further.

It will be all right as long as he doesn't come back and want to see the "Secret Annexe," since then it won't look too good for us.

Daddy has emptied a card index box for Margot and me, and put cards in it that still have one side without any writing on. It is to be a book card system; then we both put down which books we have read, who they are by, and the date.[2]

New butter and margarine rationing at table. Each person has their little bit of fat put on their plate. In my opinion the division isn't fair. The v.P.s, who always make breakfast, take one and a half times as much as they give us. My parents are much too afraid of a row to say anything about it. Pity, I think you should always give people like them tit for tat.

yours, Anne

---

*On April 22, 1943, 263, Prinsengracht was bought by F. J. Piron from M. A. Wessel. (*North Holland Land-Survey Register*, deed of purchase 3305 no. 4.)

c

You'd never guess what has happened to us now. The owner of these premises has sold the house without informing Kraler and Koophuis. One morning the new owner arrived with an architect to have a look at the house. Luckily, Mr. Koophuis was present and showed the gentlemen everything except the "Secret Annexe." He professed to have forgotten the key of the communicating door. The new owner didn't question any further. It will be all right as long as he doesn't come back and want to see the "Secret Annexe," because then it won't look too good for us.

Daddy has emptied a card index box for Margot and me, and put cards in it. It is to be a book card system; then we both write down which books we have read, who they are by, etc. I have procured another little notebook for foreign words.

Lately Mummy and I have been getting on better together, but we still *never* confide in each other. Margot is more catty than ever and Daddy has got something he is keeping to himself, but he remains the same darling.

New butter and margarine rationing at table! Each person has their little bit of fat put on their plate. In my opinion the Van Daans don't divide it at all fairly. However, my parents are much too afraid of a row to say anything about it. Pity, *I* think you should always give people like them tit for tat.

Yours, Anne

338

Thursday 4 Mar. '43.

Dear Kitty,

Mrs. v.P. has a new name, we now call her Mrs. Beverbruck. You probably won't get it, so I'll tell you: You can often hear a Mr. Beverbruck on the English radio, complaining about the halfhearted bombings of Germany. Mrs. van Pels, who is always against everyone, even Churchil and the news service, is unreservedly behind Mr. Beverbruck. We therefore thought it would be a good idea for her to marry Mr. Beverbruck, and since she felt flattered by that suggestion she is now called Mrs. Beverbruck most of the time.

We are getting a new warehouseman, the old one has to go to Germany, which is a pity but much better for us, because the new one doesn't know the house. We've always been frightened of the warehousemen.

Gandi is eating again. The black market is doing tremendous business. We'd be able | 135 | to eat till we burst if we had enough money to pay the impossible | prices. Bro. recently bought a pound of butter on the train, our vegetable man buys potatoes from the German army and brings them in sacks to our office.⁴ He knows that we are hiding and always comes during the lunch break when the warehouse staff is out.

We either can't breathe or else we keep sneezing and coughing, there is so much pepper being ground in the mills.⁶ Everyone who comes upstairs greets us with an atishoo, Mrs. v.P. declares she is simply unable to go downstairs, she'll fall ill if she has to smell any more pepper.

I don't think Daddy's business is nice at all, nothing but laxatives and pepper. A provision merchant ought to have some sweets as well!

This morning a torrent of words broke over my head yet again; it was so thunderingly full of nasty expressions that my ears rang with the Anne's bad, v.P.'s good, donderwetterwetter.*

yours, Anne

---

* Anne's rendering of the German *Donnerwetter noch einmal* (confound it all). A.J.P.

a

. . . . . .

b   136

Wednesday 10 Mar. 1943.

Dear Kitty,

We had a short circuit last evening, and on top of that the guns kept banging away all the time. I still haven't got over my fear of everything connected with shooting and planes, and I creep into Daddy's bed nearly every night for comfort. I know it's very childish but you don't know what it is like, the A.A. guns roar so loudly that you can't hear yourself speak. Mrs. Beverbruck[1], the fatalist, was nearly crying and said in a very timid little voice, "Oh, it's so unpleasant! Oh, they're shooting so hard," by which she really means "I'm so frightened!" It didn't seem nearly so bad by candlelight as in the dark; I was shivering, just as if I had a temperature, and begged Daddy to light the candle again. He was relentless, the light remained off. Suddenly there was a burst of machine-gun fire, and that is ten times worse than guns, Mummy jumped out of bed and to Pim's great annoyance lit the

| 137   candle. When he complained her answer was firm: | "After all, Anne's not exactly a veteran soldier," and that was the end of it.

c

Wednesday, 10 March, 1943

Dear Kitty,

We had a short circuit last evening, and on top of that the guns kept banging away all the time. I still haven't got over my fear of everything connected with shooting and planes, and I creep into Daddy's bed nearly every night for comfort. I know it's very childish but you don't know what it is like. The A.A. guns roar so loudly that you can't hear yourself speak. Mrs. Van Daan, the fatalist, was nearly crying, and said in a very timid little voice, "Oh, it is so unpleasant! Oh, they are shooting so hard," by which she really means "I'm so frightened."

It didn't seem nearly so bad by candlelight as in the dark. I was shivering, just as if I had a temperature, and begged Daddy to light the candle again. He was relentless, the light remained off. Suddenly there was a burst of machine-gun fire, and that is ten times worse than guns. Mummy jumped out of bed and, to Pim's annoyance, lit the candle. When he complained her answer was firm: "After all, Anne's not exactly a veteran soldier," and that was the end of it.

340

......

Have I told you about Mrs. v.P.'s other fears, I don't think so. If I am to keep you informed of all that happens in the "Secret Annexe," you must know about this too. One night Mrs. v.P. heard burglars in the attic, she heard loud footsteps and was so frightened that she woke[3] her husband just at that moment the burglars disappeared and the only sounds that Mr. v.P. could hear were the heartbeats of the frightened fatalist herself. "Oh, Putti" ([4]Mr. v.P.'s nickname)[5] they are sure to have taken the sausages and all our peas and beans and Peter, I wonder if he's still safely in bed." "They certainly won't have stolen Peter.[6] Listen, don't worry and let me go to sleep." But nothing came of that Mrs. v.P. was far too nervous to sleep another wink. A few nights after that the whole v.P. family was woken by ghostly sounds. Peter went up to the attic with a torch and scamper, scamper, what do you think was running away? A swarm of enormous rats!

138 [7]When we knew who the thieves were we let Mouschi sleep in the attic and the uninvited guests didn't come back again, at least . . . [9]not during the night. Peter went up to the loft a couple of evenings ago ([10]it was only half past 7 and still daylight) to fetch some old newspapers. He had to hold the trap door firmly to clamber down the steps, he put his hand down without looking. . . .and went tumbling down the ladder from the sudden shock and pain. Without knowing it he had put his hand on a large rat, and it had bitten him hard. By the time he reached us, as white as[15] a sheet and with his knees knocking, the blood had soaked through his pajamas. And no wonder; it's not very pleasant to stroke a large rat; and to get bitten into the bargain is really dreadful.

yours, Anne

Have I already told you about Mrs. Van Daan's other fears? I don't think so. If I am to keep you informed of all that happens in the "Secret Annexe," you must know about this too. One night Mrs. Van Daan thought she heard burglars in the attic, she heard loud footsteps and was so frightened that she woke her husband. Just at that moment the burglars disappeared and the only sounds that Mr. Van Daan could hear were the heartbeats of the frightened fatalist herself. "Oh, Putti (Mr. Van Daan's nickname), they are sure to have taken the sausages and all our peas and beans. And Peter, I wonder if he is still safely in bed?" "They certainly won't have stolen Peter. Listen, don't worry and let me go to sleep." But nothing came of that. Mrs. Van Daan was far too nervous to sleep another wink. A few nights after that the whole Van Daan family was woken by ghostly sounds. Peter went up to the attic with a torch—and scamper—scamper! What do you think it was running away? A swarm of enormous rats! When we knew who the thieves were, we let Mouschi sleep in the attic and the uninvited guests didn't come back again; at least not during the night.

Peter went up to the loft a couple of evenings ago to fetch some old newspapers. He had to hold the trap door firmly to get down the steps. He put his hand down without looking . . . and went tumbling down the ladder from the sudden shock and pain. Without knowing it he had put his hand on a large rat, and it had bitten him hard. By the time he reached us, as white as a sheet and with his knees knocking, the blood had soaked through his pajamas. And no wonder; it's not very pleasant to stroke a large rat; and to get bitten into the bargain is really dreadful.

Yours, Anne

341

a   . . . . . .

b   139 Tommy was got rid of later; we are all entertained by Boche. We have eaten so many kidney beans and haricot beans that I can't bear the sight of them any more. The mere thought of them makes me feel quite sick.

Bread is no longer served in the evenings now. Horrible air raids on Germany. Mr. v.P. is in a bad mood; the cause: cigarette shortage. Discussion over the question of whether we should, or should not, use our canned vegetables, ended in our favor.

I can't get into a single pair of shoes any more, except ski boots, which are not much use about the house. A pair of rush sandals costing 6.50 florins lasted me just one week, after which they were out of action. Perhaps Miep will scrounge something under the counter.

I must cut Daddy's hair; Pim[1] maintains that he will never have another barber after the war, as I do the job so well.[2] If only I didn't snip his ear so often!

yours, Anne

c   . . . . . .

342

Friday 12 Mar. '43[1].

Dear Kitty,

May I introduce someone to you: Mama[2] Frank, champion of youth!

Extra butter for the young; the problems of modern youth; Mummy defends youth in everything and after a certain amount of squabbling she always gets her way. A jar of pickled tongue has gone bad. Gala meal for Mouschi and Boche.

You haven't met Boche yet, although[3] he was here before we went into hiding. He is the warehouse and office cat and keeps down rats in the storerooms. His odd political name requires an explanation. For some time Messrs. Gies & Co. had two cats; one for the warehouse and one for the attic. Now it occasionally happened that the two cats met; and the result was always a terrific fight. The aggressor was always the warehouse cat; yet it was always the attic cat who managed to win—just like among nations, so the storehouse[5] cat was named the German or "Boche" and the attic cat the Englishman or "Tommy."

Tommy was got rid of later; we are all entertained by Boche.

We have eaten so many kidney beans and haricot beans that I can't bear the sight of them any more. The mere thought of them makes me feel quite sick.

Bread is no longer served in the evenings now.

Friday, 12 March, 1943

Dear Kitty,

May I introduce someone to you: Mama Frank, champion of youth! Extra butter for the young; the problems of modern youth; Mummy defends youth in everything and after a certain amount of squabbling she always gets her way. A bottle of preserved sole [A jar of pickled tongue] has gone bad: gala dinner for Mouschi and Boche. You haven't met Boche yet, although she [he] was here before we went into hiding. She [He] is the warehouse and office cat and keeps down the rats in the storerooms. Her [His] odd political name requires an explanation. For some time the firm had two cats; one for the warehouse and one for the attic. Now it occasionally happened that the two cats met; and the result was always a terrific fight. The aggressor was always the warehouse cat; yet it was always the attic cat who managed to win—just like among nations. So the storehouse cat was named the German or "Boche" and the attic cat the English or "Tommy." Tommy was got rid of later; we are all entertained by Boche when we go downstairs.

We have eaten so many kidney beans and haricot beans that I can't bear the sight of them any more. The mere thought of them makes me feel quite sick. Bread is no longer served in the evenings now.

a 97 ⎡ Daddy has just said that he doesn't feel in a good mood. His eyes look so sad again—poor soul. I can't drag myself away from a book called "The Knock at the Door" by Ina Boudier-Bakker. The story of the family is exceptionally well written. But what it says about war, writers, or the emancipation of women is not so well done, but then quite honestly I'm not awfully interested. ⎤

b 139 ⎡ Horrible air raids on Germany. Mr. v.P. is in a bad mood; the cause: cigarette shortage. Discussion over the question of whether we should, or should not, use our canned vegetables, ended in our favor.

I can't get into a single pair of shoes any more, except ski boots, which are not much use about the house. A pair of rush sandals costing 6.50 florins lasted me just one week, after which they were out of action. Perhaps Miep will scrounge something under the counter.

I must cut Daddy's hair; Pim maintains that he will never have another barber after the war, as I do the job so well. If only I didn't snip his ear so often!

yours, Anne

b 141

Thursday 18 Mar. '43.

Dearest Kitty,

Turkey is in the war. Great excitement. Waiting in suspense for the news.

c

Daddy has just said that he doesn't feel in a good mood. His eyes look so sad again—poor soul!

I can't drag myself away from a book called *The Knock at the Door* by Ina Boudier-Bakker. The story of the family is exceptionally well written. Apart from that, it is about war, writers, the emancipation of women; and quite honestly I'm not awfully interested.

Horrible air raids on Germany. Mr. Van Daan is in a bad mood; the cause—cigarette shortage. Discussions over the question of whether we should, or should not, use our canned vegetables ended in our favor.

I can't get into a single pair of shoes any more, except ski boots, which are not much use about the house. A pair of rush sandals costing 6.50 florins lasted me just one week, after which they were out of action. Perhaps Miep will scrounge something under the counter. I must cut Daddy's hair. Pim maintains that he will never have another barber after the war, as I do the job so well. If only I didn't snip his ear so often!

Yours, Anne

Thursday, 18 March, 1943

Dear Kitty,

Turkey is in the war. Great excitement. Waiting in suspense for the news.

Yours, Anne

344

a

. . . . . .

b

Friday 19 Mar. '43.

Dear Kitty,

An hour later joy was followed by disappointment. Turkey is not in the war yet. It was only a cabinet minister talking about them soon giving up their neutrality. A newspaper seller in the Dam was crying: Turkey on England's side!" The newspapers were torn out of his hands. This is how the joyful report reached us too; thousand-guilder notes have been declared no longer valid*; it is a trap for smugglers and suchlike, but even more for people who have got other kinds of "black" money and for people in hiding. If you wish to hand in a 1000-guilder note you must be able to declare, and prove, exactly how you got it.

142   They may still be used to pay taxes, but only until next week. 500-guilder notes have been declared invalid as well. Gies & Co. still hold blackmarket 1000-guilder notes, they have been paying their taxes in advance for quite some time, so that everything looked aboveboard. Pf. has received an old-fashioned foot-operated dentist's drill, I expect he'll soon give me a thorough check-over.

---

*On March 13, 1943, the German governor signed a decree declaring 500- and 1000-guilder notes invalid. This was part of a campaign to combat the black market. (*Decrees for the Occupied Netherlands*, VO 29/43, pp. 131/134.)

c

Friday, 19 March, 1943

Dear Kitty,

An hour later joy was followed by disappointment. Turkey is not in the war yet. It was only a cabinet minister talking about them soon giving up their neutrality. A newspaper [seller] in the Dam* was crying, "Turkey on England's side." The newspapers were torn out of his hands. This is how the joyful news reached us too; 500- and 1000-guilder notes have been declared no longer valid. It is a trap for black marketeers and suchlike, but even more for people who have got other kinds of "black" money, and for people in hiding. If you wish to hand in a 1000-guilder note you must be able to declare, and prove, exactly how you got it. They may still be used to pay taxes, but only until next week. Dussel has received an old-fashioned foot-operated dentist's drill, I expect he'll soon give me a thorough check-over.

---

*A square in front of the Royal Palace.

. . . . . .

For the rest, Pf. is terribly lax when it comes to obeying our rules, he not only writes letters to his wife, but also carries on a busy correspondence with various other people. As teacher of Dutch for the "Secret Annexe,"[1] Margot has to correct the letters he writes in Dutch. Daddy has strictly forbidden him to go on doing it and Margot's corrections have stopped, but I'm sure myself that it won't be long before he's writing again.

The "Führer aller Germanen" has been talking to wounded soldiers.

143   Listening-in to it was pitiful. Question and answer went something like this:

"My name is Heinrich Scheppel."

"Wounded where?"

"Near Stalingrad."

"What kind of wound?"

"Two feet frozen off and a broken joint in the left arm."

This is exactly what the frightful puppet show on the radio was like. The wounded seemed to be proud of their wounds—the more the better. One of them felt so moved at being able to shake hands with the Führer (that is, if he still had a hand!) that he could hardly get the words out of his mouth.

I dropped Pf.'s scented soap on the floor. I trod on it and a big bit has been lost. I've asked Daddy for compensation on his behalf, especially since Pf. only gets 1 bar of soap per month.

yours, Anne

The "Führer aller Germanen" has been talking to wounded soldiers. Listening-in to it was pitiful. Question and answer went something like this:

"My name is Heinrich Scheppel."

"Wounded where?"

"Near Stalingrad."

"What kind of wound?"

"Two feet frozen off and a broken joint in the left arm."

This is exactly what the frightful puppet show on the radio was like. The wounded seemed to be proud of their wounds—the more the better. One of them felt so moved at being able to shake hands with the Führer (that is, if he still had a hand!) that he could hardly get the words out of his mouth.

Yours, Anne

346

b   144

25¹ March
<u>1943.</u>
Thursday²

Dear Kitty,

Last night Mummy, Daddy, Margot and I were sitting very pleasantly together when suddenly Peter came in and whispered something in Daddy's ear, I heard something about "a barrel fallen over in the warehouse" and "someone fumbling about at the door. Margot had heard it too; but she tried to calm me down a bit because I was naturally as white as a sheet and very jittery.

The three of us waited in suspense; Daddy had meanwhile gone downstairs with Peter and a minute or 2 later Mrs. v. Pels came upstairs from the wireless, she told us that Pim had asked her to turn off the wireless and go softly upstairs. But you know what that's like, just when you want to be extra quiet, then each step of the old stairs creaks twice as loudly. 5 minutes later Pim and Peter appeared again, white to the roots of their hair, and told us their experiences:

They had hidden themselves under the stairs and waited, without success, but suddenly, yes, I must tell you, they heard two loud | bumps just as if two doors had banged here in the house; Pim was upstairs in one leap. Peter warned Pf. first, who finally landed upstairs with a lot of fuss and noise. Then we all went up in stockinged feet to the van Pels family on the next floor. Mr. v.P. had a bad cold and had already gone to bed, so we all drew up closely around his bed and whispered our suspicions to him.

| 145 (margin)

c

Thursday, 25 March, 1943

Dear Kitty,

Yesterday Mummy, Daddy, Margot, and I were sitting pleasantly together when suddenly Peter came in and whispered something in Daddy's ear. I heard something about "a barrel fallen over in the warehouse" and "someone fumbling about at the door." Margot had heard it too; but when Daddy and Peter went off immediately, she tried to calm me down a bit, because I was naturally as white as a sheet and very jittery.

The three of us waited in suspense. A minute or two later Mrs. Van Daan came upstairs; she'd been listening to the wireless in the private office. She told us that Pim had asked her to turn off the wireless and go softly upstairs. But you know what that's like, if you want to be extra quiet, then each step of the old stairs creaks twice as loudly. Five minutes later Pim and Peter appeared again, white to the roots of their hair, and told us their experiences.

They had hidden themselves under the stairs and waited, with no result at first. But suddenly, yes, I must tell you, they heard two loud bumps, just as if two doors were banged here in the house. Pim was upstairs in one leap. Peter warned Dussel first, who finally landed upstairs with a lot of fuss and noise. Then we all went up in stockinged feet to the Van Daans on the next floor. Mr. Van Daan had a bad cold and had already gone to bed, so we all drew up closely around his bed and whispered our suspicions to him.

a

. . . . . .

b

Each time Mr. v.P. coughed loudly Mrs. v.P. and I were so scared that we thought we were going to have a fit; that went on until one of us got the bright idea of giving him some codeine, which soothed the cough at once. Again we waited and waited, but we heard no more and finally we all came to the conclusion that the thieves had taken to their heels when they heard footsteps in the house, which was otherwise so silent.

Now it was unfortunate that the wireless downstairs was still turned to England, and that the chairs were neatly arranged around it; if the doors had been forced and the air-raid wardens had noticed | something and warned the police, then the results might have been very unpleasant. So Mr. v.P. got up and put on his pants, his coat and a hat and followed Daddy cautiously downstairs, Peter took up the rear armed with a large hammer in case of emergencies. The ladies upstairs (including Margot and me) waited in suspense until the gentlemen reappeared 5 minutes later and told us that all was quiet in the house. We arranged that we would not draw any water or pull the plug in the lavatory; but as the excitement had affected most of our tummies, you can imagine what the stench was like when we had each paid a visit in succession.

When something like that happens, heaps of other things seem to come at the same time, as now;[4] number 1 was that the clock at the Westertoren, which is always so

| 146

c

Each time Mr. Van Daan coughed loudly, Mrs. Van Daan and I were so scared that we thought we were going to have a fit. That went on until one of us got the bright idea of giving him some codeine, which soothed the cough at once. Again we waited and waited, but we heard no more and finally we all came to the conclusion that the thieves had taken to their heels when they heard footsteps in the house, which was otherwise so silent.

Now it was unfortunate that the wireless downstairs was still turned to England, and that the chairs were neatly arranged round it. If the door had been forced, and the air-raid wardens had noticed and warned the police, then the results might have been very unpleasant. So Mr. Van Daan got up and put on his coat and hat and followed Daddy cautiously downstairs, Peter took up the rear, armed with a large hammer in case of emergencies. The ladies upstairs (including Margot and me) waited in suspense, until the gentlemen reappeared five minutes later and told us that all was quiet in the house.

We arranged that we would not draw any water or pull the plug in the lavatory. But as the excitement had affected most of our tummies, you can imagine what the atmosphere was like when we had each paid a visit in succession.

When something like that happens, heaps of other things seem to come at the same time, as now. Number One was that the clock at the Westertoren, which I always find so reassuring, did not strike.

348

b

| 147 | reassuring, did not strike and that Mr. Voskuyl having left earlier than usual the previous evening we didn't know whether Bep had been able to get hold of the key, and had perhaps | forgotten to shut the door. However, that didn't matter so much right now, it was still evening and we were still in a state of uncertainty; although we certainly did feel a bit reassured by the fact that from quarter past 8, when the burglar had alarmed the house, until half past 10 we had not heard a sound. On further reflection it also seemed very unlikely to us that a thief would have forced open a door so early in the evening, while there were still people about in the street. Moreover, one of us had the idea that it was possible that the caretaker of the Keg firm, the warehouse next door, was still at work since, in the excitement and with our thin walls one can easily make a mistake, and what's more, one's imagination can play a big part at such critical moments.

So we all took to our beds; but none of us could get to sleep, Daddy as well as | 148 | Mummy and Mr. Pf. were awake, and | without much exaggeration I can really say that I hardly slept a wink. This morning the men went downstairs to see if the outside door was still shut, and everything was quite safe!

c

Number Two was that, Mr. Vossen having left earlier than usual the previous evening, we didn't know definitely whether Elli had been able to get hold of the key, and had perhaps forgotten to shut the door. It was still evening and we were still in a state of uncertainty, although we certainly did feel a bit reassured by the fact that from about eight o'clock, when the burglar had alarmed the house, until half past ten we had not heard a sound. On further reflection it also seemed very unlikely to us that a thief would have forced open a door so early in the evening, while there were still people about in the street. Moreover, one of us got the idea that it was possible that the caretaker of the warehouse next door was still at work since, in the excitement, and with the thin walls, one can easily make a mistake, and what's more, one's imagination can play a big part at such critical moments.

So we all went to bed, but none of us could get to sleep. Daddy as well as Mummy and Mr. Dussel were awake, and without much exaggeration I can say that I hardly slept a wink. This morning the men went downstairs to see whether the outside door was still shut, and everything turned out to be quite safe.

. . . . . .

The event, which had been far from nice, was naturally reported in every detail to the whole office, for it's easy to laugh about such things afterwards and Bep was the only one who took us seriously.*

yours, Anne

P.S. The w.c. was terribly blocked this morning and Daddy was forced to fish out all the strawberry recipes (our present toilet paper) and several kilos of muck with a long, wooden stick. The stick was later burned.

yours, Anne

149

Saturday 27 Mar. 1943.

Dear Kitty,

We have finished our Shorthand course; now we are beginning to practice speed, aren't we getting clever? I must tell you more about my time-killing subjects (I call them such, because we have got nothing else to do but make the days go by as quickly as possible, so that the end of our time here comes more quickly). I'm mad on Mythology and especially the Gods of Greece and Rome. They think here that it is just a passing craze, they've never heard of an adolescent kid of my age being interested in Mythology. Well then, I shall be the first!

Mr. v.P. has a cold or rather he has a little tickle in his throat. He makes a tremendous fuss about it. Gargling with camomile tea, painting his throat with tincture of myrrh, rubbing eucalyptus all over his chest, nose, teeth and tongue; and then getting into an evil mood on top of it all!

---

*Anne Frank has also described these events in her *Verhaaltjesboek (Tales)* under the title of "*Is er ingebroken* [Did Someone Break In]?".

We gave everyone a detailed description of the nerve-racking event. They all made fun of it, but it is easy to laugh at such things afterwards. Elli was the only one who took us seriously.

Yours, Anne

Saturday, 27 March, 1943

Dear Kitty,

We have finished our shorthand course; now we are beginning to practice speed. Aren't we getting clever? I must tell you more about my time-killing subjects (I call them such, because we have got nothing else to do but make the days go by as quickly as possible, so that the end of our time here comes more quickly); I'm mad on Mythology and especially the Gods of Greece and Rome. They think here that it is just a passing craze, they've never heard of an adolescent kid of my age being interested in Mythology. Well, then, I shall be the first!

Mr. Van Daan has a cold, or rather he has a little tickle in his throat. He makes a tremendous fuss about it. Gargling with camomile tea, painting his throat with tincture of myrrh, rubbing eucalyptus all over his chest, nose, teeth, and tongue; and then getting into an evil mood on top of it all.

350

b

| 150   Rauter, one of the German big shots, has made a speech "All Jews must be out of the German-occupied countries by July 1. Between April 1 and May 1 from March 1 to June the provinces[2] | the Province of Utrecht must be cleaned out (as if the Jews were cockroaches), between May 1 and June 1 The provinces of North and South Holland.* These wretched people are sent to filthy slaughterhouses like a herd of poor sick, neglected cattle. But I won't talk about it, I only get nightmares from such thoughts! Another good little piece of news is that the German department of the Laborers' Exchange has been set on fire by saboteurs. A few days after, the Registrar's Office went the same way. Men in German police uniform gagged the guards and[5] managed to destroy important papers.* *

yours, Anne

---

*On March 22, 1943, Hanns Albin Rauter, the head of the German SS and police in the Netherlands, told an SS gathering that all Jews would be removed from the Netherlands, province by province. "After May 1 we shall add Utrecht and finally North Holland and the city of Amsterdam." *(Het Proces Rauter,* The Hague, Nijhoff, 1952. State Institute of War Documentation, Source Publications, Trials, No. 5, p. 42.)

* *On February 10, 1943, the District Labor Exchange in Amsterdam was set on fire and on March 27 there was an attack on the office of the Amsterdam Public Registration Office. Both attacks were made to prevent the dispatch of workers to Germany and the deportation of Jews. (L. de Jong, *Het Koninkrijk der Nederlanden in de Tweede Wereldoorlog,* Vol. 6, pp. 714ff.)

c

Rauter, one of the German big shots, has made a speech. "All Jews must be out of the German-occupied countries before July 1. Between April 1 and May 1 the province of Utrecht must be cleaned out (as if the Jews were cockroaches). Between May 1 and June 1 the provinces of North and South Holland." These wretched people are sent to filthy slaughterhouses like a herd of sick, neglected cattle. But I won't talk about it, I only get nightmares from such thoughts.

One good little piece of news is that the German department of the Labor Exchange has been set on fire by saboteurs. A few days after, the Registrar's Office went the same way. Men in German police uniforms gagged the guards and managed to destroy important papers.

Yours, Anne

. . . . . .

Thursday 1 April² '43.

Dear Kitty,

I'm really not April-fooling³ (see the date) but the opposite; today I can easily quote the saying: Misfortunes never come singly." To begin with, Mr. Kleiman, the one who always cheers us up, has got a hemorrhage of the stomach and has got to stay in bed for at least three weeks. You ought to know that Mr. Kleiman suffers a great deal from hemorrhages of the stomach, and there seems to be no cure for it. Secondly, Bep has flu. Thirdly, Mr. Voskuyl is going to the Hospital next week. He has probably got an abdominal ulcer. And fourthly, the directors of the Pomosin works from Frankfurt⁷ came over to discuss the new Opekta deliveries; Daddy had discussed all the details of the conference with Kleiman, but now there isn't time to explain everything thoroughly to Mr. Kugler.

The gentlemen from Frankfurt duly arrived; even before they came Daddy was trem- | 152 bling with anxiety | as to how the talks would go. "If only I could be there, if only I was downstairs," he cried. "Why don't you go and lie with one ear pressed against the floor, then you'll be able to hear everything." Daddy's face cleared, and at half past 10 yesterday morning Margot (two ears are better than one!) and Pim took up their positions on the floor. The talks were not finished in the morning, but by the afternoon Daddy was not in a fit state to continue the listening campaign, he was half paralyzed from remaining in

Thursday, 1 April, 1943

Dear Kitty,

I'm really not April-fooling (see the date), but the opposite; today I can easily quote the saying: "Misfortunes never come singly." To begin with, Mr. Koophuis, the one who always cheers us up, has had hemorrhage of the stomach and has got to stay in bed for at least three weeks. Secondly, Elli has flu. Thirdly, Mr. Vossen is going to the hospital next week. He has probably got an abdominal ulcer. And fourthly, some important business conferences, the main points of which Daddy had discussed in detail with Mr. Koophuis, were due to be held, but now there isn't time to explain everything to Mr. Kraler.

The gentlemen who had been expected duly arrived; even before they came Daddy was trembling with anxiety as to how the talks would go. "If only I could be there, if only I was downstairs," he cried. "Why don't you go and lie with one ear pressed against the floor, then you'll be able to hear everything." Daddy's face cleared, and at half past ten yesterday morning Margot and Pim (two ears are better than one!) took up their positions on the floor. The talks were not finished in the morning, but by the afternoon Daddy was not in a fit state to continue the listening campaign.

352

. . . . . .

in so unusual and uncomfortable a position. I took his place at half past 2, as soon as we heard voices in the passage. Margot kept me company; the talk at times was so long-winded and boring that quite suddenly I fell asleep on the cold hard linoleum floor. Margot did not dare to touch me, for fear they might hear us, and talking was out of the question. I slept for a good half hour and woke with a shock, having forgotten every word of the important discussions. Luckily Margot had paid more attention.

152a

Friday 2 April 1943.

Dear Kitty,

Oh dear, I've got another terrible black mark against my name. I was lying in bed yesterday evening waiting for Daddy to come and say my prayers with me, and wish me good night, when Mummy came into my room, sat on my bed, and asked very nicely, "Anne, Daddy can't come yet. Shall I say your prayers with you tonight." "No Mummy," I answered. Mummy got up, paused⁵ by my bed for a moment, and walked slowly towards the door. Suddenly she turned around, and with a distorted look on her face said, "I don't want to be cross with you; Love cannot be forced!" There were tears in her eyes as she left the room. I lay still in bed, feeling at once that I had been horrible to push her away so rudely.

| 152b But I knew too, that I couldn't have answered | differently. It simply wouldn't work. I

He was half paralyzed from remaining in so unusual and uncomfortable a position. I took his place at half past two, as soon as we heard voices in the passage. Margot kept me company. The talk at times was so long-winded and boring that quite suddenly I fell asleep on the cold hard linoleum floor. Margot did not dare to touch me for fear they might hear us, and talking was out of the question. I slept for a good half hour and then woke with a shock, having forgotten every word of the important discussions. Luckily Margot had paid more attention.

Yours, Anne

Friday, 2 April, 1943

Dear Kitty,

Oh dear: I've got another terrible black mark against my name. I was lying in bed yesterday evening waiting for Daddy to come and say my prayers with me, and wish me good night, when Mummy came into my room, sat on my bed, and asked very nicely, "Anne, Daddy can't come yet, shall I say your prayers with you tonight?" "No, Mummy," I answered.

Mummy got up, paused by my bed for a moment, and walked slowly towards the door. Suddenly she turned around, and with a distorted look on her face said, "I don't want to be cross, love cannot be forced." There were tears in her eyes as she left the room.

I lay still in bed, feeling at once that I had been horrible to push her away so rudely. But I knew too that I couldn't have answered differently. It simply wouldn't work. I felt

b

felt sorry for Mummy, very, very sorry, because I had seen for the first time in my life that she minds my coldness. I saw the look of sorrow on her face, when she spoke of love not being forced. It is hard to speak the truth, and yet it is the truth: she herself has pushed me away, her tactless remarks and her crude jokes, which I don't find at all funny, have now made me insensitive to any love from her side. Just as I shrink at her hard[2] words, so did her heart when she realized that the love between us was[3] gone. She cried half[4] the night and didn't sleep properly at all. Daddy doesn't look at me and if he does for a second

| 152c   then I read in his | eyes the words: "How can you be so unkind, how can you bring yourself to cause your mother so much sorrow!"

Everyone expects me to apologize; but this is something I can't apologize for, because I spoke the truth, and Mummy will have to know it sooner or later anyway. I am and seem indifferent both to Mummy's tears,[6] and Daddy's looks,[7] because for the first time they are both aware of something which I have always felt. I can only feel sorry for Mummy, who has now had to discover that I have adopted her own attitude. For myself, I remain silent and aloof; I shall not shrink from the truth any longer, since the longer it is put off, the more difficult it will be for them when they do hear it!

yours, Anne

c

sorry for Mummy; very, very sorry, because I had seen for the first time in my life that she minds my coldness. I saw the look of sorrow on her face when she spoke of love not being forced. It is hard to speak the truth, and yet it is the truth: she herself has pushed me away, her tactless remarks and her crude jokes, which I don't find at all funny, have now made me insensitive to any love from her side. Just as I shrink at her hard words, so did her heart when she realized that the love between us was gone. She cried half the night and hardly slept at all. Daddy doesn't look at me and if he does for a second, then I read in his eyes the words: "How can you be so unkind, how can you bring yourself to cause your mother such sorrow?"

They expect me to apologize; but this is something I can't apologize for because I spoke the truth and Mummy will have to know it sooner or later anyway. I seem, and indeed am, indifferent both to Mummy's tears and Daddy's looks, because for the first time they are both aware of something which I have always felt. I can only feel sorry for Mummy, who has now had to discover that I have adopted her own attitude. For myself, I remain silent and aloof; and I shall not shrink from the truth any longer, because the longer it is put off, the more difficult it will be for them when they do hear it.

Yours, Anne

. . . . . .

Tuesday 27 April '43.[1]

Dear Kitty,

Such quarrels that the whole house thunders! Mummy and I, v.P. and Daddy, Mummy and Mrs. v.P., everyone is angry with everyone else. Nice atmosphere isn't it? Anne's usual list of sins has been brought out again and fully ventilated. Last Saturday the foreign gentlemen came for another visit. They remained till six o'clock, all of us sat upstairs and didn't dare move. If no one is working in the building or in the neighborhood one can hear every single step in the front office. I have the sitting fever again, sitting still as a mouse for so long certainly doesn't agree with me.

Mr. Voskuyl is already in the binnen-Gasthuis hospital. Mr.[5] Kleiman is at the office again,[6][7] the hemorrhage having stopped sooner than usual.[8] He told us[9][10] that the Registrar's Office received additional damage from the Fire Service who, instead of quenching the flames, soaked the whole place with water. I'm glad!

154   The Carlton-hotel is smashed to bits. Two British planes loaded with incendiary bombs fell right on top of the "Offizierenheim." The whole Vijzelstraat-Singel corner is burnt down.* The air raids on German towns are growing in strength every day. We don't have a single quiet night. I've got dark rings under my eyes from lack of sleep.

---

*During the night of April 26, 1943, German anti-aircraft artillery responded to an Allied attack. One of the planes came down in flames at 2:30 A.M. in Reguliersdwarsstraat, behind the Carlton Hotel. This hotel, which from the beginning of the Occupation had been requisitioned by the Germans, was destroyed by fire. (*Kroniek van Amsterdam over de jaren 1940–1945*, edited by J. F. M. den Boer and Mej. S. Duparc [Amsterdam: De Bussy, 1948], p. 98.)

Tuesday, 27 April, 1943

Dear Kitty,

Such quarrels that the whole house thunders! Mummy and I, the Van Daans and Daddy, Mummy and Mrs. Van Daan, everyone is angry with everyone else. Nice atmosphere, isn't it? Anne's usual list of failings has been brought out again and fully ventilated.

Mr. Vossen is already in the Binnengasthuis hospital. Mr. Koophuis is up again, the hemorrhage having stopped sooner than usual. He told us that the Registrar's Office received additional damage from the Fire Service who, instead of just quenching the flames, soaked the whole place with water. I'm glad!

The Carlton Hotel is smashed to bits. Two British planes loaded with incendiary bombs fell right on top of the "Offiziersheim."* The whole Vijzelstraat-Singel corner is burned down. The air raids on German towns are growing in strength every day. We don't have a single quiet night. I've got dark rings under my eyes from lack of sleep.

---

*German Officers' Club.

b   Our food is miserably poor. Dry bread and coffee substitute for breakfast. Dinner spinach or lettuce for 14 days on end. Potatoes twenty centimeters long and tasting sweet and rotten. Whoever wants to slim should stay in the "Secret Annexe"! They complain bitterly upstairs, but we don't regard it as such a tragedy.

All the men who fought in 1940 or were mobilized have been called up to work for "der Führer" as prisoners of war. Suppose they're doing that as a precaution against invasion.

yours, Anne

c   Our food is miserable. Dry bread and coffee substitute for breakfast. Dinner: spinach or lettuce for a fortnight on end. Potatoes twenty centimeters long and tasting sweet and rotten. Whoever wants to follow a slimming course should stay in the "Secret Annexe"! They complain bitterly upstairs, but we don't regard it as such a tragedy. All the men who fought in 1940 or were mobilized have been called up to work for "der Führer" as prisoners of war. Suppose they're doing that as a precaution against invasion.

Yours, Anne

2 May 1943.
Sunday

If I just think of how we live here, I usually come to the conclusion that it is a paradise compared with how other Jews who are not in hiding must be living. Even so, later on, when everything is normal again, I shall be amazed to think that we, who were so spick and span at home, should have sunk, as one can indeed call it, to such a low level. By this I mean that our manners have declined. For instance, ever since we have been here we have had one oilcloth on our table which, owing to so much use, is not one of the cleanest. Admittedly I often try to clean it with a dirty dishcloth, which is more hole than cloth and which was new before we went into hiding long ago, the table doesn't do us much credit either, in spite of hard scrubbing. The van Pelses have been sleeping on the same flannelette sheet the whole winter, one can't wash it here because the soap powder we get on the ration isn't sufficient, and besides it's not good enough. Daddy goes about in frayed trousers and his tie is beginning to show signs of wear too. Mummy's corsets have split today and are too old to be repaired, while Margot goes about in a brassiere two sizes too small for her.

Mummy and Margot have managed the whole winter with 3 vests between them, and mine are so small that they don't even come to my tummy. Certainly, these are all things which can be overcome. But still, I sometimes wonder with a shock, how are we, now going about in worn-out things, from my pants down to Daddy's shaving brush, ever going to get back to our prewar standards?

b . . . . . .

c

Saturday, 1 May, 1943

Dear Kitty,

If I just think of how we live here, I usually come to the conclusion that it is a paradise compared with how other Jews who are not in hiding must be living. Even so, later on, when everything is normal again, I shall be amazed to think that we, who were so spick and span at home, should have sunk to such a low level. By this I mean that our manners have declined. For instance, ever since we have been here, we have had one oilcloth on our table which, owing to so much use, is not one of the cleanest. Admittedly I often try to clean it with a dirty dishcloth, which is more hole than cloth. The table doesn't do us much credit either, in spite of hard scrubbing. The Van Daans have been sleeping on the same flannelette sheet the whole winter; one can't wash it here because the soap powder we get on the ration isn't sufficient, and besides it's not good enough. Daddy goes about in frayed trousers and his tie is beginning to show signs of wear too. Mummy's corsets have split today and are too old to be repaired, while Margot goes about in a brassiere two sizes too small for her.

Mummy and Margot have managed the whole winter with three vests between them, and mine are so small that they don't even reach my tummy.

Certainly, these are all things which can be overcome. Still, I sometimes realize [wonder] with a shock: "How are we, now going about in worn-out things, from my pants down to Daddy's shaving brush, ever going to get back to our prewar standards?"

Sat. 1 May 1943.

Dear Kitty,

It was Pf.[1]'s birthday. To start with he pretended it didn't matter to him, but when Miep turned up with a big shopping bag brimming over with little packages, he was as excited as a small child. His [2]Lotje had sent him eggs, butter, biscuits, lemonade, bread, cognac, gingerbread, flowers, oranges, chocolate, books and writing paper. He arranged a table full of birthday gifts which he'd have loved to leave on display for 3[7] days, the silly old fool!

Don't imagine that he's going hungry either, we discovered bread, cheese, jam and eggs in his cupboard. It's an absolute disgrace that someone we took in so hospitably, actually to save his life, should be stuffing himself now behind our backs and keeping it all for himself. After all, we've been sharing everything with him! What's even worse is that he's just as mean towards Kleiman, Voskuyl and Bep, he gives them nothing at all. In Pf.'s view the oranges | that Kleiman[13] needs so badly for his sick stomach will do his own stomach even more good.

| 156

They were banging away so much last night that 4 times I gathered all my belongings together.[16] Today I have packed a suitcase with the most necessary things for an escape. But Mummy quite rightly says: "Where will you escape to?" The whole[18] of Holland is being punished for the many strikes by the workers. Therefore a State of Siege has been declared and everyone gets one butter coupon less.* What naughty little children.

Tonight I washed Mummy's hair, not such an easy thing to do nowadays. We have to make do with sticky green soap[21] because the shampoo is finished, and secondly Mum can't comb her hair out properly because the family comb has got a mere 10 teeth.

yours, Anne

*At the end of April and the beginning of May 1943 the so-called April-May Strikes were called in protest at the removal of Dutch soldiers as prisoners of war. Apart from other "punishments," for instance the confiscation of all radio sets owned by Dutchmen, the butter ration was stopped for four weeks. (L. de Jong, *Het Koninkrijk der Nederlanden in de Tweede Wereldoorlog*, Vol, 6, p. 844.)

They were banging away so much last night that four times I gathered all my belongings together. Today I have packed a suitcase with the most necessary things for an escape. But Mummy quite rightly says: "Where will you escape to?" The whole of Holland is being punished for the strikes which have been going on in many parts of the country. Therefore a state of siege has been declared and everyone gets one butter coupon less. What naughty little children!

Yours, Anne

b   157

Tuesday 18¹ May '43.

Dear Kit,

I witnessed a terrific air battle between German and British planes. Unfortunately a couple of the Allies³ had to jump from their burning machine.⁴ Our milkman, who lives in Halfweg, saw four Canadians sitting by the roadside, one of them spoke fluent Dutch. He asked the milkman to give him a light for his cigarette and told him that the crew had consisted of 6 men. The pilot was burned to death and their 5th man had hidden himself somewhere. The German police came and fetched the four perfectly fit men. I wonder how they managed to have such presence of mind after that terrifying ⁶parachute trip!

| 158   Although it is obviously warm we have to light our fires every other day, in order to burn vegetable peelings and refuse. We can't put anything in the | garbage pails, because we must always think of the warehouseman. How easily one could be betrayed by being a little⁷ careless!

⁸All students who wish either to get their degrees this year or continue their studies are compelled to sign that they are in sympathy with everything the Germans do and approve of the New Order. 80% have refused to go against their consciences. Naturally they had to bear the consequences. All the students who do not sign have to go to a labor camp in Germany. What will be left of the youth of the country if they have all got to do hard labor in Germany?

c

Tuesday, 18 May, 1943

Dear Kitty,

I witnessed a terrific air battle between German and British planes. Unfortunately a couple of the Allies had to jump from burning machines. Our milkman, who lives in Halfweg, saw four Canadians sitting by the roadside, one of them spoke fluent Dutch. He asked the milkman to give him a light for his cigarette, and told him that the crew had consisted of six men. The pilot was burned to death, and their fifth man had hidden himself somewhere. The German police came and fetched the four perfectly fit men. I wonder how they managed to have such clear brains after that terrifying parachute trip.

Although it is fairly warm, we have to light our fires every other day, in order to burn vegetable peelings and refuse. We can't put anything in the garbage pails, because we must always think of the warehouse boy |man|. How easily one could be betrayed by being a little careless!

All students who wish either to get their degrees this year, or continue their studies, are compelled to sign that they are in sympathy with the Germans and approve of the New Order. Eighty per cent have refused to go against their consciences. Naturally they had to bear the consequences. All the students who do not sign have to go to a labor camp in Germany. What will be left of the youth of the country if they have all got to do hard labor in Germany?

359

b

| 159

Mummy shut the window last night because of all the banging; I was in Pim's bed. Suddenly Mrs. v.P. jumped out of bed above us just as if Muschi had bitten her. A loud clap followed immediately. It sounded just as if an incendiary bomb had fallen down beside my bed. I shrieked out, | light, light. Pim turned on the lamp. I expected nothing less than to see the room ablaze within a few minutes. Nothing happened. We all hurried upstairs to see what was going on. Mr. and Mrs. v.P. had seen a red glow through the open window, he thought that there was a fire in the neighborhood and she thought that our house had caught fire.⁴ When the clap came little Mrs. v.P. was already on her feet with her knees knocking. Pf. stayed upstairs smoking a cigarette, the rest of us went back to bed. Before a quarter of an hour had passed the shooting started up again. Mrs. v.P. sat bolt upright at once and then went downstairs to Pf.'s room, seeking there the rest which she could not find with her spouse. Pf. received her with the words, "Come into my bed, my child!"

⁶Which sent us off into an uncontrollable fit of laughter. The gunfire troubled us no longer, our fear was banished, as it were.

yours, Anne

c

Mummy shut the window last night because of all the banging; I was in Pim's bed. Suddenly Mrs. Van Daan jumped out of bed above us, just as if Mouschi had bitten her. A loud clap followed immediately. It sounded just as if an incendiary bomb had fallen beside my bed. I shrieked out, "Light, light!" Pim turned on the lamp. I expected nothing less than to see the room ablaze within a few minutes. Nothing happened. We all hurried upstairs to see what was going on. Mr. and Mrs. Van Daan had seen a red glow through the open window. He thought that there was a fire in the neighborhood and she thought that our house had caught fire. When the clap came Mrs. Van Daan was already on her feet with her knees knocking. But nothing more happened and we all crept back into our beds.

Before a quarter of an hour had passed the shooting started up again. Mrs. Van Daan sat bolt upright at once and then went downstairs to Mr. Dussel's room, seeking there the rest which she could not find with her spouse. Dussel received her with the words, "Come into my bed, my child!" which sent us off into uncontrollable laughter. The gunfire troubled us no longer, our fear was banished!

Yours, Anne

360

Sunday 13 June 1943![1]

Dear Kitty,

My birthday poem from Daddy is too good to keep from you[2]

As Pim usually writes verses in German, Margot volunteered to translate it. Judge for yourself whether Margot didn't do it brilliantly. After a usual summary of the events of the year, this is how it ran:

Though youngest here, you are no longer small,
But life is very hard, since one and all
Aspire to be your teacher, thus and thus:
"We have experience, take a tip from us."
"We know because we did it long ago."
"Elders are always better, you must know."
At least, that's been the rule since life began!
Our personal faults are much too small to scan;
This makes it easier to criticize
The faults of others which seem double size.
Please bear with us, your parents, for we try
To judge you fairly and with sympathy.
Corrections sometimes take against your will,

c

Sunday, 13 June, 1943

Dear Kitty,

My birthday poem from Daddy is too good to keep from you As Pim usually writes verses in German, Margot volunteered to translate it. Judge for yourself whether Margot didn't do it brilliantly After the usual summary of the events of the year, this is how it ran:

Though youngest here, you are no longer small,
But life is very hard, since one and all
Aspire to be your teacher, thus and thus:
"We have experience, take a tip from us."
"We know because we did it long ago."
"Elders are always better, you must know."
At least that's been the rule since life began!
Our personal faults are much too small to scan;
This makes it easier to criticize
The faults of others, which seem double size.
Please bear with us, your parents, for we try
To judge you fairly and with sympathy.
Correction sometimes take against your will,

Though it's like swallowing a bitter pill;
Which <u>must</u> be done if we're to keep the peace,
While time goes by till all this suffering cease.
You read and study nearly all the day,
Who might have lived in such a different way.
You're never bored and bring us all fresh air.
Your only moan is this: "What can I wear?
I have no knickers, all my clothes are small,
My vest might be a loincloth, that is all![3]
[4]

To put on shoes would mean to cut off toes,
Oh dear, I'm worried by so many woes!"
Yes, if you grow four inches more
You can't wear what you wore before.

———

There was also the bit about food but Margot could not translate it into rhyme, so I shall leave it out. Don't you think my birthday poem is good?[7] I have been thoroughly spoiled in other ways and received a lot of lovely things. Among other things a fat book on my pet subject—the mythology of Greece and Rome. I can't complain of a shortage of sweets either—everyone has broken into their last reserves. As the Benjamin of the Family in Hiding, I am really more honored than I deserve.[8] yours, Anne.

c

Though it's like swallowing a bitter pill,
Which must be done if we're to keep the peace,
While time goes by till all this suffering

                      cease.
You read and study nearly all the day,
Who might have lived in such a different way.
You're never bored and bring us all fresh air.
Your only moan is this: "What can I wear?
I have no knickers, all my clothes are small,
My vest might be a loincloth, that is all!
To put on shoes would mean to cut off toes,
Oh dear, I'm worried by so many woes!"

There was also a bit about food that Margot could not translate into rhyme, so I shall leave it out. Don't you think my birthday poem is good? I have been thoroughly spoiled in other ways and received a lot of lovely things. Among other things a fat book on my pet subject—the mythology of Greece and Rome. I can't complain of a shortage of sweets either—everyone has broken into their last reserves. As the Benjamin of the family in hiding, I am really more honored than I deserve.

Yours, Anne

b   162   Tuesday 15 June <u>1943</u>[1]

Dear Kitty,

Lots of things have happened, but I often think that all my uninteresting chatter bores you very much[2] and that you are glad not to receive too many letters.[4]

So I shall give you the news in brief.

Mr. Voskuyl has not[6] had a stomach operation: When he was on the operating table and they had opened him up, the doctors saw that he had a deadly cancer, which was far too advanced to operate. So they just stitched him up again, kept him in bed for 3 weeks and gave him good food, and then finally sent him home again. But they also made an unforgivable blunder, that is, they told the poor man exactly what was the matter with him. He is no longer able to work, sits at home surrounded by his 8 children and broods
| 163   over his | approaching death. I do pity him terribly and think it is rotten that we can't go out, otherwise I should certainly visit him frequently to cheer him up. It is a disaster for us that good old Voskuyl won't be able to keep us in touch with all that goes on, and all he hears in the warehouse. He was our best helper and security adviser; we miss him very much indeed.

c   Tuesday, 15 June, 1943

Dear Kitty,

Lots of things have happened, but I often think that all my uninteresting chatter bores you very much and that you are glad not to receive too many letters. So I shall give you the news in brief.

Mr. Vossen has not been operated on for his duodenal ulcer. When he was on the operating table and they had opened him up, the doctors saw that he had cancer, which was far too advanced to operate. So they stitched him up again, kept him in bed for three weeks and gave him good food, and finally sent him home again. I do pity him terribly and think it is rotten that we can't go out, otherwise I should certainly visit him frequently to cheer him up. It is a disaster for us that good old Vossen won't be able to keep us in touch with all that goes on, and all he hears in the warehouse. He was our best helper and security adviser; we miss him very much indeed.

363

a

......

b

It will be our turn to give up our radio next month.*¹ Kleiman has a clandestine little baby set at home, which he will let us have to take the place of our big Philips. It certainly is a shame to have to give up our lovely set, but in a house where people are hiding one daren't under any circumstances take wanton risks and so draw the attention of the authorities. We shall of course have the little radio upstairs. On top of hidden Jews, clandestine money and clandestine buyers, we can add a clandestine radio.

164   Everyone is trying to get hold of an old set, and to hand that in instead of their "source of courage." It is really true that as the news from outside gets worse, so the radio with its miraculous voice helps us to keep up our morale and to say again: "Chins up, stick it out, better times will come!"

yours, Anne

*The compulsory surrender of radio sets in Amsterdam began on May 31, 1943. *(Kroniek van Amsterdam, p. 99.)*

c

It will be our turn to hand in our radio next month. Koophuis has a clandestine baby set at home that he will let us have to take the place of our big Phillips [Philips]. It certainly is a shame to have to hand in our lovely set, but in a house where people are hiding, one daren't, under any circumstances, take wanton risks and so draw the attention of the authorities. We shall have the little radio upstairs. On top of hidden Jews, clandestine money and clandestine buying, we can add a clandestine radio. Everyone is trying to get hold of an old set and to hand that in instead of their "source of courage." It is really true that as the news from outside gets worse, so the radio with its miraculous voice helps us to keep up our morale and to say again, "Chins up, stick it out, better times will come!"

Yours, Anne

a . . . . . .

b 165

Dearest Kitty,

To return to the "upbringing" theme for a time, I must tell you that I really am trying to be helpful, friendly and good, and to do everything I can so that the rain of rebukes dies down to a light summer drizzle. It is mighty difficult to be on such model behavior with people you can't bear, especially when you don't mean a word of it. But I do really see that I get on better by shamming a bit, instead of keeping[4] my old habit of telling everyone exactly what I think (although no one ever asked my opinion or attached the slightest importance to it) and[5] Naturally I often lose my cue and simply can't swallow my rage at some injustice, so that for 4 long weeks, we hear nothing but an everlasting chatter about the cheekiest and most shameless girl on earth. Don't you think that sometimes I've

166 cause for complaint? It's a good | thing I'm not a grouser, because then I might get sour and bad-tempered. Mostly I take a humorous view of these sermons, but I can do that better when they're directed at someone else than when I am the victim myself.

I have decided (it took a great deal of thought) to let my shorthand go a bit, firstly to give me more time for my other subjects and secondly because of my eyes. I'm so miserable and wretched as I've become very shortsighted and ought to have had glasses for a long time already (ouch, what an owl I shall look) but you know of course, in hiding one cannot.

c

Sunday, 11 July, 1943

Dear Kitty,

To return to the "upbringing" theme for the umpteenth time, I must tell you that I really am trying to be helpful, friendly, and good, and to do everything I can so that the rain of rebukes dies down to a light summer drizzle. It is mighty difficult to be on such model behavior with people you can't bear, especially when you don't mean a word of it. But I do really see that I get on better by shamming a bit, instead of my old habit of telling everyone exactly what I think (although no one ever asked my opinion or attached the slightest importance to it).

I often lose my cue and simply can't swallow my rage at some injustice, so that for four long weeks we hear nothing but an everlasting chatter about the cheekiest and most shameless girl on earth. Don't you think that sometimes I've cause for complaint? It's a good thing I'm not a grouser, because then I might get sour and bad-tempered.

I have decided to let my shorthand go a bit, firstly to give me more time for my other subjects and secondly because of my eyes. I'm so miserable and wretched as I've become very shortsighted and ought to have had glasses for a long time already (phew, what an owl I shall look!) but you know, of course, in hiding one cannot. Yesterday everyone

365

. . . . . .

| 167

Yesterday everyone talked of nothing but Anne's eyes, because Mummy had suggested sending me to the oculist with Mrs. Kleiman. I shook in my shoes somewhat at this announcement, for it is[1] no small thing to do. Go out of doors, imagine it. In the street! It doesn't bear thinking about! | I was petrified at first, then glad. But it doesn't go as easily as that, as all the people who would have to approve such a step could not reach an agreement quickly. All the difficulties and risks had first to be carefully weighed, although Miep would have gone with me straight away. In the meantime I got out my gray coat from the cupboard, but it was so small that it looked as if it belonged to my younger sister. The hem has been let down and it can't be buttoned up any longer.

I am really curious to know what will come of it all, but I don't think the plan will come off because the British have landed in Sicily now and Daddy is once again expecting a "quick finish."

Bep gives Margot and me a lot of office work; it makes us both feel quite important and is a great help to her. Anyone can file away correspondence and write in the sales book, but we take special pains.

168

Miep is just like a pack mule, she fetches and carries so much. Almost every day she manages[9] to get hold of some vegetables[10] for us and brings everything in shopping bags on her bicycle. She also brings us 5 library books every Saturday. We always long[12] for Saturdays when our books come, [13]just like little children receiving a present. Ordinary people simply don't know what books mean to us shut up here. Reading, learning and the radio are our only amusements.

<u>yours, Anne</u>

talked of nothing but Anne's eyes, because Mummy had suggested sending me to the oculist with Mrs. Koophuis. I shook in my shoes somewhat at this announcement, for it is no small thing to do. Go out of doors, imagine it, in the street—doesn't bear thinking about! I was petrified at first, then glad. But it doesn't go as easily as that, because all the people who would have to approve such a step could not reach an agreement quickly. All the difficulties and risks had first to be carefully weighed, although Miep would have gone with me straight away.

In the meantime I got out my gray coat from the cupboard, but it was so small that it looked as if it belonged to my younger sister.

I am really curious to know what will come of it all, but I don't think the plan will come off because the British have landed in Sicily now and Daddy is once again hoping for a "quick finish."

Elli gives Margot and me a lot of office work; it makes us both feel quite important and is a great help to her. Anyone can file away correspondence and write in the sales book, but we take special pains.

Miep is just like a pack mule, she fetches and carries so much. Almost every day she manages to get hold of some vegetables for us and brings everything in shopping bags on her bicycle. [She also brings us five library books every Saturday.] We always long for Saturdays when our books come. Just like little children receiving a present.

Ordinary people simply don't know what books mean to us, shut up here. Reading, learning, and the radio are our amusements.

Yours, Anne

366

The best little Table[1]

Yesterday afternoon, with Daddy's permission, I asked Pf. whether he would please be so good (being really very polite) as to let me use the little table in our room 2 × a week in the afternoons from 4 o'clock till half past 5. I sit there every day from half past 2 until 4, while Pf. sleeps, but otherwise the room + table are out of bounds. Inside in our common room, there is much too much going on, it is impossible to work there and besides, Daddy likes to sit at the writing table and to work too sometimes.

So it was quite a reasonable request, and the question was put very politely. Now honestly, what do you think the very learned Pf. replied: "No." Just plain "no!"

I was indignant and refused to be put off like that, so I asked him the reason for his "No." But I was sent away with a flea in my ear. This was the barrage which followed:

"I have to work too, and if I can't work in the afternoons, then there is no time left for me at all, I must finish my task, otherwise I've started it all for nothing, anyway, you don't work seriously at anything, your mythology, now just what kind of work is that, knitting and reading are not work either, I am at the table and shall stay there!"

My reply was:

"Mr. Pf., I do work seriously and there is nowhere else for me to work in the afternoons, and I beg of you to kindly reconsider my request!" With these words the

Tuesday, 13 July, 1943

Dear Kitty,

Yesterday afternoon, with Daddy's permission, I asked Dussel whether he would please be so good (being really very polite) as to allow me to use the little table in our room twice a week in the afternoons, from four o'clock till half past five, I sit there every day from half past two till four, while Dussel sleeps, but otherwise the room plus table are out of bounds. Inside, in our common room, there is much too much going on; it is impossible to work there, and besides, Daddy likes to sit at the writing table and work too sometimes.

So it was quite a reasonable request, and the question was put very politely. Now honestly what do you think the very learned Dussel replied: "No." Just plain "No!" I was indignant and refused to be put off like that, so I asked him the reason for his "No." But I was sent away with a flea in my ear. This was the barrage which followed:

"I have to work too, and if I can't work in the afternoons, then there is no time left for me at all. I must finish my task, otherwise I've started it all for nothing. Anyway, you don't work seriously at anything. Your mythology, now just what kind of work is that; knitting and reading are not work either. I am at the table and shall stay there." My reply was:

"Mr. Dussel, I do work seriously and there is nowhere else for me to work in the afternoons. I beg of you to kindly reconsider my request!"

T

offended Anne turned her back on the very learned doctor, ignoring him completely.

I was seething with rage, and thought Pf. frightfully rude (which he certainly was) and myself very friendly.

In the evening when I could get hold of Pim I told him how it had gone off and discussed what I should do next because I was not going to give in, and preferred to clear the matter up myself. Pim told me how I ought to tackle the problem, but warned me that it would be better to leave it till the next day, as I was so het up. I let this advice go to the winds, and waited for Pf. after the dishes were done that night. Pim sat in the room next to us, which had a calming influence on me. I began:

"Mr. Pf. I don't suppose you see any point in discussing the matter any more, but I must ask you[2] to do so."

Pf. then remarked with his sweetest smile:

"I am always, and at all times, prepared to discuss this matter, but it has already been settled."

I went on talking, though continually interrupted by Pf.:

"When you first came here we arranged that this room should be for both of us; if we were to divide it correctly, you would have the morning and I all the afternoon! But I don't even ask that much; and I think that my 2 afternoons are really perfectly reasonable."

C

With these words the offended Anne turned her back on the very learned doctor, ignoring him completely. I was seething with rage, and thought Dussel frightfully rude (which he certainly was) and myself very friendly. In the evening when I could get hold of Pim, I told him how it had gone off and discussed what I should do next, because I was not going to give in, and preferred to clear it up myself. Pim told me how I ought to tackle the problem, but warned me that it would be better to leave it till the next day, as I was so het up. I let this advice go to the winds, and waited for Dussel after the dishes were done. Pim sat in the room next to us, which had a calming influence on me. I began: "Mr. Dussel, I don't suppose you see any point in discussing the matter any more, but I must ask you to do so." Dussel then remarked with his sweetest smile: "I am always, and at all times, prepared to discuss this matter, but it has already been settled."

I went on talking, though continually interrupted by Dussel. "When you first came here we arranged that this room should be for both of us; if we were to divide it fairly, you would have the morning and I all the afternoon! But I don't even ask that much, and I think that my two afternoons are really perfectly reasonable." At this Dussel jumped up

At this Pf. jumped up as if someone had stuck a needle into him:

"You can't talk about your rights here at all and where am I to go, then? I shall ask Mr. v.P. whether he will build a little compartment in the attic, then I can go and sit there. I simply can't work anywhere. With you one always gets trouble. If your sister Margot, who after all has more reason to ask such a thing, would have come to me with the same questions I | should not think of refusing, but you. . . . ." then followed some more about the mythology and the knitting, and Anne was insulted again. However I did not show it and let Pf. finish speaking:

"But you, one simply can't talk to you. You are so outrageously selfish, as long as you can get what you want, you don't mind pushing everyone else to one side, I have never seen such a child. But after all, I suppose I shall be obliged to give you your own way, because otherwise I shall be told later on that Anne Frank failed her exam because Mr. Pf. would not give up the table for her!"

It went on . . . and on and finally it was such a torrent I could hardly keep pace with it. At one moment I thought, "in a minute I'll give him such a smack in his big mouth that he'll fly up to the ceiling together with his lies," but the next moment I said to myself, "Keep calm! Such a fellow isn't worth getting worked up about." After giving final vent

as if someone had stuck a needle into him. "You can't talk about your rights here at all. And where am I to go, then? I shall ask Mr. Van Daan whether he will build a little compartment in the attic, then I can go and sit there. I simply can't work anywhere. With you one always gets trouble. If your sister Margot, who after all has more reason to ask such a thing, would have come to me with the same questions, I should not think of refusing, but you . . ." Then followed the business about the mythology and the knitting, and Anne was insulted again. However, she did not show it and let Dussel finish speaking. "But you, one simply can't talk to you. You are so outrageously selfish, as long as you can get what you want, you don't mind pushing everyone else to one side, I've never seen such a child. But after all, I suppose I shall be obliged to give you your own way, because otherwise I shall be told later on that Anne Frank failed her exam because Dr. Dussel would not give up the table for her."

It went on and on and finally it was such a torrent I could hardly keep pace with it. At one moment I thought, "In a minute I'll give him such a smack in the face that he'll fly up to the ceiling together with his lies," but the next moment I said to myself, "Keep calm! Such a fellow isn't worth getting worked up about."

to his fury, Master Pf. left the room with an expression of mixed wrath and triumph, his cape stuffed with food.

I dashed to Daddy and told him all he had not already heard of the story. Pim decided to talk to Pf. the same evening; he did just that and they talked for over half an hour. The theme of the conversation was something like this:

First of all they talked about whether Anne should sit at the table, yes or no. Daddy said he and Pf. had already discussed the subject once before, when he had professed to agree with Pf. in order not to put him in the wrong in front of the young, but Daddy had not thought it fair even then. Pf. thought that I should not speak as if he was an intruder who tried to monopolize everything, but Daddy stuck up for me firmly over that, because he had heard for himself that I had not breathed a word of such a thing. To and fro it went, Daddy defending my selfishness and my "trifling" work, Pf. grumbling continually.

Finally, Pf. had to give in after all, and I had the opportunity of working undisturbed for | two afternoons a week. Pf. looked down his nose very much, didn't speak to me for two days and still had to go and sit at the table from 5 till half past. . . . . frightfully childish.

A person of 54 who is still so pedantic and small-minded must have been made like that by nature, and will never improve.

After giving final vent to his fury, Master Dussel left the room with an expression of mixed wrath and triumph, his coat stuffed with food. I dashed to Daddy and told him all that he had not already heard of the story. Pim decided to talk to Dussel the same evening, which he did. They talked for over half an hour. The theme of the conversation was something like this: first of all they talked about whether Anne should sit at the table, yes or no. Daddy said that he and Dussel had already discussed the subject once before, when he had professed to agree with Dussel, in order not to put him in the wrong in front of the young. But Daddy had not thought it fair then. Dussel thought that I should not speak as if he was an intruder who tried to monopolize everything, but Daddy stuck up for me firmly over that, because he had heard for himself that I had not breathed a word of such a thing.

To and fro it went, Daddy defending my selfishness and my "trifling" work, Dussel grumbling continually.

Finally, Dussel had to give in after all, and I had the opportunity of working undisturbed until five o'clock for two afternoons a week. Dussel looked down his nose very much, didn't speak to me for two days and still had to go and sit at the table from five till half past—frightfully childish.

A person of fifty-four who is still so pedantic and small-minded must be so by nature, and will never improve.

Yours, Anne

. . . . . .

Friday 16 July 1943.

Dear Kitty,

Burglars again, but real this time! This morning Peter went to the warehouse at 7 o'clock as usual, and at once noticed that both the warehouse door and also the door opening on to the street were ajar. He immediately told Pim, who tuned the radio in the Private Office to Germany and locked the door; then they went upstairs together. The standing orders for such times were observed as usual: no washing, silence, everything to be finished by 8 o'clock and no lavatory. We were all very glad that we had slept so well and not heard anything. We were a bit indignant though that no one came upstairs all morning[4] and that Mr. Kleiman kept us waiting till half past 11. He told us that the burglars had pushed in the outer door with a crowbar and had forced the warehouse door. However, they did | 170 not find much to steal, so they tried their luck | upstairs. They stole 2 cash boxes containing 40 florins,[11] postal orders and checkbooks and then, worst of all, all our sugar coupons, no less than 150 florins.

The flour board was informed immediately so we might be able to wangle some new coupons perhaps, but it won't be easy.

Mr. Kugler thinks that this burglar belongs to the same gang as the ones who tried all three doors (1 warehouse and two house doors) six weeks ago, but who were

Friday, 16 July, 1943

Dear Kitty,

Burglars again, but real this time! This morning Peter went to the warehouse at seven o'clock as usual, and at once noticed that both the warehouse door and the door opening on to the street were ajar. He told Pim, who tuned the radio in the private office to Germany and locked the door. Then they went upstairs together.

The standing orders for such times were observed as usual: no taps to be turned on; therefore, no washing, silence, everything to be finished by eight o'clock and no lavatory. We were all very glad that we had slept so well and not heard anything. Not until half past eleven did we learn from Mr. Koophuis that the burglars had pushed in the outer door with a crowbar and had forced the warehouse door. However, they did not find much to steal, so they tried their luck upstairs. They stole two cashboxes containing forty florins, postal orders and checkbooks and then, worst of all, all the coupons for 150 kilos of sugar.

Mr. Koophuis thinks that they belonged to the same gang as the ones who tried all three doors six weeks ago. They were unsuccessful then.

. . . . . .

unsuccessful then. It has caused rather a stir in the building, but the "Secret Annexe" can't seem to go on without sensations like this. We were very glad of course that the typewriters and money were safe in our wardrobe.

yours, Anne

P.S. Landing in Sicily. Another step closer . . . . !

171

Monday 19 July 1943.

Dear Kitty,

North Amsterdam was very heavily bombed on Sunday. The destruction seems to be terrible, whole streets lie in ruins, and it will take a long time until all the people are dug out. Up till now there are two hundred dead and countless wounded;* the hospitals are crammed. You hear of children lost in the smoldering ruins, looking for their parents. I shudder when I recall the dull, droning rumble in the distance, which for[5] us marked the approaching[6] destruction.

---

*During the raid on North Amsterdam well over 150 people were killed and many badly wounded. (*Kroniek van Amsterdam*, p. 102.)

c

It has caused rather a stir in the building, but the "Secret Annexe" can't seem to go on without sensations like this. We were very glad that the typewriters and money in our wardrobe, where they are brought upstairs every evening, were safe.

Yours, Anne

Monday, 19 July, 1943

Dear Kitty,

North Amsterdam was very heavily bombed on Sunday. The destruction seems to be terrible. Whole streets lie in ruins, and it will take a long time before all the people are dug out. Up till now there are two hundred dead and countless wounded; the hospitals are crammed. You hear of children lost in the smoldering ruins, looking for their parents. I shudder when I recall the dull droning rumble in the distance, which for us marked the approaching destruction.

Yours, Anne

372

a ──────

. . . .

b ──────

Friday 23 July '43.

Bep is able to get hold of exercise books again just now, especially journals and ledgers, useful for my bookkeeping sister! You can buy exercise books as well, but what they're like and how long for, who knows. At the moment, all exercise books are labeled: Obtainable without coupons!" It's all rubbishy stuff, just like everything else you get "without coupons."[5]

172   An exercise book like this consists of 12 sheets of gray paper ruled with narrow lines that slant across the page. Margot is considering taking a Calligraphy Course from the same people who sent us our shorthand lessons; I have strongly advised her to, it's bound to improve one's handwriting. On no account will Mummy allow me to do it too because of my eyes, which I think is nonsense. Whether I'm doing that or something else, it all comes down to exactly the same thing.

c ──────

. . . . . .

373

a   169

As you've never been through a war, Kitty and despite all my letters know very little about life in hiding, just for fun I'm going to tell you each person's first wish when we go outside again. Margot and Mr. v. Pels long more than anything for a hot bath filled to overflowing and want to stay in it for half an hour. Mrs. v.P. wants most to go and eat cream cakes immediately, Pf. thinks of nothing but seeing his Charlotte; Mummy of her cup of coffee; Daddy is going to visit the Voskuyls; Peter the town and a cinema, while I should find it so blissful, I shouldn't know where to start!

yours, Anne

b

We asked ourselves what we should do first if ever we became ordinary people again. Margot wants a bath filled to the brim, Mummy wants to go first of all to a pastry shop, Daddy will visit Mr. Voskuyl and I should find it so glorious I shouldn't know what to do! But most of all, I long for a home of our own, to be able to move freely and to have some help with my work again at last, in other words—back to school! Bep has offered to get us some fruit. It costs next to nothing—grapes f. 5.00 per kilogram, gooseberries f. 0.70 p. lb., f. 0.50 1 peach, 1 kilogram melon¹ f. 1.50. Then you see in the newspapers every evening in bold letters, *Play fair and keep prices down!*"

c

Friday, 23 July, 1943

Dear Kitty,

Just for fun I'm going to tell you each person's first wish, when we are allowed to go outside again. Margot and Mr. Van Daan long more than anything for a hot bath filled to overflowing and want to stay in it for half an hour. Mrs. Van Daan wants most to go and eat cream cakes immediately. Dussel thinks of nothing but seeing Lotje, his wife; Mummy of her cup of coffee; Daddy is going to visit Mr. Vossen first; Peter the town and a cinema, while I should find it so blissful, I shouldn't know where to start! But most of all, I long for a home of our own, to be able to move freely and to have some help with my work again at last, in other words—school.

Elli has offered to get us some fruit. It costs next to nothing—grapes f.5.00 per kilo, gooseberries f.0.70 per pound, *one* peach f.0.50, one kilo melon f.1.50. Then you see in the newspapers every evening in bold letters, "Play fair and keep prices down!"

Yours, Anne

b   174
[= 173]

Dearest Kitty,

Nothing but tumult and uproar yesterday, we are still very het up about it all. You might really ask us does a day go by without some excitement? We had the first warning siren while we were at breakfast, but we don't give a hoot about that, it only means that the planes are crossing the coast. After breakfast I went and lay down for an hour as I had a bad headache, and then I went down to the office. It was about 2 o'clock. Margot had finished her office work at half past 2: she had not packed her things together when the sirens began to wail, so upstairs I went again with her. It was high time, for we had not been upstairs 5 minutes when the shooting starts in earnest, so much so that we went and stood in the passage. And yes, the house rumbled and shook, and down came the bombs. I clasped my "escape-bag" close to me, more because I wanted to have something to hold, than with an idea of escaping, because there's nowhere we can go and if the worst came

| 173
[= 174]

to the worst | the street would be just as dangerous as an air raid. This one subsided after ½ an hour, but the activity in the house increased. Peter came down from his lookout post in the attic, Pf. was in the main office, Mrs. v.P. felt safe in the private office, Mr. v.P. had been watching from out of the loft and we on the little landing dispersed ourselves too to watch the columns of smoke rising above the harbor. Before long you could smell burning and outside it looked as if a thick mist hung everywhere.

c

Dear Kitty,

Nothing but tumult and uproar yesterday, we are still very het up about it all. You might really ask, does a day go by without some excitement?

We had the first warning siren while we were at breakfast, but we don't give a hoot about that, it only means that the planes are crossing the coast.

After breakfast I went and lay down for an hour as I had a bad headache, then I went downstairs. It was about two o'clock. Margot had finished her office work at half past two: she had not packed her things together when the sirens began to wail, so upstairs I went again with her. It was high time, for we had not been upstairs five minutes when they began shooting hard, so much so that we went and stood in the passage. And yes, the house rumbled and shook, and down came the bombs.

I clasped my "escape bag" close to me, more because I wanted to have something to hold than with an idea of escaping, because there's nowhere we can go. If ever we come to the extremity of fleeing from here, the street would be just as dangerous as an air raid. This one subsided after half an hour, but the activity in the house increased. Peter came down from his lookout post in the attic, Dussel was in the main office, Mrs. Van Daan felt safe in the private office, Mr. Van Daan had been watching from the loft, and we on the little landing dispersed ourselves too: I went upstairs to see rising above the harbor the columns of smoke Mr. Van Daan had told us about. Before long you could smell burning, and outside it looked as if a thick mist hung everywhere.

b

Although such a big fire
is not a pleasant sight luckily for us it was all over, and we went about our respective
tasks. That evening at dinner: Another air raid alarm! It was a nice meal, but my hunger
vanished, simply at the sound of the alarm. Nothing happened and 3 quarters of an hour
later the all-clear sounded. The dishes were stacked ready to be done: Air raid warning,
ack-ack fire, an awful lot of planes. "Oh, dear me, twice in one day, that's too much,"
we all thought, but that didn't help at all; once again the bombs rained down, the other
| 175   side this time, on Skiphol, according to the British. | The planes dived and climbed, we
heard the hum of the engines and it was very gruesome, each moment I thought "one's
falling now. Here it comes."

I can assure you that when I went to bed at 9 o'clock,[6] I couldn't[7] hold my legs still.
I woke up at[8] the stroke of 12: Planes. Pf. was undressing. I didn't let that put me off,
and at the first shot, I leaped out of bed, wide awake. Into the next room until 1, in bed
at half past 1, back with Daddy at 2 and still they kept coming. They stopped firing and
I was able to go home. I fell asleep at half past 2.

7 o'clock. I sat up in bed with a start. Mr. v.P. was with Daddy. Burglars was my
first thought. I heard Mr. v.P. say "everything," I thought that everything had been stolen.
But no, this time it was wonderful news, such as we have not heard for months, perhaps
| 176   in all the war years. Mussolini has stood down, the king of | Italy has taken over the
government. We jumped for joy. After the terrible day yesterday,* at last something good
again and—hope.

---

*During the raid on Amsterdam the Fokker aircraft factory was destroyed and the raid on Schiphol,
the Amsterdam airport, started a big fire. (*Kroniek van Amsterdam*, p. 104.)

c

Although such a big
fire is not a pleasant sight, luckily for us it was all over, and we went about our respective
tasks. That evening at dinner: another air-raid alarm! It was a nice meal, but my hunger
vanished, simply at the sound of the alarm. Nothing happened and three quarters of an
hour later it was all clear. The dishes were stacked ready to be done: air-raid warning,
ack-ack fire, an awful lot of planes. "Oh, dear me, twice in one day, that's too much,"
we all thought, but that didn't help at all; once again the bombs rained down, the other
side this time, on Schiphol,* according to the British. The planes dived and climbed, we
heard the hum of their engines and it was very gruesome. Each moment I thought: "One's
falling now. Here it comes."

I can assure you that when I went to bed at nine o'clock I couldn't hold my legs still.
I woke up at the stroke of twelve: planes. Dussel was undressing. I didn't let that put me
off, and at the first shot, I leaped out of bed, wide awake. Two hours with Daddy and
still they kept coming. Then they ceased firing and I was able to go to bed. I fell asleep
at half past two.

Seven o'clock. I sat up in bed with a start. Mr. Van Daan was with Daddy. Burglars
was my first thought. I heard Mr. Van Daan say "everything." I thought that everything
had been stolen. But no, this time it was wonderful news, such as we have not heard for
months, perhaps in all the war years. "Mussolini has resigned, the King of Italy has taken
over the government." We jumped for joy. After the terrible day yesterday, at last something

---

*Amsterdam airport.

. . . . . .

b

Hope for it to end, hope for peace. Kugler called in and told us that Fokkers had been badly damaged. Meanwhile we had another air raid alarm with planes flying overhead and one more warning siren. I'm just about choked with alarms, very tired and don't feel a bit like work, but now the suspense about Italy keeps us awake and the hope that by the end of the year . . . . .

yours, Anne

177   Thursday 29 July 1943

Dear Kitty,

Mrs. v.P., Pf. and I were doing the dishes, and I was extraordinarily quiet, which hardly ever happens, so they would have been sure to notice. In order to avoid questions I quickly sought a fairly neutral topic and thought that the book: Henry from the Other Side, would meet the need. But I had made a mistake; if Mrs. v.P. doesn't pounce on me, then Mr. Pf. does. This was what it came to: Mr. Pf. had specially recommended us this book as being excellent. Margot and I thought it was anything but excellent; the boy's character was certainly well drawn, but the rest—I had better gloss over that. I said something to that effect while we were washing the dishes, but that brought me a packet of trouble:

"How can you understand the psychology of a man. Of a child is not so difficult (!).
| 178   You are much too young for a book like that; why, even a man | of 20 would not be able to grasp it." (Why did he so especially recommend this book to Margot and me?) Now Pf.

c

good again and—hope. Hope for it to end, hope for peace.

Kraler called in and told us that Fokkers has been badly damaged. Meanwhile we had another air-raid alarm with planes overhead and one more warning siren. I'm just about choked with alarms, very tired and don't feel a bit like work. But now the suspense over Italy will awaken [keeps us awake and] the hope that it will soon end, perhaps even this year.

Yours, Anne

Thursday, 29 July, 1943

Dear Kitty,

Mrs. Van Daan, Dussel, and I were doing the dishes and I was extraordinarily quiet, which hardly ever happens, so they would have been sure to notice.

In order to avoid questions I quickly sought a fairly neutral topic, and thought that the book *Henry from the Other Side* would meet the need. But I had made a mistake. If Mrs. Van Daan doesn't pounce on me, then Mr. Dussel does. This was what it came to: Mr. Dussel had specially recommended us this book as being excellent. Margot and I thought it was anything but excellent. The boy's character was certainly well drawn, but the rest—I had better gloss over that. I said something to that effect while we were washing the dishes, but that brought me a packet of trouble.

"How can you understand the psychology of a man! Of a child is not so difficult (!). You are much too young for a book like that; why, even a man of twenty would not be able to grasp it." (Why did he so especially recommend this book to Margot and me?)

b

and Mrs. v.P. continued together: "You know much too much about things that are unsuitable for you, you've been brought up all wrong. Later on, when you are older, and take no pleasure in anything, then you'll say: I read that in books 20 years ago. You had better make haste if you want to get a husband or fall in love—or everything is sure to be a disappointment to you. You are already proficient in the theory, it's only the practice that you still lack!"

Can you imagine my situation? I astonished myself by answering calmly: "You may think that I've been badly brought up, but hardly anyone would agree with you!"

I suppose it's good upbringing to always[1] try to set me against my parents, because that is what they often do, and to tell a girl of my age nothing about certain matters is admirable. I see the results of that kind of | upbringing demonstrated all too clearly.

| 179

I could have slapped both their faces at that moment as they stood there making a fool of me. I was beside myself with rage and I'm just counting the days (if only I knew when I can stop) until I'm rid of "those" people.

Mrs. v.P. is a nice one! She sets a fine example . . . she certainly sets one—a bad one. Mrs. v.P. is well known as being very pushing, selfish, cunning, calculating[2] and is never content. I can also add vanity and coquetry to the list. There is no question about it: she is an unspeakably disagreeable person. I could write whole chapters about Madame, and

c

Now Dussel and Mrs. Van Daan continued together: "You know too much about things that are unsuitable for you, you've been brought up all wrong. Later on, when you are older, you won't enjoy anything, then you'll say: 'I read that in books twenty years ago.' You had better make haste, if you want to get a husband or fall in love—or everything is sure to be a disappointment to you. You are already proficient in the theory, it's only the practice that you still lack!"

I suppose it's their idea of a good upbringing to always try to set me against my parents, because that is what they often do. And to tell a girl of my age nothing about "grown-up" subjects is an equally fine method! I see the results of that kind of upbringing frequently and all too clearly.

I could have slapped both their faces at that moment as they stood there making a fool of me. I was beside myself with rage and I'm just counting the days until I'm rid of "those" people.

Mrs. Van Daan is a nice one! She sets a fine example . . . she certainly sets one—a bad one. She is well known as being very pushing, selfish, cunning, calculating, and is never content. I can also add vanity and coquetry to the list. There is no question about it, she is an unspeakably disagreeable person. I could write whole chapters about Madame,

a   . . . . . .

b   who knows, perhaps I will someday. Anyone can put on a fine coat of varnish outside. Mrs.
         v.P. is friendly to strangers and especially men, so it is easy to make a mistake when you
         have only known her for a short time. Mummy thinks she is too stupid to waste words
         over, Margot too unimportant, Pim too ugly (literally and figuratively!) and I, after long
    180 observation—for I was never prejudiced | from the start—have come to the conclusion
         that she is all three and a lot more! She has so many bad qualities, why should I even
         begin about one of them?

                                                                                    ——yours, Anne

T   11 Will the reader take into consideration that when this story was being written the writer
         had not cooled down from her fury!*

         *Anne Frank has also described these events under the title of "*Anne in theorie* [Anne in Theory]"
         in her *Verhaaltjesboek (Tales)*.

c   and who knows, perhaps I will someday. Anyone can put on a fine coat of varnish outside.
         Mrs. Van Daan is friendly to strangers and especially men, so it is easy to make a mistake
         when you have only known her for a short time. Mummy thinks she is too stupid to waste
         words over, Margot too unimportant, Pim too ugly (literally and figuratively), and I, after
         long observation—for I was never prejudiced from the start—have come to the conclusion
         that she is all three and a lot more! She has so many bad qualities, why should I even
         begin about one of them?

                                                                                      Yours, Anne

              P.S.—Will the reader take into consideration that when this story was written the
         writer had not cooled down from her fury!

b 181

Tuesday 3 August 1943.

Dear Kitty,

Political news excellent. In Italy the Fascist party has been banned. The people are fighting the Fascists in many places—even the army is actually taking part in the battle. Can a country like that wage war against England? Our lovely radio was taken away last week, Pf. was very cross that Kugler handed it in on the appointed date. Pf. keeps sinking in my esteem, he's roughly below zero now. Everything he says about politics, history, geography and other things is such nonsense that I scarcely dare repeat it. Hitler will be forgotten by history. The port of Rotterdam is bigger than that of Hamburg. The British are idiots because they are not bombing Italy to smithereens right at this moment etc., etc.

We've just had a third air raid; I clenched my teeth to make myself feel courageous.

182   Mrs. v.P., who has always said, "just let them come," "a terrible end is better than no end at all," is the greatest coward of us all now. She was shaking like a leaf this morning and even burst into tears. When her husband, with whom she has just made it up after a week's squabbling, comforted her, the expression on her face alone almost made me feel sentimental.

[13]Mouschi has proved that keeping cats has disadvantages as well as advantages. The whole house is full of fleas, and the plague gets worse every day. Mr. Kleiman has scattered yellow powder in every nook and corner, but the fleas don't seem to mind a bit. It's making us all quite nervous; one keeps imagining an itch on one's arms, legs, and various parts of the body, which is why quite a lot of us are doing gymnastics, so as to be able to look at the back of our necks or legs while standing up. Now we're[15] being paid back for not being more supple—we're too stiff to even turn our heads properly. We gave up real gymnastics long ago.

yours, Anne

c

Tuesday, 3 August, 1943

Dear Kitty,

Political news excellent. In Italy the Fascist party has been banned. The people are fighting the Fascists in many places—even the army is actually taking part in the battle. Can a country like that wage war against England?

We've just had a third air raid; I clenched my teeth together to make myself feel courageous. Mrs. Van Daan, who has always said, "A terrible end is better than no end at all," is the greatest coward of us all now. She was shaking like a leaf this morning and even burst into tears. When her husband, with whom she has just made it up after a week's squabbling, comforted her, the expression on her face alone almost made me feel sentimental.

Mouschi has proved that keeping cats has disadvantages as well as advantages. The whole house is full of fleas, and the plague gets worse every day. Mr. Koophuis has scattered yellow powder in every nook and corner, but the fleas don't seem to mind a bit. It's making us all quite nervous; one keeps imagining an itch on one's arms, legs, and various parts of the body, which is why quite a lot of us are doing gymnastics, so as to be able to look at the back of our necks or legs while standing up. Now we're being paid back for not being more supple—we're too stiff to even turn our heads properly. We gave up real gymnastics long ago.

Yours, Anne

b 183   Wednesday 4 Aug. 1943.

Dear Kitty,

Now that we have been in the "Secret Annexe" for over a year you know something of our lives, but some of it is quite indescribable; there is so much to tell, everything is so different from ordinary times and from ordinary people's lives. But still, to give you a slightly closer look into our lives, now and again I intend to give you a description of an ordinary day. Today I'm beginning with the evening and night:

9 o'clock in the evening. The bustle of going to bed in the "Secret Annexe" begins and it is always really quite a business. Chairs are pushed about, beds are pulled down, blankets unfolded and nothing remains where it is during the day. I sleep on the little divan, which is not more than one and a half meters long. So chairs have to be used as extensions; a quilt, sheets, pillows, blankets, all fetched from Pf.'s bed where they remain

| 184   during the day. | One hears terrible creaking in the next room, Margot's concertina-bed being pulled out; again, divan, blankets and pillows, everything is done to make the wooden slats a bit more comfortable. It sounds like thunder above, but it is only: Mrs. v.P.'s bed. This is shifted to the window, you see, in order to give Her Majesty in the pink bed jacket fresh air to tickle her dainty nostrils!

c   Wednesday, 4 August, 1943

Dear Kitty,

Now that we have been in the "Secret Annexe" for over a year, you know something of our lives, but some of it is quite indescribable. There is so much to tell, everything is so different from ordinary times and from ordinary people's lives. But still, to give you a closer look into our lives, now and again I intend to give you a description of an ordinary day. Today I'm beginning with the evening and night.

Nine o'clock in the evening. The bustle of going to bed in the "Secret Annexe" begins and it is always really quite a business. Chairs are shoved about, beds are pulled down, blankets unfolded, nothing remains where it is during the day. I sleep on the little divan, which is not more than one and a half meters long. So chairs have to be used to lengthen it. A quilt, sheets, pillows, blankets, are all fetched from Dussel's bed where they remain during the day. One hears terrible creaking in the next room: Margot's concertina-bed being pulled out. Again, divan, blankets, and pillows, everything is done to make the wooden slats a bit more comfortable. It sounds like thunder above, but it is only Mrs. Van Daan's bed. This is shifted to the window, you see, in order to give Her Majesty in the pink bed jacket fresh air to tickle her dainty nostrils!

a
. . . . . .

b
9 o'clock: After Peter's finished, I step into the bathroom where I give myself a thorough wash and general toilet; it happens quite often (only in the hot months, weeks or days) that there is a tiny flea floating in the water. Then teeth cleaning, hair, curling, manicure, and my cotton-wool pads with hydrogen peroxide (to bleach black mustache hairs)—all this in under half an hour.

Half past 9: Quickly into dressing gown, soap in one hand, pottie, hairpins, pants, curlers and cotton wool in the other, I hurry out of the bathroom; but usually I am called back once for the various hairs which decorate the washbasin in graceful curls, but which | 185 are not approved of by the | next person.

10 o'clock: Put up the blackout. Good night! For at least a quarter of an hour, there is a creaking of beds and a sighing of broken springs, then all is quiet, at least that is if our neighbors upstairs don't quarrel in bed.

Half past 11: The bathroom door creaks. A narrow strip of light falls into the room. A squeak of shoes, a large coat, even larger than the man inside it—Pf. returning from his night work in Kugler's office. Shuffling on the floor for 10 minutes, crackle of paper, that is the food which has to be stowed away, and a bed is made. Then the form disappears again, and one only hears suspicious little noises from the lavatory from time to time.

c
After Peter's finished, I step into the washing cubicle, where I give myself a thorough wash and general toilet; it occasionally happens (only in the hot weeks or months) that there is a tiny flea floating in the water. Then teeth cleaning, hair curling, manicure, and my cotton-wool pads with hydrogen peroxide (to bleach black mustache hairs)—all this in under half an hour.

Half past nine. Quickly into dressing gown, soap in one hand, pottie, hairpins, pants, curlers, and cotton wool in the other, I hurry out of the bathroom; but usually I'm called back once for the various hairs which decorate the washbasin in graceful curves, but which are not approved of by the next person.

Ten o clock. Put up the blackout. Good night! For at least a quarter of an hour there is creaking of beds and a sighing of broken springs, then all is quiet, at least that is if our neighbors upstairs don't quarrel in bed.

Half past eleven. The bathroom door creaks. A narrow strip of light falls into the room. A squeak of shoes, a large coat, even larger than the man inside it—Dussel returns from his night work in Kraler's office. Shuffling on the floor for ten minutes, crackle of paper (that is the food which has to be stowed away), and a bed is made. Then the form disappears again and one only hears suspicious noises from the lavatory from time to time.

382

$\pm$ 3 o'clock: I have to get up for a little job in the metal pot under my bed, which is on a rubber mat for safety's sake in case of leakage. When this has to take place, I always hold my breath, as it clatters into the tin like a brook from a mountain. Then | the pot is returned to its place and the figure in the white nightgown, which evokes the same cry from Margot every evening: "Oh that indecent nightdress," steps back into bed. Then a certain person lies awake for about a quarter of an hour, listening to the sounds of the night.[2] Firstly, to whether there might not be a burglar downstairs, then to the various beds, above, next door, and in my room, from which one is usually able to make out how the various members of the household are sleeping, or how they pass the night in wakefulness. The latter is certainly not pleasant, especially when it concerns a member of the family by the name of Dr. Pf.

First, I hear a sound like a fish gasping for breath, this is repeated nine or ten times, then with much ado and interchanged with little smacking sounds, the lips are moistened, followed by a lengthy twisting and turning in bed and rearranging of pillows. Five minutes' perfect peace and then the same sequence of events unfolds itself at least 3 times more, after which the doctor has soothed himself to sleep again for a little while.

Three o'clock. I have to get up for a little job in the metal pot under my bed, which is on a rubber mat for safety's sake in case of leakage. When this has to take place, I always hold my breath, as it clatters into the tin like a brook from a mountain. Then the pot is returned to its place and the figure in the white nightgown, which evokes the same cry from Margot every evening: "Oh, that indecent nightdress!" steps back into bed.

Then a certain person lies awake for about a quarter of an hour, listening to the sounds of the night. Firstly, to whether there might not be a burglar downstairs, then to the various beds, above, next door, and in my room, from which one is usually able to make out how the various members of the household are sleeping, or how they pass the night in wakefulness.

The latter is certainly not pleasant, especially when it concerns a member of the family by the name of Dussel. First, I hear a sound like a fish gasping for breath, this is repeated nine or ten times, then with much ado and interchanged with little smacking sounds, the lips are moistened, followed by a lengthy twisting and turning in bed and rearranging of pillows. Five minutes' perfect peace and then the same sequence of events unfolds itself at least three times more, after [which] the doctor has soothed himself to sleep again for a little while.

a . . . . . .

b 187   It can also happen that we get a bit of shooting in the night, varying between 1 o'clock and 4. I never really realize it, until from habit I am already standing at my bedside. Sometimes I'm so busy dreaming that I'm thinking about French irregular verbs or a quarrel upstairs. It is some time before I begin to realize that guns are firing and I am still in the room. But it usually happens as described above. I quickly grab a pillow and handkerchief, put on my dressing gown and slippers and scamper to Daddy, just as Margot wrote in this birthday poem: The first shot sounds at dead of night, hush, look! A door creaks open wide, a little girl glides into sight, clasping a pillow to her side.

Once landed in the big bed, the worst is over, except if the firing is very bad.

quarter to 7: trrrrrrr—the alarm clock that raises its voice (if one asks for it and sometimes when one doesn't) at any hour of the day. Click—ping—Mrs. v.P. has turned it off. Crack—Mr. v.P. gets up. Puts on water and then full speed to the bathroom.

188   quarter past 7. The door creaks again. Pf. can go to the bathroom. Once alone I take down the blackout—and a new day in the "Secret Annexe" has begun.*

yours, Anne

---

*Under the title "*Deavond en de nacht in het Achterhuis* [Evening and Night in the 'Secret Annexe']" Anne Frank has also described these events in her *Verhaaltjesboek (Tales).*

c   It can also happen that we get a bit of shooting in the night, varying between one o'clock and four. I never really realize it, until from habit I am already standing at my bedside. Sometimes I'm so busy dreaming that I'm thinking about French irregular verbs or a quarrel upstairs. It is some time before I begin to realize that guns are firing and that I am still in the room. But it usually happens as described above. I quickly grab a pillow and handkerchief, put on my dressing gown and slippers, and scamper to Daddy, like Margot wrote in this birthday poem:

> *The first shot sounds at dead of night,*
>   *Hush, look! A door creaks open wide,*
> *A little girl glides into sight,*
>   *Clasping a pillow to her side.*

Once landed in the big bed, the worst is over, except if the firing gets very bad.

Quarter to seven. Trrrrr—the alarm clock that raises its voice at any hour of the day (if one asks for it and sometimes when one doesn't). Crack—ping—Mrs. Van Daan has turned it off. Creak—Mr. Van Daan gets up. Puts on water and then full speed to the bathroom.

Quarter past seven. The door creaks again. Dussel can go to the bathroom. Once alone, I take down the blackout—and a new day in the "Secret Annexe" has begun.

Yours, Anne

384

Thursday 5 Aug. <u>1943.</u>

Dear Kitty,[1]

Today I am going to take lunchtime:

It is <u>half past 12</u>. The whole mixed crowd breathes again. Van Maaren, the man with the dark past, and de Kok have gone home at last. Above one can hear the noise of Mrs. v.P.'s vacuum cleaner on her beautiful, one and only "rug"; Margot goes with a few books under her arm for her lesson "for children who make no progress," because that's Pf.'s attitude.

Pim goes into a corner with his inseparable Dickens to try and find peace somewhere. Mummy hurries upstairs to help the industrious housewife and I go to the bathroom to tidy it up a bit, and myself at the same time.

<u>quarter to 1</u>. The place is filling up. First Mr. Gies then Kleiman or Kugler, Bep and sometimes Miep as well.

190 <u>1 o'clock</u>. We're all sitting listening to the B.B.C., seated around the little baby radio; these are the sole times when the members of the "Secret Annexe" do not interrupt each other, because here someone is speaking even Mr. v.P. can't interrupt.

Thursday, 5 August, 1943

Dear Kitty,

Today I am going to take lunchtime.

It is half past twelve. The whole mixed crowd breathes again. The warehouse boys [men] have gone home now. Above one can hear the noise of Mrs. Van Daan's vacuum cleaner on her beautiful, and only, carpet. Margot goes with a few books under her arm for her Dutch lesson "for children who make no progress," because that's Dussel's attitude. Pim goes into a corner with his inseparable Dickens to try and find peace somewhere. Mummy hurries upstairs to help the industrious housewife, and I go to the bathroom to tidy up a bit, and myself at the same time.

Quarter to one. The place is filling up. First Mr. Van Santen, then Koophuis or Kraler, Elli and sometimes Miep as well.

One o'clock. We're all sitting listening to the B.B.C., seated around the baby wireless; these are the only times when the members of the "Secret Annexe" do not interrupt each other, because now someone is speaking whom even Mr. Van Daan can't interrupt.

. . . . . .

Quarter past 1. The great share-out. Everyone from below gets a cup of soup, and if there is ever a pudding some of that as well. Mr. Gies is happy and goes to sit on the divan or lean against the writing table. Newspaper, cup and usually cat, beside him. If one of the three is missing, he is sure to protest. Kleiman tells us the latest news from town; he is certainly an excellent source of information. Kugler comes helter-skelter upstairs—a short, firm knock on the door and in he comes rubbing his hands, according to his mood in a good temper and talkative or bad-tempered and quiet.

| 191 Quarter to 2. Everyone rises from the table and goes about his own business. Margot and Mummy to the dishes, | Mr. and Mrs. v.P. to the divan, Peter up to the attic, Daddy to the divan, Pf. too and Anne to her work. Then follows the most peaceful hour; everyone is asleep, no one is disturbed. Pf. dreams of lovely food—the expression on his face gives this away, but I don't look long because the time goes so fast and at 4 o'clock the pedantic Doctor is standing, clock in hand, because I'm one minute late in clearing the table for him.

yours, Anne

*Anne Frank has also described these events in her *Verhaaltjesboek (Tales)* under the title of *"Schaftuurtjes* [Mealtimes]."

Quarter past one. The great share-out. Everyone from below gets a cup of soup and if there is ever a pudding, some of that as well. Mr. Van Santen is happy and goes to sit on the divan or lean against the writing table. Newspaper, cup, and usually the cat, beside him. If one of the three is missing he's sure to protest. Koophuis tells us the latest news from town; he is certainly an excellent source of information. Kraler comes helter-skelter upstairs—a short, firm knock on the door and in he comes rubbing his hands, according to his mood, in a good temper and talkative, or bad-tempered and quiet.

Quarter to two. Everyone rises from the table and goes about his own business. Margot and Mummy to the dishes. Mr. and Mrs. Van Daan to their divan. Peter up to the attic. Daddy to the divan downstairs. Dussel to his bed and Anne to her work. Then follows the most peaceful hour; everyone is asleep, no one is disturbed. Dussel dreams of lovely food—the expression on his face gives this away, but I don't look long because the time goes so fast and at four o'clock the pedantic doctor is standing, clock in hand, because I'm one minute late in clearing the table for him.

Yours, Anne

b   192   Saturday 7 Aug. '43.

Dear Kitty,

An interruption in my sketches of life in the "Secret Annexe." A few weeks ago I started
to write a story, something that was completely made up and that gave me such pleasure
that my pen-children are now piling up.

Because I promised to give you a faithful and unadorned account of all my experiences,
I'll let you judge[2] whether small children may perhaps take pleasure in my tales.

Kitty*

Kitty is the girl next door. In fair weather, I can watch her playing in the yard through
our window.

Kitty has a wine-red velvet frock for Sundays and a cotton one for every day; she
has pale-blond hair with tiny braids, and clear blue eyes. Kitty has a sweet mother, but
her father is dead. The mother is a laundress; sometimes she is gone during the day,

| 193   cleaning other | people's houses, and at night she does the wash for her customers. At 11
o'clock she is still shaking out the carpets and hanging washing on the line.

Kitty has 6 brothers and sisters. The smallest screams a lot and hangs on to the skirts
of his 11-year-old sister when Mother calls "bedtime!" Kitty has a small cat which is so
black that it looks like a Moor. She takes good care of the kitten, and every evening before
bedtime, you can hear her call "Kitty, kitty, kitty!" That's how she came to be called
Kitty, which may not be her name at all, but she looks like one. Kitty also has two rabbits,
a white one and a brown one, that hop up and down in the grass under the short flight
of stairs that leads to Kitty's house. Sometimes Kitty is naughty, just like other children.
This happens mostly when she quarrels with her brothers. It's a sight to see Kitty fight
with them, she beats, kicks and even bites them and the little boys respect their sturdy
sister.

195
[= 194]   "There are errands to be done, Kitty!" Mother calls. Quickly Kitty sticks her fingers
in her ears, so that she'll be able to say honestly that she didn't hear her mother. Kitty
hates running errands, but she wouldn't lie to escape them; Kitty doesn't lie; you need
only to look into her blue eyes to know that. One of Kitty's brothers is 16 and works as
an office boy. This brother sometimes bosses the other children as if he were their father;
not even Kitty dares to contradict Peter, for she knows from experience that he is quick
with his fists but that he doesn't mind standing treat if one obeys him. Kitty loves sweets
and her sisters do too.

---

*This story can also be found in Anne Frank's *Verhaaltjesboek* under the title of "*Kaatje.*" [The
English translation is by Michel Mok (see *Anne Frank's Tales from the Secret Annex*) except for
minor differences. A.J.P.]

c   . . . . . .

b

| 194
[= 195]

Sundays, when the bell tolls, ding-dong, ding-dong, Kitty's mother and all the children go to church. Kitty prays for her dear father, who is in heaven, and also for her mother, that she may still have a long, long life. After church they go for a walk with Mummy. Kitty enjoys that a lot, they walk through the park and once in a while to the Zoo. But she'll have to wait another two months | to go to the Zoo, because they only go in September, when it costs just a quarter again, or when it is Kitty's birthday, and she can ask for a trip to the Zoo as a birthday present. Other gifts her mother cannot afford.

Often Kitty comforts her mother who, after a day's hard work, weeps in the night. Then Kitty promises her all the things she, herself, would like to have when she is grown up. Kitty wants so badly to be grown up, to earn money, buy pretty clothes, and treat her sisters to sweets, as Peter does.

But first Kitty still has to learn a lot and to go to school for a long time. Mother wants her to go to the domestic science school, but Kitty doesn't care for that idea at all. She doesn't want to work for some lady, she wants to work in a factory, like those jolly girls she sees passing by every day. In a factory you're never alone and you can have a nice gossip, and Kitty loves gossiping!

196

At school she has to stand in the corner once in a while because she talks too much, but otherwise she is a good pupil. Kitty is fond of her teacher, who is usually sweet and is terribly clever. "How hard I'll have to work before I can be so clever!" Kitty thinks, "but one can get along with less, Mother[5] always says that if I get too clever I shan't get a husband and that will be awful."[7] Kitty would like to have children later on, but not such children as her brothers and sisters. Kitty's children are going to be much sweeter and also much prettier. They will have lovely curly brown hair instead of that flaxen stuff, and they will have no freckles, which Kitty has[8] by the hundreds. Nor does Kitty want as many children as her mother has, 2 or 3, that's quite enough. But, oh, it is such a long time still, at least twice as long as she's been alive. "Kitty," her mother calls, "come here, where have | you been, naughty girl? Quick, to bed with you, you must have been sitting there dreaming again!"

| 197

Kitty sighs, for she just had been making such beautiful plans for the future.

yours, Anne

a   . . . . . .

Monday 9 Aug.
1943.

Dear Kitty,

To continue the "Secret Annexe" daily timetable. I shall now describe the evening meal.

Mr. v.P., who begins. He is first to be served, takes a lot of everything if it is what he likes. Usually talks at the same time, always gives his opinion as the only one worth listening to, and once he has spoken it is irrevocable, because if anyone dares to question it, then he flares up at once. Oh, he can spit like a cat—I'd rather not argue, I can tell you—if you've once tried you don't try again. He has the best opinion, he knows the most about everything. All right then, he has got brains, but self-satisfaction has reached a high grade with this gentleman.

Madame. Really, I should remain silent. Some days, especially if there is a bad mood coming on, you can't look at her face. On closer | examination, she is the guilty one in all the arguments. Not the subject! Oh, no, everyone prefers to keep out of that, but one could perhaps call her the starter. Stirring up trouble, that's fun. Stirring up trouble against Mrs. Frank and Anne; Margot and Mr. v.P. aren't quite so easy.

199 |

c

Monday, 9 August, 1943

Dear Kitty,

To continue the "Secret Annexe" daily timetable. I shall now describe the evening meal:

Mr. Van Daan begins. He is first to be served, takes a lot of everything if it is what he likes. Usually talks at the same time, always gives his opinion as the only one worth listening to, and once he has spoken it is irrevocable. Because if anyone dares to question it, then he flares up at once. Oh, he can spit like a cat I'd rather not argue, I can tell you—if you've once tried you don't try again. He has the best opinion, he knows the most about everything. All right then, he has got brains, but "self-satisfaction" has reached a high grade with this gentleman.

Madame. Really, I should remain silent. Some days, especially if there is a bad mood coming on, you can't look at her face. On closer examination, she is the guilty one in all the arguments. Not the subject! Oh, no, everyone prefers to remain aloof over that, but one could perhaps call her the "kindler." Stirring up trouble, that's fun. Mrs. Frank against Anne; [Stirring up trouble against Mrs. Frank and Anne.] Margot against Daddy doesn't go quite so easily. [Against Margot and Daddy it doesn't go quite so easily.]

b

But now at table, Mrs. v.P. doesn't go short, although she thinks so at times. The tiniest potatoes, the sweetest mouthful, the tenderest of everything, picking over is her system. The others will get their turn, as long as I have the best. (Just what she thinks about Anne Frank.) The second thing is talking; if only someone is listening, then it doesn't seem to matter whether they are interested or not, I suppose she thinks "Everyone is interested in what Mrs. v.P. says." Coquettish smiles, behaving as if one knew everything, giving everyone a bit of advice and encouragement, that's <u>sure</u> to produce a good impres-

| 200   sion. But if you look longer, then the good | soon wears off. One, she is industrious, two gay, three a coquette—and, occasionally, pretty: That is Gusti van Pels.

The 3rd <u>table companion.</u> One doesn't hear much from him. Young Mr. v.P. is usually quiet and doesn't draw much attention to himself. As for appetite: a danaïdean vessel, which is never full and after the heartiest meal declares quite calmly that he could have eaten double.

No. 4. Margot. Eats like a little mouse, and doesn't talk at all. Vegetables and fruit are all that go down. Spoiled, is the v.P.s' judgment; not enough fresh air and games is what we think.

c

But now at table, Mrs. Van Daan doesn't go short, although she thinks so at times. The tiniest potatoes, the sweetest mouthful, the best of everything; picking over is her system. The others will get their turn, as long as I have the best. Then talking. Whether anyone is interested, whether they are listening or not, that doesn't seem to matter. I suppose she thinks: "Everyone is interested in what Mrs. Van Daan says." Coquettish smiles, behaving as if one knew everything, giving everyone a bit of advice and encour-agement, that's *sure* to make a good impression. But if you look longer, then the good soon wears off.

One, she is industrious, two, gay, three, a coquette—and, occasionally, pretty. This is Petronella Van Daan.

The third table companion. One doesn't hear much from him. Young Mr. Van Daan is very quiet and doesn't draw much attention to himself. As for appetite: a Danaïdean vessel, which is never full and after the heartiest meal declares quite calmly that he could have eaten double.

Number four—Margot. Eats like a little mouse and doesn't talk at all. The only things that go down are vegetables and fruit. "Spoiled" is the Van Daans' judgment; "not enough fresh air and games" our opinion.

b

Beside her—Mummy. Good appetite, very talkative. No one has the impression, as with Mrs. v.P.: this is the housewife. What is the difference? Well, Mrs. v.P. does the cooking, and Mummy washes up and polishes.

Numbers 6 and 7. I won't say much about Daddy and me. The former is the most | 201 unassuming of all at table. | He always looks first to see if everyone else has something; for himself he needs nothing, the best things are for the children.

He is the perfect example, and sitting beside him, the "Secret Annexe's" "bundle of nerves."

Pfeffer. Helps himself, never looks up, eats and doesn't talk. And if one must talk, then for heaven's sake let it be about food. You don't quarrel about it, you only brag. Enormous helpings go down and the word "No" is never heard, never when the food is good and not often when it's bad.

Trousers wrapping his chest, red coat on, black patent leather bedroom slippers, and horn-rimmed spectacles. That is how one sees him at the little table, always working, never getting anywhere, alternated only by his afternoon nap, food, and—his favorite spot—the lavatory. Three, four, five times a day someone stands impatiently in front of the door and wriggles. Hopping from one foot to the other, hardly able to contain himself.

c

Beside her—Mummy. Good appetite, very talkative. No one has the impression, as [with] Mrs. Van Daan: this is the housewife. What is the difference? Well, Mrs. Van Daan does the cooking, and Mummy washes up and polishes.

Numbers six and seven. I won't say much about Daddy and me. The former is the most unassuming of all at table. He looks first to see if everyone else has something. He needs nothing himself, for the best things are for the children. He is the perfect example, and sitting beside him, the "Secret Annexe's" "bundle of nerves."

Dr. Dussel. Helps himself, never looks up, eats and doesn't talk. And if one must talk, then for heaven's sake let it be about food. You don't quarrel about it, you only brag. Enormous helpings go down and the word "No" is never heard, never when the food is good, and not often when it's bad. Trousers wrapping his chest, red coat, black bedroom slippers, and horn-rimmed spectacles. That is how one sees him at the little table, always working, alternated only by his afternoon nap, food, and—his favorite spot—the lavatory. Three, four, fives times a day someone stands impatiently in front of the door and wriggles, hopping from one foot to the other, hardly able to contain himself. Does it

a
......

b

| 202

Does it disturb him? Not a bit! From quarter past 7 till half past, from half past 12 till 1 o'clock, | from 2 till quarter past, from 4 till quarter past, from 6 till quarter past, and from half past 11 until 12. One can make a note of it—these are the regular "sittings." He won't come off or pay any heed to an imploring voice at the door, giving warning of approaching disaster!

Number 9 Isn't a member of the "Secret Annexe" family, but rather a companion in the house and at table. Bep has a healthy appetite. Leaves nothing on her plate and is not picky-and-choosy. She is easy to please and that is just what pleases us. Cheerful and good-tempered willing and good-natured, these are her characteristics.*

---

*Under the title "*Het Achterhuis van 8 aan tafel* [Eight at Table in the 'Secret Annexe']" Anne Frank has also described these events in her *Verhaaltjesboek* (*Tales*).

c

disturb him? Not a bit! From quarter past seven till half past, from half past twelve till one o'clock, from two till quarter past, from four till quarter past, from six till quarter past, and from half past eleven until twelve. One can make a note of it—these are the regular "sitting times." He won't come off or pay any heed to an imploring voice at the door, giving warning of approaching disaster!

Number nine isn't a member of the "Secret Annexe" family, but rather a companion in the house and at table. Elli has a healthy appetite. Leaves nothing on her plate and is not picky-and-choosy. She is easy to please and that is just what gives us pleasure. Cheerful and good-tempered, willing and good-natured, these are her characteristics.

Yours, Anne

392

b 203

Tuesday 10 August.
1943.

Dear Kitty,

New idea. I talk more to myself than to the others at mealtimes, which is to be recommended in two respects, firstly because everyone is happy if I don't prattle the whole time, and secondly, I needn't get annoyed about other people's opinions. I don't think my opinions are stupid and the others do; so it is better to keep them to myself. I do just the same if I have to eat something I simply can't stand: I put my plate in front of me, pretend that it is something delicious, look at it as little as I can and before I know where I am, it is gone.

When I get up in the morning, which is also a very unpleasant process, I jump out of bed thinking to myself: "You'll be back in a second," go to the window, take down the blackout, sniff at the crack of the window until I feel a bit of⁵ fresh air, and I'm awake. The bed is turned down as quickly as possible, and then the temptation is removed. Do

204 you know what Mummy calls | this sort of thing? The Art of Living. That's an odd expression. For the last week we've all been in a bit of a muddle about time, because our dear and beloved Westertoren-clock bell has apparently been taken away to the factory so that neither by day nor by night do we ever know the exact time. I still have some hope that they will think up a substitute (tin, copper or some such thing) so that the neighborhood gets reminded of the clock.

c

Tuesday, 10 August, 1943

Dear Kitty,

New idea. I talk more to myself than to the others at mealtimes, which is to be recommended for two reasons. Firstly, because everyone is happy if I don't chatter the whole time, and secondly, I needn't get annoyed about other people's opinions. I don't think my opinions are stupid and the others do; so it is better to keep them to myself. I do just the same if I have to eat something that I simply can't stand; I put my plate in front of me, pretend that it is something delicious, look at it as little as possible, and before I know where I am, it is gone. When I get up in the morning, also a very unpleasant process, I jump out of bed thinking to myself: "You'll be back in a second," go to the window, take down the blackout, sniff at the crack of the window until I feel a bit of fresh air, and I'm awake. The bed is turned down as quickly as possible and then the temptation is removed. Do you know what Mummy calls this sort of thing? "The Art of Living"—that's an odd expression. For the last week we've all been in a bit of a muddle about time, because our dear and beloved Westertoren clock bell has apparently been taken away for war purposes, so that neither by day nor night do we ever know the exact time. I still have some hope that they will think up a substitute (tin, copper or some such thing) to remind the neighborhood of the clock.

. . . . . .

[1]Whether I'm upstairs or down, or wherever I am, my feet are the admiration of all, glittering in a pair of (for these days!) exceptionally fine shoes. Miep managed to get hold of them for 27.50 florins. Wine-colored suede leather with fairly high wedge heels. I feel as if I'm on stilts and look much taller than I am. Yesterday was an unlucky day for me. I pricked my right thumb with the blunt end of a big needle. The upshot was that Margot | 205 had to peel the potatoes | for me (the silver lining and that my handwriting is clumsy.

Then I bumped my head against the cupboard door, almost fell over backwards, was given a dressing-down for all the noise I was making again, was not allowed to run water to bathe my forehead and am now going around with a giant lump over my right eye. On top of all that, the small toe of my right[6] foot caught in the pin of the vacuum cleaner It bled and was painful but I had so many other complaints that this pinprick was as nothing. [8]It's so stupid, because[9] now I'm walking about with an infected toe + [10] basilicon ointment + gauze + adhesive tape and can't put my glorious shoes on.

Pf. has endangered our lives for the umpteenth time. Miep actually brought bim a forbidden book, one which abuses Mussolini. On the way she happened to be run into | 206 by an S.S. motorcar. She lost her nerve, shouted: | Miserable wretches, and rode on. It is better not to think what might have happened if she had been forced to go to their headquarters.

yours, Anne

Whether I'm upstairs or down, or wherever I am, my feet are the admiration of all, glittering in a pair of (for these days) exceptionally fine shoes. Miep managed to get hold of them secondhand for 27.50 florins, wine-colored suede leather with fairly high wedge heels. I feel as if I'm on stilts and look much taller than I am.

Dussel has indirectly endangered our lives. He actually let Miep bring a forbidden book for him, one which abuses Mussolini and Hitler. On the way she happened to be run into by an S.S. car. She lost her temper, shouted, "Miserable wretches," and rode on. It is better not to think of what might have happened if she had had to go to their headquarters.

Yours, Anne

394

T 21

The communal duty of the day: Potato peeling![1]

One person fetches the newspapers, another the knives (keeping the best for himself of course) a third potatoes, and the fourth the water.

Pf. begins, does not always scrape well, but scrapes incessantly, glancing right and left "Does everyone do it the way he does? No! Enne, zee here; I take ze knife in mein hand like zo, scrape from ze top downvards! Nein, not like zat—like zis."

"I get on better like this, Mr. Pf.," I remark timidly.

"But still zis is ze best vay, du kannst take dies from me. Naturlich it does not matter to me, aber du should know for yourself." We scrape on. I look slyly once in my neighbor's direction. He shakes his head thoughtfully once more, (over me, I suppose) but is silent.

I scrape on again. Now I look to the other side, where Daddy is sitting; for him scraping potatoes is not just a little odd job, but a piece of precision work. When he reads,

| 22 | he has a deep wrinkle at the back of his head, but if he helps prepare potatoes, beans, or any other vegetables, then it seems as if nothing else penetrates. Then he has on his

---

c

Wednesday, 18 August, 1943

Dear Kitty,

The title for this piece is: "The communal task of the day: potato peeling!"

One person fetches the newspapers, another the knives (keeping the best for himself, of course), a third potatoes, and the fourth a pan of water.

Mr. Dussel begins, does not always scrape well, but scrapes incessantly, glancing right and left. Does everyone do it the way he does? No! "Anne, look here; I take the knife in my hand like this, scrape from the top downwards! No, not like that—like this!"

"I get on better like *this*, Mr. Dussel," I remark timidly.

"But still this is the best way. But *du kannst* take *dies* from me. Naturally I don't care a bit, *aber du* must know for yourself." We scrape on. I look slyly once in my neighbor's direction. He shakes his head thoughtfully once more (over me, I suppose) but is silent.

I scrape on again. Now I look to the other side, where Daddy is sitting; for him scraping potatoes is not just a little odd job, but a piece of precision work. When he reads, he has a deep wrinkle at the back of his head, but if he helps prepare potatoes, beans, or any other vegetables, then it seems as if nothing else penetrates. Then he has on his

395

T

"potato face," and he would never hand over an imperfectly scraped potato; it's out of the question when he makes that face.

I work on again and now just look up for a second, I know it already then, Mrs. v.P. is trying to attract Pf.'s attention. First she looks in his direction and Pf. appears not to notice anything, then she winks an eye, Pf. works on, then she laughs, Pf. doesn't look up, then Mummy laughs too, Pf. takes no notice. Mrs. v.P. has not achieved anything, so she has to manage something else. A pause and then: "Putti, do put on an apron, tomorrow I shall have to remove all the spots from your suit."

"I'm not getting myself dirty." Another moment's silence: "Putti, why don't you sit down?"

"I'm comfortable standing up and prefer it!" Pause:

"Putti, look, du spatst schon!"

"Yes, Mammy, I'm being careful!" Mrs. v.P. searches for another subject: "I say Putti, why aren't there any English air raids now?"

"Because the weather is bad Kerli!"

"But it was lovely yesterday, and they weren't flying then either."

C

"potato face," and he would never hand over an imperfectly scraped potato; it's out of the question when he makes that face!

I work on again and then just look up for a second; I know it already. Mrs. Van Daan is trying to attract Dussel's attention. First she looks in his direction and Dussel appears not to notice anything. Then she winks an eye; Dussel works on. Then she laughs, Dussel doesn't look up. Then Mummy laughs too; Dussel takes no notice. Mrs. Van Daan has not achieved anything, so she has to think of something else. A pause and then: "Putti, do put on an apron! Tomorrow I shall have to get all the spots out of your suit!"

"I'm not getting myself dirty!"

Another moment's silence.

"Putti, why don't you sit down?"

"I'm comfortable standing up and prefer it!" Pause.

"Putti, look, du spatst schon!" ("You are making a mess!")

"Yes, Mammy, I'm being careful."

Mrs. Van Daan searches for another subject. "I say, Putti, why aren't there any English air raids now?"

"Because the weather is bad, Kerli."

"But it was lovely yesterday, and they didn't fly then either."

396

T

"Let's not talk about it."

"Why, surely one can talk about it, or give one's opinion?"

"No!"

"Do be quiet, mammi'chen."

"Mr. Frank always answers his wife, doesn't he." Mr. v.P. wrestles with himself. This is his tender spot, it's something he can't take, and Mrs. v.P. begins again:

"The invasion seems as if it will never come!" Mr. v.P. goes white; when Mrs. v.P. sees that, she turns red, but goes on again: "The British do nothing!" The bomb explodes!

"And now hold your tongue, donnerwetternogeinmal!" Mummy can hardly hold back her laughter. I look straight in front of me.

This sort of thing happens nearly every day, at least if they haven't just had a very bad quarrel, because then | they both keep their mouths shut.

| 23

I have to fetch some potatoes. Go up to the attic, where Peter is busy delousing the cat. He looks up, the cat notices—pop—he has disappeared through the open window into the gutter.

Peter swears. I laugh and disappear.

C

"Let's not talk about it."

"Why, surely one can talk about it, or give one's opinion?"

"No."

"Why ever not?"

"Do be quiet, mammi'chen."

"Mr. Frank always answers his wife, doesn't he?"

Mr. Van Daan wrestles with himself. This is his tender spot, it's something he can't take and Mrs. Van Daan begins again: "The invasion seems as if it will never come!"

Mr. Van Daan goes white; when Mrs. Van Daan sees this, she turns red, but goes on again: "The British do nothing!" The bomb explodes!

"And now hold your tongue, donnerwetter-noch-einmal!"

Mummy can hardly hold back her laughter. I look straight in front of me.

This sort of thing happens nearly every day, unless they have just had a very bad quarrel, because then they both keep their mouths shut.

I have to go up to the attic to fetch some potatoes. Peter is busy there delousing the cat. He looks up, the cat notices—pop—he has disappeared through the open window into the gutter. Peter swears. I laugh and disappear.

Yours, Anne

397

263 Prinsengracht (Anne Frank Foundation.)

23   Freedom in the "Secret Annexe."[1]

half past 5. Bep comes, in order to give us our evening freedom. Immediately we begin to make some headway with our work. First, I just go upstairs with Bep, where she usually begins by having a bite in advance from our second course.

Before Bep is seated Mrs. v.P. begins thinking of things she wants. It soon comes out: "Oh, Bep, I have just one more little wish. . . . ." Bep winks at me; whoever it is that comes upstairs, Mrs. v.P. never misses a single opportunity of letting them know what she wants. It must be one of the reasons why they all dislike coming upstairs.

Bep departs. I go two floors down to have a look around. First to the kitchen then to the private office, after that the coalhole, to open the trap door for Mouschi.

After a long tour of inspection I land up in Kugler's room.

V.P. is looking in all the drawers and portfolios to find the day's post; Peter is fetching the warehouse key and Boche; Pim is hauling the typewriters upstairs; Margot is looking for a quiet spot to do her office work; Mrs. v.P. puts a kettle on the gas ring; Mummy is coming downstairs with a pan of potatoes; each one knows his own job.

C

Friday, 20 August, 1943

Dear Kitty,

The men in the warehouse go home sharp at half past five and then we are free.

Half past five. Elli comes to give us our evening freedom. Immediately we begin to make some headway with our work. First, I go upstairs with Elli, where she usually begins by having a bite from our second course.

Before Elli is seated, Mrs. Van Daan begins thinking of things she wants. It soon comes out: "Oh, Elli, I have only one little wish. . . ." Elli winks at me; whoever comes upstairs, Mrs. Van Daan never misses a single opportunity of letting them know what she wants. That must be one of the reasons why none of them like coming upstairs.

Quarter to six. Elli departs. I go two floors down to have a look around. First to the kitchen, then to the private office, after that the coalhole, to open the trap door for Mouschi. After a long tour of inspection I land up in Kraler's room. Van Daan is looking in all the drawers and portfolios to find the day's post. Peter is fetching the warehouse key and Boche; Pim is hauling the typewriters upstairs; Margot is looking for a quiet spot to do her office work; Mrs. Van Daan puts a kettle on the gas ring; Mummy is coming downstairs with a pan of potatoes; each one knows his own job.

Peter soon returns again from the warehouse. The first question is—bread: has it been forgotten. He crouches before the front office door to make himself as small as possible and crawls towards the steel lockers on all fours, gets the bread and disappears; at least wants to disappear, since before he quite realizes what has happened, Mouschi has jumped over him and gone and sat right under the writing table.

Piet looks all around—aha, he sees him there, he crawls into the office again and | 24 pulls the animal by | its tail.

Mouschi spits, Piet sighs. What has he achieved? Now Mouschi is sitting right up by the window cleaning himself, very pleased to have escaped Piet. Now Piet is holding a packet of bread under the cat's nose as a last decoy. And yes he follows and the door closes. I stood and watched it all through the crack of the door.

Mr. v.P. is cross and slams the door. Margot and I look at each other and think the same thing: "He must have lost his temper again about some stupid thing or other Kugler has done and has forgotten all about Keg.

Then we hear a step in the passage. Pf. comes in, goes to the window with a proprietorial air, sniffs. . . . . coughs, sneezes and chokes, it was pepper, bad luck. Off he goes on his way to the office. The curtains are open, that means no letter paper. He disappears with a scowl.

Margot and I look at each other again: "One page less to his sweetheart tomorrow," I hear her say, and I nod in agreement.

We continue our work. Hear once again an elephant-step on the stairs; Pf. is seeking solace in his indispensable little place.

We work on. Rat, tat, tat. Three taps means a meal!

Peter soon returns from the warehouse. The first question is—bread. This is always put in the kitchen cupboard by the Ladies; but it is not there. Forgotten? Peter offers to look in the main office. He crouches in front of the door to make himself as small as possible and crawls towards the steel lockers on hands and knees, so as not to be seen from outside, gets the bread, which had been put there, and disappears; at least, he wants to disappear, but before he quite realizes what has happened, Mouschi has jumped over him and gone and sat right under the writing table.

Peter looks all around—aha, he sees him there, he crawls into the office again and pulls the animal by its tail. Mouschi spits, Peter sighs. What has he achieved? Now Mouschi is sitting right up by the window cleaning himself, very pleased to have escaped Peter. Now Peter is holding a piece of bread under the cat's nose as a last decoy. Mouschi will not be tempted and the door closes [And yes, Mouschi is tempted and the door closes]. I stood and watched it all through the crack of the door. We work on. Rat, tat, tat. Three taps means a meal!

Yours, Anne

As the clock strikes half past eight . . . . .*[1]

Margot and Mummy are jittery: "Sh. . . Daddy, quiet, Otto, sh. . . Pim." "It is half past 8. Come back here, you can't run any more water; walk quietly!" These are the various cries to Daddy in the bathroom. As the clock strikes half past 8, he has to be in the living room. Not a drop of water, no lavatory, no walking about, everything quiet. Until the office people arrive downstairs, everything can be heard in the warehouse.

The door is opened upstairs at twenty minutes past 8 and shortly after there are three taps on the floor . . . . Anne's porridge. I climb upstairs and fetch my "puppy-dog" plate. Down again, everything goes at terrific speed: do my hair, put away my noisy tin pottie, bed in place. Hush! The clock strikes! Upstairs Mrs. v.P. has changed her shoes and is shuffling about in bedroom slippers. Mr. . . . . .Charlie Chaplin, too, all is quiet.

*This phrase is in slightly incorrect German in the original. A.J.P.

c

Monday, 23 August, 1943

Dear Kitty,

Continuation of the "Secret Annexe" daily timetable. As the clock strikes half past eight in the morning, Margot and Mummy are jittery: "Ssh . . . Daddy, quiet, Otto, ssh . . . Pim." "It is half past eight, come back here, you can't run any more water; walk quietly!" These are the various cries to Daddy in the bathroom. As the clock strikes half past eight, he has to be in the living room. Not a drop of water, no lavatory, no walking about, everything quiet. As long as none of the office staff are there, everything can be heard in the warehouse. The door is opened upstairs at twenty minutes past eight and shortly after there are three taps on the floor: Anne's porridge. I climb upstairs and fetch my "puppy-dog" plate. Down in my room again, everything goes at terrific speed: do my hair, put away my noisy tin pottie, bed in place. Hush, the clock strikes! Upstairs Mrs. Van Daan has changed her shoes and is shuffling about in bedroom slippers. Mr. Van Daan, too; all is quiet.

Now we have a little bit of real family life. | I want to read or work, Margot as well, also Daddy and Mummy. Daddy is sitting (with Dickens and the dictionary, naturally) on the edge of the sagging, squeaky bed, where there aren't even any decent mattresses: two bolsters on top of each other will also serve the purpose, then he thinks: "don't have to have them, I'll manage without!"

Once he is reading, he doesn't look up, or about him, laughs every now and then, takes awful trouble to get Mummy interested in a little story: "I haven't got time now!" Looks disappointed for just a second, then reads on again; a little later, when he comes to something extra amusing, he tries it again: "You must read this, Mummy!" Mummy sits on the "Opklap" bed, reads, sews, knits, or works, whatever she feels like. She suddenly thinks of something. Just says it quickly: "Anne, do you know . . . , Margot, just jot down . . . . After a while peace returns once more.

Margot closes the book with a clap. Daddy raises his eyebrows into a funny curve, his reading wrinkle deepens again, and he is lost in his book once more; Mummy begins to chatter with Margot, I become curious and listen too. Pim is drawn into the discussion . . .

Nine o'clock! Breakfast!

c

Now we have a little bit of real family life. I want to read or work, Margot as well, also Daddy and Mummy. Daddy is sitting (with Dickens and the dictionary, naturally) on the edge of the sagging, squeaky bed, where there aren't even any decent mattresses: two bolsters on top of each other will also serve the purpose, then he thinks: "Mustn't have them, then I'll manage without!"

Once he is reading he doesn't look up, or about him, laughs every now and then, takes awful trouble to get Mummy interested in a little story. Answer: "I haven't got time now." Looks disappointed for just a second, then reads on again; a little later, when he comes to something extra amusing, he tries it again: "You must read this, Mummy!" Mummy sits on the "Opklap"* bed, reads, sews, knits, or works, whatever she feels like. She suddenly thinks of something. Just says it quickly: "Anne, do you know . . . Margot, just jot down . . . !" After a while peace returns once more.

Margot closes her book with a clap. Daddy raises his eyebrows into a funny curve, his reading wrinkle deepens again, and he is lost in his book once more; Mummy begins to chatter with Margot, I become curious and listen too! Pim is drawn into the discussion . . . nine o'clock! Breakfast!

Yours, Anne

---

*Dutch type of bed, which folds against the wall to look like a bookcase with curtains hanging before it.

. . . . . .

Friday 10 Septem-
ber 1943.

Dear Kitty,

Every time I write to you something special seems to have happened, but they are more often unpleasant than pleasant things. However, now there is something wonderful going on:

Last Wednesday evening, 8 Sept., we sat around listening to the 7 o'clock news and the first thing we heard was as follows: Here follows the best news from whole the war: Italy has capitulered.* Italy's unconditional surrender! The Dutch program from England began at quarter past 8. "Listeners, one and a quarter hours ago I had just finished writing the chronicle of the day when the wonderful news of Italy's capitulation came in, I can tell you that I have never deposited my notes in the wastepaper basket with such joy!

"God save the King," the American national anthem and the Russian "Internationale" were played. As always, the Dutch program was uplifting, but not too optimistic.

---

*This message is in Anne's English. A.J.P.

Friday, 10 September, 1943

Dear Kitty,

Every time I write to you something special seems to have happened, but they are more often unpleasant than pleasant things. However, now there is something wonderful going on. Last Wednesday evening, 8 September, we sat around listening to the seven o'clock news and the first thing we heard was: "Here follows the best news of the whole war. Italy has capitulated!" Italy's unconditional surrender! The Dutch program from England began at quarter past eight. "Listeners, an hour ago, I had just finished writing the chronicle of the day when the wonderful news of Italy's capitulation came in. I can tell you that I have never deposited my notes in the wastepaper basket with such joy!" "God Save the King," the American national anthem, and the "Internationale" were played. As always, the Dutch program was uplifting, but not too optimistic.

The English have landed in Naples. Northern Italy has been occupied by the Germans. On Friday 3 September the truce had already been signed, the very day the English landed in Italy. The Germans rant and rave in all the newspapers about the treachery of Badoglio and the Italian emperor.

Still, we have troubles, too; it's about Mr. Kleiman. As you know, we are all very fond of him, he is always cheerful and amazingly brave, although he is never well, has a lot of pain, and is not allowed to eat much or do much walking. "When Mr. Kleiman enters, the sun begins to shine!" Mummy said only recently, and she is quite right. Now he has had to go into the hospital for a very unpleasant abdominal operation and will have to stay there for at least 4 weeks. You really ought to have seen how he said good-by to us just as usual—he might have simply been going out to do a bit of shopping

yours, Anne

c   Still we have troubles, too; it's about Mr. Koophuis. As you know, we are all very fond of him, he is always cheerful and amazingly brave, although he is never well, has a lot of pain, and is not allowed to eat much or do much walking. "When Mr. Koophuis enters, the sun begins to shine," Mummy said just recently, and she is quite right. Now he has had to go into the hospital for a very unpleasant abdominal operation and will have to stay there for at least four weeks. You really ought to have seen how he said good-by to us just as usual—he might have simply been going out to do a bit of shopping.

Yours, Anne

. . . . . .

Thursday 16 Sept. 1943.

Dear Kitty,

Relations between us here are getting worse all the time. Pf. and v.P. firm friends [1]until the next row. At mealtimes, no one dares to open their mouths, (except to allow a mouthful of food to slip in) because whatever is said you either annoy someone or it is misunderstood. Mr. Voskuyl comes to visit us now and then. What a pity that he is so ill. He doesn't make it easier for his family either, because he walks about all the time thinking: What difference can it make to me, I'm going to die anyway! I can well imagine the mood in Voskuyl's house when I think how touchy they all are even here.

[3]I swallow valerian pills every day against worry and depression, but it doesn't prevent me from being even more miserable the next day.

210   A good hearty laugh would help more than 10 Valerian pills, but we've almost forgotten how to laugh.[6] I feel afraid sometimes that from having to be so serious I'll grow a long face and my mouth will droop at the corners. The others don't get any better either, everyone looks with fear and misgivings towards that great terror, winter. Another thing which doesn't cheer us up is that the warehouseman, v. Maaren, is becoming suspicious about the Annexe. Of course anyone with any brains at all must have noticed that Miep keeps saying she's off to the laboratory, Bep to look at the records, Kleiman to the Opekta storeroom, while Kugler makes out that the "Secret Annexe" is not part of our premises but belongs to the neighbor's building.

We really wouldn't mind what Mr. v. Maaren thought of the situation if he wasn't

| 211   known to be so unreliable and if he wasn't so exceptionally inquisitive, so difficult | to fob off.

Thursday, 16 September, 1943

Dear Kitty,

Relations between us here are getting worse all the time. At mealtimes, no one dares to open their mouths (except to allow a mouthful of food to slip in) because whatever is said you either annoy someone or it is misunderstood. I swallow Valerian pills every day against worry and depression, but it doesn't prevent me from being even more miserable the next day. A good hearty laugh would help more than ten Valerian pills, but we've almost forgotten how to laugh. I feel afraid sometimes that from having to be so serious I'll grow a long face and my mouth will droop at the corners. The others don't get any better either, everyone looks with fear and misgivings towards that great terror, winter. Another thing that does not cheer us up is the fact that the warehouseman, V M., is becoming suspicious about the "Secret Annexe." We really wouldn't mind what V.M. thought of the situation if he wasn't so exceptionally inquisitive, difficult to fob off, and, moreover, not to be trusted.

......

b

      One day Kugler wanted to be extra careful, put on his coat at 20 minutes past 12, and went to the chemist round the corner. He was back in less than 5 minutes, and sneaked like a thief round the stairs leading straight to us. At a quarter past one he wanted to go again, but met Bep on the landing, who warned him that v. Maaren was in the office. He did a right-about turn and sat with us until half past 1. Then he took off his shoes and went in stockinged feet (despite his cold) to the front attic door, went downstairs step by step, and, after balancing there for a quarter of an hour to avert any creaks, he landed safely in the office, having entered from the outside. Bep had been freed of van Maaren in the meantime and came up to us to fetch Kugler, but Kugler had already been gone a long time; he was meanwhile still on the staircase with his shoes off. Whatever | 212   would the people in the street have | thought if they had seen the Manager putting on his shoes outside? Gosh! the Manager in his socks!

yours, Anne

c

      One day Kraler wanted to be extra careful, put on his coat at ten minutes to one, and went to the chemist round the corner. He was back in less than five minutes, and sneaked like a thief up the steep stairs that lead straight to us. At a quarter past one he wanted to go again, but Elli came to warn him that V.M. was in the office. He did a right-about turn and sat with us until half past one. Then he took off his shoes and went in stockinged feet to the front attic door, went downstairs step by step, and, after balancing there for a quarter of an hour to avoid creaking, he landed safely in the office, having entered from the outside. Elli had been freed of V.M. in the meantime, and came up to us to fetch Kraler, but he had already been gone a long time; he was still on the staircase with his shoes off. Whatever would the people in the street have thought if they had seen the Manager putting on his shoes outside? Gosh! the Manager in his socks!

Yours, Anne

406

Sunday 17 Oct. 1943.

Dear Kitty,

Kleiman is back again, thank goodness! He still looks rather pale, but in spite of this sets out cheerfully to sell clothes for v.P.

¹It is an unpleasant fact that the v.P.s have run right out of money, he lost his last 100 florins in the warehouse, and that gave us a lot of worry. How can 100 florins just disappear on a Monday morning in the warehouse? All sorts of suspicions. In the meantime the 100 florins have been stolen. Who is the thief?

But I was talking about their lack of money. Mrs. v.P. won't part with a thing from her pile of coats, dresses, and shoes. Mr. v.P.'s suit isn't easily disposed of, Peter's bicycle is back from the inspection. No one wanted to have it. The end of the story is not yet in sight. Mrs. v.P. will certainly have to part with her fur coat. Her idea that the business | 214 must provide for us is | absurd. They've had a terrific row upstairs about it, and now the reconciliation period of "Oh darling Putti" and "precious Kerli" has set in.

I am dazed by all the abusive exchanges that have hurtled through this virtuous house during the past month. Daddy goes about with his lips tightly pursed, when anyone speaks to him, he looks up startled, as if he is afraid he will have to patch up some tricky relationship again. Mummy has red patches on her cheeks from excitement, Margot complains of headaches. Pf. can't sleep. Mrs. v.P. grouses the whole day and I'm going round the bend! Quite honestly, I sometimes forget who we are quarreling with and with whom we've made it up.

The only way to take one's mind off it all is to study, and I do a lot of that.

yours, Anne

Wednesday 29
September 1943.

Dear Kitty,

It is Mrs. v.P.'s birthday. We gave her a pot of jam, besides coupons for cheese, meat and bread. From her husband, Pf., and the office she got things to eat and flowers. Such are the times we live in! Bep had a fit of nerves this week; she's being sent out so often, 10 x a day she has to do shopping, and she is forever being asked to fetch this and that, which means yet another errand and makes her feel that she has done something wrong! If you just think that she still has to finish her office work downstairs, that Kleiman is ill, Miep staying at home with a cold, and that she herself has a sprained ankle, love worries, and a grumbling father at home, then it's no wonder she's at her wits' end. We comforted her and said that if she puts her foot down once or twice and says she has no time, then the shopping lists will automatically get shorter.

On Saturday there was a big drama here, which exceeded in fury any that has gone before. It all started with v. Maaren and it ended in a free-for-all with sobs.⁶ Pf. complained to Mummy that he is being treated like an outcast, that none of us are friendly towards him, that after all he has done none of us any harm and a whole series of sugary blandishments that Mummy luckily didn't fall for this time telling him that he has let us all down badly and that he has given us cause for complaint more than once. Pf. promised her the moon, which hasn't come to anything yet, as usual.

⁸There is something wrong with Mr. v.P., I can see it coming on already! Daddy is angry because they're cheating us; they're⁹ keeping back meat and suchlike. Oh, what kind of explosion is hanging over us now? If only I wasn't mixed up so much with all these rows! If only I could get away! They'll drive us crazy before long!

yours, Anne

Wednesday, 29 September, 1943

Dear Kitty,

It is Mrs. Van Daan's birthday. We gave her a pot of jam, as well as coupons for cheese, meat, and bread. From her husband, Dussel, and our protectors she received things to eat and flowers. Such are the times we live in!

Elli had a fit of nerves this week; she had been sent out so often; time and again she had been asked to go and fetch something quickly, which meant yet another errand or made her feel that she had done something wrong. If you just think that she still has to finish her office work downstairs, that Koophuis is ill, Miep at home with a cold, and that she herself has a sprained ankle, love worries, and a grumbling father, then it's no wonder she's at her wit's [wits'] end. We comforted her and said that if she puts her foot down once or twice and says she has no time, then the shopping lists will automatically get shorter.

There is something wrong with Mr. Van Daan again, I can see it coming on already! Daddy is very angry for some reason or other. Oh, what kind of explosion is hanging over us now? If only I wasn't mixed up so much with all these rows! If I could only get away! They'll drive us crazy before long!

Yours, Anne

a

. . . . . .

b   213

Sunday 17 Oct. 1943.

Dear Kitty,
Kleiman is back again, thank goodness! He still looks rather pale, but in spite of this sets out cheerfully to sell clothes for v.P.

It is an unpleasant fact that the v.P.s have run right out of money, he lost his last 100 florins in the warehouse, and that gave us a lot of worry. How can 100 florins just disappear on a Monday morning in the warehouse? All sorts of suspicions. In the meantime the 100 florins have been stolen. Who is the thief?

But I was talking about their lack of money. Mrs. v.P. won't part with a thing from her pile of coats, dresses and shoes. Mr. v.P.'s suit isn't easily disposed of, Peter's bicycle is back from the inspection. No one wanted to have it. The end of the story is not yet in sight. Mrs. v.P. will certainly have to part with her fur coat.

214   Her idea that the business must provide for us is | absurd. They've had a terrific row upstairs about it, and now the reconciliation period of "Oh darling Putti" and "precious Kerli" has set in.

I am dazed by all the abusive exchanges that have hurtled through this virtuous house during the past month. Daddy goes about with his lips tightly pursed, when anyone speaks to him, he looks up startled, as if he is afraid he will have to patch up some tricky relationship again. Mummy has red patches on her cheeks from excitement, Margot complains of headaches. Pf. can't sleep. Mrs. v.P. grouses the whole day and I'm going round the bend! Quite honestly, I sometimes forget who we are quarreling with and with whom we've made it up.

The only way to take one's mind off it all is to study, and I do a lot of that
yours, Anne

c

Sunday, 17 October, 1943

Dear Kitty,
Koophuis is back again, thank goodness! He still looks rather pale, but in spite of this sets out cheerfully to sell clothes for Van Daan. It is an unpleasant fact that the Van Daans have run right out of money. Mrs. Van Daan won't part with a thing from her pile of coats, dresses, and shoes. Mr. Van Daan's suit isn't easily disposed of, because he wants too much for it. The end of the story is not yet in sight. Mrs. Van Daan will certainly have to part with her fur coat. They've had a terrific row upstairs about it, and now the reconciliation period of "oh, darling Putti" and "precious Kerli" has set in.

I am dazed by all the abusive exchanges that have taken place in this virtuous house during the past month. Daddy goes about with his lips tightly pursed; when anyone speaks to him, he looks up startled, as if he is afraid he will have to patch up some tricky relationship again. Mummy has red patches on her cheeks from excitement. Margot complains of headaches. Dussel can't sleep. Mrs. Van Daan grouses the whole day and I'm going completely crazy! Quite honestly, I sometimes forget who we are quarreling with and with whom we've made it up.

The only way to take one's mind off it all is to study, and I do a lot of that.
Yours, Anne

409

. . . . . .

Friday 29 Oct. 1943.

Dearest Kitty,

Mr. Kleiman is away again: his stomach gives him no peace. He doesn't even know whether it has stopped bleeding yet. For the first time, he was properly down when he told us that he didn't feel well and was going home.

There have been resounding rows again between Mr. and Mrs. v.P. It came about like this: the v.P.s are at the end of their money. They wanted to sell a winter coat and a suit of Mr. v.P.'s, but no one could be found for them. He wants too much for it.

One day, some time ago now, Kleiman spoke about a furrier with whom he was on good terms; this gave v.P. the idea of selling his wife's fur coat. It's a fur coat made from rabbit skins, and she has worn it 17 years. Mrs. v.P. got 325 florins for it. That sum is enormous. However, Mrs. v.P. wanted to keep the money to buy new clothes after the

| 218   war, and it took some doing before Mr. v.P. made it clear to her | that the money was urgently needed for the household.

The yells and screams, stamping and abuse—you can't possibly imagine it! It was frightening. My family stood at the bottom of the stairs holding their breath, ready if necessary to drag them apart!

All this quarreling and weeping and nervous tension are so unsettling that in the evening I drop into my bed crying, thanking heaven that I sometimes have half an hour to myself.

Friday, 29 October, 1943

Dear Kitty,

There have been resounding rows again between Mr. and Mrs. Van Daan. It came about like this: as I have already told you, the Van Daans are at the end of their money. One day, some time ago now, Koophuis spoke about a furrier with whom he was on good terms; this gave Van Daan the idea of selling his wife's fur coat. It's a fur coat made from rabbit skins, and she has worn it seventeen years. He got 325 florins for it—an enormous sum. However, Mrs. Van Daan wanted to keep the money to buy new clothes after the war, and it took some doing before Mr. Van Daan made it clear to her that the money was urgently needed for the household.

The yells and screams, stamping and abuse—you can't possibly imagine it! It was frightening. My family stood at the bottom of the stairs, holding their breath, ready if necessary to drag them apart! All this shouting and weeping and nervous tension are so unsettling and such a strain, that in the evening I drop into my bed crying, thanking heaven that I sometimes have half an hour to myself.

Mr. Koophuis is away again; his stomach gives him no peace. He doesn't even know whether it has stopped bleeding yet. For the first time, he was very down when he told us that he didn't feel well and was going home.

a . . . . . .

b

All goes well with me, except that I have no appetite. I keep being told: "You don't look at all well." I must say that they are doing their very best to keep me up to the mark. Grape sugar, cod-liver oil, yeast tablets and calcium have all been lined up. My nerves often get the better of me: it is especially on Sundays that I feel rotten. The atmosphere is so oppressive, and sleepy and as heavy as lead; you don't hear a single bird singing | 219 outside, and a deadly sultry silence hangs everywhere, | catching hold of me as if it would drag me down deep into an underworld. At such times Daddy, Mummy, and Margot leave me cold. I wander from one room to another, downstairs and up again, feeling like a songbird who has had his wings clipped and who is hurling himself in utter darkness against the bars of his cage. "Go outside, laugh, and take a breath of fresh air," a voice cries within me; but I don't even feel a response any more; I go and lie on the divan and sleep, to make the time pass more quickly, and the stillness and the terrible fear, because there is no way of killing time.

yours, Anne

c

All goes well with me on the whole, except that I have no appetite. I keep being told: "You don't look at all well." I must say that they are doing their very best to keep me up to the mark. Grape sugar, cod-liver oil, yeast tablets, and calcium have all been lined up.

My nerves often get the better of me; it is especially on Sundays that I feel rotten. The atmosphere is so oppressive, and sleepy and as heavy as lead. You don't hear a single bird singing outside, and a deadly close silence hangs everywhere, catching hold of me as if it will drag me down deep into an underworld.

At such times Daddy, Mummy, and Margot leave me cold. I wander from one room to another, downstairs and up again, feeling like a songbird whose wings have been clipped and who is hurling himself in utter darkness against the bars of his cage. "Go outside, laugh, and take a breath of fresh air," a voice cries within me, but I don't even feel a response any more; I go and lie on the divan and sleep, to make the time pass more quickly, and the stillness and the terrible fear, because there is no way of killing them.

Yours, Anne

411

. . . . . .

Wednesday 3 Nov. 1943.

Dear Kitty,

In order to give us something to do, which is also educational, Daddy applied for a prospectus from the teachers' institutes in Leiden. Margot nosed through the thick booklet at least 3 times without finding anything to her liking or to suit her purse. Daddy was quicker, and wants a letter written to the Institute asking for a trial lesson in "Elementary Latin." No sooner said than done, the lesson came, Margot set to work enthusiastically, and the course, expensive though it was, was sent for. It is much too hard for me, although I would very much like to learn Latin.

To give me something new to begin as well, Daddy asked Kleiman for a children's Bible so that I could find out something about the New Testament at last. "Do you want to give Anne a Bible for Chanuka?" asked Margot, somewhat perturbed. "Yes—er, I think St. Nicholas Day is a better occasion," answered Daddy.

221   Jesus just doesn't go with Chanuka.

Wednesday, 3 November, 1943

Dear Kitty,

In order to give us something to do, which is also educational, Daddy applied for a prospectus from the Teachers' Institute in Leiden. Margot nosed through the thick book at least three times without finding anything to her liking or to suit her purse. Daddy was quicker, and wants a letter written to the Institute asking for a trial lesson in "Elementary Latin." [No sooner said than done, the lesson came, Margot set to work enthusiastically, and the course, expensive though it was, was sent for. It is much too hard for me, although I would very much like to learn Latin.]

To give me something new to begin as well, Daddy asked Koophuis for a children's Bible so that I could find out something about the New Testament at last. "Do you want to give Anne a Bible for Chanuka?" asked Margot, somewhat perturbed. "Yes—er, I think St. Nicholas Day is a better occasion," answered Daddy; "Jesus just doesn't go with Chanuka."*

Yours, Anne

*See entry for 7 December, 1942.

a . . . . . .

b

The vacuum cleaner is broken, so I now have to brush the carpet every evening with an old sweeper. Blackout, switch on the light, light the stove and then brush the floor. "No good will come of this," I thought to myself the first time. There were bound to be complaints and actually Mummy did get a headache from the thick clouds of dust that hung whirling about in the room, Margot's new Latin dictionary was covered with dirt and Pim grumbled that the floor didn't look any different anyway. Small thanks for my pains.

The latest arrangement in the "Secret Annexe" is that the stove will be lit at half past 7 instead of half past 5 on Sunday mornings. I think it's a risky business. [5]What will the neighbors think of our[6] smoking chimney?

| 222 Just like the curtains; ever since we started hiding they've been pinned tightly up, | sometimes on an irresistible whim one of the gentlemen or ladies decides to take a look outside. Consequence: a storm of reproaches. Reply: "But no one can see." That's how every careless act begins and ends. "No one can see, no one can hear, no one pays any attention," is easily said, but is it the real truth? At the moment the storm of rows has abated, Pf. is the only one still to be quarreling with the v.P.s. [8]When he talks about Mrs. v.P., all you hear him say is: that stupid cow, or "that old heifer," and conversely Mrs. v.P. refers to our ever so learned gentleman as "that old maid," that everlastingly touchy old spinster etc. etc.

It's the pot calling the kettle black!

yours, Anne.

223

Thursday 11 Nov. 1943.

Dear Kitty,

I have a good title for this chapter:

Ode to my fountain pen
In memoriam
"From Margot's schola Latina."

My fountain pen has always been one of my most priceless possessions; I value it highly, especially for its thick nib, for I can only really write neatly with a thick nib. My fountain pen has had a very long and interesting pen-life, which I will briefly tell you about:

When I was nine, my fountain pen arrived in a packet (wrapped in cotton wool)[13] as "sample without value" all the way from Aachen, where my Grandmother, the kind donor, used to live. I was in bed with flu, while February winds howled round the house. The glorious fountain pen had a red leather case and was at once shown around to all my friends on the first day. I, Anne Frank, the proud owner of a fountain pen!

c . . . . . .

b   224   When I was ten the pen was allowed to go to school with me and the mistress went so far as to permit me to write with it. When I was eleven, however, my treasure had to be put away again,[1] because the mistress in the 6th form only allowed us to use school pens and inkpots. When I was twelve and went to the Jewish Lyceum, my fountain pen received a new case in honor of the great occasion; it could take a pencil as well, and as it closed with a zipper looked much more impressive. At thirteen the fountain pen came with us to the "Secret Annexe" where it has raced through countless diaries and compositions for me. Now I am fourteen, we have spent our last year together. · · · · · ·

——

It was on Friday afternoon after 5 o'clock. I had come out of my room and wanted to go and sit at the table to write, when I was roughly pushed on one side and had to make room for Margot and Daddy, who wanted to practice their "Latin." The fountain pen

| 225   remained on the table unused while, with a sigh, its owner con- | tented herself with a tiny little corner of the table and started rubbing beans. Bean rubbing is making moldy beans decent again. I swept the floor at a quarter to 6 and threw the dirt, together with the bad beans, into a newspaper and into the stove. A terrific flame leaped out and I thought it was grand that the fire should burn up so well when it was practically out.

All was quiet again, the "Latinites" had finished, and I went and sat at the table to continue my writing as planned,[6] but look as I might, my fountain pen was nowhere to be seen. I looked again, Margot looked, Mummy looked, Daddy looked, Pf. looked, but there was not a trace of the thing. "Perhaps it fell into the stove together with the beans!" Margot suggested. "Oh no, of course not!" I answered. When my fountain pen didn't

| 226   turn up that evening, however, we all took it that it had been burned, | all the more as celluloid is terribly[7] inflammable. And so it was, our unhappy fears were confirmed when Daddy did the stove the following morning the clip used for fastening was found among the ashes. Not a trace of the gold nib was found. "Must have melted and stuck to some stone or other," Daddy thought.

I have one consolation, although a slender one, my fountain pen has been cremated, just what I want later!

> *The clip is left.*
> *(The pen is gone)*
> *I feel bereft*
> *And put upon*
> yours, Anne.

414

· · · · · ·

Monday evening 8 November 1943.

Dear Kitty,

If you could read my pile of letters one after another,[1] you would certainly be struck by the many different moods in which these are written. It annoys me that I am so dependent on the atmosphere here, but certainly I'm not the only one—we all find it the same. If I read a book that impresses me I have to take myself firmly in hand before I mix with other people; otherwise they would think my mind rather queer. At the moment, as you've probably noticed I'm going through a spell of being depressed.

I really couldn't tell you why it is, but I believe it's just because I'm a coward, and that's what I keep bumping up against.

This evening while Bep was still here, there was a long, loud penetrating ring at the door, I turned white at once, got a tummy-ache and | heart palpitations, all from being scared!

| 228

At night, when I'm in bed, I see myself alone in a dungeon, without Mummy and Daddy. Sometimes I wander by the roadside, or our "Secret Annexe" is on fire, or they come and take us away at night and I go and lie down under my bed in despair. I see everything as if it is actually taking place and then still have the feeling that it could all happen to you very soon!

Monday evening, 8 November, 1943

Dear Kitty,

If you were to read my pile of letters one after another, you would certainly be struck by the many different moods in which they are written. It annoys me that I am so dependent on the atmosphere here, but I'm certainly not the only one—we all find it the same. If I read a book that impresses me, I have to take myself firmly in hand, before I mix with other people; otherwise they would think my mind rather queer. At the moment, as you've probably noticed, I'm going through a spell of being depressed. I really couldn't tell you why it is, but I believe it's just because I'm a coward, and that's what I keep bumping up against.

This evening, while Elli was still here, there was a long, loud, penetrating ring at the door. I turned white at once, got a tummy-ache and heart palpitations, all from fear. At night, when I'm in bed, I see myself alone in a dungeon, without Mummy and Daddy. Sometimes I wander by the roadside, or our "Secret Annexe" is on fire, or they come and take us away at night. I see everything as if it is actually taking place, and this gives me the feeling that it may all happen to me very soon!

a

. . . . . .

b

Miep often says she envies us for possessing such tranquillity here. That may be true, but she is not thinking of our fears.

I simply can't imagine that the world will ever be normal for us again. I do talk about: "After the war," but then it is only a castle in the air, something that will never really happen.

| 229 If I think back to the Merry,* my girl friends, school, fun, it is just as if another person lived it all, not me. I see the 8 of us with our "Secret An- | nexe" as if we were[3] a little piece of blue heaven, surrounded by black, black rain clouds. The round, clearly defined spot where we stand is still safe but the clouds gather more closely about us and the circle which separates us from the approaching dangers closes more and more tightly.

Now we are so surrounded by danger and darkness that we bump against each other as we search desperately for a means of escape.[7]

We all look down below, where [8]people are fighting each other, we look above, where it is quiet and beautiful, and meanwhile we are cut off by the great[9] dark mass, which will not[10] let us go either down or up, but which stands before us as an impenetrable wall; it tries to crush us but cannot do so yet.

I can only cry and implore: "Oh, if only the black circle could recede and open the way for us!"

yours, Anne

*Probably the Merwedeplein in Amsterdam. A.J.P.

c

Miep often says she envies us for possessing such tranquillity here. That may be true, but she is not thinking about all our fears. I simply can't imagine that the world will ever be normal for us again. I do talk about "after the war," but then it is only a castle in the air, something that will never really happen. If I think back to our old house, my girl friends, the fun at school, it is just as if another person lived it all, not me.

I see the eight of us with our "Secret Annexe" as if we were a little piece of blue heaven, surrounded by heavy black rain clouds. The round, clearly defined spot where we stand is still safe, but the clouds gather more closely about us and the circle which separates us from the approaching danger closes more and more tightly. Now we are so surrounded by danger and darkness that we bump against each other, as we search desperately for a means of escape. We all look down below, where people are fighting each other, we look above, where it is quiet and beautiful, and meanwhile we are cut off by the great dark mass, which will not let us go upwards, but which stands before us as an impenetrable wall; it tries to crush us, but cannot do so yet. I can only cry and implore: "Oh, if only the black circle could recede and open the way for us!"

Yours, Anne

416

. . . . . .

Thursday 11 Nov. 1943.

Dear Kitty,
I have a good title for this chapter:

Ode to my fountain pen
In memoriam
"From Margot's schola Latina."

My fountain pen has always been one of my most priceless possessions; I value it highly, especially for its thick nib, for I can only really write neatly with a thick nib. My fountain pen has had a very long and interesting pen-life, which I will briefly tell you about: When I was nine, my fountain pen arrived in a packet (wrapped in cotton wool) as "sample without value" all the way from Aachen, where my Grandmother, the kind donor, used to live. I was in bed with flu, while February winds howled round the house. The glorious fountain pen had a red leather case and was at once shown around to all my friends on the first day. I, Anne Frank, the proud owner of a fountain pen! | When I was ten, the pen was allowed to go

224

Thursday, 11 November, 1943

Dear Kitty,
I have a good title for this chapter:

ODE TO MY FOUNTAIN PEN
IN MEMORIAM

My fountain pen has always been one of my most priceless possessions; I value it highly, especially for its thick nib, for I can only really write neatly with a thick nib. My fountain pen has had a very long and interesting pen-life, which I will briefly tell you about.

When I was nine, my fountain pen arrived in a packet (wrapped in cotton wool) as "sample without value" all the way from Aachen, where my Grandmother, the kind donor, used to live. I was in bed with flu, while February winds howled round the house. The glorious fountain pen had a red leather case and was at once shown around to all my friends. I, Anne Frank, the proud owner of a fountain pen! When I was ten I was allowed to take the pen to school and the mistress went so far as to permit me to write with it.

to school with me and the mistress went so far as to permit me to write with it. When I was eleven, however, my treasure had to be put away again, because the mistress in the 6th form only allowed us to use school pens and inkpots. When I was twelve and went to the Jewish Lyceum, my fountain pen received a new case in honor of the great occasion; it could take a pencil as well, and as it closed with a zipper looked much more impressive. At thirteen the fountain pen came with us to the "Secret Annexe" where it has raced through countless diaries and compositions for me. Now I am fourteen, we have spent our last year together.

———

It was on Friday afternoon after 5 o'clock. I had come out of my room and wanted to go and sit at the table to write, when I was roughly pushed on one side and had to make room for Margot and Daddy, who wanted to practice their "Latin." The

fountain pen remained on the table unused while, with a sigh, its owner con- | tented herself with a tiny little corner of the table and started rubbing beans. Bean rubbing is making moldy beans decent again.

When I was eleven, however, my treasure had to be put away again, because the mistress in the sixth form only allowed us to use school pens and inkpots.

When I was twelve and went to the Jewish Lyceum,* my fountain pen received a new case in honor of the great occasion; it could take a pencil as well, and as it closed with a zipper looked much more impressive.

At thirteen the fountain pen came with us to the "Secret Annexe," where it has raced through countless diaries and compositions for me.

Now I am fourteen, we have spent our last year together.

It was on a Friday afternoon after five o'clock. I had come out of my room and wanted to go and sit at the table to write, when I was roughly pushed on one side and had to make room for Margot and Daddy, who wanted to practice their "Latin." The fountain pen remained on the table unused while, with a sigh, its owner contented herself with a tiny little corner of the table and started rubbing beans. "Bean rubbing" is

---

*A type of secondary school specializing in the classics, common in most continental countries.

. . . . . .

I swept the floor at a quarter to 6 and threw the dirt, together with the bad beans, into a newspaper and into the stove. A terrific flame leaped out and I thought it was grand that the fire should burn up so well when it was practically out. All was quiet again, the "Latinites" had finished, and I went and sat at the table to clear up my writing things, but look as I might, my fountain pen was nowhere to be seen. I looked again, Margot looked, Mummy looked, Daddy looked, Pf. looked, but there was not a trace of the thing. "Perhaps it fell into the stove together with the beans!" Margot suggested. "Oh no, of course not!" I answered. When my fountain pen didn't turn up that evening, however, we all took it that it had been burned, | all the more as celluloid is terribly inflammable. And so it was, our unhappy fears were confirmed when Daddy did the stove the following morning the clip used for fastening was found among the ashes. Not a trace of the gold nib was found. "Must have melted and stuck to some stone or other," Daddy thought. I have one consolation, although a slender one, my fountain pen has been cremated, just what I want later!

The clip is left,
(The pen is gone)
I feel bereft
And put upon
yours, Anne

226

making moldy beans decent again. I swept the floor at a quarter to six and threw the dirt, together with the bad beans, into a newspaper and into the stove. A terrific flame leaped out and I thought it was grand that the fire should burn up so well when it was practically out. All was quiet again, the "Latinites" had finished, and I went and sat at the table to clear up my writing things, but look as I might, my fountain pen was nowhere to be seen. I looked again, Margot looked, [Mummy looked, Daddy looked, Dussel looked,] but there was not a trace of the thing. "Perhaps it fell into the stove together with the beans," Margot suggested. "Oh, no, of course not!" I answered. When my fountain pen didn't turn up that evening, however, we all took it that it had been burned, all the more as celluloid is terribly inflammable.

And so it was, our unhappy fears were confirmed; when Daddy did the stove the following morning the clip used for fastening was found among the ashes. Not a trace of the gold nib was found. "Must have melted and stuck to some stone or other," Daddy thought.

I have one consolation, although a slender one: my fountain pen has been cremated, just what I want later!

Yours, Anne

419

. . . . . .

Wednesday 17 Nov. 1943.

Dear Kitty,

Shattering things are happening. Diphtheria reigns in Bep's home, so she is not allowed to come into contact with us for 6 weeks. It makes it very awkward over food and shopping not to mention missing her companionship. Kleiman is still in bed and has had nothing but ¹thin porridge and milk for three weeks.

Kugler is frantically busy. Luckily the business has orders to grind 2,500 kg. of pepper again. The fines imposed on us last year by the price control are so high that officially Gies & Co. may not even have that much money.

The Latin lessons Margot sends in³ are corrected by a teacher and returned, Margot writing in Bep's name. The teacher, a certain A. C. Nielson is very nice, and witty too. I expect he is glad to have such a clever pupil.

231   Pf. is very put out, none of us knows why. It began by his keeping his mouth closed upstairs; he didn't utter a word to either Mr. or Mrs. v.P. Everyone was struck by it, and when it lasted a couple of days, Mummy took the opportunity of warning him about

Wednesday, 17 November, 1943

Dear Kitty,

Shattering things are happening. Diphtheria reigns in Elli's home, so she is not allowed to come into contact with us for six weeks. It makes it very awkward over food and shopping, not to mention missing her companionship. Koophuis is still in bed and has had nothing but porridge and milk for three weeks. Kraler is frantically busy.

The Latin lessons Margot sends in are corrected by a teacher and returned, Margot writing in Elli's name. The teacher is very nice, and witty, too. I expect he is glad to have such a clever pupil.

Dussel is very put out, none of us knows why. It began by his keeping his mouth closed upstairs; he didn't utter a word to either Mr. or Mrs. Van Daan. Everyone was struck by it, and when it lasted a couple of days, Mummy took the opportunity of warning

420

b

Mrs. v.P. who, if it goes on like this, can make things very disagreeable for him.[1] Pf. said that Mr. v.P. started the silence, so he was not going to be the one to break it. Now I must tell you that yesterday it was the 16th November, the day he had been exactly 1 year in the "Secret Annexe." Mummy received a plant in honor of the occasion, but Mrs. v.P., who for weeks beforehand had made no bones about the fact that she thought Pf. should treat us to something, received nothing.

| 232   [3]Instead of expressing, for the first time, his thanks for our unselfishness[4] in taking him in, he didn't say a word. And when | I asked him, on the morning of the 16th, whether I should congratulate or condole,[6] he answered that it didn't matter to him.

Mummy, who wanted to act as peacemaker, didn't get one step further, and finally the situation remained as it was.

It is no exaggeration to say that Pf. has a screw loose. We often joke among ourselves at his lack of memory, his opinions and judgment and have many a laugh when he gets stories he has just heard completely wrong and mixes everything up.

For the rest, he answers every reproach and accusation with splendid promises, none of which he ever actually keeps.

Der Mann der hat ein grosser Geist und is so klein von Taten!

yours, Anne

c

him about Mrs. Van Daan, who, if he went on like this, could make things very disagreeable for him.

Dussel said that Mr. Van Daan started the silence, so he was not going to be the one to break it.

Now I must tell you that yesterday was the sixteenth of November, the day he had been exactly one year in the "Secret Annexe." Mummy received a plant in honor of the occasion, but Mrs. Van Daan, who for weeks beforehand had made no bones about the fact that she thought Dussel should treat us to something, received nothing.

Instead of expressing, for the first time, his thanks for our unselfishness in taking him in, he didn't say a word. And when I asked him, on the morning of the sixteenth, whether I should congratulate or condole, he answered that it didn't matter to him. Mummy, who wanted to act as peacemaker, didn't get one step further, and finally the situation remained as it was.

Der Man hat einen grossen Geist
*Und ist so klein von Taten!**

Yours, Anne

---

*(The spirit of the man is great,
  How puny are his deeds!)

421

. . . . . .

Saturday 27 November
1943.

Dear Kitty,

Yesterday evening, before I fell asleep, who should suddenly appear before my eyes but Hanneli![1] [2]

I saw her in front of me, clothed in rags, her face thin and worn. Her eyes were very big and she looked so sadly and reproachfully at me that I could read in her eyes: Oh, Anne, why have you deserted me? Help, oh, help me, rescue me from this hell!"

And I cannot help her, I can only look on, how others suffer and die, and must therefore sit idly by and can only pray to God to send her back to us. I just saw Hanneli, no one else, and now I understand. I misjudged her, was too young to understand her difficulties. She was attached to her girl friend, and to her it seemed as though I wanted to take her away. What the poor girl must have felt like, I know; I know the feeling myself so well![5]

234   Sometimes in a flash I saw something of her life, but a moment later I was selfishly absorbed again in my own pleasures and problems.

It was horrid the way I treated her, and now she looked at me, oh so helplessly, with her pale face and imploring eyes. If only I could help her! Oh, God, that I should have all I could wish for, and that she should be seized by such a terrible fate. I am not more virtuous than she; she, too, wanted what was right, why should I be chosen to live and she probably[7] to die? What was the difference between us? Why[8] are we so far from each other now?

Saturday, 27 November, 1943

Dear Kitty,

Yesterday evening, before I fell asleep, who should suddenly appear before my eyes but Lies!

I saw her in front of me, clothed in rags, her face thin and worn. Her eyes were very big and she looked so sadly and reproachfully at me that I could read in her eyes: "Oh Anne, why have you deserted me? Help, oh, help me, rescue me from this hell!"

And I cannot help her, I can only look on, how others suffer and die, and can only pray to God to send her back to us.

I just saw Lies, no one else, and now I understand. I misjudged her and was too young to understand her difficulties. She was attached to a new girl friend, and to her it seemed as though I wanted to take her away. What the poor girl must have felt like, I know; I know the feeling so well myself!

Sometimes, in a flash, I saw something of her life, but a moment later I was selfishly absorbed again in my own pleasures and problems. It was horrid of me to treat her as I did, and now she looked at me, oh so helplessly, with her pale face and imploring eyes. If only I could help her!

Oh, God, that I should have all I could wish for and that she should be seized by such a terrible fate. I am not more virtuous than she; she, too, wanted to do what was right, why should I be chosen to live and she probably to die? What was the difference between us? Why are we so far from each other now?

422

a
. . . . . .

b

Quite honestly, I haven't thought about her for months, yes almost for a year. Not completely forgotten her but then never thought about her like this until I saw her before me in all her misery. Oh, Hanneli, I hope that if you should live until the end of the war, you will come back to us and that I shall be able to take you in and do something to make up for the wrong I did you.

235   But when I am able to help her again, then she will not need my help as badly as now. I wonder if she ever thinks of me, if so, what would she feel?

Good Lord defend her, so that at least she is not[4] alone. Oh, if only You can tell her that I think lovingly of her and with sympathy, perhaps that would give her greater endurance.

I must not go on thinking about it, because I don't get any further. I only keep seeing her great big eyes and cannot free myself from them. I wonder if Hanneli has real faith in herself, and not only what has been thrust upon her?

I don't even know, I never took the trouble to ask her!

Hannelie, Hannelie, if only I could take you away, if only I could let you share all the things I[7] enjoy.

| 235a   [8]It is too late now, I can't help, or repair the wrong I have done. But I shall never | forget her again and I shall always pray for her!

yours, Anne

c

Quite honestly, I haven't thought about her for months, yes, almost for a year. Not completely forgotten her, but still I had never thought about her like this, until I saw her before me in all her misery.

Oh, Lies, I hope that, if you live until the end of the war, you will come back to us and that I shall be able to take you in and do something to make up for the wrong I did you.

But when I am able to help her again, then she will not need my help so badly as now. I wonder if she ever thinks of me; if so, what would she feel?

Good Lord, defend her, so that at least she is not alone. Oh, if only You could tell her that I think lovingly of her and with sympathy, perhaps that would give her greater endurance.

I must not go on thinking about it, because I don't get any further. I only keep seeing her great big eyes, and cannot free myself from them. I wonder if Lies has real faith in herself, and not only what has been thrust upon her?

I don't even know, I never took the trouble to ask her!

Lies, Lies, if only I could take you away, if only I could let you share all the things I enjoy. It is too late now, I can't help, or repair the wrong I have done. But I shall never forget her again, and I shall always pray for her.

Yours, Anne

423

. . . . . .

Mon. 6 Dec. '43.

Dear Kitty,

When St. Nicholas' Day approached, none of us could help thinking of the prettily decorated basket we had last year and I, especially, thought it would be very dull to do nothing at all this year. I thought a long time about it until I invented something, something to make people laugh.

I consulted Pim and a week ago we started composing a little poem for each person.

On Sunday evening at a quarter to 8, we appeared upstairs with the large laundry basket between us, decorated with little figures and bows of pink and blue carbon copy paper. The basket was covered with a large piece of brown wrapping paper on which a letter was pinned. Everyone upstairs was rather astonished at the size of the surprise package.

I took the letter from the paper and read:
            Prologue:
Santa Claus has come once more
237   Though not quite as he came before.
We can't celebrate his day
In last year's fine and pleasant way.
For then our hopes were high and bright
All the optimists seemed right
None supposing that this year
We would welcome Santa here.

c

Monday, 6 December, 1943

Dear Kitty,

When St. Nicholas' Day approached, none of us could help thinking of the prettily decorated basket we had last year and I, especially, thought it would be very dull to do nothing at all this year. I thought a long time about it, until I invented something, something funny.

I consulted Pim, and a week ago we started composing a little poem for each person.

On Sunday evening at a quarter to eight we appeared upstairs with the large laundry basket between us, decorated with little figures, and bows of pink and blue carbon copy paper. The basket was covered with a large piece of brown paper, on which a letter was pinned. Everyone was rather astonished at the size of the surprise package.

I took the letter from the paper and read:

          [Prologue:]
"Santa Claus has come once more,
Though not quite as he came before;
We can't celebrate his day
In last year's fine and pleasant way.
For then our hopes were high and bright,
All the optimists seemed right,
None supposing that this year
We would welcome Santa here.

a   . . . . . .

b   Still, we'll make his spirit live
And since we've nothing left to give
We've thought of something else to do
(And as Daddy and I lifted the wrapping paper)
Each please look inside his shoe.

——

As each owner took his shoe from the basket[2] there was a resounding peal of laughter. A little paper package lay in each shoe with the address of the shoe's owner on it. I shan't write down all the verses, for that could easily get boring. But a few of them pleased everyone so much that no doubt you will enjoy them as well.

        To Miss A.M. Frank.

When the planes appear at night
No one gets so great a fright
As little Anne, the youngest child
With fear she sometimes grows quite wild
And when the Bulldogs open up
Then little Anne, she swigs a cup
And one of her Valerian pills.
Supplies decline, but Santa will
If need be bring her a refill.
(The present was a valerian tablet.)
       To Mrs. E. Frank

Abnormal times
We have no limes
Apples or tea
No vitamin C
But be of good cheer,
Raw food is here!
Radish we eat,
All wholesome and good
So this is the food
Santa has brought
After much thought.

c   *Still, we'll make his spirit live,*
       And since we've nothing left to give,
       We've thought of something else to do
       Each please look inside his shoe."
[(as Daddy and I lifted the wrapping paper).]

     As each owner took his shoe from the basket there was a resounding peal of laughter. A little paper package lay in each shoe with the address of the shoe's owner on it.

                                        Yours, Anne

b

To Mr. P. A. v. P.
Who keeps the attic spick and span?
Peter is the very man.
Who gets the spuds, the coals for heat,
Creeps downstairs in his stockinged feet?
239   Feeds the cats downstairs, you bet
Peter never will forget.
Who fetches wood, who cleans the grate,
Washes clothes when it's late?
Piet does that and much much more
That's what Santa likes him for
Extra coupons he has found
And for him has brought them round.

To Mrs. G. v. P.
I want to knit and know just what
I have the wool, I have the lot
Enough for pants or for a vest
But first a model I request.

I started well, but now I doubt
That the material won't run out
So I unpick it and, what fun,
Knit a hairnet for my son.

Alas, the color is quite wrong,
I'll have it dyed, it won't be long!

——

Madame, before you start anew
Look what Santa has for you
He set to work despite a hitch
And even made up a new stitch!

——

I had knitted a small strip and held it up on matchsticks.

Diary of

         Anne Frank

         from 22 December 1943 to 17 April 1944.

                                        "Secret Annexe"
                                        A'dam C.

         In part letters to "Kitty."

    1   "Secret Annexe," Wednesday 22-12-'43.
         Dear Kitty,
         Daddy has tracked down another new diary for me and this one is of a respectable thickness,
         as you will see for yourself in good time. I must apologize for not having written for such
         a long time, but there are good reasons for it. I was in bed from the Saturday of last week
         until yesterday, Tuesday. Tuesday a week ago I got up for a day, but only to catch a worse
         cold. I had to put up with sore throat, sweating, compresses, little lozenges etc, etc. Now
         I am a little bit better, but it isn't all over yet.

b   240   Wednesday 22 Dec. 1943.
         Dear Kitty,
         A severe attack of flu has prevented me from writing to you until today. It's wretched to
         be ill here, when I wanted to cough   one, two, three   I crawled under the blanket and
         tried to stifle the noise. Usually the only result was that the tickle wouldn't go away at
         all; and milk and honey, sugar or little lozenges had to be brought into operation. It makes
         me dizzy to think of all the cures that were tried on me, sweating, compresses, wet cloths
         on my chest, dry cloths on my chest, hot drinks, gargling, throat painting, lying still,
         cushion for extra warmth, hot water bottles, lemon squashes, and, in addition, the ther-
         mometer every two hours.

c   Wednesday, 22 December, 1943
         Dear Kitty,
            A bad attack of flu has prevented me from writing to you until today. It's wretched
         to be ill here. When I wanted to cough—one, two, three—I crawled under the blankets
         and tried to stifle the noise. Usually the only result was that the tickle wouldn't go away
         at all; and milk and honey, sugar or lozenges had to be brought into operation. It makes
         me dizzy to think of all the cures that were tried on me. Sweating, compresses, wet cloths
         on my chest, dry cloths on my chest, hot drinks, gargling, throat painting, lying still,
         cushion for extra warmth, hot-water bottles, lemon squashes, and, in addition, the ther-
         mometer every two hours!

a   . . . . . .

b

| 241

Can anyone really get better like this? The worst moment of all was certainly when Mr. Pf. thought he'd play doctor, and came and lay on my naked chest with his greasy head, in order to listen to the sounds within. Not only did his hair tickle unbearably, but I was embarrassed | although thirty years ago, he once studied medicine and has the title of Doctor. Why should this fellow come and lie on my heart? He's not my lover after all! For that matter he wouldn't hear whether it's healthy or unhealthy inside me anyway; his ears need syringing first, as he's becoming alarmingly[4] hard of hearing. [5]But that is enough about illness. I'm as fit as a fiddle again, 1 centimeter taller, 2 lbs. heavier, pale, and with a real appetite for learning.

c

Can anyone really get better like this? The worst moment of all was certainly when Mr. Dussel thought he'd play doctor, and came and lay on my naked chest with his greasy head, in order to listen to the sounds within. Not only did his hair tickle unbearably, but I was embarrassed, in spite of the fact that he once, thirty years ago, studied medicine and has the title of Doctor. Why should the fellow come and lie on my heart? He's not my lover, after all! For that matter, he wouldn't hear whether it's healthy or unhealthy inside me anyway; his ears need syringing first, as he's becoming alarmingly hard of hearing.

But that is enough about illness. I'm as fit as a fiddle again, one centimeter taller, two pounds heavier, pale, and with a real appetite for learning.

428

a

Ausnahmsweise* (no other word will do here) everyone here is getting on well together. There's no quarreling, but it won't last long, we haven't had such peace in the home for at least half a year.

Bep is still parted from us, but her darling little sister will soon be germ-free, she was so happy with my St. Nicholas Day present that she brought me an apple, a bag of meringues, copies of Libelle etc. I also have something for Christmas for Miep and Bep. I have been saving sugar from my porridge for at least a month and for St. Nicholas Day I got a whole pound together, but I didn't realize how busy | the shops would be before St. Nicholas Day. Kleiman is now having the fondant made for Christmas. For Chanuka Margot and I got gingerbread from upstairs and I got an apron, Peter also got gingerbread and 3 meat coupons. Mr. Pf. gave Mummy and Mrs. v.P. a lovely cake, we thought that his wife had baked it, but Miep told Daddy that Mrs. Pfeffer knew absolutely nothing about the cake and that Pf. had asked her to bake it for him. With all her work, she had to do that as well! For St. Nicholas Day and Christmas we were all issued with coupons for 180 grams of oil, 1 ounce of sweets and a pot of household syrup by the rationing office. I treated Mr.⁵ Kugler, Pf., Margot, Mrs. v.P. and myself to the sweets. Actually only the ladies and the children were given sweets, because we still have 5 cards. Margot and I got a little brooch made up out of a one-cent piece; the whole thing shines beautifully, nearly all the female members of the "Secret Annexe" have one, and so has Peter. In other words, Miep, Bep, Mrs. Kleiman, Margot, Anne and Peter, and Mrs. Pf. has one as well.

Enough for today, until next time Kitty, yours,

Anne.

---

*German for "by way of exception." A.J.P.

b

There is not much news to tell you; Bep is still parted from us, we received extra oil for Christmas, sweets and syrup, the present is a brooch made out of a one-cent piece, and shining beautifully. Anyway lovely but indescribable.

It is drizzly weather, the stove smells, the food lies heavily³ on everybody's tummy, causing thunderous noises on all sides, the war at a standstill, morale rotten.

yours, Anne

c

There is not much news to tell you. We are all getting on well together for a change! There's no quarreling—we haven't had such peace in the home for at least half a year. Elli is still parted from us.

We received extra oil for Christmas, sweets and syrup; the "chief present" is a brooch, made out of a two-and-a-half-cent piece, and shining beautifully. Anyway, lovely, but indescribable. Mr. Dussel gave Mummy and Mrs. Van Daan a lovely cake which he had asked Miep to bake for him. With all her work, she has to do that as well! I have also something for Miep and Elli. For at least two months I have saved the sugar from my porridge, you see, and with Mr. Koophuis's help I'll have it made into fondants.

It is drizzly weather, the stove smells, the food lies heavily on everybody's tummy, causing thunderous noises on all sides! The war at a standstill, morale rotten.

Yours, Anne

429

Friday 24 December 1943.

Dearest Kitty,

I (whoops, that's not done!) have previously written about how very much we are affected by atmospheres here, and I think that in my own case it's been getting much worse lately. "Himmelhoch jauchzend, zu tode betrübt" certainly fits here. I am "Himmelhoch jauchzend" if I only think how lucky we are here now in comparison with other Jewish children and "zu tode betrübt" comes over me when, as happened this morning, for example, Mrs. Kleiman comes and tells us about Jopie, that she plays hockey, has friends and belongs to clubs. I don't think I'm jealous of Jopie, but I couldn't help feeling a great longing to have lots of fun myself for once, and to laugh until my tummy ached. Don't ask when we last had a good laugh, it's well over a year ago that's for sure. Especially at this time of the year with all the holidays for Christmas and the New Year, and we are stuck here like outcasts. I really ought not to write this and yet I must for once. When someone

Friday 24 Dec. <u>1943</u>.

Dearest Kitty,

I have previously written to you about how very much we are affected by atmosphere here, and I think that in my own case this trouble is getting much worse lately. "Himmelhoch jauchzend, zu Tode betrübt," certainly fits here. I am "Himmelhoch jauchzend" if I only think how lucky we are here compared with other Jewish children, and "zu Tode betrübt" comes over me for example when Mrs. Kleiman comes and tells us about Jopie's hockey club, canoe trips, theatrical performances and tea parties with friends. I don't think I am jealous of Jopie, but I couldn't help feeling a great longing to have lots of fun myself for once, and to laugh until my tummy ached. Especially at this time of the year, with all the holidays for Christmas and the New Year, and we are stuck here as if we're outcasts.

| 243   Still I really ought not to write this because it seems ungrateful but, | no matter what

Friday, 24 December, 1943.

Dear Kitty,

I have previously written about how much we are affected by atmospheres here, and I think that in my own case this trouble is getting much worse lately.

"*Himmelhoch jauchzend und zum Tode betrübt*"* certainly fits here. I am "*Himmelhoch jauchzend*" if I only think how lucky we are here compared with other Jewish children, and "*zum Tode betrübt*" comes over me when, as happened today, for example, Mrs. Koophuis comes and tells us about her daughter Corry's hockey club, canoe trips, theatrical performances, and friends. I don't think I'm jealous of Corry but I couldn't help feeling a great longing to have lots of fun myself for once, and to laugh until my tummy ached. Especially at this time of the year with all the holidays for Christmas and the New Year, and we are stuck here like outcasts. Still, I really ought not to write this, because

---

*A famous line from Goethe: "On top of the world, or in the depths of despair."

comes in from outside, with the fresh air still about him, then I could burst into tears and I wonder, whenever | will we be able to smell fresh air again?

Believe me, Kitty, if you have been shut up for 1½ years, it can indeed get too much for you some days. No matter if it's unfair and ungrateful, you can't get rid of your feelings.

Cycling again, dancing, flirting and what-have-you, how I would love that; if only I were free again! Sometimes I even think, will anybody understand me, will anybody overlook my ingratitude, overlook Jew or non-Jew, and just see the young girl in me

they think of me, I can't keep everything to myself, so I'll remind you of my opening words "paper is patient."

When someone comes in from outside, with the wind in their clothes and the cold on their faces, then I could bury my head in the blankets to stop myself thinking: When will we be granted the privilege of smelling fresh air." And because I must not bury my head in the blankets, but the reverse—I must keep my head high and be brave, the thoughts will come, not once, but oh, countless times.

Believe me, if you have been shut up for 1½ years, it can get too much for you some days. In spite of all justice and thankfulness you can't get rid of your feelings.

Cycling, dancing, whistling, looking out at the world, feeling young, to know that I'm free—that's what I long for; still I mustn't show it, because I sometimes think if all 8 of us began to pity ourselves, or went about with discontented faces, where would it lead us?

yours, Anne

it seems ungrateful and I've certainly been exaggerating. But still, whatever you think of me, I can't keep everything to myself, so I'll remind you of my opening words—"Paper is patient."

When someone comes in from outside, with the wind in their clothes and the cold on their faces, then I could bury my head in the blankets to stop myself thinking: "When ll we be granted the privilege of smelling fresh air?" And because I must not bury my head in the blankets, but the reverse—I must keep my head high and be brave, the thoughts will come, not once, but oh, countless times. Believe me, if you have been shut up for a year and a half, it can get too much for you some days. In spite of all justice and thankfulness, you can't crush your feelings. Cycling, dancing, whistling, looking out into the world, feeling young, to know that I'm free—that's what I long for; still, I mustn't show it, because I sometimes think if all eight of us began to pity ourselves, or went about with discontented faces, where would it lead us? I sometimes ask myself, "Would anyone,

431

a

who is badly in need of some rollicking fun? I don't know and I couldn't talk about it to anybody, because then I know I should cry. Crying can bring such relief, but only if you can cry on someone's shoulder and despite everything, in spite of all my theories, and however much trouble I take, each day I miss having a real mother who understands me. And that is why, with everything I do and write, I think of the Mumsie that I want to be for my children later on. The "Mumsie" who doesn't take everything that is said in general conversation so seriously, but who does take what I say seriously. I have noticed, though

| 5   I can't | explain how, that the word "Mumsie" tells you everything. Do you know what I've found, to give me the feeling of calling Mummy something which sounds like "Mumsie"? I often call her Mum; then from that comes Mums: the incomplete "Mumsie," as it were, whom I would so love to honor with the extra ie and yet who does not realize it. It's a good thing that Mums doesn't realize it, because it would only make her unhappy.

That's enough of that, writing has made my zu tode bedrübt go off a bit!

b   258

P.S. You will no doubt have noticed that I generally call Mummy Mum or Mums. That's an invention of mine in order not to have to call her "Mumsie." It's an incomplete Mumsie as it were, I would love to honor her with an extra ie, but fortunately she doesn't realize why I can't.

yours, Anne.

c

either Jew or non-Jew, understand this about me, that I am simply a young girl badly in need of some rollicking fun?" I don't know, and I couldn't talk about it to anyone, because then I know I should cry. Crying can bring such relief.

In spite of all my theories, and however much trouble I take, each day I miss having a real mother who understands me. That is why with everything I do and write I think of the "Mumsie" that I want to be for my children later on. The "Mumsie" who doesn't take everything that is said in general conversation so seriously, but who does take what I say seriously. I have noticed, though I can't explain how, that the word "Mumsie" tells you everything. Do you know what I've found? To give me the feeling of calling Mummy something which sounds like "Mumsie" I often call her "Mum"; then from that comes "Mums": the incomplete "Mumsie," as it were, whom I would so love to honor with the extra "ie" and yet who does not realize it. It's a good thing, because it would only make her unhappy.

That's enough about that, writing has made my "zum Tode betrübt" go off a bit.

Yours, Anne

432

a

— . — . — . — . — . — . — . — . — . — . — . — . —

During these days, now that Christmas is here, I find myself thinking all the time about Pim, and what he told me last year. Last year, when I didn't understand the meaning of his words as I do now. If he'd only talk about it again, perhaps I would be able to show him that I understand!

    I believe that Pim talked about it because he, who knows the secrets of so many other hearts had to express his own feelings for once; because otherwise Pim never says a word about himself, and I don't think Margot has any idea of what Pim has had to go through. | 6 Poor Pim, he can't make me think that he | has forgotten her. He will never forget. He has become very tolerant, for he too sees Mummy's faults. I hope I shall grow a bit like him, without having to go through that as well!   yours,

Anne.

b

. . . . . .

c

Saturday, 25 December, 1943

Dear Kitty,

    During these days, now that Christmas is here, I find myself thinking all the time about Pim, and what he told me about the love of his youth. Last year I didn't understand the meaning of his words as well as I do now. If he'd only talk about it again, perhaps I would be able to show him that I understand.

    I believe that Pim talked about it because he who "knows the secrets of so many other hearts" had to express his own feelings for once; because otherwise Pim never says a word about himself, and I don't think Margot has any idea of all Pim has had to go through. Poor Pim, he can't make *me* think that he has forgotten everything. He will never forget this. He has become very tolerant. I hope that I shall grow a bit like him, without having to go through all that.

Yours, Anne.

433

Monday 27 December 1943.

On Friday evening for the first time in my life I received something for Christmas.

Kleiman, Kugler and the girls had prepared a lovely surprise again. Miep had made a lovely Christmas cake, on which was written "Peace 1944." Bep had provided a pound of sweet biscuits of prewar quality.

For Peter Margot and me a bottle of yoghourt and a beer for each of the grownups. Everything was so nicely done up, and there were these nice pictures stuck on the different parcels. Otherwise Christmas passed by quickly for us.

Anne

b   . . . . . .

c

Monday, 27 December, 1943

Dear Kitty,

On Friday evening for the first time in my life I received something for Christmas. Koophuis, Kraler and the girls had prepared a lovely surprise again. Miep has made a lovely Christmas cake, on which was written "Peace 1944." Elli had provided a pound of sweet biscuits of prewar quality. For Peter, Margot, and me a bottle of yoghourt, and a bottle of beer for each of the grownups. Everything was so nicely done up, and there were pictures stuck on the different packages. Otherwise Christmas passed by quickly for us.

Yours, Anne

Wednesday 29 December 1943.

I was very unhappy again last evening. Granny and Hannelie came into my mind. Granny—oh, darling Granny, how little we understood of what she suffered, or how sweet she always was to us, how interested she was in everything that concerned us, and besides all this, she knew a terrible secret which she carefully kept to herself the whole time. How faithful and good Granny always was; she would never have let one of us down, whatever it was, however naughty I had been, Granny always stuck up for me. Granny—did you love me, or didn't you understand me either? I don't know. No one ever talked about themselves to Granny. How lonely Granny must have been, how lonely in spite of us! A person can be lonely, even if he is loved by many people, because he is still not the "One and Only" to anyone.

b   . . . . . .

c

Wednesday, 29 December, 1943

Dear Kitty,

I was very unhappy again last evening. Granny and Lies came into my mind. Granny, oh, darling Granny, how little we understood of what she suffered, or how sweet she was. And besides all this, she knew a terrible secret which she carefully kept to herself the whole time.* How faithful and good Granny always was; she would never have let one of us down. Whatever it was, however naughty I had been, Granny always stuck up for me.

Granny, did you love me or didn't you understand me either? I don't know. No one ever talked about themselves to Granny. How lonely Granny must have been, how lonely in spite of us! A person can be lonely even if he is loved by many people, because he is still not the "One and Only" to anyone.

---

*A severe internal disease.

And Hanneli, is she still alive? What is she doing? Oh, God, protect her and bring her back to us. Hanneli, I see in you all the time what my lot might have been, I keep seeing myself in your place. Why then should I often be unhappy over what happens here, | 9 shouldn't I always be glad, contented and happy, except when I think about her | and her companions in distress? I am selfish and cowardly. Why do I always dream and think of the most terrible things—my fear makes me want to scream out loud sometimes. Because still, in spite of everything, I have not enough faith in God. He has given me so much—which I certainly do not yet deserve—and I still do so much that is wrong every day!

You could cry when you think of your fellow creatures, you could really cry the whole day long. We can only pray that God will perform a miracle and save some of them. And I hope that I am doing that enough!

Anne.

. . . . . .

And Lies, is she still alive? What is she doing? Oh, God, protect her and bring her back to us. Lies, I see in you all the time what my lot might have been, I keep seeing myself in your place. Why then should I often be unhappy over what happens here? Shouldn't I always be glad, contented, and happy, except when I think about her and her companions in distress? I am selfish and cowardly. Why do I always dream and think of the most terrible things—my fear makes me want to scream out loud sometimes. Because still, in spite of everything, I have not enough faith in God. He has given me so much—which I certainly do not deserve—and I still do so much that is wrong every day. If you think of your fellow creatures, then you only want to cry, you could really cry the whole day long. The only thing to do is to pray that God will perform a miracle and save some of them. And I hope that I am doing that enough!

Yours, Anne

436

Thursday 30 December 1943.

Dear Kitty,

Ever since the last big row things have settled down here, between ourselves, Pf. and upstairs, as well as between Mr. and Mrs. v.P. But big thunderclouds are gathering again now, and all about. . . . the food. Mrs. v.P. came up with the disastrous notion of doing fewer frd. pots. in the morning but using better-quality ones. Mummy and Pf., together with us, did not agree so now we even have to divide the potatoes. And there's been something funny going on about the fat and Mummy has had to put a stop to it. If there are any interesting developments I shall | report them to you. We have been dividing most of the food recently. The meat (they have it with fat, we don't; they have soup, we don't. The potatoes (theirs peeled, ours scraped.) Extra purchases, and now the fried potatoes on top of it all.

If only we could split up completely once again!

yours, Anne.

P.S. Bep has had a picture postcard of the whole royal family copied for me. Juliana looks very young, and so does the queen. The three girls are lovely. It was terribly nice of Bep, don't you think? My fondant for the girls for Christmas went down well. Bep was also very pleased with the little tin of milk and the other St. Nicholas Day presents. I'm only glad Mummy doesn't know anything about it, I don't think that she would have approved. On 15 January it is Mr. Voskuyl's birthday, I'll give him my next little jar of plum jam. 'Bye.

b   . . . . . .

c   . . . . . .

......

Sunday 2 Jan 1944.

Dear Kitty,

This morning when I had nothing to do, I turned over some of the pages of my diary and several times I came across letters dealing with the subject "Mummy" in such a vehement way that it quite shocked me and I asked myself: "Anne, is it really you who mentioned hate, oh, Anne, how could you?" I remained sitting with the open page in my hand, and thought about it and how it came about that I should have been so brimful of rage and seemed so full of hate that I had to confide it all[3] in you. I have been trying to understand the Anne of a year back and to excuse her, because my conscience isn't clear as long as I leave you with these accusations without being able to explain, on looking back, how it happened. I suffer now—and suffered then—from moods which kept my head under water (so to speak that is) and only allowed me to see things subjectively[4] without my

| 245   being enabled to consider[6] | quietly the words of the other side, and to answer them as the words of one whom I, with my hotheaded temperament, had offended or made unhappy.

I hid myself within myself, I only considered myself and quietly wrote down all my joys, sorrows and contempt in my diary. This diary is indeed of value to me, because it has become a book of memoirs in many places, but on a good many pages I could certainly put "Past and done with."

Sunday, 2 January, 1944

Dear Kitty,

This morning when I had nothing to do I turned over some of the pages of my diary and several times I came across letters dealing with the subject "Mummy" in such a hotheaded way that I was quite shocked, and asked myself: "Anne, is it really you who mentioned hate? Oh, Anne, how could you!" I remained sitting with the open page in my hand, and thought about it and how it came about that I should have been so brimful of rage and really so filled with such a thing as hate that I had to confide it all in you. I have been trying to understand the Anne of a year ago and to excuse her, because my conscience isn't clear as long as I leave you with these accusations, without being able to explain, on looking back, how it happened.

I suffer now—and suffered then—from moods which kept my head under water (so to speak) and only allowed me to see the things subjectively without enabling me to consider quietly the words of the other side, and to answer them as the words of one whom I, with my hotheaded temperament, had offended or made unhappy.

I hid myself within myself, I only considered myself and quietly wrote down all my joys, sorrows, and contempt in my diary. This diary is of great value to me, because it has become a book of memoirs in many places, but on a good many pages I could certainly put "past and done with."

438

a

. . . . . .

b

I used to be furious with Mummy (and often still am) it's true that she doesn't understand me,[1] but I don't understand her either. She did[2] love me very much and she was tender, but as she[3] landed in so many unpleasant situations through me and as she was nervous and irritable because of other worries and difficulties, it is certainly understandable that she snapped at me.

| 246   I took it much too seriously, was offended and was rude and irritating to Mummy, which, in turn, made | her unhappy. So it was really a matter of unpleasantness and misery rebounding all the time. It wasn't nice for either of us, but it is passing. I just didn't want to see all this, and pitied myself very much; but that, too, is understandable.

Those violent outbursts on paper were only giving vent to anger which in a normal life could have been worked off by stamping my feet a couple of times in a locked room or calling Mummy names behind her back.

The period when I caused Mummy to shed tears is over, I have grown wiser and Mummy's nerves are not so much on edge. I usually keep my mouth shut if I get annoyed, and so does she, so we appear to get on much[7] better together.

I can't really[8] love Mummy in a dependent childlike way,[9]

I soothe my conscience now, with the thought that hard words are better on paper than that Mummy should carry them in her heart.

yours, <u>Anne</u>

c

I used to be furious with Mummy, and still am sometimes. It's true that she doesn't understand me, but I don't understand her either. She did love me very much and she was tender, but as she landed in so many unpleasant situations through me, and was nervous and irritable because of other worries and difficulties, it is certainly understandable that she snapped at me.

I took it much too seriously, was offended, and was rude and aggravating [irritating] to Mummy, which, in turn, made her unhappy. So it was really a matter of unpleasantness and misery rebounding all the time. It wasn't nice for either of us, but it is passing.

I just didn't want to see all this, and pitied myself very much; but that, too, is understandable. Those violent outbursts on paper were only giving vent to anger which in a normal life could have been worked off by stamping my feet a couple of times in a locked room, or calling Mummy names behind her back.

The period when I caused Mummy to shed tears is over. I have grown wiser and Mummy's nerves are not so much on edge. I usually keep my mouth shut if I get annoyed, and so does she, so we appear to get on much better together. I can't really love Mummy in a dependent childlike way—I just don't have that feeling.

I soothe my conscience now with the thought that it is better for hard words to be on paper than that Mummy should carry them in her heart.

Yours, Anne

439

Thursday 6-January 1944.

Dear Kitty,

I have three things to confess to you today, which will take a long time. But I <u>must</u> tell someone and you are the best one to tell, as I know that come what may you always keep a secret. The first is about Mummy. You know that I've grumbled a lot about Mummy, yet still tried to be nice to her again. Now it is suddenly clear to me what she lacks. Mummy herself has told us that she looked upon us more as her friends than her daughters; now that is all very fine of course, but still a friend can't take a mother's place. I need my mother as an example which I can follow, I want to be able to respect her and though my mother is an example to me in most things she is precisely the kind of example that I do not want to follow. I have the feeling that Margot thinks differently about these

| 12   things and would never be able to understand what I've just told you. | And Daddy avoids all arguments about Mummy.

. . . . . .

Wednesday, 5 January, 1944

Dear Kitty,

I have two things to confess to you today, which will take a long time. But I must tell someone and you are the best one to tell, as I know that, come what may, you always keep a secret.

The first is about Mummy. You know that I've grumbled a lot about Mummy, yet still tried to be nice to her again. Now it is suddenly clear to me what she lacks. Mummy herself has told us that she looked upon us more as her friends than her daughters. Now that is all very fine, but still, a friend can't take a mother's place. I need my mother as an example which I can follow, I want to be able to respect her. I have the feeling that Margot thinks differently about these things and would never be able to understand what I've just told you. And Daddy avoids all arguments about Mummy.

a   I imagine a mother as a woman who, in the first place, shows great tact, especially towards her children when they reach our age, and who does not laugh in my face when I cry about something—not about pain, but about other things—like "Mums" does. One thing, which perhaps may seem rather fatuous, I have never forgiven her. It was on a day that I had to go to the dentist, Mummy and Margot were going to come with me and agreed that I should take my bicycle. When we had finished at the dentist, and were outside again, Margot and Mummy told me the good news that they were going into the town now to look at something or buy something—I don't remember exactly what. I wanted to go too of course, but was not allowed to as I had my bicycle with me. Tears of rage sprang into my eyes, and Mummy and Margot burst out laughing at me. Then I became so furious that I stuck my tongue out at them in the street just as an old woman happened

| 13   to pass by, who | looked very shocked! I rode home on my bicycle and I know I cried for a long time. It is queer that of all the countless wounds Mummy has inflicted on me it is this one that burns whenever I think of how angry I was that afternoon.

The second is something that is very difficult to tell you, because it is about myself. I am not prudish, Kitty, but when they keep talking here about what they've been doing in the lavatory, I feel my whole body rise up in revolt against it.

b   . . . . . .

c   I imagine a mother as a woman who, in the first place, shows great tact, especially towards her children when they reach our age, and who does not laugh at me if I cry about something—not pain, but other things—like "Mums" does.

One thing, which perhaps may seem rather fatuous, I have never forgiven her. It was on a day that I had to go to the dentist. Mummy and Margot were going to come with me, and agreed that I should take my bicycle. When we had finished at the dentist, and were outside again, Margot and Mummy told me that they were going into the town to look at something or buy something—I don't remember exactly what. I wanted to go, too, but was not allowed to, as I had my bicycle with me. Tears of rage sprang into my eyes, and Mummy and Margot began laughing at me. Then I became so furious that I stuck my tongue out at them in the street just as an old woman happened to pass by, who looked very shocked! I rode home on my bicycle, and I know I cried for a long time.

It is queer that the wound that Mummy made then still burns, when I think of how angry I was that afternoon.

The second is something that is very difficult to tell you, because it is about myself.

441

Yesterday I read an article about blushing by Sis Heyster,* I shall try to interpret it below. Sis Heyster might have been addressing me personally; although I don't blush very easily, the other things in it certainly all fit me. She writes roughly something like this— that a girl in the years (time) of puberty becomes quiet within and begins to think about the wonders that are happening to her body. I experience that too and that is why I get

| 14   the feeling lately of being | embarrassed in front of Margot, Mummy and Daddy. Funnily enough, Margot, who is much more shy than I am, isn't at all embarrassed.

I think what is happening to me is so wonderful, and not only what can be seen on my body, but all that is taking place inside. I never discuss myself or any of these things with anybody; that is why I have to talk to myself about them. Each time I have a period, (and that has only been three times) I have the feeling that in spite of all the pain, unpleasantness and nastiness I have a sweet secret, and that is why although it is nothing but a nuisance to me in one sense of the word, I always long for the time that I shall feel that secret within me again.

*Among other things, Sis Heyster wrote instructive articles for the women's magazine *Libelle*.

. . . . . .

Yesterday I read an article about blushing by Sis Heyster. This article might have been addressed to me personally. Although I don't blush very easily, the other things in it certainly all fit me. She writes roughly something like this—that a girl in the years of puberty becomes quiet within and begins to think about the wonders that are happening to her body.

I experience that, too, and that is why I get the feeling of being embarrassed about [embarrassed in front of] Margot, Mummy, and Daddy. Funnily enough, Margot, who is much more shy than I am, isn't at all embarrassed.

I think what is happening to me is so wonderful, and not only what can be seen on my body, but all that is taking place inside. I never discuss myself or any of these things with anybody; that is why I have to talk to myself about them.

Each time I have a period—and that has only been three times—I have the feeling that in spite of all the pain, unpleasantness, and nastiness, I have a sweet secret, and that is why, although it is nothing but a nuisance to me in a way, I always long for the time that I shall feel that secret within me again.

Sis Heyster also writes that girls of this age don't feel quite certain of themselves, and discover that they themselves are individuals with ideas, thought and habits. After I came here, when I was scarcely 13, I began to think about myself rather early on and to know that I | am a person. Sometimes, when I lie in bed at night, I have a terrible desire to feel my breasts and to listen to the quiet rhythmic beat of my heart.

I already had these kinds of feelings subconsciously before I came here, because I remember one night when I slept with Jacque I could not contain myself, I was so curious to see her body, which she always kept hidden from me and which I had never seen. I asked Jacque whether as a proof of our friendship we might feel one another's breasts. Jacque refused. I also had a terrible desire to kiss Jacque and that I did. I go into ecstasies every time I see the naked figure of a woman, such as Venus in the Springer History of Art, for example. It strikes me sometimes as so wonderful and exquisite that I have difficulty not letting the tears roll down my cheeks.

If only I had a girl friend!

. . . . . .

Sis Heyster also writes that girls of this age don't feel quite certain of themselves, and discover that they themselves are individuals with ideas, thoughts, and habits. After I came here, when I was just fourteen, [just after my 13th birthday,] I began to think about myself sooner than most girls, and to know that I am a "person." Sometimes, when I lie in bed at night, I have a terrible desire to feel my breasts and to listen to the quiet rhythmic beat of my heart.

I already had these kinds of feelings subconsciously before I came here, because I remember that once when I slept with a girl friend I had a strong desire to kiss her, and that I did do so. I could not help being terribly inquisitive over her body, for she had always kept it hidden from me. I asked her whether, as a proof of our friendship, we should feel one another's breasts, but she refused. I go into ecstasies every time I see the naked figure of a woman, such as Venus, for example. It strikes me [sometimes] as so wonderful and exquisite that I have difficulty in stopping the tears rolling down my cheeks.

If only I had a girl friend!

Yours, Anne

443

a 15a Now for my third confession and this is closest to my heart. Let me begin at the beginning:

My longing to talk to someone became so intense that somehow or other I decided to speak to Peter. Sometimes if I've been upstairs into Peter's room during the day, it always struck me as very snug, but because Peter is always so retiring and would never show anyone the door, I never dared stay long, because I was afraid he might think me a terrible bore. I tried to think up all sorts of excuses for a chance to talk to him and it came yesterday. Peter has a mania for crossword puzzles at the moment and hardly does anything else all day, I helped him with them and we soon sat opposite each other at his little table, he on the chair and me on the divan.

b 247

Thursday 6 January
1944.

Dear Kitty,

My longing to talk to someone became so intense that somehow or other I took it into my head to choose Peter. Sometimes if I've been upstairs into Peter's room during the day, it always struck me as very snug, but because Peter is so retiring and would never turn anyone out who became a nuisance, I never dared stay long, because I was afraid he might think me a bore. I tried to think of an excuse to stay unobtrusively in his room and get him talking, and my chance came yesterday. Peter has a mania for crossword puzzles at the moment and hardly does anything else. I helped him with them and we soon sat opposite each other at his little table, he on the chair and me on the divan.

c

Thursday, 6 January, 1944

Dear Kitty,

My longing to talk to someone became so intense that somehow or other I took it into my head to choose Peter.

Sometimes if I've been upstairs into Peter's room during the day, it always struck me as very snug, but because Peter is so retiring and would never turn anyone out who became a nuisance, I never dared stay long, because I was afraid he might think me a bore. I tried to think of an excuse to stay in his room and get him talking, without it being too noticeable, and my chance came yesterday. Peter has a mania for crossword puzzles at the moment and hardly does anything else. I helped him with them and we soon sat opposite each other at his little table, he on the chair and me on the divan.

444

a

| 15b

And I can tell you that it gave me such a queer feeling each time I looked into his deep blue eyes, and he sat there with that mysterious laugh playing round his lips. I could read | his inward thoughts. I could see in his face that look of helplessness and uncertainty as to how to behave, and at the same time, a trace of his sense of manhood. I noticed his shy manner and it made me feel very gentle; I couldn't refrain from meeting those dark eyes again and again, and with my whole heart I almost beseeched him, oh, tell me, what is going on inside you, oh, can't you look beyond this ridiculous chatter?

But the evening passed and nothing happened, except that I told him that about blushing—naturally not what I have written, but so that he might become more sure of himself as he grew older.

When I lay in bed that night all I could do was cry, cry terribly, but having to make sure no one could hear me. In bed I thought over all the things I would say to Peter today and I couldn't stop sobbing. I fell asleep very late.

b

248

It gave me a queer feeling when I looked into his deep blue eyes and saw how embarrassed this unexpected visit had made him.

I would have liked to ask him: Won't you tell me something about yourself, won't you look beyond this ridiculous chatter? But I noticed that such questions are easier to think up than to ask.

When I lay in bed and thought over the whole situation I found it far from encouraging and the idea that I should beg for Peter's patronage was simply repellent. One can do a lot to satisfy one's longings which certainly sticks out in my case, for I have made up my mind to go and sit with Peter more often and to get him talking somehow or other.

c

It gave me a queer feeling each time I looked into his deep blue eyes, and he sat there with that mysterious laugh playing round his lips. I was able to read his inward thoughts. I could see on his face that look of helplessness and uncertainty as to how to behave, and, at the same time, a trace of his sense of manhood. I noticed his shy manner and it made me feel very gentle; I couldn't refrain from meeting those dark eyes again and again, and with my whole heart I almost beseeched him: oh, tell me, what is going on inside you, oh, can't you look beyond this ridiculous chatter?

But the evening passed and nothing happened, except that I told him about blushing—naturally not what I have written, but just so that he would become more sure of himself as he grew older.

When I lay in bed and thought over the whole situation, I found it far from encouraging, and the idea that I should beg for Peter's patronage was simply repellent. One can do a lot to satisfy one's longings, which certainly sticks out in my case, for I have made up my mind to go and sit with Peter more often and to get him talking somehow or other.

445

| 16 But you really mustn't think I'm in love with Peter—not a bit of it! If the v.P.s had had a girl instead of a boy, I should have tried to tell her something about myself and | to let her tell me things as well.

This morning, I woke up at about 5 to 7 in the morning and knew at once quite positively, what I had dreamed. I sat on a chair and opposite me sat Peter. . . . . . Schiff. We were looking together at a book of pictures by Mary Bos, in which only one page was covered with drawings, the rest had other things. The dream was so vivid that I can still partly remember the drawings. But the dream still continued, suddenly Peter's eyes and mine met and I looked into those fine velvet brown eyes for a long time, then Peter said very softly, "If I had only known, I would have come to you long before. . . . . !" I turned around brusquely because the emotion was too much for me. And after that I felt a soft, and oh, such a cool kind cheek against mine and it felt so good, so good. . . . . .

Whatever you do, don't think I'm in love with Peter, not a bit of it! If the v.P.s had had a daughter instead of a boy, I should have tried to make friends with her too.

I woke at about five to seven[2] this morning and knew at once, quite positively, what I had dreamed. I sat on a chair and opposite me sat Peter . . . . Schiff, we were looking | 249 together at a book of drawings by Mary Bos, only one side had a drawing, | on the other were all sorts of model figures. The dream was so vivid that I can still partly remember the drawings. But that was not all—the dream went on, suddenly Peter's eyes met mine and I looked into those fine, velvet brown eyes for a long time, then Peter said very softly, "If I had only known, I would have come to you long before!" I turned around brusquely because the emotion was too much for me. And after that I felt a soft, and oh, such a cool kind cheek against mine and it was so good, so good . . . . .

Whatever you do, don't think I'm in love with Peter—not a bit of it! If the Van Daans had had a daughter instead of a son, I should have tried to make friends with her too.

I woke at about five to seven this morning and knew at once, quite positively, what I had dreamed. I sat on a chair and opposite me sat Peter . . . Wessel. We were looking together at a book of drawings by Mary Bos. The dream was so vivid that I can still partly remember the drawings. But that was not all—the dream went on. Suddenly Peter's eyes met mine and I looked into those fine, velvet brown eyes for a long time. Then Peter said very softly, "If I had only known, I would have come to you long before!" I turned around brusquely because the emotion was too much for me. And after that I felt a soft, and oh, such a cool kind cheek against mine and it felt so good, so good. . . .

446

a

| 17

Then I awoke, while I could still feel his cheek against mine and still felt his brown eyes looking deep into my heart, so deep, that there he read how much I had loved him and how <u>very</u> much I still love him. Then tears | sprang into my eyes once more, and I was so sad that I had lost him again, but I was also so glad because suddenly I knew with certainty again, how much I loved Peter. The dreams of six children, a beautiful house and long journeys had gone up in smoke, but if only I could have Peter with me, oh, Petel, Petel. . . . . .

It is strange that I should often see such vivid images in my dreams here. First I saw Grandma so clearly one night that I saw how her skin was so thick, soft, wrinkled, velvety. Then Granny appeared, so that I consider her my guardian angel to whom I pray every night and send my kisses. Then came Hanneli, so clearly that I pray for her every night and she seems to be a symbol of the sufferings of all my friends and all Jews, thus when I pray for her I pray for all Jews and all those in need. And now Peter, my darling Peter —never before have I had such a clear picture of him in my mind. I need no photo of him, I can see him so, so well.

b

| 250

I awoke at this point, while I could still feel his cheek against mine and felt his brown eyes looking deep into my heart, so deep, that there he read how much I still love him. Tears sprang into my eyes once more, and I was very sad that I had lost him again, but at the same time glad because it made me feel quite certain | that Peter was still the chosen one.

It is strange that I should often see such vivid images in my dreams. First I saw Grandma so clearly one night that I could make out her thick, soft, wrinkled velvety skin. Then Granny appeared as a guardian angel; then followed Hanneli, who seems to be a symbol to me of the sufferings of all my friends and all Jews; thus when I pray for her I pray for all Jews and all those in need And now Peter, my darling Peter—I don't need a photo of him, I can see him before my eyes well enough.

c

I awoke at this point, while I could still feel his cheek against mine and felt his brown eyes looking deep into my heart, so deep, that there he read how much I had loved him and how much I still love him. Tears sprang into my eyes once more, and I was very sad that I had lost him again, but at the same time glad because it made me feel quite certain that Peter was still the chosen one.

It is strange that I should often see such vivid images in my dreams here. First I saw Grandma* so clearly one night that I could even distinguish her thick, soft, wrinkled velvety skin. Then Granny appeared as a guardian angel; then followed Lies, who seems to be a symbol to me of the sufferings of all my girl friends and all Jews. When I pray for her, I pray for all Jews and all those in need. And now Peter, my darling Peter—never before have I had such a clear picture of him in my mind. I don't need a photo of him, I can see him before my eyes, and oh, so well!

Yours, Anne.

---

*Grandma is grandmother on Father's side, Granny on Mother's side.

447

But Kitty, I don't think I ever told you the history of myself and all my boy | friends. Here it is:

When I was quite small—and only at a Kindergarten—I became attached to Sally Kimmel. He had lost his father, I believe his parents were divorced and he lived with his mother at her sister's. One of Sally's cousins was Appy and the two of them were generally together and generally dressed the same way. Appy was a slender, good-looking dark boy and Sally a short, fat, fair friendly boy, with a great sense of humor. But looks did not count with me and I was very fond of Sally for years. We used to be together a lot for quite a time, but for the rest, my love was unreturned. Until Peter crossed my path, and in my childish way I really fell in love. He also liked me very much and we couldn't be parted for one whole summer. I can still see us walking hand in hand through the streets together. Then I went into the 6th form of the Lower School and he into the First Form of the 4th-3. I would often fetch him from school, or he would fetch me and I often went

Friday 7 Jan. 1944.

Dear Kitty,

What a silly ass I am, I have quite forgotten that I have never told you the history of my great love. When I was quite small—I was even at Kindergarten I became attached to Sally Kimmel. He had lost his father and he and his mother lived with an aunt. One of Sally's cousins, Appy, was a slender, good-looking dark boy who later turned into the very picture of a screen hero and who aroused more admiration than the little, humorous fellow, Sally. We used to be together a lot for quite a long time, but for the rest, my love was unreturned, until Peter crossed my path, and in my childish way I fell for him three times over. He liked me very much, too, and we were inseparable one summer long. I can still remember us walking hand in hand through the Zuider Amstellaan together, he in a

| 252 white cotton suit and me in a short summer dress. At the end of | the summer holidays he went into 4th3 and I into the 6th form of the Lower School. He used to meet me from school and, vice versa, I would meet him. Peter was a very good-looking boy, tall,

Friday, 7 January, 1944

Dear Kitty,

What a silly ass I am! I am quite forgetting that I have never told you the history of myself and all my boy friends.

When I was quite small—I was even still at a kindergarten—I became attached to Karel Samson. He had lost his father, and he and his mother lived with an aunt. One of Karel's cousins, Robby, was a slender, good-looking dark boy, who aroused more admiration than the little, humorous fellow, Karel. But looks did not count with me and I was very fond of Karel for years.

We used to be together a lot for quite a long time, but for the rest, my love was unreturned.

Then Peter crossed my path, and in my childish way I really fell in love. He liked me very much, too, and we were inseparable for one whole summer. I can still remember us walking hand in hand through the streets together, he in a white cotton suit and me in a short summer dress. At the end of the summer holidays he went into the first form of the high school and I into the sixth form of the lower school. He used to meet me from school and, vice versa, I would meet him. Peter was a very good-looking boy, tall, handsome,

a

to his house. Peter was a very good-looking boy, tall, handsome and slim, with an earnest, calm, intelligent face. | He had dark hair and wonderful brown eyes, ruddy cheeks and a pointed nose. When he laughed a naughty glint came into his eye. When we had known each other for about 3 months, he moved into the same house as a much older boy Rolf (Peter was 3 years older than I was). He apparently drew his attention to the fact that I was very childish, and he gave me up. I adored him so that I didn't want to face it. I tried to hold on to him until I realized that if I went on running after him I should soon get the name of being boy-mad. The years passed, Peter went around with girls of his own age and soon stopped saying hello to me, but I couldn't forget him. I went to the Jewish Secondary School, almost all the boys in my class were keen on me—I thought it was fun, felt honored, but was otherwise quite untouched. Then Hello appeared who was mad on me, but I never fell in love again.

b

handsome and slim, with an earnest, calm, intelligent face. He had dark hair and wonderful brown eyes, ruddy cheeks and a pointed nose. I was mad about his laugh, above all, when he looked so mischievous and naughty!

I went to the country for the holidays and when I returned I didn't find him at his old address; he had moved in the meantime, and a much older boy lived in the same house. He apparently drew Peter's attention to the fact that I was a childish little imp, and Peter gave me up. I adored him so that I didn't want to face the truth. I tried to hold on to him until it dawned on me that if I went on running after him I should get the name of being boy-mad.

The years passed. Peter went around | with girls of his own age, and didn't even think of saying "Hello" to me any more.

I went to the Jewish Secondary School. Lots of[4] boys in our class were keen on me—I thought it was fun, felt honored, but was otherwise quite untouched. Then later on, Hello was mad about me, but, as I've already told you I never fell in love again.

c

and slim, with an earnest, calm, intelligent face. He had dark hair, and wonderful brown eyes, ruddy cheeks, and a pointed nose. I was mad about his laugh, above all, when he looked so mischievous and naughty!

I went to the country for the holidays; when I returned, Peter had in the meantime moved, and a much older boy lived in the same house. He apparently drew Peter's attention to the fact that I was a childish little imp, and Peter gave me up. I adored him so that I didn't want to face the truth. I tried to hold on to him until it dawned on me that if I went on running after him I should soon get the name of being boy-mad. The years passed. Peter went around with girls of his own age and didn't even think of saying "Hello" to me any more; but I couldn't forget him.

I went to the Jewish Secondary School. Lots of boys in our class were keen on me—I thought it was fun, felt honored, but was otherwise quite untouched. Then later on, Harry was mad about me, but, as I've already told you, I never fell in love again.

449

a

| 20

The saying says: Time heals all wounds, and so it was with me, I imagined that I had forgotten Peter and that I didn't like him a bit any more, but his memory lived on so | strongly in my subconscious mind that I had to admit to myself that I was jealous of the other girls, and that was why I didn't like him any more. This morning I knew that nothing has changed in me; on the contrary, as I grew bigger and more mature my love grew with me.

I can quite understand now that Peter thought me childish, and yet it still hurt that he had so completely forgotten me.

His face comes so clearly to mind that now I know that no one else can stay with me like he does. I love Peter with all my heart. I am still completely upset today too. When Daddy kissed me this morning, I could have cried out: "Oh, if only you were Peter!" I think of him all the time and I keep repeating to myself the whole day, "Oh, Petel, darling darling Petel......

What can help me now?[2] I must live on and pray to God that He will let Peter cross my path when I come out of here, and that when he reads the love in my eyes he will say,

| 21

"Oh Anne, if I | had only realized, I would have asked you long ago!"

b

There is a saying: Time heals all wounds, and so it was with me; I imagined that I had forgotten Peter and that I didn't like him at all any more. The memory of him, however, lived on so strongly[3] that I admitted to myself sometimes I was jealous of the other girls, and that was why I didn't like him any more. This morning I realized that nothing has changed; on the contrary, as I grew older[5] and more mature my love grew with me. His face was shown[7] so clearly to me, and I know that no one else can remain with me like he does.

254

I am completely upset by the dream. What can help me now? I must live on and pray to God that He will let Peter cross my path when I come out of here, and that when he reads the love in my eyes he will say: "Oh Anne, if I had only known, I would have come to you long before."

yours, Anne.

c

There is a saying "Time heals all wounds," and so it was with me. I imagined that I had forgotten Peter and that I didn't like him a bit any more. The memory of him, however, lived so strongly in my subconscious mind that I admitted to myself sometimes I was jealous of the other girls, and that was why I didn't like him any more. This morning I knew that nothing has changed; on the contrary, as I grew older and more mature my love grew with me. I can quite understand now that Peter thought me childish, and yet it still hurt that he had so completely forgotten me. His face was shown so clearly to me, and now I know that no one else could remain with me like he does.

I am completely upset by the dream. When Daddy kissed me this morning, I could have cried out: "Oh, if only you were Peter!" I think of him all the time and I keep repeating to myself the whole day, "Oh, Petel, darling, darling Petel . . . !"

Who can help me now? I must live on and pray to God that He will let Peter cross my path when I come out of here, and that when he reads the love in my eyes he will say, "Oh, Anne, if I had only known, I would have come to you long before!"

450

Once, when we spoke about sex, Daddy told me that I couldn't possibly understand the longing yet, I always knew that I did understand it and now I understand it fully. Nothing is so beloved to me now as he, my Petel.

———

I saw my face in the mirror and it looks quite different than at other times. My eyes look so clear and deep, my cheeks are pink—which they haven't been for weeks—my mouth is much softer; I look as if I am happy, and yet there is something so sad in my expression and my smile slips away from my lips as soon as it has come. I'm not happy because I should know that Petel's thoughts are not with me, and yet I still feel his wonderful eyes upon me and his cool, soft cheek against mine. . . . . .

Oh, Petel, Petel, how will I ever free myself of your image? Wouldn't any other in your place be a miserable substitute? I love you, and with such a great love that it can't grow in my heart any more but has to leap out into the open and suddenly manifest itself in such a tremendous way!

22 A week ago, even yesterday, if you had asked me, "Which of your friends do you consider would be the most suitable to marry? I would have answered: "Sally, for he makes me feel good, peaceful and safe!"

But now I would cry, "Petel, because I love him with all my heart and soul, I give myself completely!" But one thing, he may touch my face, but no more.

This morning I imagined I was in the front attic with Petel, sitting on the wooden window sill and after a short conversation, the two of us started to cry and then I felt his mouth and his wonderful cheek! Oh Petel, come to me, think of me, my own dear Petel!

. . . . . .

I saw my face in the mirror and it looks quite different. My eyes look so clear and deep, my cheeks are pink—which they haven't been for weeks—my mouth is much softer; I look as if I am happy, and yet there is something so sad in my expression and my smile slips away from my lips as soon as it has come. I'm not happy, because I might [should] know that Peter's thoughts are not with me, and yet I still feel his wonderful eyes upon me and his cool soft cheek against mine.

Oh, Petel, Petel, how will I ever free myself of your image? Wouldn't any other in your place be a miserable substitute? I love you, and with such a great love that it can't grow in my heart any more but has to leap out into the open and suddenly manifest itself in such a devastating way!

A week ago, even yesterday, if anyone had asked me, "Which of your friends do you consider would be the most suitable to marry?" I would have answered, "I don't know"; but now I would cry, "Petel, because I love him with all my heart and soul. I give myself completely!" But one thing, he may touch my face, but no more.

Once, when we spoke about sex, Daddy told me that I couldn't possibly understand the longing yet; I always knew that I did understand it and now I understand it fully. Nothing is so beloved to me now as he, my Petel.

Yours, Anne

451

Wednesday 12 January 1944

Dear Kitty,

Bep has been back a fortnight now, although her little sister isn't allowed to go back to school yet. Dina and Joop too are still at home; the Health Service had just forgotten about Gerda. Bep wasn't here on Monday or Yesterday, but stayed in bed with a sore throat. Last week Miep stayed home with Jan for two days with tummy upsets. The second day Jan had to go back to the office so she was able to take it easy.

Bep has promised to teach me modern dancing, Voskuyl was here on Saturday as well and it came out quite by chance that he knows "Pallada."

I have a craze for ballet and dancing at the moment and practice every evening diligently. I have made a supermodern dance frock from a pale purple petticoat with lace above and below belonging to Mummy. It's fastened round the top with a ribbon that is threaded right round the back and under the sleeves. A pink corded ribbon completes the

Wednesday 12 Jan. 1944.

Dear Kitty,

Bep has been back for a fortnight although her little sister may only go back to school next week. She herself was in bed for two days with a bad cold. Miep and Jan too were away from their work for two days—they both had tummy upsets.

I have a craze for dancing and ballet at the moment and practice dance steps every evening diligently. I have made a supermodern dance frock from a light blue petticoat edged with lace belonging to Mum. A ribbon is threaded through round the top and ties in a bow in the center, and a pink corded ribbon completes the creation. I tried in vain

Wednesday, 12 January, 1944

Dear Kitty,

Elli has been back a fortnight. Miep and Henk were away from their work for two days—they both had tummy upsets.

I have a craze for dancing and ballet at the moment, and practice dance steps every evening diligently. I have made a supermodern dance frock from a light blue petticoat edged with lace belonging to Mansa [Mum]. A ribbon is threaded through round the top and ties in a bow in the center, and a pink corded ribbon completes the creation. I tried

a | 24   creation. I've been trying in vain to convert my gym shoes into ballet shoes. | I've made quite good progress with a lot of very difficult exercises. For instance sitting on the floor holding a foot in each hand, and then lifting both legs up in the air. I have to have a cushion under me. (Here I was interrupted and continued on Thursday 13 Jan. 1944!)

All these exercises did my arms and legs no good at all. I put my left arm and my left and right leg out of joint, after 1½ days my arm was all right again, but my legs still hurt terribly. So the illusion I had of doing physical exercises every evening has vanished again.

Everyone here is reading the book Cloudless Morn at the moment, Mummy found it particularly nice because so many youth problems were discussed in it. I thought to myself rather sarcastically, take a bit of trouble with your own young people first!

I believe Mummy thinks that Margot and I have the best possible relationship with our parents, and that no one could take a greater interest in their children's lives than she.

  | 25   But quite definitely she only looks at Margot, | who I don't think ever had such problems and thoughts as I do.

---

b   to convert my gym shoes into real ballet shoes. My stiff limbs are well on the way to being supple again like they used to be. One terrific exercise is to sit on the floor, hold a heel in each hand, then lift both legs up in the air. I have to have a cushion under me otherwise my poor little behind has a rough time.

256   Everyone here is reading the book "Cloudless Morn," Mummy thought it exceptionally good since there are a lot of youth problems in it. I thought to myself rather ironically, "take a bit of trouble with your own young people first!" I believe that Mummy's eyes haven't been opened so far because she doesn't realize that our relationship with our parents is nothing like as super-perfect as she always imagines or thinks it is. I speak of our, did you notice? Margot has grown so sweet; she seems quite different from what she used to be, isn't nearly so catty these days and is becoming a real friend. Nor does she any longer regard me as a little kid who counts for nothing.

---

c   in vain to convert my gym shoes into real ballet shoes. My stiff limbs are well on the way to becoming supple again like they used to be. One terrific exercise is to sit on the floor, hold a heel in each hand, and then lift both legs up in the air. I have to have a cushion under me, otherwise my poor little behind has a rough time.

Everyone here is reading the book *Cloudless Morn*. Mummy thought it exceptionally good; there are a lot of youth problems in it. I thought to myself rather ironically: "Take a bit more trouble with your own young people first!"

I believe Mummy thinks there could be no better relationship between parents and their children [I believe Mummy thinks that Margot and I have the best possible relationship with our parents], and that no one could take a greater interest in their children's lives than she. But quite definitely she only looks at Margot, who I don't think ever had such problems and thoughts as I do. Still, I wouldn't dream of pointing out to Mummy that,

453

Still, I wouldn't dream of pointing out to Mummy that in the case of her daughters it isn't all as she imagines, because she would be utterly amazed and wouldn't know how to change anyway; I want to save her the unhappiness it would cause her, especially as I know that for me everything would remain the same anyway. Mummy certainly feels that Margot loves her much more than I do, but she thinks that this just goes in phases!

. . . . . .

in the case of her daughters, it isn't at all as she imagines, because she would be utterly amazed and wouldn't know how to change anyway; I want to save her the unhappiness it would cause her, especially as I know that for me everything would remain the same anyway.

Mummy certainly feels that Margot loves her much more than I do, but she thinks that this just goes in phases! Margot has grown so sweet; she seems quite different from what she used to be, isn't nearly so catty these days and is becoming a real friend. Nor does she any longer regard me as a little kid who counts for nothing.

a

Isn't it odd, Kitty, that sometimes I look at myself through someone else's eyes? I see quite keenly then how things are with Anne Frank. Before when I didn't think about things as much as I do now, I used to have the feeling sometimes that I didn't belong to Mummy, Pim and Margot, sometimes I would feel miserable about it for a good six months at a time until I punished myself, telling myself that it was all my own fault that I played this self-pitying role, that I didn't deserve being so fortunate.

| 26   Then came the time when I used to force myself to be | glad to get back home and to be friendly. Every morning, as soon as someone came downstairs I hoped that it would be Mummy, who would come and say good morning to me and I greeted her warmly because I really longed for her to look lovingly at me. Then she would snap at me with some remark or other and I would go off to school again feeling thoroughly disheartened, thinking that Mummy wasn't really nice after all. At 12 o'clock, when I came out of school, I would make excuses for her again because she was under so much pressure, arrive home very cheerful and most of the time the same thing would happen at lunch as

b

I have an odd way of sometimes, as it were, being able to see myself through someone else's eyes. Then I view the affairs of a certain Anne Robin at my ease, and browse through the pages of her life as if she were a stranger.

257   Before we came here[1] (when I didn't think about things as much as I do now) I used at times to have the feeling that I didn't belong to Mum, Pim, and Margot, and that I would always be a bit of an outsider, sometimes I used to pretend for a good six months that I was an orphan, until I reproached and punished myself, telling myself it was all my own fault that I played this self-pitying role, 'while I was really so fortunate. Then came the time that I used to force myself to [7be friendly. Every morning, as soon as someone came down the steep attic stairs[8] I hoped that it would be Mummy, who would come and say good morning to me. Then she made some remark or other that seemed unfriendly, and I would go off to school again feeling thoroughly disheartened. On the way home, I would make excuses for her because she had so many worries, arrive home very cheerful, chatter nineteen to the dozen, until there was a repeat of what had happened in the morning and I would leave the room wearing a pensive expression, my satchel under my arm.

c

I have an odd way of sometimes, as it were, being able to see myself through someone else's eyes. Then I view the affairs of a certain "Anne" at my ease, and browse through the pages of her life as if she were a stranger. Before we came here, when I didn't think about things as much as I do now, I used at times to have the feeling that I didn't belong to Mansa [Mum], Pim, and Margot, and that I would always be a bit of an outsider. Sometimes I used to pretend I was an orphan, until I reproached and punished myself, telling myself it was all my own fault that I played this self-pitying role, when I was really so fortunate. Then came the time that I used to force myself to be friendly. Every morning, as soon as someone came downstairs I hoped that it would be Mummy who would say good morning to me; I greeted her warmly, because I really longed for her to look lovingly at me. Then she made some remark or other that seemed unfriendly, and I would go off to school again feeling thoroughly disheartened. On the way home I would make excuses for her because she had so many worries, arrive home very cheerful, chatter nineteen to the dozen, until I began repeating myself, and [until there was a repeat of what had happened, and I] left the room wearing a pensive expression, my satchel under my arm.

455

well. Sometimes I would decide to remain cross, but when I came home from school, I always had so much to tell that my resolutions were gone with the wind again and that was all to the good! Until I would no longer wait in the mornings and feel lonely again and cry for a long time at night.

The only difference now is that since I have Mummy around me all day long I can't bear to look at her face any longer, because she is not my Mumsie and will never be!

27 Last night it suddenly all came to me and I don't know what it is, but I can never find the right moment to speak to him. And then. . . . . . I burst into tears so quickly when something like that happens and then I can't explain myself as calmly as I want to.

Now God has sent me a helper,[1] Peter . . . . . .—I just clasp my pendant, kiss it and think to myself, "What do I care about the lot of them! Peter belongs to me and no one knows anything about it!" And this way I can get over all the snubs I receive. Who would ever think here that so much can go on in the soul of a young girl?

258 Sometimes I decided to remain cross, but when I came home from school I always had so much news that my resolutions were gone with the wind and Mummy, whatever she might be doing, had to lend an ear to all my adventures.

Until the time came once more when I didn't listen for footsteps on the staircase any longer, felt lonely and at night my pillow was wet with tears.

Everything grew much worse at this point, enfin you know all about it and now I've reached the stage that I press a kiss on my golden pendant,[1] and think "what do I care about the lot of them", and make plans for the future!

yours, Anne.

P.S. You will no doubt have noticed that I generally call Mummy Mum or Mums. That's an invention of mine in order not to have to call her "Mumsie." It's an incomplete Mumsie as it were, I would love to honor her with an extra ie, but fortunately she doesn't realize why I can't.

yours, Anne.

Sometimes I decided to remain cross, but when I came home from school I always had so much news that my resolutions were gone with the wind and Mummy, whatever she might be doing, had to lend an ear to all my adventures. Then the time came once more when I didn't listen for footsteps on the staircase any longer, [felt lonely] and at night my pillow was wet with tears.

Everything grew much worse at that point; *enfin*, you know all about it.

Now God has sent me a helper—Peter . . . I just clasp my pendant, kiss it, and think to myself, "What do I care about the lot of them! Peter belongs to me and no one knows anything about it." This way I can get over all the snubs I receive. Who would ever think that so much can go on in the soul of a young girl?

Yours, Anne

a

Saturday 15 January 1944.

Dearest Kitty,

There is no point in telling you every time the exact details of our rows and arguments. It is enough if I tell you that we keep drifting further apart and increasingly ignore the wishes of the others.

| 28

Mummy's birthday is approaching, she got some sugar from Kugler which is already cause for jealousy, because there was no sugar | for Mrs. v.P.'s birthday. I know that you and everyone else must be sick of hearing about all these discussions, tears and unkind words and we are even more fed up with them. Mummy made the wish—a wish that cannot come true just now—never to see Mr. v.P.'s face again.

b   259

Saturday, 15 Jan. 1944.

Dear Kitty,

There is no point in telling you every time the exact details of our rows and arguments. Let it suffice to tell you that we have divided up a great many things such as fat and meat¹, and eat our own fried potatoes with it and that as far as the meat is concerned we no longer have to bother about the v.P.s' taste nor do we have to look in the pans for missing bits of this and that. For some time now we have been eating whole-meal bread between meals as an extra because by 4 o'clock in the afternoon we are longing for our supper so much that we hardly know how to control our rumbling tummies.

Mummy's birthday is rapidly approaching; she got some extra sugar from Kugler, which made the v.P.s jealous as Mrs. v.P. had not been favored in this way for her birthday. But what's the use of annoying each other with yet more unkind words, tears and angry

| 260

out- | bursts, as you must know that we are fed up with them even more.

Mummy has expressed the wish—one which cannot come true just now—not to see Mr. van Pels's face for a fortnight.

c

Saturday, 15 January, 1944

Dear Kitty,

There is no point in telling you every time the exact details of our rows and arguments. Let it suffice to tell you that we have divided up a great many things, such as butter and meat, and that we fry our own potatoes. For some time now we've been eating whole-meal bread between meals as an extra, because by four o'clock in the afternoon we are longing for our supper so much that we hardly know how to control our rumbling tummies.

Mummy's birthday is rapidly approaching. She got some extra sugar from Kraler, which made the Van Daans jealous as Mrs. Van Daan had not been favored in this way for her birthday. But what's the use of annoying each other with yet more unkind words, tears, and angry outbursts. You can be sure of one thing, Kitty, that we are even more fed up with them than ever! Mummy has expressed the wish—one which cannot come true just now—not to see the Van Daans for a fortnight.

457

a

I ask myself whether one would have trouble in the long run, whomever one shared a house with. Or did we have extra bad luck? At table when Pf. takes ¼ of a half-full gravy boat while all the rest are still waiting for the gravy then I lose my appetite and feel like leaping to my feet and chasing him off his chair and out of the door. Are most people so selfish and stingy then? The van Pels motto is: "If we have got enough, then the rest may have some too, but we get the best, we get it first, we get the most." Pf.'s motto is: "I take as much of everything as I want, I don't bother to look if there's any left and I tell everyone how modest I am!" I think it's a good thing that I've learned a bit about | 29 human beings here, but I feel it's enough now; Peter says the same and I would say it | even if we'd been here for only half a year instead of a year and a half. But God knows what we need and what is good for us and so we should try to make the best of our stay here.

Now I'm preaching Kitty, but I do believe that if I stay here for very long, the youth in my young woman's soul will have fled. And I did so much want to grow into a real young woman!

AnneFrank.

b

I continually ask myself whether one would have trouble in the long run, whomever one shared a house with. Or did we strike it extra unlucky? At table when Pf. takes ¼ of a half-full gravy boat and lets the rest of us simply go without gravy then I lose my appetite and feel like leaping to my feet and chasing him off his chair and out of the door.

Are most people so selfish and stingy then? The van Pels method is: "If we have got enough, then the rest may have some too; but we get the best, we get it first, we get the most!" Pf. goes a bit further still: "I take as much of everything as I want, I don't bother to look if there's any left and I tell everyone how modest I am!" I think it's all to the good | 261 to have learned a bit about human beings, | but now I think it's been enough. The war goes on just the same, whether or not we choose to quarrel, or long for freedom and fresh air, and so we should try to make the best of our stay here. Now I'm preaching, but I also believe that if I stay here for very long I shall grow into a dried-up old beanstalk. And I did want to grow into a real young woman!

yours, Anne

c

I keep asking myself, whether one would have trouble in the long run, who[m]ever one shared a house with. Or did we strike it extra unlucky? Are most people so selfish and stingy then? I think it's all to the good to have learned a bit about human beings, but now I think I've learned enough. The war goes on just the same, whether or not we choose to quarrel, or long for freedom and fresh air, and so we should try to make the best of our stay here. Now I'm preaching, but I also believe that if I stay here for very long I shall grow into a dried-up old beanstalk. And I did so want to grow into a real young woman!

Yours, Anne

458

Wednesday evening (8 o'clock!)
19 January 1944.

Dear Kitty,

I (the same old mistake!) don't know what it is, but I always notice after a dream that I've changed. In parenthesis, last night I dreamed again about Peter and saw his searching look again, but this dream was not as beautiful or as clear as the last. You know that I used to be jealous of Margot's relationship with Daddy before, there is no longer any trace of that now; I still feel hurt when Daddy treats me unreasonably because of his nerves, but then I think: "I can't really blame you people for being like that, you talk so | 30 much about children—and the thoughts of young people, | but you don't know the first thing about them!" I long for more than Daddy's kisses, for more than his caresses. Isn't it terrible of me to keep thinking about this all the time? Shouldn't I, who want to be good and kind, forgive them first of all? I even forgive Mummy, but I can hardly take it when she's being so sarcastic and laughing at me all the time.

I know that I am far from being as I ought to be; will I ever be?

AnneFrank.

P.S. Daddy asked whether I have told you about the cake. As a birthday present the office gave Mummy a genuine pre-war mocha cake. It was really lovely! But at the moment I have so little room in my thoughts for things like that.

. . . . . .

. . . . . .

459

Dearest Kit,

I wonder whether you could tell me why it is that people always try so hard to hide their real feelings? How is it that I am always quite different from what I should be in other people's company and also quite different from what I am inside? Why do people trust one another so little? Oh, I do know there must be a reason, but things are bad, very bad indeed!

Since my dream the other night I have changed, have grown up a lot, have become more of an independent being. You'll certainly be amazed when I tell you that even my attitude towards the van Pelses has changed. I suddenly see all the arguments etc. etc. in a different light, and am not as prejudiced now as I was. How can I have changed so much? I have suddenly begun to feel (where/whence I do not know myself) that if Mummy had been different, a real Mumsie, our relationship here might have been quite, quite

---

Dear Kitty,

I wonder whether you could tell me why it is that people always try so hard to hide their real feelings? How is it that I always behave quite differently from what I should in other people's company? Why do we trust one another so little? I know there must be a reason, but still I sometimes think it's horrible that you find you can confide so little in people, even in those who are nearest to you.

It seems as if I've grown up a lot since my dream the other night. I'm much more of an independent being. You'll certainly be amazed when I tell you that even my attitude towards the van Pelses has changed. I suddenly see all the arguments etc. etc. in a different light, and am not as prejudiced as I was. How can I have changed so much? Yes, you see. it suddenly struck me that if Mummy had been different, a real Mumsie, the relationship

| 263 might have been quite, quite different. It's true that Mrs. v. Pels is by no means | a nice

---

Dear Kitty,

I wonder whether you can tell me why it is that people always try so hard to hide their real feelings? How is it that I always behave quite differently from what I should in other people's company?

Why do we trust one another so little? I know there must be a reason, but still I sometimes think it's horrible that you find you can never really confide in people, even in those who are nearest to you.

It seems as if I've grown up a lot since my dream the other night. I'm much more of an "independent being." You'll certainly be amazed when I tell you that even my attitude towards the Van Daans has changed. I suddenly see all the arguments and the rest of it in a different light, and am not as prejudiced as I was.

How can I have changed so much? Yes, you see it suddenly struck me that if Mummy had been different, a real Mumsie, the relationship might have been quite, quite different.

32

different. It's true that Mrs. van Pels has a disagreeable character, but the people here can't be so bad that there isn't a good side to them too.

If Mummy wasn't so impossible during every discussion, so severe, so disapproving and so unfeminine, then all our quarrels could easily have been avoided for Mrs. van Pels with all her talking and preaching is really not as bad as she seems. True, she is stingy, selfish and stupid but still you can talk to her.

All the problems of our upbringing, of our being spoiled, the food—all, all, all could have been quite different if we'd remained perfectly open and friendly, and not always only on the lookout for something to seize on. I know exactly what you would say Kitty: "But Anne, do these words really come from your lips? From you who have had to listen to so many harsh words from the people upstairs, from you the girl who has suffered so many injustices! Yes really, they come from me. At the moment I seize every opportunity to find anything I can talk to and Mrs. v.P. despite her bad points is not really bad through and through.

person, but still I do think that if Mummy hadn't been so impossible whenever the conversation gets tricky, then half the quarrels could have been avoided. Mrs. van Pels has one good side, and that is that you can talk to her. Despite all her selfishness, stinginess and underhandedness, you can make her give in easily, as long as you don't irritate her and get on the wrong side of her. This way doesn't work every time but if you have patience you can try again and see how far you get.

All the problems of our "upbringing," of our being spoiled, the food—all, all, all, it could have been quite different if we'd remained perfectly open and friendly, and not always on the look-out for something to seize on. I know exactly what you'll say Kitty: "But Anne, do these words really come from your lips? From you who have had to listen to so many harsh words from the people upstairs, from you, the girl who has suffered so many injustices!"

264

And yet they come from me. I want to start afresh and try to get to the bottom of it all, not be like the saying "the young always follow a bad example." I want to examine the whole matter carefully myself and find out what is true and what is exaggerated. Then

It's true that Mrs. Van Daan is by no means a nice person, but still I do think that half the quarrels could be avoided if it weren't for the fact that when the conversation gets tricky Mummy is a bit difficult too.

Mrs. Van Daan has one good side, and that is that you can talk to her. Despite all her selfishness, stinginess, and underhandedness, you can make her give in easily, as long as you don't irritate her and get on the wrong side of her. This way doesn't work every time, but if you have patience you can try again and see how far you get.

All the problems of our "upbringing," of our being spoiled, the food—it could have been quite different if we'd remain perfectly open and friendly, and not always only on the look-out for something to seize on.

I know exactly what you'll say, Kitty: "But, Anne, do these words really come from your lips? From you, who have had to listen to so many harsh words from the people upstairs, from you, the girl who has suffered so many injustices?" And yet they come from me.

I want to start afresh and try to get to the bottom of it all, not be like the saying "the young always follow a bad example." I want to examine the whole matter carefully myself and find out what is true and what is exaggerated. Then if I myself am disappointed

Of course I can't tell her so, for I mustn't turn against my own family, but I'll take care not to gossip any longer and to stand up for them as much as possible.

Until now I've always thought that they were in the wrong, but we too are a very great deal to blame. We have certainly been right about the subject matter; but when it comes to handling others one expects more insight from intelligent people (which we consider ourselves to be!).

I have acquired that insight now and hope I'll have occasion to make good use of it.

AnneFrank.

P.S. I am still working hard and in particular I have recently developed a special liking for the family trees of royal houses. Once you start with that you get on very quickly. I haven't deserted my film stars either. Mr. Kugler brings me Cinema & Theater every week. 'Bye yours Anne.

if I myself am disappointed I can again follow the same path as Mummy and Daddy; if not, well I shall just try first of all to make them alter their ideas and if I don't succeed I shall stick to my own opinions and judgment.

I shall seize every opportunity to discuss openly all our disagreements with Mrs. v.P. and not be afraid of declaring myself neutral even at the cost of being called a "know-all."

I shall of course say nothing that goes against my own family, but from today there will be no more unkind gossip on my part, although this does not mean that I will ever | 265 stop defending them against all comers. | Until now I was immovable I always thought that they were in the wrong, but a large part of the blame also lay with us. We have certainly been right about the subject matter; but when it comes to handling others one expects more insight from intelligent people (which we consider ourselves to be!).

I hope that I have acquired a little drop of insight and will use it well when the occasion arises.

yours, Anne

in them I can adopt the same line as Mummy and Daddy; if not, I shall try first of all to make them alter their ideas and if I don't succeed I shall stick to my own opinions and judgment. I shall seize every opportunity to discuss openly all our points of argument with Mrs. Van Daan and not be afraid of declaring myself neutral, even at the cost of being called a "know-all." It is not that I shall be going against my own family, but from today there will be no more unkind gossip on my part.

Until now I was immovable! I always thought the Van Daans were in the wrong, but we too are partly to blame. We have certainly been right over the subject matter; but handling of others from intelligent people (which we consider ourselves to be!) one expects more insight [but one expects more insight from intelligent people (which we consider ourselves to be!) when it comes to the handling of others]. I hope that I have acquired a bit of insight and will use it well when the occasion arises.

Yours, Anne

Monday 24 Jan. 1944.

Dear Kitty,

Something has happened to me, or rather, I can hardly speak of it as an event, except that I think it is pretty crazy. Whenever anyone used to speak of sexual problems at home or at school, it was something either mysterious or revolting. Words which had any bearing on the subject were whispered, and if someone didn't understand he was laughed at. This always struck me as crazy and I thought: "Why are people so secretive and tiresome all the time whenever they talk about these things?" But as it didn't seem that I could change things, I kept my mouth shut as much as possible or only spoke on the subject when I was alone with Jacque or she [with me]. When I already knew quite a lot about it, Mummy said to me once, "Anne, let me give you some good advice; never speak about such things to boys and don't reply if they begin about it!" I replied: "No of course not! The very idea!" And I have never spoken about it to boys.

Monday 24 Jan. 1944

Dear Kitty,

Something has happened to me (or rather, I can hardly describe it as an event), except that I think it is completely crazy. Whenever anyone used to speak of sexual problems at home or at school, it was something either mysterious or revolting. Words which had any bearing on the subject were whispered and often if someone didn't understand something ⁴he was laughed at. It struck me as very odd and I often thought: "Why are these people so secretive or tiresome when they talk about these things?" But as I didn't think that I could change things, I kept my mouth shut as much as possible, or asked my girl friends for information. When I had learned quite a lot and had also⁵—Mummy said once, "Anne, let me give you some good advice; never speak about this subject to boys and don't reply if they begin about it." I remember exactly what my answer was: I said, "No of course not! The very idea!" And there it remained.

Monday, 24 January, 1944

Dear Kitty,

Something has happened to me; or rather, I can hardly describe it as an event, except that I think it is pretty crazy. Whenever anyone used to speak of sexual problems at home or at school, it was something either mysterious or revolting. Words which had any bearing on the subject were whispered, and often if someone didn't understand he was laughed at. It struck me as very odd and I thought, "Why are people so secretive and tiresome when they talk about these things?" But as I didn't think that I could change things, I kept my mouth shut as much as possible, or sometimes asked girl friends for information. When I had learned quite a lot and had also spoken about it with my parents, Mummy said one day, "Anne, let me give you some good advice; never speak about this subject to boys and don't reply if they begin about it." I remember exactly what my answer was: I said, "No, of course not! The very idea!" And there it remained.

| 35   When I came here, Daddy told me a whole lot more and I gradually gathered the rest, from books and conversations. | Peter here was never as tiresome about these things as the boys at school—a few times at first perhaps—but he never tried to draw me out. Mrs. v.P. told us that she had never talked about these things to Peter, and for all she knew neither had her husband. Apparently she didn't even know how and what he knew.

Yesterday now, when Margot, Peter and I were peeling potatoes the conversation turned to Boche. And I don't know how it came about but Peter said that Boche was a tomcat after all and added that Pf. had said the same thing, "but he had first said that she was a queen, but never mind!"

"Well," I said, "in that case I can't tell the difference either, but I have been wanting to go downstairs with you for some time so you can let me see for myself!" Peter thought

| 267   When we first came here, Daddy often told | me about things that I would really have preferred to hear from Mummy, and I found out the rest from books and things I picked up from conversations. Peter v. Pels was never as tiresome over this as the boys at school—once or twice at first perhaps—but he never tried to get me talking.

Yesterday, when Margot, Peter and I were peeling potatoes somehow the conversation turned to Boche. "We still don't know what sex Boche is, do we?" I asked

"Yes, certainly," Peter answered "He's a tom."

I began to laugh: "A tomcat that's expecting, that's marvelous!"

Peter and Margot laughed too over this silly mistake. You see, two months ago Peter had stated that Boche would soon be having a family, her tummy was growing visibly. However, the fatness appeared to come from the many stolen bones, because the children

When we first came here, Daddy often told me about things I would really have preferred to hear from Mummy, and I found out the rest from books and things I picked up from conversations. Peter Van Daan was never as tiresome over this as the boys at school—once or twice at first perhaps—but he never tried to get me talking.

Mrs. Van Daan told us that she had never talked about these things to Peter, and for all she knew neither had her husband. Apparently she didn't even know how much he knew.

Yesterday, when Margot, Peter, and I were peeling potatoes, somehow the conversation turned to Boche. "We still don't know what sex Boche is, do we?" I asked.

"Yes, certainly," Peter answered. "He's a tom."

I began to laugh. "A tomcat that's expecting, that's marvelous!"

Peter and Margot laughed too over this silly mistake. You see, two months ago, Peter had stated that Boche would soon be having a family, her tummy was growing visibly. However, the fatness appeared to come from the many stolen bones, because the children

a

that a good idea: "But he's a tom, all right," he insisted "I watched him having intercourse myself from the private office!" I must have looked a bit taken aback; I wasn't used to hearing people speak so openly about such matters, not Peter, anyway.

| 36   In the afternoon I put on my coat and went | downstairs with him. We went and stood in the conservatory, because there was no sign of Boche and Pete started calling him. "Yes," he said "Boche is a tom, all right, I can see it when he plays with me, he jumps up against me and then when he gets excited he even thinks I am a woman cat, it's really noticeable!" "I know what you mean," I said, for I had seen the same thing once with Tor, the Amendes' dog.

I wanted to ask all along whether Boche had been castrated, but I didn't dare. Peter took the words out of my mouth however: "Boche has certainly not been castrated."

"Peter," I asked "how old was Mouschi when he was castrated?"

"As soon as he came to us, very small!" And he went on whistling and calling softly but Boche didn't come. "Tell me, how do you say 'geschlechtsteil' [sex organ] in Dutch," he said then.

"Geslachtsdeel."

"No, that's not what I mean."

"Oh you mean the other thing, I don't know the word."

And then we went upstairs.

b

didn't seem to grow, let alone make their appearance! Peter just had to defend himself.

| 268   "No," he said, "you can go with me yourself | to look at him. Once when I was playing around with him, I noticed quite clearly that he's a tom."

I couldn't control my curiosity and went with him to the warehouse. Boche, however, was not receiving visitors, and was nowhere to be seen; we waited for a while, began to get cold and went upstairs again.

c

didn't seem to grow fast, let alone make their appearance!

Peter just had to defend himself. "No," he said. "You can go with me yourself to look at him. Once when I was playing around with him, I noticed quite clearly that he's a tom."

I couldn't control my curiosity, and went with him to the warehouse. Boche, however, was not receiving visitors, and was nowhere to be seen. We waited for a while, began to get cold, and went upstairs again. Later in the afternoon I heard Peter go downstairs for

465

Later in the afternoon, I heard him go downstairs again and I followed him on my own. He was standing beside the packing table playing with Boche.

"Well, here he is, do you want to see?" And suddenly he picked up the cat and showed me: "This here is the male organ and these are just a few stray hairs and that is his bottom!" The cat was turned round again and stood on the counter.

If any other boy had shown me "the male organ" like that he would have got a slap in the face, I would have been so indignant, But Peter spoke about it all in such a normal way, without any sneering or the slightest insinuation, that I felt quite normal about it too. "Were you there, when Mouschi was castrated?

b

Later in the afternoon, I heard Peter go downstairs for the second time; I mustered up all my courage to walk through the silent house alone, and reached the warehouse. Boche stood on the packing table playing with Peter, who had just put him on the scales to weigh him. "Hello, do you want to see him?" He didn't make any lengthy preparations, but picked up the animal, turned him over on to his back, deftly held his head and paws together, and the lesson began: "These are the male organs, these are just a few stray hairs, and that is his bottom."

| 269   The cat did another half turn and was standing on his | white socks once more.

If any other boy had shown me "the male organs," I would never have looked at him again. But Peter went on talking quite normally on what is otherwise such a painful subject, without meaning anything unpleasant, and in the end put me sufficiently at my ease for me to be normal too.

We played with Boche, amused ourselves well, chattered together, and finally sauntered through the large warehouse towards the door.

c

the second time. I mustered up all my courage to walk through the silent house alone, and reached the warehouse. Boche stood on the packing table playing with Peter, who had just put him on the scales to weigh him.

"Hello, do you want to see him?" He didn't make any lengthy preparations, but picked up the animal, turned him over on to his back, deftly held his head and paws together, and the lesson began. "These are the male organs, these are just a few stray hairs, and that is his bottom." The cat did another half turn and was standing on his white socks once more.

If any other boy had shown me "the male organs," I would never have looked at him again. But Peter went on talking quite normally on what is otherwise such a painful subject, without meaning anything unpleasant, and finally put me sufficiently at my ease for me to be normal too. We played with Boche, amused ourselves, chattered together, and then sauntered through the large warehouse towards the door.

a

"Yes, certainly, it doesn't take long, he was anesthetized of course."

"Do they take anything out?"

"No the doctor just cuts the sperm tube.² You can't see anything from the outside.³ Just listen to that other cat howling!" Outside there was a cat that kept miaowing day | 38 and night all through the season when the females were on heat. "That's a tom | cat for sure', I stated.

"You can't possibly tell."

"Yes, it's always the tom who calls."

"That one certainly isn't getting anywhere."

"Are dogs castrated as much as cats?"

"No, only lap dogs." Peter kept playing with the cat and wanted to show me Boche's teeth. I gathered up my courage since I wasn't feeling all that "normal" after all.

"Peter, a geschlechtsteil is a geslachtsdeel, but it has different names in male and female animals."

"I know that."

"In females it's called a vagina, I know that much, but I don't know what it's called in males."

"Yes."

"Oh well," I said again "how are you meant to know these words, most of the time you come across them by accident."

b

I always come across my information by accident in some book or other, don't you? I asked

c

"Usually, when I want to know something, I find it in some book or other, don't you?" I asked.

467

"Why on earth? I just ask upstairs. My parents know more than me and have had more experience."

Then we went upstairs.

"Things may alter", as Brer Rabbit said. Yes. Really I shouldn't have discussed these | 39 things in such a normal way | with a girl. That's not what Mummy meant when she said I mustn't discuss the subject with boys.

I wasn't quite my usual self though. When I thought about it, it still seemed rather odd.

Luckily, I know one thing at least now, that there really are young people—and of the opposite gender too—who can discuss these things quite naturally without making fun of them.

I wonder if Peter really always asks his parents. Would he really behave with them in the way he did with me yesterday? Ah, what would I know about it?!

Anne.

"Why on earth? I just ask upstairs. My parents know more than me and have had more experience."

We were already on the stairs, so I kept my mouth shut after that.

³"Things may alter," as Brer Rabbit said. Yes. Really I shouldn't have discussed these things in such a normal way with a girl. I know too definitely that Mummy didn't mean | 270 it that way when she warned me not to discuss the subject | with boys.

I wasn't quite my usual self for the rest of the day though, in spite of everything. When I remembered our talk, it still seemed rather odd. But at least I'm wiser about one thing, that there really are young people—and of the opposite sex too—who can discuss these things naturally without making fun of them.

I wonder if Peter really does ask his parents much. Would he honestly behave with them as he did with me yesterday? Ah, what would I know about it?!!!!!

yours, Anne

"Why on earth? I just ask upstairs. My father knows more than me and has had more experience in such things."

We were already on the stairs, so I kept my mouth shut after that.

"Things may alter," as Brer Rabbit said. Yes. Really I shouldn't have discussed these things in such a normal way with a girl. I know too definitely that Mummy didn't mean it that way when she warned me not to discuss the subject with boys. I wasn't quite my usual self for the rest of the day though, in spite of everything. When I thought over our talk, it still seemed rather odd. But at least I'm wiser about one thing, that there really are young people—and of the opposite sex too—who can discuss these things naturally without making fun of them.

I wonder if Peter really does ask his parents much. Would he honestly behave with them as he did with me yesterday? Ah, what would I know about it!

Yours, Anne

468

a . . . . . .

b 271

Friday 28 Jan. 1944.

Dear Kitty,

Lately I have developed a great love for family trees and genealogical tables of the royal families, and have come to the conclusion that once you begin, you want to delve still deeper into the past, and can keep on making fresh and interesting discoveries. Although I am extraordinarily industrious over my lessons, and can already follow the English Home Service quite well on the wireless, I still devote many Sundays to sorting and looking over my large collection of film stars, which is quite a respectable size by now. I am awfully pleased whenever Mr. Kugler brings the Cinema & Theater with him on Mondays; although this little gift is often called a waste of money by the less worldly members of the household, they are amazed each time at how accurately I can[2] state who[4] is in a certain

| 272

film, even after | a year. Bep, who, on her days off, often goes to the movies with her boy friend, tells me the titles of the new films each week; and in one breath I rattle off the names of the stars who appear in them, together with what the reviews say. Not so long ago, Mum said that I wouldn't need to go to a cinema later on because I knew the plots, the names of the stars and the opinions of the reviews all by heart.

c

Thursday, 27 January, 1944

Dear Kitty,

Lately I have developed a great love for family trees and genealogical tables of the royal families, and have come to the conclusion that, once you begin, you want to delve still deeper into the past, and can keep on making fresh and interesting discoveries. Although I am extraordinarily industrious over my lessons, and can already follow the English Home Service quite well on the wireless, I still devote many Sundays to sorting and looking over my large collection of film stars, which is quite a respectable size by now.

I am awfully pleased whenever Mr. Kraler brings the *Cinema and Theater* with him on Mondays. Although this little gift is often called a waste of money by the less worldly members of the household, they are amazed each time at how accurately I can state who is in a certain film, even after a year. Elli, who, on her days off, often goes to the movies with her boy friend, tells me the titles of the new films each week; and in one breath I rattle off the names of the stars who appear in them, together with what the reviews say. Not so long ago, Mum said that I wouldn't need to go to a cinema later on because I knew the plots, the names of the stars, and the opinions of the reviews all by heart.

If ever I come sailing in with a new hair style, they all look disapprovingly at me, and I can be quite sure that someone will ask which glamorous star I'm supposed to be imitating. They only half believe me if I reply that it's my own invention. But to continue about the hair style, it doesn't stay put for more than half an hour; then I'm so tired of the remarks people pass that I quickly hasten to the bathroom and restore my ordinary curly hair style.

yours, <u>Anne</u>

273

Friday 28 Jan. 1944.

Dear Kitty,

I asked myself this morning whether you don't sometimes feel rather like a cow who has had to chew over all the old pieces of news again and again, and who finally yawns loudly and silently wishes that Anne would occasionally dig up something new. Alas, I know it's dull for you, but try to put yourself in my place and imagine how sick I am of the old cows who keep having to be pulled out of the ditch again. If the conversation at mealtimes isn't over politics or a delicious meal, then Mummy or Mrs. v.P. trot out one of the old stories of their youth, which we've heard so many times before, or Pf. twaddles on about his wife's extensive wardrobe, beautiful race horses, leaking rowboats, boys who can swim at the age of 4, muscular pains and nervous patients. What it all boils down to is this, | 274 that if one of the eight of us opens his mouth, the other seven can finish the story | for

If ever I come sailing in with a new hair style, they all look disapprovingly at me, and I can be quite sure that someone will ask which glamorous star I'm supposed to be imitating. They only half believe me if I reply that it's my own invention.

But to continue about the hair style—it doesn't stay put for more than half an hour; then I'm so tired of the remarks people pass that I quickly hasten to the bathroom and restore my ordinary house-garden-kitchen hair style.

Yours, Anne

Friday, 28 January, 1944

Dear Kitty,

I asked myself this morning whether you don't sometimes feel rather like a cow who has had to chew over all the old pieces of news again and again, and who finally yawns loudly and silently wishes that Anne would occasionally dig up something new.

Alas, I know it's dull for you, but try to put yourself in my place, and imagine how sick I am of the old cows who keep having to be pulled out of the ditch again. If the conversation at mealtimes isn't over politics or a delicious meal, then Mummy or Mrs. Van Daan trot out one of the old stories of their youth, which we've heard so many times before; or Dussel twaddles on about his wife's extensive wardrobe, beautiful race horses, leaking rowboats, boys who can swim at the age of four, muscular pains and nervous patients. What it all boils down to is this—that if one of the eight of us opens his mouth,

470

b   him! We all know the point of every joke from the start, and the storyteller is alone in laughing at his witticisms. The various milkmen, grocers and butchers of the two ex-housewives have already grown beards in our eyes, so often have they been praised to the skies or pulled to pieces; it is impossible for anything in the conversation here to be fresh or new.

Still, all this would be bearable if the grownups didn't have their little way of telling the stories, with which Kleiman, Jan or Miep oblige the company, 10 times over and adding their own little frills and furbelows, so that I often have to pinch my arm under the table to prevent myself from putting them right. Little children such as Anne must never, under any circumstances, know better than the grownups, however many blunders they make and to whatever extent their imaginations run away with them.

c   the other seven can finish the story for him! We all know the point of every joke from the start, and the storyteller is alone in laughing at his witticisms. The various milkmen, grocers, and butchers of the two ex-housewives have already grown beards in our minds, so often have they been praised to the skies or pulled to pieces; it is impossible for anything in the conversation here to be fresh or new.

Still, all this would be bearable if the grownups didn't have their little way of telling the stories, with which Koophuis, Henk, or Miep oblige the company, ten times over and adding their own little frills and furbelows, so that I often have to pinch my arm under the table to prevent myself from putting them right. Little children such as Anne must never, under any circumstances, know better than the grownups, however many blunders they make, and to whatever extent they allow their imaginations to run away with them.

a

Dearest Kitty,

Although there is not much news here I mustn't neglect "Secret Annexe" affairs for the sake of my own. In the first place I wanted to say something about those who have gone "underground." Going underground and hiding have become nothing out of the ordinary for everyone and you can't imagine how much is being done by such organizations as

| 40   "Vrije-Nederland."* | Thousands and thousands of identity and ration cards are being provided, sometimes for nothing and sometimes for money. Goodness knows how many false identity cards are in circulation. Jewish acquaintances are going about under ordinary Christian names and there are certainly not many people in hiding like ourselves who have no identity cards and never go out. Bep's friend, who strictly speaking ought to be in Berlin, runs across good friends of his in the street every day and they often know where each one is hiding. Three of our milkman's sons are in the countryside etc. etc.

Vrij Nederland (The Free Netherlands) was one of the main underground newspapers; the Vrij-Nederland group was also involved with helping people in hiding. (L. de Jong, *Het Koninkrijk der Nederlanden in de Tweede Wereldoorlog*, Vol. 5, p. 814.)

---

b | 275   One favorite subject of Kleiman's and Jan's is that | of people in hiding and in the underground movement; they know very well that anything to do with other people in hiding interests us tremendously, and how deeply we can sympathize with the sufferings of people who get taken away, and rejoice with the liberated prisoner. We are quite used to the idea of people in hiding or "underground," as in bygone days one was used to Daddy's ¹bedroom slippers warming in front of the fire. There are a great number of organizations such as "The Free Netherlands" which forge identity cards, hand out money to people "underground," find hiding places for people, and work for young men in hiding, and it is amazing how much noble, unselfish work these people are doing, risking their own lives to help and save others. Our helpers are a very good example, they have pulled us through up till now and we hope they will bring us safely to dry land. Otherwise they

| 276   would have to share the same | fate as the many others who are being searched for, never have we heard one word of the burden which we certainly must be to them, never has

---

c   One favorite subject of Koophuis's and Henk's is that of people in hiding and in the underground movement. They know very well that anything to do with other people in hiding interests us tremendously, and how deeply we can sympathize with the sufferings of people who get taken away, and rejoice with the liberated prisoner.

We are quite as used to the idea of going into hiding, or "underground," as in bygone days one was used to Daddy's bedroom slippers warming in front of the fire.

There are a great number of organizations, such as "The Free Netherlands," which forge identity cards, supply money to people "underground," find hiding places for people, and work for young men in hiding, and it is amazing how much noble, unselfish work these people are doing risking their own lives to help and save others. Our helpers are a very good example. They have pulled us through up till now and we hope they will bring us safely to dry land. Otherwise, they will have to share the same fate as the many others who are being searched for. Never have we heard *one* word of the burden which we certainly must be to them, never has one of them complained of all the trouble we give.

a

You hear the wildest tales from the most reliable sources e.g.: There was a football match in Gelderland between an underground eleven and a police eleven.

In Hilversum, where new registration cards are being issued, certain hours have been set aside during which the police look the other way in order to give people in hiding a chance to collect their ration books. I still have work to do, so until next time.

AnneFrank.

b

one of them complained about all the trouble we cause. They[2] all come upstairs every day, talk to the men about business and politics, to the women about food and wartime difficulties, and about newspapers and books with the children. They put on the brightest possible faces, bring flowers and presents for birthdays and bank holidays, are always ready to help and do all they can. That is something we must never forget; although others may show heroism in the war or against the Germans, our helpers prove their heroism in their cheerfulness and affection.

The wildest tales are going around, but still they usually happened. For instance, Kleiman told us this week that in Gelderland two football elevens met, and one side consisted solely of members of | the "underground" and the other was made up of members of the police.[*] New registration cards are being handed out in Hilversum, in order that the many people in hiding may also draw rations (ration cards can only be obtained with a registration card or for 60 florins each) the officials have given instructions to those of them in the district to come at a certain time, so that they can collect their papers from a separate little table. Still, they'll have to be careful that such impudent tricks do not reach the ears of the Germans.

yours, Anne

| 277

[*] The underground paper *Trouw*, Vol. 1, No. 13, published a version of this story in November 1943, but did not say where the match was played.

c

They all come upstairs every day, talk to the men about business and politics, to the women about food and wartime difficulties, and about newspapers and books with the children. They put on the brightest possible faces, bring flowers and presents for birthdays and bank holidays, are always ready to help and do all they can. That is something we must never forget; although others may show heroism in the war or against the Germans, our helpers display heroism in their cheerfulness and affection.

The wildest tales are going around, but still they are usually founded on fact. For instance, Koophuis told us this week that in Gelderland two football elevens met, and one side consisted solely of members of the "underground" and the other was made up of members of the police. New ration books [registration cards] are being handed out in Hilversum. In order that the many people in hiding may also draw rations, the officials have given instructions to those of them in the district to come at a certain time, so that they can collect their documents from a separate little table. Still, they'll have to be careful that such impudent tricks do not reach the ears of the Germans.

Yours, Anne.

473

Sunday 30 January 1944.

Dearest Kit,

We've arrived at Sunday again; it may be true I don't mind it as much as I did at the beginning but it's still pretty boring.

I still haven't been to the warehouse, maybe I'll manage to go there soon. Last night I went downstairs all by myself in the dark having done it a few nights before with Daddy. I stood on top of the stairs, it was not too bad, lots of German airplanes were about and I realized that I was a-person-to-myself, not needing to rely on the support of others. My fear vanished, I looked up at the sky and trusted in God.

I desperately want to be alone. Daddy has noticed that I'm not quite my usual self, but I really can't tell him everything. "Leave me in peace, leave me alone," that's what I'd like to keep crying out all the time. Who knows, the day may come when I'm left alone more than I would wish!

AnneFrank.

b   . . . . . .

c   . . . . . .

Thursday 3 February 1944.

Dearest Kitty,

Invasion fever in the whole country is mounting daily. If you were here, on the one hand, you would probably feel the effect of all these preparations just as I do and, on the other, you would laugh at us for making such a fuss—who knows—perhaps for nothing! All the newspapers are full of the invasion and are driving people mad by saying that "In the event of the English landing here, the Germans will have to do all they can to defend the country; if necessary they will resort to flooding." Everywhere you can see maps on which those parts of Holland that will be under water are marked. The first question was now: What shall we do if the water in the streets rises to one meter?

Because you are sure to be interested, I will write down what answers everyone here in the "Secret Annexe" made to this question.

Thursday 3 Febr. 1944.

Dear Kitty,

Invasion fever in the whole country is mounting daily. If you were here, on the one hand,[1] you would probably feel the effect of all these preparations just as I do and, on the other, you would laugh at us for making such a fuss—who knows—perhaps for nothing!

All the newspapers are full of the invasion and are driving people mad by saying that "In the event of the English landing in Holland[3], the Germans will have to do all they can to defend the country; if necessary they will resort to flooding." With this, maps have been published in which the parts of Holland that would be under water are marked. As this applies to large parts of Amsterdam, the first question was, what shall we do if the

| 279 water in the streets rises to one meter? The answers given by | different people vary considerably.

Thursday, 3 February, 1944

Dear Kitty,

Invasion fever in the country is mounting daily. If you were here, on the one hand, you would probably feel the effect of all these preparations just as I do and, on the other, you would laugh at us for making such a fuss—who knows—perhaps for nothing.

All the newspapers are full of the invasion and are driving people mad by saying that "In the event of the English landing in Holland, the Germans will do all they can to defend the country; if necessary they will resort to flooding." With this, maps have been published, on which the parts of Holland that will be under water are marked. As this applies to large parts of Amsterdam, the first question was, what shall we do if the water in the streets rises to one meter? The answers given by different people vary considerably.

No. 1: Since people won't be able to walk or cycle any more, they will have to try and escape by wading through the water; in the end the water will | of course have become stagnant.

No. 2: People will have to try and swim. Mrs. v.P.: "I still have a bathing suit and Peter will have to learn to swim in a hurry." Reply: "If you put on a bathing cap as well and swim under water as far as you can no one will see that you are Jewish."

No. 3: What a stench there'll be; we shall probably see water rats in all the streets.

No. 4: Perhaps the whole warehouse will collapse, it's more wood than stone.

No. 5: No, all joking apart now. We shall try to get a small boat.

No. 6: No, a much better idea, each of us will get into a wooden packing case and row with a soup ladle!

No. 7: Can't we walk on stilts?

No. 8: Jan Gies won't need to. He's sure to take his wife on his back.

"As walking or cycling is out of the question, we shall have to wade through the stagnant water."

"Of course not, one will have to try and swim. We shall all put on our bathing suits and caps and swim under water as much as possible, then no one will see that we are Jews."

"Oh, what nonsense! I'd like to see the ladies swimming, if the rats started biting their legs" (That was naturally a man; just see who screams the loudest!)

"We shan't be able to get out of the house anyway; the warehouse will definitely collapse if there is a flood of water, it is so wobbly already."

"Listen, folks, all joking apart, we shall try and get a boat."

"Why bother? I know something much better we each get hold of a wooden packing case from the attic and row with a soup ladle!"

"I shall walk on stilts: I used to be an expert at it in my youth."

280 "Jan Gies won't need to, he's sure to take his wife on his back, then she'll be on stilts."

"As walking or cycling is out of the question, we shall have to wade through the stagnant water."

"Of course not, one will have to try and swim. We shall all put on our bathing suits and caps and swim under water as much as possible, then no one will see that we are Jews."

"Oh, what nonsense! I'd like to see the ladies swimming, if the rats started biting their legs!" (That was naturally a man: just see who screams the loudest!)

"We shan't be able to get out of the house anyway; the warehouse will definitely collapse if there is a flood, it is so wobbly already."

"Listen, folks, all joking apart, we shall try and get a boat."

"Why bother? I know something much better. We each get hold of a wooden packing case from the attic and row with a soup ladle!"

"I shall walk on stilts: I used to be an expert at it in my youth."

"Henk Van Santen won't need to, he's sure to take his wife on his back, then she'll be on stilts."

a

Etc. Etc. All of that may sound very funny now but the truth is far from funny.

The second question came this morning in connection with all the posters that have gone up in the streets: What do we do if the Germans start evacuating people?

No. 1: Leave the city too. Disguise ourselves as best we can.

44 No. 2: Don't go, whatever happens. Stay put! The | Germans are quite capable of driving the whole population right into Germany, where they will all die.

No. 3: Yes, we'll stay here, we're safest where we are. We'll try and fetch Kleiman and his family over here to come and live with us. We'll try and get hold of some more wood wool, then we can lie on the floor. Let's ask Miep and Kleiman to start bringing blankets here now. We'll order 50 lbs. of flour from Siemons, 60 lbs. of corn are already in the house, ground and in good condition. Let's ask Jan for another 10 lbs. of peas, we already have 70 lbs. of kidney beans, 10 lbs. of peas and 5 lbs. of marrow peas, 50 tins of vegetables, 20 tins of fish, 40 tins of milk,

b

This gives you a rough idea, doesn't it, Kit?

This chatter is all very amusing, but the truth may be otherwise. A second question about the invasion was bound to arise: what do we do if the Germans evacuate Amsterdam?

"Leave the city too, and disguise ourselves as best we can."

"Not in the street, whatever happens, stay put! The only thing to do is remain here! The Germans are quite capable of driving the whole population right into Germany, where they will all die."

"Yes, naturally, we shall stay here, since this is the safest place. We'll try and fetch Kleiman and his family over here to come and live with us. We'll try and get hold of a sack of wood wool, then we can sleep on the floor. Let's ask Miep and Kleiman to start

281 bringing blankets here now. We'll order some extra corn in addition to our | 60 lbs. Let's get Jan to try and obtain more peas and beans; we have about 60 lbs. of beans and 10 lbs. of peas in the house at present. Don't forget that we've got 50 tins of vegetables.

c

This gives you a rough idea, doesn't it, Kit?

This chatter is all very amusing, but the truth may be otherwise. A second question about the invasion was bound to arise: what do we do if the Germans evacuate Amsterdam?

"Leave the city too, disguise ourselves as best we can."

"Don't go, whatever happens, stay put! The only thing to do is remain here! The Germans are quite capable of driving the whole population right into Germany, where they will all die."

"Yes, naturally, we shall stay here, since this is the safest place. We'll try and fetch Koophuis and his family over here to come and live with us. We'll try and get hold of a sack of wood wool, then we can sleep on the floor. Let's ask Miep and Koophuis to start bringing blankets here."

"We'll order some extra corn in addition to our sixty pounds. Let's get Henk to try and obtain more peas and beans; we have about sixty pounds of beans and ten pounds of peas in the house at present. Don't forget that we've got fifty tins of vegetables."

4 kilos of milk powder, 3 bottles of salad oil, 4 preserving jars of butter, 4 preserving jars of meat, 4 jars of marmalade, 60 preserving jars of fruit, 20 bottles of tomato soup, 10 lbs. of rolled oats, 8 lbs. of rice, and no sugar. Our stocks are rather large; but when you think that we could suddenly have a great many more people to share our food, it's certainly not a lot. We have enough coal and firewood in the house; and as far as possible plenty of candles.

No. 4: Let's all make little moneybags, which could easily be hidden in our clothing, to

| 45   put our money in if we need to.

No. 5: We'll make lists and pack the most essential things into our rucksacks.

No. 6: If it gets that far we'll make an observation post in the front and the back loft.

No. 7: We may have all the supplies we need now, you know, but what if the gas and electricity pack up? Then we'll have to cook on the stove. Filter and boil our water. We'll clean out some wicker bottles now and store water in them when the time comes. We can also use three preserving pans and a washtub as water tanks.

[1]Mummy, just count up how much we've got of other food, will you:

10 tins of fish, 40 tins of milk, 10 kilos of milk powder, 3 bottles of salad oil, 4 preserving jars of butter, 4 preserving jars of meat, [2]2 wicker-covered bottles of strawberries, 2 bottles of raspberries, 20 bottles of tomatoes, 10 lbs. of rolled oats, 8 lbs. of rice and that's all.

Our stock's not too bad, but if you think that we could be having [3]visitors as well and drawing from reserves each week, then it seems more than it actually is.

We have sufficient coal and firewood in the house, also candles[4] (we've skipped Chanuka). Let's all make little moneybags, which could easily be hidden in our clothing, in case we want to take money with us. We'll make lists of the most important things to take, should we have to run for it, and pack rucksacks now in readiness.

| 282   If it gets that far, we'll put two people on watch, one in the front | and one in the back loft.

I say what's the use of collecting such stocks of food, if we haven't any water,[6] gas or electricity?

Then we must cook on the stove. Filter and boil our water. We'll clean out some large wicker bottles and store water in them. We can also use three preserving pans and a washtub as water tanks.

"Mummy, just count up how much we've got of other food, will you?"

"Ten tins of fish, forty tins of milk, ten kilos of milk powder, three bottles of salad oil, four preserving jars of butter, four ditto of meat, two wicker-covered bottles of strawberries, two bottles of raspberries, twenty bottles of tomatoes, ten pounds of rolled oats, eight pounds of rice; and that's all.

"Our stock's not too bad, but if you think that we may be having visitors as well and drawing from reserves each week, then it seems more than it actually is. We have sufficient coal and firewood in the house, also candles. Let's all make little moneybags, which could easily be hidden in our clothing, in case we want to take money with us.

"We'll make lists of the most important things to take, should we have to run for it, and pack rucksacks now in readiness. If it gets that far, we'll put two people on watch, one in the front and one in the back loft. I say, what's the use of collecting such stocks of food, if we haven't any water, gas, or electricity?"

"Then we must cook on the stove. Filter and boil our water. We'll clean out some large wicker bottles and store water in them."

478

a

No. 8: We'll have our Red Cross box, all winter coats, shoes, brandy and sugar brought over from the Amendes as soon as possible.

No. 9: We still have 1½ sacks of winter potatoes in the back spice store. That's how they go on here all day long, Daddy is planning to give Margot and me 500 florins each if matters go that far probably including dollars. Mummy and he will take 1,000 florins each.

During the meal we had the following conversation with Jan:

| 46 Gentlemen: We are afraid Jan, that the Germans | will take the whole population with them.

Jan: But that's impossible, how will they get the trains for it?

Gentlemen: Trains? Civilians will have to use shanks's pony.

J.: I don't think so, you look on the black side of everything all the time. What would be their object?

G.: What did Goebels say: "If we have to step down, we shall slam the doors of all the occupied countries behind us!"

b

We'll have our Red Cross box, all winter coats, shoes, brandy, eau de cologne and sugar brought out of safekeeping as soon as possible.

On top of that we still have 1½ sacks of winter potatoes in the spice store.

———

I hear nothing but this sort of talk the whole day long, invasion and nothing but invasion, arguments about suffering from hunger, dying, bombs, fire extinguishers, sleeping bags, Jewish vouchers, poisonous gases etc., etc. None of it is exactly cheering. Our gentlemen give pretty straightforward warnings; an example is the following conversation with Jan:

Gentlemen: We are afraid that if the Germans withdraw they will take the whole

| 283 population | with them.

J.: That is impossible, they haven't the trains at their disposal.

G.: Trains? Do you really think they'd put civilians in carriages. Out of the question. They could use shanks's pony. (per pades apostolonum Pf. always says).

J.: I don't believe a word of it, you look on the black side of everything. What would be the object in driving all the civilians along with them?

G.: Didn't you know that Goebels said, if we have to step down, we shall slam the doors of all the occupied Countries behind us!"

c

I hear nothing but this sort of talk the whole day long, invasion and nothing but invasion, arguments about suffering from hunger, dying, bombs, fire extinguishers, sleeping bags, Jewish vouchers, poisonous gases, etc., etc. None of it is exactly cheering. The gentlemen in the "Secret Annexe" give pretty straightforward warnings; an example is the following conversation with Henk:

"Secret Annexe": "We are afraid that if the Germans withdraw, they will take the whole population with them."

Henk: "That is impossible, they haven't the trains at their disposal."

"S.A.": "Trains? Do you really think they'd put civilians in carriages? Out of the question. They could use 'shank's mare.' " (*Per pedes apostolorum*, Dussel always says.)

H.: "I don't believe a word of it, you look on the black side of everything. What would be their object in driving all the civilians along with them?"

"S.A.": "Didn't you know that Goebbels said, 'If we have to withdraw, we shall slam the doors of all the occupied countries behind us'?"

479

a

J: They have said so much already!

G: Do you think the Germans are too nice for that, they simply say: If we have got to go down, then everyone else will go down as well.

J: I just don't believe it!

G: It's always the same, you don't want to see what is happening!

J: But where do you get it from, it's all just supposition.

G: We have been through it ourselves and are things any different in Russia?

J: That's quite different, you mustn't include the Jews. And no one knows what is | 47 going on in Russia, the English and the Russians are | sure to exaggerate things for propaganda purposes, just like the Germans.

b

J. They have said so much already.

G. Do you think the Germans are above doing such a thing or too humane? What they think is this: If we have to go down, then everybody in our clutches will go down with us"

J. Tell that to the Marines; I just don't believe it!

284   G. It's always the same song, no one will see danger approaching until it is actually on top of him.

J. But you know nothing definite. You just suppose.

G. We have all been through it ourselves, first in Germany and then here. And what is going on in Russia?

J. You mustn't include the Jews. I don't think anyone knows what is going on in Russia. The English and the Russians are sure to exaggerate things for propaganda purposes, just like the Germans.

c

H.: "They have said so much already."

"S.A.": "Do you think the Germans are above doing such a thing or too humane? What they think is this: 'If we have got to go down, then everybody in our clutches will go down with us.' "

H.: "Tell that to the Marines; I just don't believe it!"

"S.A.": "It's always the same song; no one will see danger approaching until it is actually on top of him."

H.: "But you know nothing definite; you just simply suppose."

"S.A.": "We have all been through it ourselves, first in Germany, and then here. And what is going on in Russia?"

H.: "You mustn't include the Jews. I don't think anyone knows what is going on in Russia. The English and the Russians are sure to exaggerate things for propaganda purposes, just like the Germans."

480

G.: We don't believe that and even if they exaggerate 100% then it's bad enough anyway, because it's a fact that in Poland and Russia Millions and millions of people have been murdered and gassed.

Kitty, I'll leave it at that, spare you further details. I myself keep very quiet and don't take any notice of all the fuss and excitement; but it would be very nice and reassuring if the Kleimans came to stay here.

I have now reached the stage that I don't care much whether I live or die, the world will still keep on turning without me; what is going to happen, will happen, and anyway it's no good trying to resist.

I trust to luck, but should I be saved, and spared from destruction, then it would be terrible if my diaries and my tales were lost.

AnneMaryFrank.

G.: Out of the question, the English have always told the truth over the wireless. And suppose they do exaggerate the news by 10%, the facts are bad enough anyway, because you can't deny that many millions of peace-loving people were just simply murdered or gassed in Poland and Russia.

285   I will spare you further examples of these conversations; I myself keep very quiet and don't take any notice of all the fuss and excitement. I have now reached the stage that I don't care much whether I live or die. The world will still keep on turning without me; what is going to happen, will happen, and anyway it's no good trying to resist.

I trust to luck and do nothing but work, hoping that all will end well

yours, Anne

"S.A.": "Out of the question, the English have always told the truth over the wireless. And suppose they do exaggerate the news, the facts are bad enough anyway, because you can't deny that many millions of peace-loving people were just simply murdered or gassed in Poland and Russia."

I will spare you further examples of these conversations; I myself keep very quiet and don't take any notice of all the fuss and excitement. I have now reached the stage that I don't care much whether I live or die. The world will still keep on turning without me; what is going to happen, will happen, and anyway it's no good trying to resist.

I trust to luck and do nothing but work, hoping that all will end well.

Yours, Anne

Tuesday 8 February 1944.

Dearest Kitty,

I can't tell you how I feel. One moment I long for peace and quiet, the next for a little fun. We are not used to laughing here any more, to laughing properly till you can't laugh any more.

This morning I did have a fit of "helpless laughter," you know, the sort we used to have at school. Margot and I were giggling like real schoolgirls.

Last night there was trouble with Mummy again. Margot was just tucking her woolen blanket around her when suddenly she jumped out of bed again and stared at the blanket; there was a pin stuck in it! Mummy had sewn a patch in the blanket. Daddy shook his head meaningfully and talked about Mummy's slipshod ways. Soon afterwards Mummy came back from the bathroom and I said by way of a joke: "You know you're a real Rabenmutter."* Naturally, she asked why and we told her about the pin. She immediately pulled her haughtiest face and said to me: "You can talk about slovenliness, when you sew, the whole floor is covered with pins. And just look at that manicure case lying around again, you | never clear that away!" I said that I hadn't used it and Margot jumped in, since she was the guilty party. But Mummy went on talking about my slovenliness until I was fed up with it and said rather abruptly: "I never mentioned slovenliness, it's always me who gets into trouble when someone else does something wrong!" Mummy shut up and barely a minute later I was obliged to give her a good-night kiss the incident may have been unimportant but things like that annoy me.

[... ... ...]**

Anne Mary Frank.

---

*Literally "raven's mother," i.e., a cruel mother. Anne Frank wrote this sentence in German. A.J.P.
**In the 47 lines omitted here Anne Frank gave an extremely unkind and partly unfair picture of her parents' marriage. At the request of the Frank family this passage has been deleted.

b   . . . . . .

c   . . . . . .

a 52

Saturday 12 February 1944.

Dear Kitty

The sun is shining, the sky is deep blue, there is a lovely breeze and I'm longing—so longing—for everything . . . . . —

To talk, for freedom, for friends, to be alone. And I do so long . . . . . to cry! I feel as if I'm going to burst, and I know that it would get better with crying, but I can't. I'm restless I go from one room to the other, breathe at the bottom of a window, feel my heart beating, as if it is saying, "Can't you satisfy my longings at last?" . . . —I believe that it's spring within me, I feel that spring is awakening, I feel it in my whole body and soul.

I have to keep myself under control—time and again, I long for my Petel, I long for every boy, even for Peter—here. I want to shout at him: "Oh say something to me, don't just smile all the time, touch me, so that I can again get that delicious feeling inside me that I first had in my dream of Petel's cheek!"

| 53   I feel completely confused, I don't know | what to read, what to write, what to do, I only know that I am longing.

yours,
Anne Mary Frank.

b 286

Saturday 12 Febr. 1944.

Dear Kitty,

The sun is shining, the sky is deep blue, there is a lovely breeze and I am longing-[1] so longing-[2] for everything . . . . To talk, for freedom, for friends, to be alone. And I do so long. . . .to cry! I feel as if I'm going to burst, and I know that it would get better with crying; but I can't. I'm restless, I go from one room to the other, breathe through the crack of a closed window, feel my heart beating, as if[5] it is saying, "Can't you satisfy my longings at last?"

I believe that it's spring within me, I feel that spring is awakening, I feel it in my whole body and soul. It is an effort to behave normally, I feel utterly confused, don't know what to read, what to write, what to do, I only know that I am longing. . . .-

yours, Anne

c

Saturday, 12 February, 1944

Dear Kitty,

The sun is shining, the sky is a deep blue, there is a lovely breeze and I'm longing—so longing—for everything. To talk, for freedom, for friends, to be alone. And I do so long . . . to cry! I feel as if I'm going to burst, and I know that it would get better with crying; but I can't, I'm restless, I go from one room to the other, breathe through the crack of a closed window, feel my heart beating, as if it is saying, "Can't you satisfy my longings at last?"

I believe that it's spring within me, I feel that spring is awakening, I feel it in my whole body and soul. It is an effort to behave normally, I feel utterly confused, don't know what to read, what to write, what to do, I only know that I am longing . . . !

Yours, Anne

Monday[1] 14[2] February
'44.

Dear Kitty,

Since Saturday a lot has changed for me. It came about like this: I longed (and am still longing) but . . . . . now something has happened, which has made it a little, just a little, less.

To my great joy (I will be quite honest about it) already this morning I noticed that Peter kept looking at me all the time. Not in the ordinary way, I don't know how, I just can't explain, but I suddenly had the feeling that he isn't as much in love with Margot as I had thought. I made a special effort not to look at him too much, because whenever I did, he kept on looking too and then—yes, then—it gave me a lovely feeling inside, but which I mustn't feel too often.

On Monday morning I had to go up to the attic to get some books for Mr. Pfeffer and Peter immediately took the opportunity to come upstairs as well. We talked about | 54 nothing of any importance; Mr. van Pels joined us and | I went downstairs again fairly soon. When I had brought Pf. his books, I had to take the [3]ones he had read back again (I could easily have put [4]it off, of course, but I didn't).

I climbed up the stairs again with my coat on and sat down on the floor on a pile of things with a cushion on top. The window was open, there was glorious sunshine and I was glad because I knew he would be back. And he did come back and told me what had happened the night before.

> I desperately want to be alone. Daddy has noticed that I'm not quite my usual self, but I really can't tell him everything. "Leave me in peace, leave me alone," that's what I'd like to keep crying out all the time. Who knows, the day may come when I'm left alone more than I would wish!
>
> AnneFrank.

. . . . . .

Sunday, 13 February, 1944

Dear Kitty,

Since Saturday a lot has changed for me. It came about like this. I longed—and am still longing—but ... now something has happened, which has made it a little, just a little, less.

To my great joy—I will be quite honest about it—already this morning I noticed that Peter kept looking at me all the time. Not in the ordinary way, I don't know how, I just can't explain.

I used to think that Peter was in love with Margot, but yesterday I suddenly had the feeling that it is not so. I made a special effort not to look at him too much, because whenever I did, he kept on looking too and then—yes, then—it gave me a lovely feeling inside, but which I mustn't feel too often.

I desperately want to be alone. Daddy has noticed that I'm not quite my usual self, but I really can't tell him everything. "Leave me in peace, leave me alone," that's what I'd like to keep crying out all the time. Who knows, the day may come when I'm left alone more than I would wish!

Yours, Anne

a

On Sunday evening everyone, with the exception of Daddy and me, was sitting beside the wireless listening to the Sunday night concert. Pf. fiddled with the knobs continually, this annoyed Peter, and the others too. When that had been going on for about half an hour Peter asked Pf. somewhat irritably if the twisting and turning might stop. Pf. answered in his usual tone: "I'm getting it all right!" Peter became angry, I don't know what exactly he said but it was rude. Mr. van Pels joined in, got angry as well and defended Peter. That was all.

| 55   Peter was in good form, he must have realized that I | sympathized with him, in any case he unburdened himself a little to me.

b   287

Monday 14¹ Febr. 1944.

Dear Kitty,

On Sunday evening everyone except Pim and me was sitting beside the wireless in order to listen to the "immortal Music of the German Masters." Pf. fiddled with the knobs continually, this annoyed Peter, and the others too. After restraining himself for half an hour, Peter asked somewhat irritably if the twisting and turning might stop. Pf. answered in his most hoity-toity manner, "I'm getting it all right." Peter became angry, was rude, Mr. v. Pels took his side, and Pf. had to give in. That was all.

The reason in itself was very unimportant, but Peter seems to have taken it very much to heart, in any case, when I was rummaging about in the bookcase in the attic he came up to me and began telling me the whole story. I didn't know anything about it, but Peter soon saw that he had found an attentive ear and got fairly into his stride.

c

Monday, 14 February, 1944

Dear Kitty,

On Sunday evening, everyone except Pim and me was sitting beside the wireless in order to listen to the "Immortal Music of the German Masters." Dussel fiddled with the knobs continually. This annoyed Peter, and the others too. After restraining himself for half an hour, Peter asked somewhat irritably if the twisting and turning might stop. Dussel answered in his most hoity-toity manner, "I'm getting it all right." Peter became angry, was rude, Mr. Van Daan took his side, and Dussel had to give in. That was all.

The reason in itself was very unimportant, but Peter seems to have taken it very much to heart. In any case, when I was rummaging about in the bookcase in the attic, he came up to me and began telling me the whole story. I didn't know anything about it, but Peter soon saw that he had found an attentive ear and got fairly into his stride.

485

"Yes and you see," he said "I don't easily say anything, because I know beforehand that I'll only become tongue-tied. I begin to stutter, turn red and twist around what I want to say. Yesterday too, I wanted to say something quite different, but once I had started, I got into a hopeless muddle. And that's frightful; I have a very bad habit, i.e. when I get angry with anyone rather than argue it out I used to get to work on him with my fists. But I quite realize that this doesn't get me anywhere; and that's why I admire you so. You are never at a loss for a word, you say exactly what you want to say to people and are not so shy."

| 288 | "Yes and you see," he said "I don't easily say anything, because I know beforehand | that I'll only become tongue-tied. I begin to stutter, turn red and twist around what I want to say, and go on until I have to break off because I simply can't find the words. That's what happened yesterday, I wanted to say something quite different, but once I had started, I got in a hopeless muddle, and that's frightful.

I used to have a bad habit; I wish I still had it now: if I was angry with anyone, rather than argue it out I would get to work on him with my fists. I quite realize that this method doesn't get me anywhere; and that is why I admire you. You are never at a loss for a word, you say exactly what you want to say to people and are never the least bit shy."

"Yes, and you see," he said, "I don't easily say anything, because I know beforehand that I'll only become tongue-tied. I begin to stutter, blush, and twist around what I want to say, until I have to break off because I simply can't find the words. That's what happened yesterday, I wanted to say something quite different, but once I had started, I got in a hopeless muddle and that's frightful. I used to have a bad habit; I wish I still had it now. If I was angry with anyone, rather than argue it out I would get to work on him with my fists. I quite realize that this method doesn't get me anywhere; and that is why I admire you. You are never at a loss for a word, you say exactly what you want to say to people and are never the least bit shy."

486

a

"Just listen", I said, generally I say things quite differently from the way I wanted to say them. I talk too much and that's no good either!"

Peter went on talking and kept coming back to Pf. I shan't write down what he said | 56 for you know my own fits of rage against Pf. only | too well. However there's one thing he said I shall repeat:

"Last night I was so jumpy, I was trembling all over, I've never been like that before; I didn't recognize myself! That didn't happen to me just like that, I'm almost never jumpy."

I felt really sorry for him. He was leaning against a potato barrel with such apparent nonchalance, while I was sitting nearly at his feet. And from his words, his gestures, his voice and his eyes I could see and tell that something was burning inside him just as it burns in me. We are more or less the same age and he isn't very sure of himself either.

b

"I can tell you you are making a big mistake," I answered, I usually say things quite differently from the way I meant to say them, and then I talk too much and far too long, | 289 and that's | something just as bad."

"Maybe, but you have the advantage that no one can tell when you are embarrassed. You don't blush and you don't go to pieces."

I couldn't help laughing to myself over this last sentence. However, I wanted to let him go on talking about himself, so I kept my amusement to myself,[2] went and sat on a cushion on the floor, put my arms around my bent knees, and looked at him attentively.

I am very glad that there is someone else in the house who can get into the same fits of rage as I get into. I could see it did Peter good to pull Pf. to pieces to his heart's content, without fear of my telling tales. And as for me, I was very pleased, because I sensed[3] a real feeling of fellowship, such as I can only remember having had with my girl friends

yours, Anne

c

"I can tell you, you're making a big mistake," I answered. "I usually say things quite differently from the way I meant to say them, and then I talk too much and far too long, and that's just as bad."

I couldn't help laughing to myself over this last sentence. However, I wanted to let him go on talking about himself, so I kept my amusement to myself, went and sat on a cushion on the floor, put my arms around my bent knees, and looked at him attentively.

I am very glad that there is someone else in the house who can get into the same fits of rage as I get into. I could see it did Peter good to pull Dussel to pieces to his heart's content, without fear of my telling tales. And as for me, I was very pleased, because I sensed a real feeling of fellowship, such as I can only remember having had with my girl friends.

Yours, Anne

487

a   57   Tuesday 15-2-44.

On Tuesday I heard from Mummy that Pf. had told her the following:

"Yesterday morning Peter came to me, said good morning and asked if I had slept well. He added that he was sorry about last night and that he hadn't really meant it so I told him that I hadn't really taken it badly either."

I thought that it had been brave of Peter to have apologized all the same, and when I was in the attic at quarter past twelve I told him so.

"Not a word of it is true!" he exclaimed. I was amazed. Why should Pfeffer have lied? We went on talking some more, about films and movie theaters, and then we went downstairs.

In the evening Mr. van Pels and Peter gave Pfeffer a terrible talking to and got themselves into a fury again. But it can't have ended so badly because Peter had some dental treatment today.

The fact is they'd decided not to talk to each other any more.

b   290

Thursday 17 Febr. 1944.

Dear Kitty,

The slight dispute with Pf. had a long sequel and it's all his own fault.

On Monday night[2] Pf. came triumphantly to Mummy and told her that Peter had asked him that same morning whether he had had a good night, and had added that he was sorry about what had happened on Sunday night and that he hadn't really meant what he'd said. Thereupon Pf. had reassured him by saying that he hadn't really taken it badly either. So everything was as right as rain again.[4]

Mummy repeated this conversation to me and I was secretly struck dumb with amazement that Peter, who was so angry with Pf., should have humbled himself so despite all his assurances.

And so I couldn't stop myself from tackling Peter, only to be told straight out by him
| 291   that Pf. had been lying. You should have seen Peter's face, | it would have been worth its weight in gold just to photograph it. Indignation about the lies, rage, [7]uncertainty about what to do next, unease and much more clearly followed each other at short intervals across his face.

I am[8] really a bit sorry that I was so hasty with my question, because it was plain to see that he wouldn't leave things as they were. And indeed my suspicions were confirmed. In the evening Mr. v.P. and Peter had a flaming row with Pf., they didn't speak to each other for two days but today the whole affair has blown over. Luckily!

c   . . . . . .

488

Wednesday 16-2-1944.
We didn't talk to each other all day long except for a few unimportant words. It was too cold to go up to the attic and anyway: it was Margot's birthday.

He came at half past twelve to look at the presents and stayed talking much longer than was strictly necessary—which he'd never have done otherwise. But in the afternoon I got my chance, because I wanted to look after Margot for just that one day in the year and so I went to fetch the coffee and after that the potatoes. I went into Peter's room; he took all his papers off the stairs at once and I asked whether I should close the trap door. "Yes," he replied "knock when you come back, then I'll open it for you." I thanked him, went upstairs, and searched at least 10 minutes in the large barrel for the smallest potatoes. Then my back began to ache and I got cold. Naturally I didn't knock, but opened the trap door myself, but still he came to meet me most obligingly, and took the pan from me. "I've looked for a long time, but couldn't find any smaller ones."

"Did you look in the big barrel?"

"Yes, I've been over them all."

By this time I was standing at the bottom of the stairs and he looked searchingly in the pan which he was still holding. "Oh, but these are first-rate," he said, and added

. . . . . .

Wednesday, 16 February, 1944

Dear Kitty,

It's Margot's birthday. Peter came at half past twelve to look at the presents and stayed talking much longer than was strictly necessary—a thing he'd have never done otherwise. In the afternoon I went to get some coffee and, after that, potatoes, because I wanted to spoil Margot for just that one day in the year. I went through Peter's room; he took all his papers off the stairs at once and I asked whether I should close the trap door to the attic. "Yes," he replied, "knock when you come back, then I'll open it for you."

I thanked him, went upstairs, and searched at least ten minutes in the large barrel for the smallest potatoes. Then my back began to ache and I got cold. Naturally I didn't knock, but opened the trap door myself, but still he came to meet me most obligingly, and took the pan from me.

"I've looked for a long time, these are the smallest I could find," I said.

"Did you look in the big barrel?"

"Yes, I've been over them all."

By this time I was standing at the bottom of the stairs and he looked searchingly in the pan which he was still holding. "Oh, but these are first-rate," he said, and added

489

when I took the pan from him, "I congratulate you!" At the same time he gave me such a gentle warm look which made a tender glow within me. I could really see that he wanted to please me, and because he couldn't deliver a long complimentary speech he spoke with his eyes. I understood him, oh, so well, and was very—grateful! It gives me pleasure even now when I recall those words and that look he gave me!

When I went downstairs, Mummy said that some more potatoes were needed, this time for supper. I willingly offered to go upstairs again. When I came into Peter's room I apologized at having to disturb him again. When I was already on the stairs he got up and went and stood between the door and the (outside) wall, firmly took hold of my arm and wanted to hold me back by force: "I'll go," he said, | "I have to go upstairs anyway!" But I replied that it really wasn't necessary and that I didn't have to get particularly small ones this time. Then he was convinced and let my arm go. On the way down, he came and opened the trap door and took the pan again. When I reached the door, I still asked, "What are you doing?" "French," he replied. I asked if I might glance through the exercises, washed my hands, and went and sat on the divan opposite him.

. . . . . .

when I took the pan from him, "I congratulate you!" At the same time he gave me such a gentle warm look which made a tender glow within me. I could really see that he wanted to please me, and because he couldn't make a long complimentary speech he spoke with his eyes. I understood him, oh, so well, and was very grateful. It gives me pleasure even now when I recall those words and that look he gave me.

When I went downstairs, Mummy said that I must get some more potatoes, this time for supper. I willingly offered to go upstairs again.

When I came into Peter's room, I apologized at having to disturb him again. When I was already on the stairs he got up, and went and stood between the door and the wall, firmly took hold of my arm, and wanted to hold me back by force.

"I'll go," he said. I replied that it really wasn't necessary and that I didn't have to get particularly small ones this time. Then he was convinced and let my arm go. On the way down, he came and opened the trap door and took the pan again. When I reached the door, I asked, "What are you doing?" "French," he replied. I asked if I might glance through the exercises, washed my hands, and went and sat on the divan opposite him.

490

We soon began talking, after I'd explained some of the French to him. He told me that he wanted to go to the Dutch E. Indies and live on a plantation later on. He talked about his home life, about the black market, and then he said that he felt so useless. I told him that he certainly had a really strong inferiority complex. He talked about the war, that the Russians and the English were bound to go to war against each other and he talked about the Jews. He would have found it much easier if he'd been a Christian and if he could be one after the war. I asked if he wanted to be baptized, but that wasn't | 61 the case either. He couldn't possibly | feel like a Christian, he said, but who was to know whether he was a Jew after the war was over and what his name was!⊛

This gave me rather a pang; it seems such a pity that there's always just a tinge of dishonesty about him. But for the rest we chatted very pleasantly about Daddy, and about judging people's characters and all kinds of things, I can't remember exactly what now.

It was quarter past five by the time I left, because Bep had arrived.

. . . . . .

We soon began talking, after I'd explained some of the French to him. He told me that he wanted to go to the Dutch East Indies and live on a plantation later on. He talked about his home life, about the black market, and then he said that he felt so useless. I told him that he certainly had a very strong inferiority complex. He talked about the Jews. He would have found it much easier if he'd been a Christian and if he could be one after the war. I asked if he wanted to be baptized, but that wasn't the case either. Who was to know whether he was a Jew when the war was over? he said

This gave me rather a pang; it seems such a pity that there's always just a tinge of dishonesty about him. For the rest we chatted very pleasantly about Daddy, and about judging people's characters and all kinds of things, I can't remember exactly what now.

It was half past four by the time I left.

491

In the evening he said something else that I thought was nice, we were talking about a picture of a film star which I'd given him once, which has now been hanging in his room for at least a year and a half. He liked it very much and I offered to give him a few more sometime. "No," he replied "I'd rather leave it like this, I look at these every day and they have grown to be my friends!"

Now I understand much better why he always hugs Muschi. He needs some affection, too, of course. I had forgotten something else that he talked about. He said: "No, I don't

| 62   know what fear is, except when I go wrong myself, but I'm | getting over that too."

Peter has a terrible inferiority complex. E.g. he always thinks that he is so stupid and we are so clever. If I help him with his French, he thanks me a thousand times. One day I shall surely turn around and say: "Oh, shut up, you are really much better at English and geography!" yours

Anne Frank.

P.S.

⊛Peter also said: "The Jews have always been the chosen people and will always be so!"
I replied: "I keep hoping that for once they've been chosen for the good!"

. . . . . .

In the evening he said something else that I thought was nice. We were talking about a picture of a film star that I'd given him once, which has now been hanging in his room for at least a year and a half. He liked it very much and I offered to give him a few more sometime. "No," he replied, "I'd rather leave it like this. I look at these every day and they have grown to be my friends."

Now I understand more why he always hugs Mouschi. He needs some affection, too, of course.

I'd forgotten something else that he talked about. He said, "I don't know what fear is, except when I think of my own shortcomings. But I'm getting over that too."

Peter has a terrible inferiority complex. For instance, he always thinks that he is so stupid, and we are so clever. If I help him with his French, he thanks me a thousand times. One day I shall turn around and say: "Oh, shut up, you're much better at English and geography!"

Yours, Anne

Thursday 17 February
<u>1944.</u>

Dearest Kitty,
This morning I was upstairs since I had promised Mrs. v.P. to read her some of my tales sometime. I began with Eva's dream, she thought that was very nice, then I read a few other things from the "Secret Annexe" that made her roar with laughter. Peter also listened to some of it (I mean during the second part) and asked if I would come to see him sometime and read him some more. I thought I'd take a chance there and then, fetched my diary and let him read the piece between Cady and Hans on God. I really can't tell what impression it made on him, he said something I can't remember, not whether it was good, but something about the idea behind it. I told him that I merely wanted to prove that I no longer wrote amusing things only. He nodded and I left the room. We'll see if I hear anything more about it!

yours
<u>Anne Frank.</u>

b   . . . . . .

c   . . . . . .

Friday 18 February
1944.

Dear Kitty,

Whenever I go upstairs now, I keep hoping that I shall see "him." Because my life now has some object and I have something to look forward to, everything has become more pleasant.

At least the object of my feelings is always there, and I needn't be afraid of rivals (except Margot). You really needn't think I'm in love, since I'm not, but I do have the feeling all the time that something fine can grow up between us, something which gives confidence and friendship. If there is half a chance, I go up to him now. It's not like it used to be when he didn't know how to begin, it's just the opposite—he's still talking when I'm half out of the room. Mummy doesn't like it much, and always says I'll be a nuisance and that I must leave him in peace. Honestly, doesn't she realize that I've got | 65   some intuition? (at least I'm using the word properly Mr. van Pels uses it rightly | and wrongly!)

She looks at me so queerly every time I go into Peter's little room. If I come downstairs from there she asks me where I've been. I think that's horrible and little by little I'm beginning to dislike her!

yours
Anne M. Frank.

. . . . . .

Friday, 18 February, 1944.

Dear Kitty,

Whenever I go upstairs now I keep on hoping that I shall see "him." Because my life now has an object, and I have something to look forward to, everything has become more pleasant.

At least the object of my feelings is always there, and I needn't be afraid of rivals, except Margot. Don't think I'm in love, because I'm not, but I do have the feeling all the time that something fine can grow up between us, something that gives confidence and friendship. If I get half a chance, I go up to him now. It's not like it used to be when he didn't know how to begin. It's just the opposite—he's still talking when I'm half out of the room.

Mummy doesn't like it much, and always says I'll be a nuisance and that I must leave him in peace. Honestly, doesn't she realize that I've got some intuition? She looks at me so queerly every time I go into Peter's little room. If I come downstairs from there, she asks me where I've been. I simply can't bear it, and think it's horrible.

Yours, Anne

Saturday 19 February
1944.

Dear Kitty,

It is Saturday again and that really speaks for itself. The morning was quiet, I spent nearly an hour preparing the meatballs upstairs but I didn't have more than a few fleeting words with "him."

At half past 2, when everyone was upstairs either sleeping or reading I went downstairs, with my blanket and everything, to sit at the desk and read or write. It was not long, just after three o'clock perhaps, before it all became too much for me, my head drooped on to my arms, and I sobbed my heart out. The tears streamed down my cheeks and I felt desperately unhappy.

Oh, if only "he" had come to comfort me. It was 4 o'clock by the time I went upstairs again, at about 5 o'clock I went for some potatoes with | fresh hope in my heart of a meeting, but while I was still smartening up my hair in the bathroom he went down to see Boche.

| 66

I wanted to help Mrs. v.P. and went upstairs with my book and everything, but suddenly I felt the tears coming back and I hurried downstairs to the lavatory quickly grabbing a pocket mirror as I passed.

There I sat then, on the lavatory, fully dressed, even though I had finished long before, while the tears made dark spots on the red of my apron, and I felt very wretched.[1] This is

. . . . . .

Saturday, 19 February, 1944

Dear Kitty,

It is Saturday again and that really speaks for itself.

The morning was quiet, I helped a bit upstairs, but I didn't have more than a few fleeting words with "him." At half past two, when everyone had gone to their own rooms, either to sleep or to read, I went to the private office, with my blanket and everything, to sit at the desk and read or write. It was not long before it all became too much for me, my head drooped on to my arm, and I sobbed my heart out. The tears streamed down my cheeks and I felt desperately unhappy. Oh, if only "he" had come to comfort me. It was four o'clock by the time I went upstairs again. I went for some potatoes, with fresh hope in my heart of a meeting, but while I was still smartening up my hair in the bathroom, he went down to see Boche in the warehouse.

Suddenly I felt the tears coming back and I hurried to the lavatory, quickly grabbing a pocket mirror as I passed. There I sat then, fully dressed, while the tears made dark spots

495

what was going through my mind: Oh, I'll never reach Peter like this, who knows, perhaps he doesn't like me at all and doesn't need anyone at all to confide in. Perhaps he only thinks about me in a casual sort of way and didn't find that bit about God very confidence-inspiring. Oh, I shall have to go on alone once more, without friendship and without Peter. Perhaps soon I'll be without hope, without comfort, or anything to look forward to again. Oh, if I could nestle my head against his shoulder and not feel so hopelessly alone and deserted!

67   Who knows perhaps he doesn't care about me at all and looks at the others in just the same way, perhaps I only imagined that it is especially for me. Oh, Peter, if only you could see or hear me, but if the truth were to prove as bad as that I really could not listen to it!

But later fresh hope and anticipation seemed to return, even though the tears were still streaming down my cheeks.

yours
Anne M. Frank.

. . . . . .

on the red of my apron, and I felt very wretched.

This is what was going through my mind. Oh, I'll never reach Peter like this. Who knows, perhaps he doesn't like me at all and doesn't need anyone to confide in. Perhaps he only thinks about me in a casual sort of way. I shall have to go on alone once more, without friendship and without Peter. Perhaps soon I'll be without hope, without comfort, or anything to look forward to again. Oh, if I could nestle my head against his shoulder and not feel so hopelessly alone and deserted! Who knows, perhaps he doesn't care about me at all and looks at the others in just the same way. Perhaps I only imagined that it was especially for me? Oh, Peter, if only you could see or hear me. If the truth were to prove as bad as that, it would be more than I could bear.

However, a little later fresh hope and anticipation seemed to return, even though the tears were still streaming down my cheeks.

Yours, Anne

496

Wednesday 23 February 1944.

Dearest Kitty,

It's lovely weather again and I've quite perked up since yesterday. My writing, the finest thing I have, is making good progress.

This morning (Thursday) when I went to the attic again, Peter was busy clearing up. He was finished very quickly and when I sat down on my favorite spot on the floor, he joined me. Both of us looked at the glorious blue of the sky, the bare chestnut tree on whose branches little raindrops shone, at the seagulls and other birds that looked like | 68 silver in the sun and | all these things moved and thrilled the two of us so much that we could not speak. He stood and I sat, we breathed the fresh air, looked outside, and both felt that the spell should not be broken. We sat quietly together for a long while and I didn't dare begin, for I couldn't start speaking about the most intimate things without any warning. As I sat there and saw how deep in thought he was, I knew then that he was a nice fellow and a real treasure.

At half past twelve we went up to the loft, during the quarter of an hour he was chopping wood we remained silent. I watched him and saw that he was so obviously

| 292

It's lovely weather outside and I've quite perked up since yesterday. Nearly every morning I go to the attic to blow the stuffy air out of my lungs; from[1] my favorite spot,[2] | the floor, I look up at the blue sky, the bare chestnut tree on whose branches the little raindrops shone, and at the seagulls and other birds gliding on the wind and looking like silver and all that moved and thrilled [4]the two of us so much that we could not speak. He stood with his head against a thick beam, and I sat down. We breathed the fresh air, looked outside, and both felt that the spell should not be broken by words. We remained like this for a long time, and when he had to go to chop wood,[5] I knew that he was a nice fellow. He climbed the ladder to the loft, and I followed; then he chopped wood for about a quarter of an hour, during which time we still remained silent. I watched him from where I stood, he was obviously doing his best to show off his strength. But I

Wednesday, 23 February, 1944

Dear Kitty,

It's lovely weather outside and I've quite perked up since yesterday. Nearly every morning I go to the attic where Peter works to blow the stuffy air out of my lungs. From my favorite spot on the floor I look up at the blue sky and the bare chestnut tree, on whose branches little raindrops shine, appearing like silver, and at the seagulls and other birds as they glide on the wind. [From my favorite spot on the floor I look up at the blue sky and the bare chestnut tree, on whose branches little raindrops shine, and at the seagulls and other birds gliding on the wind and looking like silver in the sun.]

He stood with his head against a thick beam, and I sat down. We breathed the fresh air, looked outside, and both felt that the spell should not be broken by words. We remained like this for a long time, and when he had to go up to the loft to chop wood, I knew that he was a nice fellow. He climbed the ladder, and I followed; then he chopped wood for about a quarter of an hour, during which time we still remained silent. I watched him from where I stood, he was obviously doing his best to show off his strength. But I

doing his best to show off his strength. But I looked out of the open window too, over a large piece of Amsterdam, over all the roofs and on to the far distance, fading into purple. As long as this exists, I thought, and I may live to see it, this sunshine, the cloudless skies, while this lasts, I cannot be unhappy.

| 69   And the best remedy for those who are afraid, lonely or unhappy is | to go outside, somewhere where they can be quite alone with the heavens, nature, and God. Because only then does one feel that all is as it should be and that God wishes to see people happy, amidst the simple beauty of Nature.

As long as this exists, and it certainly always will, I know that there will always be comfort for every sorrow, whatever the circumstances may be.

And I believe that nature sets all fear at rest for every trouble, even when there are bombs or gunfire.

Oh, who knows, perhaps it won't be long before I can share this overwhelming feeling of bliss with Peter.

<u>yours, Anne M. Frank.</u>

| 293   looked out of the open window too, out over a large area of Amsterdam, over all the roofs and on to the horizon which was such a pale blue that it was hard | to see the line.

"As long as this exists" I thought, "and I may live to see it, this sunshine, the cloudless skies, while this lasts, I cannot be unhappy.[1]

The best remedy for those who are afraid, lonely or unhappy is to go outside, somewhere where they can be quite alone with the heavens, nature, and God. Because only then does one feel that all is as it should be and that God wishes to see people happy, amidst the simple beauty of Nature.

As long as this[2] exists, and it certainly always will, I know that then there will always be comfort for every sorrow, whatever the circumstances. And I firmly believe that nature brings solace for every trouble.[4]

Oh, who knows, perhaps it won't be long before I can share this overwhelming feeling of bliss with someone who thinks the way I do about it.

<u>yours, Anne</u>

looked out of the open window too, over a large area of Amsterdam, over all the roofs and on to the horizon, which was such a pale blue that it was hard to see the dividing line. "As long as this exists," I thought, "and I may live to see it, this sunshine, the cloudless skies, while this lasts, I cannot be unhappy."

The best remedy for those who are afraid, lonely, or unhappy is to go outside, somewhere where they can be quite alone with the heavens, nature, and God. Because only then does one feel that all is as it should be and that God wishes to see people happy, amidst the simple beauty of Nature. As long as this exists, and it certainly always will, I know that then there will always be comfort for every sorrow, whatever the circumstances may be. And I firmly believe that nature brings solace in all troubles.

Oh, who knows, perhaps it won't be long before I can share this overwhelming feeling of bliss with someone who feels the way I do about it.

Yours, Anne

a

| 70

P.S. A thought for Peter.

We miss so much here, so very much and for such a long time now: I miss it too, just as you do. Don't think I am talking of outward things, for we are looked after extremely well in that way. No, I mean the inward things. Like you, I long for freedom and fresh air, but I believe that we have ample compensation for our pri- | vations. Let me try to explain it to you: when I sat in front of the window this morning I suddenly realized that we have had a great, great many compensations. I mean inward compensation. When I looked outside right into the depth of Nature and God, then I was happy, really happy. And Peter, so long as I have that happiness here, the joy in Nature, health and a lot more besides, all the while one has that, one can always recapture happiness.

Riches can all be lost, but that happiness in one's own heart can only be veiled, and will always bring you happiness again, as long as you live.

Just try when you are alone and unhappy or sad looking outside from the attic when the weather is nice. Not at the houses or the roofs but towards Heaven. As long as you can look fearlessly at the heavens, as long as you know that you are pure within, and that you will still find happiness.

b

. . . . . .

c

A thought:

We miss so much here, so very much and for so long now: I miss it too, just as you do. I'm not talking of outward things, for we are looked after in that way; no, I mean the inward things. Like you, I long for freedom and fresh air, but I believe now that we have ample compensation for our privations. I realized this quite suddenly when I sat in front of the window this morning. I mean inward compensation.

When I looked outside right into the depth of Nature and God, then I was happy, really happy. And Peter, so long as I have that happiness here, the joy in nature, health and a lot more besides, all the while one has that, one can always recapture happiness.

Riches can all be lost, but that happiness in your own heart can only be veiled, and it will still bring you happiness again, as long as you live. As long as you can look fearlessly up into the heavens, as long as you know that you are pure within, and that you will still find happiness.

499

Dearest Kitty,

From early in the morning till late at night, I really do hardly anything else but think of Peter. I sleep with his image before my eyes, dream about him and he is still looking at me when I awake.

I have a strong feeling that Peter and I are not so different as we would appear to be, and I will tell you why: we both lack a Mother. His is too superficial, loves flirting and doesn't trouble much about what Peter thinks. Mine does bother about me a lot but lacks tact, sensitiveness, real Motherliness.

Peter and I both wrestle with our inner feelings, we are still uncertain and are really too sensitive to be roughly treated. When that happens I want to get away or hide my feelings, throw my weight about the place, am noisy and boisterous so that everyone wishes that I was far away.

| 72   He shuts himself up, hardly talks at all, is quiet and day-dreams and in this way carefully conceals his | true self.

But how and when will we finally reach each other? I don't know quite how long my common sense will keep this longing under control

yours, <u>Anne M. Frank.</u>

b

. . . . . .

c

Sunday, 27 February, 1944

Dearest Kitty,

From early in the morning till late at night, I really do hardly anything else but think of Peter. I sleep with his image before my eyes, dream about him and he is still looking at me when I awake.

I have a strong feeling that Peter and I are really not so different as we would appear to be, and I will tell you why. We both lack a mother. His is too superficial, loves flirting and doesn't trouble much about what he thinks. Mine does bother about me, but lacks sensitiveness, real motherliness.

Peter and I both wrestle with our inner feelings, we are still uncertain and are really too sensitive to be roughly treated. If we are, then my reaction is to "get away from it all." But as that is impossible, I hide my feelings, throw my weight about the place, am noisy and boisterous, so that everyone wishes that I was out of the way.

He, on the contrary, shuts himself up, hardly talks at all, is quiet, day-dreams and in this way carefully conceals his true self.

But how and when will we finally reach each other? I don't know quite how long my common sense will keep this longing under control.

Yours, Anne

Monday 28 February '44.

Dearest Kitty,

It is becoming a bad dream—in daytime as well as at night. I see him nearly all the time and can't go to him, I mustn't show anything to anybody, must remain gay while I'm really in despair.

Peter Schiff and Peter van Pels have grown into one Peter, who is beloved and good, and for whom I long desperately. Mummy is terrible, Daddy sweet and therefore all the more tiresome, Margot the most tiresome because she expects me to wear a pleasant expression; and all I want is to be left in peace.

Peter didn't come to me in the attic. He went up to the loft and did some carpentry. At every creak and every knock some of my courage seemed to seep away and I grew more unhappy. In the distance a bell was playing: "Pure-in-body, pure-in-soul."

73   I'm sentimental—I know. I'm desperate and silly—I know that too. Oh, help me!

yours, Anne M. Frank.

Here I sit and learn all day
For Him; that is the only way!
        Rea.

. . . . . .

Monday, 28 February, 1944

Dearest Kitty,

It is becoming a bad dream—in daytime as well as at night. I see him nearly all the time and can't get at him, I mustn't show anything, must remain gay while I'm really in despair.

Peter Wessel and Peter Van Daan have grown into one Peter, who is beloved and good, and for whom I long desperately.

Mummy is tiresome, Daddy sweet and therefore all the more tiresome, Margot the most tiresome because she expects me to wear a pleasant expression; and all I want is to be left in peace.

Peter didn't come to me in the attic. He went up to the loft instead and did some carpentry. At every creak and every knock some of my courage seemed to seep away and I grew more unhappy. In the distance a bell was playing "Pure in body, pure in soul."*
I'm sentimental—I know. I'm desperate and silly—I know that too. Oh, help me!

Yours, Anne

*The bells in old clock towers play tunes.

501

Wednesday 1 March '44.

Dearest Kitty,

I have won my bottle of yoghourt for the 1st of March! Mrs. v.P. gave it to me this morning; what a pity the invasion hasn't started yet.

We've had lots of excitement again, there has been a burglary. This time things were even more complicated than last time:

When Mr. v.P. went downstairs last night as usual, he found that the communicating glass door and Kugler's door were open. He was surprised, walked through and became even more surprised when he found that the office doors, which are normally kept open, were now locked. He walked on to the main office, where there was a terrible mess, drawers had been put on top of the desk and a cupboard door was open. "There has been | 74 a burglar," | he thought and went straight downstairs to look at the front door, which was closed, the yale lock, too. Then he assumed that Bep must have left the office in a mess.

294

Wednesday 1 March
1944.

Dear Kitty,

My own affairs have been driven into the background by—a burglary. I'm becoming boring with all my burglars, but what can I do, they seem to take such a delight in paying Gies & Co. the honor of a visit. This burglary is much more complicated than the one in July '43.

When Mr. v. Pels went to Kugler's office at half past 7, as usual, he saw that the communicating glass door and the office door were open. Surprised at this, he walked through and was even more amazed to see that the doors of the little dark room were open too, and that there was a terrible mess in the main office. "There has been a burglar," he thought to himself at once, and to satisfy himself he went straight downstairs, took hold of the front door, felt the yale lock and found everything closed. Oh, then both Bep | 295 and Peter must have been very slack this evening," Mr. v.P. | decided. He remained in Kugler's room for a while, then switched off the lamp, and went upstairs, without worrying much about either the open doors or the untidy office.

Wednesday, 1 March, 1944

Dear Kitty,

My own affairs have been pushed into the background by—a burglary. I'm becoming boring with all my burglars, but what can I do, they seem to take such a delight in honoring Kolen & Co. with their visits. This burglary is much more complicated than the one in July 1943.

When Mr. Van Daan went to Kraler's office at half past seven, as usual, he saw that the communicating glass doors and the office door were open. Surprised at this, he walked through and was even more amazed to see that the doors of the little dark room were open too, and that there was a terrible mess in the main office. "There has been a burglar," he thought to himself at once, and to satisfy himself he went straight downstairs to look at the front door, felt the Yale lock, and found everything closed. "Oh, then both Peter and Elli must have been very slack this evening," he decided. He remained in Kraler's room for a while, then switched off the lamp, and went upstairs, without worrying much about either the open doors or the untidy office.

502

This morning Peter came upstairs with the news that the front door was open. Pf. told us that the projector had disappeared and v.P. now told us about the previous evening's surprise. Peter went downstairs again and locked the front door.

What exactly had happened? The thief must have had a skeleton key, because the door had not been forced. When Mr. v.P. had gone downstairs in the evening he must have hidden himself and fled as soon as v.P. went upstairs again. Then he had left the door unlocked.

This morning Peter knocked at our door early and came with the not so pleasant news that the front door was wide open. He also told us that the projector and Kugler's new portfolio had both disappeared from the cupboard. Peter was told to close the door. V. Pels told us of his discoveries the previous evening and we were all awfully worried. .

What must have happened is that the thief had a skeleton key because the lock was quite undamaged. He must have crept into the house quite early and closed the door behind him,[4] hid himself when disturbed by Mr. v.P., and, when he departed, fled with his spoils and, in his hurry, left the door open.

This morning Peter knocked at our door early and came with the not so pleasant news that the front door was wide open. He also told us that the projector and Kraler's new portfolio had both disappeared from the cupboard. Peter was told to close the door. Van Daan told us of his discoveries the previous evening and we were all awfully worried.

What must have happened is that the thief had a skeleton key, because the lock was quite undamaged. He must have crept into the house quite early and closed the door behind him, hidden himself when disturbed by Mr. Van Daan, and when he departed fled with his spoils, leaving the door open in his haste.

It's a mystery. Who can have our key. And why didn't the thief go to the warehouse. If the thief is one of our warehousemen, then he now knows that someone is in the house at night. The thief was also planning to steal the big electric clock; he had cleared the

mantelpiece in the main | office for that purpose, but he must have been disturbed.

It is all very creepy; but I didn't get into a state and realized that it's best not to get excited.

yours, Anne M. Frank.

It's a mystery. Who can | have our key? Why didn't the thief go to the warehouse? Might it be one of our own warehousemen, and would he perhaps betray us, since he certainly heard v.P. and perhaps even saw him?

It is all very creepy, because we don't know whether this same burglar may not take it into his head to visit us again, or did it give him a shock to find that there was someone walking about in the house?

yours, Anne

P.S. We should be very pleased if you could perhaps dig up a good detective for us. The first requirement of course is that he can be relied on not to betray that we are hiding here.

yours, Anne

Who can have our key? Why didn't the thief go to the warehouse? Might it be one of our own warehousemen, and would he perhaps betray us, since he certainly heard Van Daan and perhaps even saw him?

It is all very creepy, because we don't know whether this same burglar may not take it into his head to visit us again. Or perhaps it gave him a shock to find that there was someone walking about in the house?

Yours, Anne

504

Thursday 2 March '44.

Dear Kitty,

Margot and I were both up in the attic today, we were not able to enjoy it together as I had imagined I would have with Peter (or someone else). I do know though that she shares my feelings over most things!

During dish washing Bep began telling Mummy and Mrs. v.P. that she felt very discouraged at times. And what do you think they did to help her? Our tactless mother in particular can only help people out of the frying pan into the fire. Do you know what her advice was? She should try to think of all the other people who are in trouble! What is the good of thinking of misery when one is already miserable oneself? I said this too and was naturally told to keep out of this sort of conversation!

Aren't the grownups idiotic and stupid? Just as if Peter, Margot, Bep and I don't all | feel the same about things, and only a mother's love, or that of a very, very good friend, can help us.

The two mothers here just don't understand us at all! Perhaps Mrs. v.P. does a little more than Mummy! Oh, I would have so liked to say something to poor Bep, something I know from experience would have helped her; but Daddy came between us and pushed me aside very roughly. Aren't they all stupid!

I also had a talk with Margot about Daddy and Mummy, how nice things would be here if only they weren't so terribly tiresome. We'd be able to arrange evenings when everyone would give a talk in turn on a given subject. But that's a non-starter here right now. I'm not allowed to open my mouth! Mr. v.P. goes on the attack, Mummy gets all cutting and can't talk normally about <u>anything</u>, Daddy isn't interested in things like that, any more than Mr. Pf. is, Mrs. v.P. is always so much under attack that she just sits there with a red face hardly able to speak up for herself at all! And us? We aren't even allowed to have any opinions!

. . . . . .

76

Thursday, 2 March 1944

Dear Kitty,

Margot and I were both up in the attic today; although we were not able to enjoy it together as I had imagined, still I do know that she shares my feelings over most things.

During dish washing Elli began telling Mummy and Mrs. Van Daan that she felt very discouraged at times. And what help do you think they gave her? Do you know what Mummy's advice was? She should try to think of all the other people who are in trouble! What is the good of thinking of misery when one is already miserable oneself? I said this too and was told, "You keep out of this sort of conversation."

Aren't the grownups idiotic and stupid? Just as if Peter, Margot, Elli, and I don't all feel the same about things, and only a mother's love or that of a very, very good friend can help us. These mothers here just don't understand us at all. Perhaps Mrs. Van Daan does a little more than Mummy. Oh, I would have so liked to say something to poor Elli, something that I know from experience would have helped her. But Daddy came between us and pushed me aside.

Aren't they all stupid! We aren't allowed to have any opinions [Yes, they are terribly

77   Yes, they are terribly modern. We aren't allowed to have an opinion! People can tell
you to keep your mouth shut, but it doesn't stop you having your own opinion! Even if
people are still very young, they shouldn't be prevented from saying what they think!

Only great love and devotion can help Bep, Margot, Peter, and me, and none of us
here gets it. And no one, especially the stupid "know-alls" here, can understand us, because
we are much more sensitive and much more advanced in our thoughts than anyone here
would ever imagine in their wildest dreams!

Love, what is love? I believe love is something that can't really be put into words.
Love is understanding someone, caring for someone, sharing their ups and downs. And
in the long run that also means physical love, you have shared something, given something
away and received something, no matter whether you are married or unmarried, or whether
you are with child or not. It doesn't matter in the least if you've lost your honor, as long
as you know that someone will stand by you, will understand you for the rest of your
life, someone you won't have to share with anyone else!

yours,
Anne M. Frank.

78   Mummy is grumbling again at the moment—she is obviously jealous because I talk more
to Mrs. v.P. than to her nowadays, but I don't care!

. . . . . .

modern. We aren't allowed to have an opinion!]. People can tell you to keep your mouth
shut, but it doesn't stop you having your own opinion. Even if people are still very young,
they shouldn't be prevented from saying what they think.

Only great love and devotion can help Elli, Margot, Peter, and me, and none of us
gets it. And no one, especially the stupid "know-alls" here, can understand us, because
we are much more sensitive and much more advanced in our thoughts than anyone here
would ever imagine in their wildest dreams.

Mummy is grumbling again at the moment—she is obviously jealous because I talk
more to Mrs. Van Daan than to her nowadays.

506

I managed to get hold of Peter this afternoon and we talked for at least three quarters of an hour. Peter had the greatest difficulty in saying anything about himself, but he was very gradually drawn out. I didn't honestly know whether I had better go downstairs or stay upstairs. But I wanted to help him so much!

I told him about Bep and how tactless our two mothers are. He told me how his parents quarrel all the time over politics, cigarettes, and all kinds of things. As I said earlier, Peter was very shy, but not too much to let it slip out that he'd love not to have to see his parents for two years. "My father is really not nearly as nice as he looks" he said "but when it comes to cigarettes Mother is absolutely right!"

Then I talked to him about my mother. But he defended Daddy, he thought him a "first-rate chap."

79 Tonight when I was hanging up my apron after doing the dishes, he called me out and asked me not to tell them downstairs that his parents had been quarreling again and weren't talking to each other. I promised him that, although I had already told Margot. I'm sure Margot will keep it to herself.

"Now listen Peter", I said "you don't have to be afraid of me, I have learned not to talk too much, I never repeat anything you tell me."

He was pleased with that. I also told him about the terrible way we gossip and said: "Margot is absolutely right, of course, when she says I'm not being honest; because although I've decided not to gossip any more, I still love doing it about Mr. Pfeffer." "It's nice of you to tell me", he said, he started to blush and I almost became embarrassed too by his sincere compliment. Then we talked about "upstairs" and "downstairs" again; he was really rather amazed that we don't always like his parents. "Peter," I said "you know I'm always honest, so why shouldn't I tell you that we can see their faults too."

80 We promised each other to have absolute trust in each other, among other things I also said:

"I would so like to help you, Peter; can't I? You are in such an awkward position and, although you don't say anything, it doesn't mean that you don't care."

"Oh, I should always welcome your help."

"Perhaps you would do better to go to Daddy, he wouldn't let things go any further either, take it from me, you can easily tell him!"

. . . . . .

I managed to get hold of Peter this afternoon and we talked for at least three quarters of an hour. Peter had the greatest difficulty in saying anything about himself; it took a long time to draw him out. He told me how often his parents quarrel over politics, cigarettes, and all kinds of things. He was very shy.

Then I talked to him about my parents. He defended Daddy: he thought him a "first-rate chap." Then we talked about "upstairs" and "downstairs" again; he was really rather amazed that we don't always like his parents. "Peter," I said, "you know I'm always honest, so why shouldn't I tell you that we can see their faults too." And among other things I also said, "I would so like to help you, Peter; can't I? You are in such an awkward position and, although you don't say anything, it doesn't mean that you don't care."

"Oh, I would always welcome your help."

"Perhaps you would do better to go to Daddy, he wouldn't let anything go any further, take it from me; you can easily tell him!"

507

a

"Yes, he is a real pal."

"You're very fond of him, aren't you?" Peter nodded and I went on: "And he is of you too!"

He looked up quickly and blushed, it was really moving to see how these few words pleased him. "Do you think so?" he asked.

"Yes," I said "you can easily tell by little things that slip out now and then!"

Then Mr. van Pels came to do some dictating. Peter certainly is a first-rate chap too, just like Daddy!

yours, Anne M. Frank.

81
Friday 3 March 1944.

Dearest Kitty,

When I looked into the candle this evening (Friday night at 5 to 8) I felt calm and happy. Oma seems to be in the candle and it is Oma too who shelters and protects me and who always makes me feel happy again. But . . . . . there is someone else who governs all my moods and that is . . . . . Peter. When I went up to get potatoes today and was still standing on the stepladder with a pan, he at once asked, "What have you been doing since lunch?" I went and sat on the steps and we started talking; at a quarter past five (an hour later) the potatoes (which had been put down on the floor in the meantime) reached their destinations. Peter didn't say anything more about his parents; we just talked about books and about the past. Oh, the boy has such warmth in his eyes; I believe I'm pretty near to

b

. . . . . .

c

"Yes, he is a real pal."

"You're very fond of him, aren't you?" Peter nodded and I went on: "And he is of you too!"

He looked up quickly and blushed, it was really moving to see how these few words pleased him.

"Do you think so?" he asked.

"Yes," I said, "you can easily tell by little things that slip out now and then!"

Peter is a first-rate chap, too, just like Daddy!

Yours, Anne

Friday, 3 March, 1944

Dear Kitty,

When I looked into the candle this evening* I felt calm and happy. Oma [Granny] seems to be in the candle and it is Oma too who shelters and protects me and who always makes me feel happy again.

But . . . there is someone else who governs all my moods and that is . . . Peter. When I went up to get potatoes today and was still standing on the stepladder with the pan, he at once asked, "What have you been doing since lunch?" I went and sat on the steps and we started talking. At a quarter past five (an hour later) the potatoes, which had been sitting on the floor in the meantime, finally reached their destinations.

Peter didn't say another word about his parents; we just talked about books and about the past. The boy has such warmth in his eyes; I believe I'm pretty near to being in love with him.

---

*In Jewish homes candles are lit on the Sabbath eve.

being in love with him. He talked about that this evening. I went into his room, after peeling the potatoes, and said that I felt so hot. "You can tell what the temperature is by Margot and me; if it's cold we are white, and if it is hot we are red in the face," I said.

"In love?" he asked

"Why should I be in love?" my answer (or rather (better) my question) was rather silly.

"Why not?" he said and then we had to have supper.

Would he have meant anything by that question? I finally managed to ask him today whether he didn't find my chatter a nuisance; he only said: "It's okay, I like it!" To what extent this answer was just shyness, I was not able to judge. I also told him that Mummy knew about the quarrel, but not from me. Mrs. van Pels herself had told Mummy[1] that she and her husband weren't talking. He trusts and believes me, I really do think!

. . . . . .

He talked about that this evening. I went into his room, after peeling the potatoes, and said that I felt so hot.

"You can tell what the temperature is by Margot and me; if it's cold we are white, and if it is hot we are red in the face," I said.

"In love?" he asked.

"Why should I be in love?" My answer was rather silly.

"Why not?" he said, and then we had to go for supper.

Would he have meant anything by that question? I finally managed to ask him today whether he didn't find my chatter a nuisance; he only said: "It's okay, I like it!"

To what extent this answer was just shyness, I am not able to judge.

Kitty, I'm just like someone in love, who can only talk about her darling.

And Peter really is a darling. When shall I be able to say that to him? Naturally, only if he thinks I'm a darling too. But I'm quite capable of looking after myself, and he knows that very well. And he likes his tranquillity, so I have no idea how much he | likes me. In any case, we are getting to know each other a bit better. I wish we dared to tell each other much more already. But who knows, the time may come sooner than I think! I get an understanding look from him about twice a day, I wink back, and we both feel happy.

I certainly seem quite mad to talk about him being happy, and yet I feel pretty sure that he thinks just the same as I do!

yours, Anne M. Frank.

. . . . . .

Kitty, I'm just like someone in love, who can only talk about her darling. And Peter really is a darling. When shall I be able to tell him so? Naturally, only if he thinks I'm a darling too. But I'm quite capable of looking after myself, and he knows that very well. And he likes his tranquillity, so I have no idea how much he likes me. In any case, we are getting to know each other a bit. I wish we dared to tell each other much more already. Who knows, the time may come sooner than I think! I get an understanding look from him about twice a day, I wink back, and we both feel happy.

I certainly seem quite mad to be talking about him being happy, and yet I feel pretty sure that he thinks just the same as I do.

Yours, Anne

510

Saturday 4 March 1944.

Dearest Kitty,

This is the first Saturday for months and months that it hasn't been boring, dreary and dull. And Peter is the cause. This morning I went to hang up my apron when Daddy asked whether I'd like to stay and talk some French. I agreed; first we talked French, and I explained something to him, then we did some English, Daddy read out loud to us from Dickens and I was in the seventh heaven, because I sat on Daddy's chair very close to Peter.

84 I went downstairs at a quarter to 11, coming back again quickly to go to the attic. Peter jumped up to open the window upstairs, but he sat down again when I said that I could just as easily return later.

I was rather surprised, for any other time he would certainly have opened the window all the same. I wondered deep inside: "Would he prefer to go upstairs with me later?"

And indeed at half past eleven he said on the stairs that I could leave the trap door open. We talked until a quarter to 1. If, as I leave the room, he gets a chance, e.g. after a meal, and if no one can hear, he says: "Good-by, Anne, see you soon!"

Oh, I am so pleased! I wonder if he is going to fall in love with me after all? Anyway, he's a very nice fellow and no one knows what lovely talks I have with him!

Mrs. v.P. quite approves when I go and talk to him, but still she asked today teasingly, "can I really trust the two of you up there together?"

85 "Of course," I protested "really you quite insult me!"

From morn till night I rejoice that I shall be seeing Peter.

yours, Anne M. Frank.

P.S. Mustn't forget, a big load of snow fell tonight, hardly any is left now it's all thawed.

yours, A.M.F.

. . . . . .

Saturday, 4 March, 1944.

Dear Kitty,

This is the first Saturday for months and months that hasn't been boring, dreary, and dull. And Peter is the cause.

This morning I went to the attic to hang up my apron, when Daddy asked whether I'd like to stay and talk some French. I agreed. First we talked French, and I explained something to Peter; then we did some English. Daddy read out loud to us from Dickens and I was in the seventh heaven, because I sat on Daddy's chair very close to Peter.

I went downstairs at eleven o'clock. When I came upstairs again at half past eleven, he was already waiting for me on the stairs. We talked until a quarter to one. If, as I leave the room, he gets a chance after a meal, for instance, and if no one can hear, he says: "Good-by, Anne, see you soon."

Oh, I am so pleased! I wonder if he is going to fall in love with me after all? Anyway, he is a very nice fellow and no one knows what lovely talks I have with him!

Mrs. Van Daan quite approves when I go and talk to him, but she asked today teasingly, "Can I really trust you two up there together?"

"Of course," I protested, "really you quite insult me!"

From morn till night I look forward to seeing Peter.

Yours, Anne

Monday 6 March 1944.

Dear Kitty,

Isn't it funny, ever since Peter told me about his parents, I have been feeling a little bit responsible for him. It's as if the quarrels affect me as much as they do him and yet I daren't speak to him about them any longer, for fear he might not like it. And I wouldn't go too far now for all the money in the world.

I can tell by Peter's face that he thinks just as much as I do, and when Mrs. v.P. yesterday evening said scoffingly: "The thinker!" I was irritated. Peter flushed and looked very embarrassed, and I was about to explode.

| 86   Why can't these people keep their mouths shut? | You can't imagine how horrible it is to stand by and see how lonely he is and yet not be able to do anything. I can so well imagine, just as if I were in his place, how desperate he must feel sometimes in quarrels and in love. Poor Peter, he needs love very much!

When he said he didn't need any friends how harsh the words sounded to my ears. Oh, how mistaken he is! I don't believe he meant it a bit.

He clings to his manliness, to his solitude and to his affected indifference, but it's only an act, so as never, never to show his real feelings. Poor Peter, how long will he be able to go on playing this role, surely a terrible outburst must follow as a result of this superhuman effort?[6]

Oh, Peter, if only I could help you, if only you would let me! Together we could drive away your loneliness and mine!

. . . . . .

Monday, 6 March, 1944

Dear Kitty,

I can tell by Peter's face that he thinks just as much as I do, and when Mrs. Van Daan yesterday evening said scoffingly: "The thinker!" I was irritated. Peter flushed and looked very embarrassed, and I was about to explode.

Why can't these people keep their mouths shut?

You can't imagine how horrible it is to stand by and see how lonely he is and yet not be able to do anything. I can so well imagine, just as if I were in his place, how desperate he must feel sometimes in quarrels and in love. Poor Peter, he needs love very much!

When he said he didn't need any friends how harsh the words sounded to my ears. Oh, how mistaken he is! I don't believe he meant it a bit.

He clings to his solitude, to his affected indifference and his grown-up ways, but it's just an act, so as never, never to show his real feelings. Poor Peter, how long will he be able to go on playing this role? Surely a terrible outburst must follow as the result of this superhuman effort?

Oh, Peter, if only I could help you, if only you would let me! Together we could drive away your loneliness and mine!

512

The *"Secret Annexe"* (Anne Frank Foundation.)

513

I think a lot, but I don't say much. I am happy if I see him and the sun shines when I'm with him. I was very excited yesterday and while I was washing my hair I knew that he | 87 was sitting in | the room next to ours. I couldn't do anything about it; the more quiet and serious I feel inside the more noisy I become outwardly! Who will be the first to discover and break through this armor?

I'm glad after all that the v.P.s have a son and not a daughter, my conquest could never have been so difficult, so beautiful, so good, if I had not happened to hit on someone of the opposite sex.[2]

yours, Anne M. Frank.

P.S. You know that I am always honest with you and so I must tell you that I actually live from one meeting to the next. I keep hoping to discover that he too is waiting for me all the time and I'm thrilled if I notice a small, shy advance from his side. I believe he'd oh so like to say a lot just like I would, little does he know that it's just his clumsiness that attracts me so.

Oh sweetheart! (it sounds so banal, but it's not at all!)

yours, A.

b . . . . . .

c   I think a lot, but I don't say much. I am happy if I see him and if the sun shines when I'm with him. I was very excited yesterday; while I was washing my hair, I knew that he was sitting in the room next to ours. I couldn't do anything about it; the more quiet and serious I feel inside, the more noisy I become outwardly.

Who will be the first to discover and break through this armor? I'm glad after all that the Van Daans have a son and not a daughter, my conquest could never have been so difficult, so beautiful, so good, if I had not happened to hit on someone of the opposite sex.

Yours, Anne

P.S. You know that I'm always honest with you, so I must tell you that I actually live from one meeting to the next. I keep hoping to discover that he too is waiting for me all the time and I'm thrilled if I notice a small shy advance from his side. I believe he'd like to say a lot just like I would; little does he know that it's just his clumsiness that attracts me.

Yours, Anne

514

a 88

Dear Kitty,

If I think now of my life in 1942, it all feels so unreal. It was quite a different Anne Frank who enjoyed that heavenly existence from the Anne who has grown wise within these walls. Yes, it was a heavenly life. Boy friends at every turn, about 20 friends and acquaintances of my own age, the darling of nearly all the teachers, spoiled from top to toe by Mummy and Daddy, lots of sweets, enough pocket money, what more could one want?

You will certainly wonder by what means I got around all these people. Peter's word "attractiveness" is not altogether true. All the teachers were entertained by my cute answers, my amusing remarks, my smiling face and my questioning looks. That is all I was—a terrible flirt, coquettish and amusing. I had one or two advantages which kept me rather in favor. I was industrious, honest and frank. I would never have refused anyone who wanted to crib from me. I shared my sweets generously, and I wasn't conceited.

b 297

Tuesday 7 Mar. 1944.

Dear ¹Kitty,

If I [think] of my life in 1942 it feels like something unreal. It was quite a different Anne who lived that life than the one who is being brought up in the "Secret Annexe." At home, on the Merry, things look so wonderful from here, lots of boy friends and girl friends, spoiled by Mummy and Daddy, lots of sweets, enough pocket money, what more could one want?

You will certainly wonder how I got around all these people who liked me in the past. It wasn't attractiveness, far from it, it was the result of my answers, amusing remarks, questioning looks and sense of humor. That is all I was, a flirt, coquettish and sometimes amusing.³ I had some advantages which kept me rather in favor. I was industrious and honest. I would never have refused anyone who wanted to crib from me. I always admitted my mistakes and I was far from conceited. But wouldn't I really have become so in the

c

Tuesday, 7 March, 1944

Dear Kitty,

If I think now of my life in 1942, it all seems so unreal. It was quite a different Anne who enjoyed that heavenly existence from the Anne who has grown wise within these walls. Yes, it was a heavenly life. Boy friends at every turn, about twenty friends and acquaintances of my own age, the darling of nearly all the teachers, spoiled from top to toe by Mummy and Daddy, lots of sweets, enough pocket money, what more could one want?

You will certainly wonder by what means I got around all these people. Peter's word "attractiveness" is not altogether true. All the teachers were entertained by my cute answers, my amusing remarks, my smiling face, and my questioning looks. That is all I was—a terrible flirt, coquettish and amusing. I had one or two advantages, which kept me rather in favor. I was industrious, honest, and frank. I would never have dreamed of cribbing from anyone else [I would never have refused anyone who wanted to crib from me]. I shared my sweets generously, and I wasn't conceited.

515

Wouldn't I have become rather forward | with so much admiration? It was a good thing that in the midst of, at the height of, all this gaiety, I suddenly had to face reality, and it took me at least a year to get used to the fact that there was no more admiration forthcoming.

How did I appear at school? The ringleader who thought of new jokes and pranks, always "king of the castle," never in a bad mood, never a crybaby. No wonder everyone liked to cycle with me and I got their attentions.

I look now at that Anne Frank as an amusing, jokey, but superficial girl who has nothing to do with the Anne of today. What did Peter say about me? "If ever I saw you you were always surrounded by 2 or more boys and a whole troupe of girls, you were always laughing and always the center of everything!" He was quite right.

What is left of this Anne Frank? Oh, don't worry, I haven't forgotten how to laugh or to answer back readily. I'm just as good, if not better, at criticizing people, and I can still flirt and still be amusing if I wish . . . . . —That's not it though, for an evening, a few
| 90   days, or even a week I'd still like to play the fool, because life is nothing but | comedy. Then I should be dead beat and fall round the neck of anyone who talked sense. I don't

end, wouldn't this life have made me | rather forward? It was a good thing, despite everything, that in the midst of, at the height of, all this gaiety, I suddenly had to face reality, and it took me at least a year to get used to the fact that there was no more admiration forthcoming.

Now I look back at that Anne as an amusing, but very superficial girl, who has nothing to do with the Anne of today. Peter said quite rightly about me: "If ever I saw you you were always surrounded by 2 or more boys and a whole troupe of girls, you were always laughing and always the center of everything!" What is left of this girl? Oh, don't worry, I haven't forgotten how to laugh or to answer back readily. I'm just as good, or better, at criticizing people and I can still flirt if. . . . I wish. That's not it though, I'd like that sort of life again for an evening, a few days, or even a week, the life which seems so
| 299   carefree and gay. At the end of that week, I should be dead beat | and would be only too thankful to listen to anyone who began to talk about something sensible.

Wouldn't I have become rather forward with so much admiration? It was a good thing that in the midst of, at the height of, all this gaiety, I suddenly had to face reality and it took me at least a year to get used to the fact that there was no more admiration forthcoming.

How did I appear at school? The one who thought of new jokes and pranks, always "king of the castle," never in a bad mood, never a crybaby. No wonder everyone liked to cycle with me, and I got their attentions.

Now I look back at that Anne as an amusing, but very superficial girl, who has nothing to do with the Anne of today. Peter said quite rightly about me: "If ever I saw you, you were always surrounded by two or more boys and a whole troupe of girls. You were always laughing and always the center of everything!"

What is left of this girl? Oh, don't worry, I haven't forgotten how to laugh or to answer back readily. I'm just as good, if not better, at criticizing people, and I can still flirt if . . . I wish. That's not it though, I'd like that sort of life again for an evening, a few days, or even a week; the life which seems so carefree and gay. But at the end of that week, I should be dead beat and would be only too thankful to listen to anyone who began to talk about something sensible.

516

a

want followers but friends, admirers who fall not for a flattering smile but for what one does and for one's character. I don't need all that many admirers, I know myself what is good and what is bad!

The Anne of 1942 was quite different, she too was lonely, she too longed for a true girl friend but consciously or unconsciously tried to drive away the emptiness with jokes.

Now I think seriously about life, since one period of my life is already over, that of the carefree, happy-go-lucky schooldays. It will never come back, I don't want it any more, I have outgrown it. Who knows, I might have remained stuck in it, never have been able to rid myself of it!

I look upon my life up till the New Year, as it were, through a powerful magnifying glass. At home, the carefree life of a schoolgirl, with lots of fun and pleasure, but also with some emptiness. Then coming here in 1942, the setback, the quarrels, I couldn't understand it, I was taken completely by surprise and the only way I could keep up some bearing was by being impertinent. Then the first half of '43. My | inexpressible sadness, | 91 my fits of crying and my loneliness, how I began to see all my faults and shortcomings

b

I don't want followers, but friends, admirers who fall not for a flattering smile but for what one does and for one's character.

I know quite well that the circle around me would be much smaller. But what does that matter as long as one still keeps a few sincere friends?

Yet I wasn't entirely happy in 1942 in spite of everything, that's impossible, I often felt deserted, but because I was on the go the whole day long, I didn't think about it and enjoyed myself as much as I could.

Now I think seriously about life and see that one period of my life is over forever; the carefree schooldays are gone, never to return. I don't even long for them much; I have outgrown them, I can't just play the fool as my serious side is always there.

300 I look upon my life up till the New Year, as it were, through a powerful magnifying glass. The sunny ²life at home, then coming here in '42, the sudden change, the quarrels, the ³bickerings; I couldn't understand it, I was taken by surprise, and the only way I could keep up some bearing was by being impertinent. ⁴The first half of 1943, my fits of crying, the loneliness, how I slowly began to see all my faults and shortcomings, which are so

c

I don't want followers, but friends, admirers who fall not for a flattering smile but for what one does and for one's character.

I know quite well that the circle around me would be much smaller. But what does that matter, as long as one still keeps a few sincere friends?

Yet I wasn't entirely happy in 1942 in spite of everything; I often felt deserted, but because I was on the go the whole day long, I didn't think about it and enjoyed myself as much as I could. Consciously or unconsciously, I tried to drive away the emptiness I felt with jokes and pranks. Now I think seriously about life and what I have to do. One period of my life is over forever. The carefree schooldays are gone, never to return.

I don't even long for them any more; I have outgrown them, I can't just only enjoy myself as my serious side is always there.

I look upon my life up till the New Year, as it were, through a powerful magnifying glass. The sunny life at home, then coming here in 1942, the sudden change, the quarrels, the bickerings, I couldn't understand it, I was taken by surprise, and the only way I could keep up some bearing was by being impertinent.

The first half of 1943: my fits of crying, the loneliness, how I slowly began to see all

517

a

which were much greater than I ever thought. I still spoke just as much, did my utmost to turn Daddy into my confidant, failed, was alone and (nearly) every evening did nothing but cry.

Then the second half of 1943, I became a young woman, an adult in body and my mind underwent a great, a very great change, I came to know God! I started to think, to write and I discovered myself. I gained in confidence but also in sorrow because I realized that I no longer cared for Mummy and that Daddy would never become my confidant. I no longer had idle dreams, I had myself.

At the beginning of the New Year the second great change, my dream . . . . . and with it I discovered Peter, discovered a second and as hard a conflict, discovered my longing for a boy; not for a girl friend but for a boy friend. I also discovered my inward happiness and my defensive armor of superficiality and gaiety. But in due time I quieted down. Now | 92 I live only for Peter, for on him will depend very much | what will happen to me from now on!

b

great and which seemed much greater then. During the day I deliberately talked about anything and everything that was farthest from my thoughts, tried to draw Pim to me; but couldn't, alone I had to face the difficult task of changing myself, to stop the everlasting reproaches, which were so oppressive and which reduced me to such terrible despondency. Things improved slightly in the 2nd half of the year, I became a young woman and was treated more like a grownup. I started to think, and to write stories, and came to the conclusion that the others had nothing to do with me any more, they had no right to | 301 throw me about like a pendulum clock | from left to right, I wanted to change in accordance with my own desires. I realized that I could do without Mummy, completely and utterly, that was hurtful, but one thing that struck me even more was when I realized that even Daddy would never become my confidant. I trusted no one but myself any longer.

At the beginning of the New Year the second great change, my dream . . . . . and with it I discovered my boundless desire for all that is beautiful and good.

c

my faults and shortcomings, which are so great and which seemed much greater then. During the day I deliberately talked about anything and everything that was farthest from my thoughts, tried to draw Pim to me; but couldn't. Alone I had to face the difficult task of changing myself, to stop the everlasting reproaches, which were so oppressive and which reduced me to such terrible despondency.

Things improved slightly in the second half of the year, I became a young woman and was treated more like a grownup. I started to think, and write stories, and came to the conclusion that the others no longer had the right to throw me about like an india-rubber ball. I wanted to change in accordance with my own desires. But *one* thing that struck me even more was when I realized that even Daddy would never become my confidant over everything. I didn't want to trust anyone but myself any more.

At the beginning of the New Year: the second great change, my dream. . . . And with it I discovered my longing, not for a girl friend, but for a boy friend. I also discovered my inward happiness and my defensive armor of superficiality and gaiety. In due time I quieted down and discovered my boundless desire for all that is beautiful and good.

518

Oh, in the evening when I lie in bed and end my prayers with the words, "Ich danke dir, für all das Gute und Liebe und Schöne," I am filled with joy. Then I think about "das Gute" of going into hiding, of my health, of my whole being, of "das Liebe" of Peter, of that which is still embryonic and impressionable and which we neither of us dare to name or touch, and of "das Schöne" which exists in the world; the world and Nature, Beauty and everything, everything exquisite and fine.

I don't think then of all the misery, but think of the beauty that still remains. And that is also the difference between Mummy and myself. Her counsel when one feels melancholy is: "Think of all the misery in the world and be thankful that you are still alive."

And in the evening, when I lie in bed and end my prayers with the words, "Ich danke dir für all das Gute und Liebe und Schöne," I am filled with joy, then I think about "das Gute" of going into hiding, my health, and with my whole being of "das Liebe" that will come sometime, love, the future, happiness and of "das Schöne" which the world means. The world, nature, and outstanding beauty of everything, everything that is exquisite | 302 | and fine.

I don't think then of all the misery but of the beauty that still remains. This is one of the things that Mummy and I are so entirely different about. Her counsel when one feels melancholy is: "Think of all the misery in the world and be thankful that you are

And in the evening, when I lie in bed and end my prayers with the words, "I thank you, God, for all that is good and dear and beautiful," I am filled with joy. Then I think about "the good" of going into hiding, of my health and with my whole being of the "dearness" of Peter, of that which is still embryonic and impressionable and which we neither of us dare to name or touch, of that which will come sometime; love, the future, happiness and of "the beauty" which exists in the world; the world, nature, beauty and all, all that is exquisite and fine.

I don't think then of all the misery, but of the beauty that still remains. This is one of the things that Mummy and I are so entirely different about. Her counsel when one feels melancholy is: "Think of all the misery in the world and be thankful that you are

My advice is: "Go outside to the fields, enjoy nature and the sunshine, go out and try to recapture happiness in yourself and in God; think of all the beauty that's still left in and around you and be happy!" Therein lies a world of difference, the world | of difference between the two of us. What can you do about misery if you are depressed? What good is life to you if there is nothing but misery in it?

But nature, sunshine, freedom and yourself, these can all help you. There and only there can you find yourself and God.

And whoever is happy will make others happy too. He who has courage and faith will never perish in misery!

yours, Anne Mary Frank.

not sharing in it." My advice is: "Go outside, to the fields, enjoy nature and the sunshine, go out and try to recapture happiness in yourself; think of all the beauty that's still left in and around you and be happy!"

I don't see how Mummy's idea can be right, because then how are you supposed to behave if it's you that goes through the misery? Then you are lost. On the contrary, I've found that in every misfortune there is always some beauty left, if only you look for it, you will discover more and more happiness and regain your balance. And whoever is happy will make others happy too. He who has courage and faith will never perish in misery.

yours, Anne M. Frank.[4]

not sharing in it!" My advice is: "Go outside, to the fields, enjoy nature and the sunshine, go out and try to recapture happiness in yourself and in God. Think of all the beauty that's still left in and around you and be happy!"

I don't see how Mummy's idea can be right, because then how are you supposed to behave if you go through the misery yourself? Then you are lost. On the contrary, I've found that there is always some beauty left—in nature, sunshine, freedom, in yourself; these can all help you. Look at these things, then you find yourself again, and God, and then you regain your balance.

And whoever is happy will make others happy too. He who has courage and faith will never perish in misery!

Yours, Anne

Wednesday 8 March 1944.

I shall now include a few short notes Margot and I sent each other yesterday afternoon, just for the fun of it of course:

Tuesday:

Anne: I'll be happy to let you read what I've written in my diary today sometime, but I'm not ready yet. Later on, say in a month's time, if I've got any further with it, I might show it to you. Just let Mummy say I don't know anything about life then!

You know why I think you'd be interested? Because although I can't express myself properly anywhere else even in my tales, | in my diary I can completely.

| 94

It cries with pain or joy just as I sometimes do myself!

Wednesday:

Anne: Funny, isn't it, I always remember the events of the night before much later on, now I suddenly remember that Mr. Pfeffer was snoring terribly last night (it's a quarter to three on Wednesday afternoon now and Mr. Pfeffer is snoring again, that's why I remembered it of course) and that when I had to use the potty I deliberately made a lot of noise in order to put a stop to his snoring.

On top of that I heard them flying (literally!)* and dreamed of Jacque and J.** and of after-the-war and had great fun. A.

Margot:

What is better gasping for air or snoring? Did you kick up an old-fashioned row with J. and J.

Anne:

Snoring is better, because when I make a noise it stops without the person in question waking up!

Jacque and J. were the only ones involved in the postwar dream, Jacque wanted to learn shorthand | from me⁴ in the meantime though she was standing at the cooker upstairs

| 95

stirring a pan. J. was sitting on a chair next to the china cabinet wearing a knitted skirt in all sorts of colors. It looked a bit like my sun top, but there was a stitch in it!

A.

What I didn't tell Margot, but want to confess to you dearest Kitty, is that I dream a great deal about Peter. The night before last I was in our living room here, skating with that small boy from the Apollo Hall ice rink, who had come here with his little sister with the-perpetually-blue dress-and-spindly-legs. I introduced myself to him in a very affected way as: Anne Frank and asked for his name, it was: Peter. In my dream I wondered how many Peters I now know!

Then I dreamed that we were standing in Peter's room, facing each other beside the stairs. I said something to him, he gave me a kiss, but replied that he didn't like me behaving like that and that I mustn't flirt. In a desperate and pleading voice I said: "I don't flirt, Peter!"

---

*Anne Frank's play on words in the Dutch expression "*ik zie ze vliegen* [I see them flying]," which means "my imagination is running riot." A.J.P.

**At the request of the person concerned this name has been replaced by an initial chosen at random.

. . . . . .

. . . . . .

96   When I woke up I was glad that Peter hadn't said it after all.

Tonight we kissed each other again, but Peter's cheeks were very disappointing, they were not as soft as they look, but were like Daddy's cheek, the cheek of a man who already shaves.

———

This afternoon after our meal when Bep, Daddy and Pf. had already gone downstairs, I decided to tell Mrs. v.P. for once that she shouldn't be so insensitive and keep going on about Henk. She had in fact already said something to Bep like: You really ought to have married Henk, after all you like him well enough! Now you'll have to wait until he's divorced, etc. etc.

So I put my plan into practice and said: "I don't understand, Mrs. v.P., why you keep saying these things about Henk to Bep all the time. I find it incomprehensible that you don't realize how unpleasant it is for Bep." Mrs. v.P. blushed of course and said: "Surely I know best what to say to Bep; if she finds it unpleasant, she shouldn't talk about Henk so much herself!"

97   My reply was rather disdainful and cool: "All I know is that Bep finds this sort of talk very dis- | agreeable!" Soon afterwards I went downstairs.

My great achievement with Mrs. v.P. is that I'm able to keep so calm nowadays; she turns red and I remain my usual self and say precisely what I intended to say. I believe that my self-assurance often catches Mummy off her guard as well.

For you see Kitty, I may still often make mistakes, very often, in a lot of things, but I do know when it happens. And one thing that I can do very well is to say what I want to say!

However I am now terribly curious about what Peter will have to say about it, for I waited until he was there as well! Of course he may say nothing at all, but I do hope he will!

yours, Anne M. Frank.

Friday 10 March 1944.

Dearest Kitty,

In fact Peter didn't say anything, so I asked him yesterday. He didn't have anything special to say about it. Today the proverb: "Misfortunes never come singly, came to pass!" Peter just said it. I'll tell you what nastinesses we've all | been having and what probably still hangs over our heads.

98   Firstly, following on Henk and Aagje's wedding yesterday, Miep is ill. The Westerkerk, where the blessing took place, gave her a terrible cold. Vomiting, headache, sore throat and so on.

Secondly Mr. Kleiman is still not back after his last bout of gastric bleeding and so Bep is all alone in the office.

Thirdly a gentleman, whose name I shall not mention and which doesn't matter in any case, has been arrested by the police. Not only is it bad for the man in question but for us as well, because we badly need potatoes, butter and jam. We'll just call him Mr. M., he has five children under the age of 13 and another on the way. Last night we had another little fright when someone knocked on the wall next door. We were having our supper; for the rest of the evening we were all depressed and nervous.

. . . . . .

. . . . . .

99 Lately I haven't felt at all like writing about what's been going on here. I've been much more concerned with personal matters. Don't misunderstand my meaning, I'm terribly upset about what happened to poor, good Mr. M., but there isn't all that much room for him in my diary.

On Tuesday, Wednesday and Thursday I was with Peter from half past 4 to quarter past 5, when everyone else was out of the way. We did French and gossiped about a hundred and one things. I am so happy about that hour or so in the afternoon and the best of it all is that I think Peter likes me to be there too.

yours, Anne M. Frank.

Saturday 11 March 1944.

Dear Kitty,
I can't seem to sit still lately, I run from upstairs to downstairs and then from downstairs back up again. I sometimes have fits of <u>having</u> to be all by myself or at least with Peter. Poor, poor Peter, his parents have had a row again, screams and curses are reverberating again above our heads. I'm going upstairs, I <u>can't</u> help myself.

yours, Anne M. Frank.

303

Sunday 12 March 1944.

Dear Kitty,
I can't seem to sit still lately, I run upstairs and down and then back again. I love talking to Peter, but I am always afraid of being a nuisance. He has told me a bit about the past, about his parents and about himself, it's not half enough though and I ask myself every five minutes why it is that I always long for more. He used to think I was unbearable, and I returned the compliment, now I've changed my opinion, has he changed his too? I think so; still it doesn't necessarily mean that we shall become great friends, although as far as I am concerned it would make the time here much more bearable. But still, I won't drive myself mad over it, I see quite a lot of him and there is no need to bore you with it too, Kitty, because I'm miserable. On Saturday afternoon I felt in such a whirl after

Sunday, 12 March, 1944

Dear Kitty,
I can't seem to sit still lately; I run upstairs and down and then back again. I love talking to Peter, but I'm always afraid of being a nuisance. He has told me a bit about the past, about his parents and about himself. It's not half enough though and I ask myself why it is that I always long for more. He used to think I was unbearable; and I returned the compliment; now I have changed my opinion, has he changed his too?

I think so; still it doesn't necessarily mean that we shall become great friends, although as far as I am concerned it would make the time here much more bearable. But still, I won't get myself upset about it—I see quite a lot of him and there's no need to make you unhappy about it too, Kitty, just because I feel so miserable.

Sunday 12 March 1944.

Dear Kitty,

Things are getting crazier here all the time and Peter hasn't looked at me since yesterday. It's just as if he were cross with me, I do my very best not to run after him and to speak to him as little as possible, but it's all very difficult! What could it be, that often keeps him from me then often sends him to me? Perhaps I imagine that it's worse than it really is, perhaps he too has moods, perhaps tomorrow everything will be all right again!

The hardest thing of all is to keep looking normal, when I feel so dismal and sad. I have to talk, to help, sit with the others and above all I have to be cheerful! Most of all I miss Nature and a little corner where I can be alone as long as I like! I think I'm getting everything mixed up, Kitty, but then I'm completely confused:[1] on the one hand I am mad with desire for him, can hardly be in the same room, without looking at him and on the other hand I ask myself why he should actually matter to me so much, why I am not suf-

| 101 | ficient unto myself, why I can't be calm again!

Day and night, whenever I'm awake I do nothing but ask myself: "Have you left him alone enough?[2] Have you been upstairs too much? Do you talk too much about serious subjects that he's not ready to talk about yet? Does he perhaps not really like you very much? Was the whole to-do just in my imagination? Is he perhaps sorry it all happened?" And a whole lot more.

b . . . . . .

c . . . . . .

a

Yesterday afternoon, after a miserable morning, after news of arrests (of D. too now) after bad news about Bep's father and never a friendly glance from Peter, I felt in such a whirl and so under the weather that I went for a sleep, sleeping so as not to think any more. I slept till 4 o'clock and then I had to go into the living room. Oh how hard it was to answer Mummy and to explain to Daddy why I went to sleep. At the end of my wits I simply said that I had a headache, and I did have a headache but inside!

| 102   Ordinary people, ordinary girls, teen-agers | like myself will no doubt think I'm a bit

b   304   hearing a whole lot of sad pieces of news that I went and lay on my divan for a sleep. I only wanted to sleep to stop thinking.

I slept till 4 o'clock, then I had to go into the living room. I found it difficult to answer all Mummy's questions and think of some little fib to tell Daddy, as an explanation for my long sleep. I resorted to a "headache," which wasn't a lie as I had one. . . but inside!

Ordinary people, ordinary girls, teen-agers like myself will think I'm a bit cracked with all my self-pity, yes, that's what it is, but I pour out my heart to you, then for the rest of the day I'm as impudent, gay and self-confident as I can be, in order to avoid questions and getting myself down.

Margot is very sweet and would like me to trust her, but still,[3] I can't tell her everything.[4] She's a darling, she's good and pretty, but she lacks the nonchalance for conducting deep

| 305   discussions, she takes me so ser- | iously, much too seriously, and then thinks about her queer little sister for a long time afterwards, looks searchingly at me, at every word I say, and keeps on thinking: "Is this just a joke or does she really mean it?" I think that's because we are together the whole day long, and that if I trusted someone completely, then I shouldn't want them hanging around me all the time.

c

On Saturday afternoon I felt in such a whirl, after hearing a whole lot of sad news, that I went and lay down on my divan for a sleep. I only wanted to sleep to stop myself thinking. I slept till four o'clock, then I had to go into the living room. I found it difficult to answer all Mummy's questions and think of some little excuse to tell Daddy, as an explanation for my long sleep. I resorted to a "headache," which wasn't a lie, as I had one . . . but inside!

Ordinary people, ordinary girls, teen-agers like myself, will think I'm a bit cracked with all my self-pity. Yes, that's what it is, but I pour out my heart to you, then for the rest of the day I'm as impudent, gay, and self-confident as I can be, in order to avoid questions and getting on my own nerves.

Margot is very sweet and would like me to trust her, but still, I can't tell her everything. She's a darling, she's good and pretty, but she lacks the nonchalance for conducting deep discussions; she takes me so seriously, much too seriously, and then thinks about her queer little sister for a long time afterwards, looks searchingly at me, at every word I say, and keeps on thinking: "Is this just a joke or does she really mean it?" I think that's because we are together the whole day long, and that if I trusted someone completely, then I shouldn't want them hanging around me all the time.

525

cracked, but no one knows how difficult it is to be so much in love, without being loved back and to have the person you worship always around you. I wouldn't miss Peter for anything in the world, and yet I would sometimes like to be far away from him. That's silly, but understandable too, for when I have just spent an hour trying to get some order into my thoughts and feelings, and then I see him again, all my good intentions vanish at a stroke.

I am unhappy in love, countless admirers and lovable young men have begged for my favors, while I felt nothing but comradeship for them. But there were three I liked and none of the three saw anything in me.

Oh Peter, just say something at last, don't let me drift on between hope and dejection. Give me a kiss or send me out of the room, but like this I'll do something desperate. In the evening the loveliest scenes, in the morning the naked reality and that for weeks on end, every day, I'm not strong enough for that yet!

——

103   And that's just it, everyone thinks that I'm cheeky, confident and amusing, while I want nothing more than to be just Anne for one single person. I put on an act everywhere, play the clown, the minx, the daredevil, yet all I want is to show my sensitivity to just one single person, that's all. For I am sensitive, very sensitive! Margot would so much like to be my confidante, but I can't. She's a darling, she's good, and pretty, but she lacks something I need. Nor could I bear to have someone about all day long who knew what was going on inside me. I can't have my confidant around me all day long, except for . . . Peter!

What I have to bear is so hard but then I am strong. In one sense I am also self-confident, but quite differently from what people think. I know that I'm above Mummy and Mrs. v. Pels. I can't feel anything but contempt for all their actions, and awareness that I am different. I know that I have God, God and Granny and so much more and that's what keeps me going. Without the voice that keeps holding out comfort and goodness
| 104   to me I should have lost all hope long ago, without God I should long ago have | collapsed.

I know I am not safe, I am afraid of prison cells and concentration camps, but I feel I've grown more courageous and that I am in God's hands!

yours, Anne M. Frank.

When shall I finally untangle my thoughts, when shall I find peace and rest within myself again?

yours, Anne

When shall I finally untangle my thoughts, when shall I find peace and rest within myself again?

Yours, Anne

Tuesday 14 March 1944.

Dearest Kit,

Perhaps it would be entertaining for you (though not in the least for me) to hear how we are going to eat today. As the charwoman is idling about downstairs, I'm at the v.P.s' at the moment, sitting at the oilcloth table with a handkerchief steeped in some good scent (bought before we came here) over my mouth and pressed against my nose. You won't gather much from this, so let's "begin at the beginning!"

    B. and D. have been caught, so we have no coupons (apart from our five ration cards) and no fats. Because Miep and Kleiman are ill, Bep can't go out so the atmosphere is dreary and dejected, and so is the food. From tomorrow we'll be without a scrap of fat, butter or margarine and we shall probably get nothing before Saturday, when the new

| 105   coupons | are issued. Now we can't have fried potatoes for breakfast any longer, so we have porridge instead, and as Mrs. v.P. thinks we're starving, we've bought some more full cream milk. Our supper today consists of a hash made from kale that came out of the barrel. Hence the precautionary measure with the handkerchief!

Tuesday 14 Mar. <u>1944.</u>

Dear Kitty,

Perhaps it would be entertaining for you (though not in the least for me) to hear how we are going to eat today. As the charwoman is at work downstairs I am sitting on the v.P.s' oilcloth table at the moment. I have a handkerchief soaked in some good scent (bought before we came here) over my mouth and held against my nose. You won't gather much from this so let's "begin at the beginning.

    Our food coupon suppliers have been caught so we just have our 5 black-market ration cards³ and no coupons and no fats. As both Miep and Kleiman are ill, Bep hasn't time to do any shopping, so the atmosphere is dreary and dejected, and so is the food. From tomorrow we shall not have a scrap of fat, butter or margarine left. We can't have fried potatoes (to save bread) for breakfast any longer, so we have porridge instead, and

| 307   as Mrs. v.P. thinks we are starving we have bought some | extra full cream milk. Our supper today consists of a hash made from kale which has been preserved in a barrel. Hence the precautionary measure with the handkerchief!

Tuesday, 14 March, 1944

Dear Kitty,

    Perhaps it would be entertaining for you—though not in the least for me—to hear what we are going to eat today. As the charwoman is at work downstairs, I'm sitting on the Van Daans' table at the moment. I have a handkerchief soaked in some good scent (bought before we came here) over my mouth and held against my nose. You won't gather much from this, so let's "begin at the beginning."

    The people from whom we obtained food coupons have been caught, so we just have our five ration cards and no extra coupons, and no fats. As both Miep and Koophuis are ill, Elli hasn't time to do any shopping, so the atmosphere is dreary and dejected, and so is the food. From tomorrow we shall not have a scrap of fat, butter, or margarine left. We can't have fried potatoes (to save bread) for breakfast any longer, so we have porridge instead, and as Mrs. Van Daan thinks we're starving, we have bought some full cream milk "under the counter." Our supper today consists of a hash made from kale which has been preserved in a barrel. Hence the precautionary measure with the handkerchief! It's

It's incredible how kale that is probably a few years old can stink! The smell is a mixture of W.C., bad plums, preservatives + 10 rotten eggs. Ugh! the mere thought of eating that muck makes me feel sick!

Added to this, our potatoes are suffering from such peculiar diseases that out of two buckets of pommes de terre one whole one ends up on the stove. And so we amuse ourselves by searching for all the different kinds of diseases, and have come to the conclusion that they range from cancer and smallpox to measles. Oh yes, it's quite something to be in hiding during the 4th year of the war (that is for the Netherlands!). If only the whole rotten business was over!

Quite honestly, the food wouldn't matter so much to me if only things were more | 106 | pleasant otherwise. Here's the rub precisely, this boring life is | beginning to make us all boring. The following is the way we hiders respectively view the present situation:

It's incredible how kale that is probably a few years old can stink! The smell in the room is a mixture of bad plums, strong preservatives and 10 rotten eggs. Ugh! the mere thought of eating that muck makes me feel sick!

Added to this our potatoes are suffering from such peculiar diseases that out of two buckets of pommes de terre one whole one ends up on the stove. We amuse ourselves by searching for all the different kinds of diseases, and have come to the conclusion that they range from cancer and smallpox to measles! Oh, yes, it's no joke to be in hiding during the 4ᵗʰ year of the war. If only the whole rotten business was over!

Quite honestly, I wouldn't care so much about the food if only it were more pleasant | 308 | here otherwise. There's the rub, this tedious existence is | beginning to make us all bored. The following are the views of the 5 grownups on the present situation (for once I've kept to the rule that children must have no opinion.

incredible how kale can stink when it's a year old! The smell in the room is a mixture of bad plums, strong preservatives, and rotten eggs. Ugh! the mere thought of eating that muck makes me feel sick.

Added to this, our potatoes are suffering from such peculiar diseases that out of two buckets of *pommes de terre*, one whole one ends up on the stove. We amuse ourselves by searching for all the different kinds of diseases, and have come to the conclusion that they range from cancer and smallpox to measles! Oh, no, it's no joke to be in hiding during the fourth year of the war. If only the whole rotten business was over!

Quite honestly, I wouldn't care so much about the food, if only it were more pleasant here in other ways. There's the rub; this tedious existence is beginning to make us all touchy.

The following are the views of the five grownups on the present situation:

528

a

Mrs. van Pels:

The job as queen of the kitchen lost its attraction a long time ago. It's dull to sit and do nothing, or to learn English. So I go back to my cooking again, not complaining: "It's impossible to cook without any fats, and all these nasty smells make me feel sick. Nothing other than ingratitude and rude remarks do I get, I have always been the black sheep, I am always the guilty one! Moreover, according to me, the war isn't going fast enough; in the end the Germans will still win. I am afraid we shall starve: "Scheisse, Schwein, Rottzeug!"

Mr. van Pels: I must smoke and smoke and smoke, and then the food, the political situation, and Kerli's moods all don't seem so bad. Kerli is a darling wife after all!

If I haven't anything to smoke then I get ill, then I must have meat, we don't live well enough, nothing is good enough and a terrible row is bound to follow. Frightfully stupid person my Kerli is after all.

b

Mrs. v. Pels.

The job as queen of the kitchen lost its attraction a long time ago. It's dull to sit and do nothing. So I go back to my cooking again, still, I have to complain: "It's impossible to cook without any fats, and all these nasty smells make me feel sick. Nothing but ingratitude and rude remarks do I get for my services, I'm always the black sheep, always the guilty one." Moreover, according to me, very little advance is being made in the war, eventually the Germans will still win. I am afraid we're going to starve and if I'm in a bad mood I scold everyone.

Mr. v. Pels.

| 309   I must smoke and smoke and smoke, and then the food, | the political situation, and Kerli's moods all don't seem so bad. Kerli is a darling wife.

If I haven't anything to smoke then I get ill, then I have to have meat, then³ we don't live well enough, nothing is any good and a terrible row is bound to follow. Frightfully stupid person my Kerli is.

c

Mrs. Van Daan: "The job as queen of the kitchen lost its attraction a long time ago. It's dull to sit and do nothing, so I go back to my cooking again. Still, I have to complain that it's impossible to cook without any fats, and all these nasty smells make me feel sick. Nothing but ingratitude and rude remarks do I get in return for my services. I am always the black sheep, always the guilty one. Moreover, according to me, very little progress is being made in the war; in the end the Germans will still win. I'm afraid we're going to starve, and if I'm in a bad mood I scold everyone."

Mr. Van Daan: "I must smoke and smoke and smoke, and then the food, the political situation, and Kerli's moods don't seem so bad. Kerli is a darling wife."

But if he hasn't anything to smoke, then nothing is right, and this is what one hears: "I'm getting ill, we don't live well enough, I must have meat. Frightfully stupid person, my Kerli!" After this a terrific quarrel is sure to follow.

529

Peter:

Study, keep quiet, don't grumble, be no bother to anyone and do what has to be done!

Mrs. Frank:

Food is not so important, but I would still love a slice[1] of rye bread, I feel so terribly hungry.

If I were Mrs. van Pels I would have put an end to Mr. van Pels's everlasting smoking a long time ago. Now I must definitely have a cigarette because my head is swimming.

The v.P.s are terrible people. The English make a lot of mistakes. I must have a chat and be thankful I'm not in Poland!

Mrs. Frank.

Food is not very important, but I would love a slice of rye bread now, I feel so terribly hungry. If I were Mrs. v.P. I would have put a stop to Mr. v.P.'s everlasting smoking a long time ago. But[2] now I must definitely have a cigarette, because my head is swimming.

The v.P.s are terrible people; the English make a lot of mistakes, but still the war is progressing. I must have a chat and be thankful I'm not in Poland.

Mrs. Frank: "Food is not very important, but I would love a slice of rye bread now, I feel so terribly hungry. If I were Mrs. Van Daan I would have put a stop to Mr. Van Daan's everlasting smoking a long time ago. But now I must definitely have a cigarette, because my nerves are getting the better of me. The English make a lot of mistakes, but still the war is progressing. I must have a chat and be thankful I'm not in Poland."

a

Mr. Frank:

Everything's all right, I don't require anything. Take it easy, we have ample time. Give me 10 potatoes and that's enough for me. Let me put something aside for Bep. Politics are improving!

Margot Frank:

Everything is boring and horrible, that can't be helped, take it as it comes and above all don't whine. I never have any appetite, but so what!

Fritz Pfeffer:

I must get my task for today, everything must be finished on time. Political situation | 108   *outschtänding* and it | is *eempossible* that we'll be caught. I, I, I . . . . !

Anne Frank:

Keep your chin up, trust to luck, be cheerful. You can cry as much as you like in bed. We shan't starve and I hope everything will turn out well!

yours, Anne M. Frank.

b

Mr. Frank.

Everything's all right, I don't require anything. Take it easy, we've ample time. Give me my potatoes and then I will keep my mouth shut. Put some of my rations on one side for Bep. The Political situation is very promising, I'm an extreme optimist!

| 309a   Mr. Pfeffer.

I must get my task for today, everything must be finished on time. Political situation is *outschtänding* and it is *eempossible* that we'll be caught. I, I, I. . . . . !

yours, Anne

c

Mr. Frank: "Everything's all right, I don't require anything. Take it easy, we've ample time. Give me my potatoes and then I will keep my mouth shut. Put some of my rations on one side for Elli. The political situation is very promising, I'm extremely optimistic!"

Mr. Dussel: "I must get my task for today, everything must be finished on time. Political situation 'outschtänding' and it is 'eempossible' that we'll be caught.

"I, I, I . . . !"

Yours, Anne

531

263, Prinsengracht is the seventh building from the corner. (© KLM Aerocarto.)

Wednesday 15 March 1944.

Dear Kitty,

Not much to report. Miep is still very busy with the packing, Kleiman is far from well. We think that he must have had another hemorrhage because he lost consciousness.

Bep was at a piano recital at the Concertgebouw last night. A certain Telma something-or-other, a girl of 20 was playing. Tonight she is going to hear Evelyn Künneke! The weather is glorious but cold. I'm doing a great deal of English and French, I don't feel like anything else at the moment.

| 109 I have finished the first five volumes of the Forsytes. Jon reminds me in many ways of Peter, Fleur is in some ways better and worse than I am, but she is also a bit like | me. Tonight I dreamed of Peter again. We were standing together somewhere and I asked him for a lock of his hair. He agreed, and for one reason or another we kissed each other again.

I am in a good mood again, if only Saturday and Sunday never came round!

yours, Anne M. Frank.

Thursday 16 March 1944.

Dear Kitty,

It's getting more and more boring here; Bep has a bad cold a bad back and a sore throat. We are afraid she's going down with flu. What will become of us then?

The weather is lovely, superb, I can't describe it, I'll probably be going up to the attic in a minute.

I know now why I am so much more restless than Peter. He has his own room where he can work, dream, think and sleep. I am shoved about from one corner to another. I am never alone in my "double" room and yet it's something I long for so much. That is the reason too why I escape to the attic. There, and with you, I can be myself for a while.

| 110 Still, I don't want to moan about myself, on the con- | trary, I want to be brave!

. . . . . .

. . . . . .

Thank goodness they can't tell downstairs what my inward feelings are, except that I am growing cooler and more contemptuous towards Mummy daily, I'm not so affectionate to Daddy and don't tell Margot a single thing, I'm completely closed up. Above all I must maintain my outward reserve, no one must know that war still reigns incessantly within. War between desire and common sense. The latter has won up till now, yet will the former prove to be the stronger of the two? Sometimes I fear that it will and sometimes I long for it to be!

Oh it's so terribly difficult never to say anything to Peter, but I know that the first to begin must be he; there's so much I want to say and do, I've lived it all in my dreams, it is so hard to find that yet another day has gone by and none of it comes true! Yes, Kitty, Anne is a crazy child, but I do live in crazy times and under still crazier circumstances.

But, still, the brightest spot of all is that at least I can write down my thoughts and feelings, otherwise I would be absolutely stifled. I wonder what Peter thinks about all these things, I keep thinking that I can talk about it to him | one day. There must be something he has guessed about me, because he certainly can't love the outer Anne, which is the one he knows so far! How can he, who loves peace and quiet, have any liking for all my bustle and din? Could he be the first and only one to have looked through my concrete armor? And will it take him long to get there? Isn't there an old saying that love often springs from pity, or that the two go hand in hand? Is that the case with me too; because I'm often just as sorry for him as I am for myself!

I really don't honestly know how to begin, and however would he be able to, when he finds talking so much more difficult than I do? If only I could write to him, then at least I would know that he would grasp what I want to say, because it is so terribly difficult to put it into words!

yours, Anne M. Frank.

. . . . . .

. . . . . .

a   . . . . . .

b   310

Thursday 23
March[1] 1944.

Dear Kitty,

Things are running more or less normally again now. Our coupon men are out of prison again, thank goodness!

[2]Miep returned yesterday; today her husband had to take to his bed. Shivers and a temperature, the well-known symptoms of flu. Bep is better, although she still has a cough; Kleiman will have to stay at home for a long time still.

A pilot crashed near here yesterday;* the occupants were able to jump out in time by parachute. The machine crashed onto a school, but there were no children there at the time. The result was a small fire and two people killed. The Germans shot at the airmen terribly as they were coming down. The Amsterdammers who saw it nearly burst with rage and indignation at the cowardliness of such a deed. We—I'm speaking of the ladies—nearly jumped out of our skins, brr, I absolutely loathe the blasted shooting.

| 311   I often go upstairs after supper nowadays and take a breath of the | fresh evening air in Peter's room. In a dark room you can talk much more freely than when the sun tickles your face. I like it up there, sitting on a chair beside him and looking outside. V. P. and Pf. make terribly feeble remarks when I disappear into his room. "Anne's second home," they call it, or "Is it suitable for gentlemen[9] to receive young girls in semidarkness?"

---

*An American plane crashed on the Spaarndammerweg, killing three people and injuring many others. (*Kroniek van Amsterdam*, p. 124.)

c   . . . . . .

b

| 312

Peter shows an amazing wit in his replies to these so-called humorous[1] sallies. For that matter, my mama too is somewhat curious and would love to ask what we talk about, if she wasn't secretly afraid of being snubbed. Peter says it's nothing but jealousy on the part of the grownups, because we are young and we don't pay much attention to their spitefulness. Sometimes he comes and gets me from downstairs, but that is embarrassing too, because he turns simply scarlet in spite of all precautions, and can hardly get the words | out of his mouth; how thankful I am that I don't blush, it must be a highly unpleasant sensation. I also find it very tiresome that Margot has to sit downstairs by herself while I enjoy good company upstairs. [3]But what can I do about it, I would like it best if she came upstairs with me, but then she would just be a gooseberry, more or less the odd man out.

I hear a lot from all sides about the sudden friendship and I really don't know how often the talk at table hasn't been about a marriage in the "Secret Annexe" if the war should last another 5 years. How much notice do we really take of all this parental chatter? Not much, anyway, it is all so feeble. Have my parents too forgotten their own youth? It seems like it, at least they seem to take us seriously, if we make a joke and laugh at us when we are serious

yours, Anne

c   . . . . . .

a

| 112

Thursday afternoon.

This morning I really didn't know what lay in store for us. Kugler has had a call-up notice from the employment office and is to report to them for work in 6 days' time. He has now gone | to a doctor who is reliable and whom Mr. v.P. also knows and who will give him a certificate. Bep hasn't got a temperature any more but she still isn't well. Miep, according to Jan, will have to stay in bed for at least another 14 days. Kleiman hasn't had another gastric hemorrhage but a nervous breakdown! hence the fainting! So things are in a fine state here. The warehouse people are to get a day off tomorrow, so Bep will be alone in the office, if she can keep on her feet, that is. The front door will remain locked and we shall have to lie low so that the neighbors don't hear us. If Bep isn't able to come, then we'll have to be even quieter and in any case Jan will come to visit us after one o'clock.

b   313

Thursday 16 Mar. 1944.

Dear Kitty,

Phew...! Oh dear, oh dear—released from the somber scenes for a moment! Today I hear nothing but, if this or that should happen, then we are going to be in difficulties.....
if he or she should become ill, then we'll be completely isolated, then if..... enfin, I expect you know the rest, at least I presume you know the "Secret Annexers" well enough by this time to be able to guess the trend of their conversations.

The reason for all this if, if, is that Mr. Kugler has been called up to go digging in 6 days. Bep has a streaming cold and will probably have to stay at home tomorrow. Miep hasn't fully recovered from her flu yet, and Kleiman has had such a bad hemorrhage of the stomach that he lost consciousness. What a tale of woe for us!

We think that the first thing Kugler should do is find a reliable doctor, get a proper certificate and produce it at the town hall in Hilversum. The warehouse people are getting

| 314

| a day off tomorrow so that Bep will be alone in the office. If (another if) Bep has to stay at home then the door will remain locked and we shall have to be as quiet as mice so that the Keg people don't hear us, and Jan is coming to visit the deserted ones at 1 o'clock for ½ an hour, playing the role of zoo keeper, as it were.

c

Wednesday, 15 March, 1944

Dear Kitty,

Phew! Oh dear, oh dear—released from the somber scenes for a moment! Today I hear nothing but "if this or that should happen, then we are going to be in difficulties . . .
if he or she should become ill, then we'll be completely isolated, and then if . . ." *Enfin*, I expect you know the rest, at least I presume you know the "Secret Annexers" well enough by this time to be able to guess the trend of their conversations.

The reason for all this "if, if" is that Mr. Kraler has been called up to go digging. Elli has a streaming cold and will probably have to stay at home tomorrow. Miep hasn't fully recovered from her flu yet, and Koophuis has had such a bad hemorrhage of the stomach that he lost consciousness. What a tale of woe!

The warehouse people are getting a free day tomorrow; Elli can stay at home, then the door will remain locked and we shall have to be as quiet as mice, so that the neighbors don't hear us. Henk is coming to visit the deserted ones at one o'clock—playing the role

537

a

As an example of conditions outside Jan told us what he had had to eat since Saturday. On Saturday he got 3 big old carrots, Mrs. Pfeffer or he himself I don't know which cooked them with green peas and that was the meal for Saturday, Sunday and Monday. On Tuesday there were some marrow peas and on Wednesday the left-over carrot was used in a hash.

113   When we asked whether Miep's doctor had called on her again, Jan replied: "The doctor is so busy that he has had to take on an assistant in his private practice. If you ring him up and ask for a prescription to be put out ready, he says that his consulting hours are from 8 to 9 and that the prescription must be fetched at that time!"

b

For the first time in ages Jan told us something about the great wide world this afternoon. You should have seen the 8 of us around him; it looked exactly like a picture out of Grimm: Grandmother telling a story.—He talked nineteen to the dozen to his grateful audience, about food of course first of all. Mrs. Pf. one of Miep's acquaintances cooks for him. This lady was able with great difficulty to get three carrots from the vegetable man. The day before yesterday Jan

315   had carrots with green peas, yesterday he had to eat up the rest of it, today he is cooking marrow peas and tomorrow a hash will be made with the left-over carrots.

We asked about Miep's doctor. "Doctor?" asked Jan, "don't mention the doctor, I called him this morning, had his assistant on the phone, asked for a prescription for flu, the reply was that I could fetch the prescription any time between 8 and 9 in the morning. "If you have a very severe attack of flu the doctor comes to the telephone himself and says put out your tongue, say Aah. I can hear all right that your throat is inflamed. I'll write out a prescription for you to order from the chemist. Good-by.

c

of zoo-keeper, as it were. For the first time in ages he told us something about the great wide world this afternoon. You should have seen the eight of us sitting around him; it looked exactly like a picture of Grandmother telling a story. He talked nineteen to the dozen to his grateful audience about food, of course, and then Miep's doctor, and everything that we asked about. "Doctor," he said, "don't talk to me about the doctor! I rang him up this morning, had his assistant on the phone and asked for a prescription for flu. The reply was that I could come and get the prescription any time between eight and nine in the morning. If you have a very bad attack of flu, the doctor comes to the telephone himself and says 'Put out your tongue, say Aah. I can hear all right that your throat is inflamed. I'll write out a prescription for you to order from the chemist. Good-by.' And

538

a

     All in all it's a tragic business and if it weren't so tiresome for us all, it would be very interesting and funny. Still, we aren't terribly worried, we shan't die of hunger and everything will probably turn out all right and we'll land on our feet!

Anne.

b

     And that's that. A fine practice that, run by telephone only. But I don't want to criticize the doctors; after all a person has but two hands, and in these days there's an abundance of patients and very few doctors to cope with them. Still, we couldn't help laughing when Jan repeated the telephone conversation to us. I can just imagine what a

| 316

doctor's waiting room must look like nowadays. One | doesn't look down on poor panel patients any more, but on the people with minor ailments, and thinks: "Hi, you, what are you doing here, end of the line, please; an urgent case has priority!"

yours, Anne

c

that's that." A fine practice that, run by telephone only.

     But I don't want to criticize the doctors; after all, a person has but two hands, and in these days there's an abundance of patients and very few doctors to cope with them. Still, we couldn't help laughing when Henk repeated the telephone conversation to us.

     I can just imagine what a doctor's waiting room must look like nowadays. One doesn't look down on panel patients any more, but on the people with minor ailments, and thinks: "Hi, you, what are you doing here, end of the line, please; urgent cases have priority!"

Yours, Anne

539

a 109

The weather is lovely, superb, I can't describe it, I'll probably be going up to the attic in a minute. I know now why I am so much more restless than Peter. He has his own room where he can work, dream, think and sleep. I am shoved about from one corner to another. I am never alone in my "double" room and yet it's something I long for so much. That is the reason too why I escape to the attic. There, and with you, I can be myself for a while. Still, I don't want to moan about

110   myself, on the con- | trary, I want to be brave! Thank goodness they can't tell downstairs what my inward feelings are, except that I am growing cooler and more contemptuous towards Mummy daily, I'm not so affectionate to Daddy and don't tell Margot a single thing, I'm completely closed up. Above all I must maintain my outward reserve, no one must know that war still reigns incessantly within. War between desire and common sense. The latter has won up till now, yet will the former prove to be the stronger of the two? Sometimes I fear that it will and sometimes I long for it to be! Oh it's so terribly difficult never to say anything to Peter, but I know that the first to begin must be he; there's so much I want to say and do, I've lived it all in my dreams, it is so hard to find that yet another day has gone by, and none of it comes true! Yes, Kitty, Anne is a crazy child, but I do live in crazy times and under still crazier circumstances.

b   ......

c

Thursday, 16 March, 1944

Dear Kitty,

The weather is lovely, superb, I can't describe it; I'm going up to the attic in a minute.

Now I know why I'm so much more restless than Peter. He has his own room where he can work, dream, think, and sleep. I am shoved about from one corner to another. I hardly spend any time in my "double" room and yet it's something I long for so much. That is the reason too why I so frequently escape to the attic. There, and with you, I can be myself for a while, just a little while. Still, I don't want to moan about myself, on the contrary, I want to be brave. Thank goodness the others can't tell what my inward feelings are, except that I'm growing cooler towards Mummy daily, I'm not so affectionate to Daddy and don't tell Margot a single thing. I'm completely closed up. Above all, I must maintain my outward reserve, no one must know that war still reigns incessantly within. War between desire and common sense. The latter has won up till now; yet will the former prove to be the stronger of the two? Sometimes I fear that it will and sometimes I long for it to be!

Oh, it is so terribly difficult never to say anything to Peter, but I know that the first to begin must be he; there's so much I want to say and do, I've lived it all in my dreams, it is so hard to find that yet another day has gone by, and none of it comes true! Yes, Kitty, Anne is a crazy child, but I do live in crazy times and under still crazier circumstances.

540

a

| 111

But, still, the brightest spot of all is that at least I can write down my thoughts and feelings, otherwise I would be absolutely stifled. I wonder what Peter thinks about all these things, I keep thinking that I can talk about it to him | one day. There must be something he has guessed about me, because he certainly can't love the outer Anne, which is the one he knows so far! How can he, who loves peace and quiet, have any liking for all my bustle and din? Could he be the first and only one to have looked through my concrete armor? And will it take him long to get there? Isn't there an old saying that love often springs from pity, or that the two go hand in hand? Is that the case with me too; because I'm often just as sorry for him as I am for myself! I really don't honestly know how to begin, and however would he be able to, when he finds talking so much more difficult than I do? If only I could write to him, then at least I would know that he would grasp what I want to say, because it is so terribly difficult to put into words!

yours, Anne M. Frank.

b

. . . . . .

c

But, still, the brightest spot of all is that at least I can write down my thoughts and feelings, otherwise I would be absolutely stifled! I wonder what Peter thinks about all these things? I keep hoping that I can talk about it to him one day. There must be something he has guessed about me, because he certainly can't love the outer Anne, which is the one he knows so far.

How can he, who loves peace and quiet, have any liking for all my bustle and din? Can he possibly be the first and only one to have looked through my concrete armor? And will it take him long to get there? Isn't there an old saying that love often springs from pity, or that the two go hand in hand? Is that the case with me too? Because I'm often just as sorry for him as I am for myself.

I really don't honestly know how to begin, and however would he be able to, when he finds talking so much more difficult than I do? If only I could write to him, then at least I would know that he would grasp what I want to say, because it's so terribly difficult to put it into words!

Yours, Anne

541

Friday 17 March 1944.

Very dearest Darling,

Everything has in fact turned out all right after all, Bep's cold didn't develop into flu just into a sore throat and Mr. Kugler has been let off work thanks to a doctor's certificate. Things are not so nice for Mr. Kleiman who seems to have had a hemorrhage of the stomach[1] after all.

Here everything is still all-right!

114   Except that Margot and I are getting a bit tired of our parents. Don't misunderstand me, I still love Daddy just as much as ever and Margot loves Daddy and Mummy, but when you are as old as we are, you do want to decide just a few little things for yourself, you want to be independent sometimes. If I go upstairs, then I am asked what I am going to do. I'm not allowed salt, every evening regularly at a quarter past eight Mummy asks whether I ought not to start undressing, every book I read must be inspected. I must admit that they are not at all strict, and I'm allowed to read nearly everything, but we are sick of all the remarks plus all the questioning that go on the whole day long.

Friday 17 March 1944.

Dearest Kitty,

Everything is all right again. Kugler has been exempted from digging by the Court. Bep has given her nose a talking to and strictly forbidden it to be a nuisance to her today. A sigh of relief has gone through the "Secret Annexe!"

yours, Anne.

Friday, 17 March, 1944

Dear Kitty,

A sigh of relief has gone through the "Secret Annexe." Kraler has been exempted from digging by the Court. Elli has given her nose a talking to and strictly forbidden it to be a nuisance to her today. So everything is all right again, except that Margot and I are getting a bit tired of our parents. Don't misunderstand me, I can't get on well with Mummy at the moment, as you know. I still love Daddy just as much, and Margot loves Daddy and Mummy, but when you are as old as we are, you do want to decide just a few things for yourself, you want to be independent sometimes.

If I go upstairs, then I'm asked what I'm going to do, I'm not allowed salt with my food, every evening regularly at a quarter past eight Mummy asks whether I ought not to start undressing, every book I read must be inspected. I must admit that they are not at all strict, and I'm allowed to read nearly everything, and yet we are both sick of all the remarks plus all the questioning that go on the whole day long.

Something else, especially about me, that doesn't please them: I don't feel like giving lots of kisses all day long any more. I think sweet and fancy nicknames are terribly affected, I find Daddy's special liking for talk about flatulence and lavatories revolting. In short I'd really like to be rid of them for a while and that's something they can't understand. Not that we've said anything about it to them, far from it, what's the good, they wouldn't know what to make of it anyway.

Margot said last evening, "I think it's awfully | annoying, the way they ask if you've got a headache, or whether you don't feel well, if you happen to give a sigh and put your hand to your head!"

And Margot realizes for the first time that you can talk more freely about yourself to your girl friends than to your parents.

It is a great blow to us both, suddenly to realize how little remains of the confidence and harmony that we used to have at home! And it's largely due to the fact that we're all "skew-wiff" here. By this I mean that we are treated as children over outward things, and we are much older than most girls of our age inwardly. Although I'm only fourteen, I know quite well what I want, I know who is right and who is wrong, I have my opinions, my own ideas and principles, and although it may sound pretty mad from an adolescent, I feel more of a person than a child, I feel quite independent of anyone.

. . . . . .

Something else, especially about me, that doesn't please them: I don't feel like giving lots of kisses any more and I think fancy nicknames are terribly affected. In short, I'd really like to be rid of them for a while. Margot said last evening, "I think it's awfully annoying, the way they ask if you've got a headache, or whether you don't feel well, if you happen to give a sigh and put your hand to your head!"

It is a great blow to us both, suddenly to realize how little remains of the confidence and harmony that we used to have at home. And it's largely due to the fact that we're all "skew-wiff" here. By this I mean that we are treated as children over outward things, and we are much older than most girls of our age inwardly.

Although I'm only fourteen, I know quite well what I want, I know who is right and who is wrong, I have my own ideas and principles, and although it may sound pretty mad from an adolescent, I feel more of a person than a child, I feel quite independent of anyone.

543

a

| 116   I know that I can discuss things and argue better than Mummy, I know I have a less prejudiced outlook, I know that I don't exaggerate so much, I'm more precise and adroit and because of this (you may laugh) I feel superior to her | over a great many things. If I love anyone, above all I must have admiration for them, admiration and respect, and Mummy fails completely in these two requirements!

Everything would be all right, and I would make light of everything else, if only I had Peter, for I do admire him in many ways. Oh, he is such a nice, good-looking boy!

yours, Anne M. Frank.

---

b   . . . . . .

---

c   I know that I can discuss things and argue better than Mummy, I know I'm not so prejudiced, I don't exaggerate so much, I am more precise and adroit and because of this—you may laugh—I feel superior to her over a great many things. If I love anyone, above all I must have admiration for them, admiration and respect. Everything would be all right if only I had Peter, for I do admire him in many ways. He is such a nice, good-looking boy!

Yours, Anne

Saturday 18 March 1944.

Dear Kitty,

There's no one in the world I've told more about myself and my feelings than you, so I might as well tell you something about sexual matters too.

Parents and people in general are very strange when it comes to this subject. Instead of telling their daughters as well as their sons everything when they are 12 years old, they send the children out of the room during such conversations and leave them to find things out for themselves. If the parents notice later on that the children have learned things anyway, then they assume that the children know either more or less than they actually do. Why don't they then try to make good the damage and find out what the | position is?

| 117

Grownups do come up against an important obstacle, although I'm sure the obstacle is no more than a very small barrier, they believe that children will stop looking on marriage as something sacred and pure when it dawns on them that in most cases the purity is nothing more than eyewash.

For my part I don't think it's at all a bad thing for a man to bring a little experience into a marriage, it's got nothing to do with the marriage itself, has it?

When I had just turned 11, they told me about having a period, but how it really came about or what it meant I didn't find out until much later. When I was 12½ I heard some more, because Jacque was not nearly as stupid as I was. I had sensed myself what a man and a woman do when they are together; at first I thought the whole idea completely crazy, but when Jacque confirmed it for me I was quite proud of my intuition!

That it wasn't the stomach that babies came from is something else I learned from Jacque, who said simply: "The finished product comes out where | it went in!" J., Jacque

| 118

and I learned about the maidenhead and quite a few other details from a little book on sex education. I also knew that you could prevent babies from being born, but how that worked inside was still a mystery.

When I came here Daddy told me about prostitutes etc., but all in all there are still a lot of questions that haven't been answered yet.

If a mother doesn't tell her children everything, they learn it bit by bit and that must be wrong!

—

Although it is Saturday I'm not bored! That's because I sat with Peter in the attic, shut my eyes and dreamed; it was glorious!

yours, Anne M. Frank.

. . . . . .

. . . . . .

Sunday 19 March 1944.

Dear Kitty,

Yesterday was a great day for me, and this is why: after lunch everything carried on as usual, at 5 o'clock I put on the potatoes and Mummy gave me some of the blood sausage to take to Peter. I didn't want to at first but went anyway after a bit: "Peter," I said "will you accept this from us for your sandwiches?" But he wouldn't take it and I had the unhappy feeling that it was because of the quarrel still over those suspicions. Suddenly I couldn't help myself, the tears sprang into my eyes and without any prompting I put the dish down next to Mummy again and went to the w.c. to sob my heart out. By the time I had done I had decided to talk things out with Peter. Before supper the four of us sat down to help him with his crossword puzzle, so I couldn't say anything, but just as we were going to sit down to supper I whispered to him, "Are you going to do shorthand this evening, Peter?" "No," was his reply. "Then I'd like to talk to you later!" and he agreed.

So after the dishes were done I went to his room and asked him whether he had | 120 refused the blood sausage because of the | quarrel we'd had. But luckily that hadn't been the reason at all, he simply hadn't wanted to sound too eager. We talked about the quarrels and how I regard them quite differently now etc. etc. It was very warm in the room and my face was as red as a lobster's, that's why after I'd taken Margot down some water I went back upstairs to get a breath of air. For the look of things I stood by the v.P.s' window for a while but soon I went to Peter. He was standing on the left side of the open window; I went and stood on the right side, and we talked. It was much easier to talk beside the open window in semidarkness than in bright light and I believe Peter felt the same.

. . . . . .

Sunday, 19 March, 1944

Dear Kitty,

Yesterday was a great day for me. I had decided to talk things out with Peter. Just as we were going to sit down to supper I whispered to him, "Are you going to do shorthand this evening, Peter?" "No," was his reply. "Then I'd just like to talk to you later!" He agreed. After the dishes were done, I stood by the window in his parents' room awhile for the look of things, but it wasn't long before I went to Peter. He was standing on the left side of the open window, I went and stood on the right side, and we talked. It was much easier to talk beside the open window in semidarkness than in bright light, and I believe Peter felt the same.

a

We told each other so much, so very very much, that I can't repeat it all, but it was lovely, the most wonderful evening I have ever had in the "Secret Annexe."

I will just tell you briefly the various things we talked about:

First we talked about the quarrels and how I regard them quite differently now, and | 121 then about the estrangement between us and our parents. | I told Peter about Mummy and Daddy, Margot, and about myself. At one moment he asked, "I suppose you always give each other a good night kiss, don't you?"

"One, dozens, why, don't you?"

"No, I have hardly kissed anyone!" "Not even on your birthday?"

"Yes, I have then."

We talked about how we neither of us confide in our parents. How his parents thought a lot of each other and would have loved to have his confidence too, but that he didn't wish it. How I cry my heart out in bed, and he goes up into the loft and swears. How Margot and I really only know each other well for a little while, but that, even so, we don't tell each other all that much, because we are always together. Over every imaginable thing, trust, feelings and ourselves—oh, he was just as I thought.

Then we talked about 1942, how different we were then. We just don't recognize ourselves in that period any more. How we simply couldn't bear each other in the beginning. | 122 He thought it tiresome when I came to listen to the radio, | felt that I was much too talkative and unruly, and I soon came to the conclusion that I'd no time for him. I couldn't

b

. . . . . .

c

We told each other so much, so very very much, that I can't repeat it all, but it was lovely; the most wonderful evening I have ever had in the "Secret Annexe." I will just tell you briefly the various things we talked about. First we talked about the quarrels and how I regard them quite differently now, and then about the estrangement between us and our parents.

I told Peter about Mummy and Daddy, and Margot, and about myself.

At one moment he asked, "I suppose you always give each other a good night kiss, don't you?

"One, dozens, why, don't you?"

"No, I have hardly ever kissed anyone."

"Not even on your birthday?"

"Yes, I have then."

We talked about how we neither of us confide in our parents, and how his parents would have loved to have his confidence, but that he didn't wish it. How I cry my heart out in bed, and he goes up into the loft and swears. How Margot and I really only know each other well for a little while, but that, even so, we don't tell each other everything, because we are always together. Over every imaginable thing—oh, he was just as I thought!

Then we talked about 1942, how different we were then. We just don't recognize ourselves as the same people any more. How we simply couldn't bear each other in the beginning. He thought I was much too talkative and unruly, and I soon came to the

547

understand why he didn't flirt with me, but now I'm glad. He also mentioned how much he isolated himself from us all. I said too that there was not much difference between my noise and high spirits and his silence.

That I love peace and quiet too, and have nothing for myself alone, except my diary, that everyone would rather see me going than coming, Mr. Pf. most of all, and that I don't always want to be with them. How very glad he is that my parents have children and that I'm glad he is here. That I understand his reserve now and his relationship with his parents, and how I would love to be able to help him face the quarrels. "Peter, if ever you need help, will you be sure to tell me?" "You always do help me!" he replied. "How?" I asked, very surprised. "By your cheerfulness."

That was certainly the loveliest thing he said. He also told me that he no longer minded at all my coming into his room, as he had before, but liked it.

| 123   I also told him that all those little endearments between Daddy and Mummy were | empty. That you don't create trust with a little peck here and a little peck there.

Then we spoke about doing things your own way, the diary and loneliness, the difference between everyone's inner and outer selves. My mask etc.

It was wonderful, he must have grown to love me as a friend and that is enough for the time being. I am so grateful and happy, I just can't find the words. I must apologize Kitty, that my style is not up to standard today. I have just written down what came into my head!

I feel as if Peter and I now share a secret, if he looks at me with those eyes that laugh and wink, then it's just as if a little light goes on inside me. I hope it will remain like this and that we may have many, many more glorious times together!

<u>your grateful, happy Anne</u>

......

conclusion that I'd no time for him. I couldn't understand why he didn't flirt with me, but now I'm glad. He also mentioned how much he isolated himself from us all. I said that there was not much difference between my noise and his silence. That I love peace and quiet too, and have nothing for myself alone, except my diary. How glad he is that my parents have children here, and that I'm glad he is here. That I understand his reserve now and his relationship with his parents, and how I would love to be able to help him.

"You always do help me," he said. "How?" I asked, very surprised. "By your cheerfulness." That was certainly the loveliest thing he said. It was wonderful, he must have grown to love me as a friend, and that is enough for the time being. I am so grateful and happy, I just can't find the words. I must apologize, Kitty, that my style is not up to standard today.

I have just written down what came into my head. I have the feeling now that Peter and I share a secret. If he looks at me with those eyes that laugh and wink, then it's just as if a little light goes on inside me. I hope it will remain like this and that we may have many, many more glorious times together!

Your grateful, happy Anne.

548

Monday 20 March 1944.

Dear Kitty,

This morning Peter asked me if I would come again one evening, that I really didn't disturb

| 124   him and if there was | room for one there was room for two. I said that I couldn't come every evening, for they wouldn't like it downstairs, but he thought that I needn't let that bother me. Then I said that I would love to come one Saturday evening and especially asked him to warn me when there was a moon. "Then we'll go downstairs," he said "and look at the moon from there." I quickly agreed and anyway I'm not really terrified of burglars.

In the meantime a little shadow has fallen on my happiness, I've thought for a long time that Margot liked Peter quite a lot too. How much she loves him I don't know, but I think it's wretched. I must cause her terrible pain each time I'm with Peter, and the funny part of it is that she hardly shows it. I know quite well that I'd be desperately jealous, but Margot only says that I needn't pity her. "I think it's so rotten that you should be the odd one out," I added. "I'm used to that," she answered, somewhat bitterly.

| 125   I don't dare tell Peter this yet, perhaps later on, but we've got to talk about so | many other things first.

. . . . . .

Monday, 20 March, 1944

Dear Kitty,

This morning Peter asked me if I would come again one evening, and said that I really didn't disturb him, and if there's room for one there's room for two. I said that I wouldn't come every evening, because they wouldn't like it downstairs, but he thought that I needn't let that bother me. Then I said that I would love to come one Saturday evening and especially asked him to warn me when there was a moon. "Then we'll go downstairs," he answered, "and look at the moon from there."

In the meantime a little shadow has fallen on my happiness. I've thought for a long time that Margot liked Peter quite a lot too. How much she loves him I don't know, but I think it's wretched. I must cause her terrible pain each time I'm with Peter, and the funny part of it is that she hardly shows it.

I know quite well that I'd be desperately jealous, but Margot only says that I needn't pity her.

"I think it's so rotten that you should be the odd one out," I added. "I'm used to that," she answered, somewhat bitterly.

I don't dare tell Peter this yet, perhaps later on, but we've got to talk about so many other things first.

549

I had a little ticking off yesterday evening from Mummy, which I certainly deserved. I mustn't overdo my indifference and contempt towards her. So, in spite of everything, I must try once again to be friendly and to keep my observations to myself!

even Pim is different lately. He is making some attempt to stop treating me like a child and it makes him much too cool. See what comes of it! He has warned me that if I don't do any algebra, I mustn't count on getting extra lessons later. Although I could just wait and see, I do want to start again, provided I get a new book.

Enough for now, I'm full to the brim with Peter and can do nothing but look at him!

yours, Anne M. Frank.

Evidence of Margot's goodness, I received this today, March 20th, 1944.

Anne, when I said yesterday that I was not jealous of you, I was only fifty per cent honest. It is like this; I'm jealous of neither you nor Peter. I only feel[1] | *here I had skipped a page.* *See previous page.* a bit sorry that I haven't found anyone yet, and am not likely to for the time being, with whom I can discuss my thoughts and feelings. But I should not grudge it to you for that reason; one misses enough here anyway, things that other people just take for granted.

. . . . . .

I had a little ticking off yesterday evening from Mummy, which I certainly deserved. I mustn't overdo my indifference towards her. So in spite of everything, I must try once again to be friendly and keep my observations to myself.

Even Pim is different lately. He is trying not to treat me as such a child, and it makes him much too cool. See what comes of it!

Enough for now, I'm full to the brim with Peter and can do nothing but look at him!

Evidence of Margot's goodness: I received this today,

March 20th, 1944

Anne, when I said yesterday that I was not jealous of you I was only fifty per cent honest. It is like this; I'm jealous of neither you nor Peter. I only feel a bit sorry that I haven't found anyone yet, and am not likely to for the time being, with whom I can discuss my thoughts and feelings. But I should not grudge it to you for that reason. One misses enough here anyway, things that other people just take for granted.

On the other hand, I know for certain that I would never have got so far with Peter, anyway, because I have the feeling that if I wished to discuss a lot with anyone, I should want to be on rather intimate terms with him. I would want to have the feeling that he understood me through and through without my having to say much, but for that reason it would have to be someone whom I felt to be my superior intellectually, and that is not the case with Peter. But I can imagine it being so with you and Peter.

You are not doing me out of anything which is my due; do not reproach yourself in the least on my account. You and Peter can only gain by the friendship.

. . . . . .

On the other hand, I know for certain that I would never have got so far with Peter, anyway, because I have the feeling that if I wished to discuss a lot with anyone, I should want to be on rather intimate terms with him. I would want to have the feeling that he understood me through and through without my having to say much. But for that reason it would have to be someone whom I felt was [felt to be] my superior intellectually, and that is not the case with Peter. But I can imagine it being so with you and Peter.

You are not doing me out of anything which is my due; do not reproach yourself in the least on my account. You and Peter can only gain by the friendship.

a 127   My reply:
Dear Margot

    I thought your letter was exceptionally sweet, but I still don't feel quite happy about it and nor do I think that I shall.

    At present there is no question of such confidence as you have in mind between Peter and myself, but in the twilight beside an open window you can say more to each other than in brilliant sunshine. Also it's easier to whisper your feelings than to trumpet them forth out loud. I believe that you are beginning to feel a kind of sisterly affection for Peter, and that you would love to help us, just as much as I. Perhaps you shall still be able to do that sometime, although that is not the kind of confidence we have in mind. I think it must come from both sides, and I believe that's the reason why Daddy and I have never got so far. Let's not talk about it any more, but if you still want anything please write to me about it, because I can say what I mean much better on paper.

| 128   You don't know how much I admire you, and I only hope | that I may yet acquire some of the goodness that you and Daddy have, because now I don't see much difference in that sense.

Yours, Anne

b . . . . . .

c My reply:

Dear Margot,

    I thought your letter was exceptionally sweet, but I still don't feel quite happy about it and nor do I think that I shall.

    At present there is no question of such confidence as you have in mind between Peter and myself, but in the twilight beside an open window you can say more to each other than in brilliant sunshine. Also it's easier to whisper your feelings than to trumpet them forth out loud. I believe that you are beginning to feel a kind of sisterly affection for Peter, and that you would love to help him, just as much as I. Perhaps you will be able to do that sometime, although that is not the kind of confidence we have in mind. I think it must come from both sides, and I believe that's the reason why Daddy and I have never got so far.

    Let's not talk about it any more; but if you still want anything please write to me about it, because I can say what I mean much better on paper.

    You don't know how much I admire you, and I only hope that I may yet acquire some of the goodness that you and Daddy have, because now I don't see much difference between you and Daddy in that sense.

Yours, Anne

552

Anne Frank's timetable for the weekdays, Monday, Tuesday, Wednesday, Thursday and Friday, in the Spring of 1944 in the "Secret Annexe":

Wake up, between half past 6 and half past 7.

Wake Daddy, half past 7.

Get up: 7.38

Get dressed: from 7.38 to five to 8, including stripping bed, taking out curlers, taking clothes, hydrogen peroxide, comb, mirror and lotion into the living room.

Bathroom: 8 o'clock.

Finish dressing and doing hair: ± quarter past 8 Fetching potty and books etc. etc. until half past 8.

Break for reading or other quiet occupation from half past 8 to 9

Breakfast: 9 to half past 9.

Peeling potatoes: half past 9 to 10 o'clock or half past 10.

Book work; with interruptions for talking, writing up diary, chitchat and doing | 129 *nothing (sometimes coffee too at about ± quarter to 11) | from half past 10 to 12 o'clock.*

Attic: 12 o'clock to quarter to 1. Getting some air.

Domestic chores: quarter to 1–1 o'clock. By that is meant cleaning the basin.

Radio: 1 o'clock to quarter past 1.

Lunch: quarter or half past 1 to 10 to 2.

Chitchat: 10 to 2 to 2 o'clock.

German Army Bulletin: 2 o'clock to just after two.

Hanging about downstairs and upstairs till half past 2.

Working, again with various interruptions, often reading a lot, depending on the reading matter: from half past 2 to quarter to 4.

Eating sandwiches: quarter to 4–4 o'clock.

Freshening up: 4 o'clock–quarter past 4.

Drinking coffee. quarter past 4.

Fetching potatoes after coffee until just before half past 4. Coffee is served upstairs. At quarter past 4 Margot and I always go upstairs.

With Peter for French and a chat; half past 4 to quarter past 5.

Freedom, the office staff have left and the house is in chaos: quarter past 5 to 6 o'clock.

Radio: 6 o'clock to quarter past 6.

Chitchat, hanging about and doing nothing: quarter past 6 to half past 6.

130 *Supper: half past 6 to 7 o'clock.*

Dishes: 7 o'clock[3] to half past 7.

Reading, writing, talking: half past 7 to half past 8.

Getting undressed: half past 8 to ten to 9.

Bathroom: ten to 9 to quarter past 9.

Getting ready for bed: [5]quarter past 9 to half past 9.

Saying good night, lights out: half past 9–quarter to 10.

Thinking, dreaming, praying and having a good time: quarter to 10–quarter past 10.

Sleeping: quarter past 10 or half past 10 to ± 7 o'clock.

Anne Frank.

. . . . . .

. . . . . .

Dear Kitty,

I received this from Margot last evening:

Dear Anne,

After your letter yesterday I have the unpleasant feeling that you will have prickings of conscience when you visit Peter; but really there is no reason for this. In my heart of hearts I feel that I have the right to share mutual confidence with someone, but I could not bear Peter in that role yet.

| 131   However, I do feel just as you say, that Peter is a bit like a brother, but— | a younger brother; we have put out tentacles towards each other, the affection of brother and sister might grow if they touched, perhaps they will later—perhaps never; however, it has certainly not reached that stage yet.

Therefore you really needn't pity me. Now that you've found companionship, enjoy it as much as you can.

—

In the meantime it is getting more and more wonderful here, I believe Kitty, that we may have a real great Love in the "Secret Annexe." So all that teasing about marrying Peter if we stay here for a long time wasn't so silly. Don't worry, I'm not thinking of marrying him. I don't know what he will be like when he grows up, nor do I know whether we should ever love each other enough to marry.

I know now that Peter loves me, but just how, I don't yet know. Whether he only

. . . . . .

Wednesday, 22 March, 1944.

Dear Kitty,

I received this from Margot last evening:

Dear Anne,

After your letter yesterday I have the unpleasant feeling that you will have prickings of conscience when you visit Peter; but really there is no reason for this. In my heart of hearts I feel that I have the right to share mutual confidence with someone, but I could not bear Peter in that role yet.

However, I do feel just as you say, that Peter is a bit like a brother, but—a younger brother; we have put out feelers towards each other, the affection of a brother and sister might grow if they touched, perhaps they will later—perhaps never; however, it has certainly not reached that stage yet.

Therefore you really needn't pity me. Now that you've found companionship, enjoy it as much as you can.

In the meantime it is getting more and more wonderful here. I believe, Kitty, that we may have a real great love in the "Secret Annexe." Don't worry, I'm not thinking of marrying him. I don't know what he will be like when he grows up, nor do I know whether we should ever love each other enough to marry. I know now that Peter loves me, but just how I myself don't know yet.

wants a great friend, or whether I attract him as a girl or as a sister, I can't yet discover.

When he said that I always helped him over | his parents' quarrels, I was awfully glad; it was one step towards making me believe in his friendship. I asked him yesterday, what he would do if there were a dozen Annes here who always kept coming to him, his reply was, "If they were all like you, it certainly wouldn't be too bad!" He's tremendously hospitable towards me and I really believe he likes to see me.

Meanwhile he is working diligently at his French, even when he's in bed, going on until a quarter past ten. Oh, when I think about Saturday evening and recall it all, words and mood, then for the first time I don't feel discontented about myself; I mean that I would still say exactly the same and wouldn't wish to change anything, as is usually the case.

He is so handsome, both when he laughs and also when he looks quietly in front of him; he is such a darling and so good and handsome. I believe that what took him most by surprise about me was when he discovered that I'm not a bit the superficial worldly Anne that I appear, but just as dreamy a specimen, with just as many difficulties as he himself!

. . . . . .

Whether he only wants a great friend, or whether I attract him as a girl or a sister, I can't yet discover.

When he said that I always helped him over his parents' quarrels, I was awfully glad; it was one step towards making me believe in his friendship. I asked him yesterday what he would do if there were a dozen Annes here who always kept coming to him. His reply was: "If they were all like you, it certainly wouldn't be too bad!" He's tremendously hospitable towards me and I really believe he likes to see me. Meanwhile he is working diligently at his French, even when he's in bed, going on until a quarter past ten. Oh, when I think about Saturday evening and recall it all, word for word, then for the first time I don't feel discontented about myself; I mean that I would still say exactly the same and wouldn't wish to change anything, as is usually the case.

He is so handsome, both when he laughs and when he looks quietly in front of him; he is such a darling and so good. I believe what surprised him most about me was when he discovered that I'm not a bit the superficial worldly Anne that I appear, but just as dreamy a specimen, with just as many difficulties as he himself.

Yours, Anne

555

Last night after we had done the dishes I waited confidently for him to ask me to stay upstairs. But nothing happened; I went away he came downstairs to call Pfeffer to the radio, hung about the bathroom for a long time, but when Pf. took too long he went upstairs again. He paced up and down his room for a long time and went to bed early.

I was so agitated all evening that I kept running to the bathroom, washing my face with cold water, reading a bit, dreaming, looking at the clock and just waiting, waiting, waiting and listening out for him. When I fell into bed it was early but I was ready to drop.

Tonight a bath and tomorrow?

That is still so far away!

yours, Anne M. Frank.

Reply:

Dear Margot,

I think the best thing we can do is simply to wait and see what happens. It can't be very long before Peter and I come to a definite decision, either to go on as before or be different. Just which way it will go I don't know myself, and I don't bother to look beyond my own nose.

But I shall certainly do one thing, if Peter and I decide to be friends, I shall tell him that you are very fond of him too and would always be prepared to help him should the need arise. The latter may not be what you wish, but I don't care now; I don't know what Peter thinks about you but I shall ask him then.

I'm sure it's not bad—the opposite! You are always welcome to join us in the attic, or where or wherever we are; you honestly won't disturb us because I feel we have a silent agreement to talk only in the evenings when it's dark.

Keep your courage up! Like I do. Although it's not always easy, your time may come sooner than you think!

yours, Anne

---

b   . . . . . .

---

c   Reply:

Dear Margot,

I think the best thing we can do is simply to wait and see what happens. It can't be very long before Peter and I come to a definite decision, either to go on as before or be different. Just which way it will go I don't know myself, and I don't bother to look beyond my own nose. But I shall certainly do one *thing, if Peter and I decide to be friends, I shall tell him that you are very fond of him too and would always be prepared to help him should the need arise. The latter may not be what you wish, but I don't care now; I don't know what Peter thinks about you, but I shall ask him then.*

I'm sure it's not bad—the opposite! You are always welcome to join us in the attic, or wherever we are; you honestly won't disturb us because I feel we have a silent agreement to talk only in the evenings when it's dark.

Keep your courage up! Like I do. Although it's not always easy; your time may come sooner than you think.

Yours, Anne

Thursday 23 March 1944.

Dearest Kitty,

Such a tremendous amount has happened since yesterday morning that I really don't know where to start. First of all the news from outside. B. & D. have been let out of prison. The most wonderful examples are being reported from there but it's enough when I say that the Dutch People are tremendous. Brouwer's wife is expecting a baby any moment; that's why he's been let out, but the thing isn't completely over yet. Let's hope for the best!

Mr. Kleiman is not very well. His wife and all of us are not happy with his doctor. It appears that his latest stomach hemorrhage was very severe, hence his fainting.

Miep returned yesterday morning, but this morning Jan had to go to bed with a cold and shivers. Bep is a little better, although she still has a cough. A pilot crashed near here

Thursday 23
March 1944.

Dear Kitty,

Things are running more or less normally again now. Our coupon men are out of prison again, thank goodness!

Miep returned yesterday; today her husband had to take to his bed. Shivers and a temperature, the well-known symptoms of flu. Bep is better, although she still has a cough; Kleiman will have to stay at home for a long time still.

Thursday, 23 March, 1944

Dear Kitty,

Things are running more or less normally again now. Our coupon men are out of prison again, thank goodness!

Miep returned yesterday. Elli is better, although she still has a cough; Koophuis will have to stay at home for a long time still.

a

| 136

yesterday, the men were able to jump out in time by parachute. The machine crashed onto a school, | but fortunately there were no children there at the time, a few people were killed and there was a small fire. The machine must have been hit close to the Market Halls. We've never heard so much shooting before. That was because the Germans fired machine guns at the crew who had jumped out and at the plane as it came down. Ear-splitting shooting lasting ten minutes. It was absolutely terrifying.

b

A pilot crashed near here yesterday; the occupants were able to jump out in time by parachute. The machine crashed onto a school, but there were no children there at the time. The result was a small fire and two people killed. The Germans shot at the airmen terribly as they were coming down. The Amsterdammers who saw it nearly burst with rage and indignation at the cowardliness of such a deed. We—I'm speaking of the ladies—nearly jumped out of our skins, brr, I absolutely loathe the blasted shooting.

c

A plane crashed near here yesterday; the occupants were able to jump out in time by parachute. The machine crashed onto a school, but there were no children there at the time. The result was a small fire and two people killed. The Germans shot at the airmen terribly as they were coming down. The Amsterdammers who saw it nearly exploded with rage and indignation at the cowardliness of such a deed. We—I'm speaking of the ladies—nearly jumped out of our skins, I loathe the blasted shooting.

558

Now about myself.

When I was with Peter yesterday we ended up, I honestly don't remember how, by discussing sex. I had long since decided to ask him one or two things. He knows everything; when I told him that Margot and I weren't particularly well informed he was stupefied. I told him a lot about Margot and me and Mummy and Daddy, things I hadn't recently dared to ask about. He then offered to tell me things and I gratefully made use of the offer: he told me how contraceptives work and I asked him very boldly how boys could tell that they are grown up. He had to think about that for a while; then he said he would tell me in the evening. Among other things I told him | what had happened to Jacque and about how girls are completely defenseless when faced with such strong boys: "Well, you don't have to be frightened of me!" he said.

| 137

When I came back in the evening we talked at great length about the same subject and he then told me about boys. It was a bit embarrassing of course, but it was still nice to be able to talk to him about it. Neither of us had ever imagined that we would be able to speak to a girl or boy so openly about the most intimate matters.

I think that I really do know everything now. He told me a lot about "Präsentiv" methods. German.[1]*

This evening Margot and I talked about Bram and Drees in the bathroom!

This morning something really horrid was lying in wait for me: After breakfast Peter beckoned me to go upstairs with him: "That was a dirty trick you played on me!" he said "I heard what you and Margot were talking about in the bathroom yesterday, I think you just wanted to find out what Peter knew about it and then | have a good laugh!"

| 138

Well, I was flabbergasted. I did everything I could to get such a shameful idea out of his head; I could well understand how he must have felt and it's all quite untrue! "Oh no, Peter," I said I would never be so mean, I told you I'd keep my mouth shut and that's just what I'm doing. To put on an act like that and then to do such a mean thing on purpose, no Peter, that wouldn't be funny, that would be unfair. I didn't let on about anything and everything I've told you is true, won't you believe me?"

Then he promised that he did believe me, but I'm going to have to talk to him again, I did nothing else all day except fret about it. What a good thing he came straight out with what he thought, imagine if he'd gone around keeping all those awful thoughts about me to himself. What a darling he is!

Now I shall and must tell him everything!

yours,
Mary Anne Frank.[5]
mistake!

That must be from all the excitement, because my heart is beating like a sledgehammer!

yours, Anne.

---

*Anne meant *Präservativmittel*, the German word for "condom." A.J.P.

. . . . . .

. . . . . .

daarmee plezieren!"

O, ik was stomgeslagen. Met alle middelen heb
ik hem die schandelijke praat uit het hoofd
gezet; ik kan zo goed begrijpen hoe het hem
te moede moet zijn geweest en er zo niets
aanaan! "'t nee, Peter," zei ik, "zo gemeen kan
ik niet zijn, ik heb gezegd m'n mond
te houden en zal dat ook doen. Zo comedie
te spelen en met ernst zo gemeen te
doen, nee Peter, dat zou niet langer grappig zijn, dat is onfair. Ik heb niets ge-
teld wat ik je verteld heb is allemaal
waar, geloof je me?"

Hij verzekerde me dat hij me geloofde, maar
ik moet er nog eens met hem over praten.
De hele dag doe ik niets anders dan hierover piekeren. Gelukkig dat hij direct zei,
wat hij dacht, stel je voor dat hij met
zo iets gemeens van mij in zich rond-
gelopen zou zijn. Die lieve Peter!

Nu zal en moet ik hem alles vertellen!

je Margot Anne Frank.

Herziening! —

Dit komt zeker van de opwinding, want
m'n hart klopt met snokenlagen!

je Anne

Friday morning 24 March 1944.

Dearest Kitty,

I haven't told you everything, but that's all to the good or rather even better. You can't imagine how grateful I am to have been given so much even here in the "Secret Annexe."

Yesterday afternoon when I was with Peter we did English again, and we also spoke about our parents. The v.[1]P.s make such feeble remarks whenever I come out of Peter's room in the evenings and Peter says that they also whisper about it with Pf. and with each other. Peter has advised me not to take any notice of it. "Do they say anything about it downstairs as well?"

"Yes Mummy is very inquisitive, but I always manage to duck her questions."

"Presumably they said something last night as well," he continued.

"Yes of course, they said[2]: are you still there, that must have become your second home" "Pf. said to me that it's not right to receive young girls in your room so late at night, and I replied something like it was none of his | business. To my parents I said it was nothing but jealousy, that they were old while we were still young.[4] But you needn't

| 140

> I often go upstairs after supper nowadays and take a breath of the | fresh evening air in Peter's room. In a dark room you can talk much more freely than when the sun tickles your face. I like it up there, sitting on a chair beside him and looking outside. V. P. and Pf. make terribly feeble remarks when I disappear into his room. "Anne's second home," they call it, or "Is it suitable for gentlemen to receive young girls in semidarkness?" Peter shows an amazing wit in his replies to these so-called humorous sallies. For that matter, my mama too is somewhat curious and would love to ask what we talk about, if she wasn't secretly afraid of being snubbed. Peter says it's nothing but jealousy on the part of the grownups, because we are young and we don't pay much attention to their spitefulness. Sometimes he comes and gets me from downstairs, but that is embarrassing too, because he turns simply scarlet

I often go upstairs after supper nowadays and take a breath of the fresh evening air [in Peter's room]. I like it up there, sitting on a chair beside him and looking outside.

Van Daan and Dussel make very feeble remarks when I disappear into his room; "Anne's second home," they call it, or "Is it suitable for young gentlemen to receive young girls in semidarkness?" Peter shows amazing wit in his replies to these so-called humorous sallies. For that matter, Mummy too is somewhat curious and would love to ask what we talk about, if she wasn't secretly afraid of being snubbed. Peter says it's nothing but envy on the part of the grownups, because we are young and we don't pay much attention to

a worry, I (really) think it's okay." And again, when I said: "After all, you don't tell such things to everyone," (I was referring to our talks by the window), he replied: "But then you aren't everyone, are you!"

b | 312 | in spite of all precautions, and can hardly get the words | out of his mouth; how thankful I am that I don't blush, it must be a highly unpleasant sensation. |

c their spitefulness. Sometimes he comes and gets me from downstairs, but he turns simply scarlet in spite of all precautions, and can hardly get the words out of his mouth. How thankful I am that I don't blush, it must be a highly unpleasant sensation. Daddy always says I'm

Unfortunately I skipped this page, so that to continue from the last page you have to go on to the next.

¹Daddy always says I'm prudish and vain but that's not true, I'm just simply vain! I have not often had anyone tell me I was pretty. Except for C.N.,* who said I looked so attractive when I laughed.

Yesterday I received a genuine compliment from Peter, and just for fun I will tell you roughly how the conversation went:

Peter so often used to say "Do laugh, Anne!" This struck me as odd, and yesterday I asked: "Why must I always laugh?"

"Because I like it; you get such dimples in your cheeks when you laugh; how do they come, actually?"

"I was born with them. I've got one in my chin too. That's my only beauty!"

"Of course not, that's not true!"

"Yes, it is, I know quite well that I'm not a beauty; I never have been and never shall be!"

"I don't agree at all, I think you're pretty."

143 "That's not true."

"If I say so, then you can take it from me it is!"

Then I naturally said the same of him!

*At the request of the person concerned, this name has been replaced by initials chosen at random.

. . . . . .

prudish and vain but that's not true, I'm just simply vain! I have not often had anyone tell me I was pretty. Except a boy at school, who said I looked so attractive when I laughed. Yesterday I received a genuine compliment from Peter, and just for fun I will tell you roughly how the conversation went:

Peter so often used to say, "Do laugh, Anne!" This struck me as odd, and I asked, "Why must I always laugh?"

"Because I like it; you get such dimples in your cheeks when you laugh; how do they come, actually?"

"I was born with them. I've got one in my chin too. That's my only beauty!"

"Of course not, that's not true."

"Yes, it is, I know quite well that I'm not a beauty; I never have been and never shall be."

"I don't agree at all, I think you're pretty."

"That's not true."

"If I say so, then you can take it from me it is!"

Then I naturally said the same of him.

563

a · · · · · ·

b 312

> I hear a lot from all sides about the sudden friendship and I really don't know how often the talk at table hasn't been about a marriage in the "Secret Annexe" if the war should last another 5 years. How much notice do we really take of all this parental chatter? Not much, anyway, it is all so feeble. Have my parents too forgotten their own youth? It seems like it, at least they seem to take us seriously, if we make a joke and laugh at us when we are serious.
>
> yours, Anne

c

I hear a lot from all sides about the sudden friendship. We don't take much notice of all this parental chatter, their remarks are so feeble. Have the two sets of parents forgotten their own youth? It seems like it, at least they seem to take us seriously, if we make a joke, and laugh at us when we are serious.

Yours, Anne

In the evening when I heard the v.P.s opening their window I was very much in two minds; at 8 o'clock I decided to risk it. I knocked softly at the door and was received by Mr. v.P. with: "Scat, scat, get her Mouschi, get her!"

"Oh shall I go away again then?" I asked but I walked straight on through to Peter's room all the same. Mrs. v.P. was standing there and asked me straight away if I'd come for some fresh air. She stayed talking with us for a little while, but when Mr. v.P. closed the window Peter tried to turn her out. Mrs. v.P. refused to go, she wanted to stay with us. We agreed of course, but after 5 minutes she went all the same. I said that our company | 141 | wasn't all that in- | teresting anyway, but she didn't agree and said she would be coming back.

As soon as we were alone Peter said: "They really have nothing against your coming here, they'll never forbid it; I told them this evening that you would be coming any minute now!" "Oh," I said "At first I didn't really want to come." [1]Obviously taken aback, he said: "But I winked at you across the table before you went downstairs!"

[2]"Listen here, Peter," I said then "I can't come here every evening in any case." "But why not?" "I just can't, I get the creeps going upstairs. The only way round this, and it's a reasonable middle course, is for you to come downstairs and take me upstairs with you. You won't want to ask me to come every evening and I won't want to come up by myself, so that would be the best."

"But, but, but. . . . ."

"Please just do me that favor." That did it. He said straight away "Okay then." Then he asked if he would have to go through our living room. He doesn't of course, he can | 142 | simply go through |

144   the bathroom and fetch me from my room. Then he asked if he should speak loudly, my answer to that was: "Just behave naturally."

Later in the evening, he came back to the subject and said that I simply had to come: "Otherwise I get bored all on my own."

"You weren't bored before!"

"Yes but that was quite different!"

What a strange turn things have taken with us haven't they, in the beginning I really wanted to do things with you but you hated it whenever I came. Then for a whole year I almost forgot your existence, until one day I suddenly remembered that there was still such a thing as Peter."

"If you hadn't come to me then, I would certainly have come to you."

. . . . . .

. . . . . .

| 145   It's strange isn't it Kitty, that we should have discovered each other at more or less the same time. Now I can tell from everything he says and does that he is very fond of me as well. If he doesn't come up to the attic it's certainly because I | told him that I too liked to be alone now and then. I don't honestly know how things will turn out, or whether we shall always have something to talk about. But if things go further between us then we shall certainly be able to keep each other company without even talking. The only horrid thing is that Margot has to sit downstairs all by herself when I'm upstairs with Peter, but she turns a deaf ear to talk like that.

Daddy doesn't ask or say anything, but he is no longer so childish with me. Mummy knows perfectly well that I don't care much for her, the same is true of Peter's Father and Mother. And, Kitty, I've got a little bit of a feeling that I'm no longer so independent of Peter, that actually I am running after him, that I'm dependent on his favors.

If only his parents didn't behave so stupidly upstairs; it must be because they're not very keen to see me. But Peter and I never tell them what we talk about. Just imagine if they knew that we talk about such intimate subjects. To talk to a boy about having your period and a boy telling a girl about his secrets is certainly not something that happens | 146   every day. I'd like to ask Peter quite a lot more on the subject but | I'm always afraid he may think I can't talk about anything else.

I [1]would like to ask him whether he knows what a girl really looks like there. I don't think a boy is as complicated down there as a girl. You can see exactly what a naked man looks like from photographs or pictures, but you can't with women. With them the sexual parts[2] or whatever they are called are further between the legs. He probably hasn't seen a girl from so close to, to be honest I haven't either. With a boy it's much easier. How in heaven's name will I be able to explain the setup to him, since from what he said I was able to gather that he doesn't know the exact details. He was talking about the "mouth of the womb" but that's right inside, you can't see anything of that. With us it's all pretty much divided, before I was 11 or 12 years old I didn't realize that there were two inner lips as well, you couldn't see them at all. And the funniest thing of all was that I thought that the urine came out of the clitoris.

When I asked Mummy once what that stub of a thing was for, she said that she didn't | 147 | know, she still pretends to be ignorant even now!

But when the subject comes up again how in heaven's name will you be able to explain what things are like without using examples? Shall I just try it out here in the meantime? Well then get on with it! From the front when you stand up you can see nothing but hair, between your legs there are things like little cushions, soft, with hair on too, which press together when you stand up so that you can't see what's inside. When you sit down they divide and inside it looks very red and ugly and fleshy. At the very top, between the big outer lips there is a little fold of skin which turns out to be a kind of little bladder on closer inspection, that is the clitoris. Then come the small inner lips, they are also pressed against each other just like a little pleat. When they open, there is a fleshy little stump inside, no bigger than the top of my thumb. The top of it is porous, there are different little holes in it and that's where the urine comes out. The lower part looks as if it's nothing but skin, but that is where the vagina is. There are little folds of skin all over the

| 148

place, you can hardly find it. | The little hole underneath is so terribly small that I simply can't imagine how a man can get in there, let alone how a whole baby can get out. The hole is so small you can't even put your index finger in, not easily anyway. That's all it is and yet it plays such an important role!

yours, Anne M. Frank.

The following was written a few weeks ago, it doesn't count any longer, but because my verses are so few and far between I'll write it down all the same:
Once more the day has been a blight
For me just like the darkest night!

Anne. (Rea.)

Saturday 25 March 1944.

Dear Kitty,

When you change you only notice it after you have changed. I have changed and radically so, wholly and in every way. My opinions, ideas, critical outlook; outwardly, inwardly everything is changed and I can safely say, since it is true, for the better.

| 149

I once told you how difficult it was for me when I came here, from the life of | an adored little person into the harsh reality of scoldings and adults. But, Daddy and Mummy are largely to blame for my having had to suffer so much.

At home they were only too glad to let me have fun and that was fine, but they didn't have to stir me up here into the bargain and show me just "their" side in all their rows and tittle-tattle. It was wrong of them although I believe they were in the right in most of the squabbles and there is much to find fault with in the characters of the v.P.s.

There is a proverb or saying to the effect that there's always some truth in all reproaches and words spoken in anger. This applies to me as well. There was much that was true in their reproaches, I simply knew no better, even earning admiration for my amusing comments and snappy repartee. Indeed, my opponents often suffered a knock out, but that happened to me even more often inside.

. . . . . .

. . . . . .

567

It took me quite some time to catch on that the quarrel score here was fifty-fifty. But now I know how many mistakes have been made here by old and young alike.

| 150   Daddy's and Mummy's greatest fault in their deal- | ings with the v.P.s. is that they never speak to them frankly and in friendship (even if the friendliness does have to be a little bit put on).

Now I want above all to keep the peace and neither quarrel nor gossip. That's not difficult where Daddy and Margot are concerned; with Mummy however it is and that's why it's a very good thing that she should rap me over the knuckles now and then. Mr. v.P. can also be won round if you agree with him, listen to him quietly, don't say very much and above all . . . . if you reply to all his little jokes and feeble jests with some joke of your own. Mrs. v.P. can be won round by talking to her frankly and agreeing with everything. She is also very quick to admit her mistakes, which are in truth very great in number.

I know only too well that she no longer thinks as badly of me as she did at the beginning. And that's just because I'm honest and no longer keep flattering people. I want to be honest and I think that you get much further that way; on top of that it also makes you feel much better yourself.

Under no circumstances do I want to act against Daddy and Mummy; I don't want to get involved any longer in quarrels and arguments with them (luckily things have been

| 151   fairly quiet of late) but I'm | no longer going to back them through thick and thin. I have my own views even on these matters and I no longer choose to take their side all the time for appearances' sake!

Yesterday Mrs. v.P. talked to me about all this and also about the rice we gave to the Kleimans:

"We've been giving, giving and giving again, but the point came when I said: Enough is enough. If Mr. Kleiman just took the trouble he could get rice for himself, why do we have to give everything away from our supplies? The children and all of us here need it just as much," said Mrs. v.P.

"No, Mrs. v.P.," I replied "I don't agree with you. Mr. Kleiman might perhaps be able to lay his hands on some rice, but he obviously finds it a difficult business. It's not for us to criticize those who help us, we must give them everything they need if we can possibly do without it. One plate of rice per week won't do us any harm, we can eat peas and beans instead!"

| 152   Mrs. v.P. didn't see it my way, but she added | that though she disagreed with me she'd do her best to leave it there, for that was quite a different matter. Well yes, let's leave it at that, sometimes I know my place now and sometimes I still doubt it, but I'll get there eventually! You'll see!

And especially now that I have got some help, for Peter helps me make the best of a bad job. He has already said that he would like to look after me if I should fall ill, to comfort me if there is shooting or the invasion, to help me as much as he can. And the other way round too of course!

. . . . . .

. . . . . .

a

I really don't know how much he likes me and if we will ever get as far as a kiss; I don't want to force it in any case! I told Daddy that I go to see Peter a great deal and asked whether he approved, he did of course!

I also told Peter much less difficult things that I normally keep to myself; thus I told him that I want to write later on, and even if I don't become a writer I won't neglect my writing while doing some other job. Oh yes, I don't want to have lived for nothing like most people. I want to be useful or give pleasure to the people around me yet who don't really know me, | I want to go on living even after my death! And therefore I am grateful to God for giving me this gift, this possibility of developing myself and of writing, of expressing all that is in me!

I'm not rich in money or worldly goods, I'm[1] not beautiful, intelligent, or smart, but I am and I shall be happy! I have a happy nature, I like people, I'm not distrustful and would like to see all of them happy with me.

your devoted Anne M.
Frank.

| 153

b . . . . . .

c . . . . . .

569

Monday 27 March 1944.

Dear Kitty,

One very big chapter of our history in hiding should really be about politics, but as this
subject doesn't concern me personally very much I've rather let it go. So I will write a
letter devoted to politics today. It goes without saying that there are very many different
| 154 opinions on this topic, and it's even more logical that it should be a favorite subject | for
discussion at such a critical time, but—it's just simply stupid that there should be so many
quarrels over it! They may speculate, laugh, abuse, and grumble, let them do what they
will, as long as they fry in their own fat and don't quarrel, because the consequences are
usually unpleasant. The people from outside bring with them a lot of news that isn't true;
however, so far our radio set hasn't lied to us. Jan, Miep, Kleiman, Bep, and Kugler are
all up and down in their political moods, Jan least of all.

317

Monday 27 March
1944.

Dear Kitty,

One very big chapter of our history in hiding should really be about politics, but as this
subject doesn't interest me personally very much, I've rather let it go. So for once I will
devote my whole letter to politics today. It goes without saying that there are very many
different opinions on this topic, and it's even more logical that it should be a favorite
subject for discussion in such critical times, but—it's just simply stupid that there should
be so many quarrels over it! They may speculate, laugh, abuse, and grumble, let them do
what they will as long as they fry in their own fat and don't quarrel, because the consequences are usually unpleasant. The people from outside bring with them a lot of news
that is not true; however, so far our radio set hasn't lied to us. Jan, Miep, Kleiman, Bep,
| 318 and Kugler are all up and down in their poli- | tical moods, Jan least of all.

Monday, 27 March, 1944

Dear Kitty,

One very big chapter of our history in hiding should really be about politics, but as
this subject doesn't interest me personally very much, I've rather let it go. So for once I
will devote my whole letter to politics today.

It goes without saying that there are very many different opinions on this topic, and
it's even more logical that it should be a favorite subject for discussion in such critical
times, but—it's just simply stupid that there should be so many quarrels over it.

They may speculate, laugh, abuse, and grumble, let them do what they will, as long
as they stew in their own juice and don't quarrel, because the consequences are usually
unpleasant.

The people from outside bring with them a lot of news that is not true; however, up
till now our radio set hasn't lied to us. Henk, Miep, Koophuis, Elli, and Kraler all show
ups and downs in their political moods, Henk least of all.

Political feeling here in the "Secret Annexe" is always about the same. During the countless arguments about invasion, air raids, speeche's etc., etc., one also always hears the countless cries of imposs'pul or Gottes Willen, if they're going to start now however long is it going to last. It's going shplendidly, first class, good!

Optimists and pessimists and above all don't let's forget the realists who give their opinions with untiring energy and, just as with everything else, they think all the time that they're right.

| 155   It annoys a certain lady that her spouse has such un- | paralleled faith in the British, and a certain gentleman attacks his lady because of her teasing and disparaging remarks about his beloved nation! From morning till late at night, and the best thing is that they never seem to tire of it. I have made a discovery—the effects are truly stupendous, just like pricking someone with pins, who then jumps out of his skin. This is exactly how I do it, begin on politics, one question, one word, one sentence and at once they're off!

Political feeling here in the "Secret Annexe" is always about the same. During the countless arguments over invasion, air raids, speeches etc., etc one also always hears the countless cries of impossipul, Um Gottes Willen, if they are going to start now however long is it going to last. It's going schplendidly, first class, good!

Optimists and pessimists and above all, don't let's forget the realists who give their opinion with untiring energy and, just as with everything else, each one thinking he is right. It annoys a certain lady that her spouse has such unparalleled faith in the British, and a certain gentleman attacks his lady because of her teasing and disparaging remarks about his beloved nation!

| 319   From morning till late at night, and the best thing is that they | never seem to tire of it. I have discovered something—its effects are stupendous, just like pricking someone with pins and waiting to see how they jump. This is what I do: begin on politics, one question, one word, one sentence and at once they're off!

Political feeling here in the "Secret Annexe" is always about the same. During the countless arguments over invasion, air raids, speeches, etc., etc., one also always hears the countless cries of "impossible," or *Um Gottes Willen,* if they are going to start now however long is it going to last." "It's going splendidly, first class, good!" Optimists and pessimists, and, above all, don't let's forget the realists who give their opinions with untiring energy and, just as with everything else, each one thinking he is right. It annoys a certain lady that her spouse has such unparalleled faith in the British, and a certain gentleman attacks his lady because of her teasing and disparaging remarks about his beloved nation.

They never seem to tire of it. I have discovered something—the effects are stupendous, just like pricking someone with a pin and waiting to see how they jump. This is what I do: begin on politics. One question, one word, one sentence, and at once they're off!

571

Just as if the German Wehrmacht news bulletins and the English B.B.C. were not enough they started "special air raid announcements" not so long ago. In one word, magnificent; but (the reverse of the coin) often disappointing too. The British are making a non-stop business of their air attacks, but with the same zest that the Germans make a business of lying!

The radio therefore goes on at 8 o'clock in the morning (if not earlier) and is listened to at all hours of the day until 9, 10 and often 11 o'clock in the evening.

156   This is certainly a sign that the grownups have infinite patience and brains with a pretty limited power of absorption, (or rather some of them have, because I don't want to hurt anyone's feelings), one or two news bulletins would be ample per day! But the old geese, well, I've said my piece!

Arbeiter-program, Radio "Oranje," Frank Philips or Her Majesty Queen Wilhelmina, they each get their turn and an ever attentive ear, and if they are not eating or sleeping, then they are sitting around the radio and discussing food, sleep and politics. Ugh! It gets so boring, and it's quite a job not to become a dull old stick oneself. Politics can't do much more harm to the old folk!

Just as if the German Wehrmacht news bulletins and the English B.B.C. were not enough, they have recently started "special air raid announcements." In one word, magnificent, but the reverse of the coin often disappointing too. The British are making a non-stop business of their air attacks, but with the same zest that the Germans make a business of lying!

The radio therefore goes on at 8 o'clock in the morning (if not earlier) and is listened to at all hours of the day until 9, 10 and often 11 o'clock in the evening.

This is certainly a sign that the grownups have infinite patience and brains with a pretty limited power of absorption, (or rather some of them have, because I don't want to hurt anyone's feelings), one or two | news bulletins would be ample per day! But the
| 320   old geese, well, I've said my piece!

Arbeiter-program, Radio "Oranje," Frank Philips or Her Majesty Queen Wilhelmina, they each get their turn and an ever attentive ear, and if they are not eating or sleeping, then they are sitting around the radio and discussing food, sleep and politics. Ugh! It gets so boring, and it's quite a job not to become a dull old stick oneself. Politics can't do much more harm to the old folks!

C   Just as if the German Wehrmacht news bulletins and the English B.B.C. were not enough, they have now introduced "Special Air-Raid Announcements." In one word, magnificent; but on the other hand often disappointing too. The British are making a non-stop business of their air attacks, with the same zest as the Germans make a business of lying. The radio therefore goes on early in the morning and is listened to at all hours of the day, until nine, ten, and often eleven o'clock in the evening.

This is certainly a sign that the grownups have infinite patience, but it also means the power of absorption of their brains is pretty limited, with exceptions, of course—I don't want to hurt anyone's feelings. One or two news bulletins would be ample per day! But the old geese, well—I've said my piece!

Arbeiter-Programm, Radio "Oranje," Frank Phillips [Philips] or Her Majesty Queen Wilhelmina, they each get their turn, and an ever attentive ear. And if they are not eating or sleeping, then they're sitting around the radio and discussing food, sleep, and politics.

Ugh! It gets so boring, and it's quite a job not to become a dull old stick oneself. Politics can't do much more harm to the parents!

573

But I must mention one shining exception, a speech by our beloved Windston Churchil is quite perfect.

Nine o'clock on Sunday evening. The teapot stands, with the cozy over it, on the table, and the guests come in. Pfeffer next to the radio on the left, Mr. van Pels in front of it, with Peter behind him Mummy next to Mr. v.P. and Mrs. v.P. in front. Margot and | 157 | I right at the back and Daddy at the table | I know I haven't described very clearly where our places are but it doesn't matter. The gentlemen puff non-stop at their pipes, Peter listens, eyes closed with the exertion, Mummy wearing a long dark negligée, Mrs. v.P. trembling because of the planes, which take no notice of the speech but fly blithely on towards Essen, Daddy sipping tea, Margot and I sharing Mouschi in a sisterly fashion,

I must mention one shining exception, a speech by our beloved Windston Churchil is quite perfect.

Nine o'clock on Sunday evening. The teapot stands, with the cozy over it, on the table, and the guests come in. Pf. next to the radio on the left, Mr. v.P. in front of it with Peter beside him. Mummy next to Mr. v.P. and Mrs. v.P. behind him, Margot and I further behind and Pim at the table. I see I haven't described very clearly how we sit but in the | 321 | end | it doesn't really matter. The gentlemen puff away at their pipes, Peter's eyes are closed from the exertion of listening, Mummy wearing a long dark negligée and Mrs. v.P. trembling because of the planes which take no notice of the speech but fly blithely on

I must mention one shining exception—a speech by our beloved Winston Churchill is quite perfect.

Nine o'clock on Sunday evening. The teapot stands, with the cozy over it, on the table, and the guests come in. Dussel next to the radio on the left, Mr. Van Daan in front of it, with Peter beside him. Mummy next to Mr. Van Daan and Mrs. Van Daan behind him, and Pim at the table, Margot and I beside. I see I haven't described very clearly how we sit. The gentlemen puff away at their pipes, Peter's eyes are popping out of his head with the strain of listening [Peter's eyes are closed from the exertion of listening], Mummy wearing a long dark negligée, and Mrs. Van Daan trembling because of the planes, which take no notice of the speech but fly blithely on towards Essen, Daddy sipping tea, Margot

574

a

the first with a scarf round her head because of her curlers, the second in a nightdress which is much too small, too narrow and too short. It all looked so intimate, snug, peaceful, and it was too this time, but I await the consequences with horror![5]

They can hardly wait and stamp their feet, so impatient are they to find out if there won't be another row! Brr, brr as if trying to coax a cat out of her basket, they egg each other on to discord and quarrels!

b

towards Essen, Daddy sipping tea, Margot and I united in a sisterly fashion by the sleeping Mouschi, who has monopolized both our knees. Margot's hair is in curlers, I am wearing a nightdress which is much too small, too narrow and too short.

It all looks so intimate, snug, peaceful and this time it is too, yet I await the consequences with horror.

They can hardly wait, stamping their feet, so impatient are they to find out if there won't be another row. Brr, brr, like a cat coaxing a mouse out[3] of its hole, they egg each other on to discord and quarrels.

yours, Anne

c

and I united in a sisterly fashion by the sleeping Mouschi, who is monopolizing both our knees. Margot's hair is in curlers, I am wearing a nightdress, which is much too small, too narrow, and too short.

It all looks so intimate, snug, peaceful, and this time it is too, yet I await the consequences with horror. They can hardly wait till the end of the speech, stamping their feet, so impatient are they to get down to discussing it. Brr, brr, brr—they egg each other on until the arguments lead to discord and quarrels.

Yours, Anne

Tuesday 28 March 1944.

Dearest Kitty,

I could write a lot more about politics, about the news bulletin early this morning, about

| 158

Miep's and Bep's questions and so on and so forth, but I have | heaps else to tell you today.

First, Mummy has more or less forbidden me to go upstairs, because, according to her, Mrs. van Pels is jealous. Secondly, Peter has invited Margot to join us upstairs, I don't know whether it's just out of politeness or whether he really means it. Thirdly, I went and asked Daddy if he thought I need pay any regard to Mrs. v.P.'s jealousy, and he didn't think so.

What next? Mummy is cross, wants me to work inside with Pfeffer again, doesn't want to let me go upstairs and is perhaps jealous too. Daddy doesn't grudge us these times together, and thinks it's nice that we get on so well. Margot is fond of Peter too, but feels that two's company and three's a crowd.

Mummy also thinks that Peter is in love with me; quite frankly, I only wish he were, then we'd be quits and really be able to get to know each other. She also says that he

| 159

keeps on looking at me; now I suppose that's true, but still I can't help it if he looks at | my dimples and we wink at each other occasionally, can I?

. . . . . .

Tuesday, 28 March, 1944

Dearest Kitty,

I could write a lot more about politics, but I have heaps of other things to tell you today. First, Mummy has more or less forbidden me to go upstairs so often, because, according to her, Mrs. Van Daan is jealous. Secondly, Peter has invited Margot to join us upstairs; I don't know whether it's just out of politeness or whether he really means it. Thirdly, I went and asked Daddy if he thought I need pay any regard to Mrs. Van Daan's jealousy, and he didn't think so. What next? Mummy is cross, perhaps jealous too. Daddy doesn't grudge us these times together, and thinks it's nice that we get on so well. Margot is fond of Peter too, but feels that two's company and three's a crowd.

Mummy thinks that Peter is in love with me; quite frankly, I only wish he were, then we'd be quits and really be able to get to know each other. She also says that he keeps on looking at me. Now, I suppose that's true, but still I can't help it if he looks at my dimples and we wink at each other occasionally, can I?

576

I'm in a very difficult position. Mummy is against me and I'm against her, Daddy closes his eyes and tries not to see the silent battle between us. Mummy is sad, because she still really loves me, while I'm not in the least bit sad, because I'm through with her. And Peter—I don't want to give Peter up, he is such a darling and I admire him so, it can grow into something beautiful between us; why do the "old 'uns" have to poke their noses in all the time?

Luckily I'm quite used to hiding my feelings and I manage extremely well not to let them see how mad I am about him. Will he ever say anything? Will I ever feel his cheek against mine, like I felt Petel's cheek in my dream? Oh, Peter and Petel, you are one and the same! They don't understand us; won't they ever grasp that we are happy just sitting together and not saying a word. They don't understand what has drawn us together like this! Oh, when will all these difficulties be overcome? And yet it is good to overcome them, because then the end will be all the more wonderful. When he lies with his head on his arm with | his eyes closed, then he is still a child; when he plays with Mouschi or talks about him, he is loving; when he carries potatoes or anything heavy, then he is strong. When he goes and watches the shooting, or looks for burglars in the darkness, then he is brave; and when he is so awkward and clumsy, then he is just a pet.

I like it much better if he explains something to me than when I have to teach him, I would really adore him to be my superior in almost everything!

What do we care about the two Mothers, Oh but if only he would speak.

yours, Anne M. Frank.

. . . .

I'm in a very difficult position. Mummy is against me and I'm against her, Daddy closes his eyes and tries not to see the silent battle between us. Mummy is sad, because she does really love me, while I'm not in the least bit sad, because I don't think she understands. And Peter—I don't want to give Peter up, he's such a darling. I admire him so; it can grow into something beautiful between us; why do the "old 'uns" have to poke their noses in all the time? Luckily I'm quite used to hiding my feelings and I manage extremely well not to let them see how mad I am about him. Will he ever say anything? Will I ever feel his cheek against mine, like I felt Petel's cheek in my dream? Oh, Peter and Petel, you are one and the same! They don't understand us; won't they ever grasp that we are happy, just sitting together and not saying a word. They don't understand what has driven us together like this. Oh, when will all these difficulties be overcome? And yet it is good to overcome them, because then the end will be all the more wonderful. When he lies with his head on his arm with his eyes closed, then he is still a child; when he plays with Boche [Mouschi], he is loving; when he carries potatoes or anything heavy, then he is strong; when he goes and watches the shooting, or looks for burglars in the darkness, then he is brave; and when he is so awkward and clumsy, then he is just a pet.

I like it much better if he explains something to me than when I have to teach him; I would really adore him to be my superior in almost everything.

What do we care about the two mothers? Oh, but if only he would speak!

Yours, Anne

577

Wednesday 29 March 1944.

Dear Kitty,

Bolkesteyn, an M.P., was speaking in the Dutch News from London, and he said that they ought to make a collection of diaries and letters after the war. Of course they all made a rush at my diary immediately.

Just imagine how interesting it would be if I were to publish a romance of the "Secret Annexe," the title alone would be enough to make people | think it was a detective story. But, seriously, it would be quite funny 10 years after the war if people were told how we Jews lived and what we ate and talked about here. Although I tell you a lot, still, even so, you only know very little of our lives. How scared the ladies are here sometimes (for instance on Sunday they used 350 planes to drop 500,000 kg on IJmuiden)* how the

| 161

Wednesday 29 March
1944.

Dear Kitty,

Bolkesteyn, an M.P., was speaking in the Dutch News from London, and he said that they ought to make a collection of diaries and letters after the war. Of course they all made a rush at my diary immediately.

Just imagine how interesting it would be if I were to publish a romance of the "Secret Annexe." The title alone would be enough to make people think it was a detective story. But, seriously, it would be quite funny 10 years after the war if we Jews were to tell how we lived and what we ate and talked about here. Although I tell you a lot, still, even so, you only know very little of our lives.

How scared the ladies are during the air raids. For instance on Sunday when 350 British planes dropped ½ million kilos of bombs on IJmuiden,* how the houses trembled like a wisp of grass in the wind, and who knows how many epidemics now rage. You

---

*The bombing of the IJmuiden docks could be heard clearly in Amsterdam. (*Kroniek van Amsterdam*, p. 124.)

Wednesday, 29 March, 1944

Dear Kitty,

Bolkestein, an M.P., was speaking on the Dutch News from London, and he said that they ought to make a collection of diaries and letters after the war. Of course, they all made a rush at my diary immediately. Just imagine how interesting it would be if I were to publish a romance of the "Secret Annexe." The title* alone would be enough to make people think it was a detective story.

But, seriously, it would seem quite funny ten years after the war if we Jews were to tell how we lived and what we ate and talked about here. Although I tell you a lot, still, even so, you only know very little of our lives.

How scared the ladies are during the air raids. For instance, on Sunday, when 350 British planes dropped half a million kilos of bombs on Ijmuiden, how the houses trembled like a wisp of grass in the wind, and who knows how many epidemics now rage. You

---

*The original title of this diary was *Het Achterhuis*. There is no exact translation into English, the nearest being *The Secret Annexe*.

houses shake from the bombs, how many epidemics there are, such as diphtheria, scarlet fever etc. What the people eat, how they line up for vegetables and all kinds of other things, it is almost indescribable.

The doctors here are under incredible pressure, if they turn their backs on their cars for a moment they are stolen from the street, in the Hospitals there is no room for the many infectious cases, medicines are prescribed over the telephone.

Above all the countless burglaries and thefts are beyond belief. You may wonder whether the Dutch have suddenly turned into a nation of thieves. Little children of 8 and 11 years break the windows of people's homes and steal whatever they can lay their hands on, you can't leave your home unoccupied, for in | the five minutes you are away your things are gone too. Each day there are announcements in the newspapers offering rewards for the return of lost property, typewriters, Persian rugs, electric clocks, sewing machines, as well as toys, jewelry, linen and cloth. The oddest things sometimes. And wanton destruction by youths also increases by the day, the removal of electric clocks in the street, of public telephones, the smashing of windows and pilfering of bicycles, everything is broken that can be.

b | 323

don't know anything about all these things, and | I would need to keep on writing the whole day if I were to tell you everything in detail. People have to line up for vegetables and all kinds of other things; doctors are unable to visit the sick, because if they turn their backs on their cars for a moment they are stolen; burglaries and thefts abound, so much so that you wonder what has taken over the Dutch for them suddenly to have become such thieves. Little children of 8 and 11 years break the windows of people's homes and steal whatever they can lay their hands on. No one dares to leave his home unoccupied for five minutes, because if you go,[2] your things go too. Every (Each) day there are announcements in the newspapers offering rewards for the return of lost property, typewriters, Persian rugs, electric clocks, cloth, etc. Electric clocks in the street are removed, public telephones are pulled to pieces, down to the last thread.

c

don't know anything about all these things, and I would need to keep on writing the whole day if I were to tell you everything in detail. People have to line up for vegetables and all kinds of other things; doctors are unable to visit the sick, because if they turn their backs on their cars for a moment, they are stolen; burglaries and thefts abound, so much so that you wonder what has taken hold of the Dutch for them suddenly to have become such thieves. Little children of eight and eleven years break the windows of people's homes and steal whatever they can lay their hands on. No one dares to leave his house unoccupied for five minutes, because if you go, your things go too. Every day there are announcements in the newspapers offering rewards for the return of lost property, typewriters, Persian rugs, electric clocks, cloth, etc., etc. Electric clocks in the streets are dismantled, public telephones are pulled to pieces—down to the last thread. Morale among the population

310.

Woensdag 29 Maart
1944.

Lieve Kitty,

Gisteren avond sprak minister Bolkestein,
aan de Oranje-Zender erover dat er na
de oorlog een inzameling van dagboeken en
brieven van deze oorlog zou worden ge-
houden. Natuurlijk stormden ze allemaal
direct op mijn dagboek af.

Stel je eens voor hoe interessant het zou
zijn als ik een roman van het Achterhuis uit zou geven; aan de titel alleen
zouden de mensen denken, dat het een
detective-roman was. Maar nu in ernst
het moet ongeveer 10 jaar na de oorlog al
grappig aandoen als wij vertellen hoe
wij als Joden, hier geleefd, gegeten en gesproken hebben. Al vertel ik je heel veel toch
toch weet je nog maar een heel klein
beetje van ons leven af.

Hoeveel angst de dames hebben als de
bombarderen, b.v. Zondag toen 350 Engelse
machines ½ millioen kilo bommen
op IJmuiden gegooid hebben, hoe de
huizen trillen als een grassprietje in
de wind, hoeveel epidemieën hier heersen,
van al deze dingen weet jij niets af en

322

From Anne's letter to Kitty of March 29, 1944 (b)

Morale among the population can't be good either, they're all hungry, the weekly rations are not enough to stretch for 2 days except for coffee substitute. The invasion is a long time coming, and the men have to go to Germany, the children ill or undernourished, and all are wearing old clothes and old shoes. A new sole costs 7.50 florins in the black market but hardly any of the shoemakers will accept shoe repairs or customers, and if they do you have to wait 4 months for the shoes, if they haven't been stolen in the meantime.

| 163 But one thing is good; sabotage is rife everywhere, everyone knows people | with false identity cards or papers. Many people (particularly officials) will warn you when they know that a check is coming, the police quite often look the other way when it comes to coupon dealers. The people in the food offices issue ration cards all over the town to members of the "Vrij Nederland" for nothing. From the milkman to the seamstress, everyone helps, but many, very many get caught or are too careless.

Just look at our vegetable suppliers, they know that someone is hiding here and yet keep supplying us with vegetables without coupons and at normal prices. The whole of the Netherlands, all the inhabitants, all of us have been kept in a closed prison for nearly 4 years now. Every day our living space grows smaller. Will it be over soon enough, before we suffocate and die of hunger?

yours, Anne M. Frank.

Morale | among the population can't be good, everyone is hungry, the weekly rations are not enough to last for two days except for coffee substitute. The invasion is a long time coming, and the men have to go to Germany, the children are ill or undernourished, all are wearing old clothes and old shoes.

A new sole costs 7.50 florins in the black market, moreover[1], hardly any of the shoemakers will accept shoe repairs or, if they do, you have to wait 4 months, during which time the shoes often disappear.

There's one good thing in the midst of it all, which is that as the food gets worse and the measures against the people more severe, so sabotage against the authorities steadily increases. The people in the food offices, the police, officials, they all either work with their fellow citizens and help them or else they tell on them and have them sent to prison. Fortunately, only a small percentage of Dutch people are on the wrong side.

yours, Anne

can't be good, [everyone is hungry,] the weekly rations are not enough to last for two days except the coffee substitute. The invasion is a long time coming, and the men have to go to Germany. The children are ill or undernourished, everyone is wearing old clothes and old shoes. A new sole costs 7.50 florins in the black market; moreover, hardly any of the shoemakers will accept shoe repairs or, if they do, you have to wait [four] months, during which time the shoes often disappear.

There's one good thing in the midst of it all, which is that as the food gets worse and the measures against the people more severe, so sabotage against the authorities steadily increases. The people in the food offices, the police, officials, they all either work with their fellow citizens and help them or they tell tales on them and have them sent to prison. Fortunately, only a small percentage of Dutch people are on the wrong side.

Yours, Anne

a

Friday 31 March 1944.

Dear Kitty,

Think of it it's still pretty cold but most people have been without coal for about a month—unpleasant, eh!

| 164
In general public feeling over the Russian front is optimistic again, because that is terrific! | You know I don't write much about politics, but I must tell you where they are now; they are right by the Polish border and have reached the Pruth near Rumania. They are close to Odessa, they have surrounded Tarnopol etc. etc. Every evening here they expect an extra communiqué from Stalin. They fire off so many salvos in Moscow to celebrate their victories that the city must rumble and shake just about every day—whether they think it's fun to pretend the war is close at hand again or that they know of no other way of showing their joy, I don't know!

Hungary is occupied by German troops. There are still 1 million Jews there, so they too will have had it now! Nothing special here. Today was Mr. v. Pels's birthday, he got 2 small packs of tobacco, enough coffee to make a cup, which his wife had managed to save, lemon punch from Kugler, sardines from Miep, eau de cologne from us, 2 lilac branches and some tulips. And I mustn't forget a currant-and-raspberry pie, a bit sticky because of the poor flour and the absence of butter, but nice all the same.

| 165
The chatter about Peter and me has calmed down a bit now, | he's coming to fetch me this evening, nice of him don't you think, because he finds it such a bore himself! We are very good friends, are together a lot and discuss every imaginable subject. It is awfully nice never to have to keep a check on myself as I would have to with other boys, whenever we get onto precarious ground. We were talking, for instance, about blood and via that subject we began talking about menstruation etc.

He thinks we women are pretty tough, seeing that we can stand up to losing 1 to 2 liters of blood. He thinks I'm tough as well. I wonder why?

b

......

c

Friday, 31 March, 1944

Dear Kitty,

Think of it, it's still pretty cold, but most people have been without coal for about a month—pleasant, eh! In general public feeling over the Russian front is optimistic again, because that is terrific! You know I don't write much about politics, but I must just tell you where they are now; they are right by the Polish border and have reached the Pruth near Rumania. They are close to Odessa. Every evening here they expect an extra communiqué from Stalin.

They fire off so many salvos in Moscow to celebrate their victories that the city must rumble and shake just about every day—whether they think it's fun to pretend that the war is close at hand again or that they know of no other way of expressing their joy, I don't know!

Hungary is occupied by German troops. There are still a million Jews there, so they too will have had it now.

The chatter about Peter and me has calmed down a bit now. We are very good friends, are together a lot and discuss every imaginable subject. It is awfully nice never to have to keep a check on myself as I would have to with other boys, whenever we get on to precarious ground. We are talking, for instance, about blood and via that subject we began talking about menstruation. He thinks we women are pretty tough. Why on earth? My

582

We are about to go and eat, my life here has improved, greatly improved. God has not left me alone and will not leave me alone <u>yours, Anne M. Frank.</u>

Saturday 1 April 1944.

Dearest Kitty,

And yet everything is still so difficult; I expect you can guess what I mean, can't you? I am so longing for a kiss from him, the kiss that is so long in coming. I wonder if all the time he still regards me as a friend, am I nothing more?

You know and I know that I am strong, that I can carry most of my burdens alone, I have | never been used to sharing troubles with anyone, I have never clung to a mother, but now I would so love to lay my head on "his" shoulder just once and remain still.

I can't, I simply can't forget that dream of Peter's cheek, when it was all good, all so good! Wouldn't he long for it too? Is it that he is just too shy to acknowledge his love? Why does he want me with him so often? Oh, why doesn't he speak?

I'd better stop, I must be quiet, I shall remain strong and with a bit of patience the other will come too, but—and that is the worst of it—it looks just as if I am running after him; <u>I</u> am always the one who goes upstairs, <u>he</u> doesn't come to me. But that is just because of the rooms, and he is sure to understand the difficulty. Oh, yes, and there's more he'll understand.

<u>yours, Anne M. Frank.</u>

. . . . . .

life here has improved, greatly improved. God has not left me alone and will not leave me alone.

Yours, Anne

Saturday, 1 April 1944

Dear Kitty,

And yet everything is still so difficult; I expect you can guess what I mean, can't you? I am so longing for a kiss, the kiss that is so long in coming. I wonder if all the time he still regards me as a friend? Am I nothing more?

You know and I know that I am strong, that I can carry most of my burdens alone. I have never been used to sharing my trouble with anyone, I have never clung to my mother, but now I would so love to lay my head on "his" shoulder just once and remain still.

I can't, I simply can't ever forget that dream of Peter's cheek, when it was all, all so good! Wouldn't he long for it too? Is it that he is just too shy to acknowledge his love? Why does he want me with him so often? Oh, why doesn't he speak?

I'd better stop, I must be quiet, I shall remain strong and with a bit of patience the other will come too, but—and that is the worst of it—it looks just as if I'm running after him; *I* am always the one who goes upstairs, *he* doesn't come to me.

But that is just because of the rooms, and he is sure to understand the difficulty.

Oh, yes, and there's more he'll understand.

Yours, Anne

583

Monday 3 April 1944.

Dearest Kitty,

Contrary to my usual custom, I will for once write more fully about food because it has become a very difficult and important matter, not only here in the "Secret Annexe" but in the whole of Holland, all Europe, and even beyond.

In the twenty-one months that we have spent here we have been through a good many "food cycles"—you'll understand what that means in a minute. When I talk of "food cycles" I mean periods in which one has nothing else to eat but one particular dish or kind of vegetable. We had nothing but endive for a long time, day in, day out, endive with sand, endive without sand, stew with endive, boiled or en casserole; then it was spinach, and after that followed kohlrabi, salsify, cucumbers, tomatoes, sauerkraut, etc., etc.

For instance, it's really disagreeable to eat a lot of sauerkraut for lunch and supper every day, but you do it if you're hungry. However, we have the most delightful period of all now, because we don't get any greens at all. Our weekly menu for supper consists | 168   of kidney beans, pea soup, potatoes with dumplings, potato cholent and, | by the grace of God, occasionally turnip tops or rotten carrots, and then the kidney beans once again. We eat potatoes at every meal, beginning with breakfast, because of the bread shortage, but they are still a bit warm then. We make our soup from kidney or haricot beans, potatoes, Julienne soup in packets, thick chicken soup in packets, kidney beans in packets.

Everything contains beans, not to mention the bread!

. . . . . .

Monday, 3 April, 1944

Dear Kitty,

Contrary to my usual custom, I will for once write more fully about food because it has become a very difficult and important matter, not only here in the "Secret Annexe" but in the whole of Holland, all Europe, and even beyond.

In the twenty-one months that we've spent here we have been through a good many "food cycles"—you'll understand what that means in a minute. When I talk of "food cycles" I mean periods in which one has nothing else to eat but one particular dish or kind of vegetable. We had nothing but endive for a long time, day in, day out, endive with sand, endive without sand, stew with endive, boiled or *en casserole*; then it was spinach, and after that followed kohlrabi, salsify, cucumbers, tomatoes, sauerkraut, etc., etc.

For instance, it's really disagreeable to eat a lot of sauerkraut for lunch and supper every day, but you do it if you're hungry. However, we have the most delightful period of all now, because we don't get any fresh vegetables at all. Our weekly menu for supper consists of kidney beans, pea soup, potatoes with dumplings, potato-chalet [potato cholent] and, by the grace of God, occasionally turnip tops or rotten carrots, and then the kidney beans once again. We eat potatoes at every meal, beginning with breakfast, because of the bread shortage. We make our soup from kidney or haricot beans, potatoes, Julienne soup in packets, French beans [thick chicken soup] in packets, kidney beans in packets. Everything contains beans, not to mention the bread!

In the evening we always have potatoes with gravy substitute and—thank goodness we've still got it—beetroot salad. I must tell you about the dumplings, which we make out of government flour, water and yeast. They are so sticky and tough, they lie like stones in one's stomach—ah, well!

The greatest attraction each week is a slice of liver sausage, and jam on dry bread. But we are still alive and even enjoy things quite often!

yours, Anne M. Frank.

169 As you've never been through a war, Kitty and despite all my letters know very little about life in hiding, just for fun I'm going to tell you each person's first wish when we go outside again.

Margot and Mr. v. Pels long more than anything for a hot bath filled to overflowing and want to stay in it for half an hour. Mrs. v.P. wants most to go and eat cream cakes immediately, Pf. thinks of nothing but seeing his Charlotte; Mummy of her cup of coffee; Daddy is going to visit the Voskuyls; Peter the town and a cinema, while I should find it so blissful, I shouldn't know where to start!

yours, Anne

. . . . . .

In the evening we always have potatoes with gravy substitute and—thank goodness we've still got it—beetroot salad. I must still tell you about the dumplings, which we make out of government flour, water, and yeast. They are so sticky and tough, they lie like stones in one's stomach—ah, well!

The great attraction each week is a slice of liver sausage, and jam on dry bread. But we're still alive, and quite often we even enjoy our poor meals.

Yours, Anne

a

Wednesday 5 April 1944.

Dearest Kitty,

For a long time I haven't had any idea of what I was working for any more, the end of the war is so terribly far away, so unreal, like a beautiful fairy tale. If the war isn't over by September I shan't go to school any more, because I don't want to be two years behind.

| 170 Peter filled my days—nothing but Peter, dreams and thoughts until Saturday night, | when I felt so utterly miserable; oh, it was terrible. I was holding back my tears all the while I was with Peter, then laughed madly with v.P. over a lemon punch, was cheerful and excited, but the moment I was alone I knew that I would have to cry my heart out. So, clad in my nightdress, I let myself go and slipped down onto the floor, first I said my long prayer, very intently, then I cried with my head on my arms, my knees bent under me, on the bare floor completely folded up. One large sob brought me back to earth again, and I quelled my tears because I didn't want them to hear anything in the next room.

Then I began trying to talk some courage into myself. I could only say: I must, I must, I must. . . . . . Completely stiff from the unnatural position, I fell against the side of the bed and fought on, until I climbed into bed again just before half past 10. It was over!

And now it's all over, I must work, so as not to be a fool, to get on to become a journalist, because that's what I want! I know that I <u>can</u> write, a couple of my stories are good, my descriptions of the "Secret Annexe" are humorous, there's a lot in my diary

| 171 that speaks, but—whether I have real talent | remains to be seen.

b

. . . . . .

c

Tuesday, 4 April, 1944

Dear Kitty,

For a long time I haven't had any idea of what I was working for any more; the end of the war is so terribly far away, so unreal, like a fairy tale. If the war isn't over by September I shan't go to school any more, because I don't want to be two years behind. Peter filled my days—nothing but Peter, dreams and thoughts until Saturday, when I felt so utterly miserable; oh, it was terrible. I was holding back my tears all the while I was with Peter, then laughed with Van Daan over a lemon punch, was cheerful and excited, but the moment I was alone I knew that I would have to cry my heart out. So, clad in my nightdress, I let myself go and slipped down onto the floor. First I said my long prayer very earnestly, then I cried with my head on my arms, my knees bent up, on the bare floor, completely folded up. One large sob brought me back to earth again, and I quelled my tears because I didn't want them to hear anything in the next room. Then I began trying to talk some courage into myself. I could only say: "I must, I must, I must . . ." Completely stiff from the unnatural position, I fell against the side of the bed and fought on, until I climbed into bed again just before half past ten. It was over!

And now it's all over. I must work, so as not to be a fool, to get on, to become a journalist, because that's what I want! I know that I can write, a couple of my stories are good, my descriptions of the "Secret Annexe" are humorous, there's a lot in my diary that speaks, but—whether I have real talent remains to be seen.

"Eva's Dream" is my best fairy tale, and the queer thing about it is that I don't know where it comes from. Quite a lot of "Cady's Life"* is good too, but, on the whole, it's nothing!

I am the best and sharpest critic of my own work, I know myself what is and what is not well written. Anyone who doesn't write doesn't know how wonderful it is; I used to bemoan the fact that I couldn't draw at all, but now I am more than happy that I can at least write.

And if I haven't any talent for writing books or newspaper articles, well, then I can always write for myself. But I want to get on; I can't imagine that I would have to lead the same sort of life as Mummy and Mrs. v.P. and all the women who do their work and are then forgotten, I must have something besides a husband and children, something that I can devote myself to!

*"Eva's Dream" and "Cady's Life" are included in Anne Frank's *Verhaaltjesboek* (Amsterdam/Antwerp: Uitgeverij Contact, 1960). [English translations by Michel Mok and Ralph Manheim in *Anne Frank's Tales from the Secret Annex*, Doubleday & Co., Inc., 1983. A.J.P.]

I want to go on living even after my death! And therefore I am grateful to God for giving me this gift, this possibility of developing myself and of writing, of expressing all that is in me!

. . . . . .

"Eva's Dream" is my best fairy tale, and the queer thing about it is that I don't know where it comes from. Quite a lot of "Cady's Life" is good too, but, on the whole, it's nothing.

I am the best and sharpest critic of my own work. I know myself what is and what is not well written. Anyone who doesn't write doesn't know how wonderful it is; I used to bemoan the fact that I couldn't draw at all, but now I am more than happy that I can at least write. And if I haven't any talent for writing books or newspaper articles, well, then I can always write for myself.

I want to get on; I can't imagine that I would have to lead the same sort of life as Mummy and Mrs. Van Daan and all the women who do their work and are then forgotten. I must have something besides a husband and children, something that I can devote myself to!

I want to go on living even after my death! And therefore I am grateful to God for giving me this gift, this possibility of developing myself and of writing, of expressing all that is in me.

I can shake off everything if I write; my sorrows disappear, my courage is reborn! But, and that is the great question, will I ever be able to write anything great, will I ever become a journalist or a writer? I hope so, oh, I hope so very much, for I can recapture everything | when I write, my thoughts, my ideals and my fantasies.

I haven't done anything more to "Cady's Life" for ages; in my mind I know exactly how to go on, but somehow it doesn't flow from my pen. Perhaps I never shall finish it, it may land up in the wastepaper basket, or the fire. That's a horrible idea, but then I think to myself, at the age of fourteen and with so little experience, how could you write about philosophy? So I go on again with fresh courage; I think I shall succeed, because I want to write!

yours, Anne M. Frank.

. . . . . .

I can shake off everything if I write; my sorrows disappear, my courage is reborn. But, and that is the great question, will I ever be able to write anything great, will I ever become a journalist or a writer? I hope so, oh, I hope so very much, for I can recapture everything when I write, my thoughts, my ideals and my fantasies.

I haven't done anything more to "Cady's Life" for ages; in my mind I know exactly how to go on, but somehow it doesn't flow from my pen. Perhaps I never shall finish it, it may land up in the wastepaper basket, or the fire . . . that's a horrible idea, but then I think to myself, "At the age of fourteen and with so little experience, how can you write about philosophy?"

So I go on again with fresh courage; I think I shall succeed, because I want to write!

Yours, Anne

Thursday 6 April 1944.

Dear Kitty,
You asked me what my hobbies and interests were, so I want to reply, but I warn you that there are heaps of them, so don't get a shock!

First of all: writing, but that can hardly be reckoned as a hobby.

No. 2: is family trees. I have been searching for family trees of the French, German, Spanish, English, Austrian, Russian, Norwegian and Dutch royal families in all the news-

| 173 papers, books and pamphlets | I can find. I have made great progress with a lot of them, as, for a long time already, I've been taking down notes from all the biographies and history books that I read; I even copy out many passages of history.

My third hobby then is history, for which Daddy has already bought me a lot of books. I can hardly wait for the day that I shall be able to comb through the books in the public library.

No. 4 is Greek & Roman mythology. I have various books about this too. I can rattle off the 9 muses or the 7 loves of Zeus. I have the wives of Hercules etc. etc. at my fingertips.

Other hobbies are film stars, and family photos. Mad on books and reading. Have a great liking for history of art, poets and painters. I may go in for musicians later on. I have a great loathing for Algebra, Geometry and figures. I enjoy all the other school subjects, but history above all!

yours, Anne M. Frank.

. . . . . .

Thursday, 6 April, 1944

Dear Kitty,
You asked me what my hobbies and interests were, so I want to reply. I warn you, however, that there are heaps of them, so don't get a shock!

First of all· writing, but that hardly counts as a hobby.

Number two: family trees. I've been searching for family trees of the French, German, Spanish, English, Austrian, Russian, Norwegian, and Dutch royal families in all the news-papers, books, and pamphlets I can find. I've made great progress with a lot of them, as, for a long time already, I've been taking down notes from all the biographies and history books that I read; I even copy out many passages of history.

My third hobby then is history, on which Daddy has already bought me a lot of books. I can hardly wait for the day that I shall be able to comb through the books in a public library.

Number four is Greek and Roman mythology. I have various books about this too.

Other hobbies are film stars and family photos. Mad on books and reading. Have a great liking for history of art, poets and painters. I may go in for music [musicians] later on. I have a great loathing for algebra, geometry, and figures.

I enjoy all the other school subjects, but history above all!

Yours, Anne

589

a 174   <u>Tuesday 11 April 1944.</u>[1]

Dearest Kitty,

My head is spinning, I honestly don't know where to begin. Thursday (the last time that I wrote to you) was normal, Friday was Good Friday, we played a board game, on Saturday afternoon as well. These days passed quickly. On Saturday morning everyone was present, at about 2 o'clock some heavy firing started, automatic weapons the men said, besides that everything was quiet.

On Sunday afternoon, on my invitation, Peter came to my room at half past 4; at a quarter past 5 we went to the front attic, where we remained until 6 o'clock.

There was a beautiful Mozart concert on the radio from 6 o'clock until a quarter past 7. I loved it all, but especially the "kleine Nachtmusik." I can hardly listen in the room because I'm always so inwardly stirred when I hear lovely music.

On Sunday evening[6] Peter couldn't have a bath, because the tub was standing in the kitchen downstairs full of laundry. So at 8 o'clock we went to the front attic together and, in order to sit comfortably, I took along the only divan cushion that I was able to | 175 lay my hands on. We seated ourselves on a | packing case. Both the case and the cushion were very narrow, so we sat absolutely squashed together, leaning against other cases; Mouschi kept us company too, so we weren't unchaperoned. Suddenly, at a quarter to 9, Mr. v.P. whistled and asked if we had one of Mr. Pf.'s cushions. We both jumped up and went downstairs with cushion, cat and v.P.

b   . . . . . .

c   Tuesday, 11 April, 1944

Dear Kitty,

My head throbs, I honestly don't know where to begin.

On Friday (Good Friday) we played Monopoly [a board game], Saturday afternoon too. These days passed quickly and uneventfully. On Sunday afternoon, on my invitation, Peter came to my room at half past four; at a quarter past five we went to the front attic, where we remained until six o'clock. There was a beautiful Mozart concert on the radio from six o'clock until a quarter past seven. I enjoyed it all very much, but especially the "Kleine Nachtmusik." I can hardly listen in the room because I'm always so inwardly stirred when I hear lovely music.

On Sunday evening Peter and I went to the front attic together and, in order to sit comfortably, we took with us a few divan cushions that we were able to lay our hands on. We seated ourselves on one packing case. Both the case and the cushions were very narrow, so we sat absolutely squashed together, leaning against other cases. Mouschi kept us company too, so we weren't unchaperoned.

Suddenly, at a quarter to nine, Mr. Van Daan whistled and asked if we had one of Dussel's cushions. We both jumped up and went downstairs with cushion, cat, and Van Daan.

590

A lot of trouble arose out of this cushion, Pf. was annoyed because I had taken the cushion he used for a pillow and he was afraid that there might be fleas in it and made a great commotion about his beloved cushion! Peter and I put two hard brushes in his bed as a revenge for his nastiness, but they had to come out again later because he still had to use the room.

We laughed horribly over this little interlude!

Sunday evening 9 April 1944.

But our fun didn't last long; at half past 9 Peter knocked softly on the door and asked Daddy if he would just help him upstairs over a difficult English sentence. "That's a blind," I said to Margot "anyone could see through that one, I can tell from the men's voices that | 176 there's been a break-in!" I was right, | they were in the act of breaking into the warehouse. Daddy, v.P. and Peter were downstairs in a flash, Margot, Mummy, Mrs. v.P. and I stayed upstairs and waited.

Four frightened women just have to talk, so talk we did, until we heard a bang downstairs. After this all was quiet, the clock struck a quarter to 10. The color had vanished from our faces, but we were still quiet, although we were afraid. Where could the men be? What was that bang? Would they be fighting the burglars? No one knew what to think, we just waited.

10 o'clock, footsteps on the stairs, Daddy, white and nervous entered, followed by Mr. v.P. "Lights out, creep upstairs, we expect the police in the house!"

. . . . . .

A lot of trouble arose out of this cushion, because Dussel was annoyed that we had one of his cushions, one that he used as a pillow. He was afraid that there might be fleas in it and made a great commotion about his beloved cushion! Peter and I put two hard brushes in his bed as a revenge. We had a good laugh over this little interlude!

Our fun didn't last long. At half past nine Peter knocked softly on the door and asked Daddy if he would just help him upstairs over a difficult English sentence. "That's a blind," I said to Margot, "anyone could see through that one!" I was right. They were in the act of breaking into the warehouse. Daddy, Van Daan, Dussel, and Peter were downstairs in a flash. Margot, Mummy, Mrs. Van Daan, and I stayed upstairs and waited.

Four frightened women just have to talk, so talk we did, until we heard a bang downstairs. After that all was quiet, the clock struck a quarter to ten. The color had vanished from our faces, we were still quiet, although we were afraid. Where could the men be? What was that bang? Would they be fighting the burglars? Ten o'clock, footsteps on the stairs; Daddy, white and nervous, entered, followed by Mr. Van Daan. "Lights out, creep upstairs, we expect the police in the house!"

time to be frightened: the lights went out, I quickly grabbed a jacket and we were upstairs. "What has happened? Tell us quickly!" There was no one to tell us, the men having disappeared downstairs again.

Only at 10 past[1] ten did they reappear; 2 kept watch at Peter's open window, the | 177 door to the landing was closed, the swinging cupboard shut. We hung a jersey | round the night light and after that they told us:

"Peter heard two loud bangs on the landing, ran downstairs, and saw there was a large plank out of the left half of the door. He dashed upstairs, warned the "Home Guard" of the family and the four of them proceeded downstairs. When they entered the warehouse, the burglars were busy stealing, without further thought v.P. shouted "police!" a few hurried steps outside, and the burglars had fled. In order to avoid the hole being noticed by the police, a plank was put against it, but a good hard kick from outside sent it flying to the ground. The men were perplexed at such impudence, and both v.P. and Peter felt murder welling up within them, v.P. beat on the ground with a chopper, and all was quiet again. Once more a plank was put up against the hole, once more disturbance, a married couple outside shone a bright torch in and lit up the whole warehouse. "Hell!" muttered one of the men, and now they switched over from their role of police to that of burglars. The four of them raced upstairs, Pf. and v.P. snatched up the former's books, | 178 Peter opened the doors and windows of the kitchen and private office, | flung the telephone on the floor and loaded with the wash tub the four of them landed behind the swinging cupboard."

End of part one.

. . . . . .

There was no time to be frightened: the lights went out, I quickly grabbed a jacket, and we were upstairs. "What has happened? Tell us quickly!" There was no one to tell us, the men having disappeared downstairs again. Only at ten past ten did they reappear; two kept watch at Peter's open window, the door to the landing was closed, the swinging cupboard shut. We hung a jersey round the night light, and after that they told us:

Peter heard two loud bangs on the landing, ran downstairs, and saw there was a large plank out of the left half of the door. He dashed upstairs, warned the "Home Guard" of the family, and the four of them proceeded downstairs. When they entered the warehouse, the burglars were in the act of enlarging the hole. Without further thought Van Daan shouted: "Police!"

A few hurried steps outside, and the burglars had fled. In order to avoid the hole being noticed by the police, a plank was put against it, but a good hard kick from outside sent it flying to the ground. The men were perplexed at such impudence, and both Van Daan and Peter felt murder welling up within them; Van Daan beat on the ground with a chopper, and all was quiet again. Once more they wanted to put the plank in front of the hole. Disturbance! A married couple outside shone a torch through the opening, lighting up the whole warehouse. "Hell!" muttered one of the men, and now they switched over from their role of police to that of burglars. The four of them sneaked upstairs, Peter quickly opened the doors and windows of the kitchen and private office, flung the telephone onto the floor, and finally the four of them landed behind the swinging cupboard.

END OF PART ONE

a

The married couple with the torch were likely to warn the police: it was Sunday evening, easter Sunday, no one at the office on easter Monday, so no one of us could budge until Tuesday morning. Think of it waiting in such fear for two nights and a day! No one had anything to suggest, so we simply sat there in pitchy darkness, because Mrs. v.P. in her fright had unintentionally turned the lamp right out; talked in whispers, and at every creak one heard sh, sh!

It turned half past 10, 11, but not a sound; Daddy and v.P. joined us in turns. Then, a quarter past 11, a bustle and noise downstairs. Everyone's breath was audible, in other respects no one moved. Footsteps in the house, in the private office, kitchen, then. . . . . on our staircase, no one breathed audibly now, 8 hearts thumped, footsteps on our staircase, then a rattling of the swinging cupboard. This moment is indescribable:[3] [4]

| 179   "Now we are lost!" I said and could see | all fifteen of us being carried off by the Gestapo that very night.

Twice they rattled the cupboard, then a tin can fell down, the footsteps withdrew, we were saved thus far! A shiver seemed to pass from one to the other, I heard someone's teeth chattering, no one said a word, and so we sat until half past 11.

There was not another sound in the house, but a light was burning on our landing, right in front of the cupboard. Could that be because it was our secret cupboard? Perhaps the police had forgotten the light? Would someone come back to turn it off? Voices were heard, there was no one in the house any longer, perhaps there was someone on guard outside.

b

. . . . . .

c

The married couple with the torch would probably have warned the police: it was Sunday evening, Easter Sunday, no one at the office on Easter Monday, so none of us could budge until Tuesday morning. Think of it, waiting in such fear for two nights and a day! No one had anything to suggest, so we simply sat there in pitch-darkness, because Mrs. Van Daan in her fright had unintentionally turned the lamp right out; talked in whispers, and at every creak one heard "Sh! sh!"

It turned half past ten, eleven, but not a sound; Daddy and Van Daan joined us in turns. Then a quarter past eleven, a bustle and noise downstairs. Everyone's breath was audible, otherwise no one moved. Footsteps in the house, in the private office, kitchen, then . . . on our staircase. No one breathed audibly now, [eight hearts thumped,] footsteps on our staircase, then a rattling of the swinging cupboard. This moment is indescribable. "Now we are lost!" I said, and could see us all being taken away by the Gestapo that very night. Twice they rattled at the cupboard, then there was nothing [then something fell down], the footsteps withdrew, we were saved so far. A shiver seemed to pass from one to another, I heard someone's teeth chattering, no one said a word.

There was not another sound in the house, but a light was burning on our landing, right in front of the cupboard. Could that be because it was a secret cupboard? Perhaps the police had forgotten the light? Would someone come back to put it out? Tongues loosened, there was no one in the house any longer, perhaps there was someone on guard outside.

Next we did three things: we went over again what we supposed had happened, we shivered with fear, and number 3, we had to go to the lavatory. Buckets were in the attic, so we had to make do with Peter's tin wastepaper bin. V.P. went first, then came Daddy, but Mummy was too shy to face it. Daddy brought the wastepaper basket into the room, where Margot, Mrs. v.P. and I gladly made use of it, finally Mummy decided to do so too. People kept on asking for paper—fortunately I had some in my pocket! The tin

| 180 smelled ghastly, everything went on in a whisper, we were tired, | it was twelve o'clock. "Lie down on the floor then and sleep!" Margot and I were each given a pillow and one blanket. Margot lay just near the store cupboard and I between the table legs, the smell wasn't quite so bad when one was on the floor, but still Mrs. v.P. quietly brought some chlorine, a tea towel over the pot serving as a second expedient. Talk, whispers, fear, stink, flatulation, and always someone on the pot, then try to go to sleep. However, by half past 2 I was so tired that I knew no more until half past 3. I awoke when Mrs. v.P. laid her head on my feet.

"For heaven's sake, give me something to put on!" I asked. I was given something, but don't ask what—a pair of woolen knickers over my pajamas, the red jumper and black skirt, white oversocks and a pair of holey sports stockings. Mrs. v.P. sat then in the chair and her husband came and lay on my feet. I lay thinking till half past 3, shivering the whole time, which prevented v.P. from sleeping, I prepared myself for the return of the police, "then we'd have to say that we were in hiding, they would either be good

| 181 Dutch people then it's all right, or the N.S.B. then they'd have to be bought off!" |

. . . . . .

Next we did three things: we went over again what we supposed had happened, we trembled with fear, and we had to go to the lavatory. The buckets were in the attic, so all we had was Peter's tin wastepaper basket. Van Daan went first, then Daddy, but Mummy was too shy to face it. Daddy brought the wastepaper basket into the room, where Margot, Mrs. Van Daan, and I gladly made use of it. Finally Mummy decided to do so too. People kept on asking for paper—fortunately I had some in my pocket!

The tin smelled ghastly, everything went on in a whisper, we were tired, it was twelve o'clock. "Lie down on the floor then and sleep." Margot and I were each given a pillow and one blanket; Margot lying just near the store cupboard and I between the table legs. The smell wasn't quite so bad when one was on the floor, but still Mrs. Van Daan quietly brought some chlorine, a tea towel over the pot serving as a second expedient.

Talk, whispers, fear, stink, flatulation, and always someone on the pot; then try to go to sleep! However, by half past two I was so tired that I knew no more until half past three. I awoke when Mrs. Van Daan laid her head on my foot.

"For heaven's sake, give me something to put on!" I asked. I was given something, but don't ask what—a pair of woolen knickers over my pajamas, a red jumper, and a black skirt, white oversocks and a pair of sports stockings full of holes. Then Mrs. Van Daan sat in the chair and her husband came and lay on my feet. I lay thinking till half past three, shivering the whole time, which prevented Van Daan from sleeping. I prepared myself for the return of the police, then we'd have to say that we were in hiding; they would either be good Dutch people, then we'd be saved, or N.S.B.-ers,* then we'd have to bribe them!

*The Dutch National Socialist Movement.

594

"In that case, destroy the radio!" sighed Mrs. v.P. "yes in the stove!" replied her husband "if they find us, then let them find the radio as well!"

"Then they will find Anne's diary," Daddy joined in! "Burn it then," suggested the most terrified member of the party.

This, and when the police rattled the cupboard door, were my worst moments; not my diary, if my diary goes I go with it! But luckily Daddy didn't answer! There is no object at all in recounting all the conversations that I can still remember, so much was said, I comforted Mrs. v.P. who was very scared. We talked about escaping and being questioned by the Gestapo, about ringing up, and being brave.

"We must simply behave like soldiers, Mrs. v.P. If all is up now, then let's go for Queen and Country, for freedom, truth and right, just what the Dutch news from England keeps telling us. The only thing that's really awful is that we'll drag a lot of other people into trouble too!"

| 182 Mr. v.P. changed places again with his wife after an hour, and Daddy came and sat beside me. The men smoked non-stop, now and then there was a | a deep sigh, then someone went on the pot and everything began all over again.

Four o'clock, five o'clock, half past 5. Then I went and sat beside Peter and listened, we sat close against each other, so close that we could feel the quivering of each other's bodies; we spoke a word or two now and then, and listened attentively.

Inside they took down the blackout and wrote down all the points they wanted to mention to Kleiman on the telephone. For they intended to call up Kleiman at 7 o'clock and get him to send someone around. The risk that the police on guard at the door, or in the warehouse, might hear the telephone was very great, but that of the police returning was even greater.

. . . . . .

"In that case, destroy the radio," sighed Mrs. Van Daan. "Yes, in the stove!" replied her husband. "If they find us, then let them find the radio as well!"

"Then they will find Anne's diary," added Daddy. "Burn it then," suggested the most terrified member of the party. This, and when the police rattled the cupboard door, were my worst moments. "Not my diary; if my diary goes, I go with it!" But luckily Daddy didn't answer.

There is no object in recounting all the conversations that I can still remember; so much was said. I comforted Mrs. Van Daan, who was very scared. We talked about escaping and being questioned by the Gestapo, about ringing up, and being brave.

"We must behave like soldiers, Mrs. Van Daan. If all is up now, then let's go for Queen and Country, for freedom, truth, and right, as they always say on the Dutch News from England. The only thing that is really rotten is that we get a lot of other people into trouble too."

Mr. Van Daan changed places again with his wife after an hour, and Daddy came and sat beside me. The men smoked non-stop, now and then there was a deep sigh, then someone went on the pot and everything began all over again.

Four o'clock, five o'clock, half past five. Then I went and sat with Peter by his window and listened, so close together that we could feel each other's bodies quivering; we spoke a word or two now and then, and listened attentively. In the room next door they took down the blackout. They wanted to call up Koophuis at seven o'clock and get him to send someone around. Then they wrote down everything they wanted to tell Koophuis over the phone. The risk that the police on guard at the door, or in the warehouse, might hear the telephone was very great, but the danger of the police returning was even greater.

Although I'm enclosing the memorandum,* I'll copy it out again for clarity's sake:

Burglars broken in: Police have been in the house as far as *swinging bookcase;* but no further.

Burglars were apparently disturbed, forced open the door in the warehouse and escaped through the garden. Main entrance bolted, Kugler *must* have used 2nd door when he left.

(That's where Peter got the sticks from!)

The typewriter and Adding machine are safe in the black case in private office.

| 183 Also Miep's and Bep's washing is in washtub in the | *kitchen.* Only Bep and Kugler have key to 2nd door, lock possibly broken.

Try to warn Jan and fetch the key, and look round the office, must also feed the cat.

——

For the rest everything went according to plan, Kleiman was phoned, the sticks removed, the typewriter put in the case. After that we sat around the table again and waited for Jan or the police.

Peter had fallen asleep and Mr. v.P. and I were lying on the floor when we heard loud footsteps downstairs. I got up quietly: "That's Jan!"

"No, no, it's the police!" all the others said. Someone knocked on our wall, Miep whistled. This was too much for Mrs. v.P., she turned as white as a sheet and sank limply into a chair; had the tension continued one minute longer she would have fainted. Our room was a perfect picture when Jan and Miep entered, the table alone would have been worth photographing, a copy of Cinema & Theater, covered with jam and pectin against diarrhea, opened at a page of dancing girls, 2 jam pots, one half and one quarter bread roll,

*See p. 601.

. . . . . .

The points were these:

Burglars broken in: police have been in the house, as far as the swinging cupboard, but no further.

Burglars apparently disturbed, forced open the door in the warehouse and escaped through the garden.

Main entrance bolted, Kraler must have used the second door when he left. The typewriters and adding machine are safe in the black case in the private office.

Try to warn Henk and fetch the key from Elli, then go and look round the office— on the pretext of feeding the cat.

Everything went according to plan. Koophuis was phoned, the typewriters which we had upstairs were put in the case. Then we sat around the table again and waited for Henk or the police.

Peter had fallen asleep and Van Daan and I were lying on the floor, when we heard loud footsteps downstairs. I got up quietly: "That's Henk."

"No, no, it's the police," some of the others said.

Someone knocked at the door, Miep whistled. This was too much for Mrs. Van Daan, she turned as white as a sheet and sank limply into a chair; had the tension lasted one minute longer she would have fainted.

Our room was a perfect picture when Miep and Henk entered, the table alone would have been worth photographing! A copy of *Cinema and Theater*, covered with jam and a remedy for diarrhea, opened at a page of dancing girls, two jam pots, two started loaves

596

a

184

| 185

pectin, a mirror, comb, matches, ash, cigarettes, tobacco, ash tray, matches, books, a pair of pants, a torch, Mrs. v.P.'s comb, toilet paper etc., etc.

Of course Jan and Miep were greeted with shouts and tears, Jan mended the hole in the door with some deal planks and soon went off again with Miep to tell the police about the burglary. Miep had also found a letter under the warehouse door from the night watchman Sleegers, who had seen the hole and warned the police, whom he would also visit.

So we had half an hour to tidy ourselves I've never seen such a change take place in half an hour as in this half hour. Margot and I took the bedclothes downstairs, went to the w.c., washed our hands and did our teeth and hair. After that I tidied the room a bit and went upstairs again, the table there was already cleared, so we ran off some water and made coffee and tea, boiled the milk, and laid the table for lunch, Daddy and Peter emptied the pee and shitpots and cleaned them with water and chlorine, the biggest was filled to the brim and so heavy that it was hard to lift, worse still it was leaking and had to be carried inside a bucket.

At 11 o'clock we sat round the table with Jan who was back by that time, and slowly things began to be more normal and cozy again.

| Jan's story was as follows:

Mr. Sleegers was asleep, but his wife told Jan that he had found the hole in our door when he was doing his tour round the canals and that he had called a policeman, who had gone round the building with him. Mr. Sleegers is a private night watchman and cycles along the canals every evening with his two dogs. He would be coming to see Kugler on

b

. . . . . .

c

of bread [one half and one quarter bread roll], a mirror, comb, matches, ash, cigarettes, tobacco, ash tray, books, a pair of pants, a torch, toilet paper, etc., etc., lay jumbled together in variegated splendor.

Of course Henk and Miep were greeted with shouts and tears. Henk mended the hole in the door with some planks, and soon went off again to inform the police of the burglary. Miep had also found a letter under the warehouse door from the night watchman Slagter, who had noticed the hole and warned the police, whom he would also visit.

So we had half an hour to tidy ourselves. I've never seen such a change take place in half an hour. Margot and I took the bedclothes downstairs, went to the W.C., washed, and did our teeth and hair. After that I tidied the room a bit and went upstairs again The table there was already cleared, so we ran off some water and made coffee and tea, boiled the milk, and laid the table for lunch. Daddy and Peter emptied the potties and cleaned them with warm water and chlorine.

At eleven o'clock we sat round the table with Henk, who was back by that time, and slowly things began to be more normal and cozy again. Henk's story was as follows:

Mr. Slagter was asleep, but his wife told Henk that her husband had found the hole in our door when he was doing his tour round the canals, and that he had called a policeman, who had gone through the building with him. He would be coming to see

597

a

Tuesday and he would hear more then. At the police station they knew nothing of the burglary yet, but the policeman had made a note of it at once and would come and look round sometime on Tuesday. On the way back Jan happened to meet van Hoeven, our greengrocer, and told him that the house had been broken into. "I know that," van Hoeven said quite coolly. I was passing last evening with my wife and saw the hole in the door, my wife wanted to walk on, but I just had a look in (with my torch) then the thieves must have cleared off. To be on the safe side I didn't ring up the police, as with you I didn't think it was the thing to do. I don't know anything, but I guess a lot." Jan thanked him and went on. Van Hoeven obviously guesses that we are here, because he always brings the potatoes after half past twelve and before half past two. Such a nice person!*

| 186   It was 1 by the time Jan had gone and | we'd finished doing the dishes. We all went for a sleep. I awoke at a quarter to three and saw that Mr. Pfeffer had already disappeared. Quite by chance, and heavy-eyed with sleep, I ran into Peter in the bathroom; he had just come down. We arranged to meet downstairs. I tidied myself and went down. Outside the lavatory door I heard, "Pst, pst, I'm in here!" "All right, I'll be waiting!" I sat down on a chair in the kitchen but didn't have to wait long for him.

"Do you still dare to go to the front attic?" he asked, I nodded, took my pillow with a piece of cloth round it and we went up to the attic. It was glorious weather and soon the sirens were wailing, we stayed where we were. Peter put his arm around my shoulder and I put mine around his and so we remained, our arms around each other, quietly waiting until Margot came to fetch us for coffee at 4 o'clock.

---

*H. van Hoeve ran a greengrocery at 58, Leliegracht, from where he helped Jews who wanted to go, or had already gone, into hiding. Following his arrest (see also p. 659) he ended up in Vught concentration camp and four German concentration camps, all of which he survived. (Interview with Van Hoeve in *Het Parool*, 26 Feb. 1972.)

b

. . . . . .

c

Kraler on Tuesday and would tell him more then. At the police station they knew nothing of the burglary yet, but the policeman had made a note of it at once and would come and look round on Tuesday. On the way back Henk happened to meet our greengrocer at the corner, and told him that the house had been broken into. "I know that," he said quite coolly. "I was passing last evening with my wife and saw the hole in the door. My wife wanted to walk on, but I just had a look in with my torch; then the thieves cleared [off] at once. To be on the safe side, I didn't ring up the police, as with you I didn't think it was the thing to do. I don't know anything, but I guess a lot."

Henk thanked him and went on. The man obviously guesses that we're here, because he always brings the potatoes during the lunch hour. Such a nice man!

It was one by the time Henk had gone and we'd finished doing the dishes. We all went for a sleep. I awoke at a quarter to three and saw that Mr. Dussel had already disappeared. Quite by chance, and with my sleepy eyes, I ran into Peter in the bathroom; he had just come down. We arranged to meet downstairs.

I tidied myself and went down. "Do you still dare to go to the front attic?" he asked. I nodded, fetched my pillow, and we went up to the attic. It was glorious weather, and soon the sirens were wailing; we stayed where we were. Peter put his arm around my shoulder, and I put mine around his and so we remained, our arms around each other, quietly waiting until Margot came to fetch us for coffee at four o'clock.

We finished our bread, drank lemondade and joked (we were able to again), otherwise everything went normally, in the evening I thanked Peter because he was the bravest of us all.

———

187   None of us has ever been in such danger as that night. God truly protected us, just think of it—the police at our secret cupboard, the light on right in front of it, and still we remained undiscovered. "Now we are lost!" I had said softly at that moment, but we had been saved once again.

If the invasion comes, and bombs with it, then it is each man for himself, but in this case our fear was for our good, innocent Christians. "We are saved, go on saving us!" That is all we can say.

———

This affair has brought quite a number of changes with it. Pf. now sits in the bathroom in the evenings, Peter goes round the house for a checkup at 8.30 and 9.30, Peter isn't allowed to have his window open any more because a man working for Keg noticed the open window, no one is allowed to pull the plug after half past 9, Mr. Sleegers has been engaged as night watchman, this evening a carpenter working for the underground is coming to construct barricades out of our white Frankfurt beds.

Debates are going on all the time now in the "Secret Annexe." Kugler reproached us | 188 for our carelessness, and we must | never go downstairs, says Jan too. As it is we haven't told Kugler the whole truth yet.

Now everyone is going on about whether Sleegers is reliable, whether the dogs will bark if they hear someone behind the door, how the barricades should be made, and this, that and the other.

. . . . . .

We finished our bread, drank lemonade and joked (we were able to again), otherwise everything went normally. In the evening I thanked Peter because he was the bravest of us all.

None of us has ever been in such danger as that night. God truly protected us; just think of it—the police at our secret cupboard, the light on right in front of it, and still we remained undiscovered.

If the invasion comes, and bombs with it, then it is each man for himself, but in this case the fear was also for our good, innocent protectors. "We are saved, go on saving us!" That is all we can say.

This affair has brought quite a number of changes with it. Mr. Dussel no longer sits downstairs in Kraler's office in the evenings, but in the bathroom instead. Peter goes round the house for a checkup at half past eight and half past nine. Peter isn't allowed to have his window open at nights any more. No one is allowed to pull the plug after half past nine. This evening there's a carpenter coming to make the warehouse doors even stronger.

Now there are debates going on all the time in the "Secret Annexe." Kraler reproached us for our carelessness. Henk, too, said that in a case like that we must never go downstairs. We have been pointedly reminded that we are in hiding, that we are Jews in chains, chained

599

a

We have been pointedly reminded that we are in hiding, that we are Jews in chains, chained to one spot, without any rights, with a thousand duties. We Jews mustn't show our feelings, must be brave and strong, must accept all inconveniences and not grumble, must do what is within our power and trust in God.

Sometime this terrible war will be over. Surely the time will come when we are people again, and not just Jews!

Who has inflicted this upon us? Who has made us Jews different from all other people? Who has allowed us to suffer so terribly up till now? It is God that has made us as we are, but it will be God, too, who will raise us up again. If we bear all this suffering and if there are still Jews left, when it is over, then Jews, instead of being doomed, will be held up as an example. Who knows, it might even be our religion from which the | world and all peoples learn good, and for that reason and that reason only do we have to suffer now. We can never become just Netherlanders or just English or any nation for that matter, we will always remain Jews, we must remain Jews, but we want to, too.

Be brave! Let us remain aware of our task and not grumble, a solution will come, God has never deserted our people; right through the ages there have been Jews, through all the ages they have had to suffer, but it has made them strong too, the weak are picked off and the strong will remain and never go under!

| 189

b

. . . . . .

c

to one spot, without any rights, but with a thousand duties. We Jews mustn't show our feelings, must be brave and strong, must accept all inconveniences and not grumble, must do what is within our power and trust in God. Sometime this terrible war will be over. Surely the time will come when we are people again, and not just Jews.

Who has inflicted this upon us? Who has made us Jews different from all other people? Who has allowed us to suffer so terribly up till now? It is God that has made us as we are, but it will be God, too, who will raise us up again. If we bear all this suffering and if there are still Jews left, when it is over, then Jews, instead of being doomed, will be held up as an example. Who knows, it might even be our religion from which the world and all peoples learn good, and for that reason and that reason only do we have to suffer now. We can never become just Netherlanders, or just English, or representatives of any country for that matter, we will always remain Jews, but we want to, too.

Be brave! Let us remain aware of our task and not grumble, a solution will come, God has never deserted our people. Right through the ages there have been Jews, through all the ages they have had to suffer, but it has made them strong too; the weak fall but the strong will remain and never go under!

600

During that night I really felt that I had to die, I waited for the police, I was prepared, as the soldier is on the battlefield. I was eager to lay down my life for the country, but now, now I've been saved again, now my first wish after the war is that I may become Dutch! I love the Dutch, I love this country, I love the language and want to work here. And if | 190   I have to write to the queen myself, | I will not give up until I have reached my goal!

I am becoming still more independent of my parents, young as I am, I face life with more courage than Mummy; my feeling for justice is immovable, and truer than hers. I know what I want, I have a goal, have an opinion, have a religion and love. Let me be myself and then I am satisfied. I know that I'm a woman, a woman with inward strength and plenty of courage!

If God lets me live, I shall attain more than Mummy ever has done, I shall not remain insignificant, I shall work in the world for mankind!

And now I know that first and foremost I shall require courage and cheerfulness!

yours, Anne M. Frank.

191   Burglars broken in: [illegible word] police have been in the house as far as swinging cupboard; but no further.

Burglars were apparently disturbed, forced open the door in the warehouse and escaped through the garden.

Main entrance bolted, Kugler must have used 2. door when he left.

The typewriter & Adding machine are safe in black case in private off.

Also Miep's and Bep's washing is in washing place in the kitchen.

Only Bep and Kugler have key to 2. door lock possibly broken.

Try to warn Jan and fetch the key and look round the office, must also feed the cat.

. . . . . .

During that night I really felt that I had to die, I waited for the police, I was prepared, as the soldier is on the battlefield. I was eager to lay down my life for the country, but now, now I've been saved again, now my first wish after the war is that I may become Dutch! I love the Dutch, I love this country, I love the language and want to work here. And even if I have to write to the Queen myself, I will not give up until I have reached my goal.

I am becoming still more independent of my parents, young as I am, I face life with more courage than Mummy; my feeling for justice is immovable, and truer than hers. I know what I want, I have a goal, an opinion. I have a religion and love. Let me be myself and then I am satisfied. I know that I'm a woman, a woman with inward strength and plenty of courage.

If God lets me live, I shall attain more than Mummy ever has done, I shall not remain insignificant, I shall work in the world and for mankind!

And now I know that first and foremost I shall require courage and cheerfulness!

Yours, Anne

601

Friday 14 April 1944.

Dearest Kitty,

The atmosphere here is still extremely strained. Pim has just about reached boiling point, Mrs. v.P. is in bed with a cold and grumbling away, Mr. v.P. grows pale without his fags, Pf., who is giving up a lot of his comfort is full of observations, etc., etc.

There is no doubt that our luck's not in at the moment. The lavatory leaks and the washer of the tap has gone, but, thanks to our many connections, we shall soon be able to get these things put right.

——

I am sentimental sometimes, you know that, but there is occasion to be sentimental here at times, when Peter and I are sitting somewhere together, on a hard, wooden crate in the midst of masses of rubbish and dust, our arms around each other's shoulders, and very close; he with one of my curls in his hand. When the birds sing outside and you see the trees changing to green, the sun invites one to be out in the open air, when the sky is so blue, then—oh, then I wish for so much!

b   . . . . . .

c

Friday, 14 April, 1944

Dear Kitty,

The atmosphere here is still extremely strained. Pim has just about reached boiling point. Mrs. Van Daan is in bed with a cold and trumpeting away. Mr. Van Daan grows pale without his fags, Dussel, who is giving up a lot of his comfort, is full of observations, etc., etc.

There is no doubt that our luck's not in at the moment. The lavatory leaks and the washer of the tap has gone, but, thanks to our many connections, we shall soon be able to get these things put right.

I am sentimental sometimes, I know that, but there is occasion to be sentimental here at times, when Peter and I are sitting somewhere together on a hard, wooden crate in the midst of masses of rubbish and dust, our arms around each other's shoulders, and very close, he with one of my curls in his hand; when the birds sing outside and you see the trees changing to green, the sun invites one to to be out in the open air, when the sky is so blue, then—oh, then, I wish for so much!

One sees nothing but dissatisfied, grumpy faces here, nothing but sighs and suppressed complaints; it really would seem as if suddenly we were very badly off here. If the truth is told, things are just as bad as you yourself care to make them. There's no one here to set us a good example; everyone must try to master his own moods.

Every day you hear, if only it was all over!

My work, my love, courage and hope,
make me go on and help me cope!

I really believe Kits, that I'm slightly bats today, and yet I don't know why. Everything here is so mixed up, nothing's connected any more, and sometimes I very much doubt whether in the future anyone will be interested in all my tosh.

"The unbosomings of an ugly duckling," will be the title of all this nonsense; my diary really won't be much use to Messrs. Bolkesteyn or Gerbrandi

yours, Anne M. Frank

. . . . . .

One sees nothing but dissatisfied, grumpy faces here, nothing but sighs and suppressed complaints; it really would seem as if suddenly we were very badly off here. If the truth is told, things are just as bad as you yourself care to make them. There's no one here that sets a good example; everyone should see that he gets the better of his own moods. Every day you hear, "If only it was all over."

My work, my hope, my love, my courage, all these things keep my head above water and keep me from complaining.

I really believe, Kits, that I'm slightly bats today, and yet I don't know why. Everything here is so mixed up, nothing's connected any more, and sometimes I very much doubt whether in the future anyone will be interested in all my tosh.

"The unbosomings of an ugly duckling" will be the title of all this nonsense. My diary really won't be much use to Messrs. Bolkestein or Gerbrandy.*

Yours, Anne

*Two members of the wartime Dutch Cabinet-in-Exile in London.

Saturday 15 April 1944.

Dear Kitty,

"Shock upon shock;

Will there ever be an end?"

We honestly can ask ourselves that question now. Guess what's the latest: Peter forgot to unbolt the front door. The result was that Kugler and the men could not get into the house, so he had to go to Keg and force open the kitchen window. What can they be thinking? And van Maaren? Miep is also badly frightened because M. & S. have been picked up, but that's got nothing to do with us. Kugler is livid; he gets blamed for not having the doors seen to, and we make such a stupid mistake!

I can tell you, it's upset Peter frightfully. At one meal, when Mummy said she felt more sorry for Peter than anyone else, he almost started to cry. We're all just as much to blame as he is, because nearly every day we ask whether the door's been unbolted, and Mr. v.P. always asks as well. Perhaps I shall be able to console him a bit later on; I would | 195 | so love to help him!

Here follow a few more disclosures from the "Secret Annexe" about the last few weeks.

1. Miep has had flu for more than a fortnight; she was only just back on her feet when Jan got it as well. Because the doctor doesn't visit patients with ordinary flu and Jan wasn't as sick as she had been, she gave him some of the powders the doctor had made up for her and then gave him an aspirin on top of that. That's the remedy for all ailments, from feeling sick to having a headache!

2. Saturday a week ago Boche suddenly fell ill, keeping very quiet and dribbling. Miep quickly picked him up, wrapped him in a cloth, put him in her shopping bag and took him to the dog-and-cat clinic. She was given some mixture to bring back by the doctor there, because there was something wrong with Boche's insides. Peter gave him the mixture a few times but Boche very soon vanished and was out on the tiles day and night; presumably with his girl friend.

3. It didn't take long for Boche to get well again. But now his nose is all swollen and he squeals if you touch him. He was probably | 196 | given a smack somewhere when he was trying to steal something.

4. Our Mouschi's voice was broken for a few days. Just as we had made up our minds to send him to the doctor too, he was halfway better again.

5. Our attic window is kept open a little bit now at night as well; Peter and I often sit upstairs in the evenings.

6. With the aid of some rubber cement and oil paint it will be possible to do some quick repairs to our lavatory.

7. And the tap that wouldn't turn off has been replaced by another one.

b   . . . . . .

604

Saturday, 15 April, 1944

Dear Kitty,

"Shock upon shock. Will there ever be an end?" We honestly can ask ourselves that question now. Guess what's the latest. Peter forgot to unbolt the front door (which is bolted on the inside at night) and the lock of the other door doesn't work. The result was that Kraler and the men could not get into the house, so he went to the neighbors, forced open the kitchen window, and entered the building from the back. He is livid at us for being so stupid.

I can tell you, it's upset Peter frightfully. At one meal, when Mummy said she felt more sorry for Peter than anyone else, he almost started to cry. We're all just as much to blame as he is, because nearly every day the men ask whether the door's been unbolted and, just today, no one did.

Perhaps I shall be able to console him a bit later on; I would so love to help him.

Yours, Anne

605

8. Mr. Kleiman is a bit better thank goodness. He can go outside a bit and he's allowed to eat minced meat. Soon, at least as soon as his blood is up to the mark, he'll see a specialist. We can only hope that a stomach operation isn't going to be necessary.

9. Following this morning's fright we won't be opening our windows any longer before 9 o'clock. Let's hope that the head of our family will have enough sense not to leave the windows ajar day and night any more even in the summer.

| 197

10. This month we received 8 ration | cards through Br. Unfortunately, for the first two weeks dried peas and beans are all that's available instead of rolled oats or groats.

11. Mr. Pf. sits on a chair in the bathroom at night, reading. He keeps me up until half past 9 with stories about his wife and children.

12. Our latest delicacy is picalilly. If you're out of luck, all that's left in the jar is cucumbers and some mustard sauce.

13. There are hardly any vegetables. Lettuce and then more lettuce. Our meals now consist entirely of potatoes and imitation gravy.

14. The Russians have taken more than half the Crimea. The English are making no progress at Cassino. We'll have to count on the western wall.

15. There are a lot of incredibly heavy air raids.

16. In The Hague a bomb was thrown at the Pub. Registration Office. All Dutchmen are being issued with new identity cards.*

Enough for today.

yours, Anne M. Frank.

*On Tuesday 11 April 1944 the Kleykamp building in The Hague was successfully bombed. It was in this building that the State Inspectorate of the Public Registration Office kept all receipts for identity cards. (L. de Jong, *Het Koninkrijk der Nederlanden in de Tweede Wereldoorlog*. Vol. 7, pp. 797ff.)

b   . . . . . .

c   . . . . . .

Sunday 16 April 1944.

Dearest Kitty,

Remember yesterday's date, for it is a very important day in my life. Surely it is a great day for every girl when she receives her first kiss? Well, then, it is just as important for me too! Bram's kiss on my right cheek doesn't count any more, likewise the one from Woudstra on my right hand.

How did I suddenly come by this kiss? Well, I will tell you:

Yesterday evening at 8 o'clock I was sitting with Peter on his divan, it wasn't long before he put his arm round me (because it was Saturday he wasn't wearing overalls) "Let's move up a bit," I said "then I don't bump my head against the cupboard." He moved almost completely into the corner, I put my arm under his arm and across his back, and he just about buried me, because his arm was hanging on my shoulders.

Now we've sat like that on other occasions, but never so close together as yesterday. He held me firmly against him; my left breast lay against his chest; already <u>my</u> heart began to beat, but we had not finished yet.

Sunday morning, just before eleven o'clock,
16 April, 1944

Darlingest [Dearest] Kitty,

Remember yesterday's date, for it is a very important day in my life. Surely it is a great day for every girl when she receives her first kiss? Well, then, it is just as important for me too! Bram's kiss on my right cheek doesn't count any more, likewise the one from Mr. Walker on my right hand.

How did I suddenly come by this kiss? Well, I will tell you.

Yesterday evening at eight o'clock I was sitting with Peter on his divan, it wasn't long before his arm went round me. "Let's move up a bit," I said, "then I don't bump my head against the cupboard." He moved up, almost into the corner, I laid my arm under his and across his back, and he just about buried me, because his arm was hanging on my shoulder.

Now we've sat like this on other occasions, but never so close together as yesterday. He held me firmly against him, my left shoulder [my left breast] against his chest; already my heart began to beat faster, but we had not finished yet. He didn't rest until my head

He didn't rest until my head was on his shoulder and his against it. When I sat up again after about five minutes, he soon took my head in his hands and laid it against him once more. Oh, it was so lovely, I couldn't talk much, the joy was too great; he stroked my cheek and arm a bit awkwardly, played with my curls and our heads lay touching most of the time.

I can't tell you Kitty, the feeling that ran through me all the while. I was too happy for words, and I believe so was he.

We got up at half past 8, Pfeffer came in and left again with his coat, Peter put on his gym shoes, so that when he toured the house a second time he wouldn't make a noise, and I stood beside him. How I suddenly made the right move, I don't know, but before we went downstairs he kissed me, through my hair, half on my left cheek, half on my ear; I tore downstairs without looking round, and am simply longing for today

yours, Anne M. Frank.

Sunday morning, just before 11 o'clock.

b   . . . . . .

c   was on his shoulder and his against it. When I sat upright again after about five minutes, he soon took my head in his hands and laid it against him once more. Oh, it was so lovely, I couldn't talk much, the joy was too great. He stroked my cheek and arm a bit awkwardly, played with my curls and our heads lay touching most of the time. I can't tell you, Kitty, the feeling that ran through me all the while. I was too happy for words, and I believe he was as well.

We got up at half past eight. Peter put on his gym shoes, so that when he toured the house he wouldn't make a noise, and I stood beside him. How it came about so suddenly, I don't know, but before we went downstairs he kissed me, through my hair, half on my left cheek, half on my ear; I tore downstairs without looking round, and am simply longing for today!

Yours, Anne

a 200

Dear Kitty,

Do you think that Daddy and Mummy would approve of my sitting and kissing a boy on a divan—a boy of seventeen and a half and a girl of just under fifteen? I don't really think they would, but I must rely on myself over this. It is so quiet and peaceful to lie in his arms and to dream, it is so thrilling to feel his cheek against mine, it is so lovely to know that there is someone waiting for me. But there is indeed a big "but," because will Peter be content to leave it at this? I haven't forgotten his promise already, but . . . . . . he is a boy!

I know myself that I'm starting very soon, not even fifteen and so independent already is certainly hard for other people to understand, I know almost for certain that Margot would never kiss a boy unless there had been some talk of an engagement or marriage, for neither Peter nor I have anything like that in mind. I am sure too that Mummy never touched a man before Daddy. What would my girl friends or Jacque say about it if they knew that I lay in Peter's arms, my heart against his chest, my head on his shoulder and with his head and face | against mine! Oh Anne, how shameful! But honestly, I don't

| 201

b

. . . . . .

c

Dear Kitty.

Do you think that Daddy and Mummy would approve of my sitting and kissing a boy on a divan—a boy of seventeen and a half and a girl of just under fifteen? I don't really think they would, but I must rely on myself over this. It is so quiet and peaceful to lie in his arms and to dream, it is so thrilling to feel his cheek against mine, it is so lovely to know that there is someone waiting for me. But there is indeed a big "but," because will Peter be content to leave it at this? I haven't forgotten his promise already, but . . . . he is a boy!

I know myself that I'm starting very soon, not even fifteen, and so independent already! It's certainly hard for other people to understand, I know almost for certain that Margot would never kiss a boy unless there had been some talk of an engagement or marriage, but neither Peter nor I have anything like that in mind. I'm sure too that Mummy never touched a man before Daddy. What would my girl friends say about it if they knew that I lay in Peter's arms, my heart against his chest, my head on his shoulder and with his head against mine!

think it is; we are shut up here, shut away from the world, in fear and anxiety, especially just lately. Why, then, should we who love each other remain apart? Why should we not kiss each other in these times? Why should we wait till we've reached a suitable age? Why should we bother?

I have taken it upon myself to look after myself; he would never want to cause me sorrow or pain. Why shouldn't I follow the way my heart leads me, if it makes us both happy? All the same Kitty I believe you can sense that I'm in doubt, I think it must be my honesty which rebels against doing anything on the sly? Do you think it's my duty to tell Daddy what I'm doing? Do you think we should share our secret with a third person? A lot of the beauty would be lost, but would my conscience feel happier? I will discuss it with "him."

Oh, yes, there's still so much I want to talk to him about, for I don't see any use in just cuddling each other. To exchange our thoughts shows confidence and faith in each

| 202   other, | but we would both be sure to profit by it!

yours, Anne M. Frank.

. . . . . .

Oh, Anne, how scandalous! But honestly, I don't think it is; we are shut up here, shut away from the world, in fear and anxiety, especially just lately. Why, then, should we who love each other remain apart? Why should we wait until we've reached a suitable age? Why should we bother?

I have taken it upon myself to look after myself; he would never want to cause me sorrow or pain. Why shouldn't I follow the way my heart leads me, if it makes us both happy? All the same, Kitty, I believe you can sense that I'm in doubt, I think it must be my honesty which rebels against doing anything on the sly! Do you think it's my duty to tell Daddy what I'm doing? Do you think we should share our secret with a third person? A lot of the beauty would be lost, but would my conscience feel happier? I will discuss it with "him."

Oh, yes, there's still so much I want to talk to him about, for I don't see the use of only just cuddling each other. To exchange our thoughts, that shows confidence and faith in each other, we would both be sure to profit by it!

Yours, Anne

610

P.S. Yesterday morning we were up again at 6 o'clock, because the whole family had heard the burglary sounds again. Perhaps this time the victim was a neighbor of ours. When we checked at 7 o'clock our doors were shut tight, luckily!

It all turned out all right with the forgotten bolt, Kugler was incredibly inventive; he has knocked together a piece of wood out of the broken window frame. Just think, the manager of Keg's had already fetched a ladder to climb through Pf.'s open window. Kugler was only able to stop him in time because the ladder was fortunately too short.

Quarrels with Pf., not I this time but Mr. van Pels and Daddy, despite their ban he went to sit in Kugler's office again on Sunday. That is finished for good now, because the private office has been cleared for him. He is deeply offended and didn't turn up to listen to a Handel | concert on the radio.

| 203

Mr. v.P. was boiling, Mrs. v.P. and Mummy both want the correspondence with Mrs. Pf. to stop, I can't see him doing that in a hurry, although it certainly means running unnecessary risks. Our windows are now no longer opened before 9 o'clock, in the summer too we shan't be leaving them open day and night any longer; even Pfeffer's chink is banned, which was another cause for an argument.

Aunt R. must really be feeling low, she's now got a daughter and a son-in-law in Poland, her son and daughter-in-law have been picked up and L. is dead. Only P. is left (F.)

Miep is very distressed about the above situation. S.'s sister has had it, too. Luckily Miep was not involved.

On Saturday we had a visit from Kleiman. He and Kugler stayed here until a quarter to four. Kleiman is slowly getting a bit better,

yours Anne.

I must study, it's getting late,
it's already 10 to 11, Monday morning.

. . . . . .

. . . . . .

611

Diary of Anne Frank
from 17 April 1944 to

"Secret Annexe"
A'dam C.

Partly letters to "Kitty."

The owner's maxim:
Schwung muss der Mensch haben! (Zest is what man needs!)

612

18 April 1944.
Tuesday.

Dear Kitty,

Someone's been a real darling again and has torn up a chemistry exercise book for me to make a new diary, this time the someone was Margot.

Everything goes well here; last night the carpenter came back and started to screw iron plates to the front door panels. Our lavatory is working again, but we are not allowed to pull the plug before and after office hours, just to rinse afterwards with water. When the staff is about we mustn't pull the plug a lot either, because van Maaren mustn't hear us. But one gets used to everything, even to that.

Daddy's just been saying that he definitely expects large-scale operations to take place before the twentieth of May, both in Russia and Italy, and also in the West; I find it more and more difficult to imagine our liberation from here.

Yesterday Peter and I finally got down to our talk, which had already been put off | 2 for at least 10 days. I explained everything about girls | to him and didn't hesitate to discuss the most intimate things. I found it rather funny that he thought the female passage is simply left out of illustrations. That's why he wasn't able to picture the fact that it was actually positioned between the legs.

The evening ended by each giving the other a kiss, just about beside the mouth, it's really a lovely feeling!

Perhaps I'll take my diary up there sometime, to go more deeply into things for once, I don't get any satisfaction out of lying in each other's arms day in, day out, and would so like to feel that he's the same.

. . .

Tuesday, 18 April, 1944

Dear Kitty,

Everything goes well here. Daddy's just said that he definitely expects large-scale operations to take place before the twentieth of May, both in Russia and Italy, and also in the West; I find it more and more difficult to imagine our liberation from here.

Yesterday Peter and I finally got down to our talk, which had already been put off for at least ten days. I explained everything about girls to him and didn't hesitate to discuss the most intimate things. The evening ended by each giving the other a kiss, just about beside my mouth, it's really a lovely feeling.

Perhaps I'll take my diary up there sometime, to go more deeply into things for once. I don't get any satisfaction out of lying in each other's arms day in, day out, and would so like to feel that he's the same.

a   We are having a superb spring after our long, lingering winter, April is really glorious, not too hot and not too cold, with little showers now and then. Our chestnut tree is already quite greenish and you can even see little blooms here and there.

Bep gave us a treat on Saturday, by bringing 4 bunches of flowers, 3 narcissus and 1 of grape hyacinths, the latter being for me.

3   Mr. Kugler gets better and better at supplying us with journals, each week Cinema & Theater, many Prinsen [Princes] and Rijk der Vrouw [Woman's Realm], each week the Haagse Post [Hague Post], sometimes das Reich and others.

I must do some algebra, Kitty—good-by

yours, Anne M. Frank.

19 April 1944 Wednesday.

My Darling, (That is the title of a film with Dorit Kreysler, Ida Wüst and Harald Paulsen!)

Is there anything more beautiful in the world than to sit before an open window and enjoy nature, to listen to the birds singing, feel the sun on your cheeks and have a darling boy in your arms?

It is so soothing and peaceful to feel his arms around me, to know that he is close by and yet to remain silent, it can't be bad, for this tranquillity is good. Oh never to be disturbed again, not even by Mouschi!

yours, Anne M. Frank.

b   . . . . . .

c   We are having a superb spring after our long, lingering winter; April is really glorious, not too hot and not too cold, with little showers now and then. Our chestnut tree is already quite greenish and you can even see little blooms here and there.

Elli gave us a treat on Saturday, by bringing four bunches of flowers, three bunches of narcissus and one of grape hyacinths, the latter being for me.

I must do some algebra, Kitty—good-by.

Yours, Anne

Wednesday, 19 April, 1944

My darling,

Is there anything more beautiful in the world than to sit before an open window and enjoy nature, to listen to the birds singing, feel the sun on your cheeks and have a darling boy in your arms? It is so soothing and peaceful to feel his arms around me, to know that he is close by and yet to remain silent, it can't be bad, for this tranquillity is good. Oh, never to be disturbed again, not even by Mouschi.

Yours, Anne

Mein Geheimschrift!

A = □	X = Ⴒ
B = [	y = #Ġ
C =]	Z = S.
D = ⧖	
E = 1	
F = Γ	
G = L	
H = ⌐	
I = Γ	
J = [	
K =]	
L = ▣	
M = ⊓	
N = ⊓⊓	
O = ▭	
P = ⊓	
q = ⊓⊓	
R = ▭▭	
S = Δ	
T = ▽	
U = I	
V = ∇	
W = Δ	

Anne Frank.

*Ik ben aan het lezen, daarna schrijf
ik een stuk van Carry van Bruggen
nl:*

Wat gaat dat grappig hè Kitty?!

Page 4 of the new diary. The Dutch reads as follows:
New secret code!
I am busy reading, after that I'll
copy out a piece from Carry van Bruggen:

That's fun isn't it Kitty?!

Friday 21 April 1944.

Dearest Kitty,

Yesterday afternoon I was lying in bed with a sore throat, but since I was already bored on the first day and did not have a temperature, I got up again today. The sore throat has in fact almost completely "disappeared) today.

Yesterday, as you probably discovered for yourself, our Führer was 55. Today it's the 18th birthday of Her Royal Highness Princess Elizabeth of York. The B.B.C. has said she will not be declared of age yet, though it's usually the case with royal children. We have been asking ourselves what Prince this beauty is going to marry, but cannot think of anyone suitable; perhaps her sister, Princess Margaret Rose, can have Prince Baudouin of Belgium one day!

Here we are having one misfortune after another, scarcely had the outside doors been strengthened than van Maaren appeared again. In all probability it was he who stole the potato meal and wants to put the blame on to Bep's shoulders. The whole "Secret Annexe" is | understandably het up again. Bep is beside herself with anger. Maybe Kugler will have that seedy-looking character shadowed now.

| 6

This morning the valuer from Beethoven Street was here, he wanted to give us 400 florins for our chest, his other offers are too low as well in our opinion.

I want to send in to "the Prince" to see if they will take one of my stories, under a pseudonym, of course, but because all my stories so far have been too long, I don't think I have much of a chance.

Till next time darling*
yours, Anne M. Frank.

*The word "darling" is in English. A.J.P.

. . . . . .

Friday, 21 April, 1944

Dear Kitty,

Yesterday afternoon I was lying in bed with a sore throat, but since I was already bored on the first day and did not have a temperature, I got up again today. It's the eighteenth birthday of Her Royal Highness Princess Elizabeth of York. The B.B.C. has said that she will not be declared of age yet, though it's usually the case with royal children. We have been asking ourselves what prince this beauty is going to marry, but cannot think of anyone suitable. Perhaps her sister, Princess Margaret Rose, can have Prince Baudouin of Belguim one day.

Here we are having one misfortune after another. Scarcely had the outside doors been strengthened than the warehouse man appeared again. In all probability it was he who stole the potato meal and wants to put the blame on to Elli's shoulders. The whole "Secret Annexe" is understandably het up again. Elli is beside herself with anger.

I want to send in to some paper or other to see if they will take one of my stories, under a pseudonym, of course.

Till next time, darling!

Yours, Anne

Dear Kitty,

Pfeffer has not been on speaking terms with v.P. for ± 10 days and just because, ever since the burglary, a whole lot of fresh security measures have been taken. One of these is that he cannot go downstairs any longer in the evening, as I have already told you. At half past 9 every night Peter and Mr. van Pels do a last round and | after that no one may go downstairs any more. The plug may not be pulled in the lavatory any more after eight o'clock in the evening, nor in the morning at 8 o'clock. In the morning the windows can only be opened when there is a light on in Kugler's office, and no sticks may be used in the evening to prop them up. This last measure has produced sulks from Pf. He maintains that v.P. has been shouting at him, but then he has only himself to blame. He says he can manage more easily without food than without air, and that some way must be found to keep the windows open. "I shall have to speak to Mr. Kugler about it," he told me, and I said that it had nothing to do with Mr. Kugler but should be decided by all of us.

| 7

. . . . . .

Dear Kitty,

Dussel has not been on speaking terms with Van Daan for ten days and just because, ever since the burglary, a whole lot of fresh security measures have been made that don't suit him. He maintains that Van Daan has been shouting at him.

a

"Everything is being done behind my back here, I'll have to speak to your father about it." He is not supposed to sit in Kugler's office on Saturday afternoons and Sundays any more, because if the manager of Keg's should turn up he would hear him. Pf. promptly went and sat there all the same.

|8 V.P. was furious and Father went downstairs to talk to him. Naturally he kept on inventing excuses, but this time | he could not get around even Father.

Father now talks to him as little as possible, as Pf. has insulted him, none of us knows in what way, but it must have been very bad. And Pf.'s correspondence with his wife has been almost completely suspended.

Unfortunately it's the fellow's birthday next week. Having a birthday, not opening your mouth, sulking and getting presents, how does that all fit in together? In the meantime there has been another unpleasant incident, which hasn't been explained so far. Van Maaren is trying to blame Bep for all the things that have been stolen and spreads the most barefaced lies about her. A lot of potato flour has gone and more's the pity, our private chest in the front attic has been almost completely emptied.

Van Maaren probably has his suspicions about us as well; he places books and bits of paper on the very edges of things in the warehouse so that if anyone walks by they fall off. Bep isn't the last to leave any more; Kugler locks up. Kleiman, who has been here in the meantime, Kugler and the two men have been looking into the question of how to get

|9 | this fellow out of the place from every possible angle. Downstairs they think it is too risky. But isn't it even riskier to leave things as they are?

———

Mr. Voskuyl has taken a turn for the worse, he has been running a temperature of almost 104 for more than 10 days. Yesterday it was even over 105. In the mornings it is only ± 100. The doctor thinks his condition is hopeless, they think the cancer has spread to his lungs. Poor man, we would so love to help him, but no one but God⁵ can help here!

I have written a lovely story called Blurry, the Explorer,* which pleased the 3 to whom I read it very much.

I've still got a cold and have given it to Margot as well as to Mummy and Daddy. As long as Peter doesn't get it! He called me his Eldorado and wanted a kiss. Of course, I couldn't! Funny boy! But still, he's a darling.

yours, Anne M. Frank.

*This story in the *Verhaaltjesboek* was first published in Anne Frank's *Weet je nog? Verhalten en Sprookjes* (Amsterdam/Antwerp: Contact, 1949).

b

. . . . . .

c

"Everything here happens upside down," he told me. "I am going to speak to your father about it." He is not supposed to sit in the office downstairs on Saturday afternoons and Sundays any more, but he goes on doing it just the same. Van Daan was furious and Father went downstairs to talk to him. Naturally, he kept on inventing excuses, but this time he could not get around even Father. Father now talks to him as little as possible, as Dussel has insulted him. None of us know in what way, but it must have been very bad.

I have written a lovely story called "Blurr[y], the Explorer," which pleased the three to whom I read it very much.

Yours, Anne

618

Thursday 27 April 1944.

Dear Kitty,

Mrs. v.P. was in such a bad mood this morning, nothing but complaints, first there's her cold and she can't get any sweets, and so much nose-blowing is unendurable. Next, it's that the sun's not shining. That the invasion doesn't come. That we can't look out of the windows etc., etc. We all had to laugh at her; and she was sporting enough to join in. Recipe for our potato cholent modified for want of onions:

Take peeled potatoes, put them through a mincing machine. Add a little dry government flour and salt. Grease the fireproof dishes with mineral oil or ste[a]rin, bake this mixture for 2½ hours. Eat with rotten stewed strawberries. (onions not available, nor fat for the mold or the dough!)

At the moment I'm reading The Emperor Charles V, written by a professor at Göttingen university; he worked at the book for forty years. I read fifty pages in 5 days; it's | 11 impossible to do more. The book has 298 | pp.; so now you can work out how long it will take me—and there is a second volume to follow. But very interesting!

What doesn't a schoolgirl get to know in a single day! Take me for example. First I translated a piece from Dutch into English, about Nelson's last battle. After that, I went through some more of Peter the Great's war against Norway (1700–1721), Charles XII, Augustus the Strong, Stanislaus Lescinsky, Mazeppa, Von Görz, Brandenburg, Pomerania and Denmark + the usual dates.

. . . . . .

Thursday, 27 April, 1944

Dear Kitty,

Mrs. Van Daan was in such a bad mood this morning, nothing but complaints! First, there's her cold, and she can't get any lozenges, and so much nose-blowing is unendurable. Next, it's that the sun's not shining, that the invasion doesn't come, that we can't look out of the windows, etc., etc. We all had to laugh at her; and she was sporting enough to join in. At the moment I'm reading *The Emperor Charles V*, written by a professor at Göttingen University; he worked at the book for forty years. I read fifty pages in five days; it's impossible to do more. The book has 598 pages, so now you can work out how long it will take me—and there is a second volume to follow. But very interesting!

What doesn't a schoolgirl get to know in a single day! Take me, for example. First, I translated a piece from Dutch into English, about Nelson's last battle. After that, I went through some more of Peter the Great's war against Norway (1700–1721), Charles XII, Augustus the Strong, Stanislaus Leczinsky [Leszczynski], Mazeppa, Von Görz, Brandenburg, Pomerania and Denmark, plus the usual dates.

a

  After that I landed up in Brazil, read about Bahia tobacco, the abundance of coffee and the 1½ million inhabitants of Rio de Janeiro, of Pernambuco and São Paulo,[1] not forgetting the river Amazon; about Negroes, Mulattos, Mestizos(!), Whites, [2]more than fifty per cent of the population being illiterate, and the malaria. As there was still some time left, I quickly ran through a family tree; Jan the Elder, Willem Lodewijk, Ernst Casimir I, Hendrick Casimir I, right up to the little Margriet Franciska (born in 1943) in Ottawa.

| 12 12 o'clock: in the attic I continued my program | with deacons, parsons, ministers, popes and....... Phew! Till 1 o'clock.

  Just after 2, the poor child sat working (mm) again, this time studying Narrow- and broad-nosed monkeys. Kitty, tell me quickly how many toes a hippopotamus has! Then followed the Bible, Noah and the Ark, Shem, Ham and Jafeth. After that Charles V.

  Then with Peter: the Colonel, in English, by Thackeray. Heard my French verbs and then compared the Mississippi with the Missouri!

a   9

  I've still got a cold and have given it to Margot as well as to Mummy and Daddy. As long as Peter doesn't get it! He called me his Eldorado and wanted a kiss. Of course, I couldn't! Funny boy! But still, he's a darling.

  Enough for today, good-by!

  yours, Anne M. Frank.

b   ......

c

  After that I landed up in Brazil, read about Bahia tobacco, the abundance of coffee and the one and a half million inhabitants of Rio de Janeiro, of Pernambuco and Sao Paulo, not forgetting the river Amazon; about Negroes, Mulattos, Mestizos, Whites, more than fifty per cent of the population being illiterate, and the malaria. As there was still some time left, I quickly ran through a family tree. Jan the Elder, Willem Lodewijk, Ernst Casimir I, Hendrik Casimir I, right up to the little Margriet Franciska (born in 1943 in Ottawa).

  Twelve o'clock: In the attic, I continued my program with the history of the Church—Phew! Till one o'clock.

  Just after two, the poor child sat working ('hm, 'hm!) again, this time studying narrow- and broad-nosed monkeys. Kitty, tell me quickly how many toes a hippopotamus has!! Then followed the Bible, Noah and the Ark, Shem, Ham, and Japheth. After that Charles V. Then with Peter: *The Colonel*, in English, by Thackeray. Heard my French verbs and then compared the Mississippi with the Missouri.

  I've still got a cold and have given it to Margot as well as to Mummy and Daddy. As long as Peter doesn't get it! He called me his "Eldorado" and wanted a kiss. Of course, I couldn't! Funny boy! But still, he's a darling.

  Enough for today, good-by!

  Yours, Anne

620

Friday 28 April 1944.

Dear Kitty,

   I have never forgotten my dream about Peter Schiff (see beginning of January), if I think of it, I can still feel his cheek against mine now, and recall that lovely feeling that made everything good. Sometimes I have had the feeling here with Peter, but never to such an extent, until yesterday, when we were, as usual, sitting on the divan, our arms around each other's waist, then suddenly the | ordinary Anne slipped away and a 2nd Anne took her place, a second Anne who is not reckless and jocular, but one who just wants to love and be gentle. I sat pressed closely against him and felt a wave of emotion come over me, tears sprang into my eyes, the left one trickled onto his dungarees, the right one ran down my nose and also fell onto his dungarees. Did he notice? He made no move or sign to show that he did. I wonder if he feels the same as I do? He hardly said a word. Does he know that he has two Annes before him? These questions must remain unanswered. At half past 8 when Pf. had already gone through, I stood up and went to the window, where we always say good-by, I was still trembling, I was still Anne No. 2. He came towards me, I flung my arms around his neck and gave him a kiss on his left cheek, and was about to kiss the other cheek, when my lips met his and we just pressed them together. In a whirl we were clasped in each other's arms, again and again, never to leave off.

   . . . . . .

Friday, 28 April, 1944

Dear Kitty,

   I have never forgotten my dream about Peter Wessel (see beginning of January). If I think of it, I can still feel his cheek against mine now, and recall that lovely feeling that made everything good.

   Sometimes I have had the same feeling here with Peter, but never to such an extent, until yesterday, when we were, as usual, sitting on the divan, our arms around each other's waists. Then suddenly the ordinary Anne slipped away and a second Anne took her place, a second Anne who is not reckless and jocular, but one who just wants to love and be gentle.

   I sat pressed closely against him and felt a wave of emotion come over me, tears sprang into my eyes, the left one trickled onto his dungarees, the right one ran down my nose and also fell onto his dungarees. Did he notice? He made no move or sign to show that he did. I wonder if he feels the same as I do? He hardly said a word. Does he know that he has two Annes before him? These questions remain unanswered.

   At half past eight I stood up and went to the window, where we always say good-by. I was still trembling, I was still Anne number two. He came towards me, I flung my arms around his neck and gave him a kiss on his left cheek, and was about to kiss the other cheek, when my lips met his and we pressed them together. In a whirl we were clasped in each other's arms again and again, never to leave off. Oh, Peter does so need

621

14 Oh, Peter does so need tenderness. For the first time in his life he has discovered a girl, has seen for the first time that even the most irritating girls have another side to them, that they have hearts and can be different when you are alone with them.

For the first time in his life he has given of himself and, having never had a boy or girl friend in his life before, shown his real self. Now we have found each other. For that matter, I didn't know him either, like him having never had a trusted friend, and this is what it has come to[1]. . . . . . Once more there is a question which gives me no peace: "Is it right?" Is it right that I should have yielded so soon, that I am so ardent, just as ardent and eager as Peter himself? May I, a girl, let myself go to this extent?

There is but one answer: "I have longed so much and for so long—I am so lonely—and now I have found consolation."

In the mornings we behave in an ordinary way, in the afternoons more or less so (except just occasionally) but in the evenings the suppressed longings of the whole day, the happiness and blissful memories of all the previous occasions come to the surface and we only | 15 | think of each other. Every evening, after the last kiss, I would like to dash away, not to look into his eyes any more—away, away, alone in the darkness. And what do I have to face when I reach the bottom of the staircase? Bright lights, questions, and laughter; I have to swallow it all and not show a thing.

My heart still feels too much; I can't get over a shock like the one I received yesterday

. . . . . .

tenderness. For the first time in his life he has discovered a girl, has seen for the first time that even the most irritating girls have another side to them, that they have hearts and can be different when you are alone with them. For the first time in his life he has given of himself and, having never had a boy or girl friend in his life before, shown his real self. Now we have found each other. For that matter, I didn't know him either, like him having never had a trusted friend, and this is what it has come to. . . .

Once more there is a question which gives me no peace: "Is it right? Is it right that I should have yielded so soon, that I am so ardent, just as ardent and eager as Peter himself? May I, a girl, let myself go to this extent?" There is but *one* answer: "I have longed so much and for so long—I am so lonely—and now I have found consolation."

In the mornings we just behave in an ordinary way, in the afternoons more or less so (except just occasionally) but in the evenings the suppressed longings of the whole day, the happiness and the blissful memories of all the previous occasions come to the surface and we only think of each other. Every evening, after the last kiss, I would like to dash away, not to look into his eyes any more—away, away, alone in the darkness.

And what do I have to face, when I reach the bottom of the staircase? Bright lights, questions, and laughter; I have to swallow it all and not show a thing. My heart still feels too much; I can't get over a shock such as I received yesterday all at once. The Anne who

622

all at once, the Anne who is gentle shows herself too little anyway and, therefore, will not[2] allow herself to be suddenly driven into the background; Peter has touched my emotions more deeply than anyone has ever done before—except in my dreams. Peter has taken possession of me and turned me inside out; surely it goes without saying that anyone would require a rest and a little while to recover from such an upheaval? Oh Peter, what have you done to me? What do you want of me? Where will this lead us? Oh, now I understand Bep; now, now that I am going through this myself, now I understand her doubt; if I were older and he should ask me to marry him, what should I answer. Anne,

| 16 be honest! You would not be able to marry him, but yet, it would be hard | to let him go. Peter hasn't enough character yet, not enough will power, too little courage and strength. He is still a child in his heart of hearts, he is no older than I am; he is only searching for tranquillity and happiness.

Am I only fourteen? Am I really still a silly little schoolgirl? Am I really so inexperienced about everything? I have more experience than most; I have been through things that hardly anyone of my age has undergone.[3]

I am afraid of myself, I am afraid that in my longing I'm giving myself too quickly. How, later on, can it ever go right with other boys? Oh it is so difficult, always battling with one's heart and reason; in its own time each will speak, but do I know for certain that I have chosen the right time?

yours, Anne M. Frank.

......

is gentle shows herself too little anyway and, therefore, will not allow herself to be suddenly driven into the background. Peter has touched my emotions more deeply than anyone has ever done before—except in my dreams. Peter has taken possession of me and turned me inside out; surely it goes without saying that anyone would require a rest and a little while to recover from such an upheaval?

Oh Peter, what have you done to me? What do you want of me? Where will this lead us? Oh, now I understand Elli; now, now that I am going through this myself, now I understand her doubt; if I were older and he should ask me to marry him, what should I answer? Anne, be honest! You would not be able to marry him, but yet, it would be hard to let him go. Peter hasn't enough character yet, not enough will power, too little courage and strength. He is still a child in his heart of hearts, he is no older than I am; he is only searching for tranquillity and happiness.

Am I only fourteen? Am I really still a silly little schoolgirl? Am I really so inexperienced about everything? I have more experience than most; I have been through things that hardly anyone of my age has undergone. I am afraid of myself, I am afraid that in my longing I am giving myself too quickly. How, later on, can it ever go right with other boys? Oh, it is so difficult, always battling with one's heart and reason; in its own time, each will speak, but do I know for certain that I have chosen the right time?

Yours, Anne

Tuesday 2 May 1944.

Dear Kitty,

On Saturday evening I asked Peter whether he thought that I ought to tell Daddy a bit about us; when we'd discussed it a little, he came to the conclusion that I should: I was glad, for it shows that he's a good boy. As soon as I got downstairs I went off with Daddy to get some water; and while we were on the stairs I said, "Daddy I expect you've gathered that when we are together, Peter and I don't sit miles apart. Do you think it's wrong?" Daddy didn't reply immediately, then said, "No I don't think it's wrong, but you must be careful, Anne; you are in such a confined space here." When we went upstairs he said something else on the same lines.

On Sunday morning he called me to him and said: "Anne, I have thought more about what you said (I felt scared already!), it's not really very right—here in this house; I thought that you were just pals, is Peter in love?"

"Oh, of course not," I replied.

"You know that I understand both of you, but you must be the one to hold back; | 18 don't go upstairs so often, don't encourage him more | than you can help. It is the man who is always the active one in these things; the woman can hold him back. It is quite different under normal circumstances, when you are free, you see other boys and girls, you can get away sometimes, play games and do all kinds of other things; but here if you're together a lot and you want to get away you can't; you see each other every hour of the day—in fact all the time. Be careful Anne, and don't take it too seriously!"

......

Tuesday, 2 May, 1944

Dear Kitty,

On Saturday evening I asked Peter whether he thought that I ought to tell Daddy a bit about us; when we'd discussed it a little, he came to the conclusion that I should. I was glad, for it shows that he's an honest boy. As soon as I got downstairs I went off with Daddy to get some water; and while we were on the stairs I said, "Daddy, I expect you've gathered that when we're together Peter and I don't sit miles apart. Do you think it's wrong?" Daddy didn't reply immediately, then said, "No, I don't think it's wrong, but you must be careful, Anne; you're in such a confined space here." When we went upstairs, he said something else on the same lines. On Sunday morning he called me to him and said, "Anne, I have thought more about what you said." I felt scared already. "It's not really very right—here in this house; I thought that you were just pals. Is Peter in love?"

"Oh, of course not," I replied.

"You know that I understand both of you, but you must be the one to hold back. Don't go upstairs so often, don't encourage him more than you can help. It is the man who is always the active one in these things; the woman can hold him back. It is quite different under normal circumstances, when you are free, you see other boys and girls, you can get away sometimes, play games and do all kinds of other things; but here, if you're together a lot, and you want to get away, you can't; you see each other every hour of the day—in fact, all the time. Be careful, Anne, and don't take it too seriously!"

624

"I don't Daddy, but Peter is a decent boy, really a nice boy!"

"Yes, but he's not a strong character; he can be easily influenced, for good, but also for bad; I hope for his sake that his good side will remain uppermost, because, by nature, that is how he is."

We talked on for a bit and agreed that Daddy should talk to him too.

On Sunday morning in the attic he asked: "And have you talked to your father, Anne?"

"Yes," I replied "I'll tell you about it. Daddy doesn't think it's bad, but he says that here, where we're so close together all the time, clashes may easily arise."

19 "But we agreed, didn't we, never to quarrel, and I'm determined to stick to it."

"So will I Peter, but Daddy didn't think that it was like this, he thought we were pals; do you think that we still can be?"

"I can—what about you?"

"Me too, I told Daddy that I trusted you. I do trust you, Peter, just as much as I trust Daddy, and I believe you to be worthy of it. You are, aren't you?"

"I hope so (He was very shy and rather red in the face).[1]

"I believe in you Peter," I went on "I believe that you have good qualities, and that you'll get on in the world."

. . . . . .

"I don't, Daddy, but Peter is a decent boy, really a nice boy!"

"Yes, but he is not a strong character; he can be easily influenced, for good, but also for bad; I hope for his sake that his good side will remain uppermost, because, by nature, that is how he is."

We talked on for a bit and agreed that Daddy should talk to him too.

On Sunday morning in the attic he asked, "And have you talked to your father, Anne?"

"Yes," I replied, "I'll tell you about it. Daddy doesn't think it's bad, but he says that here, where we're so close together all the time, clashes may easily arise."

"But we agreed, didn't we, never to quarrel; and I'm determined to stick to it!"

"So will I, Peter, but Daddy didn't think that it was like this, he just thought we were pals; do you think that we still can be?"

"I can—what about you?"

"Me too, I told Daddy that I trusted you. I do trust you, Peter, just as much as I trust Daddy, and I believe you to be worthy of it. You are, aren't you, Peter [You are, aren't you?"]?"

"I hope so." (He was very shy and rather red in the face.)

"I believe in you, Peter," I went on, "I believe that you have good qualities, and that you'll get on in the world."

625

After that we talked about other things. Later I said, "If we come out of here, I know quite well that you won't bother about me any more"! He flared right up "that's not true Anne, oh no, I <u>won't</u> let you think that of me!"

Then we were called away.

⸺

| 20 Daddy has talked to him; he told me about it on Monday. "Your father thought that the friendship might develop into love sooner or later he said, | "but I replied that we would keep a check on ourselves!"

⸺

Daddy doesn't want me to go upstairs so much in the evenings now, but I don't want that, not only because I like being with Peter; but I have told him that I trust him, I do trust him and I want to show him that I do, which can't happen if I stay downstairs through lack of trust.

No, I'm going!"

⸺

In the meantime the Pf. drama has righted itself again, at supper on Saturday evening he apologized in beautiful Dutch. V.P. was nice about it straight away, it must have taken Pf. a whole day to learn that little lesson off by heart.

Sunday, his birthday passed peacefully. We gave him a bottle of good 1919 wine, from the v.P.s (who could give their present now after all) a bottle of picalilly and a packet of razor blades, a jar of lemon (lemonade) from Kugler a book "Little Martin" from Miep

| 21 a plant from | Bep. He treated each one of us to an egg.

<u>yours, Anne M. Frank</u>. in the evening!¹

(the food is calling!) <u>half past 6.</u>

. . . . . .

After that, we talked about other things. Later I said, "If we come out of here, I know quite well that you won't bother about me any more!"

He flared right up. "That's not true, Anne, oh no, I won't let you think that of me!"

Then I was called away.

Daddy has talked to him; he told me about it today. "Your father thought that the friendship might develop into love sooner or later," he said. But I replied that we would keep a check on ourselves.

Daddy doesn't want me to go upstairs so much in the evenings now, but I don't want that. Not only because I like being with Peter; I have told him that I trust him. I do trust him and I want to show him that I do, which can't happen if I stay downstairs through lack of trust.

No, I'm going!

In the meantime the Dussel drama has righted itself again. At supper on Saturday evening he apologized in beautiful Dutch. Van Daan was nice about it straight away; it must have taken Dussel a whole day to learn that little lesson off by heart.

Sunday, his birthday, passed peacefully. We gave him a bottle of good 1919 wine, from the Van Daans (who could give their presents now after all), a bottle of piccalilli and a packet of razor blades, a jar of lemon jam [a jar of lemon (lemonade)] from Kraler, a book, *Little Martin*, from Miep, and a plant from Elli. He treated each one of us to an egg.

Yours, Anne

626

Wednesday 3 May 1944.

Dear Kitty,

First, just the news of the week! We're having a holiday from politics there is nothing absolutely nothing to announce. I too am gradually beginning to believe that the invasion will come. After all, they can't let the Russians clear up everything; for that matter, they're not doing anything either at the moment.

Mr. Kleiman comes to the office every morning again now, his blood is still not back to normal and so he can't see the specialist. He's got a new spring for Peter's divan, so Peter will have to do some upholstering, about which, quite understandably, he doesn't feel a bit happy. Kleiman has also brought some flea powder for the cats.

Have I told you that Boche has disappeared? Simply vanished—we haven't seen a sign | 22 of him since Thursday of last week. I expect he's already in the cats' heaven, | while some animal lover is enjoying a succulent meal from him. Perhaps some little rich girl will be given a fur cap out of his skin. Peter is very sad about it. Bep has won a real victory, she's going swimming with Bertus, how long will she be able to keep it up?

Since Saturday (two weeks ago) we have been having lunch at half past 11 in the mornings once a week; so we have to last out with one cupful of porridge. From tomorrow it will be like that every day, this saves us a meal. Vegetables are still very difficult to get hold of, we had rotten boiled lettuce this afternoon. Ordinary lettuce, spinach and boiled lettuce, there's nothing else. With these we eat rotten potatoes, so it's a delicious combination!

I hadn't had a period[5] for over 2 months, but it finally started again on Sunday. Still, in spite of all the unpleasantness and bother, I'm glad it hasn't failed me any longer.

. . . . . .

Wednesday, 3 May, 1944

Dear Kitty,

First, just the news of the week. We're having a holiday from politics; there is nothing, absolutely nothing to announce. I too am gradually beginning to believe that the invasion will come. After all, they can't let the Russians clear up everything; for that matter, they're not doing anything either at the moment.

Mr. Koophuis comes to the office every morning again now. He's got a new spring for Peter's divan, so Peter will have to do some upholstering, about which, quite understandably, he doesn't feel a bit happy.

Have I told you that Boche has disappeared? Simply vanished—we haven't seen a sign of her [him] since Thursday of last week. I expect she's [he's] already in the cats' heaven, while some animal lover is enjoying a succulent meal from her [him]. Perhaps some little girl will be given a fur cap out of her [his] skin. Peter is very sad about it.

Since Saturday we've changed over, and have lunch at half past eleven in the mornings, so we have to last out with one cupful of porridge; this saves us a meal. Vegetables are still very difficult to obtain: we had rotten boiled lettuce this afternoon. Ordinary lettuce, spinach and boiled lettuce, there's nothing else. With these we eat rotten potatoes, so it's a delicious combination!

627

a —

23 As you can easily imagine we often ask ourselves here despairingly: "What, oh, what is the use of the war, why can't people live peacefully together, why all this destruction?"

The question is very understandable, but no one has found a satisfactory answer to it so far, yes, why do they make still more gigantic planes in England, still heavier bombs and then prefabricated houses for reconstruction? Why are millions spent daily on the war and not a penny on medical services, artists or on poor people? Why do some people have to starve while there are surpluses rotting in other parts of the world? Oh why are people so crazy?

I don't believe that the big men, the politicians and the capitalists alone are responsible for the war, oh no, the little man is just as guilty, otherwise the peoples of the world would have risen in revolt long ago! There's in people simply an urge to destroy, an urge to kill, to mur- | der and rage and until all mankind without exception, undergoes a great change wars will be waged, everything that has been built up, cultivated and grown will be cut down and disfigured, to begin all over again after that!

| 24

—

I have often been downcast, but never in despair; I regard our hiding as a dangerous adventure, romantic and interesting at the same time. In my diary I treat all the privations

b . . . . . .

c As you can easily imagine we often ask ourselves here despairingly: "What, oh, what is the use of the war? Why can't people live peacefully together? Why all this destruction?"

The question is very understandable, but no one has found a satisfactory answer to it so far. Yes, why do they make still more gigantic planes [in England], still heavier bombs and, at the same time, prefabricated houses for reconstruction? Why should millions be spent daily on the war and yet there's not a penny available for medical services, artists, or for poor people?

Why do some people have to starve, while there are surpluses rotting in other parts of the world? Oh, why are people so crazy?

I don't believe that the big men, the politicians and the capitalists alone, are guilty of the war. Oh no, the little man is just as guilty, otherwise the peoples of the world would have risen in revolt long ago! There's in people simply an urge to destroy, an urge to kill, to murder and rage, and until all mankind, without exception, undergoes a great change, wars will be waged, everything that has been built up, cultivated, and grown will be destroyed and disfigured, after which mankind will have to begin all over again.

I have often been downcast, but never in despair; I regard our hiding as a dangerous adventure, romantic and interesting at the same time. In my diary I treat all the privations

628

as amusing. I have made up my mind now to lead a different life from other girls and, later on, different from ordinary housewives. My start has been so very full of interest, and that is the sole reason why I have to laugh at the comical side of the most dangerous moments.

I am young and I possess many buried qualities; I am young and strong and am living a great adventure; I am still in the midst of it and can't grumble the whole day long because I don't do anything but enjoy myself!

25   I have been given a lot, a happy nature, a great deal of cheerfulness and strength. Every day I feel that I am developing inwardly, that the liberation is drawing nearer and how beautiful nature is, how good the people about me, how interesting and amusing this adventure! Why, then, should I be in despair?

yours, Anne M. Frank.

Friday 5 May 1944.

Dearest Kitty,

Daddy is not pleased with me, he thought that after our talk on Sunday I automatically wouldn't go upstairs every evening. He doesn't want any "necking," a word I can't bear. It was bad enough talking about it, why must he make it so unpleasant now! I shall talk to him today, Margot has got some good advice for me, so listen; this is roughly what I want to say:

"I believe Daddy that you expect a declaration from me, so I will give it to you. You are disappointed in me, as you had expected more reserve from me, and I suppose you

. . . . . .

as amusing. I have made up my mind now to lead a different life from other girls and, later on, different from ordinary housewives. My start has been so very full of interest, and that is the sole reason why I have to laugh at the humorous side of the most dangerous moments.

I am young and I possess many buried qualities; I am young and strong and am living a great adventure; I am still in the midst of it and can't grumble the whole day long. I have been given a lot, a happy nature, a great deal of cheerfulness and strength. Every day I feel that I am developing inwardly, that the liberation is drawing nearer and how beautiful nature is, how good the people are about me, how interesting this adventure is! Why, then, should I be in despair? ·

Yours, Anne

Friday, 5 May, 1944

Dear Kitty,

Daddy is not pleased with me; he thought that after our talk on Sunday I automatically wouldn't go upstairs every evening. He doesn't want any "necking," a word I can't bear. It was bad enough talking about it, why must he make it so unpleasant now? I shall talk to him today. Margot has given me some good advice, so listen; this is roughly what I want to say:

"I believe, Daddy, that you expect a declaration from me, so I will give it to you. You are disappointed in me, as you had expected more reserve from me, and I suppose want me to be | just as a fourteen-year-old should be, but that's where you're mistaken!

"Since we've been here, from July 1942 until a few weeks ago, I can assure you that I haven't had an easy time. If you only knew how I cried my fill in the evenings, how desperate and unhappy I was, how lonely I felt, then you would understand that I want to go upstairs! I have now reached the stage that I can live entirely on my own, without Mummy's support or anyone else's for that matter. But it hasn't just happened in a night; it's been a bitter, hard struggle and I've shed many a tear, before I became as independent as I am now. You can laugh at me and not believe me, but that can't harm me. I know that I'm a separate individual and I don't feel in the least bit responsible to any of you. I am only telling you this because I thought that otherwise you might think that I was underhand, but I don't have to give an account of my deeds to anyone but myself.

"When I was in difficulties you all closed your eyes and stopped up your ears and didn't help me; on the contrary, I received nothing but | warnings not to be so boisterous. I was only boisterous so as not to be miserable all the time. I was reckless so as not to hear that persistent voice within me continually. I played a comedy for a year and a half, day in, day out, I never grumbled, never lost my cue, nothing like that, and now, now the battle is over. I have won! I am independent both in mind and body. I don't need a mother any more, for all this conflict has made me strong!

"And now that I'm on top of it, now that I know that I've fought the battle, now I want to be able to go on in my own way too, the way that I think is right. You can't and mustn't regard me as fourteen, for all these troubles have made me older; I shall not be

b

. . . . . .

c you want me to be just as a fourteen-year-old should be. But that's where you're mistaken!

"Since we've been here, from July 1942 until a few weeks ago, I can assure you that I haven't had any [an] easy time. If you only knew how I cried in the evening, how unhappy I was, how lonely I felt, then you would understand that I want to go upstairs!

"I have now reached the stage that I can live entirely on my own, without Mummy's support or anyone else's for that matter. But it hasn't just happened in a night; it's been a bitter, hard struggle and I've shed many a tear, before I became as independent as I am now. You can laugh at me and not believe me, but that can't harm me. I know that I'm a separate individual and I don't feel in the least bit responsible to any of you. I am only telling you this because I thought that otherwise you might think that I was underhand, but I don't have to give an account of my deeds to anyone but myself.

"When I was in difficulties you all closed your eyes and stopped up your ears and didn't help me; on the contrary, I received nothing but warnings not to be so boisterous. I was only boisterous so as not to be miserable all the time. I was reckless so as not to hear that persistent voice within me continually. I played a comedy for a year and a half, day in, day out, I never grumbled, never lost my cue, nothing like that—and now, now the battle is over. I have won! I am independent both in mind and body. I don't need a mother any more, for all this conflict has made me strong.

"And now, now that I'm on top of it, now that I know that I've fought the battle, now I want to be able to go on in my own way too, the way that I think is right. You

a

sorry for what I have done but shall act as I think I can! You can't coax me into not going upstairs; either you forbid it, or you trust me through thick and through thin, but then leave me in peace as well!"

yours, Anne M. Frank.

28   ± a week ago there was a report in the paper about a man who caught hold of a cat that had entered his home uninvited and killed it with a poker. The judge sentenced him to 1 month in prison.

In this connection the following poem*
Catastrophes.

This paper your obedient servant
Receives from this source and from that
Several catty notes and strictures
And all about the neighbor's cat
The neighbor's cat digs up the garden
Scatters seeds just neatly sown
Laps up milk without a coupon
Wolfs the poor canary down
Then without your kind permission
In your house decides to stay
Steals your meat and never falters
If there is no litter tray
'Tis small wonder that your neighbor
Works himself into a state,
Not least when the cat serenely

29 *Laughs at his unhappy fate*
If he can no longer hear it
And does to death the neighbor's cat:
Two camps soon are on the warpath:
Both have got their cases pat.
Each side raises in the paper,
A major question of its own:
Why can't cats pay friendly visits?
No, why not put the cat plague down?

---

*The report was published in *De Telegraaf* on 27 April 1944 and the poem by Clinge Doorenbos appeared on 4 May in the same newspaper.

b

......

c

can't and mustn't regard me as fourteen, for all these troubles have made me older; I shall not be sorry for what I have done, but shall act as I think I can. You can't coax me into not going upstairs; *either* you forbid it, *or* you trust me through thick and thin, but then leave me in peace as well!"

Yours, Anne

.. ..
There are two sides to every question,
As this case makes clear again;
And the wise man will endeavor,
To keep his distance from the twain.
Then he'll see the next door cat
Also has another side
(Would King Solomon the Wise
To this day with us abide!)
Not because he owns a cat,
But because it is a fact,
And because he senses that
Justice is mere tit for tat.
Very likely (I'm not certain)
Solomon would have decreed:
Over quarrels draw a curtain
Peaceful be in thought and deed!
30 *Be you cat fans or cat foes,*
Let the latter buy a hose
Banish cats with water spray.
But on no account them slay;
Let the former keep his cats,
Safe as houses in his home,
For they are domestic pets,
And as such they must not roam. . . . . . .

Clinge Doorenbos.

31
Saturday 6 May 1944.

Dear Kitty,

I put my letter in his pocket before supper yesterday, according to Margot he was very upset for the rest of the evening after he read it. (I was upstairs doing the dishes!) Poor Pim, I might have known what the effect of such an epistle would be! He is so sensitive! I immediately told Peter not to ask or say anything more.

Pim hasn't yet said anything about it to me. Is that yet in store I wonder?

. . . . . .

Saturday, 6 May, 1944

Dear Kitty,

I put a letter, in which I wrote what I explained to you yesterday, in Daddy's pocket before supper yesterday. After reading it, he was, according to Margot, very upset for the rest of the evening. (I was upstairs doing the dishes.) Poor Pim, I might have known what the effect of such an epistle would be. He is so sensitive! I immediately told Peter not to ask or say anything more. Pim hasn't said any more about it to me. Is that yet in store, I wonder?

632

Here everything is going on more or less normally again. Kleiman didn't feel very well yesterday, and went home early, Miep is cross with us; she always sides with Pf. and isn't being very friendly towards us. Bep went to the hairdresser today, a new perm! What Jan, Kugler and Kleiman tell us about the prices and people outside is almost unbelievable, a ½ pound of tea costs 350 florins. A ½ pound of coffee 80 florins. Butter 35 florins per pound, an egg 1.45 florins. People pay 14 florins for an ounce of Bulgarian cigarettes! Everyone deals in the black market, every errand | boy has something to offer. Our baker's boy got hold of some sewing silk for us, 0.9 florin for a thin little skein, the milkman manages to get clandestine ration cards, the undertaker delivers the cheese. Burglaries, murders, and theft go on daily. The police and night watchmen join in just as strenuously as the professionals, everyone wants something in their empty stomachs and because wage increases are forbidden the people simply have to cheat. The police are continually on the go tracing girls of fifteen, sixteen, seventeen, 18 and older who are reported missing every day.

M.K.* is in L'aône in France. There has been terrible bombing and she wants to come home at any price. She rang one of her many friends, an airman from Eindhoven, in the middle of the night and begged him to help her. [. . .]**

M. is deeply worried about her past behavior and has asked for forgiveness in her letters. Is it any wonder that the Ks have long since been placated? It certainly isn't!

I want to try and finish the story of Ellen, the fairy.*** I can give it to Daddy for fun on his birthday, together with all author's rights. See you soon (that's not really the right phrase, in the German-language broadcasts from England they say: until you hear us again; so what I should write is, until I write again!)

yours, Anne M. Frank.

* At the request of the person concerned, this name has been replaced with initials chosen at random.
** At the request of the person concerned 24 words have been deleted.
*** Anne Frank wrote this story on four loose pages. She also revised the first part for her *Verhaalt jesboek* The story was first published in *Anne Frank. Verhalen rondom het Achterhuis* (Amsterdam/ Antwerp: Contact, 1960). The story is included in *Anne Frank's Tales from the Secret Annex* (Garden City, N.Y.: Doubleday & Co., 1983).

. . . .

Here everything is going on more or less normally again. What they tell us about the prices and the people outside is almost unbelievable, half a pound of tea costs 350 florins, a pound of coffee 80 florins, butter 35 florins per pound, an egg 1.45 florin. People pay 14 florins for an ounce of Bulgarian tobacco! Everyone deals in the black market, every errand boy has something to offer. Our baker's boy got hold of some sewing silk, 0.9 florin for a thin little skein, the milkman manages to get clandestine ration cards, the undertaker delivers the cheese. Burglaries, murders, and theft go on daily. The police and night watchmen join in just as strenuously as the professionals, everyone wants something in their empty stomachs and because wage increases are forbidden the people simply have to swindle. The police are continually on the go, tracing girls of fifteen, sixteen, seventeen and older, who are reported missing every day.

Yours, Anne

633

a

Dear Kitty,

Daddy and I had a long talk yesterday afternoon, I cried terribly and he joined in. Do you know what he said to me, Kitty? "I have received many letters in my life, but this is certainly the most unpleasant! ¹You, Anne, who have received such love from your parents, you, who have parents who are always ready to help you, who have always defended you whatever it might be, you talk of feeling no responsibility towards us! You feel wronged and deserted; no Anne, you have done us a great injustice!

"Perhaps you didn't mean it like that, but it is what you wrote; no Anne, "<u>we</u>" haven't deserved such a reproach as this!"

| 34   Oh I have failed miserably; this is certainly the worst thing | I've ever done in my life. I was only trying to show off with my crying and my tears, just trying to appear big, so that he would respect me. Certainly, I had had a lot of unhappiness, and as far as Mummy is concerned all of it is true, but to accuse the good Pim, who has done and still does do everything for me—no, that was too low for words.

It's right that for once I've been taken down from my inaccessible pedestal, that my pride has been shaken a bit, for I was becoming much too taken up with myself again. What Miss Anne does is by no means always right! Anyone who can cause such unhappiness to someone else, someone he professes to love, and on purpose, too, is low, very low!

b

. . . . . .

c

Dear Kitty,

Daddy and I had a long talk yesterday afternoon, I cried terribly and he joined in. Do you know what he said to me, Kitty? "I have received many letters in my life, but this is certainly the most unpleasant! You, Anne, who have received such love from your parents, you, who have parents who are always ready to help you, who have always defended you whatever it might be, can you talk of feeling no responsibility towards us? You feel wronged and deserted; no, Anne, you have done us a great injustice!

"Perhaps you didn't mean it like that, but it is what you wrote; no, Anne, we haven't deserved such a reproach as this!"

Oh, I have failed miserably; this is certainly the worst thing I've ever done in my life. I was only trying to show off with my crying and my tears, just trying to appear big, so that he would respect me. Certainly, I have had a lot of unhappiness, but to accuse the good Pim, who has done and still does do everything for me—no, that was too low for words.

It's right that for once I've been taken down from my inaccessible pedestal, that my pride has been shaken a bit, for I was becoming much too taken up with myself again. What Miss Anne does is by no means always right! Anyone who can cause such unhappiness to someone else, someone he professes to love, and on purpose, too, is low, very low!

And the way Daddy has forgiven me makes me feel more than ever ashamed of myself, he is going to throw the letter in the fire and is so sweet to me now, just as if <u>he</u> had done something wrong. No, Anne, you still have a tremendous lot to learn, begin by doing that first, instead of looking down on others and accusing them!

35   I have had a lot of sorrow, but who hasn't at my age? I have played the clown a lot too, but I was hardly conscious of it; I felt lonely but hardly ever in despair! I have never been in such a state as Daddy, who once ran out onto the street with a knife in his hand to put an end to it all.

I ought to be deeply ashamed of myself, and indeed I am; what is done cannot be undone, but one can prevent it happening again. I want to start from the beginning again and it can't be difficult, now that I have Peter. With him to support me I <u>can</u> and will! I'm not alone any more; he loves me. I love him, I have my books, my storybook and my diary, I'm not so frightfully ugly, not utterly stupid, have a cheerful temperament and want to have a good character!

Yes, Anne, you've felt deeply that your letter was too hard and that it is untrue. To think that you were even proud of it! I will take Daddy as my example, and I <u>will</u> improve.

yours, Anne M. Frank.

. . . .

And the way Daddy has forgiven me makes me feel more than ever ashamed of myself, he is going to throw the letter in the fire and is so sweet to me now, just as if he had done something wrong. No, Anne, you still have a tremendous lot to learn, begin by doing that first, instead of looking down on others and accusing them!

I have had a lot of sorrow, but who hasn't at my age? I have played the clown a lot too, but I was hardly conscious of it; I felt lonely, but hardly ever in despair! I ought to be deeply ashamed of myself, and indeed I am.

What is done cannot be undone, but one can prevent it happening again. I want to start from the beginning again and it can't be difficult, now that I have Peter. With him to support me, I can and will!

I'm not alone any more; he loves me. I love him, I have my books, my storybook and my diary, I'm not so frightfully ugly, not utterly stupid, have a cheerful temperament and want to have a good character!

Yes, Anne, you've felt deeply that your letter was too hard and that it was untrue. To think that you were even proud of it! I will take Daddy as my example, and I *will* improve.

Yours, Anne

Monday 8 May 1944.

Dear Kitty,

Have I ever really told you anything about our family? I don't think I have, so I will begin now. Daddy was born in Frankfurt am Main, his parents were immensely rich, Michael Frank owned a bank and became a millionaire and Alice Stern had very rich and distinguished parents. Michael Frank had not been at all rich when he was young, but he duly worked his way up. In his youth Daddy had a real little rich boy's upbringing, parties every week, balls, festivities, beautiful girls, waltzing, dinners, a large home, etc., etc. After Grandpa's death all the money was lost and after the World War and the inflation nothing was left at all. Before the war they still had quite a few rich relatives, such as Olga Spitzer in Paris and Milly Stanfield in London. And Jacob and Hermann in Luxembourg couldn't complain of lack of money either. Daddy was therefore extremely well brought up and he laughed very much yesterday when, for the first time in his fifty-five years, he scraped out the frying pan at table.

| 37   Mummy was not so rich, but was still very | well off and we listen openmouthed to the stories of engagement parties of two hundred and fifty people, private balls and dinners.

One certainly could no longer call us rich, but all my hopes are pinned on after the war, I can assure you I'm not at all keen on having a narrow cramped existence, like, say, Mummy and Margot. I'd adore to go to Paris for a year and London for a year to learn the languages and study the history of art. Compare that with Margot, who wants to be a

. . . . . .

Monday, 8 May, 1944

Dear Kitty,

Have I ever really told you anything about our family?

I don't think I have, so I will begin now. My father's parents were very rich. His father had worked himself right up and his mother came from a prominent family, who were also rich. So in his youth Daddy had a real little rich boy's upbringing, parties every week, balls, festivities, beautiful girls, dinners, a large home, etc., etc.

After Grandpa's death all the money was lost during the World War and the inflation that followed. Daddy was therefore extremely well brought up and he laughed very much yesterday when, for the first time in his fifty-five years, he scraped out the frying pan at table.

Mummy's parents were rich too and we often listen openmouthed to stories of engagement parties of two hundred and fifty people, private balls and dinners. One certainly could not call us rich now, but all my hopes are pinned on after the war.

I can assure you I'm not at all keen on a narrow, cramped existence like Mummy and Margot. I'd adore to go to Paris for a year and London for a year to learn the languages and study the history of art. Compare that with Margot, who wants to be a midwife in midwife in Palestine.

I always long to see beautiful dresses and interesting people, I want to see something of the world and do all kinds of exciting things, I've already told you this before, and a little money as well won't do any harm!

——

Miep told us this morning about the party she went to on Saturday to celebrate the engagement of her cousin. The cousin in question is 27 years old and the bridegroom is 23. The cousin is a nice, buxom girl with rich parents, the bridegroom a short, weedy boy with even richer parents. Both are only children and can therefore count on inheriting from both sides. | Miep made our mouths water telling us about the food they had: Vegetable soup with minced meat balls in it, cheese, rolls with minced meat, hors d'oevres with eggs and roast beef, cheese rolls, fancy cakes, wine and cigarettes, as much as you wanted of everything.

Miep had ten drinks and smoked 3 cigarettes; can that be the woman who calls herself a teetotaler? If Miep had all those, I wonder however many her spouse managed to knock back? Naturally all those at the party were a bit tipsy; there were two policemen from the homicide branch, who took photos of the engaged couple; you can see that we are never far from Miep's thoughts, because she memorized the addresses of these men at once, in case anything should happen at some time or other, and good Dutchmen might

| 38

. . . . . .

Palestine! I always long to see beautiful dresses and interesting people.

I want to see something of the world and do all kinds of exciting things. I've already told you this before. And a little money as well won't do any harm.

Miep told us this morning about a party she went to, to celebrate an engagement Both the future bride and bridegroom came from rich families and everything was very grand. Miep made our mouths water telling us about the food they had: vegetable soup with minced meat balls in it, cheese, rolls, hors d'oeuvre with eggs and roast beef, fancy cakes, wine and cigarettes, as much as you wanted of everything (black market). Miep had ten drinks—can that be the woman who calls herself a teetotaler? If Miep had all those, I wonder however many her spouse managed to knock back? Naturally, everyone at the party was a bit tipsy. There were two policemen from the fighting squad, who took photos of the engaged couple. It seems as if we are never far from Miep's thoughts, because she took down the addresses of these men at once, in case anything should happen at some time or other, and good Dutchmen might come in useful.

637

a

| 39

come in useful. She made our mouths water. We, who get nothing but two spoonfuls of porridge for our breakfast and whose tummies were so empty that they were positively rattling, we, who get nothing but half-cooked spinach (to preserve the vitamins!) and rotten potatoes day after day, we, who get nothing but lettuce, cooked or raw, spinach and yet again spinach in our hollow stomachs. Perhaps we may | yet grow to be as strong as Popey, although I don't see much sign of it at present!

If Miep had taken us to the party we shouldn't have left any rolls for the other guests. If we had been at the party we should undoubtedly have snatched up the whole lot and left not even the furniture in place!

I can tell you, we positively drew the words from Miep's lips, we gathered round her as if we'd never heard about delicious food or smart people in our lives before! And these are the granddaughters of a renowned millionaire, the world is a queer place!

yours, Anne M. Frank.

b

. . . . . .

c

She made our mouths water. We, who get nothing but two spoonfuls of porridge for our breakfast and whose tummies were so empty that they were positively rattling, we, who get nothing but half-cooked spinach (to preserve the vitamins) and rotten potatoes day after day, we, who get nothing but lettuce, cooked or raw, spinach and yet again spinach in our hollow stomachs. Perhaps we may yet grow to be as strong as Popeye, although I don't see much sign of it at present!

If Miep had taken us to the party we shouldn't have left any rolls for the other guests. I can tell you, we positively drew the words from Miep's lips, we gathered round her, as if we'd never heard about delicious food or smart people in our lives before!

And these are the granddaughters of a millionaire. The world is a queer place!

Yours, Anne

638

Tuesday 9 May 1944.

Dear Kitty,

I've finished my story of Ellen, the fairy. I have copied it out on nice note paper, decorated it in red ink and sewn it together. It certainly looks very attractive, but I don't really know if it's enough. Margot and Mummy have both written birthday poems.

40   We are going to be able to get almost 50 prewar petit fours from Siemons the baker.

Mr. Kugler came upstairs this afternoon with the news that Mrs. Broks wants to eat her box lunch here at 2 o'clock every afternoon from Monday onwards. Think of it! No one can come upstairs any more, the potatoes cannot be delivered, Bep can't have any lunch, we can't go to the w.c., we mustn't move and all sorts of other unpleasantnesses! We thought up the wildest and most varied suggestions to wheedle her away. Mummy told Mr. Kugler her ideas on the subject, v.P. thought that a good laxative in her coffee would be sufficient. "No," replied Kleiman "I beg of you not, then we'd never get her off the box!"

Resounding laughter "off the box," asked Mrs. v.P., "what does that mean?" An explanation followed "can I always use it?" she then asked stupidly. "Imagine it," Bep giggled "if one asked for the box in Bijenkorf's they wouldn't even understand what you mean!"

. . . . . .

Tuesday, 9 May, 1944

Dear Kitty,

I've finished my story of Ellen the fairy. I have copied it out on nice note paper [,decorated it in red ink and sewn it together]. It certainly looks very attractive, but is it really enough for Daddy's birthday? I don't know Margot and Mummy have both written poems for him.

Mr. Kraler came upstairs this afternoon with the news that Mrs. B., who used to act as demonstrator for the business, wants to eat her box lunch in the office here at two o'clock every afternoon. Think of it! No one can come upstairs any more, the potatoes cannot be delivered, Elli can't have any lunch, we can't go to the W.C., we mustn't move, etc., etc. We thought up the wildest and most varied suggestions to wheedle her away. Van Daan thought that a good laxative in her coffee would be sufficient. "No," replied Koophuis, "I beg of you not, then we'd never get her off the box!" Resounding laughter. "Off the box," asked Mrs. Van Daan, "what does that mean?" An explanation followed. "Can I always use it?" she then asked stupidly. "Imagine it," Elli giggled, "if one asked for the box in Bijenkorf's* they wouldn't even understand what you mean!"

---

*"Bijenkorf" is a large store in Amsterdam.

639

Pf. now sits down promptly at half past 12 "on the box," to continue using that expression, this afternoon I resolutely picked up a piece of pink paper and wrote on it: W.C. regulations for Mr. Pfeffer.

in the mornings 7.15–7.30
in the afternoons after 1 o'clock

at other times according to requirement!

I fastened this to the green w.c. door while he was still inside, I could easily have added: Anyone breaking this law will be locked in!

Because our lavatory can be locked from the outside as well as the inside.

Latest joke from v.P.:

After a bible lesson about Adam and Eve, a 13-year old[3] boy asked his father: "Tell me Daddy, how exactly was I born?"

"Well," answered his father "the stork lifted you out of the big sea, laid you in your mother's bed and then pecked her leg hard. That made her bleed so much she had to stay in bed for over a | week."

42

Not fully satisfied the boy asked his mother for further details. "Tell me Mummy," he asked "how exactly were you born and how was I born?"

His mother told him precisely the same story, whereupon the boy turned to the fount of all wisdom, that is to say his grandfather. "Tell me Grandpa," he said "how were you born and how was your daughter born?" And for the third time he heard the same story.

In the evening he made the following entry in his diary: "Following very careful inquiries I have had to conclude that there has been no sexual intercourse in our family for the last three generations!

I still have work to do, it's 3 o'clock already.
yours, Anne M. Frank.

P.S. I have already told you about the new charwoman, so I just want to add that this

lady is married, 60 years old and hard of hearing! | Most acceptable because of the sounds that might filter through from 8 people in hiding.

Oh Kit, it's such wonderful weather, if only I could go outdoors!
yours, Anne

. . . . . .

Oh, Kit, it's such wonderful weather, if only I could go outdoors!

Yours, Anne

Wednesday 10 May 1944.

Dear Kitty,

We were sitting in the attic doing some French yesterday afternoon when I suddenly heard water pattering down behind me, I asked Peter what it could be, but he didn't even reply, simply tore up to the loft, where the site of the disaster was, and pushed Mouschi, who, because of the wet earth box, had sat down beside it, harshly back to the right place. A great din and disturbance followed, and Mouschi, who had finished peeing by that time, dashed downstairs.[2]

Mouschi, seeking the convenience of something similar to his box, had chosen some wood shavings over a crack in the [3]porous floor of the loft, the pool had trickled down from the loft into the attic immediately and, unfortunately, landed just beside and in the barrel of potatoes.

44   The ceiling was dripping, and as the attic floor is not free from holes either, several yellow drips came through the ceiling into the dining room between a pile of stockings and a book lying on the table.

I was doubled up with laughter, it really was such a scream. There was Mouschi crouching under a chair, Peter with water, bleaching powder, and floor cloth and v.P. trying to soothe everyone. The calamity was soon over, but it's a well-known fact that cats' puddles positively stink, the potatoes proved this only too clearly and also the wood shavings, that Daddy took downstairs in a bucket to be burned. Poor Mouschi! How were you to know that peat is unobtainable?

Anne.

. . . . . .

Wednesday, 10 May, 1944

Dear Kitty,

We were sitting in the attic doing some French yesterday afternoon when I suddenly heard water pattering down behind me. I asked Peter what it could be, but he didn't even reply, simply tore up to the loft, where the source of the disaster was, and pushed Mouschi, who, because of the wet earth box, had sat down beside it, harshly back to the right place. A great din and disturbance followed, and Mouschi, who had finished by that time, dashed downstairs.

Mouschi, seeking the convenience of something similar to his box, had chosen some wood shavings. The pool had trickled down from the loft into the attic immediately and, unfortunately, landed just beside and in the barrel of potatoes. The ceiling was dripping, and as the attic floor is not free from holes either, several yellow drips came through the ceiling into the dining room between a pile of stockings and some books, which were lying on the table. I was doubled up with laughter; it really was a scream. There was Mouschi crouching under a chair, Peter with water, bleaching powder, and floor cloth, and Van Daan trying to soothe everyone. The calamity was soon over, but it's a well-known fact that cats' puddles positively stink. The potatoes proved this only too clearly and also the wood shavings, that Daddy collected in a bucket to be burned [downstairs]. Poor Mouschi! How were you to know that peat is unobtainable?

Yours, Anne

Thursday 11 May 1944.

Dear Kitty,

A new piece of drama to make you laugh:

Peter's hair was due to be cut, the hairdresser to be his mother, as usual. At 25 past 7 Peter disappeared into his room, on the stroke of half past he came out again, stripped down to his blue swimming trunks and gym shoes.

46   "Are you coming?" he asked his mother.

"Yes, but I'm still looking for the scissors!"

Joining in the search, Peter rummaged about clumsily in Mrs. v.P.'s dressing table drawer. "Don't make such a mess, Peter," she grumbled, I didn't catch Peter's reply, but it must have been rude, because Mrs. v.P. gave him a slap on the arm, he gave her one back, then she hit out as hard as she could and Peter pulled his arm back with a funny expression. "You're coming along with me, old girl!" Mrs. v.P. stayed put, Peter grabbed her by the wrists and pulled her by them right across the room, Mrs. v.P. wept, laughed, scolded and stamped, none of it helped, Peter carried his prisoner off as far as the attic stairs, where he had to let go of her. Mrs. v.P. came back to the room and sighing loudly collapsed into a chair

"The Escape of the Mother,"* I joked

"Yes, but he hurt me."

I went to look and cooled her hot, red wrists with some water. Peter, still by the stairs, grew impatient again and stepped into the room, belt in hand like a lion tamer.

| 47   But Mrs. v.P. didn't budge, she stayed where she was sitting by the | desk and looking for a handkerchief. "First you've got to apologize!" "All right, then, I offer you my apologies herewith, because it's getting late!" Mrs. v.P. had to laugh despite herself, got up and went to the door. Here she felt obliged to give us an explanation first. (us were Daddy, Mummy and myself, we were busy doing the dishes) "At home he was never like that," she said "he would have had a slap from me that would have sent him flying down the stairs (!), he has never been so rude, it's not the first time he's had a slap, but this is what modern education does for you, modern children, I would never grab my mother like that, did you ever behave like that with your mother, Mr. Frank?" She was terribly worked up, walked up and down, talked nineteen to the dozen and still hadn't gone upstairs. At long, long last off she slunk.

She hadn't been upstairs for 5 minutes when she stormed down again, cheeks puffed out, flung down her apron and when I asked if she had finished answered by saying that she was just going downstairs and then flew down like a whirlwind, probably straight

| 48   into the arms of | her Putti.

She didn't come up again until 8 o'clock, her husband came with her, Peter was taken to the attic, was given a merciless dressing down and called a few names, lout, good-for-nothing, ill-mannered, a bad example, Anne is this, Margot does that, I couldn't hear the rest.

It looks as if things have settled down again today!

yours, Anne M. Frank.

*In German in the original ("*Die Entführung der Mutter*"), no doubt a reference to Mozart's opera *Die Entführung aus dem Serail*. A.J.P.

P.S. On Tuesday and Wednesday night our beloved queen spoke to us. She is taking a holiday in order to be strong for her return to Holland. She used words like, soon, when I am back, speedy liberation, heroism and heavy burdens.

A speech by Gerbrandi followed, he has such a whining little child's voice that Mummy could not help saying "oh, dear." A clergyman, who must have pinched his voice from Mr. Edel, concluded by asking God to take care of the Jews, the people in concentration camps, prisons and in Germany.*

yours, Anne

*The address Queen Wilhelmina gave on the night of Tuesday 9 May 1944 on Radio Orange was repeated on Thursday afternoon 11 May. Her address of Wednesday afternoon 10 May was repeated that same evening. Prime Minister Gerbrandy and the Rev. J. van Dorp spoke on 10 May. (State Inst. for War Doc., *Radio Oranje-uitzendingen* [Radio Orange Broadcasts].

. . . . . .

P.S. Our beloved Queen spoke to us yesterday and this evening. She is taking a holiday in order to be strong for her return to Holland. She used words like "soon, when I am back, speedy liberation, heroism, and heavy burdens."

A speech by Gerbrandy followed. A clergyman concluded with a prayer to God to take care of the Jews, the people in concentration camps, in prisons, and in Germany.

Yours, Anne

Thursday 11 May 1944.

Dear Kitty,

Because I've left my entire "junk box" including my fountain pen upstairs and since I can't disturb their siesta (half past 2) you will have to make do with a letter written in pencil.

I'm frightfully busy at the moment, and although it sounds mad, I haven't time to get through my pile of work. Shall I tell you briefly what I have got to do? Well, then, by tomorrow I must finish reading the first book of Galileo Galileï, as it has to be returned to the library. I only started it yesterday, I'm now on p. 220, it has 320 pages in all so I shall manage. Next week I have got to read Palestine at the Crossroads and the 2nd part of Galileï. Next I finished reading the first part of the life of emperor Charles V yesterday, and it's essential that I work out all the diagrams and family trees that I have collected from it. After that I have 3 pp. of foreign words gathered from various books, which have

| 50 | all got to be recited, entered and learned.

. . . . . .

Thursday, 11 May, 1944

Dear Kitty,

I'm frightfully busy at the moment, and although it sounds mad, I haven't time to get through my pile of work. Shall I tell you briefly what I have got to do? Well, then, by tomorrow I must finish reading the first part of *Galileo Galilei*, as it has to be returned to the library. I only started it yesterday, but I shall manage it.

Next week I have got to read *Palestine at the Crossroads* and the second part of *Galilei*. Next I finished reading the first part of the biography of *The Emperor Charles V* yesterday, and it's essential that I work out all the diagrams and family trees that I have collected from it. After that I have three pages of foreign words gathered from various books, which have all got to be recited, written down, and learned. Number four is that

a

Number 4 is that my film stars are all mixed up together and are simply gasping to be tidied up, however, as such a clearance would take quite a few days, and since professor Anne, as she's already said, is choked with work, the chaos will have to remain a chaos. Next Theseus, Oidipus, Peleus, Orpheus, Jason and Hercules are awaiting their turn to be arranged, as their different deeds lie crisscross in my mind like fancy threads in a dress; it's also high time Myron and Phidias had some treatment, if they are to be placed in context. Likewise it's the same as the seven and nine years' war; I'm mixing everything up together at this rate. Yes, but what can one do with such a memory! Think how forgetful I shall be when I'm 80!

Oh, something else, the bible; how long is it still going to take before I meet the bathing Susanna? And what do they mean by the guilt of Sodom and Gomorrah? Oh, there is still | such a terrible lot to find out and to learn. And in the meantime I've left Liselotte von der Pfaltz completely in the lurch.

| 51

Kitty, can you see that I'm just about bursting?

b

. . . . . .

c

my film stars are all mixed up together and are simply gasping to be tidied up; however, as such a clearance would take several days, and since Professor Anne, as she's already said, is choked with work, the chaos will have to remain a chaos.

Next Theseus, Oedipus, Peleus, Orpheus, Jason, and Hercules are awaiting their turn to be arranged, as their different deeds lie crisscross in my mind like fancy threads in a dress; it's also high time Myron and Phidias had some treatment, if they wish to remain at all coherent. Likewise it's the same with the seven and nine years' war; I'm mixing everything up together at this rate. Yes, but what can one do with such a memory! Think how forgetful I shall be when I'm eighty!

Oh, something else, the Bible; how long is it still going to take before I meet the bathing Suzanna? And what do they mean by the guilt of Sodom and Gomorrah? Oh, there is still such a terrible lot to find out and to learn. And in the meantime I've left Lisolette [Liselotte] of the Pfalz completely in the lurch.

Kitty, can you see that I'm just about bursting?

645

I mustn't forget the latest news, M.K. is back from L'aône, and arrived here with tin hat and gas mask. For the past few weeks they did nothing over there but sit in an air raid shelter, M. was terribly frightened. And then she was longing for home [. . .]*, each evening she went to the commander of the airfield and asked him for leave, the commander was annoyed and asked if she couldn't have come before instead of after supper. "Out of the question," replied M. "I don't want to have my appetite spoiled as well." [. . .]** But because she | was the only good worker on the airfield the commander didn't want to let her go, but finally he did give in to her pleas.

| 52

The radio has said more than once that certain people, girls as well as boys, women as well as men, will be punished after the war for treason. In the Dutch underground movement there is talk about concentration camps in Dutch Guinea. For M. the best solution would be to marry a German, then she would be treated like an ordinary German citizen.

They are sure here that M. is not one hundred per cent right in the head. Just take for example the queen's photograph which she carried in her handbag to L'aône and about which she had a row with a colleague. Next to the queen there was quite probably a photograph of the Führer!

*At the request of the person concerned four words have been deleted.
**At the request of the person concerned 28 words have been deleted.

. . . . . .

. . . . . .

646

| 53   Now about something else: you've known for a long time that my greatest | wish is to become a journalist someday and later on a famous writer. Whether these leanings towards greatness (insanity!) will ever materialize remains to be seen, but I certainly have the subjects in my mind. In any case, I want to publish a book entitled het Achterhuis after the war, whether I shall succeed or not, I cannot say, but my diary will be a great help. Cady's life must also be finished; this is how I've imagined the continuation of the story, after being cured in the sanatorium Cady goes back home and continues to correspond with Hans. It's 1941, and it doesn't take her long to discover that Hans leans towards the N.S.B. and because Cady is deeply concerned about the fate of the Jews and of her friend Marianne, the two draw apart. The final break comes after a meeting where they make it up again, but then Hans gets himself another girl. Cady is deeply hurt and

| 54   decides to get a good job and to be- | come a nurse. Once she has learned how to do that, she goes at the insistence of one of her father's friends to Switzerland to do nursing in a sanatorium. During her first holiday she goes to Lake Como where she runs into Hans. Hans tells her that he got married two years before to Cady's successor, but that his wife took her life during a fit of depression.

Walking beside her he suddenly remembered how much he used to love little Cady and asked for her hand again. Cady refused, though she still loved him despite herself, her pride wouldn't let her. Hans then left and years later Cady learned that he had finished up in England where he was in poor health.

When Cady was 27, she married a well-to-do farmer, Simon, she began to like him

| 55   very much, but not as much as Hans. She had two daughters and | a son, Lilian, Judith and Nico. Simon and she were happy together, but Hans always remained in the back of Cady's mind, until one night she took her leave of him in a dream.

It isn't sentimental nonsense for it's modeled on the story of Daddy's life.

yours, Anne M. Frank.

. . . . . .

Now, about something else: you've known for a long time that my greatest wish is to become a journalist someday and later on a famous writer. Whether these leanings towards greatness (or insanity?) will ever materialize remains to be seen, but I certainly have the subjects in my mind. In any case, I want to publish a book entitled *Het Achterhuis* after the war. Whether I shall succeed or not, I cannot say, but my diary will be a great help. I have other ideas as well, besides *Het Achterhuis*. But I will write more fully about them some other time, when they have taken a clearer form in my mind.*

Yours, Anne

*The last two sentences in this letter were published in Dutch but do not appear in the diary. A.J.P.

a 56   Saturday 13 May 1944.

Dearest Kitty,

It was Daddy's birthday yesterday, Mummy and Daddy have been married nineteen years. The charwoman wasn't below and the sun shone as it has never shone before in 1944. Our horse chestnut is in full bloom, chock-full of leaves and much more beautiful than last year.

Daddy received a biography of the life of Linnaeus[1] from Kleiman, a nature book from Kugler as well, "Amsterdam by the Water" from Pf., a gigantic box from v.P., beautifully done up and almost professionally decorated, containing 3 eggs, 1 bottle of beer, 1 yoghourt, and a green tie. It made our pot of syrup seem rather small. My roses smelled lovely compared with Miep's and Bep's red carnations. He was certainly spoiled.

Fifty fancy pastries arrived from Siemons, heavenly! Daddy also treated us to spiced gingerbread, beer for the gentlemen and yoghourt for the ladies. Enjoyment all around!

yours, Anne M. Frank.

b   . . . . . .

c   Saturday, 13 May, 1944

Dearest Kitty,

It was Daddy's birthday yesterday. Mummy and Daddy have been married nineteen years. The charwoman wasn't below and the sun shone as it has never shone before in 1944. Our horse chestnut is in full bloom, thickly covered with leaves and much more beautiful than last year.

Daddy received a biography of the life of Linnaeus from Koophuis, a book on nature from Kraler, *Amsterdam by the Water* from Dussel, a gigantic box from Van Daan, beautifully done up and almost professionally decorated, containing three eggs, a bottle of beer, a bottle of yoghourt, and a green tie. It made our pot of syrup seem rather small. My roses smelled lovely compared with Miep's and Elli's carnations, which had no smell, but were very pretty too. He was certainly spoiled. Fifty fancy pastries have arrived, heavenly! Daddy himself treated us to spiced gingerbread, beer for the gentlemen, and yoghourt for the ladies. Enjoyment all around!

Yours, Anne

648

Dearest Kitty,

Just for a change (as we haven't had them for so long) I want to tell you about a little discussion that went on between Mr. and Mrs. v.P. yesterday.

Mrs. v.P.: "The Germans are sure to have made the Atlantic wall very strong indeed, in the meantime, they will certainly do all in their power to hold back the English. It's amazing how strong the Germans are!"

Mr. v.P.: "Oh yes incredibly!"

Mrs. v.P.: "Ye-es!"

Mr. v.P.: "The Germans are so strong they're sure to win the war in the end in spite of everything."

Mrs. v.P.: "It's quite possible, I'm not convinced of the opposite yet."

Mr. v.P.: "I won't bother to reply any more."

Mrs. v.P.: "Still you always do answer me, you can't resist capping me every time."

Mr. v.P. "Of course not, but my replies are the bare minimum."

"Mrs. v.P.: "But still you do reply, and you always have to be in the right!⁴ Your

| 58 prophecies don't always come true | by a long shot!"

b   . . . . . .

c

Dearest Kitty,

Just for a change, as we haven't talked about them for so long, I want to tell you [about] a little discussion that went on between Mr. and Mrs. Van Daan yesterday.

Mrs. Van Daan: "The Germans are sure to have made the Atlantic Wall very strong indeed, they will certainly do all in their power to hold back the English. It's amazing how strong the Germans are!"

Mr. Van Daan. "Oh yes, incredibly."

Mrs. Van Daan: "Ye-es."

Mr. Van Daan: "The Germans are so strong they're sure to win the war in the end, in spite of everything!"

Mrs. Van Daan: "It's quite possible, I'm not convinced of the opposite yet."

Mr. Van Daan: "I won't bother to reply any more."

Mrs. Van Daan: "Still you always do answer me, you can't resist capping me every time."

Mr. Van Daan: "Of course not, but my replies are the bare minimum."

Mrs. Van Daan: "But still you do reply, and you always have to be in the right! Your prophecies don't always come true by a long shot."

a

Mr. v.P.: "They have up till now."

Mrs. v.P.: "That's not true. The invasion was to have come last year, and the Finns were to have been out of the war by now. Italy was finished in the winter, but the Russians would already have Lemberg; oh, no, I don't think much of your prophecies."

Mr. v.P.: (standing up) it's about time you shut your mouth. I'll still show you that I'm right; sooner or later you'll have had enough of it. I can't bear any more of your grousing. You're so infuriating but you'll stew in your own juice one day."

End of Part I.

I really couldn't help laughing. Mummy too, while Peter sat biting his lip, oh, those stupid grownups, they'd do better to start learning themselves, before they have so much to say to the younger generation!

Since Friday the windows have been kept open again at night.

yours, Anne M. Frank.

b

. . . . . .

c

Mr. Van Daan: "They have up till now."

Mrs. Van Daan: "That's not true. The invasion was to have come last year, and the Finns were to have been out of the war by now. Italy was finished in the winter, but the Russians would already have Lemberg; oh, no, I don't think much of your prophecies."

Mr. Van Daan (standing up): "It's about time you shut your mouth. One day I'll show you that I'm right; sooner or later you'll get enough of it. I can't bear any more of your grousing. You're so infuriating but you'll stew in your own juice one day."

End of Part I.

I really couldn't help laughing. Mummy too, while Peter sat biting his lip. Oh, those stupid grownups, they'd do better to start learning themselves, before they have so much to say to the younger generation!

Yours, Anne

650

a 59   *What the "Secret Annexe" family is interested in.*
(Systematic survey of subjects being learned and ¹reading matter).
Mr. v.P.: learns nothing. Looks up a great deal in Knaur's Lexicon. Likes to read dectective stories, medical books, exciting and trivial romances.
Mrs. v.P.: learns English by correspondence, likes to read fictional biography & some novels.
Mr. Fr.: learns English (Dickens!) and a little Latin, never reads novels but likes serious and dry-as-dust descriptions of people and countries.
Mrs. Fr.: learns English by correspondence, reads everything except detective stories.
Mr. Pf.: Learns English, Spanish and Dutch, without noticeable results. Reads everything, agrees with the majority.
Peter v.P.: Learns English, French (written)³, Dutch shorthand, German shorthand, English commercial correspondence, woodwork, economics and some arithmetic. Reads little. Some geog.⁴
Margot Fr.: Learns English, French, Latin by correspondence, English shorthand, German shorthand, Dutch shorthand, Mechanics, Trigonometry, Solid Geometry, Physics,

| 60   *Chemistry, Algebra, Geometry, English literature, | French literature, German literature, Dutch literature, Bookkeeping, Geography, Modern History, Biology, Economics, reads everything, preferably on religion and medicine*
Anne Fr.: learns French, English, German, Dutch Shorthand, Geometry, Algebra, <u>History</u>, Geography, History of Art, Mythology, biology, Bible history. Dutch literature, loves reading biographies, dull or exciting, historical books, (novels and light reading sometimes).

b   . . . . . .

c   , ...

651

Dear Kitty,

I felt rotten yesterday, really out of sorts (unusual that for Anne!) with headache, tummy-ache and anything else you can imagine, I'm much better again today, feel very hungry but I won't touch the kidney beans we're having today.

Bep went to a wedding reception on Wednesday evening, true the bride was a widow with a 2½ year old child, but that didn't mean less fun, she drank a great deal and has a bit of a hangover, everything else passed off smoothly.

The Ans Broks danger has been staved off until next Monday, perhaps it can still be averted altogether. Miep has brought us two white blouses, the ones that have been with the seamstress for a year, the new one has turned out very nice, with a lace border on the front, sleeves and collar. The K.s are having the old trouble again, M. is never at home, must be that attractive Eindhoven, [. . .].* M. has written a rude letter to the commander in L'aône | saying that she can't come back until she gets new shoes, because she can't go around in such worn out rubbish. All goes well with Peter and me. The poor boy seems to need a little love even more than I do, he blushes every evening when he gets his good-night kiss and simply begs for another. I wonder if I'm a good substitute for Boche? I don't mind, he is so happy now that he knows that someone loves him. After my laborious conquest I've got the situation a bit more in hand now, but I don't think my love has cooled off, he's a darling, but I soon closed up my inner self from him, if he wants to force the lock again he'll have to work a good deal harder than before!

yours, Anne M. Frank.

| 62

---

*At the request of the person concerned 31 words have been deleted.

. . . . . .

Friday, 19 May, 1944

Dear Kitty,

I felt rotten yesterday, really out of sorts (unusual for Anne!), with tummy-ache and every other imaginable misery. I'm much better again today, feel very hungry, but I'd better not touch the kidney beans we're having today.

All goes well with Peter and me. The poor boy seems to need a little love even more than I do. He blushes every evening when he gets his good-night kiss and simply begs for another. I wonder if I'm a good substitute for Boche? I don't mind, he is so happy now that he knows that someone loves him.

After my laborious conquest I've got the situation a bit more in hand now, but I don't think my love has cooled off. He's a darling, but I soon closed up my inner self from him. If he wants to force the lock again he'll have to work a good deal harder than before!

Yours, Anne

a

Dear Kitty,

At long last after a great deal of reflection I have started my "Achterhuis," in my head it is as good as finished, although it won't go as quickly as that really, if it ever comes off at all.

| 63   Last evening I came downstairs from the attic and | as I entered the room saw at once the lovely vase of carnations lying on the floor, Mummy down on hands and knees mopping up and Margot fishing up my papers from the floor. "What's happened here?" I asked, full of misgivings and, not even waiting for their answer, tried to sum up the damage from a distance. My whole portfolio of family trees, writing books, textbooks, everything was drenched. I nearly wept and was so worked up that I began to speak in German, I can hardly remember what I said but Margot said that I let fly something about "incalculable loss, schrecklich, entzetslich, nie zu ergänzen," and still more. Daddy burst out laughing, Mummy and Margot joined in, but I could have cried over all the toil that was wasted, and the diagrams I'd so carefully worked out.

b

. . .

c

Saturday, 20 May, 1944

Dear Kitty,

Last evening I came downstairs from the attic and as I entered the room saw at once the lovely vase of carnations lying on the floor, Mummy down on hands and knees mopping up and Margot fishing up some [my] papers from the floor.

"What's happened here?" I asked, full of misgivings and, not even waiting for their answer, tried to sum up the damage from a distance. My whole portfolio of family trees, writing books, textbooks, everything was soaked. I nearly wept and was so worked up that I can hardly remember what I said, but Margot said that I let fly something about "incalculable loss, frightful, terrible, can never be repaired," and still more. Daddy burst out laughing, Mummy and Margot joined in, but I could have cried over all the toil that was wasted, and the diagrams I'd so carefully worked out.

653

On closer inspection the incalculable loss" didn't turn out to be quite as bad as I thought. I carefully sorted out all the papers that were stuck together and separated them in the attic. After that I hung them all up on the clothes lines to dry. It was a funny sight and I couldn't help laughing myself, Maria de Medici beside Charles the Fifth, William of Orange and Marie Antoinette, it's a "racial outrage" was Mr. v. Pels's joke on the

| 64 subject. After I'd entrusted my pamphlets into Peter's care | I went downstairs again.

"Which books are gone?" I asked Margot who was looking them over. "Algebra," Margot said. I hurried to her, but unfortunately not even the Algebra book was spoiled.

I wish it had fallen right in the vase, I've never loathed any other book so much as that one. There are the names of at least twenty girls in the front all previous owners; it is old, yellow, full of scribbles, crossings out and improvements. If I'm ever in a really very wicked mood I'll tear the blasted thing to pieces!

yours, Anne M. Frank.

. . . . . .

On closer inspection the "incalculable loss" didn't turn out to be as bad as I'd thought. I carefully sorted out all the papers that were stuck together and separated them in the attic. After that I hung them all up on the clothes lines to dry. It was a funny sight and I couldn't help laughing myself. Maria de Medici beside Charles V, William of Orange and Marie Antoinette; it's a "racial outrage," was Mr. Van Daan's joke on the subject. After I'd entrusted my papers into Peter's care I went downstairs again.

"Which books are spoiled?" I asked Margot, who was checking up on them. "Algebra," she [Margot] said. I hurried to her side, but unfortunately not even the algebra book was spoiled. I wish it had fallen right in the vase; I've never loathed *any* other book so much as that one. There are the names of at least twenty girls in the front, all previous owners; it is old, yellow, full of scribbles and improvements. If I'm ever in a really very wicked mood, I'll tear the blasted thing to pieces!

Yours, Anne

654

a

Monday 22 May 1944.

Dear Kitty,

On May 20th Daddy lost 5 bottles of yoghourt, having had a bet with Mrs. v.P. The invasion still hasn't come yet, it's no exaggeration to say that all Amsterdam, all Holland, yes, the whole west coast of Europe, right down to Spain talks about the invasion day and night, debates about it, makes bets, and . . . . . hopes.

| 65   The suspense is rising to its peak; by no means all those we regard as "good" Dutch | have stuck to their faith in the English; by no means everyone thinks the English bluff a masterly piece of strategy, oh no the people want to see deeds at last, great, heroic deeds.

Nobody sees beyond his own nose, no one thinks that the English are fighting for their own land and their own people; everyone thinks that it's their duty to save Holland as quickly and as well as they can. What obligations do the English really have?[4] how have all the Dutch earned the generous help that they seem so explicitly to expect? Oh no, the Dutch will have made a big mistake, the English, in spite of all their bluff, are certainly no more to blame than all the other countries great and small which are not under occupation. The English really won't apologize, they were sleeping while Germany was rearming, but all the other countries, especially those that bordered on Germany, also slept. You don't get anywhere by following an ostrich policy, England and the whole world have seen that only too well now, and they all, one by one, England no less than · the rest, will have to pay dearly for it.

b

. . . . . .

c

Monday, 22 May, 1944

Dear Kitty,

On May 20th Daddy lost five bottles of yoghurt on a bet with Mrs. Van Daan. The invasion still hasn't come yet; it's no exaggeration to say that all Amsterdam, all Holland, yes, the whole west coast of Europe, right down to Spain, talks about the invasion day and night, debates about it, and makes bets on it and . . . hopes.

The suspense is rising to a climax. By no means everyone we had regarded [By no means all those we regard] as "good" Dutch have stuck to their faith in the English; by no means everyone thinks the English bluff a masterly piece of strategy, oh no, the people want to see deeds at last, great, heroic deeds. Nobody sees beyond his own nose, no one thinks that the English are fighting for their own land and their own people, everyone thinks that it's their duty to save Holland, as quickly and as well as they can.

What obligations have the English towards us? How have the Dutch earned the generous help that they seem so explicitly to expect? Oh no, the Dutch will have made a big mistake, the English, in spite of all their bluff, are certainly no more to blame than all the other countries, great and small, which are not under occupation. The English really won't offer us their apologies, for even if we do reproach them for being asleep during the years when Germany was rearming, we cannot deny that all the other countries, especially those bordering Germany, also slept. We shan't get anywhere by following an ostrich policy. England and the whole world have seen that only too well now, and that is why, one by one, England, no less than the rest, will have to make heavy sacrifices.

No country is going to sacri- | fice its men for nothing and certainly not in the interests of another. England is not going to do that either. The invasion, with liberation and freedom, will come sometime; but England can choose the day, not all the occupied countries put together.

———

To our great horror and regret we hear that the attitude of a great many people towards us Jews has changed. We hear that there is anti-Semitism now in circles that never thought of it before. This news has affected all 8 of us very very deeply. The cause of this hatred of the Jews is understandable, even human sometimes, but not good. The Christians blame the Jews for giving secrets away to the Germans, for helping to betray them and for the fact that, through the fault of the Jews, a great many Christians have gone the way of so many others before them, and suffered terrible punishments and a dreadful fate. This is all true. But they should look at these things from both sides; would Christians behave differently in our place? Can a person, whether Jew or Christian, remain silent in the face

of German methods? Everyone knows that it is practically | impossible. Why, then, should people demand the impossible of the Jews?

It's being murmured in underground circles that the German Jews who emigrated to Holland and who are now in Poland will not be allowed to return here, they once had the right of asylum in Holland but when Hitler is gone they will have to go back to Germany again.

. . . . . .

No country is going to sacrifice its men for nothing and certainly not in the interests of another. England is not going to do that either. The invasion, with liberation and freedom, will come sometime, but England and America will appoint the day, not all the occupied countries put together.

To our great horror and regret we hear that the attitude of a great many people towards us Jews has changed. We hear that there is anti-Semitism now in circles that never thought of it before. This news has affected us all very, very deeply. The cause of this hatred of the Jews is understandable, even human sometimes, but not good. The Christians blame the Jews for giving secrets away to the Germans, for betraying their helpers and for the fact that, through the Jews, a great many Christians have gone the way of so many others before them, and suffered terrible punishments and a dreadful fate.

This is all true, but one must always look at these things from both sides. Would Christians behave differently in our place? The Germans have a means of making people talk. Can a person, entirely at their mercy, whether Jew or Christian, always remain silent [Can a person, whether Jew or Christian, remain silent in the face of German methods]? Everyone knows that is practically impossible. Why, then, should people demand the impossible of the Jews?

It's being murmured in underground circles that the German Jews who emigrated to Holland and who are now in Poland may not be allowed to return here; they once had the right of asylum in Holland, but when Hitler has gone they will have to go back to Germany again.

656

When one hears this one naturally wonders why we are carrying on with this long and difficult war. We always hear that we're all fighting together for freedom, truth and right! Is discord going to show itself while we are still fighting, is the Jew once again worth less than another? Oh, it is sad, very sad, that once more, for the umpteenth time, the old truth is confirmed: What one Christian does is his own responsibility, what one Jew does is thrown back at all Jews.

Quite honestly, I can't grasp that the Dutch, who are such a good, honest, upright people, should judge us like this, we, the most oppressed, unhappiest, perhaps the most pitiful of all peoples of the whole world.

68   I hope one thing only, and that is that this hatred of the Jews will be a passing thing, that the Dutch will show what they are after all, and that they will never totter and lose their sense of right, for this is unjust!

And if this terrible threat should actually come true, then the pitiful little collection of the Jews that remain in Holland will have to leave. We, too, shall have to move on again with our little bundles, and leave this beautiful country, which offered us such a warm welcome and which now turns its back on us.

I love Holland. I who, having no native country, had hoped that it would become my fatherland, and I still hope it will!

yours, Anne M. Frank.

. . . . . .

When one hears this one naturally wonders why we are carrying on with this long and difficult war. We always hear that we're all fighting together for freedom, truth, and right! Is discord going to show itself while we are still fighting, is the Jew once again worth less than another? Oh, it is sad, very sad, that once more, for the umpteenth time, the old truth is confirmed: "What *one* Christian does is his own responsibility, what *one* Jew does is thrown back at all Jews."

Quite honestly, I can't understand that the Dutch, who are such a good, honest, upright people, should judge us like this, we, the most oppressed, the unhappiest, perhaps the most pitiful of all peoples of the whole world.

I hope *one* thing only, and that is that this hatred of the Jews will be a passing thing, that the Dutch will show what they are after all, and that they will never totter and lose their sense of right. For anti-Semitism is unjust!

And if this terrible threat should actually come true, then the pitiful little collection of Jews that remain will have to leave Holland. We, too, shall have to move on again with our little bundles, and leave this beautiful country, which offered us such a warm welcome and which now turns its back on us.

I love Holland. I who, having no native country, had hoped that it might become my fatherland, and I still hope it will!

Yours, Anne

Thursday 25 May 1944.

Dear Kitty,

Bep is engaged! In itself the fact is not so astonishing although none of us is very happy about it. Bertus may be a steady, kind, sportsmanlike young man, but Bep doesn't really love him and for me that's reason enough to advise her not to get married.

69   Bep's only ambition is to work her way up and Bertus keeps pulling her down; he is a workingman without interests and without any urge to get ahead and I don't believe that Bep will be happy with that.

It's easy to understand why Bep wanted to bring this halfhearted business to an end; only 4 weeks ago she wrote him off but then she felt even more miserable and so she took him back again and now they are engaged.

There are a great many factors involved in this engagement, firstly her sick father, who likes Bertus a lot, secondly that she is the oldest of the Voskuyl girls and that her mother nags her about being a spinster, thirdly that she is still only 24 and that matters a great deal to Bep.

Mummy says she would have preferred it if Bep had just had an affair with him, I can't agree, I feel sorry for Bep and can understand how lonely she was. In any case, they can only get married when the war is over because Bertus does illegal things on the black market and neither of them has a penny or any kind of trousseau. What a dreary outlook

| 70   for Bep, whom | all of us wish so well. I only hope Bertus will change under her influence, or that Bep will yet find a nice man who is worthy of her!

yours, Anne M. Frank.

. . . . . .

. . . . . .

The same day.
There's something fresh every day. This morning v. Hoeven was picked up for having two Jews in his house. It is[1] a great blow to us, not only that those poor Jews are balancing on the edge of an abyss, it's terrible for v. Hoeven.

The world has turned topsy-turvy, the most respectable people are being sent off to concentration camps, prisons, and lonely cells, and the dregs that remain govern young and old, rich and poor. One person walks into the trap through the black market, a second through Jews or other people who've had to go "underground"; anyone who isn't one of the N.S.B.ers doesn't know what may happen to him from one day to another.

V. Hoeven is a great loss to us too. First it was Br. but v. Hoeven is even worse. Bep can't and isn't allowed to haul along our share of potatoes, so the only thing to do is to eat less. I will tell you how we shall do | that; but it's certainly not going to make things any pleasanter. Mummy says we shall cut out breakfast altogether, have porridge and bread for lunch, and for supper fried potatoes and possibly once or twice per week vegetables or lettuce, nothing else.
We're going to be hungry, but nothing is worse than being discovered.

yours, Anne M. Frank.

| 71

. . . . . .

Thursday, 25 May, 1944

Dear Kitty,
There's something fresh every day. This morning our vegetable man was picked up for having two Jews in his house. It's a great blow to us, not only that those poor Jews are balancing on the edge of an abyss, but it's terrible for the man himself.

The world has turned topsy-turvy, respectable people are being sent off to concentration camps, prisons, and lonely cells, and the dregs that remain govern young and old, rich and poor. One person walks into the trap through the black market, a second through helping the Jews or other people who've had to go "underground"; anyone who isn't a member of the N.S.B. doesn't know what may happen to him from one day to another.

This man is a great loss to us too. The girls can't and aren't allowed to haul along our share of potatoes, so the only thing to do is to eat less. I will tell you how we shall do that; it's certainly not going to make things any pleasanter. Mummy says we shall cut out breakfast altogether, have porridge and bread for lunch, and for supper fried potatoes and possibly once or twice per week vegetables or lettuce, nothing more. We're going to be hungry, but anything is better than being discovered.

Yours, Anne

659

Friday 26 May 1944

Dearest Kitty,

At last, at last I can sit quietly at my table in front of a crack of window and write you everything.

I feel more miserable than I have for months, even after the burglary I didn't feel so utterly broken. On the one hand[3] van Hoeven, the Jewish question, which is being discussed minutely over the whole house, the invasion delay, the bad food, the strain, the miserable atmosphere, my disappointment in Peter; and on the other hand, Bep's engagement, Whitsun reception, flowers, Kugler's birthday, fancy cakes and stories about cabarets, films and concerts. That difference, that huge difference, it's always there, one day we laugh and see the comical side of the situation, but the next | we are afraid, [4]fear, suspense and despair staring from our faces. Miep and Kugler carry the heaviest burden of us and all those in hiding, Miep in all she does, and Kugler through the enormous responsibility for the 8 of us, which is sometimes so much for him that he can hardly talk from pent-up nerves and strain. Kleiman and Bep look after us well too, but they can forget us at times, even if it's only for a few hours, or a day, or even two days. They have their own worries, Kleiman over his health, Bep over her engagement, which is not altogether rosy, but they also have their little outings, visits to friends, the whole life of ordinary people, for them the suspense is sometimes lifted, even if it is only for a short time, but for us it has never lifted for a moment, not for two years now and how long will it still keep bearing down on us with its almost unbearable, ever more oppressive hand?

. . . . . .

Friday, 26 May, 1944

Dear Kitty,

At last, at last I can sit quietly at my table in front of a crack of window and write you everything.

I feel so miserable, I haven't felt like this for months; even after the burglary I didn't feel so utterly broken. On the one hand, the vegetable man, the Jewish question, which is being discussed minutely over the whole house, the invasion delay, the bad food, the strain, the miserable atmosphere, my disappointment in Peter; and on the other hand, Elli's engagement, Whitsun reception, flowers, Kraler's birthday, fancy cakes, and stories about cabarets, films, and concerts. That difference, that huge difference, it's always there; one day we laugh and see the funny side of the situation, but the next we are afraid, fear, suspense, and despair staring from our faces. Miep and Kraler carry the heaviest burden of the eight in hiding, Miep in all she does, and Kraler through the enormous responsibility, which is sometimes so much for him that he can hardly talk from pent-up nerves and strain. Koophuis and Elli look after us well too, but they can forget us at times, even if it's only for a few hours, or a day, or even two days. They have their own worries, Koophuis over his health, Elli over her engagement, which is not altogether rosy, but they also have their little outings, visits to friends, and the whole life of ordinary people. For them the suspense is sometimes lifted, even if it is only for a short time, but for us it never lifts for a moment. We've been here for two years now; how long have we still to put up with this almost unbearable, ever increasing pressure?

The sewer is blocked again, so we mustn't run water or rather only a trickle; when we go to the w.c. we have to take a lavatory brush with us, and we keep | dirty[1] water in a large cologne pot. We can manage for today, but what if the plumber can't do the job alone, the municipality doesn't come until Tuesday. Miep sent us a currant cake, made up in the shape of a doll with the words "Happy Whitsun" on the note attached to it, it's almost as if she's ridiculing us; our present frame of mind and our uneasiness could hardly be called "happy."

The van Hoeven affair has made us more nervous, you hear sh from all sides again and we're being quieter over everything. The police forced the door there, so they could do it to us too! If one day we too should. . . . . . no, I mustn't write it down, but I can't put the question out of my mind today. On the contrary all the fear I've already been through seems to face me again in all its frightfulness.

This evening at 8 o'clock I had to go to the downstairs lavatory all alone; there was no one down there, as everyone was listening to the radio; I wanted to be brave, but it was difficult. I always feel much safer here upstairs than alone in that large, silent house; alone with the mysterious clattering noises from upstairs and the tooting of motor horns in the street, I have to hurry for I start to quiver if I begin thinking about the | situation.

. . . . . .

The sewer is blocked, so we mustn't run water, or rather only a trickle, when we go to the W.C. we have to take a lavatory brush with us, and we keep dirty water in a large Cologne pot. We can manage for today, but what do we do if the plumber can't do the job alone? The municipal scavenging service doesn't come until Tuesday.

Miep sent us a currant cake, made up in the shape of a doll with the words "Happy Whitsun" on the note attached to it. It's almost as if she's ridiculing us; our present frame of mind and our uneasiness could hardly be called "happy." The affair of the vegetable man has made us more nervous, you hear "ssh, shh" from all sides again, and we're being quieter over everything. The police forced the door there, so they could do it to us too! If one day we too should . . . no, I mustn't write it, but I can't put the question out of my mind today. On the contrary, all the fear I've already been through seems to face me again in all its frightfulness.

This evening at eight o'clock I had to go to the downstairs lavatory all alone; there was no one down there, as everyone was listening to the radio; I wanted to be brave, but it was difficult. I always feel much safer here upstairs than alone downstairs in that large, silent house; alone with the mysterious muffled noises from upstairs and the tooting of motor horns in the street. I have to hurry for I start to quiver if I begin thinking about the situation.

661

a

Miep has become much nicer and warmer towards us after her talk with Daddy. But I haven't told you about that. One afternoon Miep came to Daddy with a red face and asked him straight out if we thought that they were contaminated with anti-Semitism as well. Daddy was terribly shocked and talked her out of it completely, but a little of Miep's suspicion still lingers. They are fetching and carrying more for us, take more interest in our troubles, although we certainly mustn't ever be a nuisance to them. Oh what very good people they really are!

Again and again I ask myself, would it not have been better for us all if we had not gone into hiding, and if we were dead now and not going through all this misery, especially as we should be sparing the others. But we all shrink away from that too, for we still love life; we haven't yet forgotten the voice of nature, we still hope, hope about everything.

| 75   I hope something will happen soon now, shooting | if need be—nothing can crush us more than this restlessness, let the end come, even if it is hard; then at least we shall know whether we are finally going to win through or go under.

yours, Anne M. Frank.

b   . . . . . .

c

Again and again I ask myself, would it not have been better for us all if we had not gone into hiding, and if we were dead now and not going through all this misery, especially as we shouldn't be running our protectors into danger any more. But we all recoil from these thoughts too, for we still love life; we haven't yet forgotten the voice of nature, we still hope, hope about everything. I hope something will happen soon now, shooting if need be—nothing can crush us *more* than this restlessness. Let the end come, even if it is hard; then at least we shall know whether we are finally going to win through or go under.

Yours, Anne

662

Wednesday 31 May 1944.

Dear Kitty,

It was so frightfully hot on Saturday, Sunday, Monday and Tuesday that I simply couldn't hold a fountain pen in my hand, that's why it was impossible to write to you. The drains went phut again on Friday, were mended again on Saturday, Mrs. Kleiman came to see us in the afternoon and told us masses about Jopie and her being in the same hockey club as Jacque van Maarssen. On Sunday Bep came to make sure no one had broken in and stayed for breakfast, on Whit Monday Mr. Gies acted as the hide-out watchman and finally on Tuesday the windows could be opened again at last. There's seldom been such a beautiful and warm, one can even say hot, Whitsun. The heat here in the "Secret Annexe" is terrible, I will briefly describe these warm days by giving you a sample of the sort of complaints that arise:

76   ¹Saturday: "Lovely, what perfect weather, we all said in the morning, "if only² it wasn't quite so warm" in the afternoon when the windows had to be closed.

Sunday: "It's positively unbearable, this heat, the butter's melting, there's not a cool spot anywhere in the house, the bread's getting so dry, the milk's going sour, windows can't be opened, and we, wretched rejects, sit here suffocating while other people enjoy their Whitsun holiday," all this from Mrs. v.P.

Monday: "My feet hurt me, I haven't got any thin clothes, I can't wash the dishes in this heat," complaints from early morning till late at night, it was extremely unpleasant.

I still can't put up with heat and am glad that there's a stiff breeze today, and yet the sun still shines.

yours, Anne M. Frank.

. . . . . .

Wednesday, 31 May, 1944

Dear Kitty,

It was so frightfully hot on Saturday, Sunday, Monday, and Tuesday that I simply couldn't hold a fountain pen in my hand. That's why it was impossible to write to you. The drains went phut again on Friday, were mended again on Saturday; Mr. Koophuis came to see us in the afternoon and told us masses about Corry and her being in the same hockey club as Jopie.

On Sunday Elli came to make sure no one had broken in and stayed for breakfast, on Whit Monday Mr. Van Santen acted as the hide-out watchman, and, finally, on Tuesday the windows could be opened again at last.

There's seldom been such a beautiful, warm, one can even say hot, Whitsun. The heat here in the "Secret Annexe" is terrible; I will briefly describe these warm days by giving you a sample of the sort of complaints that arise:

Saturday: "Lovely, what perfect weather," we all said in the morning. "If only it wasn't quite so warm," in the afternoon when the windows had to be closed.

Sunday: "It's positively unbearable, this heat. The butter's melting, there's not a cool spot anywhere in the house, the bread's getting so dry, the milk's going sour, windows can't be opened, and we, wretched outcasts, sit here suffocating while other people enjoy their Whitsun holiday."

Monday: "My feet hurt me, I haven't got any thin clothes. I can't wash the dishes in this heat," all this from Mrs. Van Daan. It was extremely unpleasant.

I still can't put up with heat and am glad that there's a stiff breeze today, and yet the sun still shines.

Yours, Anne

Friday 2 June 1944.

Dearest Kitty,

"Anyone going up to the attic must take a large umbrella, preferably a gentleman's!"
That's for sheltering from the rain coming down. There is a saying: "High and dry, safe
| 77   and sound," | but that obviously doesn't apply to wartime (gunfire) and to people in hiding
(cat's box!) In fact Mouschi has been making it something of a habit to do his business
on some newspapers or between a crack in the floor boards, so that not only the fear of
making a clatter but the even greater dread of an apalling stench are very well founded.
If I add that the new Moortje in the warehouse suffers from the same complaint, then
everyone who has ever owned an uncivilized cat can form an idea of the sort of smells
other than pepper and thyme that are wafting about our house.

Apart from that I have a brand-new prescription against gunfire: During particularly
loud bangs hasten to the nearest wooden stairs, run up and down a few times and make
sure that you fall gently downstairs at least once. What with the scratches and the noise
of the running + falling, you are too busy to listen to the gunfire let alone worry about
it. The writer of these lines has certainly used this ideal recipe with success!

yours, Anne M. Frank.

. . . . . .

. . . . . .

Monday 5 June 1944,

Dear Kitty,

Fresh "Secret Annexe" troubles, a quarrel between Pf. and Fr. over the sharing out of the butter. Pf.'s capitulation. Mrs. v.P. and the latter very thick, flirtations, kisses and friendly little laughs, Pf. is beginning to long for women.

The v.P.s don't see why we should bake gingerbread for Kugler's birthday because we don't get any to eat ourselves. What pettiness. Tempers bad upstairs. Mrs. v.P. has got a cold. Pf. was caught with brewer's yeast tablets, while we don't get any.

The Fifth Army has taken Rome, the city has been spared devastation by both armies and air forces, and is undamaged. Tremendous propaganda for Hitler.

Very few vegetables and potatoes, a load of bread has gone rotten. Little Scraggy (name of the new warehouse cat) can't stand the pepper. She uses the cat's box as her bed and the wood wool packaging as a w.c. Impossible to keep.

Bad weather. Bombardments against the French West coast and the Pas de Calais continue.

Kleiman is about to have a new stomach operation. Dollars can't be sold, gold even less, we can see the bottom of our black chest, what are we going to live on next month?

yours, Anne M. Frank.

. . . . . .

Monday, 5 June, 1944

Dear Kitty,

Fresh "Secret Annexe" troubles, a quarrel between Dussel and the Franks over something very trivial: the sharing out of the butter. Dussel's capitulation. Mrs. Van Daan and the latter very thick, flirtations, kisses and friendly little laughs. Dussel is beginning to get longings for women. The Fifth Army has taken Rome. The city has been spared devastation by both armies and air forces, and is undamaged. Very few vegetables and potatoes. Bad weather. Heavy bombardments against the French coast and Pas de Calais continue.

Yours, Anne

Tuesday 6 June 1944.[1]

Dearest Kitty,

"This is the day,"* came the announcement over the English news at 12 o'clock and quite rightly "this is the day,"* the invasion has begun!

The English gave the news at 8 o'clock this morning: Calais, Boulogne, Le Havre and Cherbourg, also the Pas de Calais (as usual) were heavily bombarded. Moreover, as a safety measure for all occupied territories, all people who live within a radius of thirty-five km. from the coast are warned to be prepared for bombardments. If possible the English will drop pamphlets one hour beforehand.

According to German news, English parachute troops have landed on the French coast. English landing craft are in battle with the German Navy. So says the B.B.C.

| 80   Conclusion during the "Annexe" breakfast at 9 o' | clock: This is just a trial landing like Dieppe 2 years ago.

English broadcast in German, Dutch, French, etc. at ten o'clock: The invasion has begun!—that means the "real" invasion.

English broadcast in German at eleven o'clock, speech by the Supreme Commander, General Dwight Eisenhower.

The English news at twelve o'clock in English: "This is the day."* General Eisenhower said to the French people: "Stiff fighting will come now, but after this the victory. The year 1944 is the year of the complete victory, good luck."*

---

*Anne's English. A.J.P.

. . . . . .

Tuesday, 6 June, 1944

Dear Kitty,

"This is D-day," came the announcement over the English news and quite rightly, "this is the day."* The invasion has begun!

The English gave the news at eight o'clock this morning: Calais, Boulogne, Le Havre, and Cherbourg, also the Pas de Calais (as usual), were heavily bombarded. Moreover, as a safety measure for all occupied territories, all people who live within a radius of thirty-five kilometers from the coast are warned to be prepared for bombardments. If possible, the English will drop pamphlets one hour beforehand.

According to German news, English parachute troops have landed on the French coast, English landing craft are in battle with the German Navy, says the B.B.C.

We discussed it over the "Annexe" breakfast at nine o'clock: Is this just a trial landing like Dieppe two years ago?

English broadcast in German, Dutch, French, and other languages at ten o'clock: "The invasion has begun!"—that means the "real" invasion. English broadcast in German at eleven o'clock, speech by the Supreme Commander, General Dwight Eisenhower.

The English news at twelve o'clock in English: "This is D-day." General Eisenhower said to the French people: "Stiff fighting will come now, but after this the victory. The year 1944 is the year of complete victory; good luck."*

---

*Original English.

a

English news in English at 1 o'clock: (translated) 11,000 planes stand ready, and are flying to and fro non-stop, landing troops and attacking behind the lines; 4,000 landing boats + the smaller craft are plying incessantly between Cherbourg and Le Havre. English and American armies are already engaged in hard fighting. Speeches by Gerbrandy, by the Prime Minister of Belgium, king Haackon of Norway, De Gaul of France, the king | of England, and last, but not least, Churchil.

| 81

Great commotion in the "Secret Annexe." Would the long-awaited liberation about which so much has been said, but which still seems too wonderful, too much like a fairy tale, ever come true. Could we be granted victory this year, this 1944? We don't know yet, but hope lives on; it gives us fresh courage, it makes us strong again. Since we must put up bravely with all the fears, privations, and sufferings, the great thing now is to remain calm and steadfast, now we must clench our teeth rather than cry out! France, Russia, Italy, and Germany, too, can all cry out and give vent to their misery, but we haven't the right to do that yet!

b

. . . . . .

c

English news in English at one o'clock (translated): 11,000 planes stand ready, and are flying to and fro non-stop, landing troops and attacking behind the lines; 4000 landing boats, plus small craft, are landing troops and matériel between Cherbourg and Le Havre incessantly. English and American troops are already engaged in hard fighting. Speeches by Gerbrandy, by the Prime Minister of Belgium, King Haakon of Norway, De Gaulle of France, the King of England, and last, but not least, Churchill.

Great commotion in the "Secret Annexe"! Would the long-awaited liberation that has been talked of so much, but which still seems too wonderful, too much like a fairy tale, ever come true? Could we be granted victory this year, 1944? We don't know yet, but hope is revived within us; it gives us fresh courage, and makes us strong again. Since we must put up bravely with all the fears, privations, and sufferings, the great thing now is to remain calm and steadfast. Now more than ever we must clench our teeth and not cry out. France, Russia, Italy, and Germany, too, can all cry out and give vent to their misery, but we haven't the right to do that yet!

667

a

| 82

Oh, Kitty, the best part of the invasion is that I have the feeling that friends are approaching. We have been oppressed by those terrible Germans for so long, they have had their knives so at our throats, and now friends and delivery are all before us! | Now it doesn't concern the Jews any more; no, it concerns Holland, Holland and all occupied Europe. Perhaps, Margot says, I may yet be able to go back to school in September or October.

yours, Anne M. Frank.

P.S. I'll keep you up to date with all the latest news!

Anne.

This morning[1] *and also during the night straw dolls and dummies were dropped from the air behind the German positions, these dolls exploited* as soon as they hit the ground. Many paratroopers landed as well, they were all painted black so as not to attract attention at night. At 6 o'clock in the morning the first vehicles were landed after the coast had been bombarded during the night with 5,000,000 kg. of bombs. 20,000 airplanes were in action today. The German coastal batteries were all put out of action during the landing; a small bridgehead has already been formed, everything is going well, although the weather is bad.*

The army and the people are "one will and one hope."**

Anne.

---

*Anne's error in Dutch. A.J.P.
**Quotation in English. A.J.P.

b

. . . . . .

c

Oh, Kitty, the best part of the invasion is that I have the feeling that friends are approaching. We have been oppressed by those terrible Germans for so long, they have had their knives so at our throats, that the thought of friends and delivery fills us with confidence!

Now it doesn't concern the Jews any more; no, it concerns Holland and all occupied Europe. Perhaps, Margot says, I may yet be able to go back to school in September or October.

Yours, Anne

P.S. I'll keep you up to date with all the latest news!

668

Friday 9 June 1944.

Dear Kitty,

Super-duper news of the invasion. The Allies have taken Bayeuth, a small village on the French coast, and are now fighting for Caen. It is obvious that they intend to cut off the peninsula where Cherbourg lies. Every evening war correspondents give news from the battle front, telling us of the difficulties, courage and enthusiasm of the army, they report the most incredible stories, also some of the wounded who are already back in England again came to the microphone. The air force are up all the time in spite of the miserable weather. We heard over the B.B.C. that Churchil wanted to set out with the troops on D-day, however, Eisenhower and the other generals managed to get him out of the idea. Just think of it, what pluck he has for such an old man, he must be seventy at least.

The excitement here has worn off a bit; still, we're hoping that the war will be over at the end of the year, it'll be about time too. Mrs. v.P.'s grizzling is absolutely unbearable; now she can't any longer drive us crazy | over the invasion, she nags us the whole day long about the bad weather, it really would be nice to dump her in a bucket of cold water and put her up in the loft!

. . . . . .

Friday, 9 June, 1944

Dear Kitty,

Super news of the invasion. The Allies have taken Bayeux, a small village on the French coast, and are now fighting for Caen. It's obvious that they intend to cut off the peninsular [peninsula] where Cherbourg lies. Every evening war correspondents give news from the battle front, telling us of the difficulties, courage, and enthusiasm of the army; they manage to get hold of the most incredible stories. Also some of the wounded who are already back in England again came to the microphone. The air force are up all the time in spite of the miserable weather. We heard over the B.B.C. that Churchill wanted to land with the troops on D-day, however, Eisenhower and the other generals managed to get him out of the idea. Just think of it, what pluck he has for such an old man—he must be seventy at least.

The excitement here has worn off a bit; still, we're hoping that the war will be over at the end of this year. It'll be about time too! Mrs. Van Daan's grizzling is absolutely unbearable; now she can't any longer drive us crazy over the invasion, she nags us the whole day long about the bad weather. It really would be nice to dump her in a bucket of cold water and put her up in the loft.

a   —

The whole of the "Secret Annexe" except v.P. and Peter have read the trilogy "Hungarian Rhapsody"; this book deals with the life history of the composer, virtuoso and child prodigy Frans Liszt. It is a very interesting book, but in my opinion there is a bit too much about women in it; in his time Liszt was not only the greatest and most famous pianist, but also the greatest ladies' man right up to the age of 70. He lived with the Duchess Marie[2] d'Agoult, Princess Caroline[3] Sayn-Wittgenstein, the dancer Lola Montez, the Pianist Agnes Kingworth, the pianist Sophie Menter, Princess Olga Janina, Baroness Olga Meyendorff, the actress Lilla what's-her-name etc. etc. it is just endless. The parts[4] of the book that deal with music and other arts[5] are much more interesting, among those mentioned are: Schumann & Clara Wieck, Hector Berlioz, Johannes Brahms, Beethoven, | 85 Joachim, | Richard Wagner, Hans von Bülow, Anton Rubinstein, Frederic Chopin, Victor Hugo, Honoré de Balzac, Hiller, Hummel, Czerny, Rossini, Cherubini, Paganini, Mendelsohn, etc. etc.

Liszt was personally a fine man, very generous and modest about himself though exceptionally vain, he helped everyone, his art was everything to him, he was mad about cognac and about women, could not bear to see tears, was a gentleman, would never refuse to do anyone a favor, didn't care about money, loved religious liberty and world freedom.

yours, Anne M. Frank.

b   . . . . . .

c

The whole of the "Secret Annexe" except Van Daan and Peter have read the trilogy *Hungarian Rhapsody*. This book deals with the life history of the composer, virtuoso, and child prodigy, Franz Liszt. It is a very interesting book, but in my opinion there is a bit too much about women in it. In his time Liszt was not only the greatest and most famous pianist, but also the greatest ladies' man—right up to the age of seventy. He lived with the Duchess Marie d'Agould [d'Agoult], Princess Caroline Sayn-Wittgenstein, the dancer Lola Montez, the pianist Agnes Kingworth, the pianist Sophie Menter, Princess Olga Janina, Baroness Olga Meyendorff, the actress Lilla what's-her-name, etc., etc.; it is just endless. The parts of the book that deal with music and art are much more interesting. Among those mentioned are Schumann, Clara Wieck, Hector Berlioz, Johannes Brahms, Beethoven, Joachim, Richard Wagner, Hans von Bülow, Anton Rubinstein, Frédéric Chopin, Victor Hugo, Honoré de Balzac, Hiller, Hummel, Czerny, Rossini, Cherubini, Paganini, Mendelssohn, etc., etc.

Liszt was personally a fine man, very generous, and modest about himself though exceptionally vain. He helped everyone, his art was everything to him, he was mad about cognac and about women, could not bear to see tears, was a gentleman, would never refuse to do anyone a favor, didn't care about money, loved religious liberty and world freedom.

Yours, Anne

a   Suggested by an article by Prof. Dr. Sleeswijk in the Telegraaf, on bacteria and kissing.*

The Kissing Peril.
Professor Sleeswijk's sound advice:
From all kissing henceforth cease
Lest unwittingly you spread
The dreaded Sore-Throat Germ Disease
Kiss no baby in its cradle,
Nor give any a caress;

86 *As if love were now on ration,*
Daily growing less and less.
For platoons of deadly microbes
Ever ready to attack:
Travel by their millions from him
In a kiss to her and back.

- - - - - - - - - - - - - - - - - -

Let me tell you, dear Professor,
That the theory you provide
Is most perfect, but the practice
Has a much more complex side.
People sometimes have the outlook
Of the hardened fatalist:
Taking chances on bronchitis,
Rather than forgo a kiss.
They prefer themselves to please,
The more so as hygienic measures
Though a barrier to disease
Do not compensate for pleasures.
If we put it to the vote
Of old and young and big and small:
Asking what they think of kissing,
Would they like a kiss at all,
I am sure that of the voters

87 *Most would signify the view:*
He who seeks a plover's egg,
A little hardship must go through. . . . .

Clinge Doorenbos.

---

*This article was published in *De Telegraaf* on 7 June 1944 and Clinge Doorenbos's poem followed on 8 June in the same paper.

b   . . . . . .

c   . . . . . .

a

Tuesday 13 June 1944.

Dear Kit,

My birthday has gone by again, so now I'm fifteen. I received quite a lot of presents.

the 5 Springer books, a set of underwear, two belts, a handkerchief, two yoghourts, a pot of jam, 2 Honey cakes, (small size) book on botany from Mummy and Daddy, a plated bracelet from Margot, a Patria book from the v.P.s, biomalt and sweet peas from Pf., sweets from Miep, sweets and exercise books from Bep and, the high spot of all the book Maria Theresa and 3 slices of full-cream cheese from Kugler. A lovely bunch of peonies from Peter; the poor boy took a lot of trouble to try and find something but didn't have any luck.

88   There's still excellent news of the invasion in spite of the wretched [weather], the countless gales, heavy rains, and high sea. Yesterday Churchil, Smutz, Eisenhower and Arnold visited French villages which have been conquered and liberated. The torpedo boat that Churchil was in shelled the coast, he appears, like so many men, not to know what fear is; makes me envious!

b   . . . . . .

c

Tuesday, 13 June, 1944

Dear Kitty,

Another birthday has gone by, so now I'm fifteen. I received quite a lot of presents.

All five parts of Sprenger's [Springer's] *History of Art*, a set of underwear, [two belts,] a handkerchief, two bottles of yoghourt, a pot of jam, a spiced gingerbread cake, and a book on botany from Mummy and Daddy, a double bracelet [plated bracelet] from Margot, a book from the Van Daans, [biomalt and] sweet peas from Dussel, sweets and exercise books from Miep and Elli and, the high spot of all, the book *Maria Theresa* and three slices of full-cream cheese from Kraler. A lovely bunch of peonies from Peter; the poor boy took a lot of trouble to try and find something, but didn't have any luck.

There's still excellent news of the invasion, in spite of the wretched weather, countless gales, heavy rains, and high seas.

Yesterday Churchill, Smuts, Eisenhower, and Arnold visited French villages which have been conquered and liberated. The torpedo boat that Churchill was in shelled the coast. He appears, like so many men, not to know what fear is—makes me envious!

672

a

It's difficult for us to judge from our secret redoubt how people outside have reacted to the news. Undoubtedly people are pleased that the idle (!) English have rolled up their sleeves and are doing something at last. They don't realize how unfair they are when they keep saying they don't want to have an English occupation. This sort of argument boils down to saying that the English must fight, struggle and sacrifice their sons for the Netherlands and other occupied countries. The English must not stay in the Netherlands, must offer their most abject apologies to all the occupied countries, must return India to its original | owners and then return weakened and impoverished to England!

| 89

Poor idiots, who argue like that, but as I've already said, many Netherlanders must be counted among such idiots. What, I wonder, would have become of the Netherlands and her neighbors had England signed a peace with Germany, which she could have done on so many occasions? The Netherlands would have become German and that would have been that!

Any Dutch people who still look down on the English, scoff at England and her government of old gentlemen, call the English cowards, and yet hate the Germans, deserve a good shaking, perhaps it would put some sense into their woolly brains!

b

. . . . . .

c

It's difficult for us to judge from our secret redoubt how people outside have reacted to the news. Undoubtedly people are pleased that the idle (?) [(!)] English have rolled up their sleeves and are doing something at last. Any Dutch people who still look down on the English, scoff at England and her government of old gentlemen, call the English cowards, and yet hate the Germans deserve a good shaking. Perhaps it would put some sense into their woolly brains.

I hadn't had a period for over two months, but it finally started again on Saturday. Still, in spite of all the unpleasantness and bother, I'm glad it hasn't failed me any longer.

Yours, Anne

673

| 90 My head is haunted by so many wishes and thoughts, accusations and reproaches. I'm really not as conceited as so many people seem to think, I know my own faults and shortcomings better than anyone does, but the difference is that I also know that I want | to improve, shall improve and have already improved a great deal!

Why is it then, I so often ask myself, that everyone still thinks I'm so terribly knowing and forward? Am I so knowing? Is it that I really am, or that maybe the others aren't? That sounds queer, I realize now, but I shan't cross out the last sentence, because it really isn't so crazy. Everyone knows that Mrs. v.P. and Pf., my chief accusers, are both completely unintelligent. I might as well put it plainly and say "stupid!" Stupid people usually can't take it if others do better than they do; the best examples are indeed those two stupid people, Mrs. v.P. and Pf. Mrs. v.P. thinks I'm stupid because being unwell doesn't make me suffer as frightfully as she does, she thinks I'm forward because she's even more so; she thinks my dresses are too short, because hers are even shorter and that's also the reason that she thinks I'm knowing, because she's two times worse about joining in over

| 91 subjects about which she knows absolutely | nothing; the same is true of Pf. But one of my favorite sayings is: "there's no smoke without fire," and I readily admit that I'm knowing.

Now the trying part about me is that I scold myself more and am much harder on myself than anyone else; then if Mummy adds her share of advice the pile of sermons

......

Wednesday, 14 June, 1944

Dear Kitty,

My head is haunted by so many wishes and thoughts, accusations and reproaches. I'm really not as conceited as so many people seem to think, I know my own faults and shortcomings better than anyone, but the difference is that I also know that I want to improve, shall improve, and have already improved a great deal.

Why is it then, I so often ask myself, that everyone still thinks I'm so terribly knowing and forward? Am I so knowing? Is it that I really am, or that maybe the others aren't? That sounds queer, I realize now, but I shan't cross out the last sentence, because it really isn't so crazy. Everyone knows that Mrs. Van Daan, one of my chief accusers, is unintelligent. I might as well put it plainly and say "stupid." Stupid people usually can't take it if others do better than they do.

Mrs. Van Daan thinks I'm stupid because I'm not quite so lacking in intelligence as she is; she thinks I'm forward because she's even more so; she thinks my dresses are too short, because hers are even shorter. And that's also the reason that she thinks I'm knowing, because she's twice as bad about joining in over subjects she knows absolutely nothing about. But one of my favorite sayings is "There's no smoke without fire," and I readily admit that I'm knowing.

Now the trying part about me is that I criticize and scold myself far more than anyone else does. Then if Mummy adds her bit of advice the pile of sermons becomes so insur-

becomes so insurmountable that in my despair I become rude and start contradicting and then, of course, the old well-known Anne watchword comes back: no one understands me! This phrase sticks in my mind: I know it sounds silly, yet there is some truth in it. I often accuse myself to such an extent that I simply long for a word of comfort, for someone who could give me sound advice and also draw out some of my real self; but, alas, I keep on looking, but I haven't found anyone yet.

| 92   I know that you'll immediately think of Peter, won't you, Kit? It's like this: Peter loves me not as a lover | but as a friend, and grows more affectionate every day. But what is the mysterious something that holds us both back? I don't understand it myself.

Sometimes I think that my terrible longing for him was exaggerated, yet that's really not it, because if I don't go up to see him for two days, then I just long for him more desperately than ever before. Peter is good and he's a darling, but still there's no denying it, a lot disappoints me. Especially his dislike of religion and all his talk about food and various other things, don't appeal to me. Yet I feel quite convinced that we shall never quarrel now that we've made that straightforward agreement together, Peter is a peace-loving person; he's tolerant and gives in very easily. He lets me say a lot of things to him that he would never accept from his mother, he tries most persistently to remove the

. . . . . .

mountable that in my despair I become rude and start contradicting and then, of course, the old well-known Anne watchword comes back: "No one understands me!" This phrase sticks in my mind; I know it sounds silly, yet there is some truth in it. I often accuse myself to such an extent that I simply long for a word of comfort, for someone who could give me sound advice and also draw out some of my real self; but, alas, I keep on looking, but I haven't found anyone yet.

I know that you'll immediately think of Peter, won't you, Kit? It's like this: Peter loves me not as a lover but as a friend and grows more affectionate every day. But what is the mysterious something that holds us both back? I don't understand it myself. Sometimes I think that my terrible longing for him was exaggerated, yet that's really not it, because if I don't go up to see him for two days, then I long for him more desperately than ever before. Peter is good and he's a darling, but still there's no denying that there's a lot about him that disappoints me. Especially his dislike of religion and all his talk about food and various other things don't appeal to me. Yet I feel quite convinced that we shall never quarrel now that we've made that straightforward agreement together. Peter is a peace-loving person; he's tolerant and gives in very easily. He lets me say a lot of things to him that he would never accept from his mother, he tries most persistently to keep his

675

a

| 93 blots from his copy book and to keep his innermost self to himself and why am I never allowed there? By nature he is more closed-up than I am, I agree; but | I know and from my own experience, (remember the "Anne in theory" who keeps popping up) that at some time or other even uncommunicative people long just as much, if not more, to find someone in whom they can confide.

Both Peter and I have spent our most meditative years in the "Secret Annexe." We often discuss the future, the past and the present, but as I've already said, I still seem to miss the real thing and yet I know it's there!

——

I wonder if it's because I haven't been able to poke my nose outdoors for so long that I've grown so crazy about everything to do with nature? I can perfectly well remember that there was a time when a deep blue sky, the song of the birds, moonlight and flowers could never have kept me spellbound. That's changed since I've been here, e.g. at Whitsun when it was so warm, I stayed awake on purpose until half past eleven one evening in order to have a good look at the moon for once by myself, alas, the sacrifice was all in | 94 vain, as the moon gave far too much | light and I didn't dare risk opening a window. Another time, some months ago now, I happened to be upstairs one evening when the window was open. I didn't go downstairs until the window had to be shut, the dark,

b

. . . . . .

c

things in order. And yet why should he keep his innermost self to himself and why am I never allowed there? By nature he is more closed-up than I am, I agree, but I know—and from my own experience—that at some time or other even the most uncommunicative people long just as much, if not more, to find someone in whom they can confide.

Both Peter and I have spent our most meditative years in the "Secret Annexe." We often discuss the future, the past and the present, but, as I've already said, I still seem to miss the real thing and yet I know that it's there.

Yours, Anne

Thursday, 15 June, 1944

Dear Kitty,

I wonder if it's because I haven't been able to poke my nose outdoors for so long that I've grown so crazy about everything to do with nature? I can perfectly well remember that there was a time when a deep blue sky, the song of the birds, moonlight and flowers could never have kept me spellbound. That's changed since I've been here.

At Whitsun, for instance, when it was so warm, I stayed awake on purpose until half past eleven one evening in order to have a good look at the moon for once by myself. Alas, the sacrifice was all in vain, as the moon gave far too much light and I didn't dare risk opening a window. Another time, some months ago now, I happened to be upstairs one evening when the window was open. I didn't go downstairs until the window had

676

rainy evening, the gale, the scudding clouds held me entirely in their power, it was the first time in 1½ years that I'd seen the night face to face. After that evening my longing to see it again was greater than my fear of burglars, rats and raids on the house. I went downstairs all by myself and looked outside through the private office and kitchen windows. A lot of people are fond of nature, many sleep outdoors occasionally, and people in prisons and hospitals long for the day when they will be free to enjoy the beauties of nature, but few are so shut away and isolated from that which can be shared alike by rich and poor. It's not imagination on my part when I say that to look up at the | sky, the clouds, the moon and the stars makes me calm and patient. It's a better medicine than either Valerian or bromine; Mother Nature makes me small and prepared to face every blow bravely!

It has had to be that I am only able to look at nature on odd occasions and then only through dirty net curtains hanging before very dusty windows and it's no pleasure looking through these any longer, nature is just the one thing that really must be unadulterated!

. . . . . .

to be shut. The dark, rainy evening, the gale, the scudding clouds held me entirely in their power; it was the first time in a year and a half that I'd seen the night face to face. After that evening my longing to see it again was greater than my fear of burglars, rats, and raids on the house. I went downstairs all by myself and looked outside through the windows in the kitchen and the private office. A lot of people are fond of nature, many sleep outdoors occasionally, and people in prisons and hospitals long for the day when they will be free to enjoy the beauties of nature, but few are so shut away and isolated from that which can be shared alike by rich and poor. It's not imagination on my part when I say that to look up at the sky, the clouds, the moon, and the stars makes me calm and patient. It's a better medicine than either valerian or bromine; Mother Nature makes me humble and prepared to face every blow courageously.

Alas, it has had to be that I am only able—except on a few rare occasions—to look at nature through dirty net curtains hanging before very dusty windows. And it's no pleasure looking through these any longer, because nature is just the one thing that really must be unadulterated.

Yours, Anne

A question that has been raised more than once and that gives me no inner peace is why did so many nations in the past, and often still now, treat women as inferior to men? Everyone can agree how unjust this is, but that is not enough for me, I would also like to know the cause of the great injustice!

| 96   Presumably man, thanks to his greater physical strength, achieved dominance over woman from the very start; man, who earns the money, who | begets children, who may do what he wants . . . . . It is stupid enough of women to have borne it all in silence for such a long time, since the more centuries this arrangement lasts, the more deeply rooted it becomes. Luckily schooling, work and progress have opened women's eyes. In many countries women have been granted equal rights; many people, particularly women, but also men, now realize for how long this state of affairs has been wrong, and modern women demand the right of complete independence!

But that's not all, respect for woman, that's going to have to come as well! Generally, man is held in high esteem all over the world; why shouldn't women have a share in this? Soldiers and war heroes are honored and celebrated, explorers acquire immortal fame, martyrs are revered, but how many will look upon woman as they would upon a soldier?

97   There is something in the book "The Fight for Life" that has affected me deeply, along the lines that women suffer more pain, more illness and more misery than any war hero just from giving birth to children. And what reward does woman reap for coming successfully through all this pain? She is pushed to one side should she lose her figure through giving birth, her children soon leave her, her beauty passes. Women are much braver, much more courageous soldiers, struggling and enduring pain for the continuance of mankind, than all the freedom-fighting heroes with their big mouths!

In no way do I mean by this that women should turn against childbearing, on the contrary, nature has made them like that and that is all to the good. I merely condemn all the men, and the whole system, that refuse ever to acknowledge what an important, arduous, and in the long run beautiful part, women play in society.

98   I fully agree with Paul de Kruif, the author of the above-mentioned book, when he says that men must learn that birth has ceased to be something natural and ordinary in those parts of the world we consider civilized. It's very easy for men to talk, they don't and will never have to bear the miseries of women!

I believe that the idea that a woman's duty is simply[7] to bear children will change over the centuries to come and will make way for respect and admiration for one who without complaint and a lot of talk shoulders all these burdens!

—

                                                          yours, Anne M. Frank.

b   . . . . . .

c   . . . . . .

a

Dear Kitty,

New problems: Mrs. v.P. is desperate, talks of a bullet through her head, prison, hanging | 99 and suicide. She's jealous that Peter confides in me and not her, | she's offended that Pf. doesn't enter into her flirtations with him, as she'd hoped, afraid that her husband is smoking all the fur-coat money away, she quarrels, uses abusive language, cries, pities herself, laughs and then starts a fresh quarrel again. What on earth can one do with such a foolish, blubbering specimen? No one takes her seriously, she hasn't any character, she grumbles to everyone too. The worst of it is that it makes Peter rude, Mr. v.P. irritable and Mummy cynical. Yes it's a frightful situation here! There's one golden rule to keep before you: Laugh about everything and don't bother yourself about the others! It sounds selfish, but it's honestly the only cure for anyone suffering from self-pity.

Kugler has to go digging for 4 weeks in Alkmaar, he's trying to get out of it with a doctor's certificate and a letter from Opekta.

Kleiman wants to have an operation on his stomach soon. All private telephones were | 100 cut off | at eleven o'clock last night.*

yours, Anne M. Frank.

*All non-essential telephone lines were disconnected on 15 June 1944. (*Kroniek van Amsterdam*, p. 130.)

b

. . . . . .

c

Friday, 16 June, 1944

Dear Kitty,

New problems: Mrs. Van Daan is desperate, talks about a bullet through her head, prison, hanging, and suicide. She's jealous that Peter confides in me and not her. She's offended that Dussel doesn't enter into her flirtations with him, as she'd hoped, afraid that her husband is smoking all the fur-coat money away, she quarrels, uses abusive language, cries, pities herself, laughs, and then starts a fresh quarrel again. What on earth can one do with such a foolish, blubbering specimen? No one takes her seriously, she hasn't any character, and she grumbles to everyone. The worst of it is that it makes Peter rude, Mr. Van Daan irritable, and Mummy cynical. Yes, it's a frightful situation! There's *one* golden rule to keep before you: laugh about everything and don't bother yourself about the others! It sounds selfish, but it's honestly the only cure for anyone who has to seek consolation in himself.

Kraler has received another call-up to go digging for four weeks. He's trying to get out of it with a doctor's certificate and a letter from the business. Koophuis wants to have an operation on his stomach. All private telephones were cut off at eleven o'clock yesterday.

Yours, Anne

679

Friday 23 June 1944.

Dear Kitty,

Nothing special going on here. The English have begun their big attack on Cherbourg; according to Pim and v.P. we're sure to be free by Oct. 10. The Russians are taking part in the campaign, and yesterday started their offensive near Vitebsk; it's exactly 3 years to the day since the Germans attacked.

Bep's spirits are still below zero. We've hardly got any potatoes, from now on we're going to count them out for each person everyone will know what he's getting. Miep is taking a week's early vacation on Monday. Kleiman's doctors have found nothing on the X-ray photographs, now he's torn between having an operation or letting things take their course.

yours, Anne M. Frank.

101

Tuesday 27 June 1944.

Dearest Kitty,

The whole mood has changed, everything is going wonderfully. Cherbourg, Vitebsk and Slobin fell today. There are bound to be lots of prisoners and booty. 5 German generals killed at Cherbourg, 2 captured. Now the English can land what they want now they've got a harbor; the whole Contentin Peninsula 3 weeks after the English invasion! A

......

Friday, 23 June, 1944

Dear Kitty,

Nothing special going on here. The English have begun their big attack on Cherbourg; according to Pim and Van Daan, we're sure to be free by October 10. The Russians are taking part in the campaign, and yesterday began their offensive near Vitebsk; it's exactly three years to a [the] day since the Germans attacked. We've hardly got any potatoes; from now on we're going to count them out for each person, then everyone knows what he's getting.

Yours, Anne

Tuesday, 27 June, 1944

Dearest Kitty,

The mood has changed, everything's going wonderfully. Cherbourg, Vitebsk, and Sloben fell today. Lots of prisoners and booty. Now the English can land what they want now they've got a harbor, the whole Cotentin Peninsular [Peninsula] three weeks after the tremendous achievement! In the three weeks since D-day not a day has gone by without rain and gales, both here and in France, but a bit of bad luck didn't stop the enormous strength of the English and Americans from showing, and how! Certainly the "wonder weapon" is in full swing, but of what consequence are a few scratches apart from a bit of damage in England and pages full of it in the Boche newspapers? For that matter, when they really realize in "Bocheland" that the Bolshevists really are on the way, they'll get even more jittery.

| 102

All German women and children not in military service are being evacuated to Groningen, Friesland and | Gelderland with their children.* Mussert has declared that if the invasion comes here he will put on a soldier's uniform.** Does that old fatty want to do some fighting? He could have done so in Russia before now. Some time ago Finland turned down a Peace offer, now the negotiations have just been broken off again, they'll be sorry for it later, the silly fools!

How far do you think we'll be on July 27?

yours, Anne M. Frank.

*After the invasion on 6 June 1944, Seyss-Inquart ordered the families of German citizens in the Western Netherlands to move to the east of the country. (L. de Jong, *Het Koninkrijk der Nederlanden in de Tweede Wereldoorlog.* Vol. 10 a, p. 184.)
**At a large rally of the NSB on 10 June 1944 in the Amsterdam Concertgebouw, Mussert, the Dutch Nazi leader, told his audience that if the Netherlands were invaded he would volunteer for the Wehrmacht. This announcement was greeted with derision by the underground press. (L. de Jong, *Het Koninkrijk der Nederlanden in de Tweede Wereldoorlog.* Vol. 10 a, pp. 188–90.)

. . . . . .

English invasion! A tremendous achievement! In the three weeks since D-day not a day has gone by without rain and gales, both here and in France, but a bit of bad luck didn't prevent the English and Americans from showing their enormous strength, and how! Certainly the "wonder weapon" is in full swing, but of what consequence are a few squibs apart from a bit of damage in England and pages full of it in the Boche newspapers? For that matter, when they really realize in "Bocheland" that the Bolshevists really are on the way, they'll get even more jittery.

All German women [and children] not in military service are being evacuated to Groningen, Friesland, and Gelderland with their children. Mussert* has announced that if they get as far as here with the invasion he'll put on a [soldier's] uniform. Does that old fatty want to do some fighting? He could have done so in Russia before now. Some time ago Finland turned down a peace offer, now the negotiations have just been broken off again, they'll be sorry for it later, the silly fools!

How far do you think we'll be on July 27?

Yours, Anne

*Mussert was the Dutch National Socialist leader.

Friday 30 June 1944.

Dear Kitty,

Bad weather, or bad weather from one at a strech to thirty June.* Isn't that well said!
Oh yes, I have a smattering of English already; just to show that I can, I'm reading "An
Ideal Husband" with the aid of a dictionary! War going wonderfully: B̄roboisk, Mogilef̲
and Orsa have fallen, lots of prisoners.

Everything's all right here. Tempers are improving, the superoptimists are irritating,
the v.P.s are juggling with the sugar, Bep has changed her hair style and Miep has the
week off. That's the latest news!

103   I am having some really horrible nerve-treatment and in one of my front teeth too,
it's been hurting me dreadfully and was so bad that Pf. thought I was going to faint. It
wouldn't have taken much. Mrs. v.P. promptly got toothache as well!

yours, Anne M. Frank.

P.S. We've heard from Basle that Bernd took the part of Innkeeper in Minna von Barnhelm.
Artistic temperament Mummy says.

Thursday 6 July 1944.

Dear Kitty,

It strikes fear to my heart when Peter talks of later being a criminal, or of gambling;
although it's meant as a joke, of course, it gives me the feeling that he's afraid of his own
weakness. Again and again I hear from both Margot and Peter: "Yes, if I was as strong
and plucky as you are, if I always stuck to what I wanted, if I had such persistent energy,
yes then . . . . !"

---

*Anne's English. A.J.P.

. . . . . .

Friday, 30 June, 1944

Dear Kitty,

Bad weather, or *bad weather at a stretch to the thirtieth of June.** Isn't that well said!
Oh yes, I have a smattering of English already; just to show that I can, I'm reading *An
Ideal Husband* with the aid of a dictionary. War going wonderfully! Bobroisk [Bobruysk],
Mogilef [Mogilev], and Orsa have fallen, lots of prisoners.

Everything's all right here and tempers are improving. The superoptimists are triumph-
ing. Elli has changed her hair style, Miep has the week off. That's the latest news.

Yours, Anne

Thursday, 6 July, 1944

Dear Kitty

It strikes fear to my heart when Peter talks of later being a criminal, or of gambling;
although it's meant as a joke, of course, it gives me the feeling that he's afraid of his own
weakness. Again and again I hear from both Margot and Peter: "Yes, if I was as strong
and plucky as you are, if I always stuck to what I wanted, if I had such persistent energy,
yes then . . . !"

---

*In English in the original.

| 104   I wonder if it's really a good quality not to let myself be influenced. Is it really good to follow almost entirely my own | conscience?

Quite honestly, I can't imagine how anyone can say: "I'm weak," and then remain so. After all, if you know it, why not fight against it, why not try to train your character? The answer was: "Because it's so much easier not to!" This reply rather discouraged me. Easy? Does that mean that a lazy, deceitful life is an easy life? Oh no, that can't be true, it mustn't be that people can so easily be tempted by ease . . . . and by money. I thought for a long time about the best answer to give Peter, how to get him to believe in himself and, above all, to try and improve himself; I don't know whether I've got it across though.

I've so often thought how lovely it would be to have someone's complete confidence, but now, now that I am that far, I realize how difficult it is to think what the other person is thinking and then to find the <u>right</u> answer. More especially because the very ideas of "easy" and "money" are something entirely | foreign and new to me. Peter is beginning to lean on me a bit and that mustn't happen under any circumstances. It's difficult to stand on one's own feet, but it's even more difficult to stand alone with character and soul and yet to remain constant through it all.

| 105

I'm just drifting around, have been searching for days, searching for a good argument against the terrible word "easy," something to settle it once and for all.

. . . . .

I wonder if it's really a good quality not to let myself be influenced. Is it really good to follow almost entirely my own conscience?

Quite honestly, I can't imagine how anyone can say: "I'm weak," and then remain so. After all, if you know it, why not fight against it, why not try to train your character? The answer was: "Because it's so much easier not to!" This reply rather discouraged me. Easy? Does that mean that a lazy, deceitful life is an easy life? Oh no, that can't be true, it mustn't be true, people can so easily be tempted by slackness . . . and by money.

I thought for a long time about the best answer to give Peter, how to get him to believe in himself and, above all, to try and improve himself; I don't know whether my line of thought is right though, or not.

I've so often thought how lovely it would be to have someone's complete confidence, but now, now that I'm that far, I realize how difficult it is to think what the other person is thinking and then to find the *right* answer. More especially because the very ideas of "easy" and "money" are something entirely foreign and new to me. Peter's beginning to lean on me a bit and that mustn't happen under any circumstances. A type like Peter finds it difficult to stand on his own feet, but it's even harder to stand on your own feet as a conscious, living being. Because if you do, then it's twice as difficult to steer a right path through the sea of problems and still remain constant through it all. I'm just drifting around, have been searching for days, searching for a good argument against that terrible word "easy," something to settle it once and for all.

683

How can I make
it clear to them that what appears easy and attractive will drag him down into the depths,
depths where there is no comfort to be found, no friends and no beauty, depths from
which it is almost impossible to raise oneself?

We all live but we don't know the why or the wherefore. We all live with the object
of being happy; our lives are all different and yet the same. We three have been brought
up in good circles, we have the chance to learn, the possibility of attaining something, we
have all reason to hope for much happiness, but . . . . . we must earn it for ourselves. And
| 106   that is never easy. You must work and | do good, not be lazy and gamble, if you wish to
earn happiness. Laziness may <u>appear</u> attractive, but work <u>gives</u> satisfaction.

I can't understand people who don't like work, yet that isn't the case with Peter; he
just hasn't got a fixed goal to aim at, and he thinks he's too stupid and inferior to achieve
anything. Poor Boy, he's never known what it feels like to make other people happy, and
I can't teach him that either. He has no religion, scoffs at Jesus Christ, and swears, using
the name of God; although I'm not orthodox either, it still hurts every time I see how
deserted, how scornful and how poor he really is. People who have a religion should be
glad, for not everyone has the gift of believing in heavenly things. You don't necessarily
even have to be afraid of punishment after death; purgatory, hell and heaven are things
that a lot of people can't accept, but still a religion, it doesn't matter which, keeps a

. . . . . .

How can I make it clear to him that what appears easy and attractive will drag him
down into the depths, depths where there is no comfort to be found, no friends and no
beauty, depths from which it is almost impossible to raise oneself?

We all live, but we don't know the why or the wherefore. We all live with the object
of being happy; our lives are all different and yet the same. We three have been brought
up in good circles, we have the chance to learn, the possibility of attaining something, we
have all reason to hope for much happiness, but . . . we must earn it for ourselves. And
that is never easy. You must work and do good, not be lazy and gamble, if you wish to
earn happiness. Laziness may *appear* attractive, but work *gives* satisfaction.

I can't understand people who don't like work, yet that isn't the case with Peter; he
just hasn't got a fixed goal to aim at, and he thinks he's too stupid and too inferior to
achieve anything. Poor boy, he's never known what it feels like to make other people
happy, and I can't teach him that either. He has no religion, scoffs at Jesus Christ, and
swears, using the name of God; although I'm not orthodox either, it hurts me every time
I see how deserted, how scornful, and how poor he really is.

People who have a religion should be glad, for not everyone has the gift of believing
in heavenly things. You don't necessarily even have to be afraid of punishment after death;
purgatory, hell, and heaven are things that a lot of people can't accept, but still a religion,
it doesn't matter which, keeps a person on the right path. It isn't the fear of God but

684

person on the right path. It isn't the fear of God but the upholding of | one's own honor and conscience. How noble and good everyone could be if, every evening before falling asleep, they were to recall to mind the events of the whole day and consider exactly what has been good and bad. Then, without realizing it, you try to improve yourself at the start of each new day; of course, you achieve quite a lot in the course of time. Anyone can do this, it costs nothing and is certainly very helpful. Whoever doesn't know it must learn and find by experience that "a quiet conscience makes one strong!"

yours, Anne M. Frank.

Saturday 8³ July 1944.

Dear Kitty,

Broks has been in Beverwijk and managed, just like that, to get strawberries at the auction sale. They arrived here very dusty, covered with sand, but in large quantities. No less than twenty-four trays for the office people and us + the rest for Broks himself. That very same evening we preserved the first six jars and made 8 pots of jam. The next morning Miep wanted to make jam for the office people.

108   At half past 12, front door bolted, trays fetched, Peter, Daddy, v.P. clattering on the stairs, Anne, get hot water; Margot, bring a bucket; all hands on deck! I went into the kitchen, which was chock-full, with a queer feeling in my tummy, Miep, Bep, Kleiman, Jan, Daddy, Peter the families in hiding and their supply column all mingling together, and in the middle of the day too! The curtains drawn, the windows open, the loud voices

. . . . . .

the upholding of one's own honor and conscience. How noble and good everyone could be if, every evening before falling asleep, they were to recall to their minds the events of the whole day and consider exactly what has been good and bad. Then, without realizing it, you try to improve yourself at the start of each new day; of course, you achieve quite a lot in the course of time. Anyone can do this, it costs nothing and is certainly very helpful. Whoever doesn't know it must learn and find by experience that: "A quiet conscience makes one strong!"

Yours, Anne

Saturday, 8 July, 1944

Dear Kitty,

The chief representative of the business, Mr. B., has been in Beverwijk and managed, just like that, to get strawberries at the auction sale.* They arrived here dusty, covered with sand, but in large quantities. No less than twenty-four trays for the office people and us. That very same evening we bottled [the first] six jars and made eight pots of jam. The next morning Miep wanted to make jam for the office people.

At half past twelve, no strangers in the house, front door bolted, trays fetched, Peter, Daddy, Van Daan clattering on the stairs: Anne, get hot water; Margot, bring a bucket; all hands on deck! I went into the kitchen, which was chock-full, with a queer feeling in my tummy, Miep, Elli, Koophuis, Henk, Daddy, Peter: the families in hiding and their supply column, all mingling together, and in the middle of the day too!

*It is compulsory in Holland for all growers to sell their produce at public auction.

a

and banging doors, positively gave me the jitters. Are we really still supposed to be in hiding? that's what flashed through my mind, and it gives one a very queer feeling to be able to appear in the world again. The pan was full, and I dashed upstairs again. The rest of the family was seated round the table in the kitchen busy stalk-picking—at least that's what they were supposed to be doing; more went into mouths than into the bucket. Another bucket would soon be required. Peter went to the kitchen again, there were two rings at the door, the bucket stayed where it was, Peter tore upstairs, locked the cupboard doors. We were kicking our heels impatiently, couldn't turn on a tap and the strawberries

| 109

were only half washed, but the | rule: If anyone in the house, use no water, because of the noise, was strictly maintained.

At 1 o'clock arrival of Jan, it was the postman, Peter hurried downstairs again. Ting-a-ling . . . the bell, right about turn. I go and listen to see if I can hear anyone coming, first at our cupboard door and then at the top of the stairs. Finally Peter and I both lean over the banisters like a couple of thieves, listening to the din downstairs. No strange voices. Peter goes quietly down, stops halfway and calls out: Bep. No answer, one more: Bep. Peter's voice is drowned by the din in the kitchen. He runs downstairs and goes into the kitchen. I stand looking down tensely: "Get upstairs at once Peter, v. Erp is there, clear out," it was Kleiman speaking. Peter comes upstairs sighing, the cupboard door stays closed. Finally Kugler arrives at half past 1! "Oh, Dearie me, I see nothing but strawberries, strawberries at breakfast, Jan eats strawberries, Kleiman tucks into strawberries, straw-

| 110

berries stewed by Miep, Bep picks strawberry stalks, I smell straw- | berries, must have a rest from them and go upstairs—what is being washed up here . . . . strawberries The

b

. . . . . .

c

People can't see in from outside because of the net curtains, but, even so, the loud voices and banging doors positively gave me the jitters. Are we really supposed to be in hiding? That's what flashed through my mind, and it gives one a very queer feeling to be able to appear in the world again. The pan was full, and I dashed upstairs again. The rest of the family was seated round our table in the kitchen busy stalk-picking—at least that's what they were supposed to be doing; more went into mouths than into buckets. Another bucket would soon be required. Peter went to the downstairs kitchen again—the bell rang twice; the bucket stayed where it was, Peter tore upstairs, locked the cupboard door! We were kicking our heels impatiently, couldn't turn on a tap, even though the strawberries were only half washed; the rule is: "If anyone in the house, use no water, because of the noise," was strictly maintained.

At one o'clock Henk came and told us that it was the postman. Peter hurried downstairs again. Ting-a-ling . . . the bell, right about turn. I go and listen to see if I can hear anyone coming, first at our cupboard door and then creep to the top of the stairs. Finally Peter and I both lean over the banisters like a couple of thieves, listening to the din downstairs. No strange voices, Peter sneaks down, stops halfway, and calls out: "Elli!" No answer, one more: "Elli!" Peter's voice is drowned by the din in the kitchen. He goes right down and into the kitchen. I stand looking down tensely. "Get upstairs at once, Peter, the accountant is here, clear out!" It was Koophuis speaking. Peter comes upstairs sighing, the cupboard door closes. Finally Kraler arrives at half past one. "Oh, dearie me, I see nothing but strawberries, strawberries at breakfast, [Henk eats strawberries, Koophuis tucks into strawberries,] strawberries stewed by Miep, I smell strawberries, must have a rest from them and go upstairs—what is being washed up here . . . strawberries."

a

remainder are being bottled. In the evening: two jars unsealed. Daddy quickly makes them into jam. The next morning: two more unsealed. In the afternoon: 4 unsealed. V.P. hadn't brought them to thje right temperature for sterilizing, now Daddy makes jam every evening.

We eat strawberries with our porridge, skimmed milk with strawberries, bread and butter with strawberries, strawberries for dessert, strawberries with sugar, strawberries with sand. For two whole days strawberries and nothing but strawberries, then the supply was finished or in pots and under lock and key.

"I say Anne," Margot calls out "Mrs. van Hoeven has let us have some green peas, 18 pcunds." "That's nice of her," I replied. And it certainly is, but oh, the work . . . Ugh! "You've all got to help shelling peas on Saturday morning," Mummy announced when we were at table. And, sure enough, the biggest enamel pan duly appeared this morning, | 111   filled to the brim. Shelling peas is a | boring job, but you ought to try skinning the pods. I don't think many people realize how rich in vitamins, soft and tasty the pod is when the skin on the inside has been removed. However, even more important than the three above-named advantages is the fact that the quantity which can be eaten is about 3 times as much as you get when you only eat the peas. It's an exceptionally precise, finicky job

b

. . . . . .

c

The remainder are being bottled. In the evening: two jars unsealed. Daddy quickly makes them into jam. The next morning: two more unsealed and four in the afternoon. Van Daan hadn't brought them to the right temperature for sterilizing. Now Daddy makes jam every evening.

We eat strawberries with our porridge, skimmed milk with strawberries, bread and butter with strawberries, strawberries for dessert, strawberries with sugar, strawberries with sand. For two whole days strawberries and nothing but strawberries, then the supply was finished or in bottles and under lock and key.

"I say, Anne," Margot calls out, "the greengrocer on the corner has let us have some green peas, nineteen pounds." "That's nice of him," I replied. And it certainly is, but oh, the work . . . ugh!

"You've all got to help shelling peas on Saturday morning," Mummy announced when we were at table. And, sure enough, the big enamel pan duly appeared this morning, filled to the brim. Shelling peas is a boring job, but you ought to try "skinning" the pods. I don't think many people realize how soft and tasty the pod is when the skin on the inside has been removed. However, an even greater advantage is that the quantity which can be eaten is about triple the amount of when one only eats the peas. It's an exceptionally

687

pulling out the skins, perhaps it's all right for pedantic dentists or precise spice merchants, But for an impatient teen-ager like me, it's frightful. We began at half past nine, I sat down to it at half past ten, at 11 I got up again, at half past 11 I sat down. This refrain hummed in my ears: bend the top, pull the skin, remove the string, throw out the pod; bend the top, pull the skin, remove the string, throw out the pod etc. etc., they dance before my eyes, green, green, green maggots, rotten pods, green, green, green. Just for the

| 112   sake of | doing something, I keep chattering the whole morning, any nonsense that comes into my head, make everyone laugh, and feel nearly stifled by my own stupidity. But every string that I pull makes me feel more certain that I never, never want to be just a housewife only!

We finally have breakfast at 12 o'clock, but from half past 12 until quarter past 1 we've got to go skinning pods again. I'm just about seasick when I stop, the others a bit too, I go and sleep till 4 o'clock, but I'm still upset by those wretched peas.

yours, Anne M. Frank.

. . . . . .

precise, finicky job, pulling out this skin; perhaps it's all right for pedantic dentists or precise office workers, but for an impatient teen-ager like me, it's frightful. We began at half past nine, I got up at half past ten, at half past eleven I sat down again. This refrain hummed in my ears: bend the top, pull the skin, remove the string, throw out the pod, etc., etc., they dance before my eyes, green, green, green maggots, strings, rotten pods, green, green, green. Just for the sake of doing something, I chatter the whole morning, any nonsense that comes into my head, make everyone laugh, and bore them stiff [feel nearly stifled by my own stupidity]. But every string that I pull makes me feel more certain that I never, never want to be just a housewife only!

We finally have breakfast at twelve o'clock, but from half past twelve until quarter past one we've got to go skinning pods again. I'm just about seasick when I stop, the others a bit too. I go and sleep till four o'clock, but I'm still upset by those wretched peas.

Yours, Anne

Saturday 15 July 1944.

Dear Kitty,

We have had a book from the library with the challenging title of: "What Do You Think of the Modern Young Girl?" I want to talk about this subject today.

The author criticizes "the youth of today" from top to toe, without, however, condemning the whole of the young brigade as "incapable of anything good." On the contrary, she is | rather of the opinion that if young people wished, they have it in their hands to make a bigger, more beautiful and better world, but that they occupy themselves with superficial things, without giving a thought to real beauty.

²In some passages the writer gave me very much the feeling she was directing her criticisms at me, and that's why I want to lay myself completely bare to you for once and defend myself against this attack.

I have one outstanding trait in my character, which must strike anyone who knows me for any length of time, and that is my self-knowledge. I can watch myself and my actions, just like an outsider. The Anne of every day I can face entirely without prejudice, without being full of excuses for her, and watch what's good and bad about her. This self-consciousness haunts me, and every time I open my mouth I know as soon as I've spoken whether that ought | to have been different, or, that was right as it was!" There are so many things about myself that I condemn; I couldn't begin to name them all. I understand more and more how true Daddy's words were when he said: "All children

| 113 (margin)
| 114 (margin)

. . . . . .

Saturday 15 July, 1944

Dear Kitty,

We have had a book from the library with the challenging title of: *What Do You Think of the Modern Young Girl?* I want to talk about this subject today.

The author of this book criticizes "the youth of today" from top to toe, without, however, condemning the whole of the young brigade as "incapable of anything good." On the contrary, she is rather of the opinion that if young people wished, they have it in their hands to make a bigger, more beautiful and better world, but that they occupy themselves with superficial things, without giving a thought to real beauty.

In some passages the writer gave me very much the feeling she was directing her criticisms at me, and that's why I want to lay myself completely bare to you for once and defend myself against this attack.

I have one outstanding trait in my character, which must strike anyone who knows me for any length of time, and that is my knowledge of myself. I can watch myself and my actions, just like an outsider. The Anne of every day I can face entirely without prejudice, without making excuses for her, and watch what's good and what's bad about her. This "self-consciousness" haunts me, and every time I open my mouth I know as soon as I've spoken whether "that ought to have been different" or "that was right as it was." There are so many things about myself that I condemn; I couldn't begin to name them all. I understand more and more how true Daddy's words were when he said: "All children

689

must look after their own upbringing." Parents can only give good advice or put them on the right paths, but the final forming of a person's character lies in their own hands. In addition to this, I have lots of courage, I always feel so strong and as if I can bear a great deal, I feel so free and so young! I was glad when I first realized it, because I don't think I shall easily bow down before the blows that inevitably come to everyone.

But I've talked about these things so often before. Now I want to come to the chapter of: Daddy and Mummy don't understand me. Daddy and Mummy have always thoroughly spoiled me, were sweet to me, defended me against upstairs, and have done all that parents could do. And yet I've felt so terribly lonely for a long time, so left out, neglected and misunderstood. Daddy tried everything possible to check my rebellious spirit, but it was

no use, I have cured myself, by confronting myself with what was wrong | in my behavior. How is it that Daddy was never any support to me in my struggle, why did he completely miss the mark when he wanted to offer me a helping hand? Daddy tried the wrong methods, he always talked to me as a child who was going through difficult phases.[5] It sounds crazy, because Daddy's the only one who has always taken me into his confidence, and no one but Daddy has given me the feeling that I'm sensible. But there's one thing he's omitted, you see, he hasn't realized that for me the fight to get on top was more important than

. . . . . .

must look after their own upbringing." Parents can only give good advice or put them on the right paths, but the final forming of a person's character lies in their own hands.

In addition to this, I have lots of courage, I always feel so strong and as if I can bear a great deal, I feel so free and so young! I was glad when I first realized it, because I don't think I shall easily bow down before the blows that inevitably come to everyone.

But I've talked about these things so often before. Now I want to come to the chapter of "Daddy and Mummy don't understand me." Daddy and Mummy have always thoroughly spoiled me, were sweet to me, defended me, and have done all that parents could do. And yet I've felt so terribly lonely for a long time, so left out, neglected, and misunderstood. Daddy tried all he could to check my rebellious spirit, but it was no use, I have cured myself, by seeing for myself what was wrong in my behavior and keeping it before my eyes.

How is it that Daddy was never any support to me in my struggle, why did he completely miss the mark when he wanted to offer me a helping hand? Daddy tried the wrong methods, he always talked to me as a child who was going through difficult phases. It sounds crazy, because Daddy's the only one who has always taken me into his confidence, and no one but Daddy has given me the feeling that I'm sensible. But there's one thing he's omitted: you see, he hasn't realized that for me the fight to get on top was more important than all else. I didn't want to hear about "symptoms of your age," or "other

690

everything else. I didn't want to hear about symptoms of your age, or other girls, or it wears off by itself; I didn't want to be treated as a girl-like-all-others, but as Anne-on-her-own-merits and that Pim didn't understand. For that matter, I can't confide in anyone, unless they tell me a lot about themselves, and as I know nothing about Pim, I don't feel I can tread upon more intimate ground with him. Pim always adopts the older fatherly attitude, tells me | that he too has had similar passing tendencies. But he's not able to be more to me than a young girl's friend, however hard he tries. These things have made me never mention my views on life nor my well-considered theories to anyone but my diary and, occasionally, to Margot. I concealed from Daddy everything that perturbed me, never shared my ideals with him, I was aware of the fact that I was pushing him away from me.

I couldn't do anything else. I have acted entirely according to my feelings, I have acted selfishly, but I have acted in the way that was best for my peace of mind. Because I should completely lose my repose and self-confidence, which I have built up so shakily, if, at this stage, I were to accept criticisms of my half-completed task. And I can't do that even from Pim, although it sounds very hard, for not only have I not shared my secret thoughts with Pim but I have often pushed him even further from me, by my irritability.

. . . . . .

girls," or "it wears off by itself"; I didn't want to be treated as a girl-like-all-others, but as Anne-on-her-own-merits. Pim didn't understand that. For that matter, I can't confide in anyone, unless they tell me a lot about themselves, and as I know very little about Pim, I don't feel that I can tread upon more intimate ground with him. Pim always takes up the older, fatherly attitude, tells me that he too has had similar passing tendencies. But still he's not able to feel with me like a friend, however hard he tries. These things have made me never mention my views on life nor my well-considered theories to anyone but my diary and, occasionally, to Margot. I concealed from Daddy everything that perturbed me; I never shared my ideals with him, I was aware of the fact that I was pushing him away from me.

I couldn't do anything else. I have acted entirely according to my feelings, but I have acted in the way that was best for my peace of mind. Because I should completely lose my repose and self-confidence, which I have built up so shakily, if, at this stage, I were to accept criticisms of my half-completed task. And I can't do that even from Pim, although it sounds very hard, for not only have I not shared my secret thoughts with Pim but I have often pushed him even further from me, by my irritability.

691

This is a point that gives me much thought: | Why is it that Pim sometimes annoys me? So much so that I can hardly bear him teaching me, that his many affectionate ways strike me as being put on, that I want to be left in peace and would really prefer it if he dropped me a bit, until I felt more certain in my attitude towards him! Because I still have a gnawing feeling of guilt over that horrible letter that I dared to fling in his teeth when I was so wound up. Oh how hard it is to be really strong and brave in every way!

Yet this is not my greatest disappointment; no, I ponder far more over Peter than Daddy. I know very well that I conquered him instead of he conquering me. I created an image of him in my mind, pictured him as the quiet, sensitive,[4] lovable boy, who needed affection and friendship! I needed a living person to whom I could pour out my heart; I wanted a friend who'd help to put me on the right road. I achieved what I wanted, and, slowly but surely, I drew him towards me.

Finally, when I had made him feel friendly, it automatically developed into an intimacy which, on second thought, I don't think I ought to have allowed. We talked about the most private things and yet up till now we have never touched on those things that filled, and still fill, my heart and soul. I still don't quite know what to make of Peter, is he superficial, or does he feel shy, even of me? But dropping that, I committed one error in

. . . . . .

This is a point that I think a lot about: why is it that Pim annoys me? So much so that I can hardly bear him teaching me, that his affectionate ways strike me as being put on, that I want to be left in peace and would really prefer it if he dropped me a bit, until I felt more certain in my attitude towards him? Because I still have a gnawing feeling of guilt over that horrible letter that I dared to write him when I was so wound up. Oh, how hard it is to be really strong and brave in every way!

Yet this was not my greatest disappointment; no, I ponder far more over Peter than Daddy. I know very well that I conquered him instead of he conquering me. I created an image of him in my mind, pictured him as a quiet, sensitive, lovable boy, who needed affection and friendship. I needed a living person to whom I could pour out my heart; I wanted a friend who'd help to put me on the right road. I achieved what I wanted, and, slowly but surely, I drew him towards me. Finally, when I had made him feel friendly, it automatically developed into an intimacy which, on second thought, I don't think I ought to have allowed.

We talked about the most private things, and yet up till now we have never touched on those things that filled, and still fill, my heart and soul. I still don't know quite what to make of Peter, is he superficial, or does he still feel shy, even of me? But dropping that,

692

my desire to make a real friendship: I switched over and tried to get at him by developing it into a more intimate relation, whereas I should have explored all other possibilities. He longs to be loved and I can see that he's beginning to be more and more in love with me. He gets satisfaction out of our meetings, whereas they just have the effect of making me want to try it out with him again but never to touch on the subjects that I'm so longing to bring out into the daylight. I drew Peter towards me, far more than he realizes, now

he clings to me, and for the time being, I don't see any way of shaking him off | and putting him on his own feet. When I realized that he could not be a friend for my understanding, I thought I would at least try to lift him up out of his narrow-mindedness and make him do something with his youth.

"For in its innermost depths, childhood is lonelier than old age." I read this saying in some book and I've always remembered it, and found it to be true. Is it true then that grownups have a more difficult time here than we do? No. I know it isn't. Older people have formed their opinions about everything and don't waver before they act. It's twice as hard for us young ones to hold our ground, and maintain our opinions, in a time when all ideals are being shattered and destroyed, when people are showing their worst side, and do not know whether to believe in truth and right and in God.

. . . . . .

I committed one error in my desire to make a real friendship: I switched over and tried to get at him by developing it into a more intimate relation, whereas I should have explored all other possibilities. He longs to be loved and I can see that he's beginning to be more and more in love with me. He gets satisfaction out of our meetings, whereas they just have the effect of making me want to try it out with him again. And yet I don't seem able to touch on the subjects that I'm so longing to bring out into the daylight. I drew Peter towards me, far more than he realizes. Now he clings to me, and for the time being, I don't see any way of shaking him off and putting him on his own feet. When I realized that he could not be a friend for my understanding, I thought I would at least try to lift him up out of his narrow-mindedness and make him do something with his youth.

"For in its innermost depths youth is lonelier than old age." I read this saying in some book and I've always remembered it, and found it to be true. Is it true that grownups have a more difficult time here than we do? No. I know it isn't. Older people have formed their opinions about everything, and don't waver before they act. It's twice as hard for us young ones to hold our ground, and maintain our opinions, in a time when all ideals are being shattered and destroyed, when people are showing their worst side, and do not know whether to believe in truth and right and God.

693

a | 120   Anyone who claims that the older ones have a more difficult time | here certainly doesn't realize to what extent our problems weigh down on us, problems for which we are probably much too young, but which thrust themselves upon us continually, until, after a long time, we think we've found a solution, but the solution doesn't seem able to resist the weapons which reduce it to nothing again. That's the difficulty in these times, ideals, dreams and cherished hopes rise within us, only to meet the horrible truth and be shattered. It's really a wonder that I haven't dropped all my ideals, because they seem so absurd and impossible to carry out. Yet I keep them, because in spite of everything I still believe that people are really good at heart.

     I simply can't build up my hopes on a foundation consisting of confusion, misery, and death, I see the world gradually being turned into a wilderness, I hear the ever

| 121   approaching thunder, which will destroy us too, I can feel the | sufferings of millions and yet, if I look up into the heavens, I think that it will all come right, that this cruelty too will end, and that peace and tranquillity will return again. In the meantime, I must uphold my ideals, for perhaps the time will come when I shall be able to carry them out!

yours, Anne M. Frank.

b   ......

c   Anyone who claims that the older ones have a more difficult time here certainly doesn't realize to what extent our problems weigh down on us, problems for which we are probably much too young, but which thrust themselves upon us continually, until, after a long time, we think we've found a solution, but the solution doesn't seem able to resist the facts which reduce it to nothing again. That's the difficulty in these times: ideals, dreams, and cherished hopes rise within us, only to meet the horrible truth and be shattered.

     It's really a wonder that I haven't dropped all my ideals, because they seem so absurd and impossible to carry out. Yet I keep them, because in spite of everything I still believe that people are really good at heart. I simply can't build up my hopes on a foundation consisting of confusion, misery, and death. I see the world gradually being turned into a wilderness, I hear the ever approaching thunder, which will destroy us too, I can feel the sufferings of millions and yet, if I look up into the heavens, I think that it will all come right, that this cruelty too will end, and that peace and tranquillity will return again.

     In the meantime, I must uphold my ideals, for perhaps the time will come when I shall be able to carry them out.

Yours, Anne

694

Friday 21 July 1944.

Dear Kitty,

Now I'm getting really hopeful, now things are going well at last. Yes, really, they're going well! Super news! An attempt has been made on Hitler's life and not even by Jewish communists or English capitalists this time but by a thoroughbred German general, and what's more, he's a count, and still quite young. The Führer's life was saved by Divine Providence and, unfortunately, he managed to get off with just a few scratches and burns.
| 122   A few officers and generals who were with him have been killed and | wounded. The chief culprit was shot.

    Anyway, it certainly shows that there are lots of officers and generals who are sick of the war and would like to see Hitler descend into a bottomless pit, to set up a military dictatorship and make peace with the Allies, then to rearm and start the war again in about 20 years' time. Perhaps the Divine Power tarried on purpose in getting him out of the way, because it would be much easier and more advantageous to the Allies if the impeccable Germans kill each other off, it'll make less work for the Russians and the English and they'll be able to begin rebuilding their own towns all the sooner. But still,

. . . . . .

Friday, 21 July, 1944

Dear Kitty,

    Now I am getting really hopeful, now things are going well at last. Yes, really, they're going well! Super news! An attempt has been made on Hitler's life and not even by Jewish communists or English capitalists this time, but by a proud German general, and what's more, he's a count, and still quite young. The Führer's life was saved by Divine Providence and, unfortunately, he managed to get off with just a few scratches and burns. A few officers and generals who were with him have been killed and wounded. The chief culprit was shot.

    Anyway, it certainly shows that there are lots of officers and generals who are sick of the war and would like to see Hitler descend into a bottomless pit. When they've disposed of Hitler, their aim is to establish a military dictator, who will make peace with the Allies, then they intend to rearm and start another war in about twenty years' time. Perhaps the Divine Power tarried on purpose in getting him out of the way, because it would be much easier and more advantageous to the Allies if the impeccable Germans kill each other off; it'll make less work for the Russians and the English and they'll be able to begin rebuilding their own towns all the sooner.

we're not that far yet, and the last thing I want to do is anticipate the glorious events. Still, you must have noticed that what I say is the truth; for once, I'm not jabbering about high ideals.

| 123   And what's more, Hitler has even been so kind as to announce to his faithful, devoted people | that from now on everyone in the armed forces must obey the Gestapo, and that any man or any soldier who knows that one of his commanders had a part in this low, cowardly attempt upon his life may shoot him on the spot!

What a perfect shambles it's going to be. Little Johnnie's feet begin hurting him during a long march, he's snapped at by his boss, the officer, Johnnie grabs his rifle and cries out: "You wanted to murder the Führer, so there's your reward." One bang and the proud chief who had dared to tick off little Johnnie has passed into eternal life (or is it eternal death?)! In the end, whenever an officer finds himself up against a soldier, or having to take the lead, he'll be wetting his pants from anxiety, because the soldiers will have more say than they do.

| 124   Do you gather a bit what I mean, or have I been skipping too much from one subject to another? I can't help it; in anticipation of sitting on school benches next October | I feel far too cheerful to be logical! Oh, dearie me, hadn't I just told you that I didn't want to be too hopeful? Forgive me, I haven't got the reputation of being a "little bundle of contradictions" for nothing!

yours, Anne M. Frank.

. . . . . .

But still, we're not that far yet, and I don't want to anticipate the glorious events too soon. Still, you must have noticed, this is all sober reality and that I'm in quite a matter-of-fact mood today; for once, I'm not jabbering about high ideals. And what's more, Hitler has even been so kind as to announce to his faithful, devoted people that from now on everyone in the armed forces must obey the Gestapo, and that any soldier who knows that one of his superiors was involved in this low, cowardly attempt upon his life may shoot the same on the spot, without court-martial.

What a perfect shambles it's going to be. Little Johnnie's feet begin hurting him during a long march, he's snapped at by his boss, the officer, Johnnie grabs his rifle and cries out: "You wanted to murder the Führer, so there's your reward." One bang and the proud chief who dared to tick off little Johnnie has passed into eternal life (or is it eternal death?). In the end, whenever an officer finds himself up against a soldier, or having to take the lead, he'll be wetting his pants from anxiety, because the soldiers will dare to say more than they do. Do you gather a bit what I mean, or have I been skipping too much from one subject to another? I can't help it; the prospect that I may be sitting on school benches next October makes me feel far too cheerful to be logical! Oh, dearie me, hadn't I just told you that I didn't want to be too hopeful? Forgive me, they haven't given me the name "little bundle of contradictions" all for nothing!

Yours Anne

Tuesday 1 Aug. 1944.

Dear Kitty,

"Little bundle of contradictions." That's how I ended my last letter and that's how I'm going to begin this one. "A little bundle of contradictions," can you tell me exactly what it is? What does contradiction mean? Like so many words (it can be interpreted in two ways) it can mean two things, contradiction from without and contradiction from within. The first is the ordinary not giving in easily, always knowing best, getting in the last word, enfin, all the unpleasant qualities for which I am renowned, the second nobody knows about, that's my own secret.

| 125   I have already told you (said) before that I have, as it were, a dual personality. One half embodies my exuberant cheerfulness, making fun of everything, vivacity, and above all the way I take everything lightly. This includes not minding flirtation, a kiss, an embrace, a dirty joke. This side is usually lying in wait and pushes away the other, which is much better, deeper and purer. You must realize that no one knows Anne's better side and that's why most people find me so insufferable. Certainly I'm a giddy clown for one afternoon, but then for another month everyone's had enough of me. Really, it's just the same as[1]

. . . . . .

Tuesday, 1 August, 1944

Dear Kitty,

"Little bundle of contradictions." That's how I ended my last letter and that's how I'm going to begin this one. "A little bundle of contradictions," can you tell me exactly what it is? What does contradiction mean? Like so many words, it can mean two things, contradiction from without and contradiction from within.

The first is the ordinary "not giving in easily, always knowing best, getting in the last word," enfin, all the unpleasant qualities for which I'm renowned. The second nobody knows about, that's my own secret.

I've already told you before that I have, as it were, a dual personality. One half embodies my exuberant cheerfulness, making fun of everything, my high-spiritedness, and above all, the way I take everything lightly. This includes not taking offense at a flirtation, a kiss, an embrace, a dirty joke. This side is usually lying in wait and pushes away the other, which is much better, deeper and purer. You must realize that no one knows Anne's better side and that's why most people find me so insufferable.

Certainly I'm a giddy clown for one afternoon, but then everyone's had enough of me for another month. Really, it's just the same as a love film is for deep-thinking

697

a love film is for deep-thinking people, simply a diversion, amusing just for once, something which is soon forgotten, not bad, but certainly not good. I loathe having to tell you this, but why shouldn't I, if I know it's true anyway? My lighter, superficial side will always be too quick for the deeper side of me and that's why it will always win. You can't imagine how often I've already tried to push this Anne away, to slap her down, to hide her, because after all, she's only | half of what's called Anne, but it doesn't work and I know, too, how it is that it doesn't work.

| 126

I'm awfully scared that everyone who knows me as I always am will discover that I have another side, a finer and better side. I'm afraid they'll laugh at me, think I'm ridiculous, sentimental, not take me in earnest. I'm used to not being taken seriously but it's only the lighthearted Anne that's used to it and can bear it; the deeper Anne is too frail for it. Sometimes, if I really compel the good Anne to take the stage for a quarter of an hour, she simply shrivels up as soon as she has to speak, and lets Anne no. 1 take over, and before I realize it, she has disappeared.

Therefore the nice Anne is never present in company, has not appeared one single time so far, but almost always predominates when we're alone. I know exactly how I'd like to be, how I am too . . . inside. But alas I'm only like that for myself. And per- | haps that's why, no I'm sure it's the reason why I say I've got a happy nature within and why other people think I've got a happy nature without. I am guided by the pure Anne within, but outside I'm nothing but a frolicsome little goat who's breaking loose.

| 127

. . . . . .

people, simply a diversion, amusing just for once, something which is soon forgotten, not bad, but certainly not good. I loathe having to tell you this, but why shouldn't I, if I know it's true anyway? My lighter superficial side will always be too quick for the deeper side of me and that's why it will always win. You can't imagine how often I've already tried to push this Anne away, to cripple her, to hide her, because, after all, she's only half of what's called Anne; but it doesn't work and I know, too, why it doesn't work.

I'm awfully scared that everyone who knows me as I always am will discover that I have another side, a finer and better side. I'm afraid they'll laugh at me, think I'm ridiculous and sentimental, not take me seriously. I'm used to not being taken seriously but it's only the "lighthearted" Anne that's used to it and can bear it; the "deeper" Anne is too frail for it. Sometimes, if I really compel the good Anne to take the stage for a quarter of an hour, she simply shrivels up as soon as she has to speak, and lets Anne number one take over, and before I realize it, she has disappeared.

Therefore, the nice Anne is never present in company, has not appeared one single time so far, but almost always predominates when we're alone. I know exactly how I'd like to be, how I am too . . . inside. But, alas, I'm only like that for myself. And perhaps that's why, no, I'm sure it's the reason why I say I've got a happy nature within and why other people think I've got a happy nature without. I am guided by the pure Anne within, but outside I'm nothing but a frolicsome little goat who's broken loose.

As I've already said, I never utter my real feelings about anything and that's how I've acquired the name of chaser-after-boys, flirt, know-all, reader of love stories. The cheerful Anne laughs about it, answers back cheekily, shrugs her shoulders indifferently, behaves as if she doesn't care, but oh no, the quiet Anne's reactions are just the opposite. If I'm to be quite honest, then I must admit that it does hurt me, that I try terribly hard to change myself, but that I'm always fighting against a more powerful enemy.

A voice sobs within me: "There you are, that's what's become of you, you're un- | 128 charitable, you look supercilious and peevish, people you meet dislike you and | all just because you won't listen to the advice given you by your own better half." Oh, I would like to listen, but it doesn't work, if I'm quiet and serious they all think that it's a new comedy and then I have to get out of it by turning it into a joke, not to mention my own family, who are sure to think I'm ill, make me swallow pills for headaches and sedatives, feel my neck and my head to see whether I'm running a temperature, ask if I'm constipated and criticize me for being in a bad mood, I can't keep that up, if I'm watched to that extent I start by getting snappy, then unhappy, and finally I twist my heart round again, so that the bad is on the outside and the good is on the inside and keep on trying to find a way of becoming what I would so like to be and what I could be, if . . . . . there weren't any other people living in the world.

yours, Anne M. Frank.

Soit gentil et tiens courage!

As I've already said, I never utter my real feelings about anything and that's how I've acquired the name of chaser-after-boys, flirt, know-all, reader of love stories. The cheerful Anne laughs about it, gives cheeky answers, shrugs her shoulders indifferently, behaves as if she doesn't care, but, oh dearie me, the quiet Anne's reactions are just the opposite. If I'm to be quite honest, then I must admit that it does hurt me, that I try terribly hard to change myself, but that I'm always fighting against a more powerful enemy.

A voice sobs within me: "There you are, that's what's become of you: you're un- charitable, you look supercilious and peevish, people dislike you and all because you won't listen to the advice given you by your own better half." Oh, I would like to listen, but it doesn't work; if I'm quiet and serious, everyone thinks it's a new comedy and then I have to get out of it by turning it into a joke, not to mention my own family, who are sure to think I'm ill, make me swallow pills for headaches and nerves, feel my neck and my head to see whether I'm running a temperature, ask if I'm constipated and criticize me for being in a bad mood. I can't keep that up; if I'm watched to that extent, I start by getting snappy, then unhappy, and finally I twist my heart round again, so that the bad is on the outside and the good is on the inside and keep on trying to find a way of becoming what I would so like to be, and what I could be, if . . . there weren't any other people living in the world.

Yours, Anne

Anne's diary ended here. On August 4, 1944, the "Grüne Polizei" made a raid on the "Secret Annexe." All the occupants, together with Kraler and Koophuis, were arrested and sent to German and Dutch concentration camps.

The "Secret Annexe" was plundered by the Gestapo. Amongst a pile of old books, magazines and newspapers, which were left lying on the floor, Miep and Elli found Anne's diary. Apart from a very few passages, which are of little interest to the reader, the original text has been printed.

Of all the occupants of the "Secret Annexe," Anne's father alone returned. Kraler and Koophuis, who withstood the hardships of the Dutch camp, were able to go home to their families.

In March, 1945, two months before the liberation of Holland, Anne died in the concentration camp at Bergen-Belsen.

Deletions and Additions*

Most of the Deletions and Additions are minor Dutch grammatical or spelling corrections. Only those reflected in the English translation have been numbered in the text, and the corresponding numbers are circled here. The Dutch alterations have, however, been retained in this section to demonstrate the nonsubstantial nature of most of the alterations and deletions.

VERSION a

197

① The photograph is missing. The assumed caption on the opposite page reads: Annelies Marie Frank 1941/1942 (winter.) *irp*
2 [−bezitt]
3 alle≤s≥maal
4 mi[e+]<ij>n
5 nieuws[−gie]gierigheid
⑥ [−contain] ≤control≥ *ip*

198

① ≤l≥ *ip*
② <table> *ip*
③ ≤so ... more≥ *ip*
4 [*.*]
⑤ [comma+] <parenthesis>
⑥ ≤strawberry tart from Mummy≥
7 le[−e]raren

199

① [is known as] <is now> *ip*

206

1 [cr]
2 <e>en *ip*
③ [travel adventures] ≤mountain holiday≥
④ Anne <ke> *ip*
⑤ semicolon → comma
⑥ [−Day]
7 [−hij] <hoe> *(ip)*

207

1 [−een]
② <quotation marks> *ip*
③ <quotation marks> *ip*
④ stroke added to letter t *ip*
⑤ [−Betty] ≤Beppy≥ *ip*
6 ≤daar≥

208

1 zoda[−k]t
2 <G.... gebleven>
3 jo[−g] ≤ch≥ *ip*

4

4 he[−l]m
5 jo[−g] ≤ch≥ *ip*
⑥ <He ... dull.> *ip*
⑦ [−Leo Blom] ≤Jopie de Beer≥ *ip*
⑧ <What ... Annexe. > *ip*
9 rotjo[−g] ≤ch≥ *ip*
⑩ <(Admirer!) *ip*

209

① <how idiotic> <you don't forget that sort of thing> *ip*
2 [−de] ≤zijn≥ *ip*
③ [−1940] ≤1941≥
④ a → a

210

1 [−wat in] ≤in≥

211

1 [z]
2 <I ... wrong. > *ip*
3 [−gepraat.] ≤gepraat.≥
4 [−mon] ≤mon≥deling

212

1 [−op,]
② [−29] ≤30≥
③ Weis <s>

219

1 midd[g+]<a>gs

220

① [−6]

221

1 [b]
2 [c+] <C>lubje

223

① [−and there he is right, except for Ilse whom I consider | not only childish, but no longer very nice either.] ≤and there he is right, except for Ilse whom I consider | not only childish, but no longer very nice either!!!!≥

226

1 [−before morning] <afternoon>

229

1 [−jor]
2 [−ee]
3 ve[*.*+]<s>t

231

1 [−van] ≤en≥ *ip*

241

1 de[−*.*]
2 [zee]kapitein
3 ermee[−r]
4 [−hoor]
5 houd[−t]
6 ≤over≥

242

1 all[e+]<g>emeen
2 [−f] ≤v≥riend
③ ≤and friend François≥
④ Daddy ... treasure *underlined three times.*
5 b[−ij]v.
⑥ Dot added to i in German "sieht"
7 sieh[*.*]t
⑧ [−quotation marks]
⑨ [−hut]

243

① [comma+] ≤period≥[−he doesn't always look like that]
② Daddy's ... 1939. *irp*

244

1 [−Sap]
2 [−Zw]
3 [−e]
4 afge[−g]ven
5 particulier[−en] *(ii)* ≤e≥ *ip*
6 [−niet] *ip*
7 vind[*.*+]<t>
8 [−*.*]

*See p. 170f for explanation of the signs used.

245

1 [−*.*]
2 *. ...
3 kamer[−kam]tje
④ [−quotation marks]

246

1 [−mocht]
② ≤So Mr. v. P. said ... seasoning≥
3 [−m]
4 ≤en≥

247

1 na[*..*+] <a>r

250

① <22> [−28]
② underlined ip
3 [−is] ip
4 [−stelen]
5 e[−n]r
6 r[e*.*+]<u>zie

251

① [−each other] ≤me≥ ip
② <21> [−14]
3 [−z]

253

① [−then Peter went upstairs and wouldn't come b]

254

1 e≤e≥n ip

255

1 [−hij]
2 f[−ij]≤ei≥telijk

257

① [−comma]
2 sch[−ij]<ei>

258

① [−15] ≤22≥

259

1 [−zeer] ≤zijn≥ ip
② [−comma]

261

1 d[−ie] ≤oe≥ (ip)
② ≤again≥
③ [−you'll] ≤we'll≥
④ ≤obviously≥

262

1 na<ar> (ip)
2 z[−ij] <ei>

263

1 [−a]

265

1 hands[−cc]chrift

266

1 [−m]<z>ijn (ip)
2 verd[−ag]er

3 molletje[−s]
4 he[m+]<b>

267

1 zogenaamd<e> ip
2 [−s]
3 na[−ar]

268

1 Men[−ij]eer

269

1 vond[−t]
2 [−a]
3 da[−t]<n> ip

270

1 he[−b]t

272

1 da[−t]<n>

273

1 o[−p]≤m≥ ip

274

1 [−*.*]
2 worden<d> ip

276

1 me<t>

278

① <period> ip
2 ne[−i]t
3 al[−s]
4 [−ik] ≤zij≥
5 [−haar] ≤mij≥
⑥ Pim ..... Mummy isn't!!!! *underlined three times*
7 He[−e]t
8 my[−e]

279

1 gek[−e]ker
2 Me[n+]<vr>
3 z[i+]<a>t

280

1 aangren[s+]<z>ende

281

① *underlined four times*

282

1 Duits[−[ts]]−land
2 ≤en met≥
3 [−en] ≤tegen≥
4 [−5]
5 [−Aan]
6 ≤Pokkie≥
7 [−M] ≤H≥emorieten
8 [−bro]
9 he[−l]le

283

1 [−van]
2 groe≤n≥te
3 [−te]

284

1 nie<t>

285

① *underlined four times*
2 [−o]
3 [−als e]
4 [−o]
5 [−en] ≤en≥
6 [−gaan] ip
7 [−a]
⑧ *braces underlined four times*
⑨ *braces underlined four times*

286

1 [−drij]
2 e[r+]<r>
③ *underlined four times*
4 b[l→]<r>oe[−d]≤k≥
⑤ *underlined four times*

287

1 [−gehd]
2 wa[−a]s
3 [−en] ip
4 [−pep]
⑤ [p. 87b] [−Then elastic for $f3 = f8$. Then py*amas*, 2 night dresses, 1 dressing gown (summer), 1 *shoe*, gown (winter) [−1 pair] 1 small cushion for]
*The letters between * * are very difficult to make out because they are under the paper with which the lined paper has been stuck in.*

288

① f [−0,7] ≤0,75≥
2 zomer[−s]slofjes
3 [−thui] ≤goed≥
④ f [−1,5] <1,00>
⑤ [−f1,25]
6 [−z]
⑦ f [−0,]50. *underlined four times*

289

① [−4]
② f[−3,95] ≤4.−≥
③ f[1+] <2>.−
④ f[−2.−] <4.−>
⑤ *underlined four times*
⑥ *underlined three times*
⑦ *underlined twice*
⑧ *underlined three times*

293

1 kor[−s]tsluiting
2 be[−a]weging
3 vro[g+]<e>ger
4 [−*.*]
5 [−*.*]

294

1 wijde[−n]<r>
② Pim ... again *underlined three times*
③ foul *underlined three times*
④ foul *underlined three times*
5 [d→]<a>ls
6 geen
7 lekker[s+]<e> (ip)
8 m<apostrophe> [e+]<n> (ip)
9 ha[−r]nden
10 z<apostrophe> [e+]<n> (ip)

297

1 tussend[−oo] ≤eu≥r
2 [−*.*]
3 vreselijk[−e] (ip)

298

1 ro≤e≥pen
② [period →] < exclamation mark> (ip)
3 V[−r]lug

299

1 [−mag]
② <comma> (ip)
③ <comma> (ip)
4 ≤het≥ (ip)
5 wi[l+]<l>
6 Zond<a>g
7 gekr[−[o+]<e>] ≤e≥gen

300

① <umlaut> (ip)
2 schrij[−ver]≤fster≥
③ Grüne[−n] (ip)

301

1 Zwit≤s≥ers
2 [−ke]
③ [−comma]
④ underlined twice
⑤ do.
⑥ do.
⑦ do.
⑧ do.

302

1 cr≤e≥am
2 [−groot] ≤goed≥ (ip)
③ [period →] <question mark> (ip)
4 [−als] <alles> (ip)

303

1 [−*.*]
2 na[−a]tuurlijk
3 ≤gestorven zijn.≥
4 al[e+]<w>eer
5 da[−ar]≤n≥ (ip)
⑥ <comma> (ip)
7 [k+] <K>oosje (ip)
⑧ Reference marks point to page 95b
⑨ <comma> (ip)
10 ≤hebben≥ (ip)
⑪ [period→] <exclamation mark> (ip)
12 [−we]

304

1 nieuw<s> (ip)
2 Ik ... 1944 (ip)
2 kraamverzorgster[−s]
4 [−*.*]
5 [−*.*]
6 he[e+]<l>ft (ip)

305

1 [−Bep] ≤Bep≥
2 [−Lee]
③ [period+] <comma> (ip)
4 nieuw[e] (ip)
5 blunder<s> (ip)
6 her[e+]<k>ennen
7 [−lst es] ≤Zieht mann≥
8 [hen]

308

1 [−ver]
2 [−ge]
3 ≤te vragen≥ (ip)

309

1 [−land] ≤stad≥
2 land <−>levensmiddel (ip)
3 [p+] <P> (ip)
4 [−br]
5 ka[−n]≤c≥hel
6 [−ap*.*]

315

1 [−meb]
2 [−op ho]
3 [h+] <H>oeden (ip)
4 Kleiman[−n]
5 [k+] <K>ahn (ip)
6 schei[−d] (ip)
7 [p+] <P>im (ip)
8 [p+] <P>im (ip)
9 [p+] <P>im (ip)

316

1 [−en]
2 [−om]
3 beu[s+]<r>sspel
4 e≤e≥n (ip)

321

1 [−door he]
2 al[l+]<g>emene

323

1 [−maar] <toch>
② <exclamation mark> (ip)
3 <zal> moet ≤en≥
4 ≤er≥ (ip)
⑤ [period+] <exclamation mark> (ip)
6 hoo[f+]<g>heid

324

1 geraf<el>de
2 [−*.*]

444

1 [−kan]

446

1 meegebra[−[a+]<c>]≤c≥t
2 Pf[−s] <period> <apostrophe> (?)
3 moe≤s≥t
4 dis[d+]<t>ributie
⑤ ≤Mr.≥

447

1 [−vade]

450

1 Ker≤s≥t[−s]mis

451

1 Ker≤s≥t[−s]mis
2 plaat[−s]jes
3 pakke≤t≥ten

452

1 ≤mee≥ droeg
2 ≤of≥

454

1 gesplit[−z]≤s≥t
2 ≤enigszins≥
3 ≤er≥

457

1 [−5] ≤6≥
2 [−comma]
3 [−comma]

458

1 [−dood] ≤heel≥

459

1 [−voor]
2 [−ik]
3 [−g]
4 gevo≤e≥l

460

1 hart[−s]
2 ≤ik≥
3 [−e]
4 [−comma]

463

1 ≤comma≥ ip
2 ≤vanochtend≥
3 we[−e]rd
4 waar[−op] ≤in≥
5 [−z]
6 ≤ge≥deeltelijk
7 ontmoette<n> ip
8 [−had] ≤was≥
9 [−je]
10 [−gevraagd] ≤bij je gekomen≥
11 [−te trouwen] ip

464

1 [−de]
2 ≤zeer≥
3 mooi[c] ip
4 dik[−ke] ip
5 zacht[−e] ip
6 [−ribbel]
7 [−dag]
8 [−en]
9 <accent aigu; comma>

465

1 <comma> ip
2 <hij> ip
3 z[−e]≤u≥ster
4 [−comma]
5 [−zat] ≤kwam≥
6 [−5] ≤6≥

466

1 donker[−e]
2 bruin[−e]−rode
3 ≤Roll≥ ip

467

1 <(had.)> ip
② [period+] <question mark>

468

1 [−sterft] ≤glijdt≥
2 z[ie+] <ij>n
3 [−zo]
4 gel≤e≥den
5 za[l+]<t> ip

469

1 ≤licht−≥
2 [−*.*]
3 ≤geribbelde≥

470

¹ [I(?)+] <H>ier

471

¹ ≤toch≥

472

¹ to≤t≥dat
² [−daar]
³ [−*.*]
⁴ naa[−w]r
⁵ [m+] <M>oeder

473

① [−.......]

474

¹ [−comma]
² [−had] ≤heeft≥
³ behoe≤v≥en

475

¹ de[−n]
² [−*.*]

476

¹ [−m]
² kinder[−en]−
³ voor≤−≥oorlogse

479

¹ [−het] ≤dit≥
² ≤er≥
³ [d+] <D>áág

480

¹ verande[−e]ren

481

¹ aardappel[−schillen] ≤pellen≥

482

¹ [−mo]
² Mous≤c≥hi

483

¹ m[o+]<i>nste

484

¹ gecastree≤r≥d
② [−quotation marks]
③ [−quotation marks]
⁴ da[−n]≤n≥
⁵ [−*.*]
⁶ [−is] ≤heeft≥

485

¹ [m+] <M>oeder
² [−comma]
³ n[−*.*]≤a≥dacht

490

¹ mare[−s][−s]ch[*..*+]<au> sée.
² [−H]
³ [dis]

491

¹ M[−e] <apostrophe>n ip
² [−g]

492

¹ [−comma]

494

¹ aanplakbillet≤t≥en
² de[−s]
³ bone[m+]<n>
⁴ groe[−t]nten

~~495~~

¹ ≤maar≥
² [−voor]

496

¹ [− op de voorzolder]
² [−*.*]

498

¹ [m+] <M>illioenen
² [−die]
³ word[−t]

499

¹ [−7] <8>
² spr[*.*+]<o>ng
³ [−ZO]
⁴ [−B]

500

¹ ≤hyphen≥
² [−apostrophe(?) t]
³ [−apostrophe]

501

① [−Wednesday] ≤Monday≥
② [−13] [−≤16≥] ≤14≥
③ [−old]
④ ≤had read≥

503

¹ ≤zo≥
² [−ben] ≤was≥

504

¹ Lu≤i≥ster
² [−aan]
³ H[−i]ij

505

¹ [−*.*]
² [−Van] ≤Gister≥ochtend
³ [−en]
⁴ goeden ≤hyphen≥ morgen
⁵ [−zo]
⁶ [−Eigenlijk]

507

¹ [−in]
² [−ik]
³ [−die]
⁴ [−(vanavond)]
⁵ [−alleen]
⁶ [−*.*]

508

¹ H[e+]<i>j
² [−half]

509

¹ [−Ik]
² Nee[−n]
³ [−weet] ≤kent≥

510

¹ <comma> [−en]
² ≤met z'n hoofd≥

511

¹ ≤dat ik≥
² [−tuss]
³ [−parenthesis]

512

¹ [−boven]
² [−*..*]
³ ≤hand≥ spiegel

513

① [−I'll never reach Peter like this.]
² [−zeker]
³ [−en]
⁴ [−je]

515

¹ [−en]

516

¹ [−zeer] ≤veel≥
² [−verzorgd period] ≤voorzien period≥
³ ve≤r≥lang
⁴ [−vanmorgen]
⁵ [−de]
⁶ [−de]

517

¹ [−verlangen]

520

¹ [−de] ≤het≥
² weer[−r]

521

¹ [−het] ≤de≥
² [−aan]
³ afwa[−en]
⁴ [−zij] ≤zei≥ ip
⁵ [−*.*]

523

¹ ≤bent≥ ip
² ≤er≥ ip

524

¹ een[−n]
² <comma> ip
³ [−ik] ≤wij≥
⁴ we[−e]t≤en≥
⁵ [−*.*]

525

¹ [−de]
² ≤meer≥

526

① ≤Mummy≥
² [d+]<t>
³ [d+]<t>

527

¹ ≤uit≥
² ga[*.*+]<u>wer

528

¹ [−starks]

529

1 [−vers]
2 [−voor] *ip*
3 [−geen]
4 [−*comma*]
5 [−naar] ≤op≥
⑥ [*period*+] <*question mark*> *ip*

531

1 [−ik] *ip*
② [−*question mark*]
3 [−voll]
4 [−*.*]
5 [−z]
6 onbehol[p+]<l>penheid

534

1 slecht[−s]
2 [−en]
3 [−*period*]

535

1 even[−s]

536

1 denk[−t]

537

1 [−in] ≤tussen≥
2 [w+] <W>at

538

1 *ip*
2 vol[−l]gen
3 [−*comma*]
④ ≤from me≥
5 gister[−e]nacht

539

1 [−*.*]
2 [−heel]
3 al[−s]-zo-meer
4 [−die] ≤welks> naam
5 [−gel−r]ass]
6 v[−i]ijf

541

① *semicolon* → *colon*
② [*quotation marks*]
3 [−me] ≤je≥
4 [−me] ≤je≥

542

1 na[−ar]

543

1 elke[−*.*]
2 ≤nog≥
3 s[*.*+]<t>erk
4 ≤er≥
5 he[m+]<b>

545

1 [−de]

546

1 le[−vn] ≤ren≥

547

① ≤slice≥

548

1 alle[−n]≤s≥
2 [−o] unmooglik.

550

1 hee≤r≥lijk
2 [−a]
3 [−ee]

551

1 [−m] ≤M≥oeder
2 eer[−s]ste
3 [−*comma*]
4 vr[−e]ede
5 ≤achter≥
6 [−het]

554

1 [−e]

559

① [−nervous breakdown]
≤hemorrhage of the stomach≥
2 [*.*] <V>ader
3 ≤bent≥

560

1 [−*comma*]
2 [−will]
3 [−*comma*]
4 [−*comma*]

561

1 [−*.*]

562

1 sexue[−a]le
2 [−erf]
3 [de]
4 ve≤r≥telde
5 [−m]
6 [−D[−i]≤a≥t]

563

1 [−*.*]
2 [−onze]

564

1 [−gauw]
2 [−zolder] ≤vliering≥

566

1 [−p]

567

① [−room for one there was room for two]
2 bl[z+]<a>[*period*] <d>zijde

569

1 [−van]
2 [−je]
3 [−dan]

570

1 [v+] <*parenthesis*>
2 [−*dash*]
③ [−half past 6 to]
4 Toilet≤−≥opmaak
⑤ [−ro]
6 [*.*+] <k>wart

571

1 [−g]
2 [l+] <L>iefde

572

1 gast[−r]vrij

576

① ≤German *period*≥
2 lu≤r≥en
3 [−sanem]
4 niet[−s]
⑤ Mary ↔ Anne
6 A[*..*+]<n>ne

578

① [−V period]
② [−*comma*] <*colon*>
3 [−tweede] ≤zweite≥
④ [−*quotation marks*]

580

① [−*quotation marks*]
2 [−zegt] ≤zei≥

582

① [−*quotation marks*]
② [−Let's agree on it now.]

583

① [−always]
② sexual [gland] ≤parts≥
3 kit≤st≥elaar

584

1 zie[−t]
2 [−Aas]
3 m|a+|<c>[a+]≤e≥r

586

① [−beautiful]

588

1 *accent and three dots on "zij"*

589

1 [−als]
2 [−maar]
3 ≤er≥
4 ou[w+]<d>elui

590

1 daar[−naast] ≤achter≥
2 [−ik] ≤er≥

591

1 Mous≤c≥hi
2 [−gel]
3 [−va]
4 [−van]≤af≥
5 [−*question mark*] ≤*exclamation mark*≥

592

1 I[n+]<s>

593

1 [−h]
2 [−*.*]

595

¹ dokter[−r]s
² [−neen]

600

¹ b[−r]onen

601

¹ [−kunt]
² [−*.*]
³ [−we*.*]
⁴ ≤je≥

602

¹ sprook≤j≥esachtig
² [−op]
³ [−de]

604

¹ word[−*.*]
² [−zou] ≤zal≥
³ [−zou] ≤zal≥
⁴ jou≤r≥naliste

605

¹ [−en]
² [−*.*]

606

① *Underlined in pencil*
² [−Na]
³ [−en]
⁴ [−van]
⁵ beur≤s≥spel
⑥ ≤afternoon≥
⁷ [−van]
⁸ [−8]
⁹ [−d]
¹⁰ fl[u+]<o>[i+]<o>t
¹¹ vr[a+]<o>[a+]<eg>[−t]
¹² h[e+]<a>[b+]<d>[b+]<d>en

607

¹ ≤daa≤r≥na≥ alles [−was weer]
² [−Op] ≤Van≥
³ [−de]

608

① [−after] ≤10 past≥
² [−ging]
³ [−weer]
⁴ [−*.*]
⁵ [−d]
⁶ [−een]
⁷ [−het] ≤die≥
⁸ pla[−*.*]nkje
⁹ ≤be≥scheen
¹⁰ [−een]

609

¹ [−mocht]
² momen[−*.*]t
③ *semicolon → colon*
④ [*quotation marks* We Are]
⁵ [−Het]

610

¹ [−*.*]

611

¹ al[−s]
² [g+] <G>estapo
³ [−zachte] ≤diepe≥
⁴ zucht[−e]

613

¹ ≤nog≥
² [−de]

614

¹ [op+] <af>
² [−*.*]

615

¹ [−*.*]
² [−zijn]

616

¹ [−wees]
² [−zijn] ≤blijven≥
³ [−de]

617

¹ ste≤r≥ven

618

¹ schouder[−s]

619

¹ hoe≤−≥(?)[−d]ie

620

¹ [−ook]

621

¹ [−de] ≤onze≥
² [−is]
³ zit≤ten≥

622

¹ ho≤e≥kje
² [−l[i+]<e>[g+]<c>hte] ≤legde≥
³ [−comma]

623

¹ stond[−e]

624

¹ moet ↔ ik.

626

¹ [−nu]
² zu[*.*+]<s>ter
³ [−erg]
⁴ al[−s]

629

¹ ≤er≥
² da[−t]n

631

¹ gist[−r]erenmiddag
² Miss≤c≥hien
³ ge[−l]ven
⁴ [−ee]

632

¹ [−z]
² [v+] <V>ader
³ [−bij]
⁴ [−keer] ≤week≥
⑤ ≤but God≥

634

① São Paul[a+]<o>
② [−5]
³ [−d]
⁴ be[−u]urt
⁵ Daa≤r≥na

635

¹ [−elkaar]

636

① [−*exclamation mark*]

637

¹ [−*comma*]
② [−still] ≤not≥
③ [−*question mark*]

638

¹ [−*comma*]

639

① [*.*+] <*parenthesis*>

640

① ≤in the evening!≥

641

¹ Eerst[−e]
² gel≤e≥den
³ [−sp]
⁴ stoof[−*comma*] −
⑤ [−2]

642

¹ [−en]
² waa≤r≥om
³ [−voor] ≤aan≥
⁴ vol[−l]keren

643

¹ ammu[−i]seren

644

¹ [−Het]

645

¹ ≤ook≥ *ip*
² stond[−e]

647

¹ alle[−n]

648

① [−*quotation marks*]

650

¹ [−was]

651

¹ kraamver[−pleegster] ≤zorgster≥
² wel[−l]

652

¹ [−en]
² [−*.*]
³ [−het] ≤er≥
⁴ [−is]
⁵ [−de]

1 [−t]
2 we[−g]≤t≥ *ip*
③ ≤13-year old≥

655

1 z[i+]<a>t[−t]en
②[−What had happened?]
③[−silver]
4 ≤hout≥ schaafsel
5 [−de]
6 [−dat] ≤die≥
7 [−de]
8 lag [*period*+] <en *period*>

656

1 [−maar]
2 Pete[*.*+]r
3 [−*comma* (?)]
4 [−een]

660

1 to≤e≥gegaan

662

①≤Linnaeus≥

663

1 [−zal]
2 [zeker]
3 Dui[−s]t≤s≥ers
④[*quotation marks*]

664

1 [−versp]
2 [−te]

665

①*hyphen written on top of* &
2 onbelan[*.*+]<g>rijke
③≤(written)≥
④≤Some geog.≥

666

①[−Thursday]
2 [−p]
3 [e+] <E>indhoven
4 [−die] ≤hij≥
5 [−*accent grave*]

667

1 z[i+]<a>[e+]<g>
2 [−m]

668

1 unübersehbare[−r]
2 scheur[−r]

669

1 [−in]
2 [−en]
3 [−op]≤naar≥
4 [*comma*] <*question mark*>
5 [−ever]

670

1 [−na]
2 [−de]

671

1 [−S]
2 [−de]

3 ons[−*.*]
4 [−onze] [−<hun≥] ≤de≥

672

1 [−n]
2 de[−n]

673

①[−was] ≤is≥
2 [−*.*]

674

1 ≤niet≥
2 zelfs[−s]
③[−first] ≤On the one hand≥
④[−fear]

675

①≤dirty≥

676

1 [−sleep]

677

①[−*quotation marks*]
②[−*quotation marks*]
3 [−al]

678

1 [−an*.*]
2 ≤die ... heeft≥

679

1 [*.*] <J>uni
2 [−in] ≤op≥

680

①*Underlined three times: twice in ink and once in red pencil.*
2 [−tre]
3 [−in]
4 [−*.*]
5 [Eng]
6 [−Yaur]

681

1 [−Z*.*]
2 [−m]
3 ≤eerder≥
4 [−vingers] ≤nagels≥

682

①*Arrow from* This morning *to* P.S.
2 [−Ok]
3 kust[a+]<b>atterijen

683

1 ≤al≥
2 [−met] ≤gezamenlijk met≥

684

1 ≤een≥
②≤Marie≥
③≤Caroline≥
④[−The part]
⑤≤other arts≥

686

1 [v+] <f>ormaat
2 [−en]

687

1 [−v]
2 oor[*.*+]spronkelijke

688

1 ve≤e≥l[−e]
2 [−dingen] ≤wensen≥
3 ve≤e≥l[−e]
4 ve≤e≥l[−e]
5 ve≤e≥l[−e]
6 [−*.*]
7 [−*.*]
8 [−meest]
9 jurk≤en≥
10 [−d]
11 ≤een van≥
12 [−aan] ≤van≥

689

1 [*comma*+] <en>
2 [−maar] ≤toch≥
3 ik ↔ mag

690

1 m[−e] <*apostrophe*>n
2 ≤aandacht≥

691

1 [*.*+] <d>e

692

1 [−des]
2 [*comma*+] <en>
3 [−en]
4 [−bes]
5 <de>
6 [−*comma*]
⑦[−woman must simply] ≤a woman's duty is simply≥

693

1 geneesmiddel[−en]
2 dokte[*.*+]<rs>attest

694

1 [−in]

695

1 kin[*.*+]<d>eren
2 toen[*.*+]<d>ertijd
3 Hoeve[−e]r

696

1 le≤c≥s

697

1 [−al] ≤al≥
2 [−het]

698

1 [−en] ≤maar≥
2 [−toch]

699

1 [−sp]
2 na [−ar]
③[−9] ≤8≥
4 [−*.*]

700

1 deu≤r≥en
2 [−snoepte] ≤plukte≥
3 [−g[a+]<ing>] ≤ga≥

4 [−als] ⩽of er⩾
5 [−K]
6 [−B*.*p]
7 [−*.*]

701

1 aar⩽d⩾beien
2 voor⩽r⩾aad
3 [−*.*]

702

1 werk<je[−*.*]>
2 ⩽geschikt is⩾
3 ⩽een⩾
4 [−ging] ⩽ga⩾
5 st[o+]<a>[−nd]
6 g[ing] ⩽a⩾
7 gons[−de]t
8 go[e+]<o>ien
9 [−sp]

703

1 [−te]
② [−In [−many] ⩽some⩾ passages of the book I had a feeling that the author was [rightly] pointing her finger straight at me as a bad example, but in some also as a good example.]

704

1 [−heb]
2 ⩽zo⩾
3 [−me]
4 zelf[−s]
⑤ ⩽difficult⩾

705

1 [−als]
2 ⩽zou ik⩾

706

1 [−erger] ⩽meer⩾
2 ⩽over⩾
3 [−s]
④ [−good]

707

1 [−met]
2 [−*.*]
3 [−r]
4 [−armer]

708

1 [−die]
2 [−*.*]
3 [−in] ⩽aan⩾
4 ⩽hoe⩾
5 [−op haar] ip
6 [−gro]
7 ⩽de⩾

709

1 [g+] <G>
2 [−ook nog]
3 geno[*.*+]<e>g
4 brand[−bommen] ⩽wonden⩾
5 [−een] ⩽een⩾
6 ⩽te⩾
7 ⩽de⩾
8 [−willen]
9 elk[−aar] ⩽ander⩾
10 [−het] ⩽de⩾
11 opbouw[−en]

710

1 [−Int]
2 [−heeft voorts]
3 [−een]
4 [−af]
5 [−in]
6 [−heet]

711

1 [−is m'n]

712

① ⩽just the same as⩾
2 ⩽wat⩾
3 [−soort]

713

1 [−man]
2 [−e]
3 [−die]
4 d<i>e
5 ⩽naar⩾

VERSION b

200

1 ⩽in⩾
2 [−het]
③ [−try] ⩽write⩾ iri
④ Because of an inkblot only the last two letters of "people" are legible. These are scratched out in green pencil and the word "people" is added above the line, also in green pencil
⑤ Four letters missing because of an inkblot
6 [−handen]
7 [−onder]
8 [−wangen] ⩽handen⩾
9 [period+] <comma>
10 <kan het> (?)
⑪ ⩽probably nobody cares.⩾
⑫ dot of semicolon added in pencil
⑬ ⩽nor is it so.⩾
⑭ [−17] ⩽16⩾ ip
15 [−welzeker] ip
⑯ Four letters missing because of an inkblot and added above the line in green pencil
⑰ Three letters missing because of an inkblot and added above the line in green pencil

201

① ⩽outside the common round⩾
2 ⩽of⩾
3 [−ien]
4 [−ook] ip
5 ⩽ook⩾ ip
6 [−*.*]
7 [−ik]
8 [−ik]
9 [−het] ⩽ik⩾

202

① Three letters missing because of inkblot
② Five letters missing because of inkblot
3 verl[−oo]⩽ie⩾p
4 [−*.*]
5 ble[v+]<e>[e+]<f>[−n]

203

① Three letters missing because of inkblot
② Letter missing because of inkblot

③ [−We(?) console ourselves with the hope that our liberation can't be far away. Thanks to the help of Dutch Christians, *.* all of them neighbours and friends [we lived] ⩽we live⩾ as best we can and every day have fresh proof of the loyal friendship.]
④ [−Febr]

204

① [−July*.*]
② [−granny's death was a blow, but because of her incurable ip
③ [−disease it was the best possible thing.] ip
4 [−het]

205

① Saturday in pencil
2 [*.*+]<b>erust
③ ⩽for our club⩾
④ Five letters blotted out so that the word is not fully readable
5 alle twee[−r]
⑥ ⩽our⩾
⑦ [−of the club]
8 [−en]
⑨ [−Hanne]
⑩ [−that is all]
11 [−Dat is alles]
12 [−De] ip
13 [−de]
⑭ [−clubmembers]
⑮ ⩽pingpongers⩾
16 [−*.*]
17 [−ook]
⑱ Delphi or↔de Oasis
⑲ [o+]<O>as is
⑳ [−altijd] ⩽meestal⩾ ip
21 [−of]
22 <accents aigus> ip

214

① The word I and the parenthesis blotted out
② [always]
③ ⩽in some cases⩾
4 [period+]<comma> ip
⑤ [−in some cases comma]
6 [−je] ⩽mij⩾
7 [−met me]
8 [−je] ⩽mij⩾
9 [−⩽je⩾] ⩽me⩾
10 [−niets] ⩽niet veel⩾
11 [−dan] ip
12 bon[d+]<t> ip
13 vader[−s]
14 [−accents aigus on e and a of thema]
15 [−je]
16 [−*.*]
17 [−toewerken] ⩽sturen⩾
18 [−geven] ⩽bemachtigen⩾
⑲ Four letters blotted out and added above the line in green pencil
⑳ [−weiger] ⩽weiger⩾ igp
㉑ [−introduction] ⩽foundation⩾

215

① [−it really is [−terribly] mean to keep all [−30] 29 of ùs]
2 JI[−*.*]ij
③ The word even blotted out and added above the line in green pencil
4 [−en]
⑤ myself ↔ my girl friends
⑥ [−get] ⩽squeeze⩾ ip
7 [−voor] ⩽in⩾ ip
8 [−een]

⑨ [– This morning]
⑩ [– This afternoon I have been invited to Eefje de Jong's]

216

① ≤and 2 mistresses≥
2 [– een] ≤de≥
3 [– voor]
4 [– van]
⑤ *One word blotted out but partly readable*
6 [– Zorgeloos]
⑦ [– That ≤was≥ very hard, Anne Frank is widely known as a chatterbox
8 m[– e] <*apostrophe*>n
⑨ [– quotation marks]
⑩ [– a chatterbox]
11 [– het]
12 [– k]
13 [– dat] ≤daar≥ *ip*
14 ≤aan≥

217

① *Two letters blotted out so that the word is not fully readable*
2 schaterd [*.* +] <e>
3 Susann[a +]<e>

218

1 [– *comma*]
2 [– <en>] <*comma*> *igp*
3 ≤af≥lopen
④ [– lemonade] ≤drink≥ *igp*
5 [*punt* +]<*comma*> *ip*
6 [– Er] *ip*
7 [– ook] *ip*
8 *transposition ip*
9 [*period* +]<*comma*> *ip*
10 [– De] ≤welks≥ *ip*
11 [– nam ons dan ook] <ons> *ip*
12 ≤nam≥ *ip*
13 ≤Aan ...hebben≥
⑭ [– at Easter] ≤in the Easter holidays≥

219

① [– *quotation marks*]
2 [– nu]
3 [– zo]
4 zal het nu↔in 't vervolg
5 ≤zo≥
6 [– ook]
7 [– *.*]
⑧ [– at Ecfje's]
9 [– en er is geen mogelijkheid]
10 ≤is er geen mogelijk≥
11 [– m]

222

1 no[– g]≤ch≥
② [– o'clock] ≤past eight≥
3 [– weer]
4 [– aan] ≤*apostrophe* t≥
5 [– en]
6 [– out so late with a strange boy]
⑦ [– next Friday]
8 [– nu]
⑨ [– and so neither my parents nor anyone else objects] ≤no one thinks anything of that≥

224

① [– On Friday afternoon, we went]
2 ≤in≥
3 ≤tijd≥
4 [– werd] ≤is≥
5 [– t]

6 [– *.*]
7 [– niemand te te mogen]
8 [– aldoor]
⑨ [– hands]
10 [– pappi]

225

1 [– Laat]
② [– 7] ≤sevens≥
③ [– 2]
④ [– 8] ≤eights≥
⑤ [– 6] ≤sixes≥
⑥ [– my parents are unusual about things like that] ≤my parents are quite different from most≥
7 [– die] ≤zij≥
8 [– marks] ≤reports≥
9 [– dat] ≤deze 3 dingen≥
10 [– is] ≤zijn≥
11 [– Maar]
12 [i +] <I>k
13 [– toch]
14 [– kwamen] ≤moesten≥
15 [– *.*]
16 [– Lies]
⑰ ≤after a bit of persuasion≥
⑱ <properly>
19 [– daar]
⑳ ≤tiny≥
21 [– ≤is≥]
22 ≤speelt≥
23 de hele dag↔haar kleine zusje
24 [– die] ≤zo'n≥
㉕ [– My sister]
㉖ *Point of semicolon added in green pencil*
27 [– zijn]
㉘ *The word* but *has been scratched out and then restored. It is also added above the line*
29 d[– i]e
30 links≤s≥e
31 [– *comma*] <*period*>
32 [– maar ze laat niet veel van haar]
33 [– in]

226

1 [– ligt]
2 [– ≤is≥]
3 [– ≤ligt≥]
4 ≤lijkt≥
⑤ [– A whole world seems to lie] ≤Years seem to have passed≥
6 [– aan het schrijven]
7 [– *.*]
8 [– el] ≤vandaag≥
9 [– na]
10 [– meer]
11 ≤me≥
12 [– weer]
13 ≤Op de [– we] veranda≥
⑭ *Transposition but then cancelled*
15 ≤van de S.S.≥
⑯ [– *quotation marks*]

227

① [– We shan't]
2 [– doemde] [– ≤noopte≥]
3 ≤deed≥
4 [– tot]
5 [– zie] ≤hield≥
6 <me tegen *comma*>
7 [– Vanaf dit dichtsluiten]
8 [– Elke]

228

1 [– was] ≤is≥
2 [– ook]
3 medecompag[– i]on
4 [– Toen] ≤Toen≥
5 [– Margot] ≤zij≥
6 jonge[– n]

7 ≤ook≥
8 [– Talloze] ≤Dat waren [– tallozen] vele≥
9 [– l]
10 [– *.*]
11 [– andere dingen] ≤het schuilen≥
12 ≤daardoor≥
13 [– *comma*]<*period*>
14 [– Ein]
15 [– toen]
16 [– Toen] ≤Daarna≥
17 [– weer]
18 [– vrijgezel]
19 ≤daarom≥
20 hij ↔ bleef
21 [– namelijk]
㉒ ≤without being rude≥

229

① [– 11 o'clock]
2 [– al]
3 [– dicht] ≤wist≥
4 [– ik] ≤het≥
5 [– niet]
6 [– slapen] ≤zijn≥
⑦ [– we put on heaps of clothes as if we were going to the North Pole]
⑧ [– it was pouring]
⑨ ≤and still much more *comma*≥
10 [– nog steeds] ≤naar [– onbeken] voor mij onbekende verten≥
11 <Ik>
12 [– ik] ≤n.l. nog steeds≥
13 [– wat] ≤waar≥
14 [– nu]
15 wij↔ook
⑯ < adressed *period*>

230

1 [– waren]
2 afgehaald<e>
3 bedden↔afgehaalde
4 [– stond]
5 [– de]
6 [– in] ≤in≥
7 in de keuken ↔ een pond ... de kat
8 ≤alleen maar weg≥
9 [– en] <*comma*>
10 [– liepen]
11 [– We leken 3]
12 [– zo]
⑬ [– On the long walk from Merwedeplein to the Prinsengracht]

231

1 [– z]
2 [– *.*]
3 [– nu]
4 [– wat] ≤ons [– in] met≥
5 [– een]
6 [– noemde ik al]
⑦ ≤a 2 [-2] 3 year-old≥
8 [– ook] ≤allen≥
9 [– was] ≤waren≥

232

① ≤ is ≥ *igp*
② [that served as a packing place *period*]
3 [– nog]
4 trap[– je]
5 [– h*.*]
⑥ [– you still had to pass a glass door] ≤but only via a glass door≥
7 [– langs]
8 ≤door≥
9 [– trap]treden
⑩ [– Furnished with dark, large

and heavy furniture] ≤Dark, dignified furniture≥
11 [– een]
12 [– was] ≤is≥

233

① [comma] <period>
2 [– hier]
3 [– Nu]
4 [– zijn]
5 [– De simple]
6 [– een idele]
7 [– deur] ≤kamer≥
8 kleine[e +]<r>[r +]<e>
9 [– die toeg]
10 [– ingeb]
11 [– de]
12 [– Bovenaan]
13 [– apostrophe n]
14 gro≤o≥t[– e] igp
15 licht[– e] igp
16 ruime[– e] igp
17 [– kame[n +]<r>]
≤vertrek≥ igp
18 ≤In≥
⑲ Dot on letter i in green pencil.
The letters "se" have been
scratched out and replaced with an
"s" above the line.
20 [– kamer] ≤vertrek≥
21 [– zou dan ook voor vele wordt]
22 ≤en een≥
23 [– zou]
24 [– zet] ≤zal≥

234

1 [– zeer]
2 ≤dat≥
3 [– ben]
4 ≤weet je≥
5 [– B]
6 [– Da]
⑦ [and the four of us were alone again for Margot was already waiting] ≤alone igp Margot ... us≥
8 [– en] [– <comma>] ≤en op≥
9 [– I]
10 [– in]
11 [– de]
12 [– het]
⑬ [– all the v. P.s' bedclothes plus our own]
⑭ ≤clearing up≥
15 ver<r≥oeren
16 [– die] ≤zij≥
17 [– maar]
18 [– *.*]
19 [– en]
20 [– ≤en≥]
㉑ [– headaches] ≤and≥
22 [– *.*]
23 [– de]
24 [– de]
25 [– o]
26 ≤te≥

235

1 [– druk bezig] ≤in de weer≥
② ≤great≥
3 ni[o +]<e>t
4 [– toen]
⑤ [– my] ≤our≥
⑥ ≤you≥
⑦ [– to Kitty]
8 ≤om≥
⑨ [– Apart from me]
10 [V +]<v>ader
11 ≤kunnen≥
12 [– maar]
13 [– dan wel]
14 [– dit]

236

1 [– maar]
2 [– al n]
3 [– ≤al≥] ≤van tevoren al≥
4 ≤van≥
5 [– Het is hier na] ≤Daardoor ziet het er≥
6 ≤uit≥
7 [– had]
8 [– hele]
9 [– zijn] ≤waren≥
10 [– weer]
11 verschillend[– e]
12 [– werden] ≤zijn≥
13 [– nooit meer]
14 ≤nooit meer≥
⑮ [– , so Daddy says]
⑯ [– I so long for the v. P.'s arrival, it will be so]

237

1 [– d]
② ≤at night≥
3 ≤te pakken≥
④ [– that I could keep Bep back at night when she is the last to leave]
5 mand<en>(?)
6 [– er]
7 [– Die kistjes]
8 altijd[– e]
9 geroep[– j]en

238

1 [– wat]
② 16 and ↔ 13 (igp)
③ ≤right and left≥
4 [– beter]
5 [– waren] ≤wisten≥ igp
⑥ [– 8] ≤7≥
7 geworden ↔ waren

239

1 acht≤er≥gelaten
2 [– en]

240

① [a year] ≤six months≥
2 ≤jeugd – ≥kennis
3 [– d]

248

1 [– wordt] ≤is≥
2 ≤geworden≥ ip
③ ≤because a lot of houses are are being searched for hidden≥ ≤bicycles ≥ ip
4 a[– o]n
⑤ [– because the step is gone] ip
6 ≤daarna≥
⑦ [– yours, Anne.]

249

1 [– could have eaten since] ≤had managed to eat in the end≥ ip
2 harmonica≤ – ≥bed
3 [– wat] ≤h[et +]<ij>is≥ ip
4 [– is dat comma] ip
5 [– hij] ip

250

① ≤that the whole thing was a pure waste of breath≥ ip
2 ≤was≥
3 ≤er≥ ip

251

1 aanleiding≤en≥
2 [– is] [– ≤zijn≥] [– ≤is≥] ≤zijn≥
3 [– dan]
4 [– b.v.]
5 [– ver]
⑥ [– she]≤Mrs. v. P.≥
7 z[e +]<ij>
8 [– hare] [– ≤ – de≥]
9 ≤goed≥
10 k[u +]<a>n[– nen]
⑪ ≤Also≥
12 [– heeft]
13 [– he]
14 [– de≤ze≥ schone dame] ≤zij≥
⑮ Dutch ≤(I daren't say anything about ... offended.)≥
16 [– wel]
17 [– hoort] ≤zou horen≥
18 [– is het om te] ≤schateren≥
19 [– maar]
20 [– Als]
21 ≤zal als ik≥
22 [– zal ik]

252

1 eentonig<e>
2 [– semicolon]
3 [– w] ≤W≥at
4 [– in dat boek wel] ≤wel≥
5 verboden[– d]s
6 [– instaan?] ≤in dat boek staan?≥
7 [– boek]
8 [– toen die even beneden]
⑨ [– comma] <period>
10 [– dan had]
11 [h +] <H>ij
12 ≤had≥
⑬ [– hyper]
14 [– bij] ≤in≥

253

1 begrijp[– l]elijk
2 [– de]

254

1 [– pratend]
2 ≤ieder≥
3 ≤Op≥
4 [– met] ≤na≥
5 b[– l]≤e≥landde
6 D≤r≥ie

257

1 ≤divan≥bed
2 [– Afd]
3 ≤, gebeitste≥
4 [– en gebeitst]
5 [– nu]
6 [– de]
7 boven[– afdeling]
8 [– o*.*]
9 [– ook]

258

1 [– de] ≤een≥
2 [– met] ≤Het≥
3 [– is]
4 [– mee]

259

① [– We also discussed the fact that I am hardly allowed to read anything]
≤Also ... mentioned;≥

2 [−lach me]
③ [− Then we talked about p.*,*]
≤Then we talked about my ignorance of ... ≥
④ [− phijchologie]
5 ≤inderdaad≥
6 [− comma]
⑦ [− ≤words checked for spelling≥
8 [− weet u]
⑨ <(I looked ... Koenen)>
10 [− maar] ≤daar zal≥
11 [− zal daar]
⑫ ≤(including the Brokses)≥

260

1 [− aan je schreef]
2 [− hoedje] ≤mik≥

262

1 [− erg]
2 bewonder<−de>
3 [− staat ≤stond≥
4 [− zegt]
5 ≤zou zeggen≥
6 verst[−aat] ≤ond≥
7 [− de] *igp*
8 [− uit]
9 uit≤voerige antwoorden≥
10 D≤r≥eher
11 [dan]
⑫ [− if Miep couldn't]
⑬ [− replied instead]
14 [− toen ze] ≤aan de≥
⑮ [− having answered it]
16 [− h]
⑰ [asks] ≤says≥
18 [− steeds]
⑲ [− these] ≤ours≥
20 ≤er≥
21 [− meer] ≤nog een keer≥

263

1 de≤ze≥
2 ouder≤ − ≥manier
3 [− b]

264

① [− He made a few howlers, quite incredible ones]
≤But the howlers ... incredible,≥
2 [− de]
3 gol[−fjes]≤ven≥
4 [− zui]

265

1 [− goed]
2 [− leve]
③ ≤indirectly≥
4 [− ingelegd] ≤ingesloten≥
5 ≤als antwoord≥
⑥ ≤envelope≥
⑦ [− secondly]

267

1 [− Heb Een]
2 [− was ik] ≤snap≥
3 [− zo]
4 mo[−l]≤e≥t
5 [− nog]
⑥ [The others agreed with me here, they also think it's rotten.]

268

① [− this month]
② [− much]
3 [− nieu*.*verd]
4 b[*.*]<e>antwoordt
5 [− en]
6 lief[−heid]< − >

7 [− W]
⑧ [− looks and]
9 [− comma] [− <period>] <comma>
10 ≤Ik≥
⑪ *I scratched out but reinstated and also added above the line*
12 [− een] ≤de≥
⑬ ≤to my parents≥
⑭ [− take] ≤make up with≥

269

1 [− dan]
2 i[*.* +]<k>
3 [− bestig]
④ [*quotation marks*]
5 [− ontzettend] ≤verschrikkelijk≥
6 opvoedings≤ − ≥thema
7 [− de]
⑧ ≤after Mrs v.P. had finished speaking so eloquently yesterday≥
⑨ [− in such eloquent words]
10 [− want]
11 ≤U≥
12 ≤eigen≥
13 [− groente]
14 [− altijd] ≤als reden≥
15 [− voor haar] [− ≤'s avonds≥] ≤voor≥
⑯ [− not good] ≤bad≥
⑰ [− yours, Anne. continued on next p.]

270

① [− I]
② [− yet another squabble] ≤hence this sequel≥
③ [− but first this] ≤and straightaway I have to report another argument≥
④ 28 Sept. 1942 *has been scratched out, restored and scratched out again*
5 [In]
6 [m +]<M>'n
7 [− af]
8 ≤wel≥
9 [− voor] ≤hier≥
⑩ [− people] ≤Germans≥

271

1 [− wel] ≤nog≥
2 ≤het eerst≥
3 [Ik] ≤Tot nu toe≥
4 <ik>
5 schinp[− woorden] ≤partijen≥

272

1 [− met alles] ≤ in elk≥
2 [− met] ≤op≥
③ [− *quotation marks*]
4 [− op]
5 bescheiden<e>
6 [− mensen]
7 [− mijn]

273

1 [− maar]
2 ≤echter≥
3 [− opp]
4 [− daardoor]
5 gauw[− ≤er≥]
6 [− tegenover] ≤van≥
7 [− Moeder]
8 [− wendt zich]
9 [− als]
10 [− en]
11 [− noemen] ≤vinden≥

274

1 ≤willen≥
2 waar[−ui] <in>
3 ≤zou≥
4 zorg<en>
5 [− daarom] <dan>
6 [− dan] [− ≤ook≥] ≤dus moeten≥
7 sto[−l] ≤e≥l *ip*
8 [− Toen] ≤Nu≥
9 [− wat]
10 [− dat]
11 to[e +]<o>nde
12 ge[w +]<m>een
13 [− *.*]
14 [− e]
15 [− harde]
16 [− een] ≤hun≥

275

① [− silly] ≤extraordinary≥ *iri*
② <exclamation mark> *iri*
3 [− mee]
④ ≤always≥, *iri*
5 <ge>hele *iri*
6 [− ook] ≤ook≥ *iri*
7 ≤bij≥ *iri*
8 badplaats [− *.*]
9 [− in] ≤een≥ *iri*
10 [− gaan] ≤n[−i]emen≥ *iri*
11 uur[− r]
⑫ ≤He ... sufficient≥ *iri*
13 [− Pf.]
14 <comma>[cn] *iri*
⑮ [− as the best place] ≤for our scrub≥ *iri*
16 gaa[−t]<n>
17 [− altijd] *iri*
18 [− ploeteren] ≤reinigen≥ *iri*
19 ≤ons≥ [− na elkaar] *iri*
⑳ ≤awaiting her turn≥ *iri*
㉑ [comments on] ≤gazes in wonder at≥ *iri*

276

1 [− nu] ≤en≥
2 ≤gegaan≥
3 [− 't W]
4 [− 't Is] ≤'t Was≥ *iri*
5 [− het] <'t> *iri*
⑥ [− fetch] [− ≤directly≥] ≤pour my own bath water away≥ *iri*
7 [− Zo geze*.*]
8 welke[− e]
⑨ [− Last week] *iri*
10 [− bestelt] ≤beneden≥ *iri*
11 [− niet meer]
12 ≤een≥
13 [− een paar dagen] ≤overdag≥ *iri*
14 [− ook] *iri*
15 mochten ↔ we
16 ≤ook≥ *iri*

277

1 [− geden]
2 [− geco]
③ *The point of the semicolon has been added iri*
4 [− stil]
5 [− b]
6 [− haast] *iri*
7 [− geweest] *iri*
8 [− G*.*]

279

1 [− nu] *iri*
2 [− weer wat] *iri*
3 [− *period*]
④ [− *comma*] <period> *iri*
5 [w +]<W>ie *iri*

6 had[−e]
7 [−*.*]
8 [−l]

280

1 anjer[−s]s
2 [−hun] ≤de≥ *iri*
3 rokje[−s] *iri*
4 Ge[−r]lukkig
5 [−ook] *iri*
6 <accents aigus> *iri*
7 <comma> *iri*
8 <comma> *iri*
9 <comma> *iri*

281

① *Vertical stroke of the letter* t *has been added* *iri*
2 [−ik]
3 [−de]
4 perfecte[−n]
5 [−tik] ≤klik≥ *iri*
6 [−tak] ≤klak≥ *iri*
⑦ [period+] <exclamation mark> *iri*

290

① [−things] ≤news≥ *iri*
2 [−gaan] ≤worden≥
3 alle<n> *iri*
4 Man<nen>
5 [−en]
6 [−thrown together] ≤sleep together≥ *iri*
⑦ <semicolon> [−en] *iri*

291

1 [−hem] *iri*
2 [−slecht gaat, hoe] <is> ≤hoe≥ *iri*
3 [−het] ≤de≥ *iri*
④ [−Poland] ≤regions≥ *iri*
⑤ [−because all of them without exception are leaving] ≤they are sent to≥ *iri*
6 [−er] *iri*
7 [−door] *iri*
8 ≤en≥ *iri*
9 [−ze is] *iri*
10 [−zo] [−≤is ze erg≥] ≤ze is eveneens erg≥ *iri*
⑪ [−Last night] ≤Just recently≥ *iri*
12 [−daarin] [− ≤mee≥] *iri*
13 [−De arme]

292

① [tense] ≤quiet≥ *iri*
② [−, Bertus,] *iri*
③ [−now] *iri*
④ [−always] *iri*
5 kilo <apostrophe s< *iri*
6 <apostrophe> [−z'n] *iri*
⑦ [−all the] *iri*
8 [−weg] *iri*
9 ≤gaan≥ *iri*
⑩ [−almost] *iri*
11 [−gaan] ≤rijden≥ *iri*
12 [−te gaan schuilen] ≤onder te duiken≥ *iri*
13 [−'t is toch altijd] ≤aan≥ *iri*
14 [−die dat] *iri*
⑮ [−manage it> *iri*
16 [−en wachten] ≤on≥ *iri*
17 ≤te wachten≥ *iri*
18 [−nu] *iri*
19 zet[−ten] *iri*
⑳ [−fine gentlemen] ≤Green police≥ *iri*
㉑ <quotation marks> *iri*
㉒ <quotation marks> *iri*

㉓ [question mark] <exclamation mark> *iri*
24 n[i+]<e>e *iri*
25 [−en]
26 [−d]

297

1 [−*.*]
2 [−krijgen voor eventuele brand] ≤hebben tegen brandgevaar.≥ *iri*
3 [−Zo] ≤Omdat ze beneden zo≥ *iri*
4 [−als ze beneden] *iri*
5 [−dan] ≤anders≥ *iri*
6 d[−i]e *iri*
7 <parenthesis> *iri*
8 <parenthesis> *iri*
⑨ [−was startled but] *iri*
10 [−daarna] *iri*
11 de<n> *iri*
12 [−dus] ≤en≥ *iri*
13 [−ik] *iri*
⑭ ≤Who was having a meal with us≥
15 [−als] ≤wanneer≥ *iri*
16 gevaa≤r≥te
17 onde<r>zoeken
18 [−wel] *iri*

298

① ≤and≥ *iri*
2 [−Ik]
3 [−Ik] ≤En net≥ *iri*
④ [−surely]
5 [−≤met≥] *iri*
6 de<n> *iri*
7 [−nu] *iri*
8 <gegaan> *iri*
9 [−kwam] ≤wilde≥ *iri*
10 <af>halen *iri*
11 [−e]

306

① [−We]
② [−We had a glorious] ≤The celebratory≥ *iri*
③ [−was] ≤tasted≥ *iri*
④ [−We were just about to do the dishes when suddenly the lights went out. There was a short.] ≤tasted divine ... What was to be done?≥ *iri*
5 [−*.*,]
6 [−werkje] ≤karweitje≥ *iri*
⑦ [−Daddy's office lamp was responsible for the interruption] *iri*
8 [−een] ≤op≥ *iri*
9 [−brengen] *iri*

307

1 lijk[t+]<en>
② period→exclamation mark *iri*
③ [−later]
4 [−dan] *iri*
5 ≤daarvan≥ *iri*
6 [−leeg] ≤ontmeubeld≥ *iri*
7 [−helemaal] *iri*
8 ≤nog≥ *iri*
9 [−of] ≤op≥ *iri*
10 [−a]
11 se<r>vies
12 ≤ook haast≥
13 [−dan] ≤nu≥
14 [−begint]
15 [−daaruit] *iri*
16 ≤wat≥ *iri*
17 [−Nu] ≤Om≥ *iri*
18 vader <apostrophe s> *iri*
⑲ [−What is good reading for me, mother wants to set a good

example] ≤Following Daddy's good example≥ *iri*
20 ≤moeder≥ *iri*
21 [−apostrophe t] ≤apostrophe t≥
22 [−op]

308

1 [−zo] ≤in≥ *iri*
2 ≤tijd≥ *iri*

311

1 [−30 Oct. 1943] ≤7 Nov. 1942≥ *ip*
2 [−Daddy] ≤Mummy≥
3 [−dus]
4 [−niet] ≤noch≥
5 ≤hadden≥ *ip*

312

① [−be] ≤stick up≥ *ip*
2 [−dat ben ik niet anders gewend]
3 [−Z] <z>ij *ip*
4 [−semicolon] <comma> (?) *ip*
5 [−dat stemt mij]
6 [−er] ≤daar≥ *ip*
⑦ [−and sermons] *ip*
8 [−voor] *ip*
9 houd[−t]
⑩ [−for my part] *ip*
11 ander[−e]
12 ≤al≥
⑬ ≤Margot≥ *ip*
14 [−l op]
15 houd[−t]
16 [−*.*]
17 ≤toe≥
18 knap<−>
19 ≤zijn≥
20 [−hebben.] <voelen.> *ip*
21 neerzie[t] *ip*
22 m[−e]'n
㉓ [−But]

313

1 [−moeder] ≤zij≥ *ip*
② [period+] <semicolon> *ip*
③ [−in my ideas] *ip*
4 ≤zie≥ *ip*
5 [−*.*]
6 [−van dit [−bee(ii)] voorbeeld] ≤daarvan≥ *ip*
7 [−vind ik] *ip*
8 ≤terugvindt≥ *ip*
9 [−, terug] *ip*
10 [−het]
11 [−moeder] ≤haar≥ *in pencil but erased*
⑫ ≤But ... work≥ *ip*
13 [−En] ≤nog≥ *ip*
14 [−is] *ip*
15 ≤wel≥ *ip*
16 [−Ik] ≤Soms≥ *ip*
17 ≤ik≥ *ip*
⑱ [−it's all because]
19 [−s] ≤wil≥ *ip*
20 stel[t+]<l><en> *ip*

314

① [−with God mother]
② [−perhaps it's because] *ip*
3 [−Ond]
4 [−i]<I>k *ip*
5 ≤word≥ *ip*
6 [−wordt] *ip*
7 [−dat wel] ≤alles≥ *ip*
8 [−wat] *ip*
9 [−de]
⑩ ≤as I lie in bed≥ *ip*
11 [je] *ip*

¹² ben[−t]   *ip*
⑬ [−always in the company of]
≤having to put up with≥   *ip*
⑭ [−don't understand
you] ≤misinterpret my
intentions≥   *ip*
¹⁵ [−op] ≤daarom op≥   *ip*
¹⁶ <comma>   *ip*
¹⁷ [−en daarom omdat]
≤want≥   *ip*
¹⁸ ≤is≥   *ip*
¹⁹ [−luistert]   *ip*
²⁰ zal ↔ ik
㉑ [−understands] <loves>   *ip*

316

¹ [−Het]
² [−is] ≤beduidt≥   *iri*
³ [−Ne]
⁴ [−nog]

317

¹ [−n.l.]   *iri*
² [−Onze]
³ Levensmiddelenkaa≤r≥ten
⁴ [−ook] ≤eveneens≥   *iri*

318

① [alone]   *iri*
② [−maar]   *iri*
③ <comma>   *iri*
④ [−downstairs]≤the office
people≥   *iri*
⑤ ≤in sacks which≥
⑥ <parenthesis>   *iri*
⑦ <parenthesis>   *iri*
⁸ [−*.*]
⑨ [−came] ≤burst≥   *iri*
⑩ [−comma] <period>   *iri*
⑪ [that made us think we must
look for a good place for storing
our winter supplies.]   *iri*
⑫ [−The sacks couldn't be left
where they were]   *iri*
⑬ [−In the long run it's best to
keep them in the attic]
⑭ [−them] ≤our winter
store≥   *iri*
¹⁵ vertrouwde<.n.>   *iri*
¹⁶ ≤al≥
¹⁷ [−gelukkig] ≤heelhuids≥   *iri*
¹⁸ [−de] ≤no≥   *iri*
¹⁹ [−hij]
²⁰ [−trap]
²¹ [−en] <semicolon>   *iri*
㉒ [−≤when they roared
downstairs≥]   *iri*
㉓ [−≤must have≥]   *iri*
²⁴ [−bonen≥ golven   *iri*
²⁵ ≤aan≥   *iri*
²⁶ [−de]   *iri*
²⁷ [−waren] ≤zijn≥   *iri*
²⁸ [−zich]
㉙ ≤possible and impossible≥   *iri*
㉚ [−and hide there]
³¹ [−met]
³² [−bij] ≤aan≥
㉝ [−How often]
㉞ <yours, Anne>   *iri*

320

¹ gewel[l+]<d>ig
² nieuw[−e]s
③ [−quietly]
⁴ d[*.*+]<i>t   *iri*
⁵ ≤in gedachten≥   *iri*
⁶ [−of we ook] ≤om≥   *iri*
⁷ ≤te≥   *iri*
⑧ [−find] ≤hit on≥
⁹ [n+]<N>adat   *iri*
⑩ [−decided on] ≤chose≥   *iri*

¹¹ [−is]
¹² [−maar is] ≤waar hij≥   *iri*
¹³ [−met haar] ≤mee≥   *iri*
⑭ ≤that doesn't matter≥   *iri*
⑮ ≤is known to be≥   *iri*
⑯ [−≤likeable≥] ≤refined≥   *iri*
¹⁷ [−op] ≤naar≥   *iri*

326

¹ L[e+]<i>eve

328

¹ [−*.*]
² [−z]
③ [−guest and]
⁴ [−f]
⁵ [−om]
⁶ [−de]
⁷ [−de]

329

① ≤(v.P. product)≥
² [m+] <M>unt

330

¹ ≤en≥

332

¹ [−*.*]
² [−*.*]
³ [−niet]   *ip*
⁴ extra ≤−≥ persoon

333

¹ [−*.*]
② [comma+] <period>   *ip*
³ [−want]   *ip*
⁴ [z+] <Z>e   *ip*
⁵ [−n]
⑥ <, innocent≥
⁷ ≤het≥   *ip* OF
⁸ hoe[v+]<f>≤d≥en
⑨ [−If only it was all over and not
yet too late to help them.]

334

① [−keep as cheerful a face]
≤remain as cheerful≥
② ≤on the few occasions≥   *ip* OF
³ bestorm[−t]≤d≥
⁴ [t+]<d>ot   *ip* OF
⁵ [−so]
⁶ m[−a]≤e≥lancholiek

335

¹ ≤toch≥   *ip* OF
② [−Nobody]

336

¹ [−of]
² [−*.*]
³ [−d]
⁴ [−bij]

337

¹ ≤Oost−≥ Indische
² [−en] ≤en≥
³ [−is] ≤komt≥
⁴ [−*.*]
⁵ ≤er≥
⁶ voo≤r≥al

338

① [−7] [−≤8≥] ≤7≥
² [−b]

339

¹ [−p]
² [−Vol]

340

¹ <(niet ge−> ≤meende vleierij!≥
² ≤daar≥
³ [−hadden]

341

① [−Friday 10] [−≤Thursday≥]
② ≤Thursday 10≥ up
³ alle[−s]
④ [−semicolon] <colon>
⁵ [−het was dan ook]
⁶ [−aan] ≤met≥
⁷ geb≤r≥oken

342

¹ [−d]
² [−met]
③ [−used some]
⁴ des[−e]infecteermiddel.
⁵ [−of]

343

¹ [−z]
² [−van]
③ allow herself ... Anne *written
across the right-hand margin*

344

① [−Saturday] ≤Sunday≥
² ≤een≥
③ [coats] ≤toes≥
④ [−you] ≤I≥
⁵ k[u+]<a>n[−t]
⁶ [−die]
⁷ [−die] ≤de≥
⁸ [−en nu] ≤daarop≥
⁹ [−de volgende]

345

¹ ≤en≥
² [−Men] ≤Ik≥
³ hoor[−t]
⁴ [−beloer]
⁵ [−maar]
⁶ [−zien]
⑦ ≤most of≥
⑧ ≤Really≥
⁹ bui[−i]ten
¹⁰ [−grode]

346

¹ [−er] ≤voor≥
² [−voor]

347

¹ [−voor] ≤toe≥
② ≤10 minutes of≥
³ [−gaat]
④ [−Then he gets dressed very
breezily, holds on with one hand
to the chair on which my head lies
and gyrates from side to side so
that I get a headache from the
incessant jolting]
⁵ [−comma en]
⁶ [−o]
⁷ [−maar]
⁸ [−we]

348

① 194 [−2] ≤3≥
² v[−a]≤u≥llen
³ [−ook]
⁴ [−*.*]
⁵ [−Mannen]
⁶ [−Mensen]
⁷ [−het] ≤haar≥
⁸ [−weg]
⁹ [−la]

349

¹ [−om]
² [−*.*]
³ [−*.*]
⁴ voor≤bij≥gangers
⁵ [−maar]
⁶ [−We]

350

¹ [−weer]
² [−*.*]
³ [−V.]
⁴ [−s]
⁵ [−en]
⑥ [−aching] ≤pounding≥
⁷ schreeu[−u]wen

351

¹ [−v]≤V≥oel
² [−laat]
³ [−was]
⁴ behandel[t+]<d>   ip
⁵ [−Ik]
⁶ houd[−t]

352

① [−Tuesday 19[−Febr.]]
[−≤Jan 1≥]
② [−≤Tuesday≥]
≤Friday−≥   ip
≤5 Febr. 1943≥
³ [−comma]
④ [−quotation marks]
⁵ o≤n≥verschillig
⁶ [−*.*]
⑦ ≤luckily≥
⁸ [−*.*ze]
⁹ [−een]

353

¹ handtastelijk[−t]
² ≤ook≥
③ [−Recently]
⁴ [−de]

354

¹ [−Ik]
² longo≤n≥tsteking
³ z[−e]'n
④ [−weap] ≤own≥
⁵ [−De]

355

¹ [−m]
② [−what date]
³ margarine≤−≥indeling
⁴ stukje[−s]
⁵ [−is] ≤geschiedt≥

356

¹ [−*.*]
² [−brengt] ≤koopt≥
³ [−zo]
④ [−comma] <period>
⁵ [−voor]
⑥ [−house] ≤mills≥

⁷ [−*.*]
⁸ [−en]

357

① Bever[−s]bruck
² [−Dat]

358

¹ [−*.*]
² [−ze]
③ [her heart] ≤she woke≥
④ [comma+] <parenthesis>
⑤ [comma+] <parenthesis>
⑥ [−quotation marks]
⑦ [−Later]
⁸ [−nu]
⑨ ≤ .... ≥
⑩ [comma+] <parenthesis>
¹¹ moe<s>t
¹² [−je je] ≤hij zich≥
¹³ [−de]
¹⁴ [−Een]
⑮ [−snow]

359

① [−he] ≤Pim≥
② [−I]

360

① '4[−2] <3>
② [−Fl]
③ [−we've had her since]
⁴ [−zich]
⑤ [−Boche] ≤the warehouse cat≥
⁶ [−de] ≤het≥
⁷ zolder [−afdeling] ≤beest≥
⁸ [−bij]
⁹ [−m]

363

① ≤As teacher ... Annexe"≥
² [−maar ik voor]
³ [−Zo]
⁴ maronett[t+]<e>n-theater.
⁵ [−die]

364

① [−24] ≤25≥
② [−Wednesday] ≤Thursday≥
③ ≤Last night≥
⁴ [−het] ≤dat≥
⁵ ≤naar≥
⁶ ≤aan−≥belandde

365

¹ tro[−e]k
² [−kan men]
³ [−er] ≤daar≥
④ period→semicolon

366

¹ [−comma zij]
² ≤ze≥
³ [−comma]
⁴ [−a]

367

¹ gehel[*.*+]<e>
² van[−ochtend] ≤morgen≥
³ aardbeie[−i]nrecepten
⁴ [−en]
⁵ [−k] ≤c≥ ursus
⁶ [−semicolon]
⁷ [−de]
⁸ [−comma] ≤en≥

368

¹ [−*.*]
② ≤from March 1 to June the
provinces≥
³ [−J]
⁴ zi<e>k
⑤ [−buildings completely]

369

¹ [−D]
② [−July] ≤April≥
③ [−in the "Secret Annexe"]
⁴ [−*.*]
⁵ [−is] ≤heeft≥
⁶ [−p]
⑦ Frankf[−ij]urt
⁸ [−quotation marks]
⁹ [−p]
¹⁰ [−T]

370

¹ [−de]
² linole[−O]um−grond.
³ ≤me≥
⁴ [−w]
⑤ [−the door]
⁶ [−dra]
⁷ Lief[j+]<d>e
⁸ [−comma]
⁹ [−*.*]

371

¹ [−*.*]
② ≤hard≥
③ [−really]
④ [−the whole] ≤half the≥
⁵ ben↔ik
⑥ [−crying] ≤tears≥
⑦ [and Margot's]
⁸ [−hoe] ≤des te≥

372

① [−Friday 9 April 1943]
≤Tuesday 27 April '43≥
² [−in]
³ ≤de≥
⁴ [−comma zonder]
⑤ [−Mrs.] ≤Mr.≥
⑥ [−paid us a visit] ≤is at the
office again≥
⑦ [−couldn't tell us much more
about her husband]
⑧ ≤comma the hemorrhage ...
usual≥   iri
⑨ [−But she did say]
⑩ ≤He told us≥
¹¹ [−Van]
¹² [−De]

373

¹ [−D]

375

① [−F]
② [−wife]
³ boter[−e]
⁴ [−enz]
⁵ pos[*.*+]<t>papier
⁶ [−Z'n]
⑦ [−4] ≤ 3≥
⁸ [−d]
⁹ ≤zeker≥
¹⁰ [−onze]
¹¹ [−waar]
¹² ≤die≥
⑬ [−vainly keeps asking all and
sundry because they are so good
for his stomach] ≤needs so badly
... stomach≥
¹⁴ [−beter] ≤gezonder≥

15 [– In 't]
⑯ [– So as later]
17 [– p]
⑱ [– A State of Siege has been declared throughout the Netherlands : that is the punishment for all the strikes, if only they left it at that] ≤The whole≥
19 [– Er is]
20 ≤al≥
㉑ [– For a start we have no shampoo] ≤We have to ... green soap≥
22 [– a]

376

① [– 4] ≤18≥
2 [– l]
③ [– English] ≤Allies≥
④ [– or an emergency landing]
5 [– apostrophe]
⑥ [– air]
⑦ ≤a little≥
⑧ [– The latest deterrent] ?
9 [– Ale]

377

1 [– en] <comma>
2 [– dan]
3 [– het] ≤ons≥
④ [– was burning]
5 [– De] <Bij de≥
⑥ [– We]

378

① A 3 and an exclamation mark have been added underneath the 4, which has not been scratched out.
② [– I hope you won't dislike it]
③ ≤short≥ omitted from English translation
4 [– die]
5 [comma]
6 [– d]

379

1 [– apostrophe]
2 [– b]
③ [– quotation marks]
④ [– Yes if you grow four inches more, | Nothing will fit you as before]
5 [– *.*]
6 vind[– t]
⑦ [– It runs to 4 pages]
⑧ yours, Anne across the right-hand margin

380

① 194[– 4] ≤3≥ ip
② [– too much]
3 [– om het] ≤en dat≥
④ ≤and that ... letters.≥
5 [– te ontvangen]
⑥ ≤not≥
7 [– goed te eten]
8 [– comma]

381

① [– We have]
2 [– dat]
3 [– *.*]
4 [– h]
5 wonder≤ – ≥stem

382

1 [– in]
2 kunt[– s]

---

3 [– in]
④ ≤keeping ≥ ip OF
⑤ [– above all so as to m period]

383

① [– is] [– ≤was≥] ≤is≥
2 [– gaat] ≤ging≥
3 [– het]
4 [– zoom]
5 [– daar]
6 [– heel]
7 [– Op]
8 [– *.*]
⑨ [– many greens from all her acquaintances]
⑩ [scrape together]
11 [– comma]
⑫ [– wait] ≤always long≥
⑬ ≤for Saturdays when our books come≥ ip
14 [– en]

384

① iri underlined
② iri underlined

385

1 verzo[c +]<c>k[– t]
② [– him] ≤you≥

387

1 [– of]

388

1 ≤de≥
2 magazijn< – >
3 [– werd als]
④ ≤all morning≥
5 ≤ons≥
6 [– hadden comma]
7 [– *.*]
8 [– Ze waren hadden]
9 [– was] ≤viel≥
10 [– stalen]
⑪ [– giro and bank giro and bank g]
12 [– d]
13 [– die]
14 [– al]

389

1 [– 't] ≤ons≥
2 [– o*.*]
3 [– b]
4 [W +] <D>e ip
⑤ ≤tor≥
⑥ ≤approaching≥

390

1 ≤m'n≥ ip
2 ≤te≥
3 [– mag] ≤moet≥
4 [– Als]
⑤ [– It comes to 12 pages]
6 scheef≤ – ≥
7 ≤nog≥
8 [– schoo]
9 [– wat] ≤iets≥

391

① [– milon]
2 [– in de]

392

1 ≤een≥
2 [– hebben ons]
3 [– wel]

---

4 maa[*.* +]<r>
5 [– de]≤er≥
6 [– comma dan]

393

1 [– het]
2 ge[– d]zicht
3 [– maar]
4 [– het] ≤ik≥
5 [– half]
⑥ ≤o'clock≥
⑦ [– couldn't keep on my legs and when I went to bed]
⑧ [– When the clock struck 12]
9 vreselijk<e> ip

394

1 ≤de≥
2 ≤en≥
3 [– is toch] ≤houdt toch≥
4 h[e +]<u>n
5 onderw[– i]erp
6 [– m]
7 uitstekend[– e]
8 [– maar]
9 [– het] ≤de≥
10 p[*.* +]<s>ych[– isch] ≤e≥
11 [– leven]
12 [– van]

395

① ≤always≥
② ≤selfish, cunning, calculating≥

396

1 iedere≤e≥n
2 [– *.*]
③ [– parenthesis]
4 [– is]

397

1 ≤het≥
2 [– dat] ≤hem≥
3 [– Ook in alle an]
4 [– het]
5 [– comma]
6 [– d]
7 [E +]<e>nz.
8 bombardent[– *.*]
9 m[– e]'n
10 beter[– e]
11 ee[– e]n
12 rietst[– r]engel
⑬ [– It's silly but]
14 voor[b +]<d>ee[ld +]<l> ip
⑮ [– I'm] ≤we're≥
16 ≤allen≥
17 ≤staande≥
18 <De> [– E] ≤e≥chte

398

1 [– ro]

399

1 [– dagen]
2 [– hipt]
3 ≤haar≥ spelden
4 [– in]
5 ≤een≥
6 [– comma] <period>

400

1 gelui[*.* +]<d>en
② [– semicolon] <period>
3 [a +]<A>llereerst
4 [– als het]

401

1 [−tussen]
2 [−besef] ≤merk≥

402

① [−Anne]
2 [−I] ≤ɪ≥
3 [−*.*]
4 [−*.*]
5 [*.* +]<l>ijkt
6 e[−e]mmertje

403

1 *colon →period*
2 k[−r]ijk
3 [−in] ≤af≥ruim

404

1 [−in]
② [−hear] ≤judge≥
3 [−kunnen]
4 schree[−e]uwlelijk
5 [−ie]
6 hoor[−t]
7 [−men haar]

405

1 maand[−jes] ≤en≥
2 [−d]
3 [−I]
4 [−je]
⑤ [−Kit]
6 [−a]
⑦ [−Later I want to have sweet]
⑧ [−in stacks]

407

1 [−het]
2 [−h]
3 [−≤denkt≥]
4 [−zo *apostrophe*]

408

1 [−Een]
2 [s +]<S>tevige
3 [−*comma*] <*comma*>
4 bescheidenheid<ste> [−zelve]
5 [−h]

409

1 [−v]
2 ≤en≥

410

1 [−over]
2 [−naar] ≤heen≥
3 [−die]
4 [−snuif] ≤snuffel≥
⑤ [−some] ≤a bit of≥
6 [−n]

411

① [Wherever I go, sit or stand, upstairs downstairs or wherever]
2 [−dan ook]
3 de[−r]
4 [−m'n] ≤een≥
5 ≤de≥
⑥ ≤right≥
7 ≤de≥
⑧ [−Unfortunately]
⑨ [−the little toe] ≤because≥
⑩ [−*dash*] *plus sign*
11 [−n]
12 [−doods] ≤levens≥gevaar
13 [−boekje]

412

① *iri underlined*
② *iri underlined*

413

1 knipoog[−s]t

416

① *iri underlined*
② *iri underlined*
③ *iri underlined*

418

① *iri underlined*
② *iri underlined*

420

1 c[*.* +]apitulerend
2 [−e]

421

1 [−nog] ≤niet≥
2 [−nam] ≤genomen heeft≥

422

① [−for once] ≤until the next row≥
2 [−ook]
③ [−Mr. Kleiman is much better; the operation was fairly successful]
4 [−tegen]
5 [−meligheid]
⑥ [−in hiding]

423

1 [−ging]

424

① [−It's like this]
2 [−die]
3 [−'t]
4 [−draai]

425

1 [−o]
2 [−heeft]
3 [−Het ≤be≥ging weer]
4 [−woorden]
5 [−en]
⑥ [−Pf. and Mummy have fallen out]
7 [−hij]
⑧ [−there's also trouble with v. P.]
⑨ ≤they're≥

427

1 [−haast]
2 [−en m]
3 [−d]
4 g[i +] <e>gil
5 k[−a]≤u≥n
6 [−niet]

428

1 [−*.* kom er aan] ≤moeten er aan≥
2 hoor[−t]
3 [−ik]
4 [−deze]
5 [−het] ≤een≥
6 [−of iemand]
7 ≤zang≥vogel
8 [−z]
9 [−lach]
10 [−*.*]

429

1 [−aan]
2 [−en]
3 neus[−t] ≤de≥
4 [−we al]
5 [−V]

430

1 [−*.*]
2 [−e]
3 [−stoffer]
4 k[*.* +]<a>n
⑤ [−*quotation marks*]
⑥ [−this] ≤our≥
7 blij[−f]ven
⑧ [−You hear nothing but]
9 <of>
10 om[k +]<g>ekeerd
11 ketel[−t]
12 [−Ons]
⑬ ≤(wrapped in cotton wool)≥
14 [−uit]
15 [−*.*]

431

① ≤again≥
2 [−h]
3 [−werd] ≤was≥
4 hu[−h]n
5 kwa[−a]rt
⑥ ≤as planned≥
⑦ [−highly] ≤terribly≥
8 [−te]
9 ≤terug≥ vond

432

① [−I believe]
2 ≤ik≥
3 [−≤ee≥]
4 ≤een≥
5 ra[−a]re
6 [−me]
7 ≤lang *comma*≥
8 [−of] ≤en≥
9 [−ik soms] ≤soms≥
10 [−in]
11 [Al]
12 ≤ik≥
13 [−al]
14 be −[−≤belan≥]leven

433

1 [−hebt] ≤heeft.≥
2 [−*.*]
③ [−are] ≤were≥
4 [−Ons st]
5 [−het]
6 [−Op]
⑦ <*period*> [−and yet all of us have to suffer the same fate]
⑧ [−the world and]
⑨ [−black]
⑩ ≤not≥
11 ondoordringba[−a]re

437

① [−or] ≤and≥
2 [−p]
③ ≤Margot sends in≥
4 les ≤sen≥ word[t +]<e>n
5 [−Deze]

438

① ≤for him≥
2 we<r≥d
③ [−On the contrary]
④ ≤unselfishness in≥
5 ≤de≥
⑥ condole ↔ or congratulate
7 ≤voor≥

716

8 [−ons]
9 [−heeft] ≤geeft≥
10 elk[−e]
11 ve[−e]le

439
① Hanneli[−e]
② [−a Hanneli, ragged and thin in a camp where she had to labor hard]
3 ≤zelf≥
4 [−zelf]
⑤ [−*quotation marks*]
6 [−u]
⑦ ≤probably≥
⑧ [−Wher]

440
1 opneme[−me]≤n≥
2 [−*period*]
3 [−o]
④ [−utterly]
5 n → ııı
6 [−w]
⑦ [−still]
⑧ [−I have]

441
1 [−o]
2 [−In] ≤Over≥
3 Alle<n>
4 [−aanw]

442
1 ieder[−e]
② ≤from the basket≥
3 [−een schoen]

443
1 [−wat] ≤iets≥
2 luciter[−doosje] ≤stokjes≥

444
1 moc<s>t
2 kro[*.*+]<o>p
3 [−lie]
4 borst ≤lappen≥

445
1 [−ik]
2 [−tw]
3 [−*.*]
④ ≤alarmingly≥
⑤ [−Bep]
6 ≤de≥
7 [−bonesta]

446
1 [−ı]
2 [−het]
③ [−is miserably heavy] ≤lies heavily≥

447
1 [−in verho] ≤en≥
2 [−en]
3 Nieuw[−s]jaarsdagen

448
1 ≤dan≥
2 [−aan]
3 [−Of het] ≤Alle≥
4 [−hele]
5 [−je] ≤me≥
6 [−da]

455
1 [−M Hoe]
2 ≤vol≥ *ip* OF
③ ≤all≥
④ [−objectively]≤subjectively≥ *ip* OF
5 liet<en> *ip* OF
⑥ [−the other side]

456
① [−*parenthesis*] *ip*
② [−does] ≤did≥
③ ≤as (*ip*) OF she≥
4 maa[−s]r
5 [−op]
6 [−gc]bot≤ge≥vierd
⑦ ≤much≥ *ip* OF
⑧ ≤really≥ *ip* OF
⑨ [−she doesn't make me feel that she really wants to be a mother]
10 [−tro z]

461
1 ≤het≥
2 geleg≥en≥heid
3 [−*.*]
4 ≤anders≥

462
1 [−don]
2 [−dat ≤die≥]
3 [−wel]
4 ve≤r≥tel
5 ≤kijk ... heen≥
6 [−maar]
7 [1+] <1>k
8 ≤echter≥
9 [−'s]
10 [−M]
11 [−voor] ≤om≥

463
1 [−ee]
②[−7]
3 metee[−e]n
4 verschil[−d]ende
5 ontmoette<n> *ip*
6 [−w]

464
1 [−nog]
2 [*.*]
3 [−ook] ≤toch≥
4 ≤weer≥
5 [−weet] ≤wist≥
6 [−ik]
7 [−ne]
8 [−2]
9 [−een]
10 Point *added* *ip*
11 [−d d]
12 [−bi]

465
1 [−h]
2 [−was]
3 [−*.*]

466
1 ≤rood−≥bruin
2 [−k]
3 [−hij liet]
④ [−nearly all]≤lots of≥
5 [−L]

467
1 ver−[−verb]beeldde
2 [−w]
③ [−in my subconscious]
4 ≤leefde≥
⑤ [−bigger] ≤older≥
6 ≤werd≥ *ip* OF
⑦ [−appeared] ≤was shown≥
8 [−dat] ≤en≥

469
1 ≤de≥
2 we≤e≥k
3 [−was] ≤lag≥
4 ≤met kant≥
5 [−h]
6 [−lintje] ≤bandje≥
7 e≤e≥n

470
1 [−E]

472
① ≤we came here≥ *ip* OF
2 [−, to]
3 [−was] ≤speelde≥
4 [−ZO] (*ii*) ([−≤ZO≥ half] *ip* OF)
⑤ [−and that I didn't] *ip*
6 [−was dat] *ip*
⑦ [like going back home] *ip*
⑧ [−(at home!)] *ip*
9 ≤dan≥ *ip* OF

473
① [−which I wear for Peter] *ip*
2 ≤nog≥
3 [−maar]

4/4
① [−sugar] ≤meat≥
2 roggebrood[−e eet]
3 [−zich als] ≤de≥
4 [−voorlopig]

475
1 [−is]
2 [−r]
3 [−ook]
4 [−van]

477
1 [−hccl]
2 nab[−ij] ≤ei≥st

478
1 [−*.*]
2 sch≤r≥aperigheid
3 [−t]
4 [−Uit] ≤Van≥
5 [−heeft] ≤hebt≥

479
1 [−al d]
2 [−is]
3 [−hocwel] ≤ofschoon≥
4 [−hen]
4 ≤van dat≥

480
1 [−wat] ≤dat≥
2 [−als] ≤vaak werd≥ *ip* OF
2 ≤die≥ *ip* OF
④ [−then]
⑤ ≤and had also−≥ *ip* OF

481

¹ [−l]
² [−in]
³ [−We]
⁴ [−l]
⁵ [−*.*]

482

¹ [−m]
² [−wer]

483

¹ [−hield]
² d[i+]<a>t
³ [−was]
⁴ [−over]

485

¹ [−het] ≤ze≥
² [−ev]
③ [−*quotation marks*]
⁴ [−o]

486

¹ [−en]
② [−recall]
³ [−precies] ≤precies≥
④ [−acts] ≤is≥
⁵ [−tot]

487

¹ [−min]
² [−Pf. b]

488

¹ ≤diverse≥
² melkboer≤en≥
³ kruidenier<s>
⁴ [−op] ≤aan≥
⁵ [−dames]

489

① [−warm]
² [−In]
³ [−erop duidt]

490

¹ [−*comma*] <*period*>
② [−always let us]
³ verjaar[−dagen] ≤ −≥
⁴ [−*.*]
⁵ [−heeft]

492

① ≤on the one hand≥
² [−hier]
③ ≤in Holland≥
⁴ [−aangebracht]
≤gepubliceerd≥   *ip* OF
⁵ wate[−n]<r>
⁶ kwam≤en≥

493

¹ [−en] ≤of≥
² stilstaan[e+]<de>
³ [−*.*]

494

¹ [−nu]
² ≤al≥vast
³ ≤nu≥
⁴ ≤bonen≥

495

① [−Mums]
② [−4 two]
③ [−strangers]
④ [−, and as far as possible]
⁵ [−twee]
⑥ ≤water,≥
⁷ [−in doen] ≤bewaren≥   *ip* OF

496

¹ ≤staan≥   *ip* OF
² [−Zoveel]
³ [−vers]
⁴ p[e+]<a>des
⁵ G[−i]eb[e+]<i>eden

497

¹ [−in] ≤binnen het bereik van≥
² [−het]
³ pro[g+]<p>agandadoeleinden

498

¹ [−uitge] ≤ver≥moord
² [−op]
³ [−toch]

500

① [−*dash*] but left in English
version
② [−*dash*] but left in English
version
³ gevo≤e≥l
⁴ ≤de≥
⑤ [−all] ≤as if≥
⁶ vo≤e≥l

502

① [−Wednesday 16] ≤Monday
14≥
² zat[−t]en
³ [−we]
⁴ [−het]≤de≥
⁵ s≤c≥hon!
⁶ ≤en≥
⁷ [−gaf]
⁸ [−*.*]
⁹ ≤en≥

503

¹ ≤zal≥
² ≤en≥
³ [−m'n]

504

¹ [−*.*]
② [−put my arms round m]
③ ≤sensed≥   *ip* OF

505

¹ [−*.*]
② [−Tuesday morning] ≤Monday
night≥
³ [−voegde]
④ [−*quotation marks*]
⁵]vertelde] ≤briefde≥
⁶ [−door]
⑦ [−regret that he]
⑧ [−I was]

514

① [−on] ≤from≥
② [−I can see no houses, no
people, no bricks, nothing but sky,
clouds, trees, birds and nature]
³ ≤de≥
④ [−[p+]<P>eter and me]

515

① [−*quotation marks*]
② [−a blue sky] ≤this≥
³ [−hij] ≤het≥
④ [−even when there are bombs
or gunfire]

519

¹ ≤zich≥
² [−versch]
³ [−vond] ≤zag≥
⁴ [−V]
⁵ [−over]
⁶ [−of]

520

¹ Vano[−c] ≤c≥htend
² [−een de] ≤het≥
³ moe[−s]t
④ ≤closed the door behind him≥

521

¹ myster[j+]<i>e[−us geval]
² [−me] ≤ons≥
³ [−en dan]
⁴ [−me] ≤ons≥

532

① [−Anne]
² [−waren]
③ [−*comma*] <*period*>

533

¹ [−bij]
² [−he]
³ [−je lachte]
⁴ [−die]
⁵ m[−e]'n
⁶ [−paar dagen]

534

¹ [−de] ≤het≥
② [−and carefree]
③ [−reproaches]
④ [−From the winter of 1943]

535

¹ [−loden]
² [−niet]
³ [−e]
⁴ grenzenlo[o+]<z>[s+]<e>

536

¹ [−en] ≤van≥
² [−dat]
³ [−er]

537

¹ beleef[d+]<t>
² [−al]
³ [−je]
④ [−May you be very, very happy,
for then you can look
unflinchingly at all the misery and
try to help, rather than like us clap
your hands to your eyes and
exclaim: 'Don't let me see, don't
let me see, I don't want to see, I

cannot see.'] *(ii)* ≤And whoever ...
yours, Anne M. Frank≥ *(iri)*

540

¹ [m+]<h>[o+]<ee>[s+] <f>t
² [−z]
³ [toch]
⁴ vind ↔ ik
⁵ [−h]

542

¹ [−aan] ≤voor≥
² [−klaag]
③ ≤still≥
④ ≤everything≥

544

¹ [−ee*.*]
² [−lev]
③ [−*parenthesis*]

545

¹ [−kan] ≤zou≥
² [−*parenthesis*]

546

¹ [−als]
² [−het] ≤de≥
③ ≤then≥   *ip* OF

547

¹ [−doch] ≤maar≥
② ≤But≥   *ip* OF
³ [−*.*]

552

① [Mrt.] ≤March≥
② [−Kleiman is poorly]
³ [−k*.*]
⁴ [−zo]
⁵ [−H]
⁶ [−Aan] ≤In≥
⁷ kom[−t ik] [−≤men≥] ≤je≥
⁸ ≤voor≥   *ip* OF
⑨ [−young girls] ≤gentlemen≥
¹⁰ [−men]

553

① [−comical] ≤humorous≥   *ip*
OF
² [−g]
③ [−Margot is so]
⁴ [−derde] ≤vijfde≥
⁵ [−been] ≤rad≥
⁶ alle[−e]n
⁷ [−hetzelfde]

554

¹ [−5] ≤6≥
² [−*.*]
³ [−als het ware spleet]

555

¹ [−was]
² [−vo]
³ steek[−t]

556

¹ [−m]

587

¹ [−je]

588

¹ [−G]
² da[n+]<t>
³ [−aan]

589

¹ [−p]
² [−e]
³ [−ze zijn]
⁴ [−d]

591

¹ [−op het]
² [−ze]
③ [−her] ≤a mouse out≥

594

¹ [−men] ≤wij≥
² o[−r]p
³ ≤dan≥

595

¹ groente[−n]
② [−in the meantime] ≤if you
go≥

597

① [−however] ≤moreover≥
² ≤nemen≥
³ [−de]
⁴ [−is] ≤staat≥